Covering the most popular destinations in North America and Europe, *For Dummies* travel guides are the ultimate user-friendly trip planners. Available wherever books are sold or go to www.dummies.com

And book it with our online partner, Frommers.com

- ✓ **Book airfare, hotels and packages**
- ✓ **Find the hottest deals**
- ✓ **Get breaking travel news**
- ✓ **Enter to win vacations**
- ✓ **Share trip photos and stories**
- ✓ **And much more**

Frommers.com, rated the #1 Travel Web Site by PC Magazine

FOR DUMMIES®

The fun and easy way™ to travel!

U.S.A.

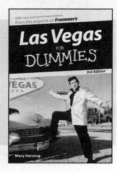

Also available:

Alaska For Dummies

Arizona For Dummies

Boston For Dummies

California For Dummies

Chicago For Dummies

Colorado & the Rockies For Dummies

Florida For Dummies

Los Angeles & Disneyland For Dummies

Maui For Dummies

National Parks of the American West For Dummies

New Orleans For Dumm

New York City For Dumr

San Francisco For Dumn

Seattle & the Olympic Peninsula For Dummies

Washington, D.C. For Dummies

RV Vacations For Dumm

Walt Disney World & Orlando For Dummies

EUROPE

Also available:

England For Dummies

Europe For Dummies

Germany For Dummies

Ireland For Dummies

London For Dummies

Paris For Dummies

Scotland For Dummies

Spain For Dummies

OTHER DESTINATIONS

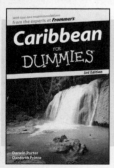

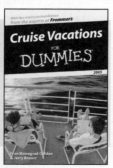

Also available:

Bahamas For Dummies

Cancun & the Yucatan For Dummies

Costa Rica For Dummies

Mexico's Beach Resorts For Dummies

Montreal & Quebec City For Dummies

Vancouver & Victoria For Dummies

Available wherever books are sold.
Go to www.dummies.com or call 1-877-762-2974 to order direct.

WILEY

Cruise Vacations

FOR

DUMMIES®

2006 EDITION

by Heidi Sarna and Matt Hannafin

WILEY

Wiley Publishing, Inc.

Cruise Vacations For Dummies® 2006

Published by
Wiley Publishing, Inc.
111 River St.
Hoboken, NJ 07030-5774
www.wiley.com

Copyright © 2006 by Wiley Publishing, Inc., Indianapolis, Indiana

Published simultaneously in Canada

No part of this publication may be reproduced, stored in a retrieval system, or transmitted in any form or by any means, electronic, mechanical, photocopying, recording, scanning, or otherwise, except as permitted under Sections 107 or 108 of the 1976 United States Copyright Act, without either the prior written permission of the Publisher, or authorization through payment of the appropriate per-copy fee to the Copyright Clearance Center, 222 Rosewood Drive, Danvers, MA 01923, 978-750-8400, fax 978-646-8600. Requests to the Publisher for permission should be addressed to the Legal Department, Wiley Publishing, Inc., 10475 Crosspoint Blvd., Indianapolis, IN 46256, 317-572-3447, fax 317-572-4355, or online at http://www.wiley.com/go/permissions.

Trademarks: Wiley, the Wiley Publishing logo, For Dummies, the Dummies Man logo, A Reference for the Rest of Us!, The Dummies Way, Dummies Daily, The Fun and Easy Way, Dummies.com, and related trade dress are trademarks or registered trademarks of John Wiley & Sons, Inc., and/or its affiliates in the United States and other countries, and may not be used without written permission. Frommer's is a trademark or registered trademark of Arthur Frommer. Used under license. All other trademarks are the property of their respective owners. Wiley Publishing, Inc., is not associated with any product or vendor mentioned in this book.

LIMIT OF LIABILITY/DISCLAIMER OF WARRANTY: THE PUBLISHER AND THE AUTHOR MAKE NO REPRESENTATIONS OR WARRANTIES WITH RESPECT TO THE ACCURACY OR COMPLETENESS OF THE CONTENTS OF THIS WORK AND SPECIFICALLY DISCLAIM ALL WARRANTIES, INCLUDING WITHOUT LIMITATION WARRANTIES OF FITNESS FOR A PARTICULAR PURPOSE. NO WARRANTY MAY BE CREATED OR EXTENDED BY SALES OR PROMOTIONAL MATERIALS. THE ADVICE AND STRATEGIES CONTAINED HEREIN MAY NOT BE SUITABLE FOR EVERY SITUATION. THIS WORK IS SOLD WITH THE UNDERSTANDING THAT THE PUBLISHER IS NOT ENGAGED IN RENDERING LEGAL, ACCOUNTING, OR OTHER PROFESSIONAL SERVICES. IF PROFESSIONAL ASSISTANCE IS REQUIRED, THE SERVICES OF A COMPETENT PROFESSIONAL PERSON SHOULD BE SOUGHT. NEITHER THE PUBLISHER NOR THE AUTHOR SHALL BE LIABLE FOR DAMAGES ARISING HEREFROM. THE FACT THAT AN ORGANIZATION OR WEBSITE IS REFERRED TO IN THIS WORK AS A CITATION AND/OR A POTENTIAL SOURCE OF FURTHER INFORMATION DOES NOT MEAN THAT THE AUTHOR OR THE PUBLISHER ENDORSES THE INFORMATION THE ORGANIZATION OR WEB SITE MAY PROVIDE OR RECOMMENDATIONS IT MAY MAKE. FURTHER, READERS SHOULD BE AWARE THAT INTERNET WEB SITES LISTED IN THIS WORK MAY HAVE CHANGED OR DISAPPEARED BETWEEN WHEN THIS WORK WAS WRITTEN AND WHEN IT IS READ.

PLEASE BE ADVISED THAT TRAVEL INFORMATION IS SUBJECT TO CHANGE AT ANY TIME AND THIS IS ESPECIALLY TRUE OF PRICES. WE THEREFORE SUGGEST THAT READERS WRITE OR CALL AHEAD FOR CONFIRMATION WHEN MAKING TRAVEL PLANS. THE AUTHOR AND THE PUBLISHER CANNOT BE HELD RESPONSIBLE FOR THE EXPERIENCES OF READERS WHILE TRAVELING.

For general information on our other products and services, please contact our Customer Care Department within the U.S. at 800-762-2974, outside the U.S. at 317-572-3993, or fax 317-572-4002.

For technical support, please visit www.wiley.com/techsupport.

Wiley also publishes its books in a variety of electronic formats. Some content that appears in print may not be available in electronic books.

Library of Congress Control Number: 2005932795

ISBN-13: 978-0-7645-9830-2

ISBN-10: 0-7645-9830-9

Manufactured in the United States of America

10 9 8 7 6 5 4 3 2 1

1B/QX/RR/QV/IN

WILEY

About the Authors

Heidi Sarna is a freelance writer living in New York City with her husband and toddler twin sons. Coauthor of *Frommer's Cruises & Ports of Call* and a contributor to several other guidebooks, she also writes regular travel columns for Frommers.com and *Porthole* cruise magazine. She has written for many magazines and newspapers, including *Gourmet, Conde Nast Traveler, Parenting, Bridal Guide,* and *Travel Weekly*.

Matt Hannafin is a freelance writer, editor, and musician based in Brooklyn, New York. Coauthor of the upcoming *1,000 Places in the U.S.A. & Canada to See Before You Die* (a sequel to the 2004 bestseller) and *Frommer's Cruises & Ports of Call,* he also writes regular travel columns for Frommers.com, the *Boston Herald,* and *Porthole* cruise magazine, and has contributed to dozens of other books, magazines, and Web sites, including *Gourmet, Travel Weekly,* and *Avid Cruiser*.

Authors' Acknowledgments

The authors would like to thank the many travel writers and experts who have contributed their opinion and expertise to this and other recent Hannafin-Sarna productions, including Christina Colon, Mike Driscoll, Art Sbarsky, Benjamin Lyons, Darlene Simidian, Rebecca Tobin, Ted Scull, Anne Kalosh, Marilyn Green, and Ken Lindley. Thanks also to Fran Golden, a good friend and author of the first several editions of this book. Lastly, big thanks go out to Rebecca Morris and Arun, Kavi, and Tejas Sarna for their eternal forbearance.

Publisher's Acknowledgments

We're proud of this book; please send us your comments through our Dummies online registration form located at www.dummies.com/register/.

Some of the people who helped bring this book to market include the following:

Editorial

Editors: M. Faunette Johnston, Production Editor; Michael Kelly, Development Editor; Naomi Kraus, Project Editor

Copy Editor: Jennifer Connolly

Cartographer: Andrew Murphy

Senior Photo Editor: Richard Fox

Cover Photos:

Front Cover: © Gary Buss/Getty Images; Alaska, Prince William Sound

Back Cover: © Neil Emmerson/ Robert Harding World Imagery/ Getty Images; Blue domed churches, Thira in the Cyclades of Greece

Cartoons: Rich Tennant (www.the5thwave.com)

Composition Services

Project Coordinators: Michael Kruzil, Jennifer Theriot

Layout and Graphics: Stephanie D. Jumper, Barbara Moore, Barry Offringa, Lynsey Osborn, Julie Trippetti

Proofreaders: Laura Albert, Leeann Harney, Carl Pierce, TECHBOOKS Production Services

Indexer: TECHBOOKS Production Services

Publishing and Editorial for Consumer Dummies

Diane Graves Steele, Vice President and Publisher, Consumer Dummies

Joyce Pepple, Acquisitions Director, Consumer Dummies

Kristin A. Cocks, Product Development Director, Consumer Dummies

Michael Spring, Vice President and Publisher, Travel

Kelly Regan, Editorial Director, Travel

Publishing for Technology Dummies

Andy Cummings, Vice President and Publisher, Dummies Technology/General User

Composition Services

Gerry Fahey, Vice President of Production Services

Debbie Stailey, Director of Composition Services

Contents at a Glance

Maps at a Glance

Table of Contents

Introduction

*Y*ou've probably seen the ads. Canoodling 60-something couples — all tanned and self-assured — sipping margaritas on deck. Smiling, perfect families splashing in pools. Groups of friends with model looks and zero body fat playing hoops. Is this for real?

We gotta be honest, not all cruise passengers are this attractive. Some are, yes, but most are just like us. Regular ol' folks that come in all shapes and sizes. If there was ever a melting pot of a vacation, a cruise is it.

And that's a part of a cruise's appeal. Considering the majority of cruise ships are huge suckers, carrying between 2,000 and 4,000 passengers apiece, it's no wonder they attract such a wide social swath. Sure, the small ships and over-the-top luxurious ones stand apart from the crowd, but most boil down to floating high-rise hotels. Before you wonder why you don't just go to a Sheraton then, consider that a cruise ship, no matter its size, has its own unique allure.

The water. Yes, you float around vast undulating seas of deep blue water. Hotels, of course, are planted firmly on the ground. Then there's the fact that you can move around and see three or four or five different countries or cities in a week. Can't take that Sheraton island-hopping, now can you?

While the newest ships are as modern as any Hyatt or Hilton, they're also steeped in maritime traditions that go back forever and lend even the most high-tech ship some old-time charm. Massive steel anchors, coils and coils of line, gangways, and that haunting moaning horn are as relevant today as they were eons ago. Basically what we're saying is that swooshing through the waves in the middle of nowhere the way our ancestors did — albeit with big diesel engines, GPS, and gin-and-tonics delivered right to our hot tubs — is a pretty cool thing to do.

We should know: Between us we've done 150 cruises or so — a few together, most apart, which is a good thing since we're married to different people — to everywhere from the tried-and-true Caribbean to far-flung mind-alternating places such as Siberia, the Galapagos, and Thailand. We have our favorites for sure, but through the years we've grown to appreciate just about all of 'em. Who can argue with a sunset melting off the bow, fruity rum drink in hand? A cruise manages to both throw you in the middle of the social fray and take you away from it all.

That all sounds fine and good, you may be saying, but what about your fears of being stuck in a small dark cabin or getting seasick? Don't worry so much. Most cabins have windows and many have private balconies too, so you can step out into the fresh sea air whenever the mood strikes. Plus, who wants to spend a lot of time in a cabin when there's so much else to do around the ship. As for feeling queasy, allow us to remind you, we're well into the 21st century. Most ships are equipped with stabilizers to keep them ultrasteady. Plus, most ships are so big that chances are you'll barely realize you're moving at all.

At its basic core, a cruise is the antidote to worry and stress. A large crew is aboard to take care of your cabin, your children, your appetite, and that sore back of yours. From spas to playrooms, sushi bars, steak houses, and movie theaters, you won't be wanting for much. And if a smaller ship is more your cup of tea, you'll find fewer amenities, but much more intimacy and really great itineraries. Pretty much, whatever it is you want out of a vacation, you can find it on one of the hundreds of ships out there, from rustic schooners to Vegas-style megaships and luxurious vessels covered in miles of marble and brocade.

The hardest part is dealing with all the "difficult choices" you'll face each day. Allow us to elaborate. Should you:

- Go to the gym and work out?
- Sit on the deck and chat with other passengers (or better yet, watch other passengers — cruise ships are prime people-watching opportunities)?
- Find a quiet place to read?
- Have a massage?
- Take a nap or watch a movie in your cabin?
- Join the men's sexy legs contest by the pool?
- Get a haircut?
- Sign up for a wine-tasting seminar?
- Take one of the organized shore excursions on days when the ship stops in port or just head off on your own?

With so much to do, you can't possibly do it all, and who needs to. If achieving your vacation nirvana means staring off into sea and doing nothing, so be it. As a wise old salt once said, "Hey, whatever floats your boat."

And one more thing, cruising is a great value vacation: For one price, you get your cabin, all your meals and entertainment, a slew of onboard activities, and the chance to visit a bunch of different places and unpack only once. Still, we have to be honest, you'll likely spring for plenty of extras once on board, from cocktails, soda, and bottled water to specialty restaurants, facials, craps, and lots more. Of course, the captain isn't _forcing_ you to buy a new dress in the ship's boutique or have your hair done; that's up to you and your willpower. For the most part, unless you're a totally penny-pinching, antisocial grouch, a cruise adds up to one heck of an attractive vacation experience.

About This Book

We want to make sure that you have a totally relaxing and memorable cruise vacation, which is why we got together to write this book. And we gotta to tell you, all those research cruises we needed to take to become such experts, well, it was just terribly grueling work . . . sweat sweat . . . groan groan.

Okay, so we can't expect sympathy. But we do want a little respect. We've done our homework so that you don't have to do. In the pages that follow, we try to anticipate every question you may have about the cruise experience and provide the answers. For first-time cruisers, we describe what to expect from the cruise experience, pre-cruise to post-cruise, with the nitty-gritty on everything from your first look at a cruise brochure or Web site to clearing customs at the end of the trip. The goal is to make the experience easy and familiar, even if you've never set foot on a ship in your life.

If you're not a first-timer, you probably picked out this book because you don't want to have to think much to plan your trip. And you won't have to if you read on. We've laid out everything you need to know in a style that is quick and easy, yet exceedingly comprehensive.

Of course, you don't have to read the whole book. And you don't have to start at the beginning either. This is a reference book. Check out the table of contents or the index and read the parts that peak your interest.

The main point of this book is to show you that a cruise is just plain fun. It's not brain surgery, for Pete's sake, to figure out that a cruise is a light and easy and, typically, quite an addictive vacation choice. From the time you walk up the gangway humming the theme from *The Love Boat* to the time you get home, dump your suitcase on the floor, and take yet another look at all those great pictures you took, it's all about pleasure. In the spirit of fun, we took the liberty of having some fun writing this book. So, c'mon aboard and enjoy the ride. If you're really not the type who likes to smile or laugh, then you may want to look for your receipt and take this book back to the store.

Dummies Post-it® Flags

As you're reading this book, you'll find information that you'll want to reference as you plan or enjoy your trip — whether it be a new ship, a must-see attraction, or a must-try tour. Mark these pages with the handy Post-it® Flags included in this book to help make your trip planning easier!

Conventions Used in This Book

This guide is designed for easy reference. We include reviews of all the best cruise lines; overviews of the most popular cruise ports in the Caribbean, Alaska, the Mediterranean, and some other destinations; and a quick-and-easy introduction to everything you're likely to experience when planning and taking a cruise. The attractions, along with telephone numbers, are often in **bold** type to draw your attention to them, and the ship names appear in *italic*. If an attraction, hotel, restaurant, or what-have-you has a toll-free number, we list that number first, in bold type, right after a tiny little telephone, which looks like this: ☎.

For sanity (ours) and brevity, whenever we talk about temperatures, the degrees are in Fahrenheit, and when we talk about prices, we mean U.S. dollars unless otherwise noted.

 People rarely pay full price for a cruise. That's why when we list sample rates, we list travel agency rates — the actual prices you'll pay — not the full brochure rate. Who knows why the lines inflate their brochure rates only to sell their cruises at a discount anyway, but it's an industry tradition and, if nothing else, makes you think you're getting a really good deal. Usually, you really are.

We list the range of brochure prices based on the following three basic types of accommodations:

✔ Inside cabin (one without windows)

✔ Outside cabin (one with windows)

✔ Suite

Foolish Assumptions

As we wrote this book, we made some assumptions about you and your needs as a traveler. We assumed the following:

✔ You may be a virgin cruiser looking for some guidance while booking your first cruise.

✔ You may be an experienced traveler who just wants some quick, easy tips about planning a cruise.

✔ You may be an experienced cruiser who wants an easy-to-use guide to the cruise lines (both big and small) and ports of call.

✔ You've cruised before in the Caribbean but want to try something new, like Alaska, the Mediterranean, New England, or western Mexico.

✔ You don't have time to wade through volumes of detailed information; you just want a book that cuts to the chase so that you can easily find a ship best suited to your unique personality.

If you fit any of these criteria, *Cruise Vacations For Dummies 2006* gives you the information you want.

How This Book Is Organized

This book is organized in a roughly chronological fashion (although you don't have to read it that way), taking you from the basics of choosing a cruise through the particulars. We detail the reasons you're going to sea: visiting great ports of call and having a ball on board as you sail from one port to the other.

Part 1: Getting Started

We start with the best of the best, our recommendations of top ships, top destinations, and top things to do on board. We get into why a cruise is a great vacation choice for most people and blow holes in some common misconceptions about cruising — that it may be too expensive or that you may get bored, for example. And we offer some suggestions of how to find the cruise and cruise experience that best suits you.

Part II: Planning Your Cruise

Part II helps you start figuring out what your trip may cost. We take you through the process of finding and booking a cruise, including when to book it and how to find a good travel agent. We also tell you what you need to know before you get on the ship — from buying travel insurance, to getting there, to packing tips, to passport requirements and how much cash to bring.

Part III: All Aboard: The Cruise Experience

Part III covers what you can expect on board during your cruise, including entertainment, food, spa offerings, shopping, gambling, and children's activities. And even though you don't want to think about it yet, this part also includes a synopsis of what you need to consider at the end of your cruise, including tipping and Customs regulations.

Part IV: Ship Shapes: The Cruise Lines and Their Ships

Part IV discusses the major cruise lines and their vessels and offers honest reviews to help you target the ship most likely to give you the vacation experience you desire.

Part V: Calling All Ports: Where to Go and Why

To find out where the ships sail from and to, check out Part V, which offers specifics on points of embarkation and ports of call. We offer advice on how to make the most of your time if you plan to stay a few days in the port city before or after your cruise, and we highlight the top attractions and best shore excursions at the major ports of call in the Caribbean, Alaska, the Mediterranean, the Mexican Riviera, Hawaii, and New England and eastern Canada.

Part VI: The Part of Tens

The Part of Tens includes our picks of the most classic onboard experiences, as well as our personal favorite stories from years of professional cruising.

Appendix: Quick Concierge

The Appendix lists toll-free phone numbers for cruise lines and airlines and a directory of top travel agencies.

Icons Used in This Book

Keep an eye peeled for these icons, which appear in the margins.

Find money-saving tips and/or great deals next to this icon.

This icon marks our choices for the best ships, destinations, and activities.

Some cruise lines, ships, and ports offer activities or features that go above and beyond. This icon gives credit where credit is due.

Watch for the Heads Up icon to identify annoying or potentially dangerous situations such as tourist traps, unsafe neighborhoods, rip-offs, and other things to be aware of.

The Kid Friendly icon reviews ship features, activities, restaurants, and ports that are particularly appealing to children or families.

Find useful advice on things to do and ways to schedule your time when you see the Tip icon.

Where to Go from Here

Now you're ready to go! Get that Hawaiian shirt out of the closet, put on a Jimmy Buffett CD, fix yourself a piña colada, and settle down to choose the cruise of your dreams. Don't worry: If your dream doesn't include loud shirts and party music, there are cruises for the Beethoven and bow tie set too!

Part I
Getting Started

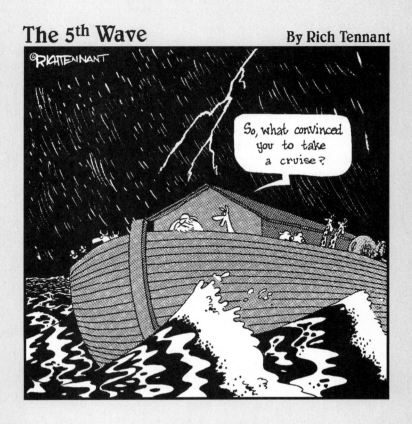

So, what convinced you to take a cruise?

In this part . . .

*T*hink of this part of the book as your quick intro course, where you discover the different kinds of cruises you can choose from, the different regions where they sail, and the differences between ship types. We also give you our picks for the best ships, lines, and experiences, and run through a list of common cruise misconceptions, shooting 'em all down like clay pigeons. Blam!

Chapter 1

Choosing Cruising: The Best of the Best

In This Chapter
▶ Picking the top cruise lines
▶ Finding the best ships to fit your interests
▶ Charting the top ports around the world

*I*n the decade-plus that we've been writing about cruises, we can't even count the number of times people have asked us, "So, what's the best cruise line?" And y'know what? We hate that question. We hate it because there's really no single answer. It's like asking, "What's the best food?" or "What's the best beer?" It all depends on your taste buds and the kind of experience you want to have. Spicy? Adventurous? Healthy? Indulgent? Or how about the cruise equivalent of a burger and a Bud?

That said, some cruise lines are clearly top-shelf, no matter what aisle in the supermarket you're browsing. And this is the chapter where you can find 'em.

You can find the "Best of the Best" icon signaling the contents of this chapter throughout the book.

The Best of the Mainstream Lines

Here's the pick of the litter among the big boys. Turn to Chapter 11 for more info.

✔ **Royal Caribbean International:** Royal Caribbean's Radiance-class ships (*Radiance, Brilliance, Serenade,* and *Jewel of the Seas*) are its most elegant vessels to date, combining a sleek, seagoing exterior; a nautically themed interior; and acres of windows. The Voyager-class ships (*Voyager, Explorer, Adventure, Navigator,* and *Mariner of the Seas*) are the archetypal activities ships and maybe the first vessels to satisfy the old "city at sea" cliché. The line's new "ultra-Voyager" ship, *Freedom of the Seas,* is scheduled to debut in April

2006 and will be an even bigger and more activity-packed ship than its Voyager-class cousins.

✔ **Princess Cruises:** Princess's huge but cozy *Diamond Princess* and *Sapphire Princess* are the line's most beautiful ships to date. They combine gorgeous exterior lines with wood-heavy, old-world lounges; an innovative dining plan; and a great covered promenade that allows you to stand right in the bow. The smaller *Coral Princess* and *Island Princess* are big winners, too, with similar décor and a smaller size that lets them traverse the Panama Canal.

✔ **Celebrity Cruises:** With their elegant modern décor, incredible spas, great service, and over-the-top alternative restaurants, Celebrity's Millennium-class ships (*Millennium, Infinity, Summit,* and *Constellation*) are some of the best mainstream megaships out there — classy yet affordable. Celebrity's older Century-class ships (*Century, Galaxy,* and *Mercury*) aren't too far behind, either.

The Best Ships for Luxury

Got some bucks to spend? Wanna be treated like Charles and Camilla? Here are your ships. Turn to Chapter 12 for all the details.

✔ **Silversea Cruises:** This line offers the best overall highbrow small ships, with top-quality cuisine, roomy suites, and over-the-top service — including complimentary and free-flowing Philipponnat champagne.

✔ **Crystal Cruises:** Crystal's dream ships offer the best of two worlds: pampering service and scrumptious cuisine on ships that are big enough to offer plenty of outdoor deck space, generous fitness facilities, four restaurants, and more than half a dozen bars and entertainment venues. Crystal's California ethic tends to keep the atmosphere more mingly and chatty than aboard the more sober ships, such as those from Seabourn and Silversea.

✔ **Cunard:** *Queen Mary 2 (QM2)* has her very own niche in the luxe market — and in the cruise market as a whole, for that matter. Although she's too enormous to offer the kind of intimate luxury you get with ships from Silversea, Seabourn, and SeaDream, she can give you a pretty close idea of what life aboard the great old ocean liners was like — a pretty luxe perk all in itself.

✔ **Seabourn Cruise Line:** Small and intimate, these quiet megayachts lavish upper-crust guests with doting service (courtesy of 157 crewmembers to just 208 guests) and very fine cuisine. Staff members greet you by name from the moment you check in, and your wish is their command.

✔ **SeaDream Yacht Club:** Even smaller and more intimate than Seabourn, SeaDream's 110-passenger yachts are also pitched to a younger and more active demographic. Elegant but casual, they carry along jet skis, mountain bikes, and kayaks for jaunts around ports such as St. Barts and Monte Carlo.

The Best Ships for Families

The trick with family cruises is offering not just family-friendly activities and entertainment, but offering things for adults to do, too, whenever they can get away from the kids. These cruise lines do. See Chapter 9 for info on family-oriented cruising activities and Chapters 11 and 12 for more about the ships.

✔ **Carnival Cruise Lines:** Carnival has made the move from party line to family line, with great kids' facilities on the Destiny-, Spirit-, and Conquest-class vessels.

✔ **Disney Cruise Line:** Well, duh. If Disney can't do family right, who can? This is the most well-developed children's program at sea. Kudos also to Disney's adult activities, even though their ships do without casinos in the interest of keeping kiddo on the straight and narrow.

✔ **Princess Cruises:** The *Coral Princess* and *Island Princess* and the Grand-class ships each have a spacious children's playroom, a sizable piece of fenced-in outside deck for toddlers, and a deck with a wading pool for older kids. Teen centers have computers, video games, and a sound system, and the ones on the Grand-class ships even have teen hot tubs and private sunbathing decks.

✔ **Royal Caribbean International:** Royal Caribbean's Voyager-class ships, with their rock-climbing walls, ice-skating rinks, in-line skating tracks, miniature golf, and full-size basketball courts, are the absolute best choice for active families — particularly those with teens. The onboard Johnny Rockets restaurants and main street–like entertainment promenades hold kids' interest pretty well, too.

✔ **Cunard:** Strange but true, the classy *QM2* also has great facilities and programs for kids, starting at age 1. Aside from Disney, no other line offers such extensive care for children so young. There's even a special daily children's teatime that's perfect as an early dinner, and programming is free up until midnight daily.

The Best Romantic Cruises

Some cruise lines cater to the amorous more than others. Here are our top picks:

✔ **Star Clippers:** With the wind in your hair and sails fluttering overhead, the top decks of the four- and five-masted *Royal Clipper* and *Star Clipper* provide a most romantic setting. Below decks, the comfy cabins, lounge, and dining room make these ships the most comfortable adventures on the sea. See Chapter 13.

✔ **Windstar Cruises:** Pure romance is a day with your loved one in a private cove or another secluded spot with one of Windstar's big sailing ships anchored offshore. Windstar offers a truly unique cruise experience, giving passengers the delicious illusion of adventure (by stopping at small coves and such), along with relatively sizable small vessels and high-quality cuisine and service. See Chapter 13.

✔ **Cunard:** Like real royalty, *QM2* was born with certain duties attendant to its station, and one of the biggest of those duties is to embody the romance of transatlantic travel and bring it into the new century. Take a stroll around that Promenade Deck, dine in that fabulous dining room, and thrill to be out in the middle of the Atlantic on nearly a billion dollars worth of Atlantic thoroughbred. See Chapter 12.

✔ **SeaDream Yacht Club:** SeaDream's small *SeaDream I* and *II* are ultraluxe in a languidly romantic sort of way, with comfy Balinese daybeds lining the teak decks, free-flowing champagne, and a table for two anytime you want it. See Chapter 12.

✔ **Windjammer Barefoot Cruises:** Well, what is romance, anyway? For some folks it's luxury and baubles. For others it's a trip cross-country on their Harley, stopping to catch the view at every scenic overlook and then finding a good bar at night. That sound like you? Windjammer's your cruise line. See Chapter 13.

The Best Party Cruises

Looking for a party at sea? Try one of these cruise lines:

✔ **Windjammer Barefoot Cruises:** Erotic tart-eating contest, anyone? Okay, so that's only on their singles cruises, but you get the idea. On regular cruises, the free rum punch, cheap beers, and visits to legendary Caribbean beach bars make sure you'll be reeling like the proverbial drunken sailor, if that's your thing. See Chapter 13.

✔ **Carnival Cruise Lines:** What, you thought Carnival's ships were called "The Fun Ships" because they could tell a good joke? Back in the day, this is where you went for a full-time party cruise. Things have toned down a lot since then, but the pool deck is still bustling, and the discos and nightspots hop until the early morning hours — especially on the short 3- and 4-night weekend cruises. See Chapter 11.

- **Royal Caribbean International:** As with Carnival, lots of Royal Caribbean's customers are in their 20s, 30s, and 40s, with short cruises drawing the hardier partiers. For an exciting Saturday-night-out-on-the-town barhopping kind of experience, the Voyager-class ships feature a multideck, boulevard-like promenade running down their centers, lined with shops, bars, cafes, and entertainment outlets. See Chapter 11.

- **Norwegian Cruise Line:** NCL's newest ships are designed to give the illusion of a night out in the big city, with ten restaurants, tons of bars, a clipboard full of activities, and some of the best entertainment at sea. An added plus: The ships all have casual dress codes and open-seating dining, creating more mingling opportunities. As on Carnival and Royal Caribbean, it's the short 3- and 4-night itineraries on their older ships that keep the party funkin' right. See Chapter 11.

The Best Small-Ship Cruises

If the big ships aren't your thing, slide on over to one of these small-ship operators, who put more of an emphasis on learning about the destination than on shopping, sightseeing, and Big Whoopin' Fun. See Chapter 13 for the scoop on each.

- **Maine Windjammer Association (Maine coast):** Owner-operated historic schooners sailing along one of the prettiest stretches of coast in the whole country — how do you top that? It's like summer camp for adults, with a rustic vibe and real, live wind in your hair.

- **Clipper, Cruise West, Lindblad, and American Safari Cruises (Baja/Sea of Cortez):** For cruise ships, Mexico's Baja Peninsula is like the bizarro Alaska. It's where the small ships (and the humpback whales) go for winter, substituting Baja's red dirt, cacti, and ruggedly beautiful coastal islands for Alaska's moss, rain forests, and glaciers.

- **Delta Queen (Mississippi River):** Mark Twain fan? Head for Delta Queen, operating three real Mississippi River stern-wheelers that look so in-place on the river that you'll think you've gone through a time warp. Bonuses? Cajun and Southern cooking, river storytelling, and a calliope to complement a music program full of Dixieland jazz and swing.

- **Lindblad Expeditions (Antarctica, Galapagos, and other exotic destinations):** This preeminent small-ship line for a really adventurous, learning-oriented experience is all the better for its recently formed alliance with the National Geographic Society. The Society gets a permanent presence on the sea, and Lindblad gets a slew of scientists, photographers, and other lecturers to wow guests.

- **Glacier Bay Cruiseline (Alaska):** Glacier Bay Cruiseline's tiny *Wilderness Explorer* and slightly larger *Wilderness Adventurer* are the best for exploring wild Alaska, carrying a fleet of sea kayaks and orienting their itineraries almost entirely toward wilderness areas, with passengers kayaking and hiking almost every day.

- **Cruise West and Clipper Cruise Line (Alaska/Russian Far East):** Want a real expedition? Cruise West's *Spirit of Oceanus* and Clipper's *Clipper Odyssey* offer 2-week cruises that sail from mainland Alaska across the Bering Sea to far-eastern Russia, also taking in remote, little-visited islands along Alaska's western coast. It's like sailing right off the map of civilization.

The Best Ships for Uncompromising Gourmands

Food and cruising go hand and hand. Find the best dining on these cruise lines:

- **Crystal Cruises:** Although all the food you get on Crystal's ships is first-class, their reservations-only Asian specialty restaurant on *Serenity* is the best at sea, with cuisine overseen by Master Chef Nobuyuki "Nobu" Matsuhisa. The accouterments help set the tone, too — chopsticks, sake served in tiny sake cups and decanters, and sushi served on thick blocky square glass platters. An Asian-themed buffet lunch, offered at least once per cruise, gives passengers an awesome spread, from jumbo shrimp to chicken and beef satays to stir-fry dishes. See Chapter 12.

- **Seabourn Cruise Lines:** Nothing quite compares to dining on the outdoor deck of Seabourn's Veranda Café, which offers casual dinners most nights. With the ships' wakes shushing just below, you have a rare opportunity to dine with the sea breezes and starry night sky surrounding you. Asian, Mediterranean, and steakhouse-style menus are featured. See Chapter 12.

- **Silversea Cruises:** Depart at sunset from port, and the windowed, candlelit Terrace Cafe alternative restaurant on each of this line's four ships becomes a window to the passing scenery and a home for some of the best food at sea. Reservations are required for the theme menus: Asian night starts with sushi and sashimi, and a French feast begins with foie gras, followed by a scallop and rata-touille salad, beef tenderloin, and a warm chocolate tart with raspberries. Excellent wines and all spirits are included in the cruise rates. See Chapter 12.

- **Radisson Seven Seas Cruises:** The award-winning chefs aboard all the line's ships produce artful culinary presentations that compare favorably to those of New York's or San Francisco's top restaurants, and the waiters are some of the industry's best. See Chapter 12.

- ✔ **Celebrity Cruises:** Among the mainstream lines, it doesn't get any better than the intimate, elegant, reservations-only alternative restaurants on Celebrity's Millennium-class ships, with their artifacts from classic Golden Age ocean liners, their doting waiters, their tableside cooking, and their musicians playing elegant period pieces. The experience takes about three hours and costs $30 a person, but it's well worth it. See Chapter 11.

- ✔ **Oceania Cruises:** Oceania's dining experience is near the top in the mainstream category, with menus created by chef Jacques Pepin, and passengers able to dine at any of four different restaurants, all of them excellent. Service is doting and fine-tuned, even at the casual semi-buffet option, offered on an outdoor terrace that's elegant and totally romantic at sunset. See Chapter 11.

The Best Ships for Spa Addicts

One company (Steiner Leisure) runs the vast majority of cruise ship spas, but facilities vary. Here are your best bets.

- ✔ **Celebrity Cruises:** Celebrity's Millennium-class and Century-class ships are at the top of the spa heap. Their huge, beautiful AquaSpa facilities manage to combine a huge repertoire of the latest wraps, packs, soaks, and massages with striking aesthetics inspired by Japanese gardens and Moorish and Turkish bathhouses. See Chapter 11.

- ✔ **Windstar Cruises:** Considering the *Wind Surf*'s intimate, 308-passenger size, she has a surprisingly large and well-accoutered spa facility, with prebookable spa packages combining six or more treatments tailored to both men and women. See Chapter 13.

- ✔ **Royal Caribbean:** The two-level spa complexes aboard the line's Voyager-class ships are among the largest and best accoutered there are, and not just for the peaceful waiting area with its New Age tropical bird-song music. The Radiance-class ships have huge, exotically themed solariums and 13 treatment rooms, including a special steam-room complex featuring heated, tiled chaise longues and special showers simulating tropical rain and fog. See Chapter 11.

- ✔ **Radisson Seven Seas:** The spas aboard the 490-passenger *Seven Seas Navigator* and 700-passenger *Seven Seas Mariner* and *Seven Seas Voyager* are some of the few not run by the ubiquitous Steiner. Instead, the French spa company Carita imports staffs and hairdressers from Parisian salons. See Chapter 12.

The Best Ports of Call

You don't spend all your cruise time on the water. The following ports are particularly intriguing:

✔ **In the Caribbean:** We like Cozumel for its wonderful Mexican flavor, party atmosphere, great buys on crafts, nearby ruins, and excellent snorkeling. Key West is a hoot-and-a-half with its raucous bars, funky history, great seafood, and cast of street performers and other characters. St. Barts is exclusive, pretty, lush, and loaded with celebrities, while St. John (U.S. Virgin Islands) is more natural, with half its land preserved as a national park. See Chapter 15.

✔ **In Alaska:** Sitka and Juneau are our favorites. Juneau has to be the prettiest state capital anywhere in America, fronted by the Gastineau Channel, backed by Mount Juneau and Mount Roberts, and otherwise surrounded by wilderness, including the huge Juneau Icefield and the Mendenhall Glacier. Sitka, a little off the beaten path, and thus less overwhelmed by cruise passengers, is a gorgeous little town packed full of Russian, American, and Tlingit Native history. See Chapter 16.

✔ **In the Mediterranean:** Venice is our favorite, a city where every view is museum-quality. For history, you can't top Athens or Rome. For quaintness, you can't beat Portofino (Italy); for dramatic port scenery, there's Santorini (Greece); and for shopping, there's Kuşadasi (Turkey), with its wonderful rugs at affordable prices, not to mention its proximity to Ephesus, an amazing ancient archeological site. Other faves include Barcelona and Istanbul — both impressively exotic. See Chapter 17.

✔ **On the Mexican Riviera:** Call us cheesy, but we like Cabo San Lucas, with its beaches, bars, beaches, bars, and beaches. For more authentic Mexican culture, give us Mazatlan's historic district, with its shady streets, opera house, and rugged coastline. And then there's Puerto Vallarta, with its lovely seaside promenade and profusion of art galleries. See Chapter 18.

✔ **In Eastern Canada and New England:** Newport, Rhode Island, is classic New England with its cobblestone streets and colorful yachts. It's no wonder America's bluebloods built so many absurdly ornate mansions here in the late 19th and early 20th centuries. If you like ships, Halifax, Nova Scotia, is maritime central, with a great museum featuring a raft of *Titanic* artifacts and tons of other shippy stuff. Perched on a cliff-top overlooking the St. Lawrence River, Quebec City, Quebec, is just about the prettiest port of call in North America, very French and full of culture. The oldest part of the city dates back nearly 400 years. See Chapter 18.

✔ **In Hawaii:** Honolulu makes a great embarkation port, with legendary Waikiki Beach, cool shopping, and the moving memorials at Pearl Harbor. For natural beauty, Kauai is hard to beat, but if your idea of fun is trekking around a bunch of volcanoes, it's the Big Island for you. See Chapter 18.

Chapter 2

Is a Cruise for Youse? The Whats, Wheres, and Whys

ruising is like comfort food — that pizza, meatloaf, baked ziti, or double cheeseburger you order when life gets too stressful. It's like a shot of Prozac mixed with a ride on the Ferris wheel. It's a mai tai in the Jacuzzi while the tiki torches dance. It's a chance to see the world while remaining in your comfort zone. It's a chance, for once in your tweaked-out 21st-century life, to not have to plan anything at all. The captain's on his bridge and all's right with the world. The only question left to answer is whether cruising is for you.

The History of Cruising, from Soup to Nuts

Time was, hardly anybody would ever say they were going on a cruise unless it was around a bay in their sailboat. Those were the old days, when stepping aboard a ship meant you had places to go and things to do, and that ship was the only way to get from point A across the ocean to point B. Sometimes that wasn't a very pleasant experience.

Cruising before cruising was cruising

In 1842, author Charles Dickens, along with 86 others, booked passage on the mail ship *Britannia,* operated by Samuel Cunard, founder of the Cunard Line. Writing in *American Notes* about his journey from Liverpool to Nova Scotia and then to Boston, Dickens described the quarters as coffinlike and his fellow passengers as of varying shades of green — though he claimed he only felt woozy, not full-on seasick.

Conditions had improved by the time Mark Twain took a transatlantic voyage on the steamship *Quaker City* in 1867. Twain described his cabin as having "room to turn around in, but not to swing a cat in, at least with entire security to the cat." In *The Innocents Abroad,* Twain wrote, "If there is one thing in the world that will make a man peculiarly and insufferably self-conceited, it is to have his stomach behave himself, the first day at sea, when nearly all his comrades are seasick."

It wasn't until late in the 19th century that shipping companies realized they could make money not just by transporting travelers, cargo, mail, and immigrants from point A to point B, but also by selling a luxurious experience at sea. Most historians agree that the first real cruise ship was P&O's *Ceylon,* which in 1881 was converted to a lavish cruising yacht for carrying wealthy, adventurous guests on world cruises. Six years later, a Scottish company launched the *St. Sunniva,* the first steamer built expressly for cruising. But cruising was still a sideline. The big money was to be had in selling passage from place to place, both for the rich and for the huddled masses booking cheap steerage berths. That was the state of things for eight decades, as the steamship era entered its golden age, weathered two world wars, and plugged along as a vital link between the continents — the only way to get from here to there and back again. It was a time when images of glamorous ship travel made their way into the popular imagination, and everyone wanted to be out at sea with the big movie stars, taking in the sea air and the giddy, tuxedo-clad nightlife.

Between the mid-1930s and the late 1950s, many steamship (and later cruise ship) traditions were born and became entrenched: shuffleboard, bridge, Ping-Pong, onboard movies, pool games, bingo, art classes, dance lessons, singles' parties, midnight buffets, and cocktails, cocktails, cocktails. Things were swingin', and everyone thought it would go on forever. They were wrong.

Entering the modern cruise era

In 1958, a sea change occurred when Pan Am flew the first nonstop jet flight from New York to Paris. In the blink of an eye, passenger liners went from being the only game in town to being a slowpoke anachronism. Shipping companies scrambled to fill berths any way they knew how, and pleasure cruising formed a big chunk of their survival strategy. It helped, but not enough — especially for older ships like the original *Queen Mary,* which had been built without air-conditioning. Within ten years, most of the world's liner fleet would be mothballed or sent to the breakers. Only the strong survived — and the innovative.

In 1966, Ted Arison, who would later form Carnival Cruise Lines, and Knut Kloster, who would later form Norwegian Cruise Line, introduced the *Sunward,* a converted car/passenger ferry that debuted as a Caribbean cruise ship. The *Sunward* began offering 3- and 4-day cruises from Florida to the Caribbean and back again, and the success of the venture quickly drew competition.

In the years that followed, established lines such as Cunard and Holland America adapted their Old World–liner mentality to cruising, while brash new lines such as Carnival rebuilt cruising from the ground up, creating the kind of fun-in-the-sun, cruise-ship-as-vacation-destination experience that's dominated the market for the past three decades. In 1977, the young cruise industry got a big boost when ABC debuted its TV series *The Love Boat,* which set up yet another new paradigm: cruise ship as romance machine. Using the real ships *Island Princess* and *Pacific Princess* (of the young Princess Cruises) as floating sets, the show was a veritable commercial for cruising, shown weekly in prime time for a full hour.

Cruising today

Today we're in another place entirely. While Carnival's vessels still offer their proven fun-ship formula, and Princess still occasionally trots out *The Love Boat* cast as spokespeople, the cruise industry has grown outward to encompass options for almost everybody. Yes, you can still do the glitzy Vegas thing, but you can also sail on ships that are nearly as grand and formal as the Golden Age ocean liners. Yes, you can do a weekend party cruise, but you can also sail to the jungles of Central America on a small expedition ship. Today's largest vessels are (get this) about four times the size of the *Titanic,* with onboard amenities such as lavish gyms and spas; intimate, reservations-only restaurants; multiple entertainment options, from big production shows to intimate music recitals; and sports options such as golf, basketball, and (on some of the Royal Caribbean ships) rock-climbing and ice skating. In 2004, Cunard introduced a planetarium aboard its new *Queen Mary 2,* while Princess started showing movies on a drive-in-style screen above the Pool Deck. Meanwhile, smaller lines began offering cruises to parts of the world you may not ever get to otherwise, such as Libya and Siberia.

Cruising: What's In It for You?

Today, people choose a cruise vacation for a variety of reasons: It's easy to plan; it's like having a full-time designated driver; you get to visit different towns and countries without having to schlep from hotel to hotel; somebody told them it was a good bargain; or their Uncle Bob told them it was a blast. Whatever your reason, you're in good company.

No matter your reason for sailing, you're buying the same basic commodity from almost all the cruise lines: relaxation. Sure, getting aboard the ship that first day can be a hassle (see Chapter 6), but after you get through that ordeal your experience should be relatively stress-free — just unpack your bags and the rest of the week is yours. No need to make dinner plans, since the kitchen crew is busy preparing more than you'll ever be able to eat — and it's included in the price. No need to buy tickets to the theater, since it's right down the corridor and free for all, just like the nightclubs and discos. No need to even carry cash, since practically all ships charge extras — bar bills, excursions, spa treatments, gift shop purchases, casino losses — to your onboard account, to be settled up later.

Pondering cruise growth conspiracy theories

In 1980, the U.S. cruise biz catered to less than a million and a half passengers — and that was at the height of *The Love Boat* buzz. By 1990, that number was up to 3.6 million, and 15 years later it's over 10 million. What's to account for the surge? More leisure time? Hardly. Americans are working more now than they ever have. Disposable income? Are you kidding, with gas over $2 a gallon? Baby boomers getting older and not being able to hoist their own packs anymore? Nope, cruise demographics have fallen over the past decade, with the average age now down around 50.

We put it down to a confluence of events. First, a ton of new ships were built over the past decade, most so much bigger and so much more technologically amazing than their predecessors that they were almost guaranteed to attract attention. Second, all those ships were in competition with each other, which meant cruises were selling for insanely low prices. Third, some cruise lines hatched really, really good advertising campaigns (yo, Royal Caribbean, good job). And fourth, the world went completely NUTS, with terrorism and wars and famine and misery and global warming and invading armies and terror alert levels and duct tape and who knows what all else; and in an environment like that, who wants to go trekking off on their own? It's the "cruise ship as protective bubble" syndrome.

Or, maybe people just like to cruise. That's another theory.

A resort by day . . .

Cruise lines learned long ago that they're not just competing with each other; they're also competing with land-based resorts. Consequently, they've pretty much figured out how to offer almost anything a land resort does, except at a speed of 20-plus knots. Most cruise ships (aside from the small adventure vessels) give you big honkin' spas armed with hot rocks, warm muds, and a slew of bizarro treatments that make you feel like warm, happy jello. They give you huge children's playrooms and teen centers designed to keep your kids occupied while you go all jellolike. When jello time is over, the ships offer activities that range from silly pool games and craft classes to lectures, computer workshops, cooking demonstrations, wine tastings, dance classes, and even scuba instruction. Depending on the ship, sports enthusiasts may find jogging tracks, volleyball, basketball, paddle tennis, water polo, aqua aerobics, rock-climbing, ice- and in-line skating, and even bungee trampolines, the latter on Royal Caribbean's *Enchantment of the Seas*. Oh, and of course there's always shuffleboard. Old habits die hard.

Want more? How about video arcades and movie theaters showing recent releases? Or live sports events beamed by satellite to the ship's sports bar? Or just lounging by the pool or on your private balcony, reading *The Da Vinci Code*. Oh, wait, you read it already? Silly us . . .

. . . A place to keep your stuff while in port

Now remember, you won't be on the ship all the time, so chuck that "I'd go nuts stuck on a ship for a week" excuse right now. Most weeklong itineraries spend two days at sea, allowing you to do all the activities we just talked about, and spend the other four days visiting ports, where you can either wander off on your own or sign up for one of the line's organized shore excursions. Generally you arrive in the morning and depart just after dinner — enough time to get a gander at the local sights, spend some time on the beach, head off into the woods looking for wildlife, or whatever it is people do in the hundreds of port cities and towns the cruise lines visit worldwide.

. . . And an urban playground by night

Nighttime is one of the liveliest times on a cruise ship. You have the multicourse dinner to look forward to, for one thing. Then, depending on the ship, you can check out the show, hit the comedy club, dance (or try to), win at the casino (or try to), sing the hits at a karaoke session (or try to), or just throw back a few stiff ones at one of a dozen bars. You can get through the night as cheaply or as expensively as you like, because even though the cruise lines have begun offering a lot of added-cost extras, the basics of the experience — food, entertainment, and most activities, are still free, free, free.

Keepin' It Fresh: What Keeps 'em Coming Back

Cruise ship years are like dog years — they don't last as long as people years. As a result, most of the ships that are carrying those 10 million annual cruisers have been launched within the past ten years, during a frantic period of construction that finally began winding down in 2005. With bookings up and the need decreasing to fill more new ships, prices — which were ridiculously low through 2003 and into 2004 — finally started leveling off in 2005. Oops! You missed the big bargains! But don't worry, it's still a good deal, and the cruise lines are busy adding other new stuff besides ships, to make sure your interest stays piqued.

Like what? Think new destinations, new activities on and off the ship, new dining options, and new entertainment. Some other trends? How about extensive refurbishments of older ships, bringing them more in line with what the newbies offer. Royal Caribbean got the ball rolling on this with its big 2003 refurb of the 1991 ship *Monarch of the Seas,* followed by redos of *Empress, Sovereign,* and *Enchantment of the Seas* — the latter of which was chopped in half and welded back together with a new midsection, increasing her size substantially. Holland America also got into the revitalization act big-time in 2004 and 2005, upgrading its older vessels to the standards of its new "Signature of Excellence" initiative, with comfier cabins, a new culinary arts center, new restaurants and Internet cafes, and vastly improved kids' and teens' facilities. Disney teen centers also got the supersizing treatment.

Speaking of Disney, and other brand names, cruise lines have been busily associating themselves with established brands over the past year, hoping to hitchhike on their name recognition. Celebrity Cruises, for example, teamed up with Cirque du Soleil to bring its brand of fantasy circus magic to the line's megaships. Norwegian Cruise Line (NCL) followed by announcing a partnership with the famed Second City improv comedy group. Over at Cunard, the cobranding was with London's Royal Academy of Dramatic Art, whose graduates and students perform short plays and offer readings, workshops, and acting classes on *QM2*'s transatlantic crossings. The ship's Cunard ConneXions learning program also includes informal talks by instructors and lecturers from Oxford University and elsewhere, while programs in the ship's planetarium have been created by NASA, the American Museum of Natural History, and others.

Finally, the cellphone trend has the most potential to annoy, while also providing a real cost saving to travelers. It used to be that the only way to call home from a ship was via satellite phone at a cost of $8 or $9 a minute. In 2004 and 2005, though, Costa, NCL, Royal Caribbean, Celebrity, and Crystal's *Crystal Serenity* all installed technology that allows passengers use of their cellphones out at sea, at a cost of roughly $1.70 per minute. At press time, Carnival, Holland America, and MSC were also looking into the matter, so expect evvvverybody to have phones beeping soon. We reap what we sow.

Seeing the world

You can cruise around North America, Central America, South America, Europe, Scandinavia, Asia, Africa, the Middle East, the South Pacific, Australia, New Zealand, and even the Arctic and Antarctica — pretty much wherever there's water. If you've got a few months (and bucks), there are even world cruises that take you all the way around the globe. In this book, we highlight the most popular cruising regions: the Caribbean and Mexican Riviera for classic fun-in-the-sun vacations; Alaska for the wilderness, wildlife, Native culture, and scenery; the Mediterranean for history; eastern Canada and New England for charm and fall foliage; and Hawaii for, well, paradise.

Travelers on a longer leash can sail to the edges of the cruise world, hitting historic and politically edgy locales such as Libya, Lebanon, and Syria; exotic stops such as Vietnam, Tahiti, and Morocco; totally bizarro spots such as Siberia; and all-American waterways such as the Mississippi River and the Erie Canal.

Sailing from everywhere

We're New Yorkers, so we're busy and important and stressed-out and don't like to be hassled any more than we already are, ya know? That's why we're thrilled that we can now hop on our bikes or grab a cab and be at the passenger-ship terminals in Manhattan or Brooklyn in about ten minutes. Is that great or what? No flying, no long security lines, and no shelling out hundreds of bucks for tiny airplane seats and no free lunch.

That's the idea behind the so-called **alternative homeporting** or **homeland cruising** deployments the cruise lines have been following over the past few years. Last count, there were more than 20 homeports on the U.S. mainland, from where you could sail to Bermuda, New England, eastern Canada, Florida, the Bahamas, the Caribbean, Alaska, Hawaii, Mexico, and Europe. Moving beyond the traditional homeports in, for example, Florida, other cities that host big cruise ships on a regular basis include Anchorage (AK), Baltimore (MD), Bayonne (NJ), Boston (MA), Charleston (NC), Galveston (TX), Los Angeles (CA), New York (NY), Norfolk (VA), Philadelphia (PA), San Diego (CA), Seattle (WA), and Whittier (AK) are all hosting big cruise ships on a regular basis, and we're not even mentioning the countless other cities that serve as homeports for the small, specialized ships. The upshot is that unless you live in Nebraska, there's a good chance you can drive to your ship, saving yourself both time and money. And even if you do fly, the alternative homeports give you an opportunity to check out more of the country, rather than just sailing from Miami for the umpteenth time.

Appealing to all types of travelers

Who cruises? According to the cruise lines' central marketing group, the average cruise passenger is 50 years old, but 26 percent of cruisers are under 40. Eighty-three percent of cruise passengers are married, with an average household income of about $99,000.

Although demographics vary from cruise line to cruise line and sometimes from ship to ship, there's a ship for pretty much any kind of person who's looking for one. The mainstream lines are the great generalists, providing something for just about everyone — which, along with their generally reasonable prices, explains why they're the big choices for multigenerational family travel.

If you're pickier but still have a hankering for the sea, consider a luxury line or a specialty small-ship line, the former tailored to the connoisseur mindset, the latter mostly to public radio types who want a human-scale learning experience. A few lines defy categorization, such as small sailing-ship line Windjammer. Let's just say they attract iconoclasts.

Appealing to all wallet sizes

So the $64,000 question is, do cruises cost $64,000? Nope.

Though prices have been climbing after the inverse bubble that reigned from 2001 to 2003, at press time rates for weeklong Caribbean and Mexican Riviera cruises were still starting at around $600 per person based on double occupancy (two people sharing a cabin). Starting rates for Alaska cruises were between $750 and $850, and Mediterranean cruises started at around $1,000. Shorter cruises typically start at about $299 for a 3-night sailing, while prices for weeklong luxury and small-ship cruises typically start around $2,000 per person and up (sometimes way, way up) from there.

Your fare includes your accommodations, three meals a day (or six, if you can eat that much), a plethora of onboard activities, use of pools and gyms, nighttime entertainment, and travel among interesting ports of call. Overall, it adds up to great value and convenience — but don't assume everything's included. Travel expenses to and from the ship are generally not. Nor are shore excursions (except aboard some small-ship adventure lines), and they can easily cost $500 or more during the week. Bar drinks aren't included except aboard some luxury lines, and can run . . . well, that depends on you, as does the amount you're willing to risk in the casino or drop in the spa for a facial, massage, or mud wrap. Gratuities for the crew are not included on most lines, which pay their service staff minimal salaries on the assumption that they'll make most of their pay in tips. Generally, expect to tip about $70 to $100 per person during a weeklong cruise. (For more on tipping, see Chapter 4.)

To beef up their bottom lines, cruise lines push a slew of added-cost extras such as intimate alternative restaurants, specialty coffees, name-brand ice cream, fresh flowers, golf-swing analysis, wireless Internet connection, wine tastings, custom-tailored suits, specialty exercise classes (boxing, spinning, Pilates, yoga, tai chi, and the like), and personal training sessions. These extras could run your tab up into the stratosphere if you succumb, but therein lies the trick: *They're optional.* Aside from gratuities, which you really should leave to keep your karma balanced, you could step aboard a ship, spend not one red cent extra during your whole trip, and still have a great time. It's all up to you.

Answering the Cruise Naysayers

Maybe you want to go on a cruise (you're reading this book, after all), but your significant other is putting up resistance with one excuse or another. We've heard most of them, and have found that those excuses are often based on long-held misconceptions. Here are the most common excuses, and our patented Matt-and-Heidi answers to beat them back with.

I'll be bored!

When people tell you this, they probably think they'll be on the ship 24/7. Not so. Unless you take a transatlantic crossing with no port calls, you're off the ship almost as much as you're on, observing places and cultures you may never have seen before. Typical weeklong cruises spend four of their six full days in port, with the other two at sea, either because it takes a while for the ship to get to its next port or just for the heck of it. We've found, through long experience, that being on vacation can be really, really tiring, so a couple days at sea are a good thing, letting you loll around and rest up. Do you see us complaining about having to sit at the bar and drink beer all day? You do not.

I'll get fat!

Although the rumor is that most people gain about five pounds on a weeklong cruise, you only do that if you, uh, sit around at the bar and drink beer all day . . . or hit every eating opportunity — of which, admittedly, there are many. Way many. So to paraphrase Goethe, repeat after us: "Self-restraint is the first mark of the master." And if you can't forego dessert or that plate of nachos between meals, at least make deals with yourself: If I eat that, I won't take the elevators today. If I drink that, I'll go to the gym for an hour, or sign on for a challenging shore excursion, like mountain biking, kayaking, or hiking.

I'll get seasick!

Well, then you don't have to worry about getting fat, do you? But honestly, folks, most cruise ships nowadays are so large and well stabilized that you can barely tell you're on water. You probably won't have any problems unless you're extremely sensitive or the ship passes through rough water. In some places you hardly ever get rough seas — Alaska's Inside Passage, for example, which, like the name says, is inside, meaning protected by barrier islands from the ocean's waves.

If you do feel queasy, try taking an over-the-counter medication such as Dramamine or Bonine. Most ships stock medicines for less sea-hardy passengers, and you can sometimes get them free from the purser's office. You can also ask your doctor to prescribe for you the Transderm patch. Alternative remedies include ginger capsules (available at health food stores) and acupressure wristbands, which most pharmacies carry and which our frequently seasick friend Cindy swears by.

Cruise ships are too crowded!

Two answers to that one: First, that's just not true of all big ships, and second, you can't even generalize by saying the ships with the most passengers are the most crowded. We've spent weeks on huge ships, such as Royal Caribbean's 3,114-passenger *Explorer of the Seas,* and have been amazed at how uncrowded they were. Put it down to good design. On the other hand, we've felt squeezed on much smaller ships that were just not as well designed. To get a rough idea of how crowded a ship will feel, divide its tonnage by its total passenger capacity to arrive at the passenger-to-space ratio.

 If you're really concerned about crowds, book aboard a small ship, most of which carry fewer than 100 passengers. There aren't as many diversions on board, but that's kind of the point: On these ships, people go to get focused on the places they're visiting, not diverted from them. Small-ship cruises almost always cost more than megaship cruises, but you tend to have fewer onboard costs. Sometimes excursions are even included in the rates.

Cruise ships aren't safe!

As we were putting together this book, a 70-foot rogue wave smacked into NCL's *Norwegian Dawn* off the coast of Florida. Seventy feet! That's like, seven stories. That's a *big* wave. It made all the newspapers, and much was made of the fact that water was sloshing around in 62 cabins, but the fact was that the only real damage was to a few forward-facing windows, which broke under the impact and let in all that water. There was no structural damage at all. So figure, if a ship can shrug off a 70-foot wall of water smacking into it, it's pretty safe. When it comes to fire safety, cruise ships operate under international rules known as Safety of Life at Sea (SOLAS), which enforce rigorous standards for fireproofing and safety equipment.

To make sure ships are up to safety snuff and comply with emergency-response requirements, the Coast Guard conducts rigorous quarterly inspections of all ships operating from U.S. ports. To check out what those requirements are, visit the consumer section of the Coast Guard's Web site at www.uscg.mil/hq/g-m/cruiseship.htm. To make sure passengers know what to do in case there is an emergency, ships are required to hold an emergency safety drill within the first 24 hours of sailing. Everyone aboard is required to participate, trying on their orange life jackets and trotting out to their assigned lifeboat stations.

They let anybody on those things. There's no security!

Way wrong. Waaaaaay wrong. We make our living writing about ships and are no strangers to the ports in New York, but even we've been turned away when someone forgot to put our name on the official list. That was true before 9/11, and it's even truer now.

Between 2001 and 2004, new regulations went into effect that mandated a no-visitors policy (excepting passengers and others on a pre-approved list); x-ray of all hand-carried bags; screening of checked bags; the use of sniffer dogs; a security zone of at least 300 feet around all cruise ships, plus concrete barriers; patrol boats and sometimes Coast Guard escorts at some ports; and the screening of all ship's stores, mail, and cargo before they're brought aboard. Many of these systems were already in place at most cruise lines and ports, so passengers generally didn't notice much difference. Other changes have been made in the back office, including a rule that ships must submit a complete list of passengers and crew to the Coast Guard 96 hours before arriving at a U.S. port. Internationally, new regulations issued by the International Maritime Organization (IMO) require all ports around the world to operate within a consistent framework to address security issues.

Smoking at sea . . . or not

While you may picture the classic sailor as a leathery tan guy with a cigarette hanging out of his mouth, today he'll likely be sipping a diet soda and wearing sunscreen. Like most places shoreside in America, all ships covered in this book prohibit smoking in all restaurants, theaters, and many other public places such as shops and the library. If you want to light up, most bars and lounges have smoking sections, and you're free to have a cig out on deck. You can also have a butt in your cabin or on your balcony.

Now, if you're looking for a nonsmoking cabin because you're concerned with the lingering smells from a previous smoker, with a few exceptions, you're out of luck. The vast majority of cruise lines do not designate cabins smoking or nonsmoking (with the exception of Disney, which designates all cabins nonsmoking). Why? It's impossible to control (honestly, there is no real way to stop someone from booking a nonsmoking cabin and then keep them from smoking anyway). Further, it would be a big fat headache for the cruise lines' inventory department — how many cabins should be set aside for smokers? Do they sit empty if not enough smokers book the cruise? Luckily, cabins are cleaned well between cruises, if necessary by shampooing the rug and using air purifiers. Matt, a fairly smoke-sensitive nonsmoker, can't recall ever walking into a cabin and smelling residual smoke.

On board, all the major cruise lines have their own security forces, who monitor people as they come aboard (passengers, crew, delivery people, and contractors) and who keep an eye out during the cruise. We're not just talking about the kind of rent-a-cops you see at your local convenience store, either. Some lines have hired former Navy SEALs as top-level security consultants, and have hired Gurkhas, the famed Nepalese fighters, to assist officers at the gangway and be on hand as needed.

On a day-to-day basis, passengers may notice ship security mostly when boarding, both initially and at the ports of call. Most cruise lines photograph passengers digitally at embarkation and then match pictures to faces every time they get back aboard thereafter. Digital passcards also allow them to tell instantly who's aboard at any given time.

What if I get sick!?

Nearly every ship carrying more than 100 passengers has a medical facility staffed by a doctor and a nurse who are ready to handle health emergencies. The biggest ships now carry two doctors and between two and four nurses to handle the large number of passengers, and some facilities have become quite elaborate. Just like at home, a ship's medical center has set office hours, but doctors are on call 24 hours a day should an emergency arise. Most shipboard ailments are fairly minor, such as seasickness, a sprained ankle, or the flu (ships stock antibiotics for the latter), but the doctors can also perform minor surgery if necessary. Should you develop a serious medical problem, you're taken off the ship at the nearest port for treatment or possibly flown by helicopter to a hospital. The latter can cost big bucks, so if you're at risk of medical problems while away, you should invest in travel insurance to cover away-from-home emergencies. (For details about travel insurance, see Chapter 4.)

Most small ships (those discussed in Chapter 13) don't carry onboard medical staff when sailing coastal, river, or geographically close inter-island cruises, because they can evacuate sick passengers quickly. Usually, some crewmembers have nursing or first-aid experience. Small ships always carry doctors when sailing more far-flung international itineraries.

And what's with that Norwalk virus?

The stomach bug known as Norovirus (also known as Norwalk-like virus) made a lot of headlines between 2003 and 2005 when outbreaks caused nausea, vomiting, and diarrhea on several ships. Here's the scoop: Norovirus is an extremely common bug that hits about 23 million Americans every year, mostly on land. It's also extremely contagious. According to the Centers for Disease Control (CDC), people infected with Norovirus can pass the bug on from the moment they begin feeling sick to between three days and two weeks after they recover, and they can pass it on hand-to-hand — meaning the cruise ship outbreaks were probably caused by contagious passengers coming aboard and touching a banister. No matter how clean the cruise lines keep their ships — and they keep them pretty darn clean — they can't catch every germ. Our advice? Take your cruise, but wash your hands frequently.

If you're particularly neurotic about cleanliness, the Centers for Disease Control and Prevention (CDC) regularly inspects cruise ships arriving at U.S. ports for conditions and practices that could lead to food contamination, and grades the vessels, with 86 the minimum passing mark. How ships score is posted at www.cdc.gov/nceh/vsp.

What if I need to stay in touch?

Don't worry about it. We live in a world where people are obsessed with staying in touch, so you can bet the cruise lines have gotten on board with the issue — and figured out how to make a few bucks on it. Onboard cellphone service is the newest thing, available on Costa, NCL, Royal Caribbean, Celebrity, and Crystal's *Crystal Serenity,* and probably coming to most other lines soon. In addition, all but the smallest small ships have an Internet center for surfing and e-mailing (costing between 50¢ and $1.50 per minute), and most ships offer satellite news on in-room televisions. Many also continue the tradition of printing a daily news sheet with headlines from major newspapers and/or wire services. And as a last resort if you absolutely have to get through to someone, almost all ships offer direct-dial satellite phone service from your cabin, though it costs an arm and a leg. People can call you on the ship, too, though that also entails a large fee.

Chapter 3

Choosing Your Ideal Cruise

· ·

In This Chapter

▶ Taking the measure of your tastes
▶ Choosing the right length of cruise
▶ Deciding on your destination
▶ Getting romantic with a cruise
▶ Cruising solo
▶ Getting aboard gay and lesbian cruises
▶ Finding a cruise that caters to wheelchair users

· ·

As we say in Chapter 1, that "What's the best cruise line?" question is the same as asking, "Where's the best place to go on vacation?" The answer to the latter, of course, is going to be different depending on who you are and what you like to do on vacation. For instance, we're fairly sure the pope wouldn't want the same kind of vacation as, say, Hugh Hefner. And they probably wouldn't like the same kind of cruise either.

We've been out there. We've seen the pope's kind of cruise and we've seen Hef's, and everything in between, too. We've schlepped our suitcases onto just about every kind of passenger vessel there is, from adventure ships in Alaska to megaships on the Mexican Riviera, sailing ships in New England and the Mediterranean, and practically everything that floats in the Caribbean. So while you may get all goo-goo-eyed over the cruise lines' snazzy brochures, with their snazzy models sipping snazzy cocktails under a snazzy sun, remember that they aren't your best tools for making choices about a ship or destination. *We are,* and in this chapter we give you the lowdown on some strategies for finding a cruise that fits you like a glove.

Choosing Your Cruise

Almost all cruises can be divided up into three basic categories — mainstream cruises, luxury cruises, and adventure and educational cruises — though within each category there are various subdivisions.

Mainstream cruises

These are the cruises you see in TV commercials, with giant ships cruising around to people-pleasing ports while up to 3,000 passengers partake of the amazing bells and whistles the cruise lines have developed over the past decade: rock-climbing walls, ice-skating rinks, pottery studios, planetariums, multi-million-dollar art collections, water parks, up to ten different onboard restaurants, suites like Park Avenue apartments, and spas that make you want to melt. And don't forget all the rest: the pool, the gym, the kids' programs, and the constant activities. For all that, these are also the most affordable ships, with cruises frequently starting around $500 a week per person.

Among the mainstream lines, the onboard vibe ranges from party central to country-club casual. The latter companies frequently promote themselves as "premium" lines — and sometimes they even deserve the term, with a more refined atmosphere and better cuisine and service than their more mass-market cousins. Though in many cases the premium lines operate ships that are comparable in size and amenities to the mass-market ships, some premium lines have stuck with smaller, more intimate vessels of the type that were more common in the early to mid-1990s.

Other distinctions within the mainstream world? Well, consider the following alternatives:

- **Family cruises:** Some cruise lines specialize in family vacations, planning activities for all age groups. Naturally, they attract the biggest crowds during summers, holidays, and other school break periods.

- **Party cruises:** On these voyages — often three or four nights long, covering a long weekend — it's all about energy, with passengers grooving to the pool band all afternoon (often fueled by the day's drink specials), then staying up dancing and lounging late into the night.

- **Romantic cruises:** Almost any cruise can be romantic if you're in the right frame of mind, but some sure do help you get in the mood. Some lines also promote romance with onboard wedding, honeymoon, or vow-renewal packages.

See Chapter 11 for details on all the mainstream lines.

Luxury cruises

Almost every cruise line uses the word "luxurious" in its advertising, but only a few really are. With mostly small and intimate vessels, these true luxury lines are the closest thing you can find to a five-star hotel, catering to discerning travelers who don't blink at paying top dollar to be pampered with exceptional service, refined décor, luxurious accommodations, a sophisticated ambience, and fine French, Italian, and Asian cuisine that often rivals that of respected shoreside restaurants. There are generally fewer organized activities — folks attracted to this kind of experience presumably want a quieter, more self-motivated cruise — but when activities and entertainment are offered, you can bet they're more dignified than on the mass-market ships. No hairy-back contests here. No way.

With the exception of Cunard's *Queen Elizabeth 2* (*QE2*) and *Queen Mary 2* (*QM2*) and Crystal's *Crystal Harmony* and *Crystal Serenity,* these high-end vessels tend to be on the smallish and more intimate side, carrying between 100 and 1,000 passengers. You're not likely to feel lost in the crowd, and the staff gets to know your likes and dislikes early on. The onboard atmosphere is much like a private club, with guests trading traveling tales and meeting for dinner and drinks — the latter often included in the cruise price, as these lines are much more all-inclusive, price-wise, than your usual mass-market and premium lines. But of course, you pay for all that inclusiveness, with prices rarely dipping lower than $2,000 per person, per week.

Though the luxury lines are more alike than they are different, we can still think of them in a few distinct groupings:

- ✔ **Old-money lines:** And by "old" we mean the passengers as much as their money.

- ✔ **Active luxury lines:** The focus may be on taking out a Waverunner or sailboard more than on putting on a tux for evening cocktails.

- ✔ **Family luxury lines:** While kids are a rarity on most luxury lines, the larger Crystal ships sometimes attract as many as 100 children on holiday cruises, and have playrooms to keep them occupied. Cunard's *QM2* sees even more underage passengers, all the way down to age one. The youth staff even includes two or three British nannies who have completed a special two-year program in England.

See Chapter 12 for details on all the luxury lines.

Adventure and educational cruises

If getting in-depth knowledge about a destination tops your list of priorities, a small-ship cruise may be for you. These ships rarely carry more than 200 passengers, and rather than overwhelming you with unrelated activities and whoop-de-do, they tailor almost everything about the trip toward furthering your knowledge about the place you're visiting. You can attend informal lectures, participate in guided nature walks or history tours, go kayaking or tidepooling, or simply stand out on deck and look — most of these ships sail coastal or river routes, so you can usually find an abundance of nature right off the port bow.

Though their ships are small, these trips usually aren't cheap, with the most expensive ones hovering in the $4,000 range for a week. Midrange small-ship operators take the nut down to about $2,500, while a few operators of sailing ships (like Windjammer Barefoot and the Maine Windjammer Association) offer some trips for $500.

Within the small-ship world you can find a few variants:

- ✔ **Learning cruises:** Some lines go full-throttle into the educational aspects of travel, with onboard experts from leading nature publications offering lectures and helping with interpretation of the natural world. Others focus on history.

- ✔ **Active-adventure cruises:** Did you know you could take cruises that avoid civilization almost entirely, putting you out in pristine coves where you can kayak all day, or on uninhabited islands where you can hike the shoreline and head into the interior? It's like the anti-cruise, but because it's offered on a boat, it counts.

- ✔ **Sailing ships:** Four lines in this book offer cruises on ships with actual sails, though how much they actually rely on those sails for propulsion varies from "some" to "completely." The feel of real sailing pretty much mirrors that equation, too, though the simple fact that there *are* sails makes these cruises special.

Gauging Your Time Away

Though cruises are available that range from two nights to several months, weeklong itineraries are the industry's bread-and-butter, and are also a nice round number around which to wrap your vacation. Most ships sailing weeklong itineraries depart on a Saturday or Sunday afternoon and return early the following Saturday or Sunday. However, booking a 3- or 4-night getaway is a good alternative to a full-week cruise — especially if you're traveling by ship for the first time or simply don't have the cash for a longer cruise. Many cruise lines offer an array of pre- and post-cruise packages that make it easy to plan a weeklong land-sea vacation, with (for instance) three nights at sea and four at a hotel in Miami or Disney World.

 With only one major exception (Disney), the shorter the cruise, the more party-oriented the passengers tend to be — something to keep in mind if you're looking for a quiet time.

Picking a Destination

At least as important as deciding what kind of cruise experience you want is deciding where you want to go. The most popular cruising region in the world is the Caribbean and the Bahamas, followed by the Mediterranean, Alaska, the Mexican Riviera (also known as western Mexico), other European destinations, Hawaii, South America, Bermuda, and eastern Canada/New England. See Part V for specifics on each destination.

Here's the hot sheet on each destination:

- ✔ **The Caribbean:** Fun, sun, beaches, colonial history, Mayan ruins (on itineraries that include ports in Mexico and Belize), tropical landscapes, seafood, and drinks with little umbrellas in them

- ✔ **The Mediterranean:** History, culture, occasional big party scenes (think Ibiza, Palma, and so on), and gorgeous scenery (think Greek Isles)

- ✔ **Alaska:** Massive glaciers, massive whales, massive forests, massive sky, massive salmon, rich Native Alaskan culture, good microbrews, and the remnants of Russian colonial history and U.S. frontier culture

- ✔ **The Mexican Riviera:** The Caribbean for left-coasters, with as much sun, as much fun, some great Mexican culture and history, and a whole heck of a lot of tequila

- ✔ **Other European destinations:** History and culture in the Baltics, gorgeous fjords in Scandinavia, beautiful scenery in the British Isles, and total European charm on river and barge cruise routes in France, Germany, and Belgium

- ✔ **Hawaii:** Paradise, paradise, paradise, beaches, incredible scenery, volcanoes, Hawaiian history and culture, surfing, ukeleles, aloha shirts, amazing coffee, and drinks served in hollowed-out coconuts

- ✔ **South America:** Urban culture, Amazon mystery, the Girl from Ipanema, suntan oil, rain forests, incredible music, rum

- ✔ **Bermuda:** British men in shorts, powdery pink sand beaches, great golf courses, friendly atmosphere, shopping for English wool and Irish linens, and great history

- ✔ **Eastern Canada/New England:** New England charm, whales, lobster pots, Victorian mansions, lighthouses, historical sites, and fall foliage

Warming up to a Caribbean cruise

If you want a tan — and some palm trees, rain forests, interesting cultures, and great shopping — consider cruising in the Caribbean. The biggest draw is the climate, which is so temperate that cruises run year-round, but there's also (depending on the island) volcanic peaks, Mayan ruins, winding mountain roads, beautiful tropical flowers, great beaches, and a laid-back vibe. On a big ship in the Caribbean, expect to visit three to five islands during a 7-night cruise, which leaves one to three days spent at sea — your chance to participate in shipboard activities or just relax.

Typical itineraries

Most Caribbean cruises are a week long, though you can also find 5-, 6-, 8-, 9-, 10-, and 11-night sailings. You can also find shorter 3- and 4-night cruises, though these often concentrate on port in the Bahamas (which are technically not in the Caribbean at all, though they may as well be, climate-wise), either visiting Nassau and/or Freeport or stopping at one of the cruise lines' private Bahamian islands.

Itineraries usually stick to one region of the Caribbean, either **eastern** (typically calling on some combination of the U.S. Virgin Islands, Puerto Rico, St. Martin, and the Bahamas), **western** (usually Grand Cayman, Jamaica, Key West, either Cozumel/Playa del Carmen, Calica, or Costa Maya [Mexico], and sometimes ports in the Central American countries of Belize and Honduras), or **southern** (less defined, but often departing from San Juan, Puerto Rico, and visiting Aruba, Curaçao, Barbados, St. Lucia, Antigua, and/or Grenada). Small-ship cruises frequently visit the less-developed islands, mostly in the eastern and southern Caribbean, including the beautiful British Virgin Islands and ports such as St. Barts, Dominica, Nevis, and the tiny islands of the Grenadines.

In addition to the usual Florida homeports (Miami, Ft. Lauderdale, Port Canaveral, and Tampa), Caribbean cruises are also sailing these days from San Juan, Puerto Rico; Galveston and Houston, Texas; Mobile, Alabama; Norfolk, Virginia; Charleston, South Carolina; New York, New York; and other ports. Smaller, more adventure-oriented lines offer Caribbean itineraries that depart from the Caribbean islands themselves (you fly to the island to catch the ship) and visit less-touristed ports.

We go into greater detail about Caribbean itineraries in Chapter 15.

Caribbean sailing seasons

Caribbean cruises sail year-round, with the greatest number of ships operating between late October and April.

High season runs from the third week in January to right around the Easter/spring-break period. The sailings most likely to sell out, however, are those during school holidays, such as Christmas and New Year's and during the summer season. You're sure to see lots of families aboard then, and lots of kids.

If you're anxious about hurricane season, which runs from approximately June 1 to November 1 in the Caribbean, you can take solace in the readiness of modern satellite warning systems to alert ships to any danger. Although ships usually have plenty of time to steer clear, you may be in for a slightly bumpier ride and a cancelled shore excursion or two, especially if you've booked activities like snorkeling. In extreme cases, your ship may have to change course, skipping one or more of the islands on its planned route. Sometimes the ship can arrange to visit another port on those days. Sometimes you just get another day at sea.

In some rare instances, brewing or active storms may prevent a ship from returning to its homeport, and you may have to take a longer trip back from another port. In cases like this, the cruise line covers any added costs of getting you home.

Acting Alaskan: Heading north to the 49th state

Need we say it? Travelers don't go to Alaska for fun in the sun. Even in August it's frequently cold enough to warrant a fleece pullover and a raincoat. Instead, they go because it's there, and it's *big,* full of enormous glaciers, unbelievably enormous mountains, huge humpback whales leaping from the sea, bald eagles soaring overhead, and forests that seem to go on forever. The culture of Alaska's Native peoples figures in, too, with the Tlingit, Haida, and Tsimshian tribes influencing daily life in Southeast Alaska (the site of most Alaska cruises) and the Athabascan, Aleut, Alutiq, Yu'pik, Cu'pik, and Inupiaq peoples figuring in the life of the Interior and northern coastal areas.

Days on an Alaskan cruise are typically spent either exploring one of the ports (on your own or via shore excursions such as kayaking, mountain biking, river rafting, helicopter or floatplane flightseeing, salmon fishing, or dog sledding) or cruising around one of the state's myriad natural wonders, including Glacier Bay National Park, Tracy Arm Fjord, or prime whale-watching areas. Unlike on a Caribbean cruise, there's actually something destination-oriented to do on days at sea here.

Because they're harder to get to, and generally cost more than a cruise in the Caribbean or the Mexican Riviera, Alaskan cruises tend to attract an audience in the 55-plus age group, though increasing numbers of families have also been sailing north in recent years.

Typical itineraries

Most Alaska cruises concentrate on the Southeast Alaska panhandle, a string of islands that stretches from Ketchikan in the south to Yakutat in the north, with British Columbia to the east and the vast reaches of interior Alaska and Canada's Yukon Territory to the north.

Cruises round-trip from Seattle or Vancouver, British Columbia, are typically known as **Inside Passage** cruises, for the waterway that connects Southeast Alaska's thousands of islands. Highlights of most itineraries include glaciers (famous Glacier Bay or several others), the old prospector town of Skagway, state capital Juneau, and boardwalked Ketchikan in the south. Small-ship cruises frequently visit much smaller towns and wilderness areas on the Inside Passage, and some avoid civilization almost entirely.

Cruises that sail north- or southbound between Vancouver and either Seward and Whittier (both of which serve as port towns for Anchorage) also sail through the Inside Passage, but are often known as **Gulf of Alaska** cruises, in recognition that their route frequently takes in the sights on that body, including College Fjord and Hubbard Glacier.

We detail the best things to see and do at Alaska's ports in Chapter 16.

Alaskan sailing seasons

Cold weather the rest of the year limits Alaska's tourist season to the summer (generally mid-May through mid-Sept), although smaller ships may venture out as early as late April. The warmest months are June, July, and August, when temperatures generally range from 50 to 80 degrees during the day with a slight dip at night. Temperatures on the water can feel considerably colder. During the shoulder-season months (May and Sept), travelers can take advantage of lower rates.

Meandering the Mediterranean

The Mediterranean — whose ports include Barcelona and Palma in the west and Athens and Turkey in the east, plus everything in between — is a destination for people who appreciate history and culture. Your journey introduces you to buildings, monuments, and sometimes whole cities that date back thousands of years; small towns where you can sit at a cafe and take in the local scene; and high culture — from some of the world's greatest art museums to some of its finest gourmet restaurants, plus excellent shopping (if the value of the dollar ever gets close to the Euro again, that is). The ports are close together, so large ships may stop at a different port every day, or even visit two ports in a single day, one in the morning and another in the afternoon. Frequently, you may also stay in a port late into the evening (giving you a chance to check out the nightlife) or even stay for two days, giving you longer to get a feel for the place. Many Mediterranean itineraries last longer than one week, and having more than one sea-day a week is rare.

Sailing in Europe provides a much more diverse experience than you can find in the Caribbean or Alaska, and the ship's passenger mix reflects the international flavor. Your fellow travelers are likely to be an assortment of older passengers, younger couples, families, and honeymooners, often from several continents.

Activities center on museum hopping, touring ancient ruins, and absorbing a cultural landscape steeped in history. Depending on the ship, activities may also include water sports.

Typical itineraries

Mediterranean itineraries vary greatly, but most ships leave from Barcelona, Athens, Istanbul, Rome (actually Civitavecchia, which is a port near Rome), or Venice. Some small ships sail from the Greek Isles or from smaller ports in Turkey or France.

Cruises range from 3-day sailings around the Greek Isles to 10- or 12-day voyages that visit ports in both the eastern and western Mediterranean. Also available are plenty of 7-day options that focus on a single region.

Three regions make up the cruising territory of most lines: the western Mediterranean, the Greek Isles/eastern Mediterranean, and the Riviera.

Some ships offer itineraries that take in all the areas; others concentrate on a particular locale.

The area typically described as the **western Mediterranean** stretches from Barcelona (or sometimes Lisbon, Portugal, over on the Atlantic) to Civitavecchia, and includes port calls in Spain, France, and Italy.

The **Greek Isles/eastern Mediterranean** area includes the Aegean Sea and sometimes the Adriatic, with ports including Piraeus (near Athens), the Greek Isles (Rhodes, Santoríni, Mykonos, and so on), and Kuşadasi and/or Istanbul (both in Turkey). Some cruises also visit Venice and Dubrovnik, Croatia.

Riviera itineraries include such French ports as Nice, Cannes, and Saint-Tropez; the tiny country of Monte Carlo; and small Italian Riviera ports such as Portofino. Riviera cruises may also include Rome (Civitavecchia).

On a smaller ship, you hit some of the same ports as the big ships do, but you may also stop at smaller towns such as Portofino and Portoferraio in Italy.

See Chapter 17 for details on all the major Mediterranean ports.

Mediterranean sailing seasons

The Mediterranean cruise season generally runs from April through November, although some operators cruise there year-round. Temperatures in-season can reach 80 degrees or higher, but nice breezes along the coast help refresh you. Greece and Turkey are the hottest, and if you don't enjoy warmer weather, you should visit these countries from April to June or mid-September through the end of October.

Doing the Romantic Cruise Thing

Imagine leaning against the rail with your new spouse, sipping champagne as a picture-perfect Technicolor sunset paints the horizon. That's a winner in almost everybody's book, and it's why cruises are such a hot pick for honeymooning couples.

Besides their inherent romance, cruises are a good honeymoon choice for a more prosaic reason: Many of them depart on Sunday, meaning couples who marry on Saturday can leave the next day, and let their parents and bridal parties worry about cleaning up.

Getting married aboard ship

Bet you think ship captains can conduct weddings any time they please, right? Wrong. That's a common misconception, and in truth the only cruise ship captains today that conduct regular ceremonies are aboard Princess's Diamond-, Coral-, and Grand-class ships. Those vessels even have cute little wedding chapels, and your friends back home can watch the ceremony via an Internet webcam.

More common, however, is for ships to bring a clergyman or a civil official on board at an embarkation port to conduct your ceremony, either in a public room decorated for the occasion or (aboard the aforementioned Princess ships and Royal Caribbean's Voyager-class ships, Carnival's Spirit-class ships, and NCL's *Norwegian Sun, Star, Dawn,* and *Pride of America*) at a dedicated onboard wedding chapel. Your friends can come aboard to see you get hitched, then either see you off on your honeymoon cruise or come along for the ride.

You can also get married shipboard at a port of call, such as a Caribbean island. Some lines also help you arrange a wedding off-ship in the islands, on the beach, by a tropical waterfall, or in some other scenic spot.

Wedding packages generally start around $750 for shipboard ceremonies and usually include the services of an officiant (though you can bring your own if you prefer), a bouquet and boutonniere, champagne and keepsake glasses, a wedding cake, and the services of a photographer (but not the photos themselves — those cost extra, should you choose to buy them). The $750 package offered by Carnival — one of the big leaders in shipboard weddings — accommodates eight people including the bride and groom. Prices go up from there based on the complexity and size of your reception (from a simple open bar and hors d'oeuvres to a formal meal) and by port, with the top price being $2,145. Additional guests can be accommodated at a rate of $24 per person. You can also arrange for a ceremony off-ship in port, at higher prices.

Keep in mind that you need to make arrangements for the ceremony, the reception, and your wedding license well in advance. Some lines have special wedding departments that help you with the details; others rely on outside wedding coordinators.

Honeymooning at sea

Some lines lure honeymooners by offering freebies such as a special cake in the dining room one night, or an invitation to a private cocktail party. But you (or someone who likes you a lot) can also book a variety of honeymoon/anniversary packages. NCL's $79 Honeymoon Package, for example, includes champagne and strawberries at embarkation, a dinner for two with complimentary wine at the ship's specialty restaurant, an invitation to a cocktail party, a keepsake photo, and canapés in your cabin one evening. Bump up to the $229 Deluxe Package and you also get breakfast in bed one morning and two 25-minute massages at the spa. All the mainstream lines offer similar deals, with more expensive packages adding spa treatments, more champagne, chocolate-covered strawberries, shore excursions, and the like. If you're interested, sign up for a package when you book your cruise, or soon after.

Renewing your vows

Some lines also offer vow-renewal packages for couples who'd like to celebrate their marriage all over again. Princess offers vow-renewal packages that run from $205 to $485, the former including the ceremony, an orchid bouquet and boutonniere, a bottle of champagne and souvenir champagne glasses, a framed formal portrait of the ceremony, a commemorative certificate signed by the captain, and a framed photo of the ceremony; the latter adding a champagne breakfast in bed, two terry-cloth robes, a visit to the spa for half-hour massages or facials, canapés or petit fours in your stateroom every evening, and a personalized invitation from the captain to visit the bridge while in port.

Going Solo

Like life in general, cruising tends to be a couples' sport, with most cabins occupied by husband-and-wife teams age 40-something and up. If you're a single traveler — whether you're sailing just for a nice getaway or to try and meet Mr. or Ms. Right — things get a little more complicated.

In the old ocean-liner days, ships often had cabins designed for people traveling solo, but those are very rare these days, and cruise lines now base their revenue expectations on two paying customers sharing every cabin. That's why solo passengers generally get socked with something called the *single supplement,* which is a fancy way of saying the cruise line charges you more than if you were sailing with another person in the cabin. The supplement can add 50 percent or more to the usual per-person fare, though some lines are quietly foregoing or reducing these charges if a ship isn't filling up — though of course there's no way to predict this kind of thing.

You can avoid the supplement by sailing with a friend, of course, and Holland America and Windjammer Barefoot Cruises can even find you a friend through their cabin-share programs, which match you with a (same-gender) roommate. If it turns out they can't find you one, you can probably get the cabin at the regular double-occupancy rate anyway.

If you're looking for romance on your cruise, here are a few guidelines:

- ✔ Short cruises, such as Carnival and Royal Caribbean's 3- and 4-day Bahamas and Mexico sailings, attract a lot of singles and have a real partying atmosphere. If the bar scene is your scene, these cruises may work for you.

- ✔ Windjammer Barefoot Cruises offers singles cruises a couple times a year, with the numbers of men and women carefully balanced. Most lines don't go that far, but most ships do host singles get-togethers the first day of the cruise to let you know who's in the same boat as you (so to speak).

> ✔ Some travel agents also arrange singles cruises, booking blocks of cabins aboard large ships and setting up singles parties for their guests. These companies include **Cruiseman** (☎ 800-889-7683; www.cruiseman.com) and **SinglesCruise.com** (☎ 800-393-5000; www.singlescruise.com).

Booking Gay/Lesbian Cruises

Snapshot from one of our most recent cruises: Woman, having imbibed considerably, running up to two male passengers and yelling, "Are you guys GAY? That's so GREAT! I love you guys!" It's that kind of fun that can make gay- and lesbian-oriented charter cruises attractive.

A number of specialized travel agencies (listed below) either charter full ships outright or reserve blocks of cabins with cruise lines that are known to be particularly gay-friendly. Full-charters typically program many of their own activities and bring aboard their own entertainers to augment the ship's entertainment staff. Hosted group trips typically have cocktail parties for group members and specially programmed activities on board and in port.

> ✔ **Atlantis Events Inc.,** 9200 Sunset Blvd., Suite 500, West Hollywood, CA 90069 (☎ **800-628-5268** or 310-859-8800; www.atlantisevents. com), offers all-gay charters with lines such as Celebrity, Royal Caribbean, and NCL. Past guest performers have included Patti LuPone, Cybill Shepherd, and Chaka Khan.

> ✔ **Friends of Dorothy Travel,** 1177 California St., Suite B, San Francisco, CA 94108-2231 (☎ **800-640-4918** or 415-864-1600; www. fodtravel.com), offers many full-gay charters with lines such as Celebrity, NCL, and the ultraluxe SeaDream Yachts, as well as hosted tours on the *QM2* and other ships.

> ✔ **Olivia Cruises and Resorts,** 4400 Market St., Oakland, CA 94608 (☎ **800-631-6277** or 415-962-5700; www.olivia.com), offers full-ship charters targeted specifically to the lesbian community, mostly aboard Holland America's ships. Recent guest performers have included k. d. lang, the Indigo Girls, Wynonna Judd, Shawn Colvin, and Melissa Etheridge, plus the cast of Showtime's *The L Word*.

> ✔ **Pied Piper Travel,** 330 West 42nd St., Suite 1804, New York, NY 10036 (☎ **800-874-7312** or 212-239-2412; www.piedpipertravel.com), offers hosted gay cruises that include visits with the local gay community at various ports of call.

> ✔ **R Family Vacations,** 2 Washington Ave., Nyack, NY 10960 (☎ **866-732-6822;** www.rfamilyvacations.com), was **founded by Rosie O'Donnell's partner Kelli O'Donnell and gay travel veteran Gregg Kaminsky.** Trips are targeted to the gay and lesbian family market.

✔ **RSVP Vacations (☎ 800-328-7787;** www.rsvpvacations.com**),** offers full-ship charters on lines such as Holland America and Star Clippers. All sailings are targeted to gay men and lesbians, and bring aboard their own guest performers. RSVP works through more than 10,000 different travel agencies, which can be located by calling the toll-free number or checking the Web site above.

Rolling Around on Deck: Cruises for Wheelchair Users

It used to be that travelers with mobility problems had a terrible time at sea, but over the past decade most ships have been built with accessibility in mind. Ships now commonly feature two dozen or more wheelchair-accessible cabins at a variety of price points, and practically all decks and public rooms are accessible via elevators and ramps.

Some lines do more than others. Holland America, for example, has a system in place to comfortably transfer wheelchair passengers to tenders (small boats) so that they can go ashore with everyone else in places where the ship can't dock. The system uses lifts and guests don't have to leave their wheelchairs during the process. Some Princess ships have handicapped-accessible pools, which also use lifts.

Once you've narrowed your focus to a few cruise lines or ships, contact the lines' special services desks and get the full scoop on their accessibility. Be aware that some lines require that travelers with a disability be accompanied by a fully mobile companion. Passengers with chronic illnesses may have to present a doctor's note stating clearance for travel. When you talk with a prospective line, consider these issues:

✔ What wheelchair-accessible cabins are available? How are they equipped? Are they near the elevators?

✔ Are there a good number of elevator banks spaced around the ship, and are the buttons low enough to reach?

✔ Are all public rooms wheelchair accessible? Will you have to maneuver over lips in doorways?

✔ At the ports of call, does the ship pull into dock or use tenders to go ashore? Can the tenders handle wheelchairs?

✔ Does the line have any special procedures for boarding and disembarking travelers with disabilities from its ships?

✔ Are shore excursions on your itinerary able to accommodate wheelchair passengers?

If you're on a ship that still does traditional fixed-seating dining, make sure the cruise line knows that you use a wheelchair. That way they can put you at a table that doesn't require too much maneuvering to get to.

A handful of travel agencies specialize in booking cruises for disabled travelers. **Accessible Journeys,** 35 W. Sellers Ave., Ridley Park, PA 19078 (☎ **800-846-4537** or 610-521-0339; www.disabilitytravel.com), publishes a newsletter and can provide licensed healthcare professionals to accompany travelers who require aid.

Part II
Planning Your Cruise

The 5th Wave   By Rich Tennant

"Don't worry, they may be called St. Croix, St. Thomas, and St. John, but you're not required to act like a saint while you're there."

In this part . . .

*H*ere's where the plastic hits the counter. We run you through the cruise-booking process; clue you in on the difference between using an online service and booking with Babs, your friendly neighborhood travel agent; fill you in on things such as cabin selection and travel insurance; and go through all the little pre-trip details you need to take care of, like getting a passport, packing for the weather, and figuring out how you keep in touch with the folks at home.

Chapter 4

Booking and Money Matters

. . . .

In This Chapter

▶ Reading between the lines: Finding the best cruise fares

▶ Budgeting for onboard extras

▶ Finding ways to save on your fare

▶ Counting on professionals to get the best deal

▶ Deciding on the perfect cabin for you

▶ Considering air travel, meal time, and pre- and post-cruise lodging

▶ Preparing for the worst: Cancellations and insurance

▶ Paying (by credit card, of course) for your cruise

▶ Making sure you get what you've paid for

. . . .

*O*kay, it's not brain surgery. But the truth is, cruise rates aren't always easy to get a handle on. Fares are constantly in flux based on the whims of supply and demand. At press time, people were traveling like mad and demand was high. So the price of a cruise today is likely not to be the same as it was a month ago or what it will be six months down the road.

So what does this mean? Book early. After preaching in previous years that booking at the last minute would land you the best deal, the sermon is over. There are always exceptions — slow periods like September and October and non-holiday weeks in November and December — but today your best strategy is booking early, say four to six months out.

As for the actual booking process, cruise lines still tend to do what they've been doing for years, relying on traditional travel agents (and now on agent Web sites) to sell their product. Because the lines keep building new ships and adding more ports, working with a plugged-in travel agent to keep everything straight is a smart move. For this and other booking and financial issues, this chapter has you covered.

Poking Holes in the Cruise Price Mirage

Just like the airbrushed Barbie and Ken dolls dancing and lounging all over the cruise lines' brochures, the prices printed in those brochures for some strange reason just aren't real, so feel free to ignore them. You'll always pay less, except aboard some of the specialized small-ship lines. Cruise line Web sites, on the other hand, print relatively realistic rates, comparable (more or less) to what you get from a travel agency.

We've partnered with a real live travel agency — Nashville–based **Just Cruisin' Plus** (☎ **800-888-0922;** www.justcruisinplus.com) — to show you the actual prices people are paying for cruises aboard all the ships in this book. Check this out: The brochure rate for a 7-night western Caribbean cruise aboard Princess Cruises' beautiful *Caribbean Princess* is $1,239 for a low-end outside cabin. In reality, however, during our sampling period (June 2005 cruises, priced in mid-Apr), we got that same cabin for $649. Can you say huge difference?

In the ship-review chapters (Chapters 11–13), we show what consumers actually pay for the lowest-priced inside cabins (ones without windows), the lowest-priced outside cabins (with windows), and the cheapest suites aboard each ship. Remember that cruise ships generally have many different categories of cabins within the basic divisions of inside, outside, and suite, all priced differently. The rates we list represent the *lowest-priced* (which usually equates to smallest) in each division. If you're interested in booking a roomier, fancier cabin or suite, the price will be higher, with rates for high-end inside cabins being close to those for low-end outsides, and rates for high-end outsides being close to those for low-end suites.

Remember that rates are always subject to the basic principles of supply and demand. The sample rates in this book are meant as a guide only — the price you pay may be higher or lower, depending on when you book, when you choose to travel, whether any special discounts are being offered by the lines, and a slew of other factors. All rates are cruise-only, per person, based on double occupancy, and, unless otherwise noted, include port charges (the per-passenger fee each island charges the cruise line for entry). Government fees and taxes are additional.

Counting Extra Costs

Here's some good news. Like few other luxuries, the price of a cruise has *not* kept up with the pace of inflation. And who's complaining? Cruises today cost less — when adjusted for inflation — than they did in the 1970s. So just how do all those big fat cruise lines stay in business then, poor things? Don't feel sorry for them. They do just fine by building new ships, rounding up more passengers, and piling on the extras offered for sale on board.

Remembering what's not included

Your cruise fare includes accommodations, meals, and entertainment, but keep in mind what's *not* included when you budget. First, there's the cost of getting to the ship (whether by plane or car), and the cost of extras, from piña coladas and soft drinks to Swedish massages, tuxedo rentals, and spinning classes. Plan on being very enticed by shopping, both aboard ship and in port, and figure out whether you want to book the ship's organized shore excursions, which can really add up. Decide if you need a hotel room before or after the cruise, and if you want to add a few days on to your trip to, say, tour Rome or chill out in Miami.

Figuring in tips

Although technically you choose how much you want to tip the crew (unless you sail on one of those rare "no tipping" ships), the cruise lines are happy to offer guidelines. In fact, most just add gratuities right on to your bill to the tune of about $70 per week (or $10 per day) per person to cover tips for your waiter, bus person, and room steward. Some lines suggest children pay only half of this amount. If you're not happy with the service, or were so impressed you want to tip extra, you can go down to the reception desk at any point and change the amount of the gratuities to be charged to your account.

 Don't worry about tipping bartenders unless they're *really* good listeners — on most ships, your bar tab includes a 15 percent gratuity. For spa treatments, a 15 percent tip is typically charged directly to your bill. If not, you can write one in (or not, if your shiatsu wasn't up to par).

Budgeting for shore excursions

Shore excursions are sightseeing tours that help you make the most of your time at the ports your ship visits; however, they can add a hefty sum to your vacation costs, ranging from about $30 for a short bus or walking tour to $400 or more per person for flightseeing by plane or helicopter. You may not stay in port long enough to take more than one tour, but the costs can still add up pretty fast.

Some tours are worth the money, particularly for active tours, such as those involving kayaking or mountain biking, or for tours that take you far beyond the port city (often a better option than going it alone in a cab, seeing as you need to get back to the ship at a specific time).

 Be aware that sometimes a shore trip means seeing the sights from a packed tour bus with some ho-hum spiel and a stop for souvenirs. Sometimes. Not always. If you're suspicious, ask for more details of the itinerary from your ship's shore excursions desk.

 A little planning early on can save you big bucks and help you avoid regrets about missing out on something cool later. Before you set sail, read up on your cruise's ports of call and figure out what you may want to see at those places (the chapters in Part V of this book can help).

Adding up admission costs and then comparing the cost of doing it your way with the cost of doing it their way can help you determine whether to go the excursion route or not. For example, Heidi has saved money and avoided the sweaty group tour thing by taking taxis to sites such as Pompeii, where you can rent headset audio tours and explore solo.

You can book shore excursions on board or, in most cases, in advance on the cruise line Web sites, with your tickets waiting in your cabin when you arrive. If you change your mind, sometimes the cruise lines allow you to cancel or switch tours. Read the fine print carefully. If you book on the ship, you can ask the shore excursion staff questions first or attend one of the so-called port lectures, which typically come off more like sales pitches for the ship's tours and the stores in port that the cruise lines partner with. Tours are huge moneymakers for cruise lines, and the role of the onboard tour folks is to get you to buy.

Paying taxes and port charges

When comparing cruise prices, note whether taxes, port charges, and other government fees are included in the total fare. They usually are, but if not, you may pay up to $200 or more extra per person on a typical one-week cruise. You can find information on whether such charges are included or not in most cruise brochures and Web sites. If you don't find the info there, ask your travel agent or call the cruise line.

Estimating onboard costs

Cruise lines make a huge chunk of their revenue on board. Don't be surprised when you first board, particularly on a big mass-market ship, if everyone seems to be selling something, from the bar staff with the enticing umbrella drinks to the roving photographer to the salespeople promoting everything from cellulite treatments to scratch-off lottery cards, fresh flowers, bottles of wines, and art auctions.

Unless you have superhuman willpower, you'll probably buy at least one cute professional photo of you and the kids by the pool, or a sweatshirt with the ship's logo, or the cocktail someone so kindly offers you the minute you step aboard, or that relaxing massage, video arcade games, and so on. Just like a hotel or a theme park, a cruise offers tons of potential extras. Make sure and budget for them.

Be aware that the ship's fancy alternative restaurant may charge a service fee of as much as $30 a head, and in most cases you'll pay extra for treats such as an espresso, cappuccino, or gourmet ice cream. Turn to Chapter 7 to find out more about the finer points of at-sea dining.

Table 4-1 lists some average prices — that may vary by ship — that can help you determine how much to set aside to cover onboard costs.

Table 4-1	Typical Costs of Cruise Extras
Service	**Charge**
Alternative dining (service charge)	$10 to $30
Babysitting for two kids	$8 to $10 per hour
Beer	$3.50 to $6
Cruise line souvenirs	$3 to $50
Dry cleaning (per item)	$2.50 to $7.50
E-mail (per minute)	50¢ to $1.50
Haircut (men)*	$30
Haircut (women)*	$45 to $75
Massage (50 minutes)*	$99 to $128
Mixed drinks	$3.95 to $6.75 (and up)
Phone calls (per minute)	$6.95 to $15.95
Photos (5 × 7)	$6.95 to $9.95
Shore excursions	$30 to $400 (and up)
Soft drinks	$1.50 to $2.50
Wine with dinner	$15 to $300 per bottle

* Standard prices of Steiner, which has contracts to provide spa and beauty services on most ships.

After you calculate your cruise fare (figuring in discounts, port charges, and additional taxes and fees) and cost of transportation, plan on setting aside $50 to $100 per person per day, not including tips, to cover other expenses. If you want to take that $400 helicopter tour, buy a bauble in the ship's jewelry store, or indulge in fine champagne and cognac, you need to budget more.

If you plan to gamble, have bucks on hand for the ship's casino. And don't forget to set aside money to spend at the ports.

Paying up when the party's over

The cruise-bill fairy visits your cabin late on the last full day of the cruise with your final bill, slipping it under your door or leaving it on your bed. If you find any error or if you want to pay by cash, traveler's check, or personal check, you need to go stand in line at the purser's or

Keeping tabs on your spending

You should keep track of your shipboard expenditures so that you aren't surprised when you get the final tab at the end of your voyage. You can do this by keeping your receipts — you get one every time you sign with your onboard credit card. On some lines, you can also take advantage of the interactive television features in your cabin, which allow you to review your account regularly at the push of a button or two. And you always have the option of stopping by the purser's desk to check the ship's listing of your expenditures (you may have to wait in line to do this, particularly late in the cruise).

guest relations desk with your cruisemates. If it all adds up right and you simply want it billed to your credit card, you don't have to lift your weary head from the pillow.

Saving Bucks on Your Booking

Naturally, the biggest cost of your cruise is the cruise itself, so this section explores the best strategies for saving.

Booking early, booking smart

You don't have to book your cruise a year in advance, but we advise booking at least a few months in advance because cruise lines today are generally offering their best prices to those who book ahead. Company policies vary, and cruise lines don't necessarily state in their brochures or on their Web sites how far out you need to book to get the early-bird rate, or even what that early-bird rate is. But given that cruise prices are based on supply and demand — and demand is up these days, to levels not seen since before 9/11 — cruise lines don't have to do as much last-minute wheeling and dealing as in years past. In fact, at press time, cruise fares overall were somewhat higher than in the past few years.

Not only can you often save money by booking well in advance, but you can also have your best shot at getting your first choice of cabin. The best and cheapest cabins are the first to sell out.

So how early is early? Lines usually announce their itineraries 10 to 14 months before a sailing. Though last-minute discounts still exist, if you don't want to take a chance, these days it usually pays to book longer cruises and cruises to places such as Europe and Asia farther out, about six to nine months in advance. It's a good idea to book shorter cruises and cruises to the Caribbean three to six months in advance.

If a better deal comes along after you book at the early-bird rate, there's a chance the cruise line may make good and give you the lower rate *if* you happen to notice the rate change. Of course, you or your travel agent must ask for the lower rate; the cruise lines generally don't notify you and they're not obligated to do so.

Keep in mind that most last-minute deals are completely nonrefundable; if you book a week before the cruise, for example, the full fare is due upfront and you get zip back if you change your mind a few days later.

Taking a risk by booking late

If a ship approaches the sailing date with empty berths — which still happens considering the number of new ships that cruise lines are building these days — the cruise line naturally gets a little antsy and starts rolling out the last-minute discounts. If you're able to just pick up and go with short notice, look for the deals in newspapers and online anywhere from four to eight weeks before the cruise is due to depart. Sometimes last-minute fares can be pretty darn enticing — try $399 or $499 per week — especially during slow travel periods, such as late fall.

On the other hand, you may not have a variety of cabins to choose from, and although the cruise fare may be great, you may have a hard time getting a good deal on last-minute airfare. If you can drive to the ship, the last-minute route can be quite appealing.

Choosing off-season cruising

Another surefire way to cut the cost of your cruise is to book slightly off season — in what's known as the *shoulder season* (the front and back ends of a high season) or in a low season. Table 4-2 lists the shoulder seasons for key cruise locales.

Table 4-2 Off Seasons for Some Popular Destinations

Dream Cruise Spot	Best Times for Savings
Alaska	April, May, and September
Bermuda	May and September
Caribbean	September to right before Christmas, the first and second weeks of January, and April to June
Europe	April, May, September, and October

Cruise lines often offer the best bargains for fall cruises because the September to mid-December time period (with the exception of Thanksgiving week) is traditionally the cruise lines' slowest.

Going on an introductory or repositioning cruise

When a cruise line moves one of its ships from one region to another each season, say from New England to the Caribbean or from the Caribbean to Alaska, it typically offers repositioning cruises at a discounted price. Some experienced cruisers love these cruises, not only because they're cheap, but also because they tend to include more days at sea than typical itineraries. That said, many people hate the idea of spending more days at sea than in port.

Likewise, the lines tend to offer cut rates when they introduce a new ship or move into a new cruising region. So it pays to keep track of what's happening in the industry when you look for a deal. Check cruise line brochures and Web sites, and sites such as www.Frommers.com, where you can get a free cruise newsletter packed with news, features, and deals e-mailed to you twice a month.

Packing more people into your cabin

Into togetherness? Enjoy rubbing elbows (and just about everything else) with friends and loved ones? You can pay less by booking extra people in your cabin.

Here's how the cruise lines pull it off: They book the first two passengers at the regular fare and give the third and fourth passengers a pretty big discount. And if your extra passengers happen to be your kids, the line may offer rates just for them. For example, kids under age 2 go free on Norwegian Cruise Line, and Disney charges children under 3 $139 for a 7-night cruise.

Going with a group

One of the best ways to get a cruise deal is to book as a group, so you may want to gather family for a reunion or convince your friends or colleagues that they need a vacation, too.

A group is generally a minimum of 16 people in eight cabins. The savings include not only a discounted rate but also at least the cruise portion (but not the air) of the 16th ticket is free (on some upscale ships, you can negotiate one free ticket for groups of eight or more). You and the gang can split the savings from the free ticket or maybe hold a drawing to see who sails for free. If your group is large enough, you may also get some freebies from the cruise line, such as a cocktail party, cabin upgrade, or onboard credit vouchers to use in gift shops, spas, and more.

Sharing with another single

Cruise lines want to get the most out of every available cabin, so they base rates on double-occupancy and often require singles who want to room alone to pay what they call a *supplement*. This is no bargain. Supplements can range from 120 percent of the per-person double-occupancy rate to an outrageous 200 percent.

As an alternative, if you're willing to share quarters, a few lines, including Holland America and Windjammer Barefoot Cruises, guarantee to match you up with a same-gender roommate. You score big-time if the line fails to find you a roommate, because that means you get to enjoy having the whole cabin to yourself at the cheaper shared rate. If you're a real cheapskate (and glutton for punishment), save by signing up for a shared quad (a room for four), available on some ships.

Using your seniority

Don't keep your age a secret. A few lines shave a percentage off the top for passengers 55 and older, and you get that rate even if you share your cabin with a younger passenger. You don't have to be a member of a senior citizens group (such as the AARP), but it doesn't hurt. Sometimes memberships get you extra savings.

Paying in advance

Cruise lines love to get your cash as early as possible. So some of the pricier lines offer discounts to folks who pay their whole cruise fare ahead of time. Silversea Cruises, for example, offers 5 percent off.

Looking for free extras

Some cruise promotions may include extra treats such as pre-cruise hotel packages and/or cabin upgrades. Some lines may even give you an onboard credit to buy stuff on the ship, such as drinks and massages. In some cases, you may even see an offer of free airfare (normally with European sailings).

Reaping repeater perks

If you enjoy your first cruise, try it again: Cruise lines appreciate repeat business, so if you sail on a line you've traveled with before (even if you were just a kid with your parents), let the line or your agent know that you've come back for another round. The line may provide special discounts or at least extra onboard amenities. If they leave truffles by your bedside on your second cruise, imagine what kind of perks you could get for your tenth cruise anniversary! Some of the high-end lines actually give away a free cruise if you've racked enough days at sea.

Booking your next cruise while sailing your last one

When they still have your undivided attention, and you're deep in that vacation high, cruise lines often offer incentive deals to bring you back another time. Be sure to ask if you can combine the discount the line offers on board with other deals it may offer later. Your travel agent can still handle your reconfirmation and tickets as long as you tell the line who your travel agent is when you sign up for your next cruise.

Booking back-to-back cruises

People who get hooked on cruises like most of us get hooked on potato chips are in luck. By booking back-to-back cruises (where the same ship covers two different routes, one right after the other), you can get up to 50 percent off the second cruise. You may even be able to combine short cruises (such as Carnival's 3-day cruise to the Bahamas with its 4-day cruise to Cozumel and Key West). You lengthen your vacation and increase the number of ports you see along the way, all while saving money — in fact, if you go for two weeks, you may get a third week free. Ka-ching, ka-ching!

Finding the deals

All the deals we mention in this section are terrific, you say, but how can you discover which lines offer special rates? Certainly it pays to keep an eye on the travel section of your Sunday newspaper and surf Web sites such as www.Frommers.com, but remember that some of these discounts are easier to spot than to assess (for example, a deal may only be for certain dates or certain cabins, and you may not be able to combine it with other discounts). Given the number of variables that can affect how much you save, you probably still want to consult a cruise-savvy travel agent (in person, on the Web, or by phone) before you make your booking. And it pays to comparison shop, too.

Finding the Best Deals via Travel Agents and the Web

To find the best deals and figure out which ship and itinerary is best for you, consult with an experienced travel agent to seal the deal. Among your choices are Web-based cruise sellers and more traditional travel agencies. The former rely on their sites for actual bookings, while the latter use their Web sites as glorified advertising space to promote their offerings, doing all actual business in person or over the phone.

With a few exceptions, cruise lines have direct online-booking engines but we don't recommend using them. Why? Because agents and Web-based sellers may have negotiated group rates with the lines, be part of a consortium with whom a line is doing an upgrade promotion, or have other deals going that enable them to offer you lower rates. In fact, cruise lines encourage you to use a travel agency, too, and the lines report that about 90 percent of their bookings come in that way.

Pricing the differences

As far as cruise prices go, there's no absolutely quantifiable difference between the real live travel agents (whether your hometown brick-and-mortar mom-and-pop agency or a big anonymous mega-agency) and Internet-based cruise sellers.

In 2004 and 2005, the major lines started doing something they had talked about for years, offering all agencies, large or small, the same rates — a major coup for small agencies who have been struggling to keep up with the Expedias of the world. Further, some lines have said they would have no dealings with any agency that publicly (via print or Web advertising) doled out rebates to clients — that is, gave their customers additional discounts by sacrificing some of their own commissions. Still, don't think there aren't any loopholes. For example, at press time, Royal Caribbean was offering one of its top-producing agencies bottles of wine for any clients booking Royal Caribbean. Other agencies have offered gift cards, free insurance, or other incentives to customers in lieu of reduced rates.

Relying on Web sites for research

Most Web sites give you only a menu of ships and itineraries to select from, plus a basic search capability that takes into account only destination, price, length of trip, and date, without consideration of the type of cruise experience each line offers. There's no one to answer your questions. That's fine if you know exactly what you want, and are comfortable on the computer. If, on the other hand, you have limited experience with cruising and with booking on the Web, it may be better to see a traditional agent, who can help you wade through the choices and answer your questions.

Before you actually book your cruise, use the Web for research to help figure out what you want. Cruise the lines' Web sites as well as those of travel agencies and online magazines such as www.Frommers.com, www.CruiseCritic.com, and www.Cruisemates.com. They're all great ways to educate yourself.

Letting travel agents lead the way

Most of us would agree that a live person, whether on the phone or in person, can offer better customer service than a computer screen. This is especially so given that pricing doesn't vary that much across all types of cruise agencies.

When it comes time to sign on the dotted line, a good agent — someone who's sailed on or inspected a variety of ships and booked many customers aboard in the past — can tell you which cabins have their views obstructed by lifeboats, which cabins are near loud areas such as discos and the engine room, which ships and itineraries you should avoid if you're not looking for a party vibe, and what the major differences are between cabin categories. An experienced cruise agent can tell you about special promotions (like free bottles of wine) and help out and act as an intermediary should any problems arise with your booking, order special extras such as a bottle of champagne in your cabin when you arrive, and in general make your planning easy.

Buyer beware!

Keep in mind that if you hear of a deal that sounds too good to be true, as the saying goes, it probably is. If you get a solicitation by phone, fax, mail, or e-mail that doesn't sound right or if your agent gives you the heebie jeebies, contact your state consumer protection agency or local office of the Better Business Bureau (www.bbb.org). You can also call the cruise line directly and ask them about the agency. And be wary of working with any company, be it on the phone or the Internet, that refuses to give you its street address. Here are some more tip-offs:

✔ **Beware of snap recommendations.** When agents suggest a cruise line without asking you a single question first about your tastes, beware. They're probably just interested in making a commission from a line that pays them the highest rates.

✔ **Always use a credit card to pay for your cruise.** It gives you more protection in the event the agency or cruise line fails. When your credit card statement arrives, make sure the payment was made to the cruise line, not the travel agency. If you find that payment was actually made to the agency, it's a big red flag that something's wrong. If you insist on paying by check, you'll be making it out to the agency, so it may be wise to ask if the agency has default protection. Many do.

✔ **Always follow the cruise line's payment schedule.** Never agree to a different schedule the travel agency comes up with. The lines' terms are always clearly printed in their brochures and usually require an initial deposit, with the balance due no later than 75 to 45 days before departure. If you're booking two months or less before departure, the full payment is usually required at the time of booking.

✔ **Keep on top of your booking.** If you fail to receive a document or ticket on the date promised, ask about it immediately. If you're told that your reservation was canceled because of overbooking and you must pay extra for a confirmed and rescheduled sailing, demand a full refund and/or contact your credit card company to stop payment.

Finding a good travel agent

So, how do you know if an agent is any good? Some are little more than order-takers, who may never even have been on a cruise themselves. One usually helpful resource is an agent referred to you by a reliable friend or acquaintance. This is particularly valuable these days, when agents are being pressed to squeeze more profit from every sale, making some of them less likely to take the time to discuss options.

When searching for a good agent, it can't hurt if an agent is an Accredited Cruise Counselor (ACC), Master Cruise Counselor (MCC), or Elite Cruise Counselor (ECC), designations doled out by the Cruise Lines International Association (CLIA), an industry trade organization. Many of the cruise lines' Web sites list preferred agencies (generally broken down or searchable by city or state), as does the CLIA site at www.cruising.org. Many of the most reliable agencies are also members of agent groups, such as Virtuoso and Signature Travel Network. In this book's appendix, we list some of the best agencies and the major cruise-selling Web sites.

Choosing Your Cabin

When it comes right down to it, choosing a cabin is really a question of money. If you've got big bucks, you're gonna get the penthouse. If you've got just a few bucks, don't fret, there are decent choices for you, too. From a windowless lower-deck cabin with upper and lower bunks to a 1,400-square-foot suite with a butler and mile-long private veranda, cruise ships can offer a dozen or more stateroom categories that differ by size, location in the ship, amenities, and, of course, price.

For the most part, and especially on small ships, where most cabins are virtually identical, cabins on higher decks are still generally more expensive, and outside cabins (with windows or balconies) are more expensive than inside cabins (those without). Outside cabins whose windows are obstructed by lifeboats are cheaper than ones with good views. Figure 4-1 shows a sample deck plan with some other considerations when choosing a cabin.

For a closer look at a ship, go online for a virtual tour of its cabins and public rooms. Most cruise lines offer an assortment of photos, videos, and/or 360-degree tours online, but to save time, go to the **Cruises Only** Web site, www.cruisesonly.com, which has visuals on almost all the mainstream and luxe ships reviewed in this book. Click on <u>Cruise Lines</u>, and then click on the little camera icons next to each ship. Remember that cruise lines tend to show off their fancier suites and cabins in these tours, and low-end staterooms, when shown, are photographed with a wide-angle lens that makes them look much bigger than they really are.

Evaluating cabin size

Inch for inch, cruise ship cabins are smaller than hotel rooms. Of course, having a private balcony attached to your cabin, as many do, makes your living space that much bigger. Figure 4-2 shows sample cabin floor plans.

A roomy standard cabin is about 170 to 180 square feet, although some of the smallest are about 85 to 100 square feet. Disney has some of the more spacious standard cabins at sea, at 226 square feet (they call them "family suites," but they're still the most common accommodation aboard their ships). Carnival and Holland America's are about 185 square feet, with some going up to a roomy 197 and 220 square feet, respectively. By way of comparison, equivalent standard cabins on a good number of ships in the Norwegian and Royal Caribbean lines are quite a bit smaller — try 120 to 160 square feet. Cabins on the small-ship lines such as Windjammer, Clipper, and American Canadian Caribbean Line can be very snug — on the order of 70 to 100 square feet.

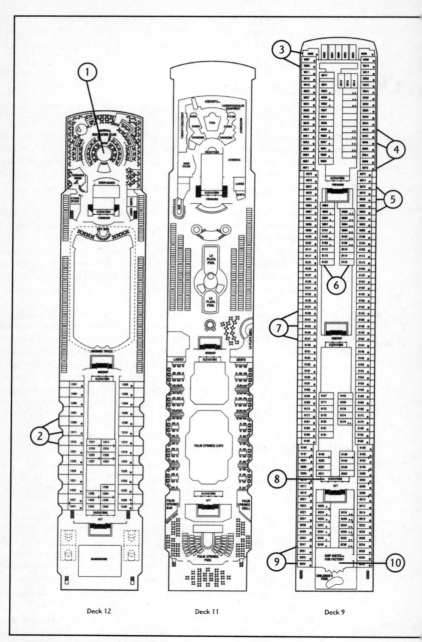

Figure 4-1: A sample deck plan.

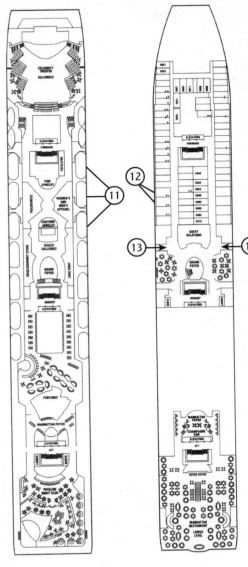

Deck 7

Deck 5

Cabin Choice Considerations

1 Make note of public areas that may be loud — the ship's disco, for example. Although the nightclub on this ship is far from any cabins, it doesn't hurt to request that your cabin not be close to or below such a sleep-inhibitor.

2 Upper-deck cabins are not a good bet if you're susceptible to seasickness because the upper decks feel more of the sea's motion.

3 The motion-sickness warning also holds for cabins in the ship's bow.

4 Outside cabins without verandas are represented as undivided rectangles.

5 Outside cabins with verandas show up as divided rectangles.

6 You can save big by booking an inside cabin without windows.

7 The cabins least affected by the motion of the sea are amidships, especially cabins amidships on the lower levels.

8 The cabins next to elevator shafts may be noisy. Of course, they're also very convenient.

9 Cabins in the stern can be affected by the motion of the sea, and also are prone to vibrations from the ship's engines.

10 Cabins near children's areas may be fairly noisy during the day.

11 Lifeboats sometimes obstruct the view from cabin windows. The lifeboats on this illustrated ship are near public rooms, so private cabins aren't affected.

12 Ideally, disabled vacationers have cabins near the ship's entrance **(13)** and an elevator.

(The Mercury's *deck plan is provided by Celebrity Cruises.)*

Typical outside cabins
- Twin beds (can often be pushed together)
- Upper berths for extra passengers fold into walls
- Bathrooms usually have showers only (no tub)
- Usually (but not always) have televisions and radios
- May have portholes or picture windows

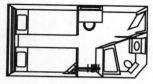
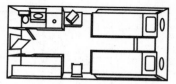

Typical suite configurations
- Queen-size or double beds
- Sitting areas (sometimes with sofa beds for extra passengers)
- Large bathrooms, usually with tub
- Refrigerators (sometimes stocked, sometimes not)
- Stereos and televisions with VCRs are common
- Large closets
- Large windows or outside verandas

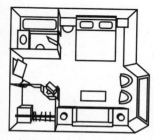
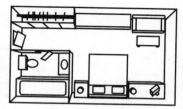

Figure 4-2: Sample cabin layouts.

All standard cabins on the high-end lines are roomy — in fact, many of the high-end ships are "suite only," measuring between about 250 and 300 square feet, not including the balcony space. Across the board, from mainstream to luxe, the top suites and penthouses are obviously the most spacious, some as large as 2,000 and 3,000 square feet (and more).

If your budget calls for something a little smaller, think of your cabin like a bedroom in a large house. It'll be mostly a place you use only for sleeping, showering, and changing clothes. Out beyond the door, vast acres of public spaces await, full of diversions.

Getting the scoop on inside cabins versus outside cabins

Whether you really plan to spend time in your cabin is a question that should be taken into account when deciding whether to book an inside cabin or an outside cabin (that is, one without windows or one with windows or a balcony). If you plan to get up bright and early, hit the buffet breakfast, and not stop till the cows come home, you can probably get away with booking an inside cabin and save yourself a bundle. Inside cabins are generally not as bad or as claustrophobic as they sound. Many, in fact — such as those aboard most of the Carnival and Celebrity fleets — are the same size as the outside cabins, and most cruise lines design and decorate them to provide an illusion of light and space.

If, on the other hand, you want to lounge around and take it easy in your cabin, maybe ordering breakfast from room service and eating while the sun streams in — or, better yet, eating out *in* the sun, on your private veranda — then an outside cabin is definitely a worthwhile investment.

 If you want a view of the sea, be sure when booking that your window or balcony doesn't just give you a good view of a lifeboat or some other obstruction (and remember, there are likely to be balconies on the deck right above your balcony, so they're more like porches than actual verandas). Some cruise line brochures tell you which cabins are obstructed, and a good travel agent or a cruise line's reservation agent can tell you which cabins on a particular ship may have this problem.

Considering other cabin matters

Unless you're booking at the last minute (like a few weeks or less before sailing), as part of a group, or in a cabin-share or cabin-guarantee program (which means you agree to a price, and find out your exact cabin at the last minute), you can work with your agent to pick an exact cabin.

Need a bathtub rather than just a shower? That narrows your choices on most ships. Want connecting cabins so that you and your kids, friends, or relatives can share space? Most ships have 'em, but they sometimes book up early, as do cabins with third or fourth berths (usually pull-down bunks or a sofa bed). Almost all ships have cabin TVs these days, but a few don't. Want an elevator close by, to make it easy to get between decks? Is the view out the cabin's windows obstructed by lifeboats or other ship equipment? Most importantly, keep cabin position in mind if you suffer from seasickness. A midships location on a middle deck is best because it's a kind of fulcrum point, the area least affected by the vessel's rocking and rolling in rough seas.

Booking Your Airfare

Except during special promotions, airfare is rarely included in cruise rates for Caribbean, Alaska, Mexico, and New England/Canada cruises, though it often is on Europe and Asia itineraries. So if you can't drive to your port of embarkation and need to fly to get to Miami, New York, Southampton, or Rome, you have to either purchase airfare on your own through an agent or online, or buy it as a package with your cruise. The latter is often referred to as an air add-on or air-sea package.

Here are the benefits of booking your airfare through the cruise line:

- ✔ When you book through the cruise line, you usually get round-trip transfers between the airport and the ship.

- ✔ A uniformed cruise line employee is in the airport to direct you to the right bus, and your luggage is taken from the airport to the ship.

- ✔ The cruise line knows your airline schedule and, in the event of delayed flights and other unavoidable snafus, does what they can to make sure you get to the ship. For instance, during the abnormally fierce hurricane season in fall 2004, those who had booked the cruise lines' air were given priority when it came to rebooking. People who book their air transportation and transfers separately are on their own.

With pros, there are bound to be cons. Here are the downsides to booking your airfare through the cruise line:

- ✔ Odds are it's more expensive to book through the cruise line than on your own. In the past, cruise lines offered more competitive fares, but the airlines aren't giving them the bulk discounts they used to, meaning prices have gone up. Consequently, fewer passengers are now booking the lines' air packages.

- ✔ If you book through the lines, you probably can't use any frequent-flier miles you've accumulated.

- ✔ The air add-on could mean a circuitous route — with indirect legs and layovers — before you arrive at your port of embarkation.

If you arrange your own air transportation, make absolutely sure that airfare is not included as part of your cruise contract. Though rare, if it is, you're often granted a deduction (usually around $250 per person) off the cruise fare. Passengers who book their own flights can still buy transfers from the airport to the ship through their cruise line, but it's often cheaper to take a taxi, such as in Miami and Fort Lauderdale.

Arranging for Dinner Reservations and Special Diets

Though most ships have casual, walk-in restaurants that don't require reservations, most also still offer at least one outlet that operates the traditional way with fixed early and late seating times. In this case, when you book your cruise you must choose an early or late seating for dinner, and sometimes even put in a request for the size table you're interested in (tables for two, four, eight, ten, and so on). Early usually means a 6 p.m. seating, while late is anywhere between 8 and 8:30 p.m. Families with young children often choose the early seating. The later seatings allow you to linger a little longer over your meal, with no rush set up for another group. For a more detailed discussion, see Chapter 7.

 On all but the smallest luxury ships, it's almost impossible to reserve a table for two, considering the sheer numbers requesting the same. Still, it can't hurt to ask.

Most ships now offer vegetarian meals and health-conscious choices as part of their daily menus. If you follow any other special diet — whether low-salt, low-fat, heart-healthy, kosher, halal, or any other — or if you have certain food allergies, make this known to your travel agent when you book, or at least 30 or more days before the cruise, and make sure your diet can be accommodated at all three meals (sometimes special meal plans cover only breakfast and dinner). If you're sailing on a small ship and have special food needs, definitely tell your agent.

Booking Pre- & Post-Cruise Hotel Stays

Cruise lines often offer hotel packages in the cities of embarkation and debarkation, and because most of these cities are tourist attractions in their own right, you may want to spend some time in New York, Oahu, or London before you sail, or drive to Disney World from Port Canaveral. The cruise lines' package deals usually include hotel stays and transportation from the hotel to the ship (before the cruise) or from the docks to the hotel (after the cruise). Compare what the line is offering with what you may be able to arrange on your own.

Considering Cancellations and Insurance

Given today's geopolitical situation, it pays to have a handle on a cruise line's cancellation and insurance policies. What should you do if the cruise you've booked is canceled before it departs? A cruise can be canceled because of shipyard delays (if you've booked an inaugural cruise), the outbreak of an infectious disease, mechanical breakdowns (such as nonfunctioning air-conditioning or an engine fire), the cruise line going out of business, act of war, or an impending hurricane.

Luckily, given today's competitive market, cruise lines have been making big efforts to appease disappointed passengers, whether they bought insurance or not. Typically, a line will reschedule the canceled cruise and offer passengers big discounts on future cruises — after all, they don't want the bad press they'd get if they cheated hundreds or thousands of people. There are, however, no set rules on how a line will compensate you in the event of a cancellation.

If the shoe's on the other foot and you need to cancel, you can generally get a refund — most lines give you every cent back if you cancel at least two to three months before your departure date, although details vary from line to line. If you cancel closer to departure, you can usually get a partial refund up until about 15 days before the cruise. After that, you won't get any refund at all, even if you cancel for medical reasons. Exceptions? In early 2003, in response to the impending war with Iraq and the general uneasiness in the Middle East, many lines liberalized their cancellation and insurance policies for their European cruises, and, in some cases, all their itineraries, in order to encourage bookings.

If you're just worried about missing the ship, go a day early and spend your money on a hotel and nice dinner instead. If you're worried about medical problems occurring during your trip, on the other hand, travel insurance may be more vital.

Except for the small coastal cruisers described in Chapter 13, most cruise ships have an infirmary staffed by a doctor and a nurse or two; but in the event of a dire illness, the ship's medical staff can only do so much. Therefore, you may want a policy that covers emergency medical evacuation and, if your regular insurance doesn't cover it, the potential cost of major medical treatment while away from home.

Cruise line policies versus third-party insurers

A good travel agent can tell you about policies sold through the cruise lines and ones sold independently of the lines. Both have pros and cons. No matter which you choose, it's absolutely crucial to read the fine print because terms vary from policy to policy.

✔ Both kinds typically reimburse you in some way when your trip is affected by unexpected events (such as canceled flights, plane crashes, dockworkers' strikes, or the illness or death of a loved one, as late as the day before or day of departure) but not by "acts of God," such as hurricanes and earthquakes (the exception being if your home is made uninhabitable, putting you in no mood to continue with your cruise plans).

✔ Both also typically cover cancellation of the cruise for medical reasons (yours or a family member's); medical emergencies during the cruise, including evacuation from the ship; lost or damaged luggage; and a cruise missed due to airline delays (though some only cover delays over three hours).

✔ Neither kind of policy reimburses you if your travel agent goes bankrupt, so using a travel agent you're very familiar with or who has been recommended to you is the safest precaution you can take. (And, of course, *always use a credit card,* never a check. If a corrupt travel agent cashes it, or a decent one just goes out of business, then you could get screwed.)

✔ Most cancellation policies also do not cover cancellations due to work requirements.

Third-party coverage

Even though agents get a commission for selling both cruise line policies and independent policies, most agents and industry insiders believe that non–cruise line policies are the best bet because some will issue insurance to those with pre-existing medical conditions if the condition is stable when purchasing the insurance (a doctor would have to verify this if you ever made a claim) and if you purchase the policy within 14 days of your initial deposit on the cruise. They also offer supplier-default coverage that kicks in if a cruise line goes bankrupt, which a handful did between 2000 and 2003.

Though bankruptcies are rare, a well-connected travel agent should see the writing on the wall months before a cruise line fails — commissions slow or stop being paid, phone calls aren't returned, and industry trade publications report on any problems — and tip you off. The less customer-service-driven cruise sellers may not stop pushing a troubled cruise line, however, selling these lines up to the very last minute.

According to the Fair Credit Billing Act, if you paid by credit card (and again, you should), you can generally get your money back if you dispute the charge within 60 days of the date the charge first appears. If you paid in full four months before the cruise, you're likely out of luck going this route and may have to resort to litigation.

Policies are available from reputable insurers such as **Access America,** Box 71533, Richmond, VA 23286 (☎ 866-807-3982; www.accessamerica. com), and **Travel Guard International,** 1145 Clark St., Stevens Point, WI 54481 (☎ 800-826-4919; www.travelguard.com), whose Web sites maintain lists of the lines they cover (or no longer cover); these are helpful in figuring out which lines may be considered financially shaky.

Cruise line coverage

Cruise lines offer their own policies, many of them administered by New York–based BerkelyCare (☎ **800-453-4069**). If you opt for this type of policy out of sheer convenience (the cost is added right onto your cruise fare), keep in mind that they do not cover you in the event of a cruise line bankruptcy (though using a credit card can save you here; see the "Cruise line policies versus third-party insurers" section earlier in this chapter) or for cancellation of your cruise due to pre-existing medical conditions. Some lines' policies, including Carnival, Costa, Silversea, and Crystal, issue a cruise credit for the penalty amount if a medical claim is deemed pre-existing, and issue you cash if you cancel for a covered reason.

Generally, the cancellation penalty imposed by the cruise line would be 100 percent of the cruise fare, for example, if you cancel a few days before the cruise (assuming you've paid in full), or it could be just $300 if you cancel right after making the initial cruise deposit.

Sounds like the third-party policies win hands down, right? Well, to make it just a little more complicated, a handful of cruise line policies are actually better in some areas than outside policies. For example, Princess Cruises has an insurance policy that allows you to cancel for all the reasons that an outside policy would (illness, injury) and get cash reimbursement or they will let you cancel for any reason whatsoever (from fear of flying to a bad hair day) up until the day of departure and have 75 percent to 90 percent of the normal penalty for canceling your cruise applied toward a future trip. Norwegian, Celebrity, Royal Caribbean, and Silversea offer similar "any reason" policies.

Putting Down a Deposit

If you book at the last minute, you typically pay in full when making your reservation. If you book several months or more ahead of time, then you pay a deposit to secure the booking. Depending on the policy of the line you selected, the amount is either fixed at a predetermined amount or represents a percentage of the ticket's total cost. The length of time cruise lines hold a cabin without a deposit is getting shorter by the minute. It seems pretty clear, in this age of near-obsessive "shopping around," that the cruise lines are doing their part to discourage it. It used to be a cruise could be held for a week before you had to plunk down cash; most lines have now shortened this window to one to three days (exceptions include exotic itineraries that aren't ultracompetitive). Carnival, for instance, now requires a deposit within 24 hours.

The balance of the cruise price is due anywhere from about 60 to 90 days before you depart; holiday cruises may require final payments earlier, perhaps 90 days before departure.

Credit card payments are made directly to the cruise line, but payments by check are made out to the agency, which then passes payment on to the cruise line. As we've said repeatedly in this chapter, it's preferable by far to pay by credit card, for the added protection it offers.

Reviewing Your Tickets

Carefully review your ticket, invoice, itinerary, and/or vouchers to confirm that they accurately reflect the departure date, ship, and cabin category you booked. The printout usually lists a specific cabin number; if it doesn't, it designates a cabin category. Your exact cabin location will then be assigned to you when you board ship.

Chapter 5

Ticking Off Your Pre-Cruise Checklist

*Y*our cruise is paid for and you think you're ready to go. But are you? Before you head to the airport, you may have some chores to do. Do you have the ID you need to get on board? Are your cruise tickets and other documents all in order? Have you figured out your spending-money situation so that you can pay for stuff on board and at the ports? You need a checklist. Wow! You're in luck. We've made one for you right here. (Well, not an actual one, but you get the general idea.)

Identifying Yourself

Ah, the old days. Not long ago we watched the 1970s disaster movie *Airport,* and there was a scene in which Helen Hayes cons her way onto a departing jet by saying her son had dropped his wallet before he boarded. Could she go aboard to give it to him? Sure, they said. Go on through.

It ain't that way anymore. Today you not only need a photo ID to get on the plane to your ship, you need the right ID to get aboard ship, too, and you probably need a passport, too — and not only when you're going somewhere far off, such as Europe or Asia.

For decades, U.S.-based cruise ships have operated under rules that permitted U.S. citizens to travel to Canada, Mexico, and the Caribbean without need of a passport, but that all seems to be changing. As of mid-2005, new rules proposed by the U.S. departments of State and

Homeland Security were set to do away with that loophole, meaning even passengers taking weekend jaunts to the Bahamas will soon need a passport — no ifs, ands, or buts.

Called the Western Hemisphere Travel Initiative, the rule change is part of the Intelligence Reform and Terrorism Prevention Act of 2004, and at press time was in a review period and probably on track to passage. If implemented according to the proposed timeline, all U.S. citizens traveling to the Caribbean, Bermuda, and Central and South America will be required to carry passports as of December 31, 2005. After December 31, 2006, the rules would cover travelers to Mexico and Canada as well (thus affecting Mexican Riviera and Canada/New England cruises, as well as any Alaska cruises that begin or end in Vancouver), and after December 31, 2007, passports would be required for all air, sea, and land border crossings, period.

The bottom line? Get a passport if you're planning any kind of cruise that leaves U.S. territorial waters. Don't dilly-dally either, since U.S. passport services are likely to be deluged when and if the new rules take effect. Passport applications generally take six to eight weeks to process, though expedited service is also available (see below).

If you don't currently have a passport, the State Department Web site (http://travel.state.gov/passport) provides information on obtaining one. Current fees are $97 for citizens age 16 and older, $82 for younger than age 16.

To get a passport for the first time (or if you have an expired passport issued more than 15 years ago, or issued while you were under 16), you need to go in person to one of 6,000 passport acceptance facilities located throughout the country, bringing two photographs of yourself, proof of U.S. citizenship (an expired passport, certified birth certificate, naturalization certificate, certificate of citizenship, or consular report of birth abroad), and a valid form of photo ID, such as a driver's license. Acceptance facilities include many federal, state, and probate courts, post offices, some public libraries, and a number of county and municipal offices. Find the one nearest you using the State Department's search page at http://iafdb.travel.state.gov.

Citizens who need a new passport for travel within two weeks may visit any of the 13 regional passport agencies listed at http://travel.state.gov/passport/about/agencies/agencies_913.html. Appointments are required, and you need to bring a completed passport application (downloadable at http://travel.state.gov/passport/forms/forms_847.html), appropriate ID, proof of citizenship (see list above), and two regulation passport-size photos. Expedited service costs $60 plus any mailing fees, above and beyond the regular application fees.

If you don't live near a passport center, you can apply for expedited service at a local passport acceptance facility, located in post offices, courthouses, and so on, and then follow up through overnight mail.

You can renew an expired passport through the mail as long as you were over age 16 when it was issued and still have the same name (or can provide legal documentation of a name change), and your old passport is undamaged and was issued within the past 15 years. Forms are downloadable at `http://travel.state.gov/passport/forms/forms_847.html`. Fees for renewal are currently $67. Expedited renewal services are available for an additional $60 plus mailing costs.

 When traveling, carry a photocopy of your passport in a separate piece of luggage from your real one. If you lose your passport while abroad, go directly to the nearest U.S. embassy or consulate. Bring all the forms of identification you have so that the officials can start generating you a new passport.

Reviewing Your Cruise Documents

Your tickets and other cruise documents usually arrive in your mailbox about a month before your cruise. Sometimes, however, they don't get to you until a week before your cruise. Plenty of important items are included, such as the following:

✔ Your airline tickets (if you bought them from the cruise line)

✔ A boarding document that contains your cabin assignment (or at least your cabin category) and sometimes your dining table assignment

✔ Boarding forms to fill out

✔ Luggage tags

✔ Vouchers for transportation between the airport and the port (if you arranged for this option)

✔ A booklet describing the shore excursions available on your trip, which you may be able to book ahead of time

✔ Another booklet with emergency phone numbers and answers to frequently asked questions, such as what kind of power outlets are in your cabin, what kind of laundry services are available, and so on

Read through your documents carefully and verify the info. Confirm that your cabin category is correct, as well as your dining preferences (on ships that still do formal, fixed-seating dining). Check that your airline tickets show the correct flights and arrival times. And definitely make sure that you've got enough time to reach the port at least a few hours before the ship is scheduled to depart.

When the big day arrives, keep your cruise documents with you in your purse, briefcase, or carryon.

Paying Up: Paper or Plastic?

Cruising is like Monopoly: Through the whole thing it feels like you're playing with funny money. It's only at the end that reality hits.

Spending on board

With the exception of some of the small ships discussed in Chapter 13, cruise vessels operate on a cashless basis from day to day. What that means is that everything you buy on board, from bar drinks to shore excursions to spa treatments and dinners at extra-cost restaurants, is put on your tab, to be paid at the end of the trip.

Most ships issue you an onboard charge card, which works as described in the following paragraphs. The exceptions are some small ships (carrying 100 or fewer passengers) that just ask for your cabin number to keep an account of onboard purchases.

Shortly before or after you first come aboard, a purser or check-in clerk takes an imprint of your credit card and issues you your onboard charge card, which, on most ships, also serves as your room key and as your cruise ID. You also have the option of using cash, traveler's checks, or sometimes personal checks to pay your account. If you decide to pay cash, you probably have to put down a deposit of at least $250.

On the last night of your cruise, you get an itemized account of all you've charged. If you don't dispute the charges, they're automatically billed to your credit card. If you're paying in cash or if you dispute any charge, you need to stop by the office of the ship's cashier or purser. There may be a long line, so don't go if you don't have to.

The only time you may need cash on board is at the end of the cruise, when (depending on the cruise line's policies) you may be leaving tips for your cabin steward, dining steward, and other staff. You may also want to keep some cash on hand to use in the laundry room (if your ship has one). In general, you need cash for the casino, but often ships allow you to charge gambling dollars to your shipboard account, up to a certain amount per day.

If you find that you need more cash, some ships have their own ATMs — often located, not surprisingly, in the casino. The ATMs give out U.S. dollars, though fees are typically higher than ATMs on shore.

Settling up on shore

Almost all the stores at the ports take credit cards, and most restaurants do, too, but you need some cash on hand to pay for taxis, to buy small items and snacks, and to tip tour guides. Small bills are best.

Pretty much all the Caribbean, Mexican, and Canadian ports we describe in Part V accept U.S. dollars. If you want to use the local currency, you can often find ATMs, bureaux de change, and banks close to the docks. ATMs are your best bet, as their exchange rates are most favorable — just be sure you have some idea of the exchange rate ahead of time, so you know how much you're taking out. In Europe, you need to convert your dollars to euros (or pounds, in Britain).

To check conversion rates before your trip, use the "Quick Cross Rates" table and currency calculator at www.xe.com.

Using ATMs means that you don't have to carry large amounts of traveler's checks or cash from the United States, but we usually carry some cash anyway, as an emergency reserve.

Before you leave home, be sure any cash you intend to access is in the checking part of your account if your ATM card allows you to access from both savings and checking — some foreign machines allow you to withdraw only from your checking account and don't offer you the option of transferring money between accounts.

You can find ATMs at most ports — even the tiny ones. Don't take out more money than you need that day or you may end up with a bunch of bills that you have to convert back at the end of your trip. Also, remember that you can't convert coins, so spend those first.

Personal checks are pretty much useless for cruise travel purposes, except as accepted on your ship (check with the cruise line for its policy on personal checks).

Decking Yourself Out: What to Pack

Some people worry about packing for vacations. Don't. Seriously, you probably have everything you need right in your closet. Over the past several years, cruises have gotten more and more casual, attire-wise.

Understanding shipboard dress codes (such as they are)

Back around the dawn of the 21st century, Norwegian Cruise Line (NCL) looked at the cruise business, saw that pretty much every line had stuck with a mix of formal, informal, and casual nights for the past, oh, hundred years, and then said, "Screw it. We're going casual." The move created an avalanche, with many other lines either toning down or scrapping their own dress codes.

Today, no matter what the itinerary, you can find people spending their days in T-shirts, polo shirts, shorts or khakis, plus casual dresses for women and sweat shirts or light sweaters to compensate for the air-conditioning. The vibe is about the same on the luxury lines, though those polos and khakis probably sport better labels. If you're going on an Alaskan or other cold-weather cruise, pack sweat shirts or fleece, jeans, comfortable (and preferably waterproof) walking shoes, and a light jacket and/or a waterproof jacket. In the evenings, people typically dress up, but not to the tux-and-gown level they used to. A lot of mainstream lines still have two traditional formal nights during any 7-night itinerary, but most men opt for dark suits over real formalwear, while women dress in cocktail dresses, sequined jackets, gowns, or the like. Some other lines are ditching the formal concept entirely. The closest NCL comes is an "optional formal" captain's cocktail night, though it's totally up to you what you decide to wear — just no shorts in the dining rooms, please. On lines such as Windstar and Oceania, the dressiest thing you may ever see is a sport jacket.

On lines that still have delineated formal, informal, and casual nights, here's the scoop:

✔ **Formal nights:** Imagine what you'd wear to a nice wedding: tuxedos or dark suits for men; cocktail dresses, sequined jackets, gowns, or other fancy attire for women.

✔ **Informal (or semiformal) nights:** Suits or sport jackets and ties for men; stylish dresses or pantsuits for women.

✔ **Casual nights:** Decent pants and collared shirts for men, and maybe a sport jacket; dresses, skirts, or pantsuits for women.

Suggested dress for the evening is usually printed in the ship's daily schedule. Cruise lines also usually describe their dress codes in their brochures, on their Web sites, and in one of the booklets you get with your cruise tickets.

Aboard all the small-ship lines we discuss in Chapter 13, it's very rare to see anything dressier than a sport jacket at any time, and those usually appear only for the captain's dinner. Most of these lines are all-casual all the time.

Planning for appliances and other odds and ends

If you plan to bring electronic devices, check the information you receive with your tickets to find out about the power situation on board. Not all ships use 110 current (although most in North American fleets do). Even if the ship is 110, you may find only two-pronged jacks rather than three-pronged, so you may need an adapter. And if you stay at a foreign hotel before or after your cruise, you may need a converter kit and different plugs.

Most ships provide hair dryers, though they're frequently low-powered models. If you use one regularly, and have a lightweight model, it can't hurt to bring it along. Just be careful where you plug it in. Some cabin outlets won't handle heat-producing devices such as dryers, curling irons, and the like.

Here are some other things for you to consider:

✔ Most cabins come with toiletries such as soap and shampoo, and sometimes conditioner and lotion, although you still may want to bring your own favorite products. If you forget something, all but a few of the smallest ships have a shop on board selling razor blades, toothbrushes, sunscreen, film, and other sundries, usually at inflated prices.

✔ Except for the small ships, most vessels have a laundry service and some dry cleaning, too, with generally about a 24-hour turnaround time. A price list will be in your cabin. Some ships also have self-service laundry rooms.

✔ Most ships have a telephone wake-up service, but you may prefer to bring your alarm clock.

✔ Don't bother with a beach towel. Most cruise lines provide them for you to take ashore.

✔ A couple of large freezer-style, reclosable plastic bags come in handy for protecting your camera and/or binoculars if you participate in water activities, such as kayaking. And you can also use them to pack damp bathing suits for the trip home.

✔ If you want to bring your own gear for sports such as golf or scuba diving, check with your airline how to transport such items.

✔ Bring plenty of film, memory disks, and/or batteries for your camera, and blank cassettes for your camcorder. Merchants will gouge you for this stuff at touristy areas.

✔ Learn from our mistakes: Don't take brand-new shoes that you haven't worn in. (Or pack a bunch of adhesive bandages if you do.)

✔ Airport security forbids the use of locks on your luggage. If you're worried about your bags just popping open, you can secure the zippers with keychain rings. Security can take them off easily if they need to get in.

Packing your carryon

Your carry-on bag (whether you're carrying it on the plane or just onto the ship) should contain everything you think you may need for the day, in case your checked luggage is delayed. Be sure to pack the following:

✔ Big Important Documents, including your passport, driver's license, airline tickets, cruise tickets, boarding forms, and claim checks for airport parking

✔ Currency, including credit and debit cards and cash and/or traveler's checks

✔ House and car keys

- Valuables, such as jewelry, binoculars, cameras, iPods or Walkmen, and video equipment

- Eyeglasses and any prescription medicines you may need during your trip

- A change of clothes

- Motion-sickness medication if you think you may need it, plus hard candy or chewing gum if you have problems with plugged ears on takeoff and landing

- Snacks if you're flying one of those Scrooge-like airlines that have cut back on food service over the past few years

Keeping in Touch at Sea

In case you're worried about staying in touch with loved ones, work, or the sports scores while you're away, calm down. Today it's easy — some people would say too easy — to stay connected while at sea. Whatever happened to getting away from it all, anyway? In addition to the news channels on most cabin TVs, some ships still maintain the old tradition of printing the day's top news stories and slipping them under passengers' doors each morning. And then, of course, there are all the gadgets . . .

Cellphone service

Beginning in 2004, technology became available that allows cellphone users to make and receive calls while aboard ship, even when far out at sea. Today, Costa Cruises has the *Costa Fortuna, Atlantica, Europa, Romantica,* and *Tropicale* wired up; Norwegian Cruise Line, Royal Caribbean, and Celebrity are all set to offer cell service fleetwide soon after this book goes to press; Crystal Cruises' *Crystal Serenity* has it going on; and other lines are eyeing the possibility. Our prediction? Everybody but the small-ship lines will offer cellular service within a couple years.

The service, usually offered by a company called Wireless Maritime Service, is available to most passengers with GSM phones that operate at 900 MHz and 1900 MHz, which are common in the United States. In addition to regular voice and text messaging, the service — which kicks in when a ship sails beyond range of shoreside towers — lets passengers with data-capable GSM/GPRS devices access data services such as e-mail and picture messaging. Passengers are billed by the carrier to which they subscribe at roaming rates set by that carrier, just as if they were roaming on land instead of at sea. Expect something in the ballpark of $1.70 per minute.

Satellite phones

As they have for years, cruise ships continue to offer satellite phone service from their cabins, usually for about $8 or $9 per minute, though it can climb as high as $15 a minute.

In addition to cabin sat-phones and cell service, each ship has a central phone number, fax number, and e-mail address, which you can sometimes find in the cruise line's brochure and usually in the documents you get with your tickets. Distribute these to family members or friends in case they have to contact you in an emergency, but be sure they know the numbers are only for emergencies, since they can easily cost $30 to $40 for just a minute or two.

It also can't hurt to leave behind the numbers of the cruise line's headquarters and/or reservations department, both of whom can put people in touch with you in an emergency situation.

Internet and e-mail at sea

Aside from most of the small, adventure-oriented ships in Chapter 13, pretty much every cruise ship has an Internet center where passengers can surf and e-mail to their wallet's content, at rates calculated on a per-minute basis (usually between 50¢ and $1) or in pre-purchased blocks (say, $40 for a 3- or 4-night cruise or $90 for a 7-night cruise).

E-mail access is usually available through the Web via your Earthlink, AOL, Hotmail, Yahoo!, or other personal account. Some lines also let you set up an account aboard ship, if you don't have your own.

Many ships built over the past several years (including the newest Celebrity, Crystal, Costa, Holland America, NCL, Oceania, Royal Caribbean, Cunard, Radisson, SeaDream, and Silversea ships) have been wired with dataports in all, most, or some cabins and suites, allowing passengers who travel with laptops to log on in privacy. The cost for these services tends to be higher than access in the Internet centers.

Wireless Internet (Wi-Fi) is another new trend, offered aboard all the Carnival, Holland America, NCL, and Princess vessels, usually in the atrium and other designated public rooms. A few ships — the small luxury ships of Seabourn and the huge new *Carnival Valor* — offer wireless access everywhere on board. To take advantage of this service, you must have a wireless card for your laptop (or you can rent a card, or a laptop), then purchase minutes either as you need them or in packages of 33 to 500 minutes.

Confirming Your Flight

Air arrival and departure times are always subject to change, so take a minute to call and confirm your flight a day or two before your departure. You can also call the day you're scheduled to leave, to avoid having to wait around the airport if your flight is delayed.

 If you follow any special diets, whether vegetarian, kosher, or otherwise, call the airline in advance to make sure you'll be fed appropriately on the plane. Different airlines require different lead times to arrange special meals, but you can bet on the minimum being 24 hours in advance. Call early.

Get to the airport early. For domestic flights, plan to get there two full hours before your plane is scheduled to depart. For international flights, you may want to get in a little earlier than that. In the worst-case scenario, it saves you stress if lines are long at check-in and security. If lines are short, it gives you time to drink beer and eat nachos at the airport bar. So what's the downside?

Remembering Other Important Stuff

Some things to keep in mind before you walk out the door:

- ✓ Read all the pre-trip material the cruise line provides you. Do you have all the requisite IDs? Also, fill out (or at least think about filling out) the boarding forms they sent. You can also do this on the plane, or when waiting at the terminal.

- ✓ Make photocopies of your passport, your airline tickets, and any credit cards you plan to use just in case they get separated from you for any reason. Pack the copies in your luggage separately from the actual documents (which should be in your carryon). You may also want to leave another set of copies with a friend.

- ✓ Write down the ship's phone number (it should be included with your cruise documents), and leave the number and a copy of your itinerary with a friend or relative.

- ✓ Put luggage tags on your bags. The cruise line will send you a set with your cruise documents, which you have to fill out with your departure date and port, cabin number, and so on and affix to each bag so they can be delivered to your cabin.

- ✓ Be sure to put your name and address *inside* your bags, too, just in case your luggage tags fall off.

- ✓ Don't carry scissors, razor blades, or any other sharp objects in your hand luggage. Ditto for grenades, poison gas, or toxic waste. You can pack the former in your checked luggage, but not the latter. Regulations on what you can and can't bring with you on the plane seem to be changing all the time. The latest no-go? Cigarette lighters. We've even been stopped for a tiny little wrench, no more than three inches long. Seems you can't bring any tools onto a plane. Who knew?

- ✓ If no one will be at home while you're away, you may want to call the post office and arrange for it to hold your mail. Ditto for any newspapers you have delivered.

Chapter 6

Embarkation Day

In This Chapter

▶ Making your way to port
▶ Preparing to board ship
▶ Finding your cabin and getting your bearings
▶ Donning the orange
▶ Getting your head into cruise mode

Is your day-to-day life as stressful as ours? If so, that cruise you signed up for months ago has probably snuck right up on you. Look at that! It starts tomorrow, and here you are reading this chapter just now. Luckily, there's nothing about the boarding process that you won't be able to negotiate with aplomb after you get through this patented Matt-and-Heidi "Coming Aboard" Aplomb-O-Mizer. Ready, get set . . .

Getting to Your Port of Embarkation

So you're about to begin your trip. Because the cruise lines are home-porting their ships in several dozen places now instead of from just a few hub cities, you may be driving or flying to your ship.

Pack your suitcases and don't forget to attach an ID tag with your name and address, and maybe your cellphone number. Attach the bag tags your cruise line sent you, too, which include your sailing date and cabin number.

If you're flying

Call the airline before you leave home to ensure that your flight is on schedule. Also, allow yourself ample time at the airport to check your bags and get through security screening.

Keep your tickets, cruise documents, passport and other identification, keys, valuable items, and medicines in a bag you can carry onto the plane and ship with you, rather than check through. You may also want to pack a light change of clothes, as a precaution in case you and your checked luggage get separated.

When you arrive at your destination airport, cruise line representatives stand at the ready at baggage claim, holding signs bearing your line's or ship's name, and wait to direct you to buses bound for the terminal. You probably already paid for bus transfers to the ship when you bought your cruise. If not, you can arrange them now or take a taxi.

If you've flown to another country, you need to clear Immigration and Customs, which includes showing your passport and any forms you were given on the plane. Follow the appropriate signs. The cruise line reps will be waiting when you get through the checkpoints.

Arranging transfers through the cruise line

If you booked transfers to the ship through the cruise line, the man or woman with the sign directs you and your bags to the bus or van that takes you to the ship. If you haven't done so already, fill out the luggage tags the cruise line sent with your tickets (listing your ship name, sailing date, and cabin number), and put one on each of your bags. The bus driver usually asks for your transportation voucher, which you also received with your cruise documents. After you arrive at the port, you have to ID your luggage and check it in. You usually find an army of porters to assist you (for a suggested tip of about $2 per bag) and another army of cruise line employees waiting to direct you to the check-in desks.

Handling transfers on your own

If you didn't book the cruise line transfers, gather your luggage from the baggage area and head to the pier via taxi or whatever other mode of transportation you've arranged.

Find out in advance what the trip from the airport to the port should cost to avoid getting ripped off. Many airports post information like that on their Web sites. Don't forget to put the luggage tags (displaying your ship name, sailing date, and cabin number) from the cruise line on your bags.

Some cities have multiple piers, and you can help your cab driver by having the pier number and directions to the ship handy. The cruise line should include this information with your documents. If not, you can get it in advance by contacting the line.

Dealing with a delayed flight

If your flight is delayed, don't panic. Let the airline personnel know that you're a cruise passenger who has a ship to catch that day. They may be able to put you on a different flight. If you've bought air transportation through the cruise line, the airline may already know you have a cruise to catch and will try to make other arrangements, and the cruise line will probably be tracking your progress as well. In any case, have the cruise line's emergency number handy (it's listed in your cruise documents) just in case you or the airline needs to get in touch. If there's a forced overnight, the airline typically pays for your hotel room. If there's a weather delay, air/sea guests are given priority on standby flights to the port of embarkation, but airlines are unlikely to provide hotel accommodations.

If you haven't booked your air travel with the cruise line, you need to work with the airline to catch your ship in the next port, as well as contact the cruise line to tell them about your situation. In cases like this, it helps if you've bought travel insurance that includes a trip-delay benefit. See Chapter 4 for more information about travel insurance.

Dealing with lost luggage

If you and your luggage get separated in transit, tell your airline you're about to board a cruise. If they can't get it to you before your ship departs, they'll ship it to your first port of call. If you don't get missing luggage the first night, you can get an overnight kit, with such items as a toothbrush, toothpaste, and a razor, from the purser's office.

If you've checked your luggage in with the ship but it never shows up in your cabin, contact the reception desk. Most likely your luggage tags fell off and your bags are waiting somewhere on board.

If you're driving

If you've driven to the port, it's just a matter of parking and trundling your luggage into the terminal. Most ports have secure parking available on-site (or at least close by), usually costing $10 to $12 per day.

Checking In at the Pier

What happens when you reach the cruise terminal depends on the ship, but the check-in process can sometimes be slow as molasses — though sometimes it's smooth as silk.

Preparing to board

If it's still morning or early afternoon, don't feel rushed. Remember, another shipload of passengers is probably just getting off from the ship's last trip, and cabins still need to be cleaned, supplies loaded, and paperwork and Customs documents completed properly before you can board. Even if your ship has been berthed since 6 a.m., new passengers are often not allowed on board until about 1 p.m., though cruise lines are increasingly offering a preboarding option — which means you can get on at 11 a.m. or noon, have lunch, and start checking out the ship, though your cabin probably won't be ready till early afternoon.

Beyond the simple joy of feeling that your vacation has started, coming aboard early affords you some advantages, such as getting choice appointment times at the spa, signing up for popular shore excursions, and getting reservations for dinner at the alternative restaurants. Note, though, that a lot of cruise lines are offering pre-booking options for some or all of these, so you may be able to sign up online or over the phone before you even sail. (See Chapter 4 for details.)

Whether you board early or late, you have to wait in some kind of line to get your paperwork cleared. Before you do, make sure that you fill out all the documents the cruise line sent you — the ones marked "Be sure to fill these out in advance." You may also want to tidy yourself up a bit, because there's sure to be a ship's photographer lurking somewhere nearby to take one of those "coming aboard" shots. We're of two minds on this: Heidi thinks they're fun to look at later in the ship's gallery, even if you don't buy them (for $7–$10 a pop); Matt thinks he's some kind of secret agent who shouldn't be photographed under any condition, so he waves the photographer off every time. And the lesson is, whether you want your picture taken or not is up to you. You're under no obligation to pose.

Checking in

During the check-in process, a cruise line rep examines your tickets and ID and sets you up with a shipboard ID and an onboard account.

Regarding IDs, proposed new State Department and Homeland Security regulations mean you almost certainly need a passport to go on any cruise that visits a foreign port, even if it's just the Bahamas. If you're sailing an Alaska cruise, you may need one, too, if the ship departs from or ends in Vancouver. See Chapter 5 for more info about getting your passport. On itineraries that visit multiple countries, your ship often holds your passport to facilitate clearance procedures. Don't worry. It's normal. You get your passports back when you go ashore.

Shipboard accounts are essentially credit cards you use for everything you buy on board: drinks, shore excursions, spa treatments, and so on. To set 'em up, the cruise line rep usually takes an imprint of your credit card, though you also have the option of leaving a cash or traveler's check deposit (usually $250) and settling the difference at the end of your cruise. Usually, the shipboard ID you're issued at check-in doubles as your onboard charge card. Often it's also your room key. If not, you either get your key now or pick it up in your cabin where it should be waiting.

Keep your shipboard ID with you at all times. Not only do you need it for any purchases you make on board (except aboard some small ships, where they just jot down your name when you buy something), but you also need it as ID every time you get on or off your ship in port.

On ships that still follow traditional fixed-seating dining, check-in is often when you get your dining-room table assignment, too (see Chapter 7 for more about this), though you may also have received it with your tickets. Either way, make sure your seating time (early or late), table size, and choice of smoking or nonsmoking section (where applicable) are as you want. If not, talk to someone now. If your ship is following a more casual dining approach, you don't have to worry about any of this.

If you booked a suite or have mobility problems, you may get priority check-in and embarkation. Otherwise, boarding lines generally form alphabetically by last name.

Stepping aboard and checking out your digs

All passengers must clear security just before boarding ship. This involves stepping through a metal detector, having your hand luggage X-rayed, and handing over your shipboard ID for the first time so that you're officially counted as "on board." From here, a crewmember directs you (and maybe even escorts you) to your cabin, where it makes sense to spend a little time checking things out. Your cabin steward may stop by to see that everything is okay and that you know how everything works: the air-conditioning and heating (assuming the system is individually controlled), the TV, the safe (if your cabin has one), the shower, the telephone, and any other nifty gadgets. Let the steward know if anything seems amiss, or if you have any special needs — extra pillows, for example — or whether you want the beds separate or pushed together.

Don't be put off by the big WHOOSH!!! of the toilet. Ships typically use vacuum toilets, which sound as if they could drag you down if you're not careful. Don't put any foreign objects into the bowl other than the toilet paper provided — they can clog up the works, creating what's technically known as *a big mess*.

A daily program in your cabin tells you what's on tap for the rest of the day, including meal times and dress codes, where applicable.

Your bags may not arrive at your cabin until after the ship leaves the pier, but don't be concerned. On the bigger ships, the crew may have to deliver 5,000 or more bags, which can take time. Because of this, dinner on the first night is always casual. If you start to worry as the night goes on, give the purser's office a call.

A few other bits of info you should know:

- ✔ Tap water on ships is potable, but it may have a strong chlorine taste. Many ships also leave bottled water in the cabins, but just because it's there doesn't mean it's free. Ditto for items in the mini-bar, unless you're sailing on a really swanky vessel. A card somewhere nearby should indicate the prices.

- ✔ Directions near the phone tell you how to make calls to other passengers and ship personnel, as well as how to dial home from the ship (though there are cheaper options — see Chapter 5).

- ✔ You should find a little binder detailing ship services, including room service. There should also be a Do Not Disturb sign (important for nappers), forms and bags for the ship's laundry and dry cleaning services (offered on all but the smallest ships), and probably a deck plan showing what's where on your vessel.

✔ Most ships have personal safes somewhere in the cabin. Some lock with a numerical code that you program in, while others recognize your key card. They're not big, but they're more than adequate for storing your passports, plane tickets, jewelry, and other valuables. If your ship doesn't have personal safes, you can check valuables at the purser's desk.

Exploring the Ship

We suggest you spend some of your time on the first day exploring the ship. Carry your shipboard credit card (in case you want to buy a drink), your cabin key, and a deck plan. If there's no deck plan in your cabin, ask at the reception desk. Some ships — especially the really big ones — offer guided tours on embarkation day, but what's the fun in that? We much prefer just wandering around and scoping out cozy nooks and comfortable barstools, and maybe grabbing a bite at the welcome-aboard buffet.

Getting a jump on your fellow passengers

You may have been able to pre-book shore excursions, spa times, and reservations at the ship's alternative restaurant before your cruise (see Chapter 4 for more about this), but if not, now's the time to get in line so that you don't get shut out of the best spots. This is especially important if you've got your eye on a specialized shore excursion that's limited to only a certain number of guests, or if you want a prime time slot such as an appointment with the hair stylist right before dinner on formal nights, or a massage appointment at midafternoon on a day at sea.

If you prefer to keep your week flexible, note that you don't have to sign up for anything early if you don't want to. You can generally sign up for shore excursions until the day before they're scheduled, and can some-times get an appointment at the spa at the last minute.

While you're at the spa, you may be asked if you'd like a tour to get acquainted with what the facility offers. This translates as "Look at all the good things we can do for you. Give us your money. Giiiive ussssss yourrrrr mooooooneeeeeeey." Keep your willpower shields up unless you're in a buying mood. Ditto for the pitches you often hear at the shore excursion manager's shore talks, which often give a pretty heavy pitch to certain shops on shore that you just *have* to hit. Yah. Right. Oh, and speaking of separating passengers from their money, note that the casino and shops are closed until the ship is actually at sea, in accor-dance with government regulations. Sometimes the swimming pool is also covered until after embarkation. But of course that's free.

If your ship has a library of videos or DVDs for watching in your cabin, you may also want to drop by there early to get the best selection.

Sailing away

You may want to be on the deck, drink in hand, when the ship leaves the pier. The nostalgic appeal alone makes it worthwhile ("Arrivederci! Don't forget to write!"), but some ships offer complimentary champagne to sweeten the deal.

Attending the Safety Drill

Ships are required by law to hold a safety drill within 24 hours of departure, and most lines get it out of the way either right before or right after sailing out of port. Attendance is mandatory, and stewards often check your cabin to make sure you're not hiding out.

In your cabin, you should find a bright-orange life jacket for each passenger, including special ones for any kids in your cabin (if they're not there, let your cabin steward know immediately). Features on the jackets include a whistle and a light that turns on automatically when it hits water.

The ship's daily program lists the time of your drill, and the captain also makes several announcements over the ship's PA as drill time gets close. When you hear the signal (seven short blasts on the ship's alarm whistle, followed by one long blast), collect your life jacket and follow the signs to your designated muster station, whose number is written both on the back of your cabin door and on your life jacket. You go to this place in case of a real emergency, too. Ship staff is posted in corridors and stairways to direct you, if you don't know exactly where you're going.

Although some drills are very brief, others can go on for a half-hour or more. Sorry, no drinks allowed, but we've had fun during long drills by taking pictures of each other in our puffy orange vests, looking like the Michelin Man.

Gearing Up for the Days Ahead

In general, life on a big ship can follow a kind of bipolar logic: On the one hand, you're taking a trip to visit some places you haven't seen before; on the other, you may get into such a cruise zone that you don't want to leave the ship, shuttling from pool to lounge to buffet to spa to virtual-golf simulator to basketball court to lecture to sports bar. Try for the middle path. It works for Buddhism, so it should work for you.

The following two sections detail what you can expect when the ship is in port and at sea.

One if by land: Days ashore

Map out your days in port to make sure you see all that the destination offers. Decide ahead of time whether you want to take an excursion or go off on your own; whether there are cultural attractions, natural wonders, or shopping zones that pique your interest; and whether you want to lunch locally or on the ship. (Check out the chapters in Part V for specifics on the ports of call.) To make sure that you don't miss the boat — literally — take careful note of your ship's departure time.

At some ports, your ship docks in or near the center of town. At others, you dock in a far-off passenger or commercial port and have to take a taxi or bus to town. At still other ports, there's no dock at all, so your ship anchors offshore and shuttles passengers back and forth via a small boat called a *tender*. To catch a lift on a tender, you usually go to a lounge area and take a number. Although you get a lower number and get ashore earlier if you get to the lounge earlier, the lines tend to be longer first thing in the morning, so sometimes you're better off lingering over a second cup of coffee than rushing to the lounge to wait in line. If you signed up in advance for a shore excursion, you're assigned a time and place to meet, and get priority group debarkation.

Don't feel like you have to get off at every port of call, but you may want to at least stretch your legs and get some exercise. On big ships especially, some people stay on the ship, which takes on a haunting yet appealing aura when the crowds disappear. The pool may be closed, but you can still sit on the Sun Deck, take spa treatments, use the gym (which is less crowded on port days), play cards, eat lunch, and enjoy some quiet time. On port days, the ship generally offers fewer organized activities, but you can still find offerings such as movies, live music poolside, a few seminars, and maybe a sports competition or two.

Two if by sea: Days at sea

If you sail on a big ship, brace yourself for a staggering array of sea-day activities, especially in the Caribbean and Mexican Riviera, where typical offerings include exercise classes, lectures, movies, beauty seminars (such as "How to Fight Cellulite"), pool games, dance classes, and contests that range from golf putting to hairy backs and knobby knees (the hairiest and knobbiest win).

Sea days on Alaskan cruises are a bit more destination-oriented, with the ships visiting glaciers and areas known for exemplary whale-watching. Wildlife and glacier experts are often on board to explain more about the area's natural wonders. Other activities may be closed or at least pared down when the ship is scheduled to cruise in and around the more extravagant natural wonders, such as Glacier Bay, Tracy Arm Fjord, or Hubbard Glacier.

Sea days in other cruise regions are similar to the above. As a general rule, small ships rarely spend entire days at sea unless they're exploring natural areas (such as Glacier Bay).

An onboard who's who

So, just who are all those people walking around in the spiffy uniforms anyway?

✔ **Captain:** The big boss (may also be referred to as The Master); he's in charge.

✔ **Staff captain:** Second in command; normally in charge of navigation and safety.

✔ **Hotel manager:** In charge of passenger services, including restaurants, bars, and accommodations. If you need someone to complain to in these areas, the buck stops here.

✔ **Chief engineer:** In charge of all the onboard machinery, including the engines.

✔ **Purser:** In charge of information and financial matters. This person delivers your bill at the end of the cruise.

✔ **Chief steward:** In charge of making sure all cabins and public rooms are cleaned and maintained.

✔ **Cabin stewards:** The people who clean the cabins.

✔ **Head chef or chef de cuisine:** In charge of the kitchen (galley) and the menus.

✔ **Maitre d':** In charge of the dining room operation.

✔ **Dining stewards:** A fancy name for waiters.

✔ **Assistant waiters:** Used to be known as busboys.

✔ **Sommeliers:** Wine experts who take your wine order and take you through the whole sniffing, sipping, nodding ritual; handled by the dining steward on many ships.

✔ **Cruise director:** In charge of all activities and entertainment; also acts as the ship's emcee.

✔ **Shore excursion director:** In charge of land tours; also often the port lecturer.

✔ **Entertainment director:** Heads the show team.

✔ **Doctor:** In charge of medical care.

Part III

All Aboard: The Cruise Experience

The 5th Wave

By Rich Tennant

©RICHTENNANT

"Oh look! Isn't that Raoul, the ship steward you refused to tip after he fished your watch out of the pool?"

In this part . . .

This is what cruising is all about: drinking beer in the hot tub, loading a mountain of food onto your buffet platter, and joining really stupid pool games. No, wait, *this* is what cruising is all about: going to a wine-tasting session; eating sushi at a small, high-toned Asian restaurant; and attending a lecture on the history of transatlantic passenger sailing. No, wait, *this* . . . well anyway, whatever cruising is about for you, we cover it here, along with practicalities such as how to navigate embarkation day and how to navigate the cruise lines' variety of programs for kids and teens.

Chapter 7

Wining and Dining

In This Chapter

▶ Finding food, nearly all the time
▶ Checking out traditional dining
▶ Considering alternative dinner options
▶ Doing breakfast and lunch

*F*ood. We're all obsessed with it in one way or the other. And the cruise lines sure haven't been shy about capitalizing on it. A cruise ship is a veritable feeding frenzy; only your willpower stands between you and a few new pounds. To please all palates and schedules, you'll find that food is available 24 hours a day, if not more — from pizza, burgers, and soft ice cream to buffets that seem endless and candlelit meals in dark cozy restaurants. Except for the very smallest 100-passenger ships, the bigger the ship the more eating opportunities you can find. On the largest megaships, expect eight to ten different venues. Aside from one or two more traditional dining rooms, you can find a casual buffet restaurant open all day, plus specialty outlets ranging from sushi bars to steakhouses, diner-style burger joints, romantic French restaurants, and the list goes on. As if that's not enough, 24-hour room service is standard, and often the pickins include pizza delivery.

Though overeating is pretty difficult to avoid, you don't have to gain an extra five pounds on a weeklong cruise. Ships offer healthier options for noshing, such as fruit and fish, plus most ships have great well-stocked gyms and fitness classes. Better yet, you can vow to take the stairs and not the elevator. On today's huge ships, that's quite an opportunity to burn calories. In port, sign up for active stuff such as biking and kayaking, and just you see, you may actually return home a skinnier version of your former self. Do we see a Jenny Craig endorsement in your future?

Never a Food-Free Moment

Endless: The key word for cruise ship eating. Check out this typical meal schedule to understand what's meant by that old joke, "You come on as a passenger and you leave as cargo":

- **Early risers:** (6:30 a.m.) Coffee and simple pastries

- **Buffet breakfast:** (7:30–11 a.m.) Daily specials, sweet rolls, fruit, eggs, bacon, French toast, cereal, oatmeal, omletes, yogurt, croissants, coffee, juice, and tea

- **Breakfast in the dining room:** (Main seating begins around 7 a.m.; late seating around 8 or 9 a.m.) Full breakfast, including omelets, eggs, French toast, pancakes, breakfast meats, potatoes, fish, cereal, oatmeal, fruit, yogurt, and juices

- **Pizza:** (11 a.m.–11 p.m.) Serving up fresh pies all day; some outlets also have salads

- **Buffet lunch:** (11:30 a.m.–3 p.m.) Full hot and cold lunch offerings, including salad bar, pasta station, and grill for burgers

- **Lunch in the dining room:** (Main seating at noon; late seating at 1:30 p.m.) Full luncheon with a rotating menu of hot dishes, salads, sandwiches, pastas, grilled items, and desserts

- **Afternoon tea:** (3:30–5 p.m.) Tea and cake or cookies

- **Snack time:** (All afternoon) Ice cream and fat-free frozen yogurt

- **Buffet dinner:** (5:30–11 p.m) Casual setting and hot and cold entrees, sometimes focused on a theme cuisine like Asian or Italian; carved beef, ham, or turkey; desserts; salads; cold meats; breads; cheeses; and fruit

- **Dinner in the dining room:** (Early seating at 6 p.m.; late seating at 8:15 p.m.) Gourmet cuisine, including popular international and American dishes served in seven courses with desserts

- **Midnight buffet:** (Guess!) Extravagant offerings of hot and cold entrees, desserts, salads, cold meats, breads, cheeses, and fruit

Still hungry? Well, seek out the coffee bars many ships have that dispense specialty drinks such as espressos and cappuccino, plus gourmet ice cream and fancy pastries. Some bars also offer caviar with all the trimmings. Just keep in mind, all of this stuff will cost you extra.

The Take on Traditional Dining

Like a big resort, you can find multiple dining options on most ships these days. The traditional set-up, where guests reserve the early or late seating in one of the main dining rooms, is still offered on most ships. The ship takes care of assigning you to a table that seats four, six, eight, or more people, who you share dinner with every evening in the main dining room.

Ships offer a very limited number of tables for two, so don't expect to snag one, though it can't hurt to ask.

If you go the traditional way because maybe you like the prospect of meeting your fellow shipmates, sitting at a table with eight seats gives you enough variety among your companions that you don't get bored. This also allows you to steer clear of a bore or some other person at the table you really don't like. Don't feel that the chair you sit in the first night needs to be your place every night — the ship assigns you to a table, not a specific seat. Go crazy by choosing a different seat each night to get the most out of the opportunity to mingle.

Don't panic if you end up sitting next to some obnoxious type who chews with his mouth open and keeps shouting "What's with all these forks?" Try to change your table by speaking with the maitre d' (greasing his palm may help). You can also request a larger or smaller table by visiting the maitre d' station on the first day of the cruise.

Dining course by course

Traditional dining aboard a cruise ship provides more than a five- to seven-course meal; it serves as one of the main social events of the day. With the multiple courses served at a relaxed pace and your table dressed in china, silver, fresh flowers, and starched linens, you can't get further from a fast-food experience.

Expect to be at your table for at least an hour and a half. Here's what you're likely to find:

- ✔ Overall, count on continental (international) cuisine in the dining room — think steaks, chicken, fish, and pasta.

- ✔ The courses consist of an appetizer, soup, salad, main course (with starch and vegetables), and dessert, and on some ships pasta, fruit, and cheese courses as well.

- ✔ Most lines provide at least one healthy selection in each category, sometimes even listing the fat, salt content, and number of calories on the menu. A few lines, including Carnival and Crystal, have joined the low-carb craze, offering special menu items for followers of low-carb diets.

- ✔ Most ships feature daily vegetarian selections.

- ✔ Children's menus are common.

- ✔ On some nights, the ship builds the menus around a theme, such as Caribbean or Italian night.

Feel free to make a culinary request if you have an urge for something in particular, but remember that the chef can prepare dishes only with what's available in the larder (no running out to the grocery store here). Make your requests the day before so that the chef can prepare.

Considering what to wear

Most 7-night cruises include two formal nights, where the dress code suggests men wear suits or tuxes, and for the ladies, fancy dresses or pant suits. Of course, one person's formalwear may be wildly different from another's (believe us, we've seen it all!). A good rule of thumb is to wear what you'd wear to a wedding (not your own silly, but someone else's).

To skip the dressy duds, hit the more casual dining venues on formal nights (see the next section), where you can get away with much more casual garb, such as chinos and polo shirts. In general, lines discourage jeans and shorts at dinner ship-wide, but we see that, too; it's at the maitre d's discretion whether you have to go back to your cabin and change into something deemed more presentable.

A Sea of Other Dining Options

If this traditional dining stuff sounds too regimented for you, no problem, most ships have supplemented the traditional set-up with other more flexible options as well. You can find at least one, if not many, casual venues operating nightly without fixed seating times. Norwegian Cruise Line, for example, operates all of its restaurants like this — you decide where, when, and with whom you want to dine. On Princess ships, you have the choice to either dine the traditional way or with open seating, but you must pick one option when you book your cruise.

These lines, and just about every other line, too, give you the option (depending on the ship you choose) of dining in a smaller gourmet restaurant. These venues are intimate and more like a fine restaurant on land, with a higher level of service (usually the ship's best waiters are sent to these spots), more expertly prepared food, and plenty of tables for two, so you don't have to sit with other passengers. The lines usually decorate them in upscale décor and focus on one type of cuisine — Italian, Asian, French, and steakhouses are the most popular. You typically have to pay a service fee ($10–$30 per head) and reserve your table in advance (do so early on in the cruise or you may not get a spot).

Many ships also offer a free casual alternative dinner option — an open-seating, no-reservations-required, casual dress affair, most often in the main buffet restaurant. Sometimes the buffet spread is supplemented with a short menu of simple food such as steaks, grilled fish, pasta, and salads. Generally, this option is available until late, sometimes past midnight.

Of course, the ultracasual alternative is room service. The menu may be limited, but you don't have to put on your formal duds — or any duds at all!

Cruise lines with the best taste

Kudos to these cruise lines for their excellent cuisine. If you're a foodie, you'll want to go with one of these lines, as they offer the best gourmet cuisine at sea.

- **Crystal:** The best Asian food afloat, as well as ultratasty cuisine all around. A guest chef series brings celebrity chefs aboard. Plus, you'll find Kosher dishes and low-carb choices are always available.

- **Seabourn:** Celebrity chef Charlie Palmer consults on cuisine that reflects California and Pacific Rim influences but also includes favorites such as broiled lobster and beef Wellington.

- **SeaDream:** This line does just about everything right, with the chefs using fresh ingredients in creative ways. And no special request gets denied.

- **Radisson Seven Seas:** Combining traditional and new cuisine, Seven Seas menus are tops. The *Seven Seas Mariner* and *Seven Seas Voyager* also have specialty restaurants overseen by chefs from the prestigious French cooking school, *Le Cordon Bleu.* On some sailings, these chefs offer cooking classes.

- **Silversea:** French-influenced recipes and great steaks cooked to order, as well as themed buffets, guest chefs, and a specialty restaurant by Spain's renowned chef Joachim Koeper. Service is first rate.

Although not quite as extravagant, these lines are also worth a mention:

- **Cunard:** On the *Queen Mary 2,* Cunard assigns you to a restaurant based on your cabin category, and if you're in the Queen's or Princess Grill, expect the best. Celebrity chef Todd English also has his first shipboard restaurant on this vessel.

- **Oceania:** Excellent alternative dining at a steakhouse and Italian restaurant, each with beautiful décor and huge portions.

- **Celebrity:** Consulting chef Michel Roux creates a meal that lasts a luxurious three hours and thrills the palate for the reservations-only alternative restaurants on the *Millennium, Infinity, Summit,* and *Constellation.*

- **Windstar:** Top Los Angeles restaurateur Joachim Splichal consults on fresh and creative menus that go way beyond what you may expect from a sailing ship.

Making special dietary requests

If you have any special dietary needs, make arrangements with the ship when you book your cruise. After you board, check with the maitre d' your first day out to make sure that the kitchen got your request. Some lines offer kosher menus and most have vegetarian, low-fat, low-salt, or sugar-free options.

Satisfying your beverage preferences

If you're a soda junkie, no need to break the bank; many lines have a deal where you can buy a prepaid drink pass, instead of doling out the usual $1.50 to $2 a pop (excuse the pun). Often you're issued a special drink card or given a special cup that you use for unlimited refills of fountain soda (mind you, canned sodas are not included in these promotions). Typically, the price is $35 to $45 for an adult soda card for a weeklong cruise. Prices are lower for children.

Unsure about how to select wine? Consult the wine steward (if your ship has one) or find out whether the ship offers a wine tasting seminar during the cruise. A small fee is typically involved for the seminar (probably $5 or $10), but you get to sample several varieties, and if you find something you like, you can order on the spot (a waiter delivers your wine later to your table in the dining room). You may even get to buy the wine at a discount.

Digging into Breakfast and Lunch

Breakfast and lunch in the dining room are multicourse events. Menus generally change daily. As with dinner, the service isn't rushed, making the meal more about having an experience and less about filling your belly. If you're in a hurry or just don't want to deal with the formalities, you can take advantage of the casual buffet — often located near the Pool Deck.

For lunch, you may have a deck-side grill option with hot dogs, burgers, and chicken. And the newest ships offer even more: On Royal Caribbean's giant *Voyager of the Seas* and its sister ships, for example, a **Johnny Rockets** diner caters to cruisers who crave a good burger and shake. The Disney ships have a poolside snack bar serving chicken fingers, fries, and other tasty fast-food treats.

Mastering dining room etiquette

Even the most socially polished cruisers may need some pointers on shipboard dining. Here are the highlights:

Do's

Display good manners in the dining room by following these tips:

- **Arrive in the dining room on time.** Dining hours are listed in the daily program.

- **Display your understanding of what the members of the dining staff do.** Order from the waiter, not the bus boy.

✔ **Offer wine to the others at your table.** If your tablemates are as polite as you are, one of them will order the next night's bottle.

✔ **If you don't finish your bottle of wine, ask your waiter to have it corked.** You can have it held for the next night.

✔ **Consider the waiter's suggestion about menu items or specials.** The waiter can tell you the most popular menu items.

Don'ts

To keep from embarrassing yourself or your dining companions, don't do the following:

✔ **Don't start eating until the waiter serves everyone at your table.** This is good etiquette no matter where you dine.

✔ **Don't show up dressed inappropriately for the evening.** Check your daily bulletin for the dress code for the evening and prepare accordingly.

✔ **Don't use the incorrect silverware.** Use your silverware moving from the outside in. The first fork on the left is the one that you use for the first course.

✔ **Don't feel as if you have to eat a meal you don't like.** Feel free to send food back and ask for something else if you don't like your selection.

✔ **Don't smoke.** Just about all ships have completely nonsmoking dining rooms.

Chapter 8

Filling Your Days: Onboard Activities and Entertainment

. . . .

In This Chapter

▶ Getting the daily scoop

▶ Lounging and playing by day

▶ Getting educated on board

▶ Gearing up for onboard sports

▶ Checking out evening entertainment options

▶ Making time for faith

. . . .

Yaaaaawn! Is it morning already? You open your eyes. Yep, there's light coming in around those drawn shades. No alarm clock, of course. You're on vacation, why would you set one? And if it's a day at sea, you don't have anywhere to be if you don't want to. You shuffle across the room, throw open the shades. Hey! There's an ocean out there? Your head hurts a little from all that champagne last night, but that's nothing some scrambled eggs and a few minutes in the sauna won't cure. Now let's see, what to do after that? Go swimming? Take a class? Watch a movie? Where's that daily planner? Let's see what there is to do . . .

Digging into the Daily Bulletin

On all but the smallest ships, a daily bulletin is typically delivered to your cabin each evening, advising you of everything that's going on the next day, and other info pertinent to onboard life such as the following:

　✔ The day's activities and live entertainment

　✔ Hours of operation for the bars and shops (with sales and specials noted)

- ✔ The evening dress code, if there is one

- ✔ Listings of in-cabin TV programs and movie presentations

- ✔ A schedule of exercise classes and fitness/wellness lectures

- ✔ Details about upcoming ports of call (such as shopping hot spots and top attractions)

- ✔ Facts about the region you're sailing through

- ✔ All-aboard time, if the ship is spending a day in port

Etcetera, etcetera, etcetera, and, like your local newspaper at home, "advertising" supplements may be stuffed in with the bulletin, promoting special deals at the ship's shops, spa promotions, and other ways to part you from your cash.

Depending on the line you sail with, your bulletin may offer up to 50 activities every day, designed so that everybody on board can find something that suits their tastes. Other ships offer almost no activities, catering instead to an audience that likes to do things at their own pace.

Doing Absolutely Nothing at All

On days at sea especially, you're faced with something most folks don't often get in their day-to-day lives: a full day to do anything you want, at any time you want. You may respond by going into zombie hammock opium-den mode, so blissed-out from the sun, the lack of responsibility, and the motherly rocking of the ship that you can't even rise out of your deck chair. And why should you? We've gotten in this mode more times than we can remember, and recommend it highly.

Lounging at the pool

The Pool Deck is the center of daytime activity on most warm-weather itineraries: a spinning vortex of goofy poolside games, live music, hot tubs, and eternal piña coladas. Most modern megaships have enough deck chairs to go around, but claim a spot early if you want to be at pool-central all day. Be fair, though: Don't just put your towel and book on a chair then walk away for hours. Other folks deserve a chance, too.

Surprisingly, you may not actually swim much at all while on board — most ship pools are just too small. The pool, then, is more of a place for taking a quick cooling dip or a long, leisurely soak while you check out the other passengers in their swimsuits.

If you're more into the idea of relaxing in the sun and reading a book, the Pool Deck probably isn't for you. For that, you can usually find an abundance of chairs on the uppermost deck and sometimes the Promenade or Boat Deck, or in hidden little nooks in the stern that get little foot traffic. A few cruise lines, such as Disney, Princess, Royal Caribbean, and

Carnival (on their Spirit-class ships), have gotten hip to the notion that some people prefer their pool experience to be calm and quiet, and have provided a separate adults-only pool where, at least in theory, kids are excluded. Though be warned that it doesn't always work out that way.

Sleuthing out the cinema

Most of the larger cruise ships either have dedicated movie theaters or (more commonly) show recent-release films in the main theater. Disney Cruise Line, whose ships offer marvelous movie theaters with stadium seating, big screens, comfy chairs, and first-run films (from Disney-owned studios, of course), is the unquestioned leader here. Some Holland America ships have dedicated movie theaters, too, with free popcorn.

Hiding out in your cabin

If you prefer a really quiet day or you spent too much time in the sun the first day, there's nothing saying you have to leave your cabin at all. Room service can bring you enough food and drink to choke a horse, and all but the smallest ships show recent-release films and sometimes classics on their cabin TVs, as well as TV shows from A&E, the Discovery Channel, ESPN, HBO, History & Biography, and TNT. Some ships have programming available in several languages, to suit a diverse clientele.

Some of the newer ships (including those in the Royal Caribbean and Celebrity fleets) also offer pay-per-view options, ranging from G to X ratings. Other ships have installed DVD players in their cabins, with movies available for checkout from the ship's library.

Another viewing option is, well, you. A few ships videotape activities to make sure that no one misses anything, and replay them on the TV system. You may be able to watch yourself doing the limbo at a poolside party from your own room — which may make for good or bad viewing, depending on the kind of night you had. Holland America videotapes cooking demonstrations at its onboard Culinary Arts Centers and beams them into cabin TVs afterward.

Learning as You Lounge

Most ships, whether mainstream megaships, ultraluxury vessels, or small adventure-oriented craft, offer at least some lectures, demonstrations, and seminars, sometimes on general subjects and sometimes on subjects matched to your sailing region. Topics may include the following:

- ✔ **History and culture:** The history of transatlantic cruising on a transatlantic cruise, for example, or a lecture on Alaskan Native culture while sailing the Inside Passage.
- ✔ **Natural history and marine biology:** Maybe rain forest ecology while sailing Central America, a lecture on volcanoes while sailing in Hawaii, or a lesson in whale behavior in Alaska.

- **Computer applications:** Sometimes practical ones such as word processing or spreadsheet software; sometimes more creative ones such as photo-imaging or Web design software.

- **Health and nutrition:** Including weight-loss and diet seminars.

- **Lifestyle topics:** Including personal investing, handwriting analysis, or scrapbook creation.

- **The arts:** Digital photography workshops are big these days, joining old favorites such as flower arranging. Princess Cruises also offers ceramics workshops on some of its ships.

- **The "classics":** Classes in napkin-folding, vegetable-carving, scarf-tying, and mixology have been offered aboard cruise ships since Eisenhower was president.

Think of these classes more as fun and informative diversions than as something you can add to your resume. On the other hand, they can sometimes provide a good first insight into something you can pursue further after you get home.

In addition to these kinds of lectures, many cruise lines also offer regular guided explorations in several other fields.

- As part of their **guest lecturer** programs, cruise lines often invite famous or simply notable speakers aboard to speak on their subject of expertise. For example, Norwegian Cruise Line (NCL) had former Florida senator and presidential aspirant Bob Graham aboard one of its Alaska cruises in summer 2005, speaking about the importance of good intelligence in international relations. Other speakers are less well known. Princess, for instance, used to regularly host a former Scotland Yard detective who had decades of stories from the underworld, and knew how to tell them.

- **Dance classes** are usually available, most frequently in salsa, country, and ballroom styles. Most are taught by the ship's onboard entertainers.

- **Cooking demonstrations** are all the rage with cruise lines, often presented like you see them on TV, complete with model kitchen and video monitors for an up-close view of the preparations. Holland America is particularly big on these, with special theaters installed for this purpose aboard nearly all of their ships.

- Similarly, many lines offer **wine-tasting seminars,** conducted by the ship's sommeliers or sometimes by guest experts. Royal Caribbean's *Navigator of the Seas* and *Mariner of the Seas* both have wine bars created in association with Mondavi and several other California vineyards. Classes in wine appreciation are held there throughout the week, and passengers can stage their own tastings by ordering special "wine flight" tasting menus.

- On most megaships and many luxury ships, staff from the gym, spa, and beauty salon offer seminars on **health, beauty,** and **fitness,** with topics including skin and hair care, detox for weight loss, and wrinkle reductions. These seminars are free, but their ulterior motive is convincing you to sign up for expensive treatments or personal-training sessions. Go anyway if you're interested; you can just say no to the rest.

✔ In general, the ultraluxury lines have the most refined and interesting **enrichment programs.** Crystal, for example, offers classes developed with the Society of Wine Educators, Berlitz, Pepperdine University, Sotheby's, Barnes&Noble.com, and other notable institutions, all of which provide lecturers on topics such as food and wine, arts and entertainment, business and technology, lifestyle (including interior design, book clubs, and language instruction), and wellness. The wine and food seminars include cocktail making, wine appreciation, chocolate, spa cuisine, and — one close to our hearts — beer essentials.

Aboard Cunard's *Queen Mary 2,* transatlantic crossings offer a similar program developed in association with Oxford University, featuring talks on history, global politics, cultural trends, theater, science, music, literature, and more.

✔ The small, adventure-oriented ships frequently offer a daily round of informal lectures by their **onboard naturalists and historians,** sometimes once a day (usually after dinner), sometimes several times a day.

✔ And, sometimes, there are lectures that come out of left field. Aboard **Royal Caribbean**'s Voyager-class vessels, for instance, resident Krooze Komics offer lectures on clown history and techniques, and teach classes in juggling. How fun is that?

Most lectures and some classes are free, though others (such as wine tastings and many computer classes) may carry a small fee.

Feeling the Burn

Yo, gym rats, don't think cruise ships are going to let you down. Back in the day (think *Titanic*), ship gyms were stuck down somewhere between the kitchen and the bilge, and looked like, well, gyms — the kind they had back then: dark, sweaty, with weights and those things that looked like bowling pins and those machines with the big strap that you put around your waist and just sorta jiggled around.

All that's changed over the past ten years or so. Beginning in the early to mid-1990s, the gyms on new ships migrated from below sea level to premium spots way up on the top decks, with all the newest equipment, trendy fitness classes, and wraparound windows to provide a view. Spas also became big business, as cruise lines capitalized on wellness trends, and several lines also began building larger onboard sports areas, from miniature golf to virtual golf to basketball and even ice-skating.

Pumping iron

Gyms on the megaships typically have a dozen or more treadmills and just as many step machines, stationary bikes, and elliptical trainers, plus aerobics rooms, saunas, full circuits of weight machines, racks of dumbbells, and the usual gym amenities: locker rooms, piles of towels, and cold, cold water. The best gym facilities are on Carnival's Conquest-, Spirit-, and Destiny-class ships; Princess's Grand- and Coral-class ships; NCL's *Dawn, Spirit, Star, Jewel, Sun,* and *Pride of Aloha;* Royal Caribbean's Radiance- and Voyager-class ships; Holland America's Vista-class ships; and Celebrity's Millennium-class ships.

Working out on your own is always free, as are most basic aerobics and stretching classes. Trendier classes — such as spinning, Pilates, yoga, boxing, tai chi, or self-defense — usually cost about $10 or $12 a class, with some ships offering unlimited weeklong passes (for around $70), as well as personal training sessions (also around $70 or $75).

Almost every ship offers some kind of jogging track, either a dedicated one with a track-type surface or simply a continuous loop of regular decking.

As a general rule, the smaller the ship, the smaller the gym, though there are exceptions. Windstar's 308-passenger *Wind Surf* has a surprisingly large gym and spa facilities, while the gyms on Princess's otherwise glorious *Diamond* and *Sapphire Princess* are too small considering the ships' 2,670-passenger size. The really small adventure-oriented ships rarely have gyms at all, but they compensate with off-ship options such as kayaking and hiking.

Getting a game going

If sports are your thing (either the team or the individual variety), plan to book aboard one of the really big ships. Royal Caribbean's enormous Voyager-class ships (the biggest in the world next to Cunard's *QM2*) have everything from a full-size basketball court to an outdoor rock-climbing wall, an in-line skating track, a running track, an ice-skating rink, miniature golf, and a virtual golf simulator (see more about golf in the "Hitting the links" section later in this chapter). The rock-climbing walls proved so popular they're now a bonafide RCI icon, and were added to the entire fleet. Other Royal Caribbean ships have cool sports options of their own. During her 2005 refurbishment, *Enchantment of the Seas* was outfitted with bungee trampolines.

Hitting the water

The small luxury ships are best for people who want to hit the water right from the vessel. All the Windstar, Seabourn, and SeaDream ships and Star Clippers' *Royal Clipper* have retractable watersports platforms that can be lowered from the stern when the ship is at anchor in calm waters, letting passengers windsurf, kayak, sail, water-ski, go on banana-boat rides, and sometimes swim and snorkel right from the ship. SeaDream's 110-passenger yachts even carry jet skis.

Hitting the links

Over the past few years, a lot of cruise lines have ramped up their golf offerings, adding hundreds of golf shore excursions as well as onboard instruction, virtual golf, pro shops, and other amenities.

Almost all the major cruise lines offer some of these, but Carnival (www.carnivalgolf.com), Holland America (www.hollandamericagolf.com), Celebrity (www.celebritycruisesgolf.com), Seabourn (www.seabourngolf.com), Princess (www.princessgolf.com), and Silversea (www.silverseagolf.com) go the extra mile, featuring programs created by Florida's Elite Golf Cruises (www.elitegolfcruises.com) that offer instruction, guided golf excursions in almost every port of call, computer simulators that mimic play on some of the world's great courses, professional onboard club fitting (with options to rent or buy), and other pro shop–style extras.

On its new Hawaii-based ships, Norwegian Cruise Line has created a major golf program that offers excursion packages at several courses each day, bookable either singly or as a package deal. Golf shoes and a variety of Callaway clubs are available for rent on board, and golf equipment and accessories are for sale in the onboard pro shop.

SeaDream Yacht Club's 110-passenger vessels are also equipped with golf simulators as well as Orlimar titanium drivers and irons. Royal Caribbean offers golf simulators and miniature golf on their Radiance- and Voyager-class ships, plus *Splendour* and *Legend of the Seas*, and golf excursions in select ports.

Sitting down for sports

All this talk about sports got you tired? Or, alternately, are you just more of an indoor sports kinda person?

Pub-sport enthusiasts can get their kicks on a number of ships. All NCL ships have dartboards in their pubs, while Royal Caribbean's Radiance-class ships have gyro-balanced pool tables. Practically every ship has a card room where you can expect bridge to be the most popular game. Some ships carry a bridge instructor on board and offer tournaments. The card rooms often provide decks of cards. According to one of our spies, there's a brisk pick-up trade in Texas Hold 'Em poker in the card rooms on NCL's Hawaii-based ships, which lack a casino due to Hawaiian gambling restrictions. Shhhh. Mum's the word.

Most megaships and some mid-size ships have sports bars with large-screen TVs broadcasting ESPN and whatever live games are available that day. Carnival's recently launched *Carnival Liberty* and Princess's *Golden, Star,* and *Caribbean Princess* all have giant 300-square-foot digital TV/movie screens mounted out on their Pool Decks, where they broadcast the big games as well as movies and other programming. Waiters bring drinks and popcorn.

Getting rubbed up at the spa

Trivia question: What's more sybaritic than lying in your underwear in a warm, dark room while a good-looking young man or woman rubs oil over your whole body?

Answer: Nothing. Nothing that's legal, anyway.

Cruise ship spas went from simple massage rooms in the early '90s to progressively more amazing New Age paradises as the years went on. Today the best are perched on top decks, boast great views from eight or ten treatment rooms, are decorated in soothing Asian and North African motifs, and offer a menu of massages (including regular massage and the popular hot-stone massage), facials, aqua-therapies, mud packs, and other esoteric procedures that make you drool, plus beauty treatments such as teeth whitening and the more standard manicure/pedicure.

Call it a monopoly if you will, but most cruise ship spas on most of the cruise lines are run by one company: London-based **Steiner Leisure.** There aren't many exceptions. NCL, Oceania, and Silversea's spas are operated by a company called Mandara, but (what a surprise . . .) they're owned by Steiner, too. Companies bucking the Steiner monopoly include Cunard (whose *QM2* spa is run by Canyon Ranch) and Radisson Seven Seas (whose spas are run by Carita), plus Star Clipper's sailing ship *Royal Clipper,* whose spa is run in-house.

In general, you won't find too many bargains at onboard spas, whose rates tend to be high. As for the quality of the treatments, they vary depending on the talent of the person administering them. We've had some amazing massages on board, as well as some blissfully esoteric treatments: Matt's round of aqua-therapy aboard Celebrity back in the late '90s still makes him tingle. On the other hand, that Ionithermie treatment, which supposedly makes you lose inches as it's happening, didn't do much for us except provide a lot of laughs afterward.

Here's a sampling of treatments and their standard Steiner rates:

- ✔ 25-minute Swedish massage: $60 to $72

- ✔ 50-minute full-body massage: $89 to $128

- ✔ 75-minute hot stone massage: $142 to $190

- ✔ 50-minute facial: $89 to $109

- ✔ Manicure: $25 to $44

- ✔ Pedicure: $40 to $61

Frequently, passengers — especially women passengers — are subjected to a sales pitch at the end of their treatment, suggesting various creams, exfoliants, toners, moisturizers, and masks that help you look like Christy Turlington when you get home. Buy if you want, but feel free to say nope, no way, not interested. You're in charge.

Rates for identical treatments can vary by as much as $20 from ship to ship. Payment is charged to your onboard account, and usually doesn't include a tip for the therapist. Ask to make sure, though, before you add one.

 Make your spa appointments early, especially if you're sailing on a megaship. If you don't head to the spa to sign up early, you risk being relegated to a bad time slot — either very early in the morning, very late in the evening, or (worst of all) during a port day when it would conflict with your shore plans. On some ships, you can call from your stateroom telephone to make an appointment. A few ships — Princess's *Caribbean Princess* and *Sapphire Princess* and Silversea's *Silver Cloud, Wind, Shadow,* and *Whisper* — have systems that let guests prebook their spa treatments before they sail. Ditto for Cunard's *Queen Mary 2,* though it's only open to guests in the top-class suites and previous Canyon Ranch customers. It's good to be king. Reportedly, Steiner Leisure is working on a prebooking system that it will eventually use aboard all the ships on which it runs spas, though it's still in development.

Entertaining Yourself after Dark

Evenings are when cruise ships begin to take on the romantic aura of the old ocean liners, as passengers dress up (even if they don't do the tux-and-gown thing as much as they used to), step out, and join the champagne slipstream. After dinner you can take in a show, listen to some music, maybe hit the dance floor, or head for the casino. The mainstream lines' megaships have a multitude of options; small luxe ships, such as those of Seabourn, SeaDream, and Silversea, have fewer, but that goes along with their quieter, more refined vibe. The quality of entertainment, of course, varies from line to line and from ship to ship.

Taking in a show

Big-ship cruising means high-tech shows that feature dazzling laser-lighting effects, pyrotechnics, video backdrops, actors "flying" in and out, and large casts of singers and dancers performing everything from Stephen Sondheim and Andrew Lloyd Webber medleys to Elvis tunes and even, occasionally, something written in the past ten years. Cruise lines spend millions of dollars on each extravagant production, though whether you get jazzed by it or not really depends on your taste. If you don't dig brassy arrangements, constant motion, nubile young Vegas-style dancers smiling and lip-synching away, and flashy solo singers bouncing between high notes, you probably won't like these either.

Occasionally, of course, something amazing pops up. Disney, for example, offers absolutely the best shows at sea, with characters and stories based on its parent company's classic films. Recent shows on NCL are also standouts, with strong soloists and really original staging, choreography, and choice of material. Carnival and Royal Caribbean are also reliably strong; the latter's Voyager-class ships have a niche show all their own: full-on ice shows in their skating rinks, with choreography and special effects similar to those in the main theaters. Royal Caribbean's sister-line, Celebrity Cruises, offers shows and other enter-tainment created by fantasy circus troupe Cirque du Soleil. Cunard takes a different tack aboard *QM2,* programming performances by graduates of Britain's Royal Academy of Dramatic Arts, as well as some more stan-dard song-and-dance revues.

Most ships offer productions twice a night to correspond with tradi-tional first and second seating dinner times; usually you see the show after dinner, but, on some nights, you may have the option of checking it out before. On lines that have deformalized the dining experience (notably Princess and Norwegian), shows may be scheduled only once a night and repeated later in the week.

Hitting the vaudeville circuit

On some nights, ships may offer various variety acts instead of (or in addition to) the big production revues. What to expect? Think magic shows complete with the old saw-the-assistant-in-half routine; acrobatic acts and aerialists who fly around on ropes strung from the theater's ceiling (always a big hit); jugglers; ventriloquists; and, most commonly of all, comedians, many of whom work on cruise ships regularly, meeting the vessels in various ports and then getting off in others to catch up with their next floating gig. Comedy acts may perform either in the main theater or in a second performance space, sometimes doing PG- and R-rated material at an early show and then running the X up the mast at an adults-only midnight performance. Expect the best humor on the mainstream ships. Carnival has been known for its comedians for years, and Norwegian Cruise Line recently announced a partnership with the famed Second City improv comedy group, who do shows weekly on the line's *Norwegian Dawn,* sailing out of New York.

Ritzier lines, such as Crystal and Cunard, and premium mainstream lines, such as Holland America and Celebrity, often feature classical pianists or violinists, though they tend to stick to familiar, ear-catching pieces. Lines with a European character, such as Costa and MSC, tend to program light-classical performances as well, typically sticking to pianists or operatic soloists. The small adventure-oriented ships typi-cally have little or no formal entertainment on board, though some bring aboard local musicians and/or dancers in various ports — a practice also followed by some of the mainstream and luxe lines on some itineraries. In Hawaii, for example, NCL does a once-a-week show of Polynesian music and dance.

Occasionally, ships carry some well-known singers and other perform-ers, such as Maureen McGovern, Joel Grey, and Lorna Luft. You may also see some excellent performers who may not be household names or a singer who was famous back in the day crooning oldies but goodies. On a Seabourn cruise, we found Phillip Huber — he created and manipulated the puppets for the hit cult film *Being John Malkovich* — and his Huber Marionettes.

Lounging around

As ships have gotten bigger, music venues have multiplied. On the biggest Royal Caribbean and Carnival ships, you may find eight or nine choices at night, from background guitar to karaoke, from sing-a-long piano bars to classical chamber groups. Lounge entertainment varies not only from ship to ship, but also from room to room on the same ship, providing enough variety to please most passengers. You'll likely find at least one band playing dance tunes, a soloist or duo playing background music in the atrium, an upbeat electric band playing by the pool, and often a pianist taking requests at a piano bar. Holland America always has an afternoon high tea featuring a string trio or quartet, while Royal Caribbean has a Latin-themed bar on several of their ships, with Latin-tinged music. Ditto for NCL's *Norwegian Dawn,* which has had an excellent small salsa band aboard every time we've sailed.

Channeling your inner diva

If you fantasize about being the next Sinatra, Streisand, J-Lo, or Seinfeld, your ship has come in: Virtually all large ships have passenger talent shows, with a sign-up early in the cruise and a final performance in the main theater or a smaller lounge later in the week. Remember to pack your sheet music (although the ship's accompanist may be able to wing it), and if you want to do a stand-up comedy act, mind your audience: If you've got a G-rated audience, save the X-rated jokes for the hot tub later on.

On a smaller scale, most large ships offer karaoke several times during the trip. For the uninitiated, karaoke involves people taking turns singing to recorded backing tracks of popular songs (from oldies to new pop hits), as lyrics scroll across a monitor. You choose the song from a book and the emcee calls you up when it's your turn. Everyone gets into the spirit at these sessions, and no one — regardless of talent level — should be embarrassed or fear getting the hook.

Carnival recently introduced a new show on some of its vessels that merges the talent-show and karaoke concepts. Dubbed "Carnival Legends," it goes a little something like this: Guests — any guests, whether they can really sing or not — sign up for the show, pick an alter-ego (Elvis, James Brown, Madonna, Gloria Estefan, Britney Spears, or one of several others), then rehearse their number with the ship's band and show dancers. Then it's lights, camera, action, and they're performing in full costume in the main lounge, with sets, lighting effects, and a full audience to complete the picture. The show debuted aboard the line's *Imagination* and has proved so popular that other Carnival ships will be introducing it soon. Start rehearsing now.

Keeping the Faith

Amid all the activities and entertainment, some ships also manage to find a place for religious services.

Depending on the ship and the presence of clergy on board, most lines offer a Sunday nondenominational service, and some lines (including Costa and Cunard) offer Catholic mass regularly. On Christian and Jewish holidays, large ships may bring clergy aboard to lead services. Some ships have chapels, and Cunard's *QE2* has a synagogue as well. For regular Friday-night Jewish Sabbath services, many ships provide prayer books, yarmulkes, challah, and wine, but the passengers conduct the service themselves, with one passenger agreeing to be the leader.

Chapter 9

Catering to the Kids: Activities for Children and Teens

In This Chapter

▶ Discovering that cruises can be kid-friendly, too
▶ Sneaking a peek at babysitting and childrens' and teens' programs
▶ Informing your kids about cruise ship rules
▶ Identifying the best cruises for families

*W*hile we may have never gotten further than a Holiday Inn at the beach, kids these days sure do get around. Cruises to the Caribbean, Alaska, and Europe have become classic must-do family vacations. Hundreds and hundreds of kids and teens — sometimes more than a thousand — cruise the decks on a typical big-ship cruise these days. In fact, about 1 million of the nearly 9 million North Americans who took a cruise in 2004 were passengers under the age of 17. If you've got kids of your own, this is great news (just ask Heidi, who schlepped her toddler twin boys on a dozen cruises before their third birthday). If you don't plan on traveling with kids, well, sure hope you like the little buggers (otherwise, you may want to consider a small ship instead, where there tend to be far fewer tots in tow).

That said, because most kids on a cruise are happy as clams in the children's areas, you won't see them running around the rest of the ship as much as you may expect. This is a good thing. Read on for the lowdown on what ships are offering for families these days.

Kids Are People, Too — And They Cruise

For years now, cruise lines have catered to families, and the amenities get better with each new ship launched. Playrooms are larger and activities are more varied, with science and art projects supplementing the standard pizza parties and scavenger hunts. Cruise lines are smart. They know that kids cruising today will be the adult cruisers of tomorrow, and they want to get them hooked early.

Just how many families are cruising with their kids these days? Are you sitting down? Try 1,000 to 1,200 kids and teens on the biggest ships, especially during summer vacation and holiday times. A Royal Caribbean executive told us that as many as 1,500 to 1,800 kids and teens will be typical on the jumbo-sized *Freedom of the Seas* when the ship debuts in spring of 2006. Holy moley!

The newer ships of the mass-market lines, including Disney (surprise, surprise), Royal Caribbean, Carnival, Norwegian, and Princess, go all out with facilities for kids of all ages. Holland America and Celebrity offer decent facilities, too. All have playrooms; the best are stocked with goodies such as ball bins and climbing mazes, plus lots of games, toys, and computers. Teen centers are typical, with many designed to look as stylish as adult lounges. Geez, when we were kids, we used to get excited by a vending machine and a swimming pool. Anyway, that was then, this is now. You can also find video arcades, kids-only splash pools, and lots of kid-friendly snack areas serving tasty junk food such as ice cream, pizza, burgers, and chicken fingers. Kids' menus are pretty standard in the main dining rooms as well, as are high chairs.

Even some of the ultraluxe lines such as Cunard and Crystal do their bit to cater to families. Both lines have playrooms on their ships along with supervised activities whenever demand warrants it.

Children's activities are included in the cruise fare, though you pay for extras like late-night babysitting (usually offered after 10 p.m.) and shore excursions.

 Though so many are, not *all* ships are kid-friendly. Many times older ships (say, from the early '90s), have small, outdated playrooms. Some ships, usually the smaller adventure and luxury vessels, don't have any children's playrooms or activities, and in a few cases, disallow kids outright. For example, American Canadian Caribbean Line doesn't permit children under 14. And for luxury lines such as Silversea and Seabourn that technically allow kids, they certainly don't cater to them, and they expect, as do the other passengers, that children who come on board be seen and not heard.

You find the most kids on ships in the Caribbean, but other regions are gaining ground, too. In Alaska, the glaciers, Native culture, and wildlife are interesting and educational for kids. Europe, too, is becoming more popular with family cruisers. Aside from the port experience, kids on a European cruise are often mingling with kids in the playroom who speak English only as a second language, if at all, so your kids may actually learn something about other cultures. (Explain this to your children in advance so that they don't think the other kids are unfriendly.) On all itineraries, it's more and more common to see multiple generations traveling together: children, parents, and grandparents. An added bonus of course is that grampy and grammy are built-in babysitters!

It's Kids' Stuff

Cruise lines set up their programs by age, similar to a summer camp, so that children can be involved in age-appropriate activities with their peers. The programs start with children ages two or three (with the exception of Disney and Cunard, you yourself are the program for a child younger than two) and often require that toddlers are potty-trained. Keep in mind, some cruise lines require that their youth counselors have degrees in education or phys ed. Other lines don't have such high standards, though don't worry, a dishwasher from the galley won't be watching over your little tykes either. As far as figuring out the ratio of youth staff to kids, most don't have one. Typically, a cruise line looks at the passenger manifest weeks before a cruise and can assess how many counselors to have given the number of kids on board.

 There's no way a cruise line can guess how many of the kids on board actually come to the playrooms and participate in the activities. (Heidi's boys have been the only ones in the playroom, with a counselor all to themselves, and they've also been two of maybe 40 or 50 kids in their age group, being supervised by four or five counselors.) Most lines have a "no turn away" policy and accepts all kids who want to participate. During busy periods, like summertime and holiday weeks, this policy means that playrooms during supervised activity times can be crowded. To ease the congestion, smaller groups break off to take walks around the ship or to do activities like drawing or painting elsewhere, such as at a quiet, unused part of the Promenade Deck.

The roster of kids' activities varies from line to line, but the pickins are better than ever. Here's a sampling of what to expect from the big cruise lines:

- ✔ Try your hand at cool science experiments with magnets and bubbles, or make a volcano (Royal Caribbean).
- ✔ Whip up ice-cream sundaes.
- ✔ Discover stuff about animation (Disney) and ocean and marine life (Princess).
- ✔ Do some water coloring (Carnival).
- ✔ Have your face painted.
- ✔ Play computer games ala PlayStation 2 and Xboxes.
- ✔ Surf the Net (teens only).
- ✔ Go on a backstage tour of the theater or get a peek at the galley.
- ✔ Design your own T-shirt.

> ✔ Take dance lessons.
>
> ✔ Show off your acting skills in a talent show.
>
> ✔ Include parents in special family activities such as pizza making.

 Supervised activities may not be offered between about 5 and 7 p.m. each day, so counselors can take a break and grab dinner. They usually resume again between about 7 and 10 p.m. (after this, the babysitting program kicks in and parents are charged an hourly rate). The exceptions to this schedule include pizza parties and special dinners the counselors host once or twice per cruise, typically around 6 p.m. Afterwards, the children are escorted back to the playroom for most activities. Most parents are psyched for the break (though Heidi actually enjoys picking mac and cheese out of her hair) and the chance to get an early start on their evenings out.

 Caribbean and Bahamas sailings of the mainstream cruise lines typically include visits to these lines' private beaches in the Bahamas, where watersports, barbeque lunches, and music are among the offerings for passengers. Most private beaches also have kids' areas of some kind, sometimes with a playground or water park, and supervised activities. The best for families are Disney's Castaway Cay, Holland America's Half Moon Cay, Royal Caribbean's CocoCay, and Princess' Princess Cays. We offer more details on these private beaches in Chapter 15.

Family Friendly? (Or Get Us off This Thing!)

As we've just been explaining (we hope you were paying attention), many cruises are great family vacations. But not all ships offer the same facilities and programs. Age minimums can vary. So can the hours of operation. The babysitting set-up and the scope of play areas and activities can also differ. So read on for the nitty gritty and don't be shy about grilling your travel agent for details, too. Most cruise line Web sites also list their programming details.

Checking out program availability and hours

Some ships offer children's programs only seasonally — during the summer and holiday periods when most families travel. Other programs run year-round, namely those of the big-ship lines. Find out if the ship offers the advertised program during the time you plan to sail.

 Some ships operate programs for a specific age category only if a minimum number of kids of that age are on board; this number varies, but is likely about 10 or 20. Find out if your cruise has such restrictions to avoid a tantrum (yours) once on board.

Most programs shut down during meal times, and they may not be offered during port calls. So if you want to take a shore excursion, you may have to bring the kids along, which can get expensive because most lines don't offer substantially cheaper rates for kids' excursions.

Keeping it real for teens

Even if your teens have vowed to mope in the cabin, dressed in black, to protest the weeklong separation from their significant others back home, they may eventually break down and want to meet the other teens. All the big-ship lines have attractive teen centers where your precious ones can hang out, pose, and make snide remarks about each other. Activities such as dances, parties, and karaoke are typically on the agenda, and give teens the green light to chill with peers and avoid parents — a bonus for all concerned.

 So that your lovely adolescent offspring can stay in touch with pals back home, just about every ship that carries more than 100 or so passengers offers Internet access. The big megaships have an Internet center with at least 15 computers, and often twice that number, that operates around the clock, or nearly so. In some cases, teen centers have a private computer nook with Internet access.

Keeping the kids close, if not in close quarters

Obviously bigger is better. If you can afford it, opt for a suite or two connecting cabins (most ships have some) to avoid getting in each other's hair. Family togetherness is all well and good, but after seven days in a space no bigger than your kitchen, you don't want to have to vote someone out of the cabin. Many ships now offer a handful of family suites, in addition to a selection of minisuites and regular suites that offer more space for families (but are also more expensive than standard cabins). But if you're all social butterflies flitting from one activity to another, you may only use the cabin to sleep. If that's the case, you can survive with four in a standard cabin (and save some dough to boot). At the very least, though, consider a cabin with a balcony; the extra living space can go a long way.

 If you need a crib, request one when booking your cruise, they're complimentary. Many cabins, but not all, have minifridges and some have bathtubs, and just about all ships have 24-hour room service for ordering cartons of milk, sandwiches, and snacks.

Knowing who's watching your kids

Most children's programs are designed so that kids — depending on their ages — can come and go. Planned activities are certainly less restrictive than day-care facilities at home. Many programs require that kids under a certain age (usually somewhere between 9 and 13) must be signed in and out of the activity area or playroom by a parent, though policies on this may vary. If you grant your older kids wandering privileges, emphasize that the casino is off limits (officially, at least). Find out, too, if the ship requests that unsupervised children not visit the spa, gym, disco, or other adult-oriented areas; typically these areas do not allow children under 16 or 18 to enter. You may want to consider investing in hand-held walkie-talkies so that you and the kids can keep tabs on each other (though they're incredibly annoying to everyone else around you).

 Most of the big-ship lines give parents of young children (say under about 8 years old) the use of pagers, so they can be summoned if the child needs them (and sometimes to alert you that you need to come up to the playroom and change a dirty diaper).

Even on ships with extensive children's programs, you're still responsible for your children's safety at the pool. There are rarely lifeguards, so for safety reasons, most programs don't take kids to the swimming pool.

 All cruise ships carrying more than a few hundred passengers have a doctor on board, and often several nurses. Though you can visit them in the infirmary on board if need be (there is a fee), it's best to also bring any special medications your children may need. It's also smart to pack a simple first-aid kit, complete with a thermometer and basic medicines, so you don't have to bother seeing the doctor for minor ailments. Also, you may want to check your insurance to find out whether it covers you in the unlikely event that someone needs to be transported ashore (as in the case of appendicitis). Definitely take the time to tell your kids how important it is to wash their hands frequently; it's the best prevention against gastrointestinal problems and other diseases.

Babysitting on board

Want to get through your formal dinner without cutting up anyone's food? A few lines offer private babysitting in your cabin between the hours of about 8 p.m. and 1 a.m., by an off-duty female crewmember (usually a cabin stewardess). Rates are generally about $10 an hour for two children, and there's usually a two-hour minimum. More common is group babysitting in the playroom, which runs about $8 to $10 an hour for two kids. Check with your travel agent ahead of time to make sure your cruise line's policies haven't changed.

 The private babysitting is offered based on availability, which means don't dawdle. Heidi always heads to the reception desk within a few hours of boarding to make her requests. Also, with group babysitting, some ships may impose a cap on the numbers allowed into it, so inquire within a few hours of boarding if this is important to you.

Following the Rules

Okay, so a ship is only so big. It's a confined environment, so kids can get themselves into only so much trouble. Nevertheless, you still need to drill your kids on basic safety procedures before setting sail. The number-one rule: Don't lean on the railings of open decks or verandas.

Although most railings are high enough to not be of major concern for nonclimbing little kids, make a strict rule about it to be on the safe side — particularly if you have active kids.

Another important rule is to make sure that your children don't go to the pool without telling you, because most ships don't have lifeguards. Pools with waterslides often have staff members regulating the flow of traffic, but they don't get paid to watch for little ones swimming unsupervised.

Make sure your children take the onboard safety drill seriously and that they understand the safety information you and the ship provide. (Check out Chapter 6 for more safety drill info.) Also, check that your cabin has appropriately sized life jackets.

As on any vacation, have your children memorize the home base information — the ship's name and their cabin and deck numbers — in case you get separated during the voyage.

Taking Notes: The Best Family Cruises

The top lines for family travelers offer not only great supervised pro-grams for kids, but also special play areas and facilities. All the major big-ship lines are family friendly to a large degree, and offer free super-vised activities daily, babysitting service evenings at an hourly rate, and children's menus (à la hot dogs, burgers, and pasta) in some or all of their restaurants. Starting with the best, we've listed the top lines for families. (Check out Part IV for more info on these lines.)

Disney Cruise Line

The undisputed big cheese of family fun, both the *Disney Magic* and *Disney Wonder* take top billing for their kids' facilities and family-friendly ships (cabins are large and feature split bathrooms). An incredible 15,000 square feet is dedicated to children's areas (nearly half a deck), more than twice that of the largest spaces on the Royal Caribbean or Carnival fleets. Beloved Disney films are shown and the line's live enter-tainment is exceedingly family friendly and incorporates Disney charac-ters into fun musicals on high-tech stages.

At least 50 counselors supervise the fun — far more than any other line, and thus counselor-to-kid ratios are better.

Some 1,000 kids or so per cruise is par for the course. Activities for five age groups between 3 and 17 are offered nearly nonstop from 9 a.m. to midnight daily in two huge play spaces, a teen center, and a nursery. All play areas are open to babies/toddlers if accompanied by a parent.

> ✔ The Oceaneer Club (ages 3–7, with separate activities for ages 3–4 and 5–7), is a kid-proportioned playroom with a Captain Hook theme. Kids can climb and crawl on the bridge, ropes, and rails of

a giant pirate ship, as well as on jumbo-size animals, barrels, and a sliding board; get dressed up from a trunk full of costumes; dance with Snow White and listen to stories by other Disney characters; or play in the kiddie computer room.

✔ The interactive Oceaneer Lab across the hall offers kids (ages 8–12, divided into ages 8–9 and 10–12) a chance to work on computers, learn fun science with microscopes, build from an enormous vat of Legos, do arts and crafts, hear how animation works, and create their own radio show.

To keep things fresh, new activities are being introduced all the time — some 24 in 2004, for example — for the 3 to 12 set.

✔ For teens (ages 13–17), a new teen hangout, called The Stack on the *Magic* and Aloft on the *Wonder,* is three times the size of the old digs and more isolated from parents. The centers have two separate rooms, one with video screens for movies and the other a disco with a teens-only Internet center. Dance parties, karaoke, trivia games, improv comedy lessons, and workshops on photography are offered for teens on all cruises, with even more options on 7-night sailings.

✔ Though not complimentary like the programming for older kids, for an hourly rate you can drop off your littlest ones, ages 3 months to 3 years, at the Flounder's Reef Nursery. Hours are 6 p.m. to midnight daily, and a few hours during the morning and afternoon. No other line offers such extensive care for babies. The room has toys and games, plus eight cribs and a one-way porthole that allows parents to check on their kids without the little ones seeing them. The price is $6 per child per hour, and $5 for each additional child in a family (with a two-hour minimum). Space is limited here, so reserve your spots as early as possible. The child-to-counselor ratio is four to one, and counselors do change diapers (though you must supply them).

Each ship has a video arcade, though it's really cramped compared to most. Kids can eat lunch and dinner with counselors in the Topsider and Beach Blanket buffet restaurants all but the first evening of the cruise.

Disney doesn't offer private in-cabin babysitting like some lines do during evening hours (so parents can dine alone), but along with Cunard they are the only line offering complimentary activities and group care until midnight (or later) in the Oceaneer Club and Lab for ages 3 to 12. Other lines charge for this after 10 p.m.

When the ship calls on Castaway Cay, Disney's private island in the Bahamas, kids can head for Scuttle's Cove, where there are barrels to crawl through, a giant whale-dig site to explore, and more. Kids' counselors are on hand to supervise the fun if the parents want to head to Serenity Bay, the adults-only beach. For families who want to play together, there are bike rentals and lots more.

Royal Caribbean International

Exceedingly well rounded for families, the Royal Caribbean fleet offers big spacious playrooms, teen rooms, plus lots of cool diversions for all ages, such as the rock-climbing walls offered on all ships. There's even more on the line's newest Freedom-, Voyager- and Radiance-class ships, including miniature golf. The innovative line was the first to introduce parent and infant/toddler playgroups, a great thing until your tots are 3 and old enough to join the ship's drop-off programming. With its new *Freedom of the Seas,* the line really went overboard for kids offering truly the best outdoor pool space at sea in the form of a giant water park with cannons, sprays, and jets set against a backdrop of colorful cartoony characters. The line also revamped an older ship, *Enchantment of the Seas,* and it now boasts four bungee trampolines, two suspension bridges, and a splash pool with water jets.

Though all of Royal Caribbean's ships are well equipped, the *Freedom* takes top billing for its water park, and the Radiance-class ships and *Voyager, Adventure,* and *Explorer* get big points for their water slides and kids' pools. The *Navigator* and *Mariner* have some 6,000 square feet more than the other ships in the Voyager class, and *Navigator* is also popular for its Ben & Jerry's ice-cream parlor. Other cool stuff in the fleet includes an ice-skating rink and in-line skating track on all the Voyager-class ships, plus a mini science museum on the *Explorer.* Kids can visit the small labs staffed by scientists from the National Oceanographic and Atmospheric Administration, the University of Miami, and elsewhere.

Year-round and fleetwide, Royal Caribbean offers its Adventure Ocean supervised kids' programs for five age groups between 3 and 17. While at sea, the programs run from 9 a.m. to noon, 2 to 5 p.m., and 7 to 10 p.m.; while in port, drop-off starts 30 minutes before the first shore excursion is scheduled until 5 p.m., and then 7 to 10 p.m. Aside from the more typical stuff to do, the line's Adventure Science activities invite kids to have fun and actually learn something by doing simple science experiments appropriate to their age group. Same deal with Adventure Art, which is all about playing with crayons, modeling clay, glitter, glue, markers, and paint.

For participating in events, kids earn Adventure Ocean Coupons, which they can trade in for gifts.

Following are some more activities available for specific age groups:

 ✔ Aquanauts (ages 3–5), do hands-on science experiments with water, magnets, and gummy candies. Art projects include mask-making (themed to the cruise itinerary) and pottery. Other things to do include ice-cream parties, face painting, talent shows, and playing with superheroes. The line's new Sail into Story Time program uses popular children's books such as *Where the Wild Things Are* and *The Very Hungry Caterpillar* as a basis for fun hands-on activities and arts and crafts. For example, after reading *Where the Wild Things Are,* they're turned loose for a supervised "wild rumpus." Hey, better here than at home. . . .

- ✔ Explorers (ages 6–8), do some of the same stuff Aquanauts do, but also scavenger hunts, dance parties, and bingo. The Story Time program with this age group uses *The Stinky Cheese Man* and *Do Pirates Take Baths?* as a theme for activities and arts and crafts.

- ✔ Voyagers (ages 9–11), do science and art programs geared to their age group, plus stuff such as reggae beach parties, backstage theater tours, sports tournaments, and more.

- ✔ Navigators (ages 12–14), do cool things such as learn how to be a DJ, sports contests (sometimes pitting boys against girls . . . oohhh, how romantic!!), karaoke, toga and pool parties, and video game competitions.

- ✔ For older teens (ages 15–17), each ship has a teen disco and a video arcade. Some of the ships, including the *Mariner, Navigator, Monarch,* and *Sovereign of the Seas* have three new teen-only areas, including a nightclub, TV room, and dedicated teen sun deck. There are also separate teen Internet centers reserved for ages 12 to 17 and huge video arcades.

- ✔ Babies and toddlers get their due, too. RCI recently partnered with Fisher-Price to offer supervised "play dates" for babies and toddlers (6 months to 3 years) along with their parents. The 45-minute play sessions for two age groups (Aqua Babies, 6–18 months, and Aqua Tots, 18 months to 3 years) are offered on all but embarkation day, and incorporate music, storytelling, and a variety of Fisher-Price toys.

Royal Caribbean offers two babysitting options: slumber party–style group babysitting for children 3 to 12 in the playroom nightly between 10 p.m. and 1 a.m., and from noon until sailing on days the ship is in port ($5 per hour per child); and private, in-cabin babysitting for kids 12 months and up, which is available from off-duty crewmembers 8 a.m. to 2 a.m., and should be booked at least 24 hours in advance through the purser's desk ($8 per hour for up to two siblings).

Among the best trained in the biz, male and female youth staff all have four-year college degrees in education, recreation, or a related field, plus they're trained in CPR and first aid.

Dinner with the youth counselors is offered on three nights of a 7-night cruise (and once or twice on shorter cruises) in the Windjammer buffet restaurant, Solarium cafe, or Johnny Rockets diner (depending on the ship). Dinner runs from 6 to 7 p.m.

Royal Caribbean's newest ships — *Voyager, Explorer, Adventure, Mariner, Navigator, Radiance, Brilliance, Serenade, Jewel,* and *Freedom* — have special family cabins that can accommodate six. Cabins on the older vessels tend to be pretty small, although some can hold a third or fourth passenger in upper berths.

Royal Caribbean's drinking age fleetwide is 18 years old for wine and beer when the ship sails in international waters, but parents have to sign a waiver stating their awareness of this rule. If parents don't sign, the age is 21.

Carnival Cruise Lines

Those wild, frat boy (and girl) singles who used to define Carnival as the party-hardy fun-ship line seem to have settled down, gotten married, and had kids. Who would have guessed that Carnival would morph into a family cruise line? And one of the best ones. The latest offerings include spa treatments tailored to teens, and art, science, and exercise-oriented activities geared to young children.

But don't get us wrong, Carnival is still a fun line for adults, too. It's just that the line's extensive kids' facilities and programming give parents plenty of opportunity to break away and party by the pool with a bucket of beers.

The line estimates that about 500,000 kids will have sailed aboard its ships in 2005, which they claim is a whopping 400 percent more children under 18 than in 1995. Some 800 children per cruise is pretty normal, with as many as 1,000 on Christmas and New Year's cruises. Lots of kiddies are around in summer, too, when it's difficult to find a kid-free hot tub. The Conquest-class ships (*Conquest, Glory, Valor,* and *Liberty*), the largest and newest in the fleet, offer the best kids' digs, occupying some 6,000 square feet. The playroom has an arts-and-crafts station, video wall, computer lab, PlayStation 2 game units, and toys from play kitchens to mini sliding boards, farm sets, and more. The separate and sprawling teen center has a video wall and soda bar flowing into a huge video arcade with three air hockey tables and more than 20 machines.

The playroom and video arcade on the Spirit-class ships (*Carnival Miracle, Spirit, Legend,* and *Pride*) are tucked away in the far forward reaches of the bow on decks 4 and 5. Playrooms are divided into three sections connected via tunnels and offer sand art, a candy-making machine, a computer lab with a handful of iMacs and PlayStation 2s, and plenty of other diversions.

The Destiny-class vessels (*Destiny, Triumph,* and *Victory*) have two-level indoor/outdoor playrooms. The Fantasy-class ships (*Ecstasy, Fantasy, Fascination, Imagination, Inspiration,* and *Sensation*) have two playrooms, though they're boxy and cramped compared to the line's newer Fantasy-class ships (*Elation* and *Paradise*).

The Camp Carnival program offers supervised kids' activities on sea days just about straight through from 9 a.m. to 10 p.m. (and 2–10 p.m. on port days) for ages 2 through 14 in four age groups. All of the 10 to 16 counselors are trained in CPR and first aid, and they organize the fun and games on each ship.

✔ Toddlers (ages 2–5) can get into face painting, computer games, puzzles, fun with clay, picture bingo, pirate hat–making, and pizza parties.

✔ For juniors (ages 6–8), there's PlayStation 2, computer games, ice-cream parties, story time and library visits, T-shirt coloring, and swimming. Young kids will also enjoy cavorting with Carnival's "Fun Ship" Freddy, a big fuzzy red, white, and blue mascot who shows up to say hello and pose for photos.

✔ For intermediates (ages 9–11), there are scavenger hunts, trivia and bingo, Ping-Pong, video-game competitions, arts and crafts, computer games, dance classes, and talent shows.

✔ Teen clubs are geared to 12 to 14 year olds (the cruise director's department schedules activities for the 16–18 set), and are quite elaborate on the newest ships. Besides karaoke parties, computer games, scavenger hunts, talent shows, card and trivia games, and Ping-Pong, teens can watch movies there and go to dance parties. Most ships are also equipped with iMacs, but there is no Internet center for teens only like some ships offer.

"Homework help" sessions are available for kids who need to keep up while on vacation. The line also has new educational activities for the various age groups that include art projects with papier-mâché, oil paintings, and watercolors; music appreciation, which gets kids acquainted with different musical instruments; science projects where kids can make their own ice cream and create mini helicopters; and a fitness program that encourages today's couch-potato computer-head kids to actually get up and run around.

The entire fleet has video arcades (the newest ships have virtual-reality games and air-hockey tables), children's wading pools, and for bigger kids there's that great corkscrew slide at the main pool of each ship. Other pluses include a supervised kids' mealtime in the buffet restaurant between about 6 and 7 p.m. nightly except the first evening and sometimes last evening(s) of the cruise. A turndown service for kids includes complimentary chocolate-chip cookies on their pillows at bedtime on formal nights.

When parents want to party (or at least take an adults-only break), free supervised children's activities are offered from 7 to 10 p.m. nightly. After that, group slumber party–style babysitting kicks in for ages 4 months through 11 years till 3 a.m. in the playroom (most lines only allow kids ages 2 or 3 plus into the group babysitting). No private babysitting is available. There's also group babysitting between 8 a.m. and noon on port days for the under-2 set, for $6 per hour for the first child, $4 per hour for each additional child. On sea days between noon and 2 p.m., you can also drop off children under two at the rate above, or parents may use the playroom with their babies for these two hours at no charge.

A handful of strollers are available for rent fleetwide for $25 for 7- and 8-night cruises (less for shorter cruises) as well as a limited number of bouncy seats, travel swings, and Game Boys. If you need to rely on a stroller, bring your own, because there's no guarantee you can get a rental.

Norwegian Cruise Line

With each new ship the line introduces, the kids' digs get better. Though every ship in the fleet has at least a playroom, the facilities on the newer ships *Dawn, Star, Jewel, Spirit, Sun,* and *Pride of America* are the winners hands down. They boast huge spaces that include a separate teen center and a wading pool, as well as a large, well-stocked playroom with areas for movie-watching, arts and crafts, and computers. The *Dawn, Star,* and *Jewel* have wonderful spaces with a huge climbing maze and ball bin combo indoors and a private kids' pool and hot tub area outside with a fun, wacky theme.

On sea days, the playrooms are open 9 a.m. to noon, 2 to 4:30 or 5 p.m., and 7 to 10 p.m.; on port days the hours are 7 to 10 p.m. Once per 7-night cruise, kids can dine with counselors between 6 and 7 p.m., and then go directly to the playroom.

The line's Kids Crew program offers year-round supervised activities for children ages 2 to 17, divided into four age groups.

- ✔ Junior Sailors (ages 2–5) can enjoy arts and crafts, face painting, story time, LEGOs, pizza making, treasure hunts, and movies.

- ✔ First Mates (ages 6–9) do the things above plus scavenger hunts, painting, sports, and storytelling.

- ✔ Navigators (ages 10–12) also enjoy board games, the video arcade, sports, and parties.

- ✔ Teens (ages 13–17) do what this age group does best: hang out. The newer ships have a teen disco, plus there are movies, parties, card games, sports, and PlayStation 2s.

For kids 5 to 17 with a penchant for performing, the line's Junior Star Seeker passenger talent competition is a big hit. Those who want to participate are given three minutes to perform before a panel of judges, and the ship awards the winners a free NCL cruise.

When the free activities wind down at 10 p.m., group babysitting kicks in for kids aged 2 to 12 nightly until 1 a.m. (and also 9 a.m.–5 p.m. on port days) for $5 per child per hour, plus $3 an hour for each additional child. You must sign up for babysitting in advance (the day before ideally). Counselors do not do diapers; parents are given beepers so that they can be alerted when it's time for the dirty work. Private babysitting is not available.

The fleet's *Wind, Dream, Majesty, Sky,* and *Sun* each have a Kids Korner playroom, and the *Pride of Aloha* and *Sun* also have kiddie pools and teen centers.

The *Star, Dawn, Sun, Jewel,* and *Pride of Hawaii* have a separate section for kids in their buffet restaurants, complete with adorable mini chairs, tables, and buffet line (Heidi's boys loved this area on the *Dawn!*).

Princess Cruises

It really shouldn't come as a surprise that the Love Boat line, born of flirty doctors and poolside trysts, would eventually produce some great family ships. Though Princess isn't the first line that comes to mind when you think family cruising, it's for no lack of really good facilities.

The line's newest ships — the Grand-, Diamond-, and Coral-class ships — have impressive facilities. Each has a spacious indoor/outdoor children's playroom with a splash pool, an arts-and-crafts corner, game tables, and computers or game consoles, plus a teen center with computers, a dance floor, and a music system. These also have totally huge virtual-reality centers (that many adults also can't resist). The two-story playrooms on *Golden* and *Grand* have a large fenced-in outside deck dedicated to kids only, including a teen section with a hot tub and private sunbathing area. The new *Caribbean Princess,* as well as the rest of the Grand- and Coral-class ships and *Sun* and *Dawn,* have a great fenced-in outdoor playspace for toddlers, complete with a fleet of three-wheelers. And the new *Coral, Island, Diamond,* and *Sapphire Princess* have a small swimming pool for adults adjacent to the outdoor kids' deck, so parents can relax (sort of) while supervising their kiddies next door.

Parents can rent walkie-talkies through the purser's desk if they want two-way communication with their kids.

Princess's program offers activities supervised by a staff of counselors year-round for three age groups. On sea days, the free activities are offered from 9 a.m. to noon, 2 to 5 p.m., and 7 to 10 p.m.; on port days the hours are 8 a.m. to 5 p.m. (including lunch) and 7 to 10 p.m.

- ✔ Princess Pelicans (ages 3–7) and Princess Pirateers (ages 8–12) get their own areas of the playroom, and have stuff such as arts and crafts, scavenger hunts, game tournaments, movies and videos, coloring contests, scavenger hunts, pizza and ice-cream parties, karaoke, dancing, tours of the galley or behind the scenes at the theater, and hula parties complete with grass skirts.

  All play areas are open to babies/toddlers if accompanied by a parent.

- ✔ Teens (ages 13–17) can act cool while they get into shipboard Olympics, T-shirt painting, karaoke, Ping-Pong and basketball tournaments, Nintendo, and teenage versions of *The Dating Game.*

The line's three older, smaller ships — the *Regal, Tahitian,* and *Pacific* — don't have extensive kids' facilities, and their activities programs are available only when 20 or more children ages 3 to 17 are on board.

On some cruises, kids and teens can actually learn more than how to lip synch to Britney Spears songs. Designed in conjunction with the California Science Center, kids can do hands-on activities on Mexican Riviera sailings, from stargazing to studying ocean and coral reef habitats, building and racing sailboats, launching rockets, and dissecting gooey squid. Budding naturalists can take a gander at the activity books and other learning materials provided by the National Wildlife Federation. These opportunities were designed to complement the line's Junior Ranger program in Alaska and the Save our Seas environmental program, which operates fleet-wide. Children who participate get a Pete's Pal stuffed animal to take home.

Twice per cruise, kids can dine with counselors, so parents get a break. Younger kids can then be taken straight to group babysitting in the children's center (available nightly 10 p.m.–1 a.m. for kids 3–12; $5 per hour, per child). Teens have their own group night in one of the main dining rooms, complete with photographs and an after-dinner show. Princess does not offer private in-cabin babysitting.

While Princess offers really good facilities and amenities for parents and children, it's not a line that's totally gung ho about catering only to families. Therein lies a big advantage — Princess ships aren't overrun with children. In fact, a Princess reservations agent told us that they cap the total number of kids under 18 at about 14 to 15 percent of a ship's capacity. On a recent cruise, Heidi took her young sons on the 3,100-passenger *Caribbean Princess* (3,782 maximum occupancy) that maxed out at about 600 children, which is a far cry from the 800 to 1,200 kids under 17 that lines such as Carnival, Disney, and Royal Caribbean routinely see. Sure, she has kids of her own, but Heidi is the first to admit she still doesn't want to cruise with hordes of other kids. Princess offers a great middle ground.

Celebrity Cruises

We love Celebrity. The line is a pro at pleasing adults with its gorgeous ships, innovative entertainment and dining, and top spas. And though they're hardly as kid-focused as some of the lines mentioned earlier in this chapter, they do a pretty good job of catering to children, too. All the ships in the fleet have a playroom with great features, but the line's four newest and biggest Millennium-class ships (which also include the *Constellation, Infinity,* and *Summit*) take top honors. Each has an indoor/outdoor playroom complex that includes a fenced-in outdoor soft-surface jungle gym and a wading pool, plus inside a computer room, movie room, an arts-and-crafts area, and video arcade. Teens get a separate center.

Supervised activities are offered year-round. During kid-intensive times, namely holidays and summers, activities are geared toward four age groups. Hours are 9 a.m. to noon, 2 to 5 p.m., and 7 to 10 p.m. Plus, on formal nights during holiday weeks, kids can dine with counselors between about 6 and 7 p.m., while parents get a break.

- ✔ Ship Mates (ages 3–6) can go gaga over treasure hunts, clown parties, T-shirt painting, dancing, movies, ship tours, mask-making and parades around the ship, and ice-cream-sundae-making parties.

- ✔ Cadets (ages 7–9) have all of the above plus computer games.

- ✔ Ensigns (ages 10–12) may enjoy karaoke, computer games, board games, trivia contests, arts and crafts, movies, and pizza parties.

- ✔ Teens (ages 13–17, and divided into two groups, 13–15 and 16–17), who don't think themselves too cool to participate, can join talent shows, karaoke, pool games, and trivia contests. The Century-class and Millennium-class ships have attractive teen discos/hangout rooms (on the *Zenith,* bars and lounges are used for teen activities before they're opened for adults).

For the 3 to 12 set, Celebrity recently introduced Celebrity Science Journeys, which expose kids to fun and educational activities daily, from learning about insects and thunderstorms, to listening to dolphins and whales communicate under water. There is also summer-stock theater presentations, which involve three age groups: the Ship Mates and Cadets sing, dance, and act, and the Ensigns direct and produce the plays.

 For toddlers under age 3, parents can borrow a "treasure box" from the playroom, which includes toys and books (though the under-3 set is not allowed to use the playrooms with or without parents).

Group babysitting in the playroom is available for ages 3 to 12 every evening from 10 p.m. to 1 a.m. for children ages 3 to 12, and between noon and 2 p.m. on port days, for $6 per child per hour. Private in-cabin babysitting in the evening by a female crewmember is available on a limited basis for $8 per hour for up to two children (kids must be at least 6 months old); make your request 24 hours in advance.

 The drinking age on Celebrity sailings is 18 for beer and wine whenever a ship is in international waters, but parents have to sign a waiver stating their awareness of this rule. If parents don't sign, the age is 21.

Holland America Line

In the old days, Holland America was pretty much an old folks' line. In the past few years, though, Holland America has made a great effort to ditch this rep. The biggest change to the Club HAL program of late is the lowering of the age minimum from 5 down to 3 (which will be fleetwide by year-end 2006).

When enough are on board, kids are divided into three age groups. You can find the most children on cruises during summers and holiday weeks — for example, as many as 300 to 400 kids aboard the new

Vista-class ships (*Zuiderdam, Oosterdam,* and *Westerdam*), especially in the Caribbean. Otherwise, around 100 to 200 is typical. Every ship has at least one full-time Club HAL youth director on board.

When demand warrants, typically during summers and holidays, program hours are 9 a.m. to noon, 2 to 5 p.m., and 7 to 10 p.m.

- ✔ Kids (ages 3–7) can enjoy storytelling, arts and crafts, face painting, pizza and ice-cream parties, ship tours, and bingo.

- ✔ Children (8–12), there's golf ball putting, sports tournaments, scavenger hunts, movies, karaoke, air hockey, foosball, and Internet access.

- ✔ Teens (13–17) are getting a lot of respect from Holland America. New teen areas are designed to look like an artist's loft, with a big-screen TV, Internet access, video games, karaoke, and a music system. A private sun deck outdoors has lounge chairs, a 9-foot-high waterfall, snack machines, and a music system. Activities there include dance parties, luaus, and sporting games. These areas will be fleetwide by year-end 2006 (with the exception of the line's smallest ship, the *Prisdendam,* and a few ships that will have only the indoor area).

Maasdam and the newer Vista-class ships have dedicated "KidZone" playrooms and separate teen centers, and the other vessels are having them installed (fleetwide by year-end 2006). Until then, those without play areas will use multipurpose rooms for kids' activities when necessary. The dedicated centers are definitely an improvement, and have computers, a large-screen TV for movies, and toys and games. All ships have a small video arcade.

Group babysitting is offered daily for the 3 to 12 set between 10 p.m. and midnight (and fleetwide by end 2006), at $5 an hour per child; in-cabin babysitting is offered fleetwide if a crewmember is available, at $8 an hour per child and $5 for each additional child.

If you sail in the Caribbean, the line has its own private island, called Half Moon Cay. It's an awesome place for families, with a kids' aqua park on the beach (complete with slides and water cannons), plus neat excursions for the family, from horseback riding to snorkeling with stingrays.

Aside from stops at Half Moon Cay, the line does not offer kids' activities in port.

A couple surprise contenders

Aside from all these big-ship lines — which for the most part are all things to all people of all ages — a handful of lines that you may think don't give a hoot about pleasing families really are quite family friendly.

Cunard connotes pomp and circumstance, *God Save the Queen,* and scones. But snotty noses? Ball bins? Xboxes? Indeed, the *Queen Mary 2* is about tradition, taste, and elegant things, but Cunard's new grande dame offers one of the most comprehensive kids' programs at sea. Complimentary activities are offered all day long until midnight for children as young as one (most lines only start their programming at ages two or three). The youth staff includes a couple of British nannies that have completed a special two-year program in England.

The comfy playroom at the aft of deck 6 can be divided up to accommodate different age groups. Just outside on deck is a small wading pool and another play gym.

- ✔ For kids (ages 1–6), there are plenty of toys, arts and crafts, a play gym, and a ball bin, plus a separate nursery with cribs and toddler beds for naptime.

- ✔ For the 7 to 12 set, half of the playroom is stocked with beanbag chairs, board games, TVs, and Xboxes for video-game playing.

- ✔ Teens do stuff around the ship such as behind-the-scenes tours and watching movies in the theater. Plus, teenagers with a cerebral side will totally enjoy the ship's cool planetarium, gym, and extensive library and bookshop.

All play areas are open to babies/toddlers if accompanied by parent.

Dining options include the King's Court buffet restaurant and the special children's tea offered daily from 5 to 6 p.m. in the Chef's Galley.

Moving 180 degrees away from finger sandwiches and stiff upper lips is **Windjammer Barefoot Cruises,** all rum swizzles and tube tops. Adventurous kids who can part with their laser tag and Game Boys for a week, will embrace the freewheeling fun of a Windjammer tall ship, whose fleet sails through the more picturesque parts of the Caribbean. These ships are like summer camp for the whole family, only here, parents can unwind with a Red Stripe while the wind catches the sails and pushes the ship into the next day of adventure.

For ages 6 to 17, three of the fleet's five eccentric sailing ships offer "Junior Jammer" kids programs during the summer.

On itineraries in the Bahamas, Costa Rica, and the southern Caribbean islands of Aruba, Bonaire, and Curacao, the *Legacy, Polynesia,* and *Amazing Grace* have counselors for two main age groups (6–11 and 12–17) who supervise activities between 9 a.m. and 9 p.m. daily in empty cabins or in unused public rooms.

- ✔ Younger kids get to do arts and crafts, face paint, hair braid, build sand castles, knot tying, hoist the sails, and visit the bridge.

- ✔ Teens can do stuff such as sailing, snorkeling, volleyball, navigating, and kayaking.

- ✔ There are even introductory scuba classes for 8- to 10-year-olds and 11- to 16-year-olds.

One child between 6 and 11 sails free May through early August when sharing a cabin with parents.

 Though none of Windjammer's ships carries more than 122 passengers (double occupancy), so many families are drawn to this quirky line that 30 or 40 kids per cruise during the summer is par for the course. That nearly qualifies as a kiddie mob considering how small these ships are. And the ultra-casual, "anything goes" atmosphere puts to rest any fear of the kids disturbing the neighbors. With flip-flops and tank tops about as formal as it gets, who's going to complain about a little noise?

Part IV
Ship Shapes: The Cruise Lines and Their Ships

The 5th Wave   By Rich Tennant

"Do I like arugula? I love arugula! One of my favorite vacations was a cruise to arugula."

In this part . . .

The kind of ship you pick for yourself says something about your personality — just as does the kind of house you live in or car you drive. In this part, we review all the major cruise lines and a healthy selection of the smaller, more niche-oriented players, giving you the scoop on everything from 3,000-passenger megaships to six-passenger schooners. Which one's for you? Though we focus primarily on ships that sail the major cruise regions (the Caribbean, Alaska, and the Mediterranean), we also include details on the ships' other itineraries, from the Far East to Antarctica and off in every other direction you can name.

Chapter 10

Vetting Your Vessel: The How-to of Comparative Cruise Shopping

In This Chapter

▶ Using our reviews to find the right ship for you

▶ Investigating varying itineraries

▶ Keying in on ship specifications

▶ Interpreting the prices listed in the reviews

Some people say cruise ships are all the same. Other people yell back at them, telling them they're nuts. The first people get all huffy, "But it's true! They're all just these giant slab-sided beasts where you eat and drink till you pop." The second people shout back, "You moron, what about the smaller, high-end ships, where it's like you're on a quiet, private yacht?" First people say, "Yeah, well I can't afford that!" Second people say, "So? Then book on one of the premium mainstream lines; they're much more high-toned, like old-fashioned ocean liners." First people say, "Who needs high-toned? I want adventure!" Second people say, "So go to Maine and sail on a schooner. You can even help hoist the sails!" First people say, "What, you think you know everything?" Second people say, "Yeah, of course we do. We wrote the *For Dummies* book, didn't we?"

So, there you have it. Different ships for different folks, and to give you some idea of which is which, we use a kind of shorthand in the following chapters to help you sort ships according to your tastes. This chapter explains all those categories and what the different ratings and labels mean. Reading through this chapter saves you time by giving you key words and phrases to look for in the reviews so that you can find the cruise lines and ships that best fit your tastes and those of your spouse or other cruise companions.

Getting a Handle on the Big Picture

Each cruise line review begins with two shorthand notes about the kind of experience the line offers, one ephemeral and one concrete.

Type of cruise

This note refers to the more ephemeral cruise experiences that a ship has to offer. Here we break down the three major categories of cruise lines we discuss in Chapter 3, and suggest a bit more detail about what to expect on a particular cruise.

Mainstream cruises are the big boys of the cruise biz, with mostly giant ships offering the latest attractions designed to appeal to the widest variety of travelers. "Premium" lines are ginned-up mainstreamers, offering a more refined experience but without the super polish (or super-high prices) of the true luxury lines. Among the mainstream and premium lines, some ships tend to offer cruises geared more to **families, party types,** or **romantic types,** though you may be surprised at how many are able to offer all three. We use the description **resort ships** to refer to those that are just good all-around vessels with a range of activities and entertainment for everybody, though they may also appeal to families, partiers, and romantic types, too.

Luxury cruises are really luxurious — in other words, they walk the walk rather than just talking the talk. After all, almost every cruise line claims that they're luxurious, while few really are. Those are the ones that stick to the highest standards: exceptional service, refined décor, luxurious accommodations, a sophisticated ambience, and truly fine cuisine. They also tend to sail more wide-ranging itineraries, rarely doing the kind of season-long round-trip cruises from the same homeports, the way mainstream ships do. That gives you a much wider range of destinations from which to choose. Another perk? Though their prices are higher, they also tend to be more inclusive than mainstream rates, often covering wines and spirits, gratuities, and sometimes some shore excursions. There are a few adjectives we can think of to differentiate between the luxury lines. On **old-money lines,** very traditional passengers enjoy a very traditional experience. On **active luxury lines,** the focus may be on taking out a Waverunner or sailboard rather than on putting on the tux for evening cocktails. **Family luxury lines** attract a lot of younger couples who sometimes sail with their kids.

Adventure and educational cruises are your best bet if you're after an experience that prizes in-depth learning about a destination's nature and culture more than quick port calls and onboard relaxation. These ships rarely carry more than 200 passengers, and usually have naturalists and historians aboard to interpret what you're seeing. Within the small-ship world, most lines break down into one of three subcategories. **Learning cruises** go full-throttle into the educational aspects of travel, with onboard experts from leading nature publications offering lectures and helping with nature interpretation. **Active adventure cruises** also offer naturalists and historians, but focus more on getting passengers out into nature, programming kayaking, hiking, and trips by inflatable landing craft. **Sailing ships** are just that — ships with sails, some of them offering passengers the chance to help haul the lines and pull up the centerboard.

Ship size/style

The size and type of a ship you choose can make a huge difference in the kind of experience you ultimately have. Fortunately, you have a tremendous range to choose from. Options run the gamut from giant megaships to the tiniest of tiny vessels — some carrying fewer than 20 passengers. The following list gives you a handle on the various shapes and styles of ships that fall under each designation.

Note: A ship's size is expressed not in actual 2,000-pound tons but in *gross registered tons (GRTs),* a figure that measures enclosed, interior space used to produce revenue on a vessel (cabins, dining areas, lounges, video game rooms, and so on). Tonnage, in ship terms, is a measure of volume rather than weight. One gross registered ton actually represents 100 cubic feet of enclosed, revenue-generating space.

- ✔ **Megaships:** When the word "megaship" came into common usage in the late 1990s, it meant ships that were up around 80,000 GRTs. Those ships still count as mega, but today the megaship category also includes vessels literally twice that size, ranging up to Cunard's *Queen Mary 2,* at 151,400 GRTs, and Royal Caribbean's new *Freedom of the Seas,* which is expected to be around 160,000 GRTs when she launches in mid-2006. Megaships carry from about 1,750 to more than 3,000 passengers.

  Big on glitz, megaships promote loads of activities, attract families and a large share of the under-50 crowd, offer large public rooms (including fancy casinos and fully equipped gyms), and provide a wide variety of meal and entertainment options. They tend to visit crowd-pleasing ports, but in many ways the ships themselves are the big attraction, with the ports as an added bit of fun.

  Most ships in the fleets of Carnival, Celebrity, Costa, Disney, Norwegian Cruise Line (NCL), Princess, and Royal Caribbean are megaships, though some of these lines also maintain smaller and frequently older ships as well. Holland America's fleet is currently split between an older generation of midsize vessels and newer megas.

- ✔ **Traditional-style ships:** These ships are modern with a traditional-style twist, often in the midsize range (carrying around 700 to 1,500 passengers). They generally provide subdued, old-fashioned décor and an onboard atmosphere geared primarily to older and/or more tradition-minded passengers. Many Holland America ships fit into this category, as do Oceania's 684-passenger ships.

✔ **Modern midsize ships:** These ships run about the same size as the traditional-style midsize vessels but with a more contemporary décor and ambience. Some are simply smaller equivalents of their megasized sisters, providing the same kind of party atmosphere but with fewer partiers — Royal Caribbean's *Empress of the Seas* fits that description, as do several of the older NCL ships. Other vessels, such as Celebrity's *Zenith,* provide a more stylish, less party-oriented experience. Ditto for luxurious ships such as Radisson Seven Seas' luxurious *Seven Seas Voyager* and *Seven Seas Mariner* and Crystal's *Crystal Symphony* and *Crystal Serenity,* the latter of which are downright glamorous. Luxe lines Silversea and Radisson also have smaller midsize ships carrying around 400 to 500 passengers.

✔ **Small ships:** Small ships can negotiate shallow waters, which enables them to reach ports that larger ships can't manage. Often running at a more relaxed pace, smaller ships tend to have fewer children on board. In addition, the combination of smaller public space and less entertainment creates an atmosphere in which you spend a lot of time talking to other passengers. Some small ships (such as the Seaborn and SeaDream vessels) are among the most luxurious afloat, whereas others (such as those operated by American Canadian Caribbean and Glacier Bay Cruiseline) are among the most rustic. The rest fall somewhere in between.

✔ **Sailing ships:** If you dream of doing the Errol Flynn thing, or if you're a purist when it comes to taking to the seas, a sailing ship may be your ticket. Sailing ship experiences run the gamut among the lines currently in operation: from the authenticity of the Maine Windjammers (many of which are more than 100 years old, and work on sail power alone) to the modern yacht stylings of Windstar, which operates some of the largest and most technically advanced sailing ships ever built. Windjammer Barefoot Cruises, down in the Caribbean, offers a bare-boned but raucous sailing adventure, while Star Clippers is more high-toned yet still casual. More than with any other type of cruising, if this is the type of cruise for you, you know it. No one is wishy-washy about a sailing ship. You either love them or you don't.

Note that except for the Maine Windjammers, none of the sailing ships we review in Chapter 13 operate on sail power alone; all also have engines, which often account for most of the ship's propulsion and are a necessary evil if you want to keep any kind of regular schedule.

In a few cases, a ship falls between a couple of different categories, or it seems so unusual in one way or another that it doesn't *exactly* fit into one of these categories. We place these ships in what we think is the nearest fit.

Grasping the Ins and Outs of Itineraries

Every cruise line review lists where all of its ships will sail in 2006, as far out as we were able to get before this book went to press. Because cruise lines tend to do some last-minute jostling, itineraries are subject to change. Be sure to check with a travel agent or with the lines' Web sites for day-by-day listings of the ports each itinerary visits, and verify sailing dates before you go too far in your planning.

The number of days we list for each cruise represents the number of full days (including nights) you spend on board — we don't count the hour or two you're on board on the last day of your cruise, waiting to get off the ship. For example, cruises that begin and end on a Sunday count as 7-day cruises, even though some cruise line brochures may refer to them as 8-day itineraries.

Understanding the Significance of Specifications

So you can compare different ships, we also include a table with each cruise line review that lists their ships' vital statistics: size, passenger capacity, number of crew, number of cabins, tonnage, and length.

To get a rough idea of how crowded a ship feels, divide its tonnage by its total passenger capacity to arrive at the passenger/space ratio. To get an idea of how personal the service is, divide the total number of passengers by the total number of crew to get the passenger/crew ratio.

Getting a Handle on Prices

As we note in Chapter 4, people hardly ever pay full price for a cruise (unless they're booking with some of the small niche lines, which are the exception that proves the rule). Cruise line brochure prices are typically wildly inflated, representing what the line's executives dream about pocketing from each booking. In reality, they charge only a fraction of that — sometimes as little as 50 percent. Prices listed on the cruise lines' Web sites are usually a lot closer to reality, but we've gone one step further by having a travel agent, Nashville's **Just Cruisin' Plus** (☎ **800-888-0922;** www.justcruisinplus.com), investigate every single ship in this book and tell us what their customers were actually paying during a common sampling period (June 2005 cruises, priced in mid-Apr). Other travel agencies and online sites will generally offer similar rates.

Because ships offer itineraries of varying lengths (making it difficult to compare prices), we've listed the sample prices as **per diems.** In other words, what you see are *daily per-person rates* for a cruise. To figure out what your total cost would be, just multiply that by the number of days in the itinerary.

When you look at a cruise line's brochure or Web site, you're likely to see that they offer sometimes a dozen or more different levels of staterooms, but at the most basic level they can all be broken down into three basic types:

- **Inside cabins:** Cabins without windows

- **Outside cabins:** Cabins that may have portholes, picture windows, or even private balconies

- **Suites:** Ranging from glorified staterooms with an extra seating area to presidential-size mansions that may have more square footage than your house, usually with a large private balcony or two

The sample rates include per diems for the *lowest-priced option* in those three categories. Generally speaking, the largest and most desirable inside cabins are priced closer to the rate we list for the lowest-level outside cabins; the largest and most desirable outside cabins are priced closer to the rate we list for the lowest-level suite; and the biggest suites are far, far higher priced than what we list for the low-level suites.

Because this book covers many different cruise regions, our sample prices may not be an exact reflection of what you can expect to pay in some regions. Cruises in Alaska, Hawaii, and the Mediterranean, for example, are almost always more expensive than comparable cruises in the Caribbean and the Mexican Riviera. These prices are meant as a guide only and are in no way etched in stone — the price you pay may be higher or even lower, depending on when you choose to travel, when you book, what specials the lines are offering, and a slew of other factors.

Rates are generally cruise only (without airfare or hotel rooms), per person, and based on double occupancy. In cases where extras are included in the cruise fare, we mention it. Unless noted otherwise, prices listed include port charges (the per-passenger fee that ports charge for ships to dock), but not government taxes.

Chapter 11

Mainstream Ships

· ·

In This Chapter

▶ Introducing the major mainstream cruise lines and ships
▶ Getting the lowdown on the mainstream cruising experience
▶ Previewing the best new ships

· ·

*T*he ships we feature in this chapter range from classic old ocean liners to the biggest new megaships — some of them nearly four times the size of the *Titanic,* but with technological features that are more at home on the International Space Station.

If luxury ships are more your style, see Chapter 12. At the other end of the spectrum, for a more down-to-earth experience, check out Chapter 13, where we discuss smaller adventure and expedition-type vessels.

What Makes Mainstream Ships Tick

Because the ships in this chapter may carry upwards of 2,000 or 3,000 passengers, getting stuck in some lines is inevitable — at the buffet, for example, or when getting off the ship in port — though some megaships are so well-designed that things rarely get backed up. The upside to all that bigness? More options. Some ships these days are so gigantic that they can offer more diversions than your average small town, but even ships that aren't *so* enormous probably fit that description, too. Mainstream ships have the classics — swimming pools, health clubs and spas, nightclubs and bars, movie theaters, casinos, shops, kids' play-rooms, and open decks. You can also find sports decks, virtual golf, computer rooms, cigar clubs, martini bars, and sometimes learning centers that offer classes that range from history to theater arts. Ship design has come so far that, even on vessels carrying 3,000 or more passengers, you can still find nooks to get away from it all. You may even find yourself wondering where all those other people are.

Mainstream ships have large dining rooms and buffet areas that serve as much food with as much variety and at almost as many times as a 24-hour New York diner — and with better views to boot. Many offer formal nights when you can dine in your tux or gown if you like, while others are casual 24/7. Beyond their large traditional restaurants, most mainstream ships these days also offer some combination of intimate, romantic, alternative restaurants; casual restaurants where you can grab a hamburger, hot dog, veggie burger, or a slice of pizza; buffets stuffed to the gills with everything from cold cuts to Indian food; ice-cream parlors; caviar bars; and specialty coffee and snack bars. Wash it all down with a drink — maybe from the ship's wine, champagne, or martini bars, or with a few beers at the sports bar.

You can find onboard activities such as games and contests, classes and lectures, and a variety of entertainment options, including large-scale production shows, quiet pianists, not-so-quiet dance bands, operatic recitals, magicians, comedians, and more.

The ships generally offer a comfortable cruising experience, with your well-being overseen by virtual armies of service employees. Ship stabilizers ensure that you have a fairly smooth sailing experience, too.

In the cabins, you can find many of the typical accoutrements of modern American life: TVs (and sometimes DVD players), telephones, hair dryers, and sometimes dataports, minibars, private safes, and fuzzy bathrobes. The cabins themselves range from cubbyholes to absolutely *enormous* suites. You may choose to upgrade from a typical window cabin to one with a private veranda so that you can lounge out in the open air — clothed or unclothed, it's up to you. (Though some aren't completely private. Careful! Unless you don't care . . .)

Where the Mainstream Ships Go

Mainstream is as mainstream does, so the itineraries of the biggest ships tend to include mostly tried-and-true ports — nothing too far out of the, well, mainstream, but that's not necessarily bad, especially if you're looking for a good time. Wherever the megaships dock, expect lots of shopping, drinking, and eating options, plus huge lists of shore excursions to take you far away from those things: out into the jungles, up into the mountains, under the sea, or sometimes deep into history.

Some smaller ships also visit less-crowded ports, away from the typical tourist crowds. The smaller the ship, the more easily it's able to do this — it can get into smaller harbors, and there's no possibility its passengers will overwhelm the town with their numbers.

As we note in Chapter 10, the rates we list here are sample per diems that approximate the actual per-day prices passengers were paying as this book went to press. The rates you find may be higher or even lower, depending on market fluctuations. To arrive at an approximation of your full vacation's cost, just multiply the per diem by the number of nights in the itinerary.

Carnival Cruise Lines

3655 NW 87th Ave., Miami, FL 33178-2428; ☎ *800-CARNIVAL (800-227-6482);* www. carnival.com

> ✔ **Type of cruise:** Family, party, resort, romantic
>
> ✔ **Ship size/style:** Modern, glitzy megaships

The king of cruise, Carnival has been dishing up fun at sea since company patriarch Ted Arison launched the *Mardi Gras* way back in 1972. The assets of parent company, Carnival Corporation, are mind-blowing (and growing); all told, the company has a stake in 12 cruise brands, for a combined fleet of 77 ships, with many more in the works.

More than 30 years and some 21 ships later, Carnival has evolved and improved, though the core remains the same: let-your-hair-down fun on outrageously themed ships. The line attracts a real mix — from those with beer bellies and tattoos to types with graduate degrees and Gucci loafers. A Carnival ship is the ultimate American melting pot.

Bob Marley blasts from the Pool Deck as happy campers young and old swig Buds and drink in that wild Carnival take on a classic Caribbean vacation. Sure, you can now find sushi and wine bars, but the ships are still all about partying into the wee hours and over-the-top flamboyance — where else would you find a Marilyn Monroe manikin or King Tut's tomb decorating a lounge? Carnival puts its whimsical spin on themes from ancient Egypt and Greece to the Renaissance, New Orleans, Billie Holiday, and Neil Armstrong. The One Small Step disco on the *Valor,* for example, is a tribute to Armstrong's walk on the moon. White mini-volcanolike craters several feet tall glow with LED lighting, the ceiling is a sea of twinkling lights, and the floor is made from moonlike white marble and granite, and covered, of course, with astronaut "footprints."

While food and service are pretty much average — not surprising considering the large numbers served — that doesn't stop the line from trying to offer a higher-quality vacation. Recent enhancements include switching from plastic to china in the buffet restaurants, and equipping cabins with thicker towels, duvets, and more TV channels. These extra touches along with the line's other assets — large cabins, professional service, lots of entertainment, and great kids' facilities — keep the masses coming back for more. And boy has Carnival cashed in. Table 11-1 shows Carnival's itineraries and sample fares.

Carnival offers a *Vacation Guarantee* program: Any guest dissatisfied with the cruise while on board can disembark at the first non-U.S. port of call and receive a refund for the unused portion of their fare, plus reimbursement for air transportation back to the ship's homeport. To qualify, passengers must inform the ship's purser before their first port of call.

Table 11-1	Carnival Itineraries and Sample Fares
Ship/Fares *(per person/day)*	**Itineraries**
Carnival Conquest $76 inside; $97 outside; $190 suite	**7-night western Caribbean:** Round-trip from Galveston, TX, year-round
Carnival Destiny $76 inside; $97 outside; $183 suite	**7-night southern Caribbean:** Round-trip from San Juan, PR, year-round
Carnival Glory $76 inside; $97 outside; $200 suite	**7-night eastern and western Caribbean** (alternating weekly): Round-trip from Port Canaveral, FL, year-round
Carnival Legend $75 inside; $94 outside; $181 suite	**8-night southern and western Caribbean** (alternating weekly): Round-trip from Ft. Lauderdale, FL, Oct–Apr; **8-night Caribbean:** Round-trip from New York, NY, Apr–Oct
Carnival Liberty $81 inside; $100 outside; $187 suite	**6- and 8-night western Caribbean:** Round-trip from Ft. Lauderdale, FL, year-round
Carnival Miracle $71 inside; $93 outside; $197 suite	**7-night western Caribbean:** Round-trip from Tampa, FL, year-round
Carnival Pride $83 inside; $104 outside; $200 suite	**7-night Mexican Riviera:** Round-trip from Long Beach, CA, year-round
Carnival Spirit $77 inside; $96 outside; $209 suite	**8-night Mexican Riviera:** Round-trip from San Diego, CA, Jan–Apr and Oct–Dec; **12-night Hawaii:** Ensenada, Mexico, to Honolulu, HI, and Honolulu to Vancouver, BC, Apr; **7-night Gulf of Alaska:** North- or south-bound (alternating weekly) between Vancouver, and Whittier/Anchorage, AK, May–Aug; **7-night Alaska Inside Passage:** Round-trip from Vancouver, May and Sept
Carnival Triumph $86 inside; $107 outside; $214 suite	**7-night eastern and western Caribbean** (alternating weekly): Round-trip from Miami, FL, year-round
Carnival Valor $74 inside; $96 outside; $193 suite	**7-night eastern and western Caribbean** (alternating weekly): Round-trip from Miami, FL, year-round
Carnival Victory $71 inside; $93 outside; $186 suite	**7-night eastern and western Caribbean** (alternating weekly): Round-trip from Miami, FL, year-round

Ship/Fares (per person/day)	Itineraries
Celebration $63 inside; $76 outside; $196 suite	**4- and 5-night Bahamas/Key West:** Round-trip from Jacksonville, FL, year-round
Ecstasy $67 inside; $84 outside; $190 suite	**4- and 5-night western Caribbean:** Round-trip from Galveston, TX, year-round
Elation $64 inside; $77 outside;$183 suite	**7-night western Caribbean:** Round-trip from Galveston, TX, year-round
Fantasy $67 inside; $82 outside; $155 suite	**3- and 4-night Bahamas:** Round-trip from Port Canaveral, FL, year-round
Fascination $62 inside; $75 outside; $155 suite	**3-night Bahamas and 4-night western Caribbean** (alternating itineraries): Round-trip from Miami, FL, year-round
Holiday $72 inside; $92 outside; $212 suite	**4- and 5-night western Caribbean:** Round-trip from Mobile, AL, year-round
Imagination $72 inside; $94 outside; $214 suite	**4- and 5-night western Caribbean:** Round-trip from Miami, FL, year-round
Inspiration $76 inside; $94 outside; $218 suite	**4- and 5-night western Caribbean:** Round-trip from Tampa, FL, year-round
Paradise $77 inside; $97 outside; $195 suite	**3-night Ensenada and 4-night Ensenada/Catalina Island** (alternating itineraries): Round-trip from Long Beach, CA, year-round
Sensation $72 inside; $92 outside; $210 suite	**4- and 5-night western Caribbean:** Round-trip from New Orleans, LA, year-round*

* Deployment affected by Hurricane Katrina disaster. Contact cruise line for updates.

Dining

Like most everything about Carnival, the quality and choice of the food have improved over the years. Still, don't expect gourmet. Geared toward a middle-American audience, just like its mainstream peers, you can find plenty of the basics — steaks, fish, and pasta — to go with choices such as sushi and Chinese food. Each ship has a main dining room or two that operate the traditional early and late seatings, plus a casual buffet restaurant operating nearly round the clock (including dinner nightly). An intimate reservations-only supper club/steakhouse features live music and the ships' most expertly prepared meals, with a $25 per person cover, on the line's newer ships: *Carnival Spirit, Pride, Legend, Conquest, Glory, Valor, Miracle,* and *Liberty.* For casual, try pizza, calzones, and Caesar salads available 24 hours a day; late-night buffet spreads; patisseries for fancy coffees (for a charge); and room service.

There's no shortage of bars, many with a healthy dose of Carnival's wacky design whimsy (try oyster shell wallpaper and furry bar stools).

Activities and entertainment

You won't be bored if big, flashy stage shows are your bag. Carnival doesn't hold back, with lavish sets and casts of 8 to 16 cast members decked out in over-the-top costumes. Live six- to ten-piece orchestras accompany the dancers and lead singers. During a typical weeklong cruise, comedians, jugglers, acrobats, blaring poolside pop bands, country-and-western bands, classical string trios, pianists, and big bands are a part of the mix. The theaters on the Destiny-class, Spirit-class, and Conquest-class ships are spectacular three-deck extravaganzas, and the casinos are so large you may think you've died and gone to Vegas; but even aboard its smaller, older ships, Carnival consistently offers some of the most fun and flamboyant entertainment extravaganzas afloat.

Speaking of wacky, Carnival's big on silly poolside games, such as belly-flop contests and pillow fights. Doesn't get much more cerebral than that, though arts and crafts classes are occasionally offered along with stuff like game shows, dancing lessons, and art auctions.

There's plenty of time to enjoy the Carnival experience, given that the line's typical 7-night Caribbean cruises include three days at sea (and just three ports). Of course, this schedule also means passengers have more time to spend, spend, spend in the ships' shops, bars, casinos, and spas (cha-ching, cha-ching for Carnival's coffers).

For kids

Among the top lines for kids, Camp Carnival delivers fun for toddlers through teens. The newest Conquest-class ships (see Figure 11-1) have the biggest and best digs with awesome teen centers and video arcades, but the entire fleet has good playrooms and the line's signature snaking water slide on the Pool Deck. Complimentary activities are scheduled nearly all day long. For an hourly fee, group babysitting for ages 4 months through 12 is offered nightly, plus for a few hours on port days.

When they turn down the cabins each night, room stewards get goofy by making bathroom towels into fluffy animals and displaying them on the beds. (You can even buy a book in the ship's gift shop that shows you how to do these tricks at home!)

(Photo: Carnival Cruise Lines)

Figure 11-1: *Carnival Conquest*

Fleet facts

The **Carnival Destiny** was, in her first year (1996), the biggest ship in the world, and she offers the "wows" you'd expect of a ship her size, including huge spa and gym areas. The **Carnival Triumph** and **Carnival Victory** are the *Carnival Destiny's* slightly bigger siblings. A stretched version of these ships, the **Carnival Conquest,** debuted in the fall of 2002, and three sisters entered service in successive years: the **Carnival Glory, Valor,** and **Liberty.** These ships are about 60 feet longer, with tonnage of 110,000 GRTs, and boast massive kids' and teen areas.

In 2001, the line introduced a relatively small (by megaship standards) class of ship: the 2,124-passenger, 84,000-ton **Carnival Spirit,** which boasts an outdoor promenade and a supper club. **Carnival Pride, Carnival Legend,** and **Carnival Miracle** arrived in the years following. These vessels all offer the most successful design elements of Carnival's earlier classes of ships, including many bars and lounges.

Carnival's Fantasy-class ships — the **Ecstasy, Elation, Fantasy, Fascination, Imagination, Inspiration, Paradise,** and **Sensation** — differ in their wacky décor but otherwise are the exact same size and have identical layouts and Carnival's roomy cabin size. They're good party ships, though a tad aged. If there was botox for cruise ships, these guys could probably use a shot. The **Celebration** and **Holiday** are the older, non-megaships in the Carnival fleet. They seem really ancient and out of date compared to their newer fleetmates, but they have roomy cabins and are often priced cheaper than the line's other ships. Table 11-2 shows the current fleet specifications.

Table 11-2	Carnival Fleet Specifications					
Ship	**Entered Service**	**Passengers**	**Crew**	**Total Cabins**	**Tonnage**	**Length in Feet**
Carnival Conquest	2002	2,974	1,160	1,487	110,000	952
Carnival Destiny	1996	2,642	1,000	1,321	101,353	893

(continued)

Table 11-2 *(continued)*

Ship	Entered Service	Passengers	Crew	Total Cabins	Tonnage	Length in Feet
Carnival Glory	2003	2,974	1,160	1,487	110,000	952
Carnival Legend	2002	2,124	920	1,062	88,500	960
Carnival Liberty	2005	2,974	1,160	1,487	110,000	952
Carnival Miracle	2004	2,124	920	1,062	88,500	960
Carnival Pride	2001	2,124	920	1,062	88,500	960
Carnival Spirit	2001	2,124	920	1,062	88,500	960
Carnival Triumph	1999	2,758	1,050	1,379	102,000	893
Carnival Valor	2004	2,974	1,160	1,487	110,000	952
Carnival Victory	2000	2,758	1,050	1,379	102,000	893
Celebration	1987	1,486	670	743	47,262	733
Ecstasy	1991	2,040	920	1,020	70,367	855
Elation	1998	2,040	920	1,020	70,367	855
Fantasy	1990	2,040	920	1,020	70,367	855
Fascination	1994	2,040	920	1,020	70,367	855
Holiday	1985	1,452	669	726	46,052	727
Imagination	1995	2,040	920	1,020	70,367	855
Inspiration	1996	2,040	920	1,020	70,367	855
Paradise	1998	2,040	920	1,020	70,367	855
Sensation	1993	2,040	920	1,020	70,367	855

Celebrity Cruises

1050 Caribbean Way, Miami, FL 33132; ☎ *800-437-3111 or 305-539-6000;* www.celebrity.com

> ✔ **Type of cruise:** Family, resort, romantic

> ✔ **Ship size/style:** Modern, stylish midsize and megaships

We'll just admit it right now, we're in love with Celebrity. Who could resist the most elegant big ships in the industry? Celebrity offers a refined experience, but isn't stuffy. There's plenty of fun to be had and lots of activities to keep you busy, but you can always find a quiet spot, too, for some good old-fashioned R & R. Each ship is glamorous and comfortable, mixing sleekly modern and Art Deco styles and throwing in cutting-edge art collections to boot.

Hands down, Celebrity has the best vessels in the mid-priced category — the *Century, Galaxy, Mercury* (see Figure 11-2), and especially the newer *Millennium, Infinity, Summit,* and *Constellation.* Celebrity gets the "best of" nod in a lot of categories: The AquaSpas on the line's megaships are tops, the art collections the most compelling fleetwide, the décor the most original, and the onboard activities and entertainment among the most varied. Dining-wise, Celebrity shines with its dashing alternative restaurants on the Millennium-class ships, the best at sea for both quality of food and their gorgeous décor. Table 11-3 shows Celebrity's itineraries and sample fares.

From its beginnings, the polite and professional staff has been a cut above the competition and contributes greatly to the elegant mood. Passengers, who range in age from 20-something honeymooners to retirees, are pampered in a low-key, non-invasive way. Like all the big-ship lines, Celebrity offers lots for its passengers to do, but Celebrity steers away from the standards. Innovative entertainment includes roving a cappella groups, while expert-led seminars on topics such as astronomy, photography, personal investing, and history offer a little more cerebral meat than the usual. The latest: acupuncture and holistic healing theme cruises and Cirque du Soleil–inspired shows.

Art is an important aspect of the Celebrity experience. It's everywhere on board and no other line in the industry comes close to offering collections as intriguing. The *Summit,* for example, has *Woman With Fruit,* a large bronze of a rotund woman by noted Colombian artist Fernando Botero (the sculpture overlooks the ship's thalassotherapy pool area), as well as an ART sculpture by LOVE artist Robert Indiana. There are also originals on the ships by David Hockney, Jasper Johns, Jeff Koons, David Levinthal, Liza Lou, Andy Warhol, and many others.

Dining

Michel Roux, Celebrity's famous culinary consultant and one of the top French chefs in Britain, guides all Celebrity cuisine. His talents and legacy shine brightest in the intimate alternative dining venues on the Millennium-class ships, where you can have just about the best dining experience available at sea.

The *Millennium* has a special reservations-only dining room with a great feature: hand-carved wood panels that were created for the *Olympic* (sister ship to the *Titanic*) and graced that vessel's A La Carte restaurant from 1911 to 1935. The dining experience in the restaurant created around these panels is leisurely and luxurious, styled after liners cruising in the Golden Age of sea travel (although be prepared to enjoy it for three hours). The line offers comparably fine restaurants with intriguing

Table 11-3	Celebrity Itineraries and Sample Fares
Ship/Fares *(per person/day)*	**Itineraries**
Century $100 inside; $118 outside; $300 suite	**7-night eastern Caribbean:** Round-trip from Ft. Lauderdale, FL, Jan–Feb; alternates with **9- and 10-night western Caribbean:** Round-trip from Miami, FL, Jan–Apr and Dec; **7- and 12-night Scandinavia/Russia:** Round-trip from Amsterdam, Netherlands, Aug; **10- and 11-night Mediterranean:** Round-trip from Barcelona, Spain, Sept–Oct; **4- and 5-night western Caribbean:** Round-trip from Miami, Nov–Dec
Constellation $125 inside; $142 outside; $500 suite	**7-night southern Caribbean:** Round-trip from San Juan, PR, Jan–Mar and Dec; **9- and 12-night Bermuda/Caribbean:** Round-trip from Bayonne, NJ, Mar–Apr; **14-night Scandinavia/Russia and British Isles/Norway:** Round-trip from London, UK, May–Aug; **10- and 11-night eastern/southern Caribbean:** Round-trip from Ft. Lauderdale, FL, Nov–Dec
Galaxy $143 inside; $157 outside; $321 suite	**11- and 12-night Panama Canal:** Round-trip from Galveston, TX, Jan–Apr; **10- and 11-night Mediterranean:** Round-trip from Rome, Italy, May–Nov; **7- and 11-night southern Caribbean:** Round-trip from San Juan, PR, Dec
Infinity $136 inside; $157 outside; $550 suite	**7-night eastern Caribbean:** Round-trip from Ft. Lauderdale, FL, Jan–Apr and Dec; **12-night Mediterranean:** East- or westbound between Venice, Italy, and Barcelona, Spain, May–Nov
Mercury $103 inside; $115 outside; $330 suite	**8-, 10- and 11-night Mexican Riviera:** Round-trip from San Diego, CA, Jan–Apr and Oct–Dec; **7-night Alaska Inside Passage:** Round-trip from Seattle, WA, May–Sept; **3- and 4-night Pacific Northwest:** Round-trip from Seattle, Sept–Oct
Millennium $100 inside; $139 outside; $275 suite	**14- and 15-night South America:** Round-trip from Buenos Aires, Argentina, and between Buenos Aires and Valparaiso, Chile, Jan–Mar and Nov–Dec; **10- and 11-night Mexican Riviera:** Round-trip from San Francisco, CA, Apr; **12-night Alaska Inside Passage:** Round-trip from San Francisco, May; **7-night Alaska Inside Passage:** Round-trip from Vancouver, BC, June–Aug; **14-night Hawaii:** Round-trip from San Diego, CA, Oct
Summit $133 inside; $172 outside; $607 suite	**13- and 14-night Hawaii:** Round-trip from Los Angeles, CA, Jan, Mar–Apr, Oct, and Dec; **14-night Panama Canal:** East- or westbound between Ft. Lauderdale, FL, and Los Angeles, Feb and Nov; **7-night Gulf of Alaska:** North- or southbound between Vancouver, BC, and Seward/Anchorage, Alaska, May–Sept

Ship/Fares (per person/day)	Itineraries
Zenith $171 inside; $179 outside; $436 suite	**4- and 5-night western Caribbean:** Round-trip from Miami, FL, Jan–Apr; **7-night Bermuda:** Round-trip from Bayonne, NJ, Apr–Oct; **10-night western Caribbean:** Round-trip from Tampa, FL, Nov–Dec

décor on the *Infinity, Summit,* and *Constellation.* The cost at these venues is $30 per person, and is totally worthwhile. Feast on appetizers such as a tartare of salmon garnished with quail eggs or goat cheese soufflé with tomato coulis, followed by entrees such as shrimp scampi flambéed in Armagnac or rack of lamb coated with mushroom duxelles and wrapped in a puff pastry. For dessert, try saying no to the chocolate soufflé or a plate of Michel Roux's favorite bite-size desserts.

On all but the *Zenith,* the ships' main dining rooms are lovely two-deck-high affairs with a dramatic staircase at the center sharing the attention with floor-to-ceiling windows facing the ships' wake — quite a sight on a moonlit night. Cuisine here is good, on par with other big-ship lines. Each ship also has a buffet restaurant operating for all meals, but unlike other big ships, waiters carry your tray to a table. Dinner is served here most nights (including a sushi bar), but reservations are requested.

There's also a specialty coffee bar — the Cova Cafe — and each Millennium-class ship has a Spa Cafe in a corner of the thalassotherapy pool area serving a light and healthy breakfast (such as fresh fruit and bagels and lox) and lunch (including raw veggie platters, vegetarian sushi, and pretty tuna or chicken salads). Several nights a week around midnight, waiters roam the public areas and lounges with upscale canapés and hors d'oeuvres such as fish tempura and roasted garlic lemon chicken. At least once per cruise fleetwide, the line offers what it calls Elegant Tea, an impressive event in which white-gloved waiters serve tea, finger sandwiches, scones, and desserts from rolling trolleys. The line's 24-hour room service allows passengers to order off the lunch and dinner menus during those hours.

Activities and entertainment

Like in so many other areas, Celebrity excels with its wide variety of activities and entertainment. Its complimentary enrichment lectures are offered on all cruises. Up to four featured speakers/performers may include caricature artists (on weeklong Caribbean and Bermuda sailings), naturalists (on Alaska, Hawaii, and South America sailings), chefs from well-regarded shoreside restaurants, and wine experts who offer onboard seminars and tastings. From time to time, actors, politicians, and journalists also sail aboard and hold talks. Other innovative activities include the line's Acupuncture at Sea program. On all cruises, doctors specializing in Oriental medicine give free talks on acupuncture and other holistic health treatments and offer acupuncture and medicinal herbal treatments (for a fee) for pain management, smoking cessation, weight loss, stress management, and other ailments.

You can find more standard fare such as wine tastings, horse racing, bingo, bridge, art auctions, trivia games, arts and crafts, cooking demos, computer classes, dancing lessons, and lots of great spa treatments.

 With the exception of the *Zenith,* Celebrity's ships each feature the AquaSpa, a water-centered spa that's the equal of anything else the industry offers. They all have a thalassotherapy pool, a kind of giant New Age hot tub where water jets hit different parts of your body as you relax. Decorated beautifully — with a Japanese motif on the *Century* and *Galaxy,* for example — the spas also offer some of the most innovative spa treatments at sea. From a Hawaiian Four Hands massage (yes, two therapists work on you at once) to Rasul (a medicinal mud and steam bath treatment) or a frangipani body wrap, how could you resist?

Celebrity has partnered with fantasy circus troupe Cirque du Soleil. The observation lounges on *Constellation* and *Summit,* the two ships that at press time were offering the show, are transformed for two hours every evening into "The Bar at the Edge of the Earth," where guests engage in interactive performances (as opposed to a straight stage show) with surreal Cirque characters. Typically, one or two performers are from the company's actual traveling circus, while the rest are from the ship's entertainment staff. Otherwise, Celebrity continues to offer some nice, understated entertainment touches such as strolling a cappella groups, harpists, and classical trios performing in various parts of each ship.

The line also offers a taste of more standard entertainment fare, with Broadway-style musical reviews; performances by magicians, comedians, and cabaret acts; and passenger talent shows. Head for the disco one night, or skip out completely and retire to one of the many cozy dark lounges for a quiet evening, among the best being the elegant and plush Michael's Club piano lounges.

For kids

The *Millennium, Constellation, Infinity,* and *Summit* are the best fit for families, each with an indoor and outdoor play area, though every ship in the fleet has a playroom and all but the *Zenith* have teen centers. Some supervised activities are offered year-round, though during holidays and summers there's more: complimentary activities are geared toward four age groups between the ages of 3 and 17. Group babysitting and private in-cabin sitting are available for an hourly fee nightly for ages 3 to 12.

(Photo: Matt Hannafin)

Figure 11-2: *Mercury*

Fleet facts

The oldest Celebrity ship, the **Zenith,** is a fine ship if you're looking for something smaller than average, but when the company moved into the megaship business, it topped itself with the impressive **Century,** and then topped itself again with the **Galaxy** and again with the **Mercury,** which will undergo a $55 million facelift in spring 2006. The line's 91,000-ton, French-built Millennium-class ships continue the trend. These vessels — the **Millennium, Infinity, Summit,** and **Constellation** — are just plain stunning: comfortable, beautifully designed, and full of lovely rooms and varied diversions, such as an Internet center, a music library, and extensive high-fashion shopping opportunities. The *Infinity, Summit,* and *Constellation* have a conservatory complete with benches and orchids (the *Millennium* has a smaller version) — a botanical garden at sea, a respite from the hustle and bustle of daily sea life.

In general, the cabins on Celebrity ships are all good-sized and decorated nicely (though not as big as Carnival's cabins, for example). All cabins fleetwide (with the exception of the *Zenith*) have minifridges. The ships' penthouse suites are very large and quite pleasing on the eyes, and all suites reap the services of a butler and other perks such as free champagne and the option of booking a massage in your cabin. Table 11-4 shows the current fleet specifications.

Table 11-4		Celebrity Fleet Specifications				
Ship	*Entered Service*	*Passengers*	*Crew*	*Total Cabins*	*Tonnage*	*Length in Feet*
Century	1995	1,750	843	875	70,606	807
Constellation	2002	1,950	999	975	91,000	964
Galaxy	1996	1,896	900	935	77,713	858
Infinity	2001	1,950	999	975	91,000	964
Mercury	1997	1,896	900	935	77,713	860

(continued)

Table 11-4 (continued)

Ship	Entered Service	Passengers	Crew	Total Cabins	Tonnage	Length in Feet
Millennium	2000	1,950	999	975	91,000	964
Summit	2001	1,950	999	975	91,000	964
Zenith	1992	1,374	645	687	47,225	682

Costa Cruises

200 South Park Rd., Suite 200, Hollywood, FL 33021-8541; ☎ *800-462-6782;* www.costacruises.com

> ✔ **Type of cruise:** Resort, family, party

> ✔ **Ship size/style:** Megaships and modern midsize ships

The origins of Costa are in Italy, and even though the company is now owned by Miami-based Carnival Corporation, its origins show in nearly everything it offers, from food to entertainment to decorative elements and the many Italian-speaking crewmembers. Onboard activities include festive Roman toga parties on Caribbean sailings, carnival and circus nights in Europe, and audience-participation shows with a distinctly European flavor. The line doesn't design its cruises strictly for an American audience, and therein lies its charm.

As the number-one cruise line in Europe, Costa boasts a modern fleet that just keeps getting bigger. Between June 2003 and November 2004, it launched three new megaships — the *Costa Mediterranea* and the sister ships *Costa Fortuna* and *Costa Magica.* Two more are in the works: the 112,000-ton, 3,800-passenger *Costa Concordia* (due summer 2006) and an as-yet-unnamed sister ship scheduled for spring 2007.

The cruises draw a good age mix, including honeymooners and families, many of whom are attracted to the line's atmosphere of festive fun. A good number of Italian-Americans are among the clientele on Caribbean sailings. On European sailings, Americans make up only about 20 percent of the passenger mix, which is predominantly Italian but also includes French, German, and British citizens, among others. That leads to some loooooooong strings of announcements, which sometimes need to be repeated in five different languages. The European mix also means that many passengers smoke like chimneys, though smoking is officially banned in all main dining rooms and main showrooms on all vessels. Table 11-5 shows Costa's itineraries and sample fares.

Table 11-5   Costa Itineraries and Sample Fares

Ship/Fares (per person/day)	Itineraries
Costa Allegra $91 inside; $118 outside; $214 suite	**11-night western Caribbean:** Round-trip from Miami, FL, Jan–Mar
Costa Atlantica $102 inside; $127 outside; $227 suite	**5-night Mediterranean:** Round-trip from Genoa, Italy, May; **11-, 12-, 13-, and 14-night northern Europe:** Round-trip from Amsterdam, Netherlands, June–Sept; **10-night Mediterranean/Egypt:** Round-trip from Genoa, Sept–Dec
Costa Classica $121 inside; $150 outside; $264 suite	**11-night Mediterranean/Egypt/Libya:** Round-trip from Genoa, Italy, Jan–Apr; **11-night Mediterranean/Canary Islands:** Round-trip from Genoa, Jan–Apr
Costa Concordia Rates not available	**7-night western Mediterranean:** Round-trip from Rome, Italy, July–Nov; **10- and 11-night Mediterranean/Egypt:** Round-trip from Genoa, Italy, Nov–Dec
Costa Europa $114 inside; $143 outside; $243 suite	**10- and 11-night Mediterranean/Canary Islands:** Round-trip from Genoa, Italy, Feb–Dec; **10- and 11-night Mediterranean/ Egypt/Libya and Egypt/Cyprus/Greece:** Round-trip from Genoa, Feb–Dec; **11-night Black Sea:** Round-trip from Genoa, May, July, and Sept
Costa Fortuna $109 inside; $145 outside; $245 suite	**10- and 11-night Mediterranean/Egypt:** Round-trip from Genoa, Italy, Jan–Mar; **7-night western Mediterranean:** Round-trip from Genoa, Apr–Nov; **10- and 11-night Mediterranean/Egypt:** Round-trip from Genoa, Nov–Dec
Costa Magica $128 inside; $157 outside; $371 suite	**7-night eastern and western Caribbean:** Round-trip from Ft. Lauderdale, FL, Jan–Apr and Nov–Dec; **7-night Bermuda:** Round-trip from Ft. Lauderdale, Apr; **7-night northern Europe:** Round-trip from Copenhagen, Denmark, May–Sept; **8-night Spain/Portugal:** Round-trip from Genoa, Italy, Sept–Oct
Costa Marina Rates not available	**7-night eastern Mediterranean:** Round-trip from Trieste, Italy, June–Sept
Costa Mediterranea $86 inside; $100 outside; $214 suite	**7-night eastern and western Caribbean:** Round-trip from Ft. Lauderdale, FL, Jan–Apr and Dec; **7-night eastern Mediterranean:** Round-trip from Venice, Italy, May–Nov
Costa Romantica $100 inside; $122 outside; $216 suite	**9-, 10-, and 22-night South America:** Round-trip from Sao Paolo, Brazil, Jan–Mar and Dec; **5-, 6- and 7-night Mediterranean:** Round-trip from Genoa, Italy, Apr; **7-night eastern and western Mediterranean:** Round-trip from Rome, Italy, May–Nov

(continued)

Table 11-5 *(continued)*	
Ship/Fares (per person/day)	*Itineraries*
Costa Victoria $123 inside; $171 outside; $283 suite	**3-, 4-, 6-, and 7-night South America:** Round-trip from Sao Paolo, Brazil, Jan–Feb and Dec; **7-night eastern Mediterranean:** Round-trip from Venice, Italy, Mar–Nov

* *Itineraries not marketed to North Americans have not been included in this table.*

Dining

Costa's food, oddly enough, is only average, though the line's pastas and pizza are very tasty and plentiful, and presented in an authentically Italian style. On theme nights, staffers may dress as gondoliers and present red roses to all the women. Aside from the main restaurants, alternative dining venues include reservations-only alternative restaurants aboard most of the line's vessels, offering Mediterranean dishes such as rigatoni served with lobster and tomatoes, or grilled lamb chops (for a cover charge of $23 per person). A Tuscan steakhouse menu is also available. Other noshing includes pizza cafes and patisseries serving espresso, chocolates, and pastries.

Activities and entertainment

More than anything else, Costa is known for its exuberant (and often Italian-inspired) activities, with three nights per 7-night cruise given over to Italian and Mediterranean themes. A cast of extremely energetic and shockingly attractive activities coordinators (known as the "animation staff") keep the atmosphere hopping into the wee hours.

The Roman Bacchanal Toga Night ends with a hysterical show that's half slapstick vaudeville and half *American Idol.* After each act, Julius Caesar and the audience decide whether to send the performers to the buffet or throw them to the lions. Yes, it's Italian à la Disney, but if you down enough Campari, it all sort of starts to work, and the next time your Filipino cabin steward greets you with *"Buongiorno!"* you may find yourself buongiorno-ing right back.

The Costa experience also includes an almost-daily Catholic mass at each ship's chapel. Those who worship at the temple of golf can attend a Golf Academy at Sea program on Caribbean cruises, in which guests take onboard clinics and private lessons with PGA pros, participate in putting competitions, and play at some of the Caribbean's best courses.

For kids

Costa's kids' programs aren't as extensive as those available on other lines such as Disney and Royal Caribbean, but how many lines offer Italian language classes? Each ship has a playroom and carries at least two full-time youth counselors to supervise kids' activities, which are offered for ages 3 to 17 for two or three age groupings, depending on demand. Group babysitting is offered nightly (for a fee) if parents want to catch a show or do cocktails.

(Photo: Costa Cruise Lines)

Figure 11-3: *Costa Atlantica*

Fleet facts

Costa Allegra began life as a freighter back in the 1960s and was completely transformed into a passenger cruiser in the 1990s, with a contemporary Italian look. Outside, she still maintains the profile of a tough, classic working ship, albeit in bright cruise-ship white. Ditto for ***Costa Marina,*** another '60s-vintage ship that was totally overhauled in the '90s, by the same architect.

Costa Classica and sister-ship ***Costa Romantica*** are stylish vessels built in the early 1990s, *Classica* with a modern, contemporary décor and *Romantica* with a warmer, more woody look. ***Costa Europa*** was extensively reconfigured and remodeled when she joined the Costa fleet. Though she's not very old in human-years, she has the solid feel of an old ocean liner.

Costa Victoria ushered Costa into the megaship era back in 1996 and remains a sleek and stylish ship, with bright interiors, a seven-story atrium, and a dramatic four-story lounge that's reminiscent of spaces aboard the great old deco liners, albeit with a lot of chrome and glass. In 2004, 246 of her cabins were retrofitted with balconies. Megaship ***Costa Atlantica*** (see Figure 11-3) was the first in the fleet built with a large number of private verandas (nearly 65 percent of the ship's outside cabins). The vessel's decks are named after films by the great director Federico Fellini, and its Café Florian is modeled after the landmark 18th-century Venetian cafe of the same name, with gilt moldings and intricate wall and ceiling murals. *Atlantica's* sister ship, ***Costa Mediterranea,*** has a dance motif and a similarly bright, festive décor.

Costa's two most recent megaships, ***Costa Fortuna*** and ***Costa Magica,*** are somewhat like Carnival ships with an Italian slant. They're the largest passenger ships in Italian maritime history — at least until summer 2006, when the 112,000-ton *Costa Concordia* debuts. Table 11-6 shows the current fleet specifications.

Table 11-6		Costa Fleet Specifications				
Ship	*Entered Service*	*Passengers*	*Crew*	*Total Cabins*	*Tonnage*	*Length in Feet*
Costa Allegra	1992	820	450	410	28,500	616
Costa Atlantica	2000	2,112	920	1,056	85,000	957
Costa Classica	1991	1,308	650	654	53,000	722
Costa Europa	1986	1,494	650	747	54,000	798
Costa Fortuna	2003	2,700	998	1,359	105,000	976
Costa Magica	2004	2,700	998	1,359	105,000	976
Costa Marina	1990	760	389	382	25,500	616
Costa Mediterranea	2003	2,114	920	1,057	85,000	960
Costa Romantica	1993	1,356	610	678	53,000	722
Costa Victoria	1996	1,928	800	964	54,000	817

Disney Cruise Line

P.O. Box 10210, Lake Buena Vista, FL 32830; ☎ *888-325-2500;* www.disneycruise.com

> ✔ **Type of cruise:** Family, resort

> ✔ **Ship size/style:** Modern, stylish megaships with the Disney touch

Just about everything Mickey's gloved hand touches turns to gold, and the company's pair of elegant cruise ships is no exception. The *Disney Magic* (see Figure 11-4) and *Wonder* manage to be both classic and ultramodern, designed to evoke the grand transatlantic liners but also decked out in some great family features.

In creating the line, Disney (being Disney) tried to rewrite the book on cruising and has succeeded with several of its innovations, which, by the way, you pay 20 to 80 percent more for compared to many other big-ship lines, according to Charlie Funk, co-owner of Just Cruisin' Plus in Nashville. But you get a lot for the higher price tag. The ships' cabins are larger than the industry average and are designed with families in mind (many come with a bathroom divided into two separate compartments: one for the toilet and another for the shower/bath). In the dining department, guests can rotate among a set of cool themed restaurants. Unique Disney-inspired entertainment, as you may expect, is among the best in the industry and includes original Broadway-style shows, first-run films (shown in a real movie theater), and even an occasional movie premiere at sea (coinciding with the movie's land opening). A stage show, *The*

Golden Mickeys, takes the audience through the history of Disney films and animation in an Academy Award–type format. The line's kids' programs are the best at sea and include a nursery for babies and toddlers as young as 3 months, awesome teen areas, and free supervised activities until midnight daily.

WOW! What else could parents and kids ask for? Of course enjoying all this assumes you can appreciate the mouse and all the wholesome family values he stands for (the ships have no casino, for example). That said, the company has successfully infused the ships and the experience with a subtler dose of Disney iconography than you may expect. For example, Mickey and his pals only make a few schedule appearances during the cruise, and the cool Art Deco– and Art Nouveau–inspired design takes center stage (and not Mickey's face).

The ships carry 1,754 passengers at the rate of two per cabin, but since Disney is a family company and its ships were built expressly to carry three, four, and five people in virtually every cabin, the ship could theoretically carry a whopping 3,325 passengers. About 1,000 kids and teens are aboard any given sailing. Passengers are usually spread out around the ship, so it doesn't feel that crowded except for the often-packed kids pool area and the cramped buffet restaurant.

If you want a taste of land and sea, you can easily combine Disney's 3- and 4-night cruises aboard *Disney Wonder* with a Disney theme park and hotel package to create a weeklong combo vacation, with bus transportation between the parks and port included. Table 11-7 shows Disney's itineraries and sample fares.

Dining

Disney's dining scheme is like no other. Guests rotate among three different restaurants, each with a whimsical design theme that keeps the kids (and parents) from getting bored. The Animator's Palette restaurant is the most entertaining, given the whole room changes colors throughout the meal (it's all magic, of course). Parrot Cay has a bright jungle theme, while Lumiere's (on *Wonder*) and Triton's (on *Magic*) are the more elegant venues. Of course, all the restaurants have great kids' menus, and friendly servers are used to catering to the kids.

If adults want a night out alone in a cozy, dimly lit venue, Palo's is the place ($10 per person). It serves tasty northern Italian food and gets booked up fast, so make a reservation pronto when you first board. Other noshing opps include a buffet restaurant, open for breakfast, lunch and sometimes dinner. It's small and cramped though.

The ships excel in the snack department, with the poolside Pluto's Dog House guaranteed to be a big hit. Who can argue with chicken tenders, fries, burgers, nachos, bratwurst, and other quick snacks served from lunch through the dinner hour. There's also pizza, ice cream, 24-hour room service, and a specialty coffee bar.

Table 11-7	Disney Itineraries and Sample Fares
Ship/Fares (per person/day)	Itineraries
Disney Magic $114 inside; $151 outside; $197 suite	**7-night eastern and western Caribbean** (alternating weekly): Round-trip from Port Canaveral, FL, year-round
Disney Wonder $130 inside; $180 outside; $210 suite	**3- and 4-night Bahamas:** Round-trip from Port Canaveral, FL, year-round

Free fountain soda. All other big-ship lines — Carnival, Royal Caribbean, Norwegian, and so on — charge for them.

Activities and entertainment

Disney's fresh, family-oriented take on entertainment and activities includes, of course, plenty of Disney-inspired stuff. Broadway-style stage shows in the well-equipped Walt Disney Theatre include various musical medleys of Disney classics. Other options include audience-participation game shows, karaoke, and themed after-dinner deck parties. There's a movie theater too, plus activities during the day such as wine tastings, galley tours, bingo, and informal lectures and seminars on all sorts of things, from animation to nautical themes, Disney history, home entertaining, and cooking. Talks from people involved with Disney's Broadway, film, and television productions are also often featured. The Pool Deck with its three pool areas (one each for kids, families, and adults) is always bustling. In fact, on sunny sea days, look out, the kids' pool area feels like a sardine can.

Sure Disney caters to families, but you'd be surprised how many folks without kids like the Disney experience, including honeymooners. To offer them, and their parents, too, some kid-free down time, the ships shave off an adults-only (18 and older) entertainment area at one end of the ship. Here you can find a jazz bar, a dance club, and a combination sports pub and karaoke bar. There's also Palo's restaurant and even an adults-only pool area (though the occasional kid wanders through). The gym and spa are also reserved for adults most of the time.

For kids

As you'd expect, the ships excel in this area. From three months on up, children are catered to. Babies get their own nursery (for an hourly fee), kids get two gigantic playrooms, and teens have a private complex all to themselves. Complimentary supervised activities are offered until midnight daily, with some 50 youth counselors running the show (many more than the other lines offer). There is no private in-cabin babysitting.

Disney's private island in the Bahamas, Castaway Cay, is included on nearly all itineraries and is a cruise highlight. The ship docks right at the island, so no riding shuttle boats back and forth from the ship. The kids' area will have them squealing with delight over the barrels to crawl through, the giant whale-dig site to explore, and more. Adults will fall in love with the adult beach area sequestered away at one end of the island, complete with rustic bar and massage cabanas. For the whole family, there are watersports and even bikes for rent.

 Kids under 3 who travel as a third, fourth, or fifth passenger and share a cabin with two adults pay $99 for a 3- or 4-night cruise and $139 for a 7-night cruise.

(Photo: Disney Cruise Line)

Figure 11-4: *Disney Magic*

Fleet facts

The two Disney ships are nearly identical. Both pay tribute to the classic ocean liners with their deep blue hulls, twin smokestacks, and updated classic décor — Art Deco on the *Magic* and lighter Art Nouveau on the *Wonder*. Cabins are bigger than standard and have minifridges and an abundance of storage space; the 82 suites are particularly plush. Table 11-8 shows the current fleet specifications.

Table 11-8	Disney Fleet Specifications					
Ship	*Entered Service*	*Passengers*	*Crew*	*Total Cabins*	*Tonnage*	*Length in Feet*
Disney Magic	1998	1,754	950	875	83,000	950
Disney Wonder	1999	1,754	950	875	83,000	950

Holland America Line

300 Elliot Ave. West, Seattle, WA 98119; ☎ ***800-426-0327;*** www.hollandamerica. com

> ✔ **Type of cruise:** Family, resort, romantic
>
> ✔ **Ship size/style:** Traditional-style midsize ships

Holland America (HAL) has been around for a looooong time, in fact, more than 130 years. Though its ships are as modern and high-tech as any others in the business, the line has managed to hang on to more of its seafaring history and tradition than any line today except Cunard.

Though the line has moved away from catering to a seniors-only crowd and focused on attracting a broader market, the ships still offer an old-world elegance for a mellow crowd. With a few exceptions (namely the *Zuiderdam* and *Oosterdam* of the line's newest Vista class), décor is understated and the vibe is subdued. Lots of fresh flowers, seafaring memorabilia, and Indonesian fabrics and woodcarving evoke Holland's relationship with its former colony. These classic touches, along with moderate size of most ships, are quite refreshing in this age of shock 'em glitz and over-the-top scale. New or old, big or small, the Holland America vessels are exceedingly handsome, their navy-blue hulls are well maintained, and the ships have excellent (and remarkably similar) layouts that ease passenger movement.

Holland America is in the midst of a fleetwide $225 million upgrade program it calls "Signature of Excellence." By the time this book goes to press in late 2005, most ships will have been refitted with enhanced dining, cabins, service, and activities (the *Veendam, Maasdam,* and *Oosterdam* get facelifts in 2006). Cabin improvements include flat-panel plasma TVs, DVD players, plush mattresses, massage showerheads, salon-quality hair dryers, and more. Suites get new duvets, fully-stocked minibars, and personalized stationery, and all suite guests will have access to a 24-hour concierge service and lounge. In addition to an expanded lecture series, each ship will get a special demonstration kitchen for food and wine events. HAL's pre-Vista-class vessels will gain a combination lounge, library, coffee shop, and Internet cafe. Kids' facilities will also be upgraded, and the spas will be enhanced to match the well-equipped Greenhouse Spas introduced on the Vista-class ships. Table 11-9 shows Holland America's itineraries and sample fares.

The line makes a conscious effort to appeal to single travelers, with a guaranteed share program for nonsmoking singles (of the same sex). Also, gentlemen hosts are brought on sailings of 14 days or more to socialize with single female passengers who want company.

Dining

Cuisine has improved over the years, and is comparable to what you may find on the other mainstream lines. The highlight of the dining options are the ship's formal restaurants, which are elegant two-story affairs that offer four seatings and feature live music. Aside from standards such as broiled lobster tail, grilled salmon, and filet mignon, you can find light options on the menu as well as vegetarian options (Matt, our resident vegetarian, went gaga recently over the tofu stroganoff).

Table 11-9   Holland America Itineraries and Sample Fares

Ship/Fares (per person/day)	Itineraries
Amsterdam $107 inside; $133 outside; $459 suite	**30-night Hawaii, Tahiti, and Marquesas Islands:** Round-trip from San Diego, CA, Jan; **15-night Hawaii:** Round-trip from San Diego, or between San Diego and Ensenada, Mexico, Feb–Apr; **10-night northern Europe:** Round-trip from Copenhagen, Denmark, May–Aug; **10-night Canada/New England:** North- or southbound between New York, NY, and Montreal, QB, Sept–Oct; **10-night southern Caribbean/Panama Canal:** Round-trip from Ft. Lauderdale, FL, Oct–Dec
Maasdam $118 inside; $118 outside; $307 suite	**10- and 11-night eastern/southern Caribbean:** Round-**10-** **and 11-night eastern/southern Caribbean:** Round-**Canada/New England:** North- or southbound between Boston, MA, and Montreal, QB, May–June and Aug–Sept; **17- and 18-night Iceland/Scandinavia:** East- or westbound between Boston, and Rotterdam, Netherlands, July
Noordam $145 inside; $166 outside; $508 suite	**10- and 11-night eastern Caribbean:** Round-trip from New York, NY, Feb–Apr and Oct–Dec; **10-night western Mediterranean:** Round-trip from Rome, Italy, May–Sept
Oosterdam $114 inside; $114 outside; $317 suite	**7-night Mexican Riviera:** Round-trip from San Diego, CA, Jan–Apr and Oct–Dec; **7-night Alaska Inside Passage:** Round-trip from Seattle, WA, May–Sept
Prinsendam $226 inside; $240 outside; $552 suite	**108-night world cruise:** Ft. Lauderdale, FL, to New York, NY, Jan–Apr (segments also bookable in South America, Africa, India, and Europe); **34-night trans-atlantic/Africa/Europe:** Fort Lauderdale to Dover, UK, May–June (15- and 20-night transatlantic segments also bookable); **13-, 14-, 16-, 18-, and 21-night northern Europe:** Round-trip from Amsterdam, Netherlands; London, UK, to Amsterdam; and Amsterdam to Lisbon, Portugal, June–July; **16-night Mediterranean:** Lisbon to Rome, Italy; Rome to Istanbul, Turkey; Istanbul to Athens, Greece; and Athens to Lisbon, Aug–Oct; **46-night Africa:** Lisbon to Cape Town, South Africa, Oct–Nov (22-night segment also bookable); **24-night Africa/South America/Caribbean:** Cape Town to Ft. Lauderdale, Nov; **14-night eastern/southern Caribbean and 16-night Caribbean/Amazon:** Round-trip from Ft. Lauderdale, Dec
Rotterdam $166 inside; $187 outside; $460 suite	**16- and 20-night South America:** Between Valparaiso, Chile, and Rio de Janeiro, Brazil, Jan–Mar and Nov–Dec; **10, 12-, 14-, and 15-night Mediterranean:** Sailing Lisbon, Portugal, to Athens, Greece; Athens to Venice, Italy; Venice to Athens; Athens to London, UK; London to Copenhagen, Denmark; Copenhagen to Rotterdam, Netherlands; Rotterdam to Copenhagen; Copenhagen to London; Rotterdam to Athens; Venice to Athens; and Athens to Lisbon, Apr–Oct

(continued)

Table 11-9 *(continued)*

Ship/Fares (per person/day)	Itineraries
Ryndam $110 inside; $110 outside; $654 suite	**14-night eastern/southern Caribbean:** Round-trip from Tampa, FL, Jan–Apr; **7-night Alaska Inside Passage:** North- or southbound between Vancouver, BC, and Seward/Anchorage, May–Sept; **10-night Mexican Riviera:** Round-trip from San Diego, CA, Oct–Dec
Statendam $136 inside; $186 outside; $400 suite	**14-night Australia/New Zealand:** Round-trip from Auckland, New Zealand, or between Auckland and Melbourne, Australia, Jan–Feb and Oct–Dec; **16-night Indonesia/Philippines/New Guinea:** Sydney, Australia, to Hong Kong, Mar; **14-night China/Japan:** Between Hong Kong and Osaka/Kyoto, Japan, Mar–Apr; **19-night Japan/Russia/Alaska:** Osaka/Kyoto to Vancouver, BC, May; **7-night Alaska Inside Passage:** North- or southbound between Vancouver and Seward/Anchorage, AK, May–Sept; **27-night South Pacific:** Vancouver to Auckland, Sept
Veendam $121 inside; $164 outside; $360 suite	**7-night western Caribbean:** Round-trip from Tampa, FL, Jan–Apr and Oct–Dec; **7-night Alaska Inside Passage:** North- or southbound between Vancouver, BC, and Seward/Anchorage, AK, May–Sept
Volendam $136 inside; $166 outside; $343 suite	**10-night southern Caribbean:** Round-trip from Ft. Lauderdale, FL, Jan–Mar and Oct–Dec; **7-night Alaska Inside Passage:** Round-trip from Vancouver, BC, May–Sept
Westerdam $114 inside; $114 outside; $339 suite	**7-night eastern and western Caribbean:** Round-trip from Ft. Lauderdale, FL, Jan–Apr and Oct–Dec; **7-night Alaska Inside Passage:** Round-trip from Seattle, WA, May–Sept
Zaandam $143 inside; $195 outside; $421 suite	**10-night Panama Canal:** Round-trip from Ft. Lauderdale, FL, Jan–Apr; **7-night Alaska Inside Passage:** Round-trip from Seattle, WA, May–Sept; **10-night Mexican Riviera:** Round-trip from San Diego, CA, Oct–Dec; **15-night Hawaii:** Round-trip from San Diego, Oct–Dec
Zuiderdam $86 inside; $100 outside; $188 suite	**7-night eastern Caribbean:** Round-trip from Ft. Lauderdale, FL, Jan–Mar and Oct–Dec; **7-night Alaska Inside Passage:** Round-trip from Vancouver, BC, May–Sept

The Pinnacle Grill is an alternative restaurant that offers what the line calls Pacific Northwest cuisine. Choices include crab cakes, salmon, wild mushroom ravioli, and premium beef cuts, all complemented with regional wines. The cover charge here is $20 per person. On a recent *Westerdam* cruise, the service was top rate and the food exceeded our expectations — make reservations as early as possible when you board.

For the casual diner, all ships have attractive and well-stocked buffet restaurants that are open nearly round-the-clock, including dinner nightly. Pizza and ice-cream stations are open till late afternoon, a taco bar is open during lunch, and a poolside grill serves hamburgers, hot dogs, veggie and turkey burgers, and a special of the day, such as knockwurst or spicy Italian sausage.

Once per cruise there's a fancy High Tea (a rarity these days); the other days there's a more casual tea service, and you can find free hot canapés served in some of the bars/lounges during the cocktail hour (none of the other mainstream lines do this). Room service is offered 24 hours a day.

There's also a specialty coffee bar, a nightly spread of snacks in the buffet restaurant around midnight, and one gala dessert buffet every week featuring lots of chocolate things plus marzipan, creampuffs, and other diet busters.

Activities and entertainment

Though there's a greater variety of things to do than ever, Holland America still attracts a mostly early-to-bed crowd. You can head to the disco or enjoy after-dinner cocktails or a show, but don't expect to be joined by half the ship doing the same thing as you might on Royal Caribbean, Norwegian, Carnival, or even Princess.

Even if most passengers aren't partying into the wee hours, most sample the ships' varied roster of things to see and do. Production shows include fairly lavish sets and choreography complete with lasers and fancy costumes (though we scold the line for not having a live orchestra for these shows on the Vista-class ships, where we're told there isn't enough space). There are also passenger and crew talent shows and live music in various lounges. Activities are plentiful and may include dance lessons, cooking demonstrations, wine tastings, bingo, ship tours, and country-western and '50s parties. There's also some tomfoolery on the Pool Deck, so head out there if goofy relay races make you laugh.

On 7-night Alaska cruises, Native artists demonstrate traditional arts such as ivory and soapstone carving, basket weaving, and mask making as part of the line's Artists in Residence program, created under the auspices of Anchorage's Alaska Native Heritage Center. Another program offered during visits to Glacier Bay brings a member of the Huna tribe aboard to talk about the land, which the Huna have called home for centuries. In Hawaii and Mexico, cultural dancers perform.

For kids

To make good on its pledge to cater to a wider audience, Holland America recently lowered the age minimum of its Club HAL complimentary kids' activities from 5 down to 3 (which will be fleetwide by year-end 2006). When enough kids are on board (usually holidays and summers), activities are offered for three age groups between 3 and 17. Though you rarely see more than 300 or 400 kids aboard any ship, the new playrooms and cool indoor/outdoor teen centers are pretty impressive (and will be added fleetwide by year-end 2006). Group babysitting is offered for an hourly rate between 10 p.m. and midnight daily for the 3 to 12 set, plus private in-cabin sitting is also available.

 In the Caribbean, the line has its own private island, called Half Moon Cay. It's an awesome place for families, with a kids' aqua park on the beach (complete with slides and water cannons), plus neat excursions for the family, from horseback riding to snorkeling with stingrays.

 Especially useful if traveling with children, most cabins on all ships have bathtubs (on other lines, typically only suites have tubs), and standard cabins are among the largest in the mainstream segment.

Figure 11-5: *Volendam*

(Photo: Holland America Line)

Fleet facts

The *Statendam, Maasdam, Ryndam,* and *Veendam* are attractive mid-size ships built in the mid-1990s, just before the ultrajumbo ships were launched. Though mellow by today's in-your-face standards, they're all-around appealing ships, with enhanced spa and children's facilities, Internet cafes, alternative dining restaurants, and other perks.

The flagship *Rotterdam VI* is a bigger vessel that sets new standards for ship design, although the basic layout of its public rooms is similar to that on the Statendam-class sisters. The *Volendam* (see Figure 11-5) and *Zaandam* combine features of both the Statendam-class and *Rotterdam VI*, with a bit more pizzazz thrown in to appeal to a younger crowd. For example, the *Zaandam*'s music theme includes a wacky mix of instruments on display, from a gigantic pipe organ in the atrium to a collection of guitars autographed by Iggy Pop, the Rolling Stones, and Queen, and a saxophone that President Clinton played in Holland.

The *Amsterdam* is a sister ship to the *Rotterdam VI* and is the first ship in the fleet with a high-tech, environmentally friendly propulsion system that provides a smoother ride than the usual rumbling diesels. The *Prinsendam* is the line's smallest ship; it's cozy, couples-oriented, relatively elegant, and features big, fancy suites.

Holland America went mega in September of 2002, with its largest ship to date: the 85,000-ton, 1,848-passenger *Zuiderdam,* which was later joined by the virtually identical *Oosterdam, Westerdam* (the third ship in the line's history to have that name), and coming in early 2006, *Noordam.* These Vista-class ships are bigger, with more public spaces (such as a dedicated disco, sports bar, and the fleet's largest spas), and brighter (in the case of the *Zuiderdam,* maybe too bright and hip). Table 11-10 shows the current fleet specifications.

Wheelchair-accessible tenders are available on all the ships.

Table 11-10   Holland America Fleet Specifications

Ship	Entered Service	Passengers	Crew	Total Cabins	Tonnage	Length in Feet
Amsterdam	2000	1,380	647	690	61,000	780
Maasdam	1993	1,266	557	633	55,000	720
Noordam	2006	1,848	800	924	85,000	951
Oosterdam	2003	1,848	800	924	85,000	951
Prinsendam	1988	794	428	394	38,000	669
Rotterdam VI	1997	1,316	593	658	61,000	780
Ryndam	1994	1,266	557	633	55,000	720
Statendam	1993	1,266	557	633	55,000	720
Veendam	1996	1,266	557	633	55,000	780
Volendam	1999	1,440	647	720	63,000	780
Westerdam	2004	1,848	800	924	85,000	951
Zaandam	2000	1,440	647	720	63,000	780
Zuiderdam	2002	1,848	800	924	85,000	951

MSC Cruises

6750 N. Andrews Ave., Fort Lauderdale, FL 33309; ☎ *800-666-9333;* www.msc cruises.com

✔ **Type of cruise:** Resort, party

✔ **Ship size/style:** Modern midsize ships, with megaships on the way

MSC Cruises is a relatively young cruise line, born back in 1990 as the cruise arm of Mediterranean Shipping, the world's second-largest container-shipping company. Like Costa, the line stresses its Italian roots, but in a less flashy, "Si, we're Italian; would you like some espresso?" kind of way. MSC started with a few old-time ocean cruisers (which it now calls its "classic fleet"), but has been in overdrive since 2003, launching two purpose-built ships, buying two vessels at auction, and placing orders for a new generation of megaships, one for delivery in June 2006 and another for 2007.

 MSC's "modern fleet" (the four ships typically marketed to North Americans) appeals to travelers who want a more traditional style of cruise, with smaller, more human-scale ships; traditional dining rituals; few gimmicks; and lots of socializing. Activities are fun and group-oriented, and the ships' modest sizes mean staff may greet you by name after a day or two.

Passengers' typical age range is mid-40s and up, and MSC's Mediterranean itineraries tend to carry 85 percent European and 15 percent North Americans and "other." Unlike Costa, though, which is all about activities, MSC's "quiet ship" approach means there are few announcements during the day, so you're not subjected to an endless stream of translations. In the Caribbean, announcements are made in two languages, English and Italian (in that order). Passenger nationalities on Caribbean itineraries are the exact opposite of European sailings, with Americans dominating. Also at diametrically opposed poles is the issue of kids, with European itineraries tending to carry a lot of them, but Caribbean ones seeing very few. Table 11-11 shows MSC's itineraries and sample fares.

Dining

Dining service is traditional, with a very European sensibility — which means courteous and professional rather than U.S.-style "Hey everybody, my name's George!" overfriendly. When the line began its big push on the American market, we heard some complaints about slow and indifferent service (and experienced some of the same ourselves), but the line's put a lot of effort into training since then. Ditto for the way the line handles varying European and American tastes. In late 2004, some American peculiarities — such as automatic after-dinner coffee, bagels at breakfast, and a love of artificial sweeteners — were not easily accommodated, but changing the dynamic so that all passengers would get "the best of both worlds" was tops on the new management's list.

On the line's "modern fleet," two formal dining rooms serve open-seating breakfast and lunch and a traditional dinner in two fixed seatings, with an emphasis on Italian cuisine. An Italian regional specialty is featured every night, with descriptive menu information. Casual dining is also available in the buffet restaurant at breakfast and lunch. There's also a standard grill on the Pool Deck during the day, and Italian specialty snacks are available at night. At the witching hour, the line offers one of the few daily midnight buffets left in the industry.

Table 11-11	MSC Itineraries and Sample Fares
Ship/Fares (per person/day)	**Itineraries**
Armonia $140 inside; $172 outside; $268 suite	**7-night South America:** Round-trip from Rio de Janeiro, Brazil, Jan–Feb; **3- and 4-night South America:** Round-trip from Rio de Janeiro, Feb–Mar; **11-night Mediterranean:** East- or westbound between Genoa and Venice, Italy, May and Nov; **7-night Mediterranean:** Round-trip from Venice, May–Oct; **11-night Mediterranean:** Round-trip from Venice, Oct
Lirica $78 inside; $106 outside; $228 suite	**11-night western Caribbean:** Round-trip from Fort Lauderdale, FL, Jan–Apr; **7-night Baltic capitals:** Round-trip from Copenhagen, Denmark, June–Aug; **7-night Norwegian fjords:** Round-trip from Copenhagen, June–Aug; **11-night Mediterranean:** Round-trip from Genoa, Italy, Sept
Melody $125 inside; $149 outside; $225 suite	**8-night South America:** Round-trip from Rio de Janeiro, Brazil, Jan–Feb; **9- and 10-night South America:** Round-trip from Rio de Janeiro, Jan–Feb; **11-night Mediterranean:** Round-trip from Genoa, Italy, Mar–Oct; **7-night Mediterranean:** Round-trip from Genoa, May–Sept
Monterey	Not marketed to North Americans
Musica $212 inside; $248 outside; $517 suite	**7-night Mediterranean:** Round-trip from Venice, Italy, July–Oct; **11-night Mediterranean:** Venice to Genoa, Italy, Oct
Opera $78 inside; $106 outside; $256 suite	**7-night eastern Caribbean:** Round-trip from Fort Lauderdale, FL, Jan–Apr; **6-night Mediterranean:** Round-trip from Genoa, Italy, Apr; **7-night Mediterranean:** Round-trip from Rome, Italy, May–Oct; **11-night Mediterranean:** Round-trip from Genoa, Oct–Nov
Rhapsody $130 inside; $155 outside; $210 suite	**7-night Norwegian fjords:** Round-trip from Amsterdam, Netherlands, June–Aug; **7-night Scotland/England:** Round-trip from Amsterdam, June–Aug; **11-night Mediterranean:** Round-trip from Genoa, Italy, Sept–Oct
Sinfonia $135 inside; $171 outside; $299 suite	**11-night Mediterranean:** Round-trip from Genoa, Italy, Jan–Apr; **12-night Mediterranean eclipse cruise:** Round-trip from Genoa, Mar; **7-night Mediterranean:** Round-trip from Genoa, Apr–Oct; **11-night Mediterranean:** Round-trip from Genoa, Oct–Nov

Activities and entertainment

Activities, led by a young "animation team," tend toward the traditional, many of them with a European sense of fun. During the day, expect games by the pool (including water polo and treasure hunts), dance lessons, and an occasional informal lecture in one of the lounges. At night, stage shows range from ho-hum production numbers to pretty interesting segments that draw on European circus traditions, featuring contortionists, acrobats, and stilt performers. Special shows may also feature operatic soloists or magicians. Elsewhere, the animation team leads participatory games in a lounge, while music, dancing, casino gambling, and piano bar entertainment are available around the ships.

For kids

Each ship has a cute (though smallish) children's center, while other kid-centric activities around the ship may include "baby disco" and balloon-tying shows. Private babysitting (for a fee) can be arranged through the main desk.

(Photo: MSC Cruises)

Figure 11-6: *Opera*

Fleet facts

While MSC's U.S. sales office markets all its ships to Americans, the emphasis is definitely on the "modern fleet," the *Opera, Lirica, Sinfonia,* and *Armonia.*

The sister ships ***Lirica*** and ***Opera*** (see Figure 11-6) are straightforward midsize vessels without any bizarre attractions or gimmicks — no planetariums, rock-climbing walls, or mythological design schemes. Expect to spend your days exploring the ports and then getting together in the various lounges at night to talk and relax in a quiet environment. Long and low, both vessels seem a lot larger than they really are. Cabins are adequate if small; cabin showers are downright tiny.

Another pair of sister ships, the ***Armonia*** and ***Sinfonia,*** are almost identical to *Lirica* and *Opera,* having been designed and built by the same French shipyard. Both from a distance and while on board, you can hardly tell the difference between them.

MSC's so-called "classic fleet" is made up of vessels that have been around for a while, and are mostly marketed to Europeans. Fans of classic liners may enjoy them, though. The ***Melody*** is most familiar to American audiences, having sailed for years as the Big Red Boat

Atlantica for now-defunct Premier Cruises. The ***Rhapsody*** sailed as Cunard's *Cunard Princess* until 1995. The ***Monterey*** is by far the oldest ship in the fleet, having launched in 1952 and gone through several owners before landing with MSC in the early 1990s.

MSC has two new 2,550-passenger megaships currently on order, one (named *Musica*) for delivery in June 2006, the second in 2007. Table 11-12 shows the current fleet specifications.

Table 11-12		MSC Fleet Specifications				
Ship	Entered Service	Passengers	Crew	Total Cabins	Tonnage	Length in Feet
Armonia	2001	1,586	760	795	58,600	824
Lirica	2003	1,586	760	795	58,600	824
Melody	1982	1,064	530	532	35,143	672
Monterey	1952	566	290	288	20,046	563
Opera	2004	1,756	800	878	58,600	824
Rhapsody	1977	780	370	383	16,852	541
Sinfonia	2002	1,586	760	795	58,600	824

Norwegian Cruise Line

7665 Corporate Center Dr., Miami, FL 33126; ☎ *800-327-7030;* www.ncl.com

✔ **Type of cruise:** Resort, family, party

✔ **Ship size/style:** Megaships and modern midsize ships

Norwegian Cruise Line (NCL) moved into the megaship age in 1999 with *Norwegian Sky.* Since it was bought by Star Cruises of Malaysia in 2000, NLC has transformed into one of the most innovative players in the cruise biz. Along with a seemingly never-ending stream of ever-larger megaships, NCL has been shaking up the industry with several major initiatives. The "Freestyle Cruising" concept broke with cruise ship tradition to offer a more casual experience, with open-seating, restaurant-style dining, and a resort-casual dress code (though an occasional optional formal night is thrown in for good measure). The idea was to shake off the stuffiness of traditional cruising and make the experience more like a land-based resort vacation. The experiment worked, because stuffy it ain't: For proof, look no further than *Norwegian Dawn*'s salsa bands and the bright paintings that adorn the white hulls of the line's newer vessels.

The Freestyle concept extends all the way through your cruise. For example, if you're not in a hurry to leave on the last day, the ships offer Freestyle debarkation, giving you time to have a leisurely breakfast and disembark up until about 10 a.m., rather than hustling off early as most lines require you to do.

NCL also innovated with its "Homeland Cruising" concept, berthing vessels in homeports up and down the U.S. seaboards and thus letting more people drive to their ship rather than fly. In maybe its biggest innovation, the line reversed a decades-long trend in the U.S. cruise industry by actually registering and staffing some of its ships in the United States, a move that brought considerable additional costs (U.S. taxes and payrolls are higher than those overseas), but also made them the only large cruise ships in compliance with U.S. cabotage laws, which forbid foreign-flagged and -staffed ships from sailing itineraries composed solely of U.S. ports. What's that mean in English? It means NCL's *Pride of Aloha* (see Figure 11-7) and *Pride of America* are the only ships — period — that can offer all-Hawaii itineraries from a homeport in Honolulu. Anyone else who sails Hawaii has to either set off from a Mexican homeport or include the islands on a longer cruise that also visits foreign ports, options that each entail many days at sea.

Fleetwide, NCL's onboard atmosphere is informal, upbeat, and well suited to casual types, party-makers, and first-time cruisers. The line attracts a lot of passengers under 50 (slightly older in Europe) and a good many families with kids, especially during summers and holidays. Passengers in general are price-conscious and more active than those aboard lines such as Holland America, Celebrity, and Princess. Table 11-13 shows NCL's itineraries and sample fares.

Dining

Know how, on dry land, there are those little restaurants with only a few tables and a short menu that is just to die for? While down the road are those huge gilded-palace restaurants with a menu that goes on forever, but where the food is more average? NCL's dining experience is more like the latter. We're not saying it's bad; it just isn't gourmet. It's mainstream — just fine, and sometimes very good. The French and Continental food at the Le Bistro specialty restaurant? Yum. Those Indian spreads they sometimes put out in the buffet? Double-yum.

You sure can't fault them for offering options, though: The newest ships have *ten different restaurants* on board, including Italian, Asian, sushi, French, steakhouse, and Tex-Mex, plus snack and sandwich options, ice-cream parlors, and an occasional chocoholic buffet.

On the newest NCL ship, the *Pride of America,* you can dine at the two main restaurants (the Art-Deco Skyline Restaurant and the Liberty Restaurant, which looks like an old-time political rally), or choose among several intimate, extra-cost dinner options: the Lazy J Texas Steakhouse, where waiters serve in cowboy hats; Jefferson's Bistro, an

Table 11-13 — NCL Itineraries and Sample Fares

Ship/Fares (per person/day)	Itineraries
Norwegian Crown $140 inside; $144 outside; $373 suite	**14-night Chilean fjords:** Between Valparaiso, Chile, and Buenos Aires, Argentina, Jan–Feb; **13- and 14-night eastern and southern Caribbean:** Round-trip from Philadelphia, PA, Mar–Apr; **5-, 6-, and 7-night Bermuda:** Round-trip from Philadelphia, Apr–June; **7-night Bermuda:** Round-trip from New York, NY, June–Oct
Norwegian Dawn $116 inside; $126 outside; $543 suite	**7-night Florida/Bahamas:** Round-trip from New York, NY, May–Aug; **7-night Canada/New England:** Round-trip from New York, Sept–Oct; **10-night eastern Caribbean:** Round-trip from New York, Jan–Apr and Oct–Dec; **11-night western Caribbean:** Round-trip from New York, Jan–Mar and Oct–Dec
Norwegian Dream $134 inside; $141 outside; $406 suite	**7-night western Caribbean:** Round-trip from Houston, TX, Jan–Apr; **12-night northern Europe:** Round-trip from London, UK, May–Sept
Norwegian Jewel $162 inside; $168 outside; $518 suite	**7-night eastern and western Caribbean:** Round-trip from Miami, FL, Jan–Apr; **7-night western Mediterranean:** Round-trip from Barcelona, Spain, May–Aug; **12-night Mediterranean/Egypt/Greek Isles:** Barcelona to Istanbul, Turkey; Istanbul to Athens, Greece; Athens to Istanbul; and Istanbul to Barcelona, Sept–Oct
Norwegian Majesty $110 inside; $122 outside; $383 suite	**7-night western Caribbean:** Round-trip from Charleston, SC, Jan–Apr; **7-night Bermuda:** Round-trip from Boston, MA, May–Oct; **7-night Bermuda:** Round-trip from Charleston, Oct–Nov
Norwegian Spirit $136 inside; $143 outside; $458 suite	**10- and 11-night eastern and southern Caribbean:** Round-trip from New York, NY, Jan–Feb and Oct–Dec; **7-night Florida/Bahamas:** Round-trip from New York, Feb–May; **6-night Florida/Bahamas:** Round-trip from New York, May–Sept; alternates with **8-night eastern Caribbean:** Round-trip from New York, May–Sept
Norwegian Star $113 inside; $123 outside; $421 suite	**8-night Mexican Riviera:** Round-trip from Los Angeles, CA, Jan–Apr; **7-night Alaska Inside Passage:** Round-trip from Seattle, WA, May–Sept
Norwegian Sun $149 inside; $185 outside; $496 suite	**7-night western Caribbean:** Round-trip from New Orleans, LA, Jan–Apr*; **7-night Alaska Inside Passage:** Round-trip from Seattle, WA, May–Sept
Norwegian Wind $106 inside; $106 outside; $331 suite	**10-night Hawaii/Kiribati:** Round-trip from Honolulu, HI, Jan–Mar; **7-night Alaska Inside Passage:** Round-trip from Vancouver, BC, May–Sept

(continued)

Table 11-13 *(continued)*

Ship/Fares (per person/day)	Itineraries
Pride of Aloha $139 inside; $196 outside; $711 suite	**7-night Hawaii:** Round-trip from Honolulu, HI, year-round
Pride of America $164 inside; $211 outside; $622 suite	**7-night Hawaii:** Round-trip from Honolulu, HI, year-round
Pride of Hawai'i Rates not available	Not yet announced, but probably 7-night Hawaii, round-trip from Honolulu, year-round

* Deployment affected by Hurricane Katrina disaster. Contact cruise line for updates.

elegant venue modeled after the third president's Monticello home and serving French cuisine; and East Meets West, a pan-Asian restaurant with attached sushi/sashimi bar and teppanyaki room. Late at night, the Cadillac Diner serves burgers, shakes, and other diner fare 24 hours.

All the restaurants on all NCL ships follow an open-seating policy each and every evening, allowing you to dine whenever you like within the 5:30 to 10 p.m. window, dressed however you like (within limits), and sitting with whomever you want rather than having a table preassigned.

The night of the captain's cocktail party is officially an "optional formal" night, giving folks who like to dress up a chance to shine. If you prefer, you can just don the slacks and polo, of course. Your choice.

As aboard most lines, the smaller, finer restaurants carry a cover charge that ranges from $12 to $20 per person. Dining service is about what you find on the other mainstream lines — generally good, with occasional lapses. But service is consistently speedy and efficient in the cabin-service, room-service, and bar departments.

Activities and entertainment

High-energy folks, take note: You always have something to do aboard NCL's activity-packed ships. You can take dance lessons; sit in on a cooking demo, beauty seminar, or talent show; play bingo, shuffleboard, or basketball; attend an art auction or wine tasting (the latter for $10 per person); and on some cruises, sit in on enrichment lectures. In Hawaii, *Pride of Aloha* and *Pride of America* offer activities with a Hawaiian arts and culture theme, such as hula lessons and Hawaiian bead-making.

All the ships feature spas offering Eastern- and Western-influenced treatments, with the spa facilities on the newest ships really standing out in the style department. All the vessels also offer sports bars with ESPN coverage of games, and extensive sports and fitness facilities, including full-size basketball courts. Gyms fleetwide are open 24 hours.

Onboard entertainment includes excellent (and surprisingly inventive) Vegas-style musical productions, some themed on Indian Bollywood musicals or Miami Latin culture. Smaller acts are also outstanding, from the always-awesome singer Jane L. Powell (an NCL regular) and her excellent accompanying band to talented piano players and comedians. On *Dawn,* each cruise features improv comedy nights with members of the famed Second City comedy troupe, whose alumni include Bill Murray, Mike Myers, John Belushi, and Gilda Radner. On the Hawaii ships, one night a week is devoted to Polynesian music and dance. Name performers are also occasionally aboard for short stints.

Other entertainment options include a "Star Seeker" show that's like *American Idol* at sea, plus tucked-away lounges for more intimate entertainment, including pianists and cabaret acts. Music for dancing is popular aboard all the ships and takes place before or after shows, and each ship has a late-night disco.

Gamblers take note: Because of Hawaiian law, *Pride of Aloha* and *Pride of America* do not have casinos aboard, nor any kind of gambling.

For kids

NCL's Kids Crew program offers year-round supervised activities for kids 2 to 17, divided into four age groups. Activities for younger kids include treasure hunts, face painting, magic shows, arts and crafts, sports competitions, dances, and cooking classes. Each ship has a playroom, but those on the newer *Dawn, Star, Spirit, Sun,* and *Pride of America* are the best by far, huge spaces that also include a separate teen center and a wading pool. *Dawn, Star,* and *Jewel* have wonderful spaces with huge climbing mazes and two ball bins, plus a kids pool and hot tub outside. Group babysitting for ages 2 to 12 is offered nightly, for a fee. Private babysitting is not available.

Kids under age 2 travel free.

Figure 11-7: *Pride of Aloha*

Fleet facts

NCL's fleet divides pretty nicely into three groups: the U.S.-flagged NCL America ships, the foreign-flagged megaships, and the 1980s- and 1990s-vintage midsize ships.

The NCL America fleet has two ships, going on three. *Pride of Aloha* was originally born as NCL's first megaship, *Norwegian Sky.* In 2001, she went in for a top-to-toe refit that turned her into the first of the line's all-Hawaii, all-the-time ships. Interiors were Hawaiianized with bright floral colors, Hawaiian artwork, charming Hawaiian souvenir items from the 1950s, and other references to Hawaiian culture and history, from orchids to outrigger canoes, beaches, fish, waterfalls, colonial plantations, surfing, and famous figures who traveled there. Few traces of *Norwegian Sky* remain except (unfortunately) for her tiny cabins. Oh, well. Otherwise she's great.

Pride of America is as all-American as her name, with an all-U.S. crew and decorative motifs that range from the Great Seal of the United States (on the marble floor of the Capitol Atrium reception area) to huge photos of the Grand Canyon, Monument Valley, the Golden Gate Bridge, the Chicago Skyline, and other American landmarks. Cabins tend to be on the small side. Insides are only 132 square feet, while standard outsides (without balconies) max out at 144. Storage space is limited, but bathrooms are adequately sized. Another Hawaii ship, *Pride of Hawai'i,* is scheduled to launch in summer 2006.

NCL's other megaships, the foreign-flagged *Norwegian Spirit, Norwegian Star, Norwegian Dawn,* and *Norwegian Jewel,* are real knockouts, offering between eight and ten different restaurants apiece, elegant spaces such as Gatsby's Champagne Bar (on *Dawn*); fun ones like an outdoor Bier Garten (on *Spirit* and *Star*); large, fanciful observation lounge/discos; great spas; huge and completely kid-centric playrooms; and Kid's Cafés in the buffet restaurants (complete with tiny chairs and a miniature buffet counter). *Norwegian Spirit* is slightly smaller than her sisters and has a slightly different layout. Two sister ships of *Norwegian Jewel* are scheduled to debut in 2007.

Norwegian Sun was NCL's second megaship after *Norwegian Sky,* and blazed the trail that the later ships followed, with 9 restaurants, 12 bars, and everything designed with casual cruising in mind.

Norwegian Crown, Norwegian Majesty, and sister ships *Norwegian Dream* and *Norwegian Wind* are from the late '80s and early '90s. The clock's ticking on them, with plans in place to transfer them to NCL's Asian parent company, Star Cruises. They're not the most modern kids on the block, and they have some pretty small cabins, but they do have their charming spots. *Dream* and *Wind,* for example, have these totally great sports bars, with booths and giant-screen TVs. They look like you should drive up to them in your old Chevy Nova. Table 11-14 shows the current fleet specifications.

Table 11-14	NCL Fleet Specifications					
Ship	Entered Service	Passengers	Crew	Total Cabins	Tonnage	Length in Feet
Norwegian Crown	1988	1,062	470	531	34,250	614
Norwegian Dawn	2002	2,224	1,318	1,120	91,740	965
Norwegian Dream	1992	1,748	614	874	50,760	754
Norwegian Jewel	2004	2,376	1,200	1,188	92,100	965
Norwegian Majesty	1992	1,462	570	731	40,876	680
Norwegian Spirit	1999	1,996	920	1,120	76,800	879
Norwegian Star	2001	2,240	1,100	1,120	91,000	965
Norwegian Sun	2001	2,002	968	1,001	77,104	853
Norwegian Wind	1993	1,748	700	874	50,764	754
Pride of Aloha	1999	2,002	750	1,001	77,104	853
Pride of America	2005	2,146	1,000	1,073	81,000	926
Pride of Hawai'i	2006	2,400	1,000	1,188	92,100	965

Oceania Cruises

8300 NW 33rd Street, Suite 308, Miami, FL 33122; ☎ *800-531-5658;* www.oceania cruises.com

✔ **Type of cruise:** Premium, country-club casual, gourmet

✔ **Ship size/style:** Mini-midsize, low-key casual

Oceania stands out with its calm, casual onboard atmosphere, superb dining, and long, interesting itineraries. All three of its ships sport a lovely sort of British hotel look: very traditional in their public areas and comfy in the cabins, with little or no glitz. On board, the vibe is floating country club: totally low-key, with few organized activities, small-scale entertainment, an always-casual dress code, and outrageously comfortable cabin beds. Despite such luxe-travel touches, you can still get Oceania's cruises on the cheap, at prices that are frequently in the same ballpark as the mainstream lines. Combine those low prices with the ships' smallish size and overall quality and you have a cruise line that doesn't fit comfortably in any of the regular cruise niches. Maybe the closest we can come is to say it's like a younger, less polished version of luxe line Radisson Seven Seas.

On board, service balances precision with friendliness, and is close to the kind of understated professionalism you see on the real luxury lines. Because of the relatively small number of passengers, it's also more personal than you find aboard the megaships. Stewards greet you by name, and bartenders remember your favorite drink after the first day.

Because of the relative length of Oceania's itineraries (mostly 12 and 14 days), and maybe because of the low-key atmosphere, passengers tend to be older and want a quiet vessel where they can entertain themselves, enjoy the ports, and linger over dinner. Couples in their mid-40s and up who want that kind of experience wouldn't be out of place on board, but party types would, as would kids — this isn't a line tailored to families. It's also not a line tailored to smokers, with smoking prohibited everywhere but in two small patches of the Pool Deck and the nightclub. Table 11-15 shows Oceania's itineraries and sample fares.

Oceania offers frequent two-for-one deals and often bundles airfare into their rates. Check out the line's Web site for details.

Dining

Dining is one of Oceania's best features, with menus created by renowned chef Jacques Pepin, four dinner venues with reliably enjoyable atmosphere and flavor, and an always casual, dress-as-you-want, dine-when-you-want (within a three-hour window) format.

The Grand Dining Room, the main restaurant on each ship, serves five-course, French-inspired meals, with tables for two, four, and more, and a string quartet provides music at dinner. Main courses may include faves such as lobster tail butterfly or beef Wellington, or surprises such as sautéed sea bream filet and pheasant breast ballotine stuffed with morel mushrooms. In each ship's stern are two alternative restaurants: Toscana for Mediterranean-style cuisine and the Polo Grill for steakhouse fare. Both offer décor and ambience appropriate to their menus, as well as great views of the ship's wake — very beautiful at sunset. The same can be said, only more so, for the Terrace Cafe. During the day it's just an outdoor seating area for the indoor buffet, but at night its tables are set with linens and hurricane-lamp candles. Regional Spanish and Mediterranean specialties are the fare, along with other ethnic dishes and home-style favorites.

Activities and entertainment

Don't book this line looking for a lot of guided play, though the ships do program a light menu of enrichment lectures (often themed around the sailing region), fitness and computer classes, karaoke, health and beauty seminars led by the spa and salon staff, plus games such as bingo and shuffleboard. The casino is nicely sized for this ship and has slots, blackjack, and roulette. Spa services (all the usual) and fitness equipment (plenty of variety and quantity to go with a good schedule of organized fitness programs) are available in nice rooms, with the outside spa pool and seating area providing a nice touch.

Table 11-15   Oceania Itineraries and Sample Fares

Ship/Fares (per person/day)	Itineraries
Insignia No inside cabins; $150 outside; $300 suite	**15-night South America:** Between Valparaiso, Chile, and Buenos Aires, Argentina, or Rio de Janeiro to Manaus, Brazil, Jan–Mar; **14-night South America/Caribbean:** Manaus to Barbados, Mar; **10- and 12-night Mediterranean:** Between Rome, Italy, and Athens, Greece; Rome to Barcelona, Spain; Rome to Venice, Italy; Venice to Lisbon, Portugal; and Barcelona to Lisbon, Apr–May and Sept–Nov; **12-night British Isles:** Lisbon to London, UK, and round-trip from London, June; **10- and 14-night northern Europe:** London to Stockholm, Sweden; between Stockholm and Copenhagen, Denmark; and Stockholm to London, July–Aug
Nautica $173 inside; $207 outside; $500 suite	**15-night Asia:** North- or southbound between Hong Kong and Singapore and Hong Kong and Bangkok, Thailand, Jan–Mar; **24-night Asia:** Bangkok to Beijing, China, Feb; **35-night Asia/Europe:** Hong Kong to Athens, Greece, Mar; **10-, 12-, and 14-night Mediterranean:** Between Athens and Istanbul, Turkey; Athens and Rome, Italy; Rome and Istanbul; Istanbul and Venice, Italy; Venice and Barcelona, Spain; and Barcelona and Athens, May–Nov
Regatta $100 inside; $120 outside; $250 suite	**10- and 12-night southern Caribbean:** Round-trip from Miami, FL, Jan–Feb; **16-night Mexico/Panama Canal:** East- or westbound between Miami, and Los Angeles, CA, Jan–Feb; **14-night western Caribbean:** Round-trip from Miami, Mar; **10- and 14-night Mediterranean:** Between Barcelona, Spain, and Athens, Greece; Athens and Istanbul, Turkey; Istanbul and Venice, Italy; Venice and Barcelona; London, UK, and Rome, Italy; Rome and Barcelona; and Barcelona and Lisbon, Portugal, Apr–May; **14-night northern Europe:** East- or westbound between London and Stockholm, Sweden, May–Aug

On the entertainment front, the line can boast really good music, with a 12-piece jazz band performing afternoons and evenings and quality pianists playing standards in the martini bar before dinner. Other entertainment includes low-key shows in the main lounge: classical pianists, magicians, and sometimes music and dance performances by local groups brought aboard for the evening.

For kids

There are no special kids' facilities on these ships, since there are rarely any kids aboard.

(Photo: Oceania Cruises)

Figure 11-8: *Regatta*

Fleet facts

Oceania lucked out with its ships. All three were built for now-defunct Renaissance Cruise — ***Regatta*** (see Figure 11-8) and ***Insignia*** in 1998, ***Nautica*** in 2000 — and were still almost brand-new when Oceania got hold of them not long after. A bit of refurbishment got them up to speed for the kind of cruises the new line planned to offer. These are comfortable and spacious ships decorated mostly in warm, dark woods and rich fabrics. They're traditional and sedate, with an emphasis on intimate spaces rather than the grand, splashy ones on most megaships.

Décor throughout stresses dark wood-grain paneling, fluted columns, ornate faux-iron railings, gilt-framed paintings, Oriental-style carpets, and deep-hued upholstery. In the bow, the spacious, woody Horizons lounge has floor-to-ceiling windows and brass telescopes. It's used for dancing in the evening and for high tea and other functions in the afternoon. Evening entertainment is presented in a club-style 345-seat show lounge with lots of comfy tables for four. A smallish but comfortable casino offers blackjack, poker tables, roulette, and slots, while the next-door Martini Bar is probably our favorite space on board, with a gentlemen's-club décor, a long martini menu, and jazz and standards in the evening. The ships' libraries are some of the loveliest at sea, with comfy seating, excellent lighting, a faux garden skylight, and marble fireplace.

Cabins are straightforward spaces with a hint of modern European hotel: plain off-white walls, dark wood trim and furniture, and rich carpeting. Of the 342 staterooms, 280 are essentially the same size (150–165 sq. ft.), and of those, 170 have balconies. Bathrooms are small, though they provide enough shelf and counter space, plus adequate amenities. Table 11-16 shows the current fleet specifications.

The best thing about the cabins are the beds, which Oceania calls "Tranquility Beds" for good reason. Each is delightfully firm and fitted with 350-thread-count Egyptian linens, a plush comforter/silk-cut duvet, and probably the best fluffy down pillows we've ever used. We'd love to get hold of a couple. Wonder if they'll fit in our suitcases?

Table 11-16	Oceania Fleet Specifications					
Ship	Entered Service	Passengers	Crew	Total Cabins	Tonnage	Length in Feet
Insignia	1998	684	400	342	30,200	594
Nautica	2000	684	400	342	30,200	594
Regatta	1998	684	400	342	30,200	594

Princess Cruises

24305 Town Center Dr., Santa Clarita, CA 91355; ☎ *800-PRINCESS (800-774-6237);* www.princess.com

> ✔ **Type of cruise:** Family, resort, romantic
>
> ✔ **Ship size/style:** Modern, stylish megaships with a couple of small-ish and midsize, traditional-style ships as well

This line gets an A for its all-around appeal. More mellow than a Carnival or Royal Caribbean cruise, you're likely to find more action than on Holland America. The line has great family facilities, yet you won't find a thousand kids aboard like on some other lines. Princess straddles a middle ground in just about everything it does, and it works just fine for many people. You can chill out with a book in the library, join a bridge tournament, or head for the Pool Deck or disco for more action. You can even play miniature golf aboard many ships or take a spin in the pottery-making studio. The line excels in the dining department too, with many options and flexible timings. Though Princess has some of the industry's largest ships, they've been designed well so that passengers are spread out and the vessels rarely feel as large as they really are (for example, the line favors multiple one-story dining rooms as opposed to giant two- and three-story affairs).

Whether you're old enough to have actually watched *The Love Boat* in the '70s and '80s, or have just seen reruns, you may know that the vessels used in the series were Princess's *Pacific Princess* and *Island Princess*. To this day, Gavin "Captain Stubing" MacLeod acts as occasional pitchman for the line. The twin 640-passenger vessels, however, left the fleet in 1999 and 2002, respectively, though their names have since been assigned to new vessels. Lusty history or not, don't expect the Princess ships of today to be havens for swingin' singles (you can't believe everything you see on TV). They tend to attract, couples, families, and a large number of seniors.

The more you cruise, the more you get. The line's Captain's Circle loyalty program issues specially colored onboard keycards and cabin-door nameplates to past cruisers (gold after taking 1 to 5 cruises, platinum after 5, and elite after 15), so staffers know to be extra helpful. Platinum Captain's Circle members also get expedited embarkation and free

Internet access throughout their cruise. Elite members receive free laundry and dry-cleaning services, a complimentary wine-tasting class, 10 percent off in the onboard gift shops, and more.

Though the line offers worldwide itineraries, Princess (along with Holland America) has been particularly strong in Alaska for decades. Through its affiliate, Princess Tours, it offers more than 40 different cruisetour itineraries in conjunction with its Gulf of Alaska and Inside Passage voyages, visiting Denali National Park, Fairbanks, the Kenai Peninsula, Wrangell–St. Elias National Park, Canada's Yukon Territory, and distant Prudhoe Bay on Alaska's north coast. Guests on land tours stay in five Princess-owned wilderness lodges and travel via motor coach and the line's domed Midnight Express train cars. Table 11-17 shows more Princess itineraries, as well as sample fares.

Dining

The food is typically tasty, but hardly memorable; what registers is the dining system. The line's Personal Choice Dining program allows passengers two options: dining at a set time with set dining companions in one of the ship's two or three main restaurants, or just wandering in at any time during a 4½-hour window to be seated by the maitre d'. No matter how you choose to dine, you can always find healthy choices, vegetarian options, and a kids' menu.

If you're not sure which option you may prefer once you're on board, sign up for traditional, because it's easier to switch to anytime dining than it is to go the other way 'round.

The *Diamond Princess* and *Sapphire Princess* offer an even more flexible set-up than the rest of the ships. Each has one main 500-seat dining room for traditional-seating guests and four smaller, 230-seat restaurants for anytime dining, which serve a different themed cuisine.

Fleetwide, you can also find a buffet restaurant operating around the clock (including full sit-down meals until 4 a.m.), including for dinner daily, as well as smaller, more intimate alternative restaurants, including an Italian trattoria and steakhouse restaurant on the Grand-class ships as well as the *Pacific* and *Tahitian Princess;* trattoria and New Orleans–style restaurants on *Coral* and *Island Princess;* and a steakhouse and free sit-down pizzeria on the Sun-class ships. *Diamond* and *Sapphire Princess* also feature the Italian trattoria, with its eight-course meals, in addition to their Italian-themed dining rooms. The *Regal* offers a sit-down pizzeria only. Prices are $20 per person at the trattoria and $15 at the steakhouse. Reservations are recommended.

Unlike the no-dress-code dress code that's part of Norwegian's "Freestyle" dining plan, Princess maintains the tradition of holding two formal nights per week, with the other nights designated smart casual (khakis and polo or button-down shirt are fine for men; ladies, you know what to do).

Table 11-17	Princess Itineraries and Sample Fares
Ship/Fares (per person/day)	*Itineraries*
Caribbean Princess $80 inside; $93 outside; $300 suite	**7-night eastern Caribbean:** Round-trip from Ft. Lauderdale, FL, year-round; **7-night western Caribbean:** Round-trip from Ft. Lauderdale May–Oct
Coral Princess $125 inside; $145 outside; $332 suite	**10-night Panama Canal:** Round-trip from Ft. Lauderdale, FL, Jan–Apr; **7-night Gulf of Alaska:** North- or southbound between Vancouver, BC, and Whittier/Anchorage, AK, May–Sept
Dawn Princess $90 inside; $110 outside; $245 suite	**10-night Mexican Riviera:** Round-trip from San Francisco, CA, Jan–May; **7-night Alaska Inside Passage:** Round-trip from Seattle, WA, May–Sept
Diamond Princess $128 inside; $128 outside; $458 suite	**12-night Australia/New Zealand:** North- or southbound between Sydney, Australia, and Auckland, New Zealand, Jan–Apr; **7-night Gulf of Alaska:** North- or southbound between Vancouver, BC, and Whittier/Anchorage, AK, May–Sept
Golden Princess $93 inside; $108 outside; $307 suite	**7-night southern Caribbean:** Round-trip from San Juan, PR, Jan–Apr; **12-night Mediterranean/Greek Isles:** East- or westbound between Venice and Rome, Italy, May–June and Sept–Oct; **10-night British Isles and western European capitals:** Round-trip from London, UK, July–Aug; **12-night Egypt/Aegean:** Round-trip from Rome, Nov
Grand Princess $78 inside; $93 outside; $300 suite	**7-night western Caribbean:** Round-trip from Galveston, TX, Jan–Apr; **12-night Mediterranean:** Between Rome and Venice, Italy; Venice and Barcelona, Spain; May–Oct
Island Princess $150 inside; $178 outside; $493 suite	**15-night Hawaii:** Round-trip from Los Angeles, CA, Jan–Apr; **7-night Gulf of Alaska:** North- or southbound between Vancouver, BC, and Whittier/Anchorage, AK, May–Sept
Pacific Princess $216 inside; $226 outside; $291 suite	**21-night Pacific:** Sydney, Australia, to Osaka, Japan, Apr; **12-night Japan/China:** Osaka to Beijing, China, May; **16-night China/Southeast Asia:** North- or southbound between Beijing and Bangkok, Thailand, May–Sept; **15-night South and Southeast Asia:** East- or westbound between Bangkok and Mumbai, India, Aug–Sept; **27-night Africa/India/Southeast Asia:** Bangkok to Cape Town, South Africa, Sept; **28-night South Africa/Indian Ocean/Australia:** Cape Town to Sydney, Oct; **20-night South Pacific:** Sydney to Papeete, Tahiti, Nov; **21-night South Pacific/Andes:** Papeete to Aruba, via the Panama Canal, Nov; **15-night South America:** Aruba to Lima, Peru, Dec

(continued)

Table 11-17 *(continued)*

Ship/Fares (per person/day)	Itineraries
Regal Princess $100 inside; $110 outside; $255 suite	**21-night Antarctica:** Rio de Janeiro, Brazil, to Valparaiso, Chile, Jan; **13-night South America/Cape Horn:** East- or westbound between Buenos Aires, Argentina, and Valparaiso, Chile, Jan–Mar; **12-night Caribbean/Amazon:** North- or southbound between Ft. Lauderdale, FL, and Manaus, Brazil, Apr; **10-night Alaska Inside Passage:** Round-trip from San Francisco, CA, May–Sept
Sapphire Princess $93 inside; $114 outside; $300 suite	**7-night Mexican Riviera:** Round-trip from Los Angeles, CA, Jan–Apr; **7-night Gulf of Alaska:** North- or southbound between Vancouver, BC, and Whittier/Anchorage, AK, May–Sept
Sea Princess $100 inside; $114 outside; $264 suite	**14-night southern Caribbean:** Round-trip from Barbados, Jan–Apr; **14-night Mediterranean:** Round-trip from Southampton, UK, May–Aug; **7-night France/Portugal/ Channel Islands:** Round-trip from Southampton, May; **7- and 14-night Scandinavia:** Round-trip from Southampton, June–Aug
Star Princess $78 inside; $93 outside; $300 suite	**7-night western Caribbean:** Round-trip from Ft. Lauderdale, FL, Jan–Apr; **10-night Scandinavia/Russia:** Round-trip from Copenhagen, Denmark, May–Sept
Sun Princess $114 inside; $171 outside; $456 suite May–Sept	**10-night eastern and southern Caribbean** (alternating itineraries): Round-trip from Ft. Lauderdale, FL, Jan–Apr; **7-night Alaska Inside Passage:** Round-trip from Seattle, WA,
Tahitian Princess $130 inside; $150 outside; $285 suite	**10-night Polynesia:** Round-trip from Papeete, Tahiti, Jan–Apr

In the snack department, aside from 24-hour room service, there's a specialty coffee bar, a poolside grill doling out burgers and pizza, and an ice-cream bar serving Häagen-Dazs and Princess's house brand for a charge (the bad news: no free frozen yogurt like most ships offer).

Though you can order room service and eat out on your balcony any time you choose, if you want to be served by a waiter and eat something more interesting than a turkey sandwich or some pizza, just cough up $50 per person and bon appetite! Offered on the Grand-class ships, you can have a table set up on your balcony with a tablecloth, hurricane candle lamp, and champagne. While the waiter is setting everything up, you and your better half can have a complimentary cocktail in one of the ship's bars. On all the ships, you can order a fancy breakfast served on the balcony for $25 per couple.

Activities and entertainment

You've got no excuse for being bored, that's for sure. A wide variety of activities include miniature golf, virtual golf, and basketball/volleyball, all available on the Grand-class ships and the *Coral, Island, Diamond,* and *Sapphire Princess.* The Grand-class ships have gigantic virtual/video game rooms, while the *Caribbean* and *Grand Princess* (see Figure 11-9) have giant LED movie screens on deck showing movies, sporting events, and other popular shows. Plus, aside from standards such as bingo, dancing lessons, and poolside bellyflop contests, in the Caribbean, guests can earn PADI scuba-diving certification while on board. A fleetwide enrichment program, called ScholarShip@Sea, offers classes in cooking, computer skills, finance, photography, and pottery making. Large-group seminars are free, while small-group and individual classes, unfortunately, carry a charge of around $20 to $25 per person. Charges for paint-your-own ceramics are calculated based on the piece you create. When it comes to evening entertainment, the choices include the standard Vegas-style song and dance revues, plus comedy routines, live music, and more innovative stuff such as the *American Idol*–style "Princess Idol" competition that gives Princess passengers their moment in the spotlight.

In Alaska, rangers, naturalists, and guest lecturers present talks and slide shows on such topics as the Iditarod sled-dog race, the wildlife and ecology of Glacier Bay and the Tongass National Forest, oceanography and marine life, glaciers, Native Alaskan cultures, and Alaskan history.

 You can book your spa appointments online before your cruise if you're sailing on the *Caribbean Princess* or *Sapphire Princess* — a real boon considering how long the lines can be when you have to sign up for a massage on board.

 Want the big boss to tie your knot? Princess is the only line where the captain himself conducts legal weddings aboard ship. The ceremonies take place on *Coral, Island, Diamond,* and *Sapphire Princess* and the four Grand-class ships, all of which have wedding chapels on board. (Other lines have wedding chapels, too, but the captain is nowhere to be seen.) Book yours far in advance; the captain doesn't have time to do more than a handful per cruise.

For kids

 The line's newest ships — the Grand-, Diamond- and Coral-class ships — have great indoor/outdoor facilities and complimentary supervised activities, including some great educational ones, for ages 3 to 17. Group babysitting is offered nightly at an hourly rate between 10 p.m. and 1 a.m.

(Photo: Princess Cruises)

Figure 11-9: *Grand Princess*

Fleet facts

The Grand- and Sun-class ships offer many of the cruise industry's best amenities — from the giant movie screens on deck of the *Caribbean* and *Grand Princess,* to the miniature golf courses many ships have, and the ships' varied and flexible dining options. The medical centers on the Grand-class ships have tele-medicine facilities that allow shipboard doctors to link to land-based hospitals for consultations. Overall, décor is pleasant, but nothing exotic; safe beiges and blues dominate, and the art work isn't memorable. Designed by Renzo Piano, the architect who did the Centre Pompidou in Paris, the *Regal Princess* is the line's oldest and one of its smallest ships, along with the two other Explorer-class ships, *Tahitian* and *Pacific Princess,* which at 30,277 tons, are tiny, compared to the rest of the fleet, and spend their time in the South Pacific.

In summer of 2006, the *Crown Princess,* a sister to the *Caribbean Princess,* will enter service, and a third sister, *Emerald Princess,* is slated to debut in spring 2007.

If you book a suite on any of the Princess ships, you get extras such as free Internet access, dry cleaning, and laundry; complimentary corsage and boutonniere on formal nights; and other perks, including free portrait sessions with the ship's photographer or en suite afternoon tea. Table 11-18 shows the current fleet specifications.

Table 11-18	**Princess Fleet Specifications**					
Ship	*Entered Service*	*Passengers*	*Crew*	*Total Cabins*	*Tonnage*	*Length in Feet*
Caribbean Princess	2004	3,100	988	1,550	116,000	952
Coral Princess	2002	1,970	900	987	92,000	964
Dawn Princess	1997	1,950	900	975	77,000	856
Diamond Princess	2003	2,670	1,100	1,337	116,000	952
Golden Princess	2001	2,600	1,100	1,300	109,000	951

Ship	Entered Service	Passengers	Crew	Total Cabins	Tonnage	Length in Feet
Grand Princess	1998	2,600	1,100	1,300	109,000	951
Island Princess	2003	1,970	900	987	92,000	964
Pacific Princess	2002	670	373	334	30,277	592
Regal Princess	1991	1,590	696	795	70,000	811
Sapphire Princess	2004	2,670	1,100	1,337	116,000	952
Sea Princess	1998	1,950	900	975	77,000	856
Star Princess	2002	2,600	1,200	1,301	109,000	951
Sun Princess	1995	1,950	900	975	77,000	856
Tahitian Princess	2002	670	373	334	30,277	592

Royal Caribbean International

1050 Caribbean Way, Miami, FL 33132; ☎ *800-327-6700;* www.royalcaribbean.com

> ✔ **Type of cruise:** Resort, family, party
>
> ✔ **Ship size/style:** Megaships, and some really *huge* ones at that

What kind of cruise line puts an ice-skating rink on a ship? Royal Caribbean (RCI), and none other. In 1999, this megacruise line (number two in the world-domination contest behind megalithic Carnival) introduced the *Voyager of the Seas,* shown in Figure 11-10. At the time, it was by far the largest passenger ship ever built. Four sister ships followed, and even though they've since been eclipsed in the size race by one-off ocean liner *Queen Mary 2,* they're still damn big, with each offering more bells, whistles, and innovations than some cruise lines have in their entire fleet.

To judge by their extremely successful advertising campaign ("Get Out There!" "Lust for Life!" Yuppies on glaciers! Yuppies kayaking!), you'd think this line was all about action, and you'd almost sorta kinda be right. While the ads definitely have elements of ad-industry hype, RCI really does offer a more youthful, energetic product than a lot of other cruise lines, delivering fun, humor, a touch of class, and a bit of "feel the burn" active excitement, all at reasonable mainstream prices.

The line is one of our top mainstream picks (especially for the Voyager- and Radiance-class ships, which among other things have some of the industry's best spas), and is a top choice for both families and party people.

Passengers range from ages 30-something and up, with most hailing from the U.S., a chunk from Canada, and a smaller chunk from elsewhere, especially Latin America and Asia. Though they're looking for good times, they're more karaoke than wet T-shirt (though shorter 3- and 4-night cruises from Miami and Los Angeles tend to attract a more partying crowd). Who wouldn't like RCI? People who want a really upscale experience (these are mainstream vessels, after all); people who hate crowds (all told, their biggest ships carry more than 5,000 people, including crew — though they're so well designed you sometimes wonder where all those people are); people who want a quiet cruise experience without the distraction of a lot of programmed activities.

Royal Caribbean doesn't accept booking from travelers under 21 unless they're sharing a room with an adult over 25. Exceptions are made for young married couples and for families who book connecting cabins so that the kids can have their own.

The ships are well run and the product consistent, with armies of well-trained staff to keep things running efficiently — no small feat on ships this large. Dining, bar, and cabin service is all surprisingly good given the sheer number of passengers with whom crewmembers must deal.

Fleetwide, the décor skews toward contemporary, with some nautical touches on the newer Radiance-class ships and some leftover chrome and '80s/'90s glitz on the older ships. All told, though, the RCI ships are a lot calmer in the ornamentation department than, say, Carnival and Costa. Many public areas are outstanding, including elaborate health clubs, spas, relaxing Solarium pools, huge theaters and smaller show lounges, enormous boulevard-like atriums on the Voyager ships, and the trademark Viking Crown Lounges, which sit atop the ships like airport control towers. While the big new vessels get all the press, RCI hasn't forgotten its older ships, spending millions to retrofit them with features that were developed for the more recent vessels. Table 11-19 shows RCI's itineraries and sample fares.

Dining

Royal Caribbean's cuisine falls in the "pretty tasty" to "impressively good" range, with a lot of options (though not as many as at Norwegian) and some pretty amazing venues. The Voyager ships' main dining rooms are probably the most impressive at sea — huge, three-level affairs with enormous chandeliers and the grand feel of a European opera house. RCI has stayed with traditional early- and late-seating dinners, with guests dining at assigned tables. As with the other mainstream lines, there are also many casual and specialty dining options. You can dine at Italian specialty restaurants on the Voyager- and Radiance-class ships and the recently refurbished *Empress of the Seas* (for a $20 surcharge), or at a steakhouse on the Radiance-class ships and the Voyager-class vessels *Navigator, Mariner,* and *Enchantment of the Seas* (also $20 per

Table 11-19   RCI Itineraries and Sample Fares

Ship/Fares (per person/day)	Itineraries
Adventure of the Seas $121 inside; $143 outside; $368 suite	**7-night southern Caribbean:** Round-trip from San Juan, PR, year-round
Brilliance of the Seas $130 inside; $145 outside; $385 suite	**10- and 11-night Panama Canal:** Round-trip from Miami, FL, Jan–Apr and Nov–Dec; **12-night Mediterranean:** Round-trip from Barcelona, Spain, May–Oct
Empress of the Seas $93 inside; $109 outside; $351 suite	**11-night eastern and southern Caribbean:** Round-trip from San Juan, PR, Jan–Apr and Nov–Dec; **3- and 4-night eastern Caribbean:** Round-trip from San Juan, Jan–Apr
Enchantment of the Seas $124 inside; $157 outside; $547 suite	**4- and 5-night western Caribbean:** Round-trip from Ft. Lauderdale, FL, year-round
Explorer of the Seas $123 inside; $128 outside; $336 suite	**7-night eastern and western Caribbean** (alternating weekly): Round-trip from Miami, FL, year-round
Freedom of the Seas $193 inside; $221 outside; $357 suite	**7-night western Caribbean:** Round-trip from Miami, FL, year-round
Grandeur of the Seas $89 inside; $100 outside; $300 suite	**7-night western Caribbean:** Round-trip from New Orleans, LA, Jan–Apr and Dec*; **5-night Bermuda:** Round-trip from Baltimore, MD, May–Nov; alternates with **9-night western Caribbean:** Round-trip from Baltimore, May–Nov
Jewel of the Seas $117 inside; $133 outside; $350 suite	**8-night eastern Caribbean:** Round-trip from Ft. Lauderdale, FL, Jan–Apr and Nov–Dec; alternates with **6-night western Caribbean:** Round-trip from Ft. Lauderdale, Jan–Apr and Nov–Dec; **12-night Scandinavia/Russia:** Round-trip from Harwich, UK, May–Aug; **12-night British Isles/Norwegian fjords:** Round-trip from Harwich, June–July; **10-night Bermuda/Caribbean:** Round-trip from Boston, MA, Sept–Oct

(continued)

Table 11-19 *(continued)*

Ship/Fares (per person/day)	Itineraries
Legend of the Seas $93 inside; $114 outside; $483 suite	**7-night western Caribbean:** Round-trip from Tampa, FL, Jan–Apr and Nov–Dec; **4-night Channel Islands/France:** Round-trip from Southampton, UK, Apr–May and Aug; **7-night western Europe:** Round-trip from Southampton, May, Aug, and Sept; **14-night Spain/Portugal/Channel and Canary Islands:** Round-trip from Southampton, May; **14-night Mediterranean:** Round-trip from Southampton, May–Sept; **10-night Canary Islands:** Round-trip from Southampton, Aug and Oct; **11-night Spain/Portugal/Channel Islands:** Round-trip from Southampton, Sept
Majesty of the Seas $67 inside; $75 outside; $310 suite	**3- and 4-night Bahamas:** Round-trip from Miami, FL, year-round
Mariner of the Seas $116 inside; $135 outside; $336 suite	**7-night eastern and western Caribbean** (alternating weekly): Round-trip from Port Canaveral, FL, year-round
Monarch of the Seas $80 inside; $87 outside; $345 suite	**3-night Ensenada and 4-night Ensenada/Catalina/San Diego** (alternating itineraries): Round-trip from Los Angeles, CA, year-round
Navigator of the Seas $124 inside; $150 outside; $336 suite	**7-night eastern and western Caribbean** (alternating weekly): Round-trip from Miami, FL, year-round
Radiance of the Seas $138 inside; $163 outside; $300 suite	**7-night eastern and western Caribbean** (alternating weekly): Round-trip from Miami, FL, Jan–Apr; **7-night Gulf of Alaska:** North- or southbound between Seward/Anchorage, AK, and Vancouver, BC, May–Sept; **14-night Hawaii:** Round-trip from San Diego, CA, May and Sept; **6-night western Caribbean:** Round-trip from Ft. Lauderdale, FL, Oct–Dec; alternates with **8-night eastern Caribbean:** Round-trip from Ft. Lauderdale, Oct–Dec
Rhapsody of the Seas $80 inside; $94 outside; $300 suite	**7-night western Caribbean:** Round-trip from Galveston, TX, year-round
Serenade of the Seas $108 inside; $123 outside; $343 suite	**7-night southern Caribbean:** Round-trip from San Juan, PR, Jan–Apr and Oct–Dec; **7-night Alaska Inside Passage:** Round-trip from Vancouver, BC, May–Sept; **11-night Hawaii:** Honolulu, HI, to Ensenada, Mexico, Oct

Ship/Fares (per person/day)	Itineraries
Sovereign of the Seas $67 inside; $75 outside; $300 suite	**3- and 4-night Bahamas:** Round-trip from Port Canaveral, FL, year-round
Splendour of the Seas $72 inside; $86 outside; $280 suite	**4- and 5-night western Caribbean:** Round-trip from Galveston, TX, Jan–Apr; **7-night Greek Isles and Greek Isles/Turkey:** Round-trip from Venice, Italy, May–Oct
Vision of the Seas $78 inside; $93 outside; $271 suite	**3-night Baja:** Round-trip from Los Angeles, CA, Jan; **7-night Mexican Riviera:** Round-trip from Los Angeles, Jan–Apr and Sept–Dec; **7-night Alaska Inside Passage:** Round-trip from Seattle, WA, May–Sept
Voyager of the Seas $108 inside; $128 outside; $336 suite	**7-night eastern and western Caribbean** (alternating weekly): Round-trip from Miami, FL, Jan–Apr and Nov–Dec; **7-night Mediterranean:** Round-trip from Barcelona, Spain, May–Nov; **3-night Mediterranean:** Round-trip from Barcelona, Nov

* Deployment affected by Hurricane Katrina disaster. Contact cruise line for updates.

person). The Voyager-class ships have '50s-style **Johnny Rockets** diners right out on deck, serving burgers and the like for a $3.95 per-person service charge (plus $3.60 a pop for milkshakes). Casual breakfast, lunch, and dinner are also available from the large buffet restaurant on each ship.

Activities and entertainment

These ships are activity-central. Fleetwide, you can find rock-climbing walls (with multiple climbing tracks and training available) plus lots of typical cruise fare: dancing lessons, art auctions, bingo, shuffleboard, spa and beauty demonstrations, wine tastings (at an elaborate wine bar on *Navigator* and *Mariner*), oddball crafts/hospitality classes such as napkin folding, and deck games, including "horse race" gambling and outrageous poolside games like the men's sexy legs contest.

Sports facilities vary by ship: ice-skating rinks and in-line skating tracks on the Voyager-class ships; combo basketball/volleyball courts on the Radiance-, Voyager-, and Vision-class ships; and several ships (the Radiance and Voyager classes as well as *Splendour* and *Legend of the Seas*) feature miniature-golf. The line's Golf Ahoy program offers golf shore excursions in more than two dozen ports. Shipboard gyms are well equipped fleetwide, with specialized fitness classes such as yoga and cardio-kickboxing available for $10 per person. The line's spas offer the usual range of massages, facials, and other beauty treatments.

Entertainment-wise, Royal Caribbean spends big bucks on its shows, high-tech productions that feature singers, dancers, live bands, and frequent headliners and guest artists, including aerialists, comedians, and name performers such as the Platters and the Drifters). Atrium bars feature live music, often classical trios, and the new Latin-themed Bolero's bars (aboard *Navigator, Mariner, Monarch, Sovereign,* and *Empress*) serve a mean mojito and have Latin music into the night.

Royal Caribbean is big on wedding packages, with many a vow made in the Voyager-class ships' wedding chapels (though you can only get married there when the ships are in port).

For kids

Royal Caribbean offers year-round supervised kids' programs fleetwide, with activities for kids aged 3 to 17 (divided into four age groups). Each ship has a kids' playroom and facilities for teens, though the facilities on the Voyager- and Radiance-class ships are far better than those on the line's older vessels, which are among the best at sea for kids. Among other activities, several learning programs offer fun exploration of science, art, and reading. Group babysitting for kids 3 and up is available nightly and from noon until sailing on days the ship is in port (for a fee). Private, in-cabin babysitting for kids 6 months and up is available from off-duty crewmembers 8 a.m. to 2 a.m.

(Photo: Royal Caribbean International)

Figure 11-10: *Voyager of the Seas*

Fleet facts

The line's superstars are definitely its Voyager-class ships: ***Voyager, Explorer, Adventure, Navigator,*** and ***Mariner of the Seas.*** It's pretty easy to describe what they've got: everything. They're the ones with the ice-skating rinks and in-line skating tracks; the miniature golf courses and golf simulators; the 1950s-style diner sitting right out on deck; the regulation-size basketball courts; the huge two-level gyms and spas; the gorgeous three-level main restaurants; the rock-climbing walls that have become one of Royal Caribbean's most distinguishing features; and, perhaps most significantly, the only ships at sea with a four-story, Main Street–like promenade running more than a football field's length down their center, lined with bars, shops, and entertainment lounges. Three decks of inside cabins have bay windows from which their occupants can view the street scene below. More than any other ship ever built, these really do live up to the old "city at sea" cliche.

That is, at least the next generation of Voyager-class ships. The first, dubbed *Freedom of the Seas,* is essentially a Voyager-plus, with all that the older ships offer plus new features such as a sprawling water park, full of spray cannons, water jets, gushers, and sculptural water guns set off by sensors and other triggers; a pair of giant cantilevered hot tubs extending 12 feet out over the edge of the ship, some 112 feet above the sea; and a pool with views down into the ship's main atrium. *Freedom of the Seas* is set to debut in May 2006, with her first sister ship arriving in spring 2007 and another due in early 2008.

The Radiance-class ships, *Radiance, Brilliance, Serenade,* and *Jewel of the Seas,* are more classic than innovative in their onboard experience, while offering a lot of the fun and games of the Voyager class, including rock climbing and miniature golf. They're Royal Caribbean's most elegant vessels to date, with shippy lines and nautical interior décor, full of dark wood paneling, caramel-brown leathers, and deep-sea-blue fabrics and carpeting. Outside, their sleek profiles are covered in 110,000 square feet of glass, providing views from public rooms like the Viking Crown Lounge, the piano bar, the Champagne Bar, and other spaces — handy for letting scenery in on Alaska itineraries.

The Vision-class ships, *Vision, Splendour, Grandeur, Rhapsody, Enchantment,* and *Legend,of the Seas,* were once paradigms on cruise ship modernity, but were so quickly eclipsed by their giant Voyager cousins that now they seem almost quaint. That's not a fair comment, of course. They're still pretty fine ships, with an open, light-filled feel and many of the same amenities offered by the line's newer, larger ships, including great solariums, pools, hoppin' discos, and sprawling outdoor decks. To keep them up to date, Royal Caribbean has retrofitted them all with rock-climbing walls, and some are scheduled for major surgery. As this book was being written, *Enchantment of the Seas* was literally being sawn in half and then welded back together with a new midsection, increasing her size and amenities substantially and adding a water park similar to the one coming on *Freedom of the Seas.* The nearby Sports Deck will include four bungee trampolines where guests strap into a harness connected to bungee cords, to keep them from flying overboard.

On the downside to these ships, their standard cabins are on the small side, a failing common to Royal Caribbean's older vessels — including the Sovereign-class ships, *Sovereign, Majesty,* and *Monarch of the Seas,* which all sail inexpensive 3- and 4-night cruises on the East and West Coasts. A decade and a half of hard use has given all three of these vessels their share of bumps, but Royal Caribbean's been busy scrubbing them up over the past two years, refurbishing and rebuilding many of the interiors on *Monarch* and *Sovereign.*

The line's oldest ship, *Empress of the Seas,* also got major elective surgery in 2004, updating the décor of her lobbies, elevators, corridors, and other public areas and transforming some of her lounge spaces into additional dining, entertainment, and fitness areas. She doesn't look half bad, particularly for short cruises, though her cabins are small and worn. Table 11-20 shows the current fleet specifications.

Table 11-20	Royal Caribbean Fleet Specifications					
Ship	**Entered Service**	**Passengers**	**Crew**	**Total Cabins**	**Tonnage**	**Length in Feet**
Adventure of the Seas	2001	3,114	1,176	1,557	142,000	1,020
Brilliance of the Seas	2002	2,100	857	1,050	90,090	962
Empress of the Seas	1990	1,602	668	800	48,563	692
Enchantment of the Seas	1997	2,252	840	1,126	80,700	989
Explorer of the Seas	2000	3,114	1,176	1,557	142,000	1,020
Freedom of the Seas	2006	3,600	1,360	1,800	158,000	1,112
Grandeur of the Seas	1996	1,950	760	975	74,140	916
Jewel of the Seas	2004	2,100	857	1,050	90,090	962
Legend of the Seas	1995	1,804	720	902	69,130	867
Majesty of the Seas	1992	2,350	825	1,175	73,941	880
Mariner of the Seas	2003	3,114	1,176	1,557	142,000	1,020
Monarch of the Seas	1991	2,350	825	1,175	73,941	880
Navigator of the Seas	2002	3,114	1,176	1,557	142,000	1,020
Radiance of the Seas	2001	2,100	857	1,050	90,090	962
Rhapsody of the Seas	1997	2,000	765	1,000	78,491	915
Serenade of the Seas	2003	2,100	857	1,050	90,090	962
Sovereign of the Seas	1988	2,852	840	1,138	73,192	880
Splendour of the Seas	1996	1,804	720	902	69,130	867
Vision of the Seas	1998	2,000	765	1,000	78,491	915
Voyager of the Seas	1999	3,114	1,176	1,557	142,000	1,020

Chapter 12

Luxury Ships

● ●

In This Chapter

▶ Discovering how luxury cruises are different
▶ Comparing the luxury lines

● ●

A cruise on a luxury ship isn't like other cruises. Erase all images of conga lines and buckets of beer — a luxury cruise bears little resemblance to a giant megaship. Luxury ships are smaller. Service is more attentive. Food tastes better. Cabins are larger and have better amenities. Itineraries are almost always superior. The list goes on. Oh, they cost more, too. A lot more.

The Lowdown on the High End

If all you've heard about cruises is that they're glitzy floating Vegas resorts full of napkin-folding, bingo-playing, pizza-eating, beer chuggers, well, forget all that and start with a blank slate. The luxury ships reviewed in this chapter are the best of the best, if best to you means eating on elegant china and sipping a rare vintage from a crystal glass. If you appreciate a sophisticated waiter who lifts a silver lid from your chateaubriand, then your ship has come in. Standard cabins on a luxury ship are usually all suites, outfitted with walk-in closets, stocked minibars, and marble bathrooms large enough to offer a tub, shower, and double sinks. Expect extras such as slippers, bathrobes, and fancy shampoos from the likes of Molton Brown and Acqua di Parma.

Most of the luxury vessels are small and intimate, carrying between 100 and 700 guests. And even on the bigger luxury ships (Cunard's *QE2* and *QM2,* and Crystal's *Symphony* and new *Serenity*), you're unlikely to feel lost in a crowd. The vibe on a luxury ship is one of exclusivity. Passengers are like members of a private club of experienced travelers who like the good life and are willing to pay for it. Passengers are mostly adults over the age of 50, although you may see some kids on the *QM2* and the Crystal ships, which have children's facilities (most luxury lines have a minimum age of 1 to sail).

Like their mainstream cousins, luxury ships have pools, gyms, and spas. Dining is the best you can find at sea, and dinner is served with much

The little extras (really add up)

The ultraluxury ships treat passengers like royalty. Their fares are more all-inclusive, so while you pay more, you get more, too. Here's a list of some of the things included in the luxury cruise rates:

✔ **Booze:** Seabourn, SeaDream, and Silversea (unlimited spirits, wine, and champagne); Radisson Seven Seas (wine with dinner)

✔ **Free stocked minibar:** Radisson Seven Seas, Seabourn, Silversea, SeaDream (beer and soft drinks only), Crystal (top suites only), and Cunard (top suites only)

✔ **A special shore excursion:** Seabourn, SeaDream, and Silversea

✔ **Tips:** Included on Seabourn, SeaDream, Silversea, and Radisson Seven Seas

✔ **Unlimited soda/bottled water:** Crystal, Seabourn, SeaDream, Silversea, and Radisson Seven Seas

✔ **Watersports:** Seabourn and SeaDream

✔ **Other goodies:** Godiva pillow chocolates nightly (Silversea), cotton logo pj's (SeaDream), CD of classic jazz (Seabourn), luggage tags and document portfolio (Seabourn offers Tumi versions)

pomp and circumstance. More effort goes into the preparation of meals and the scope goes beyond the standard pasta, salmon, and steaks you get on the mainstream lines. On the luxe lines, a fancy afternoon tea is a daily norm, as are complimentary pre-dinner canapés in the lounges (which few mainstream lines offer). Entertainment and organized activities are more limited than on mainstream ships (with the exception of Crystal and Cunard), and most guests on luxury ships like it that way. They prefer cocktails in a piano bar after dinner and chatting about stocks or recent travels over sweating it up in a disco or sprinting between the casino and the X-rated comedian in a lounge.

What to wear, what to wear, what to wear? With the exception of SeaDream Yacht Club (which has a no-jackets-required policy), it's a good idea to bring a tux (ladies, pack your fancy dresses) for formal nights; people on these ships tend to dress for dinner. Other days feature a mix of informal nights, when men need to wear a jacket and tie, and casual nights, when button-down shirts are fine for men, with or without a jacket. Women can wear nice skirts, pants, or dresses on these evenings. All the luxury lines also have at least one casual dining venue, where there's absolutely no need for a suit or jacket. Exceptions: On Seabourn and Crystal, ties are optional on all but formal nights.

Most luxury lines (with the exception of Cunard) can accommodate two or three passengers only per cabin (not including big suites and penthouses, of course). So if you're set on bringing the kids, for example, in the standard staterooms on the SeaDream, Radisson, Seabourn, Silversea, and Crystal ships, the third person/child sleeps on the couch or a roll-away (if there's space for them at all). If you've got a larger family, you have to spring for two staterooms or a larger suite. As Seabourn spokesman Bruce Good told us: "Seabourn suites are designed to accommodate two guests. A child can be accommodated on a couch in some suites or we do have a couple of rollaways that can be used, but it really compromises the experience."

Around the World They Go

Where don't they go should be the question. Luxury ships tend to globe-trot and offer a more eclectic and varied itinerary schedule than the mainstream ships we discuss in Chapter 11. They often sail from a different homeport every week or stay in one region only long enough to offer a few itineraries and then move on to another part of the world. Because most luxury ships are substantially smaller than the big mainstream ships, they can and do visit smaller, less accessible ports.

You want the world? Then you gotta pay. A typical luxury cruise will run you about $300 to $600 per person a day, more if you book the penthouse. Still, keep a lookout for deals, the luxury lines offer special promotions, too, from free airfare to the port of embarkation to two-for-one deals. It's a good idea to book a luxury cruise through an agency that specializes in them. See Chapter 4 for recommended agencies.

Crystal Cruises

2049 Century Park East, Suite 1400, Los Angeles, CA 90067; ☎ *800-446-6620;* www.crystalcruises.com

> ✔ **Type of cruise:** Gourmet, luxury, resort, romantic
>
> ✔ **Ship size/style:** Modern, midsize luxury ship

Offering the best of both worlds, Crystal gracefully straddles the line between active big ship and refined small one. The *Crystal Symphony* and the newer *Crystal Serenity* (see Figure 12-1) dole out top-of-the-line service and cuisine, plus lots of outdoor deck space, generous fitness facilities, tons of activities, multiple restaurants (including the best Asian venues at sea), bars, and entertainment venues.

Unlike Seabourn's small ships, which tend to be more calm and staid, this Japanese-owned, Los Angeles–based line lives by a more sociable California ethic, and its large passenger capacity tends to keep things mingly, chatty, and fairly active.

You'll find both dark wood-paneled rooms and light pastel ones, along with plenty of marble, glass, fresh flowers, and potted plants. The newer

Serenity has deeper, richer colors; the *Symphony* sports more of the lighter champagnes, grays, whites, and blues, especially in the atrium, where things are a tad on the shiny side with chrome and brassy railings.

The downside to all of this upside is that most cabins on both these ships are quite a bit smaller than those on Silversea, Seabourn, and Radisson. Sure, you can book a suite or penthouse that's bigger, but the price for sailing on a larger ship with more to do is that the standard staterooms are on the cozy side. Table 12-1 shows Crystal's itineraries and sample fares.

Dining

It's tops, especially if you love Asian food. In addition to the formal dining room that operates with an early or late seating system, there are alternative restaurants (Italian and Asian), plus a poolside grill, an indoor cafe, and a casual restaurant that has a theme luncheon buffet, such as Asian, Mediterranean, or South American/Cuban.

The line's Asian venues are among the best at sea. *Symphony*'s Jade Garden showcases the Asian cuisine of Wolfgang Puck's acclaimed Santa Monica restaurant, Chinois on Main. And Master Chef Nobuyuki "Nobu" Matsuhisa, known for his restaurants in New York, Miami, L.A., London, Paris, and other cities, partnered with Crystal to create menus for *Serenity*'s Sushi Bar and its Pan-Asian restaurant Silk Road. Dishes feature Nobu's eclectic blends of Japanese cuisine with Peruvian and European influences. On the *Serenity*'s Penthouse Deck, you can even get Nobu room service.

All menus include light and low-fat options as well as vegetarian, low-carb, sugar-free, gluten-free, and kosher foods. Of course, 24-hour room service is offered.

Activities and entertainment

You can find a lot to do on the Crystal ships. Entertainment runs the gamut from classical concertos by accomplished pianists to comedy and the classic cruise Vegas-style song and dance revues. From time to time, celebrity entertainers, such as Carol Channing, Tommy Tune, Robert Klein, and Marvin Hamlisch, are featured. Each ship also has lounges for dancing to live music as well as a fairly lively casino, a dark and cozy piano bar, a cigar bar, and a movie theater.

No other line has as much, with complimentary computer classes on every cruise (and private ones available for an hourly fee), plus dozens of theme sailings focused on food and wine, art, film, jazz music, wellness, and other subjects. There are always several enrichment lectures on each cruise, such as a historian presenting a slide show and speaking about the Panama Canal and how it was built, a former ambassador speaking about regional politics, or a movie critic talking to guests about Hollywood films.

Table 12-1	Crystal Itineraries and Sample Fares
Ship/Fares (per person/day)	*Itineraries*
Crystal Serenity $290 inside; $367 outside; $802 suite	**7-night Mexican Riviera:** Round-trip from Los Angeles, CA, Jan; **106-night world cruise:** Los Angeles to London, UK, Jan–May (segments bookable in South America, South Pacific, Australia/New Zealand, Africa, and Europe); **10-night France/Spain/Channel Islands:** Round-trip from London, May; **10-night northern Europe/British Isles:** Round-trip from London, May; **10- and 11-night British Isles:** Round-trip from London, May–Sept; **11- and 14-night northern Europe:** London to Stockholm, Sweden; Stockholm to Copenhagen, Denmark; and Copenhagen to London, June–Aug; **11-night Mediterranean:** London to Monte Carlo, Monaco; Monte Carlo to Venice, Italy; Venice to Rome, Italy; Rome to Athens, Greece; Athens to Monte Carlo; and Monte Carlo to Lisbon, Portugal, Sept–Nov; **7-, 10-, and 14-night eastern Caribbean:** Round-trip from Miami, FL, Nov–Dec
Crystal Symphony $300 inside; $363 outside; $968 suite	**11-night Panama Canal:** North- or southbound between Miami or Ft. Lauderdale, FL, and Caldera, Costa Rica, Jan–Feb and Nov; **11-night Caribbean/Amazon:** Miami to Manaus, Brazil, Feb; **14- and 15-night South America:** Manaus to Buenos Aires, Argentina, and west- or eastbound between Buenos Aires to Valparaiso, Chile, Mar–Apr; **16-night South America:** Bueno Aires to Miami, Apr; **7-, 10-, and 12-night Mediterranean:** Lisbon, Portugal, to Athens, Greece; Athens to Venice, Italy; Venice to Monte Carlo, Monaco; Monte Carlo to Venice; Venice to Athens; Athens to Rome, Italy; and Rome to Venice, May–Aug; **7-night New England/Canada:** Round-trip from New York, NY, Sept; **11-night New England/Canada:** Round-trip from New York, or north- or southbound between New York and Montreal, QB, Sept–Oct; **14-night Mexican Riviera:** Round-trip from Los Angeles, CA, Dec

You can find group (for free) and private (for a fee) dancing and golf lessons, plus music lessons, language classes, and tai-chi. Both ships offer a nice-size gym, feng-shui inspired spas, paddle-tennis courts, Ping-Pong, a jogging circuit, golf-driving nets, and a putting green.

In a huge computer lab, a complimentary 30-course computer curriculum is offered on all cruises, with topics such as a basic introduction to using the computer, understanding the Internet, and creating spreadsheets. Private lessons are also available for $50 an hour.

For kids

Though no Disney, Crystal does its part for families looking for a luxury getaway. Each ship has a playroom outfitted with PlayStation video games and personal computers among other goodies, plus there's a teen center and video arcade. When demand warrants it — typically during holidays and summers in Alaska — supervised activities are run for three age groups between 3 and 17. Private in-cabin babysitting is offered nightly for an hourly fee for children 6 months to 12 years.

If your bambinos are still on jar food, no need to lug a suitcase full (like Heidi has done on several occasions). With advance notice, the ship can order what you need at no charge and have it waiting. Or, the chef will puree organic food for your baby.

Crystal frequently offers kids-sail-free promotions, especially on its Alaska itineraries.

Figure 12-1: *Crystal Serenity*

(Photo: Crystal Cruises)

Fleet facts

Handsome ships by any standard, the ***Crystal Serenity*** and ***Crystal Symphony*** have some of the highest space-per-passenger ratios of any cruise ships in the industry. The two are exceedingly roomy, and the *Serenity* even more so; she's 38 percent bigger than *Symphony,* but carries only 15 percent more guests. The *Serenity* boasts expanded spa and fitness areas and more dining venues, entertainment lounges, and penthouses (the biggest four are each a whopping 1,345 sq. ft.). In early 2004, the *Symphony* received a $12 million facelift to most areas of the ship. If you're lucky enough to stay in one of the penthouse suites, you'll be treated to the services of male butlers.

Rates include unlimited nonalcoholic drinks everywhere aboard, from cappuccino to soda and bottled water. There's also now a pillow menu — what will they think up next? Table 12-2 shows current fleet specifications.

Table 12-2		Crystal Fleet Specifications				
Ship	Entered Service	Passengers	Crew	Total Cabins	Tonnage	Length in Feet
Crystal Serenity	2003	1,080	655	550	68,000	820
Crystal Symphony	1995	940	545	480	51,044	781

Cunard Line

24303 Town Center Dr., Ste. 200, Valencia, CA 91355-0908; ☎ *800-7CUNARD (800-728-6273);* www.cunard.com

> ✔ **Type of cruise:** Luxury, elegant, classic, romantic

> ✔ **Ship size/style:** Megaship ocean liner

The oldest name in the cruise biz, Cunard offered the first regularly scheduled service across the Atlantic way back in the 1840s, and today it's the only passenger line still doing so, aboard some of the few true ocean liners still going. A niche market catering to nostalgists and aviophobes, you ask? To a point, but what's wrong with that? In its public persona, Cunard is all about tradition, stressing the built-tough strength and history-minded opulence of its great ships and the old-fashioned British formality of its onboard experience.

For the past few decades, Cunard passengers have tended to be traditionalists as well — older, well-traveled folks who appreciate the line's history and slightly frumpled graciousness. On transatlantic voyages, passengers ceased being primarily British long ago (Americans are the line's top customers there), but with the huge launch of the huge *Queen Mary 2* (see Figure 12-2), Carnival Corp. signaled that Cunard was open for even more new business. That ship got so much press that it's now once again hip to go transatlantic by water instead of plane.

QM2 provides one of the most distinctive luxury experiences you can get, appealing to both romantic types and (surprisingly) families, especially on summer Atlantic crossings.

Queen Mary 2 (also known as *QM2*) replaced Cunard's legendary *Queen Elizabeth 2* (also known as *QE2*, the iconic name by which it's been known since its 1969 launch) on the line's transatlantic routes almost immediately after her launch. *QE2* now sails from a homeport in Southampton, UK, carrying primarily British passengers. A third queen, dubbed *Queen Victoria,* is currently under construction and set to debut in 2007. At 85,000 GRTs, she'll still be a substantial vessel, though nowhere near the mind-boggling size of the 151,400-ton *QM2*.

Sail Cunard to experience an inkling of how people traveled a century ago, with grand interiors and a sense of empirical exceptionalism — rule Britannia, Britannia rules the waves, and all that. Sail *QM2* to see the best built and probably most technologically advanced passenger ship in the world, to be the envy of your friends, or to just stand there and say, "Gee, it's big." Sail *QE2* for a real dose of history. Table 12-3 shows Cunard's itineraries and sample fares.

QM2's fares frequently include airfare deals. Transatlantic crossings, for example, come bundled with one-way return airfare, though we hear that deal may disappear in the future. Stay tuned.

Dining

Like *QE2, QM2* works on a vestigial multiclass system left over from the ocean liner days. Back then, first-class passengers could go their whole voyage and hardly see anyone booked in second-class or steerage. Today, however, the separation is only noticeable in a few spots on board. Essentially, cabin level determines where one dines: Passengers in the top suites dine in special restaurants, while everyone else dines in the main Britannia dining room (a gorgeous spot, far more grand than the suite guests' more quietly posh Queens Grill and Princess Grill) or in one of the alternative venues — such as Todd English, a branch of celebrity Boston chef English's Olives restaurant.

The two grill restaurants serve dinner in a single seating, while Brittania has early and late seatings. All three also serve breakfast and lunch in open seatings. Food sticks close to tradition, with entrees that may include roasted prime rib, grilled lobster with garden pea risotto, and pheasant with haggis and port wine sauce. Health-conscious dishes designed by Canyon Ranch Spa (which also runs *QM2*'s onboard spa) are available as a matter of course. For casual dining, *QM2*'s King's Court is an enormous buffet that's partitioned off at night to create three separate restaurants: a grill-type carvery, an Italian restaurant, and a pan-Asian restaurant. All are free, and reservations are recommended.

Activities and entertainment

QM2 boasts an impressive list of guest lecturers, including experts from Oxford University, *Architectural Digest, Gourmet* magazine, and other institutions and publications. Course listings for the Oxford University lecture program (presented on the transatlantic crossings) are available 90 days ahead of each sailing on the Cunard Web site. Passengers can also take advantage of the largest library at sea (most ship libraries are pretty pitiful, but truly, this one rocks), as well as a maritime history trail that snakes around the ship, an amazing spa operated by Canyon Ranch, a Monte Carlo–style casino, and an honest-to-God planetarium, with 3-D presentations created by New York's Museum of Natural History and the Smithsonian's National Air and Space Museum.

Table 12-3	Cunard Itineraries and Sample Fares
Ship/Fares (per person/day)	**Itineraries**
QE2 $233 inside; $279 outside; $2,893 suite	**6-night transatlantic:** Southampton, UK, to New York, NY, Jan*; **109-night world cruise:** Round-trip from New York, Jan–Apr (segments bookable in North America, Australia/ New Zealand, Asia, India, Europe); **3-, 5-, 7, 10-, 12-, 13-, 14-, 16-, and 18-night Europe:** Mediterranean, northern Europe, Channel Islands, and Canary Islands itineraries round-trip from Southampton, May–Oct and Dec; **28-night Caribbean/ Central America:** Round-trip from Southampton, Nov–Dec
QM2 $229 inside; $296 outside; $750 suite	**12-night Caribbean/Panama:** Round-trip from New York, NY, Jan; **38- and 36-night South American odyssey:** New York to Los Angeles, CA, Jan–Feb, and Los Angeles to New York, Mar–Apr, with segments of various lengths bookable along the route; **3-night Ensenada:** Round-trip from Los Angeles, Feb; **11-night Hawaii:** Round-trip from Los Angeles, Feb; **6-night transatlantic:** East- or westbound between New York and Southampton, UK, Apr–Nov*; **8-night transatlantic:** East- or westbound between New York and Hamburg, Germany, July–Aug; **12-night Mediterranean:** Round-trip from Southampton, June, July, and Sept; **4- and 5-night Canada/ New England:** Round-trip from New York, July and Sept; **12-night Canada/New England:** Round-trip from New York, Sept–Oct; **7-night southern and western Caribbean** (alternating weekly): Round-trip from Ft. Lauderdale, FL, Nov–Dec

* For 6-day transatlantic crossings, fares including one-way airfare.

Entertainment runs the gamut from plays featuring graduates of Britain's Royal Academy of Dramatic Arts to some pretty run-of-the-mill song-and-dance revues. There's also a variety of music, including jazz, classical, and dance music of the old-fashioned and new-fashioned kind (presented in the adjoining Queen's Ballroom and G32 disco).

For kids

Most luxury ships have little for kids, but *QM2* is a major exception to that rule, offering a program and facilities for kids as young as age 1. There's a nursery with ten crib/toddler-bed combos for napping tots, playrooms and an outdoor play area, activities for several different age groups, and a staff of real British nannies and activities counselors. The kids' center is open long hours, too (until midnight), so parents can take advantage of the ship's dining options in peace. There's even a special children's tea daily from 5 to 6 p.m. in the Chef's Galley.

(Photo: Cunard Line)

Figure 12-2: *Queen Mary 2*

Fleet facts

Launched to tremendous fanfare in early 2004, the **Queen Mary 2** was the first true ocean liner built since Cunard minted *QE2* back in 1969. What's that mean? It means strength, speed, and extraordinary sea-keeping abilities — all essential ingredients to maintaining a schedule on the sometimes brutal North Atlantic.

Inside, the ship is pretty spectacular, its public rooms impressive for both their range and quality. Even after being aboard six days on the Atlantic, you might still find spots you've never seen before. Our favorites? The classic deco-style Chart Room for drinks before dinner; the forward-facing Commodore Club with its clubby atmosphere; the grand Queen's Room ballroom on formal night; and the forward observation deck on deck 11, just below the bridge — probably the best spot aboard when sailing out of New York Harbor, *QM2*'s western terminus when sailing transatlantic. Other great spots? The spa and library, the elegant Veuve Clicquot champagne bar, the lively Golden Lion Pub, and the Winter Garden, a light, airy space designed to provide an outdoor garden feel on long transatlantic voyages.

As for *QE2,* she sails on as indomitably as ever, touching down seemingly everywhere. She's no kid, having sailed more than 5.3 million nautical miles and carried nearly 3 million passengers (as of her 36th birthday, in 2005), but she's a real grande dame, with some gorgeous public spaces mixed amid a charmingly old-fashioned, mazelike layout. Think more Anne Bancroft than Catherine Zeta-Jones. Table 12-4 shows current fleet specifications.

Table 12-4	Cunard Fleet Specifications					
Ship	*Entered Service*	*Passengers*	*Crew*	*Total Cabins*	*Tonnage*	*Length in Feet*
QE2	1969	1,740	1,000	931	70,327	963
QM2	2004	2,620	1,253	1,310	151,400	1,132

Radisson Seven Seas Cruises

600 Corporate Dr., Suite 410, Fort Lauderdale, FL 33334; ☎ **800-477-7500** *or 800-285-1835;* www.rssc.com

   ✔ **Type of cruise:** Luxury, gourmet, romantic

   ✔ **Ship size/style:** Midsize, modern, luxury ships

Radisson Seven Seas offers a cruise experience that's upscale but not uptight — homey and comfortable, with outstanding service, great cuisine, and itineraries that range the world, from the Alaska and the Caribbean to Tahiti and Antarctica. Honestly upscale but without pretense, it's the perfect cruise line for people who have sailed with mainstream or premium lines and are looking to step up.

The line appeals primarily to well-heeled passengers in their 50s and up, with a few younger passengers and honeymooners peppering the mix. Though the typical Radisson passenger has refined tastes, he or she also appreciates the line's less formal ambience, which is comfortably casual and laid-back during the day.

The line's ships are modern and midsized, with the twin *Seven Seas Mariner* (see Figure 12-3) and *Seven Seas Voyager* carrying 700 passengers apiece and *Seven Seas Navigator* carrying 490. Radisson also currently charters two ships, one sailing in Tahiti and the other on occasional Antarctica cruises.

Service is some of the best you can find in the cruise business. Restaurant waiters are gracious and professional, cabin stewardesses deft and unobtrusive, and room service fast and efficient. Bar staff often remembers your drink order after the first day. Like most of the other luxury lines, Radisson bundles gratuities into the cruise fare. Table 12-5 shows Radisson's itineraries and sample fares.

For all that it offers, Radisson's rates are often surprisingly low, with good early-booking discounts, two-for-one deals, and free or discounted airfare almost always available.

Dining

Radisson's cuisine is superb, complemented by complimentary red and white house wines. Main dining room and alternative restaurants operate on an open-seating basis — sit where you want, when you want (though the alternative restaurants require that you make reservations). In the main restaurants, meals are elaborate and elegant, with main entrees that may include dishes such as zucchini-wrapped chicken breast stuffed with olives and tomatoes, herb-crusted roast leg of lamb, and fresh fish.

Aboard *Seven Seas Mariner* and *Voyager,* passengers have the choice of three alternative restaurants: the 110-seat Signatures, directed by chefs

Table 12-5	Radisson Seven Seas Itineraries and Sample Fares
Ship/Fares (per person/day)	*Itineraries*
Paul Gauguin No inside cabins; $286 outside; $750 suite	**7-, 10-, 12-, 14-, and 17-night South Pacific:** Round-trip from Papeete, Tahiti, year-round
Seven Seas Mariner No inside cabins; $385 outside; $424 suite	**12-night South America:** Ft. Lauderdale, FL, to Manaus, Brazil, Jan; **17-night South America:** Manaus to Buenos Aires, Argentina, Jan; **20-night South America:** Buenos Aires to Lima, Peru, Feb; **13-night South America:** Lima to Ft. Lauderdale, Feb; **7-night eastern Caribbean:** Round-trip from Ft. Lauderdale, Mar; **9-night western Caribbean:** Round-trip from Ft. Lauderdale, Mar; **15-night Panama Canal:** Ft. Lauderdale to San Francisco, CA, Apr; **26-night Tahiti/ Hawaii:** Round-trip from San Francisco, Apr–May; **7-night Gulf of Alaska:** North- or southbound between Vancouver, BC, and Whittier/Anchorage, AK, May–Sept; **14-night North Pacific:** Whittier/Anchorage to Tokyo, Japan, Sept; **14-night Asia:** Tokyo to Hong Kong; Hong Kong to Singapore; Singapore to Sydney, Australia, Sept–Nov; **15-night Australia/New Zealand:** Sydney to Auckland, New Zealand, Nov; **18-night South Pacific:** Auckland to Los Angeles, CA, Nov; **10-night Mexican Riviera:** Round-trip from Los Angeles, Dec; **14-night Panama Canal:** Los Angeles to Ft. Lauderdale, Dec
Seven Seas Navigator No inside cabins; $372 outside; $469 suite	**10-night eastern and western Caribbean:** Round-trip from Ft. Lauderdale, FL, Jan; **4-, 5-, 6-, and 7-night eastern Caribbean:** Round-trip from San Juan, PR, Jan–Mar; **7-night western Caribbean:** Round-trip from Ft. Lauderdale, Mar; **11-night Bermuda/Colonial America:** Round-trip from Ft. Lauderdale, Apr; **7-night Mediterranean:** Madeira, Portugal, to Monte Carlo, Monaco; Monte Carlo to Rome, Italy; Athens, Greece, to Venice, Italy; Venice to Monte Carlo; Monte Carlo to Venice; Venice to Athens; Athens to Istanbul, Turkey; Istanbul to Athens; and Rome to Nice, France, Apr–May and Aug–Oct; **3-night Mediterranean:** Round-trip from Rome, May; **14-night western Mediterranean:** Monte Carlo to Copenhagen, Denmark, June; **7-night Baltics:** North- or southbound between Stockholm, Sweden, and Copenhagen, July; **10-night western Europe:** Dover, UK, to Monte Carlo, Aug; **7- and 10-night western Caribbean:** Round-trip from Ft. Lauderdale, Nov–Dec; **11-night eastern Caribbean:** Round-trip from Ft. Lauderdale, Nov–Dec

Ship/Fares (per person/day)	Itineraries
Seven Seas Voyager $351 suite	**108-night world cruise:** Los Angeles, CA, to Ft. Lauderdale, FL, Jan–Apr (segments in Australia/New Zealand, Asia, and Europe bookable separately); **6- and 7-night Mediterranean:** Madeira, Portugal, to Monte Carlo, Monaco; Monte Carlo to Rome, Italy; Rome to Venice, Italy; Venice to Rome; Rome to Monte Carlo; Rome to Athens, Greece; Athens to Rome; Monte Carlo to Athens; Athens to Monte Carlo, May and Sept–Oct; **10- night western Europe:** Monte Carlo to Dover, UK, June; London, UK, to Monte Carlo, Sept; **12-night Baltics:** Dover to Stockholm, Sweden, June; **7-night Baltics:** North- or southbound between Copenhagen, Denmark, and Stockholm, June–Aug; **11-night British Isles:** Copenhagen to London, Aug; **7-night eastern and western Caribbean** (alternating weekly): Round-trip from Ft. Lauderdale, Nov–Dec

from Paris's famed Le Cordon Bleu cooking school; Latitudes, serving pan-Asian "Indochine cuisine"; and La Veranda, serving Mediterranean and North African dishes in a casual setting. *Seven Seas Navigator*'s single alternative is Portofino, an indoor/outdoor Italian restaurant.

Activities and entertainment

As aboard almost all the luxury ships, entertainment and activities are limited and low-key, with passengers preferring to enjoy their vacation at their own pace. Offerings do include lectures by former diplomats, writers, anthropologists, and naturalists, often speaking on a topic relevant to the region you're sailing — for example, Colonial America on New England/Canada cruises. You can also take dance lessons; attend a wine tasting or art auction; play cards, bingo, or bridge (with instructors sailing on all cruises); or take a computer class (aboard *Mariner* and *Voyager*).

 The line also offers great spas, run by French company Carita of Paris and staffed by therapists and hairdressers imported from Parisian salons.

 As of mid-2005, Radisson has introduced a fleetwide program of science-related activities created by oceanographer Jean-Michel Cousteau. Cousteau himself presents talks, lectures, and shore excursions on select cruises; on others, experts from his Ocean Futures Society lead informal workshops and discussions on marine life and undersea habitats. Passengers may watch their dives via live TV uplinks. On other cruises, Radisson offers a series of cooking workshops led by chefs trained in the Le Cordon Bleu cooking method. The cost for the full workshop series is $395 per person.

Most evening entertainment is low-key, as aboard most luxury ships. You can choose from musical revues in the show lounges, music in other public rooms, and occasional performances from local entertainers who come aboard to perform. A headline entertainer (usually a soloist or comedian) sails with each cruise. Radisson also programs occasional themed sailings — a Doo-Wop cruise featuring The Platters, for example, or a "Spotlight on Classical Music" cruise.

For kids

Like the other luxury lines, Radisson, in general, isn't geared toward children, though summer Alaska and Bermuda sailings (and select holiday cruises) do offer a kids program for kids 6 to 17, divided into two age groups. On other cruises, an ad-hoc kids program is put together if enough kids are aboard to require it. Private babysitting may be arranged (for a fee) with off-duty crewmembers.

(Photo: Radisson Seven Seas Cruises)

Figure 12-3: *Seven Seas Mariner*

Fleet facts

The all-suite *Seven Seas Mariner* was the first vessel built by any line to offer a private balcony in every stateroom. She was also designed to be super-spacious, with a higher passenger-space ratio (the amount of interior space per passenger, mathematically speaking) than any cruise vessel besides Silversea's *Silver Shadow* and *Silver Whisper* — and she ain't that far behind them. Sister ship *Seven Seas Voyager* is very nearly as spacious, trading a few square feet for an improved layout of public rooms. Improved also are the stateroom bathrooms, which are among the roomiest and most comfortable on any cruise ship today. The same bathrooms actually debuted with Radisson aboard *Seven Seas Navigator.* Smaller than her two newer fleetmates, she has attractive public spaces and all-suite, all-outside accommodations, 90 percent of them with private balconies.

The small, beautifully appointed *Paul Gauguin* was built to sail around Tahiti year-round, and is under a charter contract to Radisson through January 2007. Radisson also charters an expedition ship called *Explorer II* (previously *Minerva*) for annual January sailings in Antarctica. Table 12-6 shows current fleet specifications.

Table 12-6	Radisson Seven Seas Fleet Specifications					
Ship	**Entered Service**	**Passengers**	**Crew**	**Total Cabins**	**Tonnage**	**Length in Feet**
Paul Gauguin	1998	320	211	160	19,200	513
Seven Seas Mariner	2001	700	447	350	50,000	675
Seven Seas Navigator	1999	490	324	245	33,000	560
Seven Seas Voyager	2003	700	447	350	46,000	670

Seabourn Cruise Line

6100 Blue Lagoon Dr., Suite 400, Miami, FL 33126; ☎ *800-929-9391;* www.seabourn.com

> ✔ **Type of cruise:** Gourmet, luxury, romantic

> ✔ **Ship size/style:** Small luxury ships

Calling itself The Yachts of Seabourn, this line makes the most of its ships' small and intimate size. Peers Silversea and Radisson may have newer ships, but they're larger. With 157 crewmembers to just 208 guests, service is very personal; staff members greet you by name from the moment you check in. They indulge guests with special little extras such as free mini-massages on deck and soothing Eucalyptus oil baths drawn in suites upon request.

The ships' small size also allows guests to mingle easily with each other and crew, and enjoy mellow pursuits such as trivia games and presentations by guest lecturers. The petite ships are able to visit less-touristed ports that larger ships may not be able to access, and the wealthy, well-traveled clientele likes that exclusivity. Many have traveled with Seabourn before, and they come back again and again for the excellent food, wine, and the overall genteel surroundings.

The line's roots are Norwegian: The captains are Norwegian, you may find your suite minibar stocked with bottles of Norwegian Ringnes pilsner, and there's no denying the ships' décor is very Scandinavian, with its cool, almost icy sea of pastels.

The cruise fare includes tips, wine and spirits, and one special shore excursion (such as a private visit to a museum after hours). Table 12-7 shows Seabourn's itineraries and sample fares.

Single travelers can get run-of-the-ship discounts, whereby Seabourn picks your cabin based on availability, and you save big bucks; reap 10 percent savings for combining two cruises; repeat passengers get

Table 12-7	Seabourn Itineraries and Sample Fares
Ship/Fares (per person/day)	*Itineraries*
Seabourn Legend No inside cabins; $357 outside; $591 suite	**14-night Panama Canal:** North- or southbound between Ft. Lauderdale, FL, and Caldera, Costa Rica, Jan–Mar and Nov–Dec; **7-night southern Caribbean:** Round-trip from St. Thomas, USVI, Mar–Apr; **5- and 7-night eastern Caribbean:** East- or westbound between Ft. Lauderdale and St. Thomas, Mar–Apr; **9-night Mediterranean:** Lisbon, Portugal, to Rome, Italy, May; **5-night Cote D'Azur:** Monte Carlo, Monaco, to Barcelona, Spain, May; **7-night Mediterranean:** Rome to Monte Carlo; Barcelona to Monte Carlo; Monte Carlo to Rome; and Monte Carlo to Barcelona, May–Oct; **14-night Mediterranean:** Round-trip from Monte Carlo, July; **7-night Cote D'Azur:** Monte Carlo to Barcelona, Aug and Oct; **8-night Spain/France:** Monte Carlo to Malaga, Spain, Oct
Seabourn Pride No inside cabins; $427 outside; $1,066 suite	**18-night South America:** Ft. Lauderdale, FL, to Valparaiso, Chile, and Valparaiso to Buenos Aires, Argentina, Jan–Feb; **7-night South America:** Buenos Aires to Rio de Janeiro, Brazil, Feb; **13-night Brazil:** Rio de Janeiro to Manaus, Brazil, Feb; **16-night Amazon/Caribbean:** Manaus to Ft. Lauderdale, FL, Feb–Mar; **12-night Spain/Morocco:** Round-trip from Lisbon, Portugal, Mar; **9-night Spain/Morocco:** Lisbon to Monte Carlo, Monaco, Apr; **14- and 18-night Mediterranean:** Monte Carlo to Istanbul, Turkey, and Istanbul to Lisbon, Apr–May; **14-night "Rivers of western Europe":** Lisbon to London, UK, May; **14-night Norway/North Cape:** London to Copenhagen, Denmark, June; **12-night Baltics:** Round-trip from Copenhagen, June–Aug; **9-night Norwegian fjords:** Round-trip from Copenhagen, June–July; **15-night Norwegian fjords/British Isles:** Copenhagen to London, Aug; **8-night Canada/New England:** North- or southbound between Gloucester, MA, and Quebec City, QB, Oct; **12-night U.S. East Coast:** Gloucester to Nassau, Bahamas, Oct; **7-night eastern Caribbean:** Barbados to Ft. Lauderdale, Nov–Dec; **7-night southern Caribbean:** Round-trip from Barbados, Nov–Dec

Ship/Fares (per person/day)	Itineraries
Seabourn Spirit No inside cabins; $258 outside; $525 suite	**17-night Spice Islands/Great Barrier Reef:** Hong Kong to Cairns, Australia, Jan; Cairns to Singapore, Mar; **14-night Australia/New Zealand:** Cairns to Christchurch, New Zealand, Jan; **14-night New Zealand/Fiji:** North- or south bound between Christchurch and Lautoka, Fiji, Feb; **14-night Australia/New Zealand:** Auckland, New Zealand, to Cairns, Mar; **16-night India/Arabian Sea:** Singapore to Dubai, Apr; **12-night Egypt:** Dubai to Alexandria, Egypt, Apr; **12-night Greek Isles/Turkey:** Alexandria to Rome, Italy, May; **7-night Mediterranean/Aegean/Adriatic:** Rome to Athens, Greece; Athens to Istanbul, Turkey; Istanbul to Venice, Italy; and Venice to Rome, May–Nov; **14-night Black Sea:** Istanbul to Venice, July; **16-night Red Sea/Africa:** Alexandria to Mombasa, Kenya, Nov; **16-night Africa/Seychelles:** Mombasa to Singapore, Nov; **14-night Thailand/Vietnam:** North- or southbound between Singapore and Hong Kong, Dec

5 percent discounts if booking your next cruise on board your current one; and rack up 140 days of sailing with Seabourn and get a free cruise!

Dining

Celebrity restaurateur Charlie Palmer, of New York's Aureole fame, is behind the ships' menus, with the ships' chefs training in Palmer's shoreside restaurants. Needless to say, cuisine in each ship's two restaurants is a highlight of a Seabourn cruise. Even the breakfast buffets are exceptional. The best setting may be the outside decks of the Veranda Café, with the churning wake shushing just below you. This venue also has indoor seating, and breakfast and lunch are offered in a combination of buffet and table-service. Every evening, a theme menu is offered. Reservations are required and don't forget to request a table outdoors if that's your desire.

The ships have one main dining room with open seating for all meals. This is the more formal of each ship's two dining venues and service is as good as it gets on the high seas: attentive, unobtrusive, and professional.

Aside from a vegetarian selection and a lighter choice on all menus, if you've got ideas of your own, just ask. If the chef has the ingredients on board, your wishes will be met. On formal nights in the Restaurant, tuxes and sequins are the uniform of choice, while you can get away with a jacket (and no tie) in the Veranda Café.

One night on each warm-weather itinerary there is an over-the-top buffet dinner served out on deck by the pool and a silver-service beach barbecue in remote ports — we're talking china and linen, and, of course, champagne and caviar. The 24-hour room service includes the option of ordering off the restaurant menus during normal lunch or dinner hours. Feeling indulgent? Jumbo shrimp and caviar can be ordered poolside, or anywhere else for that matter, at no charge.

Activities and entertainment

The Seabourn ships are sociable because of their small size, but don't offer too much in the way of organized activities and entertainment. That's how the guests like it. By day, there are trivia contests, galley tours, computer classes, wine tastings, and the ever-popular Liar's Club.

At least one and often two guest lecturers per cruise discuss upcoming ports as well as other random topics. Noted chefs, scientists, historians, authors, or statesmen may be aboard, or maybe a wine connoisseur, composer, anthropologist, TV director, or professor, presenting lectures and mingling with guests. From time to time, the line brings aboard celebrities; past guests have included actor Alan Arkin, journalist Bernard Kalb, *Jeopardy* host Alex Trebek, and author Paul Theroux.

Each ship has two roomy entertainment lounges where a cabaret singer, solo instrumentalist, quartet, or maybe a comedian performs. Before dinner, a pianist plays and sings for guests enjoying cocktails in The Club; adjacent is the tiny casino with a handful of card tables and slots.

The *Seabourn Legend* (see Figure 12-4), *Pride,* and *Spirit* each have a teak-decked platform hidden in their hulls that, when lowered, provides a launching point for water sports. Sunfish sailboats, kayaks, snorkeling gear, high-speed banana boats, and water skis are available for use.

For kids

These ships are geared to adults and there are no special programs for kids (bring your nanny). In a pinch, you may be able to negotiate private in-suite babysitting with an off-duty crewmember.

(Photo: Seabourn Cruise Line)

Figure 12-4: *Seabourn Legend*

Fleet facts

All the cabins on the **Legend, Pride,** and **Spirit** are suites with either 5-foot-wide picture windows or sliding glass doors with railings offering sea views and breezes (only the top six Owner's Suites have proper balconies). All suites also have new Bose Wave radio/CD players (a library of music and book CDs is available on board) and flat-panel TVs and DVD players (to be added to the suites by early 2006). Each also has a complimentary bar set-up, walk-in closet, and marble bathroom.

Though not exactly spring chickens in the youth-obsessed cruise industry, Seabourn has kept up appearances with the occasional nip and tuck. Sliding glass doors were added to 36 suites on each ship a few years back, for example, and the gyms were increased in size in 2003 to make room for classes such as yoga and Pilates. Table 12-8 shows current fleet specifications.

Table 12-8	Seabourn Fleet Specifications					
Ship	*Entered Service*	*Passengers*	*Crew*	*Total Cabins*	*Tonnage*	*Length in Feet*
Seabourn Legend	1992	208	157	100	10,000	439
Seabourn Pride	1988	208	157	100	10,000	439
Seabourn Spirit	1989	208	157	100	10,000	439

SeaDream Yacht Club

2601 South Bayshore Dr., Penthouse 1B, Coconut Grove, FL 33133; ☎ **800-707-4911**; www.seadreamyachtclub.com

> ✔ **Type of Cruise:** Luxury (country club chic), romantic

> ✔ **Ship size/style:** Small, yacht-like

Size does matter. And in the case of the two ships from SeaDream Yacht Club, *SeaDream I* and *SeaDream II* (shown in Figure 12-5), smaller is decidedly better. These ships are exclusive and yachty — you'll find lots of hardwood floors, Oriental carpets, and exotic floral arrangements — and also offer some cool stuff to do for those active 40- to 60-somethings attracted to SeaDream's version of the good life, which promises "an extraordinary, ultra-luxury, mega-yachting experience not currently available." With each ship carrying 110 guests in 55 suites (with 89 crewmembers at your beck and call), these small ships offer a really intimate, personalized trip. Excellent service and fine dining are the big draws, along with a "yacht casual" dress code (no jackets are required, though some wear them). Table 12-9 shows SeaDream's itineraries and sample fares.

At only 344 feet long, these twins can slip into ports that other ships couldn't even hope to, including docking curbside in places such as Monte Carlo. The ships were built in the 1980s, and the space ratio is

Table 12-9	SeaDream Itineraries and Sample Fares
Ship/Fares **(per person/day)**	**Itineraries**
SeaDream I No inside cabins; $377 outside; $1,131 suite	**4-, 6-, 7-, and 9-night eastern and southern Caribbean:** Round-trip from San Juan, PR, and between San Juan and St. Thomas, USVI, St. Thomas and St. Martin, and St. Martin and San Juan, Jan–Apr; **3-night Mediterranean:** Malaga, Spain, to Nice, France, May; **4-night Mediterranean:** Round-trip from Nice, May; **7-night Mediterranean:** Round-trip from Nice; round-trip from Venice, Italy; Nice to Monte Carlo, Monaco; Venice to Athens, Greece; Athens to Venice; Athens to Istanbul, Turkey; Istanbul to Athens; Venice to Dubrovnik, Croatia; Dubrovnik to Venice; Dubrovnik to Athens; Athens to Antalya, Turkey; Alexandria, Egypt, to Athens; Athens to Naples, Italy; Athens to Palma de Mallorca, Spain; and Palma to Seville, Spain, June–Nov; **3-, 6-, and 7-night eastern/southern Caribbean:** Round-trip from St. Thomas, Nov–Dec
SeaDream II No inside cabins; $377 outside; $1,138 suite	**4-, 6-, 7-, and 9-night eastern/southern Caribbean:** Round-trip from St. Thomas, USVI, Barbados, and Antigua, and between West Palm Beach, FL, and St. Thomas, St. Thomas and Barbados, St. Thomas and St. Martin, and Antigua and Barbados, Jan–Apr; **7-night Mediterranean:** Madeira, Portugal, to Barcelona, Spain; Nice, France, to Rome, Italy; round-trip from Rome; Rome to Athens, Greece; Athens to Genoa, Italy; Monte Carlo, Monaco, to Nice; Rome to Barcelona; round-trip from Barcelona; Barcelona to Seville, Spain; Seville to Tenerife, Canary Islands, Apr–Nov; **6-, 7-, and 8-night eastern/southern Caribbean:** Round-trip from San Juan, PR, Barbados, or St. Thomas, or between San Juan and Barbados or Barbados and St. Thomas, Nov–Dec

smallish by today's standards. Cruisers don't have tons of inside public space, but SeaDream refitted the ships to provide plenty of excellent outside space, with such touches as queen-size Sun Beds.

SeaDream offers occasional special promotions, such as save 25 percent when booking two or three consecutive sailings. They also do "Sail with Friends" promotions, where you buy four staterooms and get a fifth one free, or you buy two to four cabins and get a percentage off each one.

Dining

The vibe on board may be casual and carefree, but the food and wine are seriously good. Open-seating dining is offered from 7:30 to 10 p.m. in the main restaurant on deck 2, though it's not always easy to snag a table for two. For something more interesting, you can venture "out" for dinner by requesting a spot in advance at one of several private alcoves on deck 6, or even on the bridge. The partially covered, open-sided Topside Restaurant on deck 5 serves breakfast and lunch daily, with guests choosing from a buffet or menu. Menus include a healthy option as well as a vegetarian entree, and the galley will prepare special requests provided that the ingredients are on board.

Lavish beach barbecues, called the Caviar and Champagne Splash, are offered on Jost Van Dyke and Virgin Gorda. Sit back and enjoy the show as 20-something European stewards in Hawaiian shirts hop into the surf from a zodiac boat carrying a life preserver that doubles as a floating serving tray for an open tin of sevruga Malossol caviar. Two stewards perform ceremonial running front flips into the surf with champagne bottles in hand, and then pop off the corks in unison. Ta daaaaa! This, plus grilled lobster tails and barbecued spare ribs on the beach, and lots more. The feast is served under umbrellas at tables set with proper china and hotel silver brought ashore by the staff.

Aside from 24-hour room service, there are sandwiches and snacks at the Topside restaurant throughout the day and/or poolside. Rates include unlimited spirits, wine and soft drinks, though, oddly, cabin minifridges are stocked only with complimentary beer and soft drinks.

Activities and entertainment

Like real yachts, you are meant to spend your SeaDream days up on the open decks or exploring port. Itineraries are designed so that ships stay overnight in three-quarters of the ports they visit (such as St. Barts and St. Tropez). SeaDream's rationale? "There's no sense in leaving a port at 5 if it doesn't start really happening till 11." And the ship's crew is more than happy to get in on the action. Crewmembers, and sometimes even the captain, lead free personalized excursions in port. Join the captain on a kayaking or snorkeling jaunt to a quiet Virgin Gorda cove, meet up with the chef to scout for local produce, or follow the bartender for a night out to a local watering hole.

By day, most people who remain aboard are tanning or canoodling on a cushy Sun Bed poolside, drink in hand — the setting is totally romantic. Some spend time in the gym or Asian-influence spa. There's also a small library, and staterooms keep couch potatoes content with DVD and CD players, flat-screen TVs, and Internet accessibility (which you can also find in the library).

Tunes are served up nightly on a white glass-topped Yamaha in the piano bar. Several nights a week in the main salon, a cabaret singer with digitized accompaniment keeps things hopping (relatively) for listeners and dancers. On a few cruises in the Caribbean, local bands are brought on for the night. And for private tunes, you can borrow an MP3 player loaded with music from the reception desk.

Some guests have a nightly date with the small casino on deck 4, while many others prefer to hang out at the Top of the Yacht Bar for before- and after-dinner drinks. On one evening during each cruise, a screen is set up on deck for a movie under the stars, which passengers can view from poolside (or even from the pool).

 The ships carry aboard sea kayaks, Sunfish, and WaveRunners that can be accessed from each ship's watersports marina when docked in calm seas. There are also mountain bikes, a golf simulator, and Segway Human Transporters (they're upright two-wheel *Jetsons*-like scooters that you can use in port for $49 an hour).

For kids

Like the other small luxury ships, these are not geared to kids. There are no babysitting services or child-related activities (if you've got young kids and can't resist trying SeaDream, bring a nanny, like Heidi did). Teens, on the other hand, may enjoy the cruises' emphasis on water-sports and unstructured activities.

(Photo: SeaDream Yacht Club)

Figure 12-5: *SeaDream II*

Fleet facts

Standard cabins on the **SeaDream I** and **II** measure 195 square feet, just a tad larger than Carnival's standard cabins (though, of course, much more plush). Sixteen are convertible to a double-sized room — called a Commodore Club Stateroom — by booking two connecting rooms (essentially creating a suite with two bathrooms and a living room). At 490 square feet, the one Owner's Suite is extremely luxurious. None of the staterooms have private balconies, though all have ocean views and were refurbished a few years back, offering luxurious Belgian linen, plus tech stuff such as CD and DVD players, and a flat-screen TV with Internet capability. The bathrooms are stocked with Bulgari toiletries. Rates include all spirits, wine, tips, and some shore excursions. Table 12-10 shows current fleet specifications.

Table 12-10	SeaDream Fleet Specifications					
Ship	Entered Service	Passengers	Crew	Total Cabins	Tonnage	Length in Feet
SeaDream I	1984	110	89	55	4,260	344
SeaDream II	1985	110	89	55	4,260	344

Silversea Cruises

110 E. Broward Blvd., Fort Lauderdale, FL 33301; ☎ **800-722-9055;** www.silversea.com

▮ ✔ **Type of cruise:** Gourmet, luxury, romantic

▮ ✔ **Ship size/style:** Modern, smallish luxury ships

The champagne — Philipponnat Royale Reserve — is flowing on Silversea's four ships, and the suites' marble bathrooms are stocked with Italian Acqua di Parma bath products. Tables are set with Christofle silver and Schott-Zwiesel crystal, and beds are made up with fine Irish bed linens by Hilden and soft down pillows. Need we go on? Fine-tuned and genteel, a Silversea cruise aims to please the most discerning and well-traveled cruise lovers in the world. The food and service are the best at sea, and the ships' Italian-style décor is warm and inviting. No expense was spared in their design.

A most noteworthy program is Silversea's new and unique Personalized Voyages, which allows passengers to create their own itineraries and get on and off at select ports (you pay a daily rate, with a 5-night minimum stay required). Table 12-11 shows Silversea's itineraries and sample fares.

If you pay in full at least six months in advance, you get 5 percent off; repeat cruisers can save 5 to 10 percent on select cruises, combinable with other discounts; and there are often special deals for singles.

Dining

If you're a foodie and a ship lover, a Silversea cruise is a must. Well prepared and presented, the creative chefs continually come up with great dishes in each ship's three restaurants. Each has a formal open-seating venue and two more casual options; most evenings, all three venues are open for dinner. The main dining rooms are elegant affairs with live music and small dance floors, but the line really shines in the Terrace Cafe, one of the ships' two reservations-required alternative dinner restaurants. Fixed-themed menus may include a Provence night, which starts with foie gras carpaccio and smoked duck Margret, and leads to five more courses, not counting the petit fours at the very end. By day, the indoor/outdoor Terrace Cafe is the ships' casual spot for bountiful

Table 12-11	Silversea Itineraries and Sample Fares
Ship/Fares (per person/day)	*Itineraries*
Silver Cloud No inside cabins; $451 outside; $556 suite	**7-, 8-, 9-, 11-, 12-, 14-, 15-, and 16-night South America:** Round-trip from Buenos Aires, Argentina; Buenos Aires to Valparaiso, Chile; Valparaiso to Buenos Aires; Valparaiso to Ushuaia, Argentina; Ushuaia to Buenos Aires; Buenos Aires to Rio de Janeiro, Brazil; and Rio de Janeiro to Barbados, Jan–Mar; **7-, 10-, and 12-night Mediterranean:** Lisbon, Portugal, to Genoa, Italy; Genoa to Barcelona, Spain; Lisbon to Monte Carlo, Monaco; Monte Carlo to Rome, Italy; and Rome to Alexandria, Egypt, May and Oct; **9-, 10-, 11-, 12-, and 15-night northern Europe:** Barcelona, Spain, to London, UK; London to Stockholm, Sweden; round-trip from Copenhagen, Denmark; Copenhagen to London; Stockholm to London; and London to Lisbon, May–June and Aug–Sept; **7-night northern Europe:** North- or southbound between Stockholm and Copenhagen, June–Sept; **9-night Mediterranean/Middle East/North Africa:** Alexandria to Port Said, Egypt, Nov; **8-, 9-, 11-, and 14-night Africa/Indian Ocean:** Port Said, Egypt, to Dubai; round-trip from Dubai; Dubai to Mumbai, India; Mumbai to Singapore, Nov–Dec; **16-night Southeast Asia/Australia:** Singapore to Sydney, Australia, Dec
Silver Shadow No inside cabins; $458 outside; $564 suite	**13- and 15-night Australia/New Zealand:** Auckland, New Zealand, to Sydney, Australia, and Sydney to Fremantle, Australia, Jan; **14-night Southeast Asia/Australia:** Fremantle to Singapore, Feb; **8-, 9-, 10-, and 14-night Asia:** Singapore to Hong Kong; Hong Kong to Bangkok, Thailand; Bangkok to Singapore; and Hong Kong to Tokyo, Japan, Feb–May; **14-night North Pacific:** Tokyo to Anchorage, AK, May; **10-night Gulf of Alaska:** Anchorage to Vancouver, BC, June; **9-, 10-, and 12-night Alaska Inside Passage:** Between Vancouver and Seattle, WA; round-trip from Seattle; and round-trip from San Francisco, CA; June–Aug; **9- and 12-night Pacific Coast:** San Francisco to Vancouver (Aug), and Vancouver to Los Angeles, CA (Sept); **9-night Mexican Riviera:** Round-trip from Los Angeles, Sept; **17-night Panama Canal:** Los Angeles to Miami, FL, Sept; **7-, 9-, and 14-night eastern/southern Caribbean:** Miami to Barbados; round-trip from Barbados; Barbados to San Juan, PR; San Juan to Ft. Lauderdale, FL; Ft. Lauderdale to Barbados; Barbados to Ft. Lauderdale; and round-trip from Ft. Lauderdale, Oct–Dec; **12-night western Caribbean/Central America:** Round-trip from Ft. Lauderdale, Nov

Ship/Fares (per person/day)	Itineraries
Silver Whisper No inside cabins; $261 outside; $322 suite	**7- and 9-night eastern/southern Caribbean:** Ft. Lauderdale, FL, to Barbados; Barbados to Ft. Lauderdale; Ft. Lauderdale to Antigua; round-trip from Antigua; and Antigua to Ft. Lauderdale, Jan–Feb; **4-night southern Caribbean:** Barbados to Barbados, Jan; **15-night Panama Canal:** Ft. Lauderdale, to San Diego, CA, Feb; **10-night Mexican Riviera/Central America:** San Diego to Puerto Caldera, Costa Rica, Mar; **10-night Central America/southern Caribbean:** Puerto Caldera to San Juan, PR, Mar; **4-night eastern Caribbean:** Round-trip from San Juan, Mar–Apr; **7-night eastern Caribbean:** Round-trip from San Juan, Apr; **7-, 10-, and 11-night Mediterranean:** Las Palmas, Spain, to Barcelona, Spain; Barcelona to Nice, France; Nice to Rome, Italy; Rome to Venice, Italy; Venice to Athens, Greece; Athens to Venice; Venice to Rome; Rome to Barcelona; Barcelona to Monte Carlo, Monaco; and Barcelona to Villefranche, France, May–July and Sept; **11- and 12-night northern Europe:** Dover, UK, to Copenhagen, Denmark, and Monte Carlo to Dover, July; **7-night northern Europe:** North- or southbound between Copenhagen and Stockholm, Sweden, Aug; **9- and 14-night northern Europe:** Amsterdam, Netherlands, to Barcelona, and Copenhagen to Amsterdam, Sept; **12-night Mediterranean/North Africa:** Villefranche to Port Said, Egypt, Oct; **14- and 15-night Africa/ Indian Ocean:** Dubai to Singapore and Port Said to Dubai, Oct–Nov; **12-night Asia:** Singapore to Hong Kong; Hong Kong to Bangkok, Thailand; and Bangkok to Singapore, Nov–Dec; **14-night Southeast Asia:** Round-trip from Singapore, Dec
Silver Wind No inside cabins; $368 outside; $748 suite	**7-night South America:** Ushuaia, Argentina, to Valparaiso, Chile, Jan; **8-, 9-, 10-, and 14-night Africa/ Indian Ocean:** Cape Town, South Africa, to Port Louis, Mauritius; Port Louis to Mombasa, Kenya; Mombasa to Dubai; round-trip from Dubai; and Dubai to Port Said, Egypt, Jan–Feb; **7-night Mediterranean:** Barcelona, Spain, to Rome, Italy; Rome to Venice, Italy; Venice to Rome; Barcelona to Rome; Rome to Barcelona; Barcelona to Genoa, Italy; Athens, Greece, to Rome; and Rome to Monte Carlo, Monaco, Apr, June–Aug, and Oct; **9-night Mediterranean:** Las Palmas, Spain, to Lisbon, Portugal; Venice to Monte Carlo, Monaco; Istanbul, Turkey, to Venice; Istanbul to Athens; Monte Carlo to Lisbon; and Lisbon to Las Palmas, Mar, May, July, Oct–Nov; **10-, 12-, and 15-night Mediterranean:** Lisbon to Barcelona; Monte Carlo to Villefranche, France; Athens to Barcelona; Genoa to Venice; Athens to Lisbon; Villefranche to Venice; and Rome to Istanbul, Mar–Sept; **8-, 9-, 10-, and 16-night South America:** Rio de Janeiro, Brazil, to Buenos Aires, Argentina: round-trip from Buenos Aires; Buenos Aires to Valparaiso, Chile; and Buenos Aires to Ushuaia, Argentina, Nov–Dec

buffet breakfasts and lunches. All restaurants have plenty of tables for two, though in the main dining room, you may have to wait for one.

The other alternative venue is a new Relais & Chateaux (a guide that rates the top restaurants and hotels around the world) venture overseen by world-famous chef Joachim Koerper. Called Saletta on *Wind* and *Cloud* and Le Champagne on *Shadow* and *Whisper,* a fixed menu is offered and dining here is included in the cruise price — only the vintage wines are added to the bill. Intimate and elegant dining spaces, they're perfect for private dinner parties.

The wine list in the dining room is superb, with several complimentary wines suggested at each meal from more than 40 choices. You can also purchase one of the wines not included in the complimentary list — a $745 1990 Château Margaux, anyone?

Once per cruise, passengers are invited into the galley for the traditional galley brunch. Plus, poolside you can stay in your suit and nosh on burgers, sandwiches, and salads. The line's 24-hour room-service menu includes such decadent choices as caviar and jumbo shrimp cocktail. You can also order off The Restaurant's menu during its dinnertime hours and have your meal served in your suite course-by-course.

Activities and entertainment

After a lovely day touring, say, Singapore or Stockholm, guests dress for dinner and enjoy low-key socializing over cocktails in the piano bar. For something a bit more razzmatazz, you can find casinos on each, plus attractive two-level show lounges with small-scale song-and-dance revues and performances by classical musicians and other artists.

By day, you can enjoy cruise standards such as trivia games, card tournaments, golf putting/driving (there are special golf cruises with PGA pros on the *Shadow* and *Whisper*), wine-tasting seminars, and stretch and aerobics classes. Or, you can feed your brain and take in one of Silversea's impressive enrichment lectures. At least one guest speaker is featured on every sailing. They include guest lecturers from a wide range of disciplines, including the likes of Fred McLaren, a retired Navy captain and professor, who does a slide show and talk on his adventures diving 12,500 feet down in a Russian MIR submersible to explore the remains of the *Titanic*. Other lecturers include Lynn Sherr, ABC News correspondent and author; *The New Yorker* cartoonist Bruce McCall; and Brian Jones, who together with his Swiss colleague Bertrand Piccard, pulled off one of the most daring feats in aviation history — the first circumnavigation of the earth in a hot air balloon.

The line's culinary theme cruises (there were four in 2005), in partnership with Relais & Châteaux, are hosted by Relais Gourmands chefs and feature demos and tastings in the ships' new Viking Cooking Schools, which include Viking cooking stations so that guests can cook along with the guest chefs. There are also a number of theme cruises hosted by famous vintners.

The ships' Balinese-inspired Mandara spa beckons with its flower-strewn copper foot bowls, warm massage rocks, and other Asian-inspired treatments. To avoid waiting in line to experience it, you can book your treatments online before your cruise.

For kids

As you may expect, these are not kid-centric ships in any way, shape, or form. There are no organized activities or playrooms for kids, though you may be able to arrange in-cabin babysitting during evenings if a crewmember is available. If your kids are young, though, do yourself a favor (and everyone else's) and bring a nanny.

(Photo: Silversea Cruises)

Figure 12-6: *Silver Whisper*

Fleet facts

The appealing all-suite cabins on all four Silversea ships have walk-in closets and marble bathrooms, and most have balconies. At 285 square feet, the standard suites are slightly bigger on the newer **Whisper** (see Figure 12-6) and **Shadow** than on the **Cloud** and **Wind** (248 square feet), and their bathrooms are among the best at sea, with double sinks, separate long tub and shower, and yummy Acqua di Parma bath products. The biggest suites are apartment-sized and come with features such as three bathrooms and two balconies. The top suites also enjoy butler service, plasma-screen TVs, Bang & Olufsen or Nakamichi 3 CD stereo systems, afternoon canapés, and free laundry service. Fares include all wines, spirits, champagne, stocked minibar, tips, free shuttles from ports to city centers, and on select cruises, a special shore-side cultural event. Table 12-12 shows current fleet specifications.

Table 12-12	Silversea Fleet Specifications					
Ship	*Entered Service*	*Passengers*	*Crew*	*Total Cabins*	*Tonnage*	*Length in Feet*
Silver Cloud	1994	296	212	148	16,800	514
Silver Shadow	2000	382	295	194	28,258	610
Silver Whisper	2001	382	295	194	28,258	610
Silver Wind	1995	296	212	148	16,800	514

Chapter 13

Small and Sailing Ships

In This Chapter
▶ Reading the charts on alternative cruising experiences
▶ Introducing the major small ships and sailing ships

*O*h, woe is you. You have a hankering to travel by sea, but you've read over the preceding couple of chapters and found yourself thinking, "Well, that seems like it would really suck." The megaships sound too Vegas for you (or Cancun, or Miami, or any other high-octane resort), and the luxury ships sound too hoity-toity tea-at-three.

Well, you've come to the right place. The ships in this chapter are none of that. The smallest ships of those we review in Chapter 11 carry 342 passengers, the biggest ship in this chapter carries only 436 — and the smallest carries (get this) 6. That, all by itself, means you get a completely different cruise experience with these ships — more personal, more flexible, and more low-key.

 The downside is that because most small and sailing ships carry few passengers and operate in popular niche markets, they don't play the same constant discounting game as the big lines. Often, the prices they list in their brochures are exactly what you end up paying — and those prices are almost always higher than the mainstream lines to begin with.

 You can find a few bargains among cruises on these ships. Most small-ship lines offer some kind of early-booking discounts, and sometimes offer deals on specific sailings. Some lines (especially the sailing-ship lines) offer very attractive rates and frequent deals. Lastly, remember to think in terms of the big money picture when weighing the affordability of these lines: In contrast to most megaship experiences, where you end up spending hundreds extra on shore excursions and extra-cost onboard attractions, on small ships you often visit places you can explore on your own, or where excursions are included.

What Makes the Small Ships Tick

In a word, place — a sense of place, the idea that you're not just skimming like a rock on water from island to island, collecting a few trinkets along the way but never really getting a feel for what you're seeing. On a small ship you're down near the waterline, on a vessel small enough that it can stop for an hour at a small fishing village, or sail up canals and rivers to historic small towns, or pull up along a coastline to watch a mama bear and her cubs.

For the most part, activities center around the destination, too, whether they involve hearing lectures about the region's history and culture or just standing on deck with the ship's resident naturalists, scanning for whales or rare birds. The larger the vessel, the more likely it is to program occasional other activities as well, such as exercise classes, food-preparation demonstrations, or watersports — the latter sometimes offered right from the docked ship, via a floating sports platform. Small ships often include some or all excursions in their rates, too — whether that's a visit to an Eskimo village in northern Alaska or a stop at a beach in the Virgin Islands for barbecue and games.

Meals are usually served in a single dining room, though a few of the larger small ships also have a small buffet or other secondary option. Everyone on board is usually able to dine together, and there's never such a thing as assigned seats on a small ship — it's always open-seating. Dress is always casual: no dress codes here, and hardly anybody ever does more than a sport jacket or nice dress, even for the captain's cocktail party. Service is generally friendly and casual, with staff often covering several jobs: cabin steward in the morning, waiter by night, and luggage-handler at the beginning and end of the trip. End-of-voyage tipping is usually done on a pooled basis: You just leave some cash in an envelope, and the crew splits it between them after you're gone.

After-dinner entertainment is limited, usually consisting of nothing more than an ad hoc crew talent show or maybe a musician or two. Some ships also bring aboard local musicians and dancers when they stay late in port, and others may use the after-dinner hour for an informal lecture or to talk about the next day's port or sailing region.

Because small ships are, by definition, small, your cabin probably won't be overly spacious. Some small ships do offer suites or deluxe cabins if you have a yen for yardage (and the bucks to pay for it), but expect little variation among cabins on any of these ships. Expect little in the way of amenities, too: Many small ships don't have TVs in the cabins, for example, and bathrooms are usually very small.

A few things to consider about the small-ship experience:

- ✔ Few small ships have stabilizers, so things may get bumpy if you're sailing in rough open water. On the other hand, many small ships stick to protected coastal waters and bays, so open-water sailing may not be an issue on your itinerary.

- ✔ Very few small ships have elevators, so they aren't a good option if you have mobility problems.

✔ With few exceptions, none of the small-ship lines offers room service. Those that do include Windstar's ships, Delta Queen's ships (limited breakfast menu only), American West's ships (breakfast and sometimes dinner for suite passengers only), and Star Clipper's *Royal Clipper* (suite guests only).

✔ No small ships are really geared toward children, though a few do offer special family-oriented sailings, and one (Windjammer Barefoot) offers a children's program on some sailings.

✔ Most small ships don't carry a medical staff on board when sailing coastal or river itineraries. Instead, any passenger who becomes seriously ill or injured is evacuated quickly to a medical facility on shore. Doctors are usually carried on open-sea voyages.

Bear in mind that small-ship lines often measure their ships' gross register tonnage or GRTs (a measure of internal space, not actual weight) differently than the large lines. There's not even a definite standard within the small-ship market, so the best way to compare ship sizes is to just look at the number of passengers on board.

American Canadian Caribbean Line

461 Water St., Warren, RI 02885; ☎ *800-556-7450;* www.accl-smallships.com

✔ **Type of cruise:** Adventure/educational, gourmet

✔ **Ship size/style:** Small, luxurious yachts

No-frills and offbeat, this family-owned New England line attracts super casual, L.L.Bean types looking to explore new places. The down-to-earth older crowd appreciates ACCL's lack of glitz and gimmicks, as well as unpretentious features such as a BYOB policy.

All told, American Canadian Caribbean is a delightfully rare find. It's one of the few lines that designs, builds, maintains, and markets its own ships. If you sail this line, you're guaranteed an unusual, "what you see is what you get" experience: friendly, homespun, and visiting some places few other ships go. Each vessel's unusually shallow 6½-foot draft combines with other patented innovations to allow it to sail in narrow, shallow waterways and nudge directly up onto pristine, dockless shores, disembarking passengers via a ramp that extends from the bow.

With an innovative, exploratory design, the extremely informal small ships won't win any awards for décor (they are, in fact, about the most bare-bones vessels you can find in terms of amenities, service, and meals), but that's not what they're all about. Instead, this is a line that gets passengers close to the real life of the regions it visits, whether you want to explore historic American towns and check out fall foliage along the Erie Canal, visit tiny islands such as Bequia in the Caribbean, or play connect the dots among New England's islands. Table 13-1 shows ACCL itineraries and sample ACCL fares.

Passengers sailing solo can take advantage of a "Willing to Share" program, in which the line pairs you with another solo passenger, thus avoiding the 175 percent rate you'd pay if booking a cabin just for yourself. If another solo is not aboard, you get the cabin for the cheaper rate anyway. On the other side of the spectrum, when three passengers share one of the ships' tiny cabins, each gets a 15 percent discount.

Dining

Basic, all-American food is well prepared, folksy, presented by friendly down-home crew, and as far away from fancy as you can get. Meals are served promptly at 8 a.m., noon, and 6 p.m., and are an opportunity for passengers to mix and mingle, as dining is open seating, communal-style for all meals, at tables primarily seating eight. Each meal has one entrée choice, and anyone wanting an alternative meal (such as chicken instead of beef) can be accommodated only if he or she notifies the kitchen before 10 a.m. Passengers following special diets, such as vegetarian, can also be accommodated with advance notice.

Fresh fish is common on Caribbean and Central America itineraries, especially those that include Belize. One cook told us about a fisherman in St. Lucia who paddled up to the ship and asked if they'd like to buy some fresh tuna. When the cook asked how he'd know it was fresh, the man said, "Give me ten minutes," then went off and caught one. The same fisherman now supplies the line whenever its ships are in port.

Occasional theme nights offer dishes from Italy, the Caribbean, the American West, and other regions, and there's usually a barbecue on the top deck at least once per cruise, weather permitting. Tea, coffee and hot chocolate are available round the clock, and fresh fruit, snacks, and fresh-baked cookies and muffins are served between meals.

The line's BYOB policy is a real money-saving system for passengers — a bottle of rum we bought in Panama City, for example, cost less than $5 — about the cost of one drink on most ships. Passengers' beer and wine are labeled and stored in a cooler near the bar, which also has separate shelves for liquor bottles. Soft drinks, along with tonic and soda water, are provided free of charge at the bar. On the first and last night of each cruise, hour-long welcome and goodbye parties feature an open bar (for all drinks but beer), as well as jumbo-shrimp cocktails, smoked salmon, or something similar.

Activities and entertainment

Amusement is mostly of the do-it-yourself variety, such as board games, puzzles, cards, reading, and chatting with the other passengers. Otherwise, you can find occasional informal lectures, a few printed quizzes, cooking demonstrations, and bridge and galley tours, and that's

Table 13-1   ACCL Itineraries and Sample Fares

Ship/Fares (per person/day)	Itineraries
Grande Caribe $210 inside; $238 outside; no suites	**14-night Intracoastal Waterway:** North- or south-bound between Warren, RI, and Stuart, FL, Nov 2005 and Apr; **11-night Virgin Islands and eastern/southern Caribbean:** Round-trip from St. Thomas, USVI, or between St. Martin and Antigua, Dec 2005–Feb; **11-night Bahamas:** Round-trip from Nassau, Bahamas, Mar–Apr; **7-night Chesapeake Bay:** Between Baltimore, MD, and Alexandria, VA, May; **12-night Erie Canal:** Round-trip from Warren, June–July and Sept–Oct; **5-night New England Islands:** Round-trip from Warren, July–Aug
Grande Mariner $205 inside; $233 outside; no suites	**14-night Intracoastal Waterway:** North- or southbound between Warren, RI, and Stuart, FL, Nov 2005 and May and Nov; **11-night Panama Canal:** Round-trip from Panama City, Panama, Dec 2005–Jan; **7- and 11-night Belize:** Round-trip from Belize City, Belize, Feb–Mar; **7-night Colonial Intracoastal:** North- or southbound between Jacksonville, FL, and Charleston, SC, Apr; **15-night Erie Canal/Great Lakes:** West- or eastbound between Warren and Chicago, IL, June and Aug; **6-night Lake Michigan:** Round-trip from Chicago, June–Aug; **5-night New England Islands:** Round-trip from Warren, Sept; **12-night Erie Canal:** Round-trip from Warren, June–July and Sept–Oct
Niagara Prince $205 inside; $233 outside; no suites	**14-night Mississippi:** New Orleans, LA, to Chicago, IL, May*; **6-night Lake Michigan:** Round-trip from Chicago, June–July; **15-night Erie Canal/Great Lakes:** West- or eastbound between Warren, RI, and Chicago, June; **7-night Maine Coast:** Round-trip from Portland, ME, July–Sept; **10-night Hudson River/Lake Champlain:** Round-trip from Warren, Sept–Oct; **14-night Intracoastal Waterway:** Warren to Stuart, FL, Nov

* Deployment affected by Hurricane Katrina disaster. Contact cruise line for updates.

about it. River, canal, and coastal cruises concentrate on visits to historically rich Colonial ports, plus exploration of the region's flora and fauna, with area guides and naturalists leading visits to wildlife sanctuaries and parks. In the Caribbean and Central America, the platforms at the stern of the ships let passengers step right into the water for snorkeling, swimming, kayaking, or taking a ride in a 24-passenger glass-bottom boat, used to view coral formations and tropical fish.

The amount of time spent at each port varies from a few hours to an entire morning or afternoon, and the ship usually remains anchored or docked at night, allowing passengers to explore restaurants and/or nightspots ashore.

Select cruises, including those to Belize, typically carry full-time naturalists aboard, but the line does not consistently have the variety or quality of onboard experts you may find on more outdoors- and learning-oriented lines such as Glacier Bay, Lindblad, and Clipper.

Evenings, the BYOB cocktail hour is a time for songs (accompanied on the lounge piano, assuming there's a passenger aboard who plays), announcements, and an occasional informal talk about an upcoming sight or experience. A movie from the ship's video collection is usually shown after dinner on the large-screen TV in the lounge, and sometimes, local entertainers, such as Dixieland bands on Mississippi River itineraries and Garifuna dancers in Belize, are invited aboard for an evening or perform for passengers in port.

For kids

These are totally not family friendly, with an age minimum of 14. Teens older than that had better be pretty good at entertaining themselves or really intellectually curious to be good candidates for an ACCL trip.

(Photo: ACCL)

Figure 13-1: Grande Mariner

Fleet facts

Though sisters *Grande Mariner* (see Figure 13-1) and *Grande Caribe* are definitely the most comfortable and appealing vessels the line has ever built, they're still as basic as cruise ships come, with tiny, spartan cabins (that means no TVs) and no-fuss décor. Same deal and then some for the smaller, older *Niagara Prince,* which has an even tighter layout. No one books these ships expecting luxury, though. Seaworthy and practical, they all have the innovative exploratory features for which ACCL is known. The ships have a top-deck lounge and outdoor sitting space, plus a dining room below. No cabins are wheelchair accessible. See Table 13-2 for fleet specifications.

Table 13-2		ACCL Fleet Specifications				
Ship	*Entered Service*	*Passengers*	*Crew*	*Total Cabins*	*Tonnage*	*Length in Feet*
Grande Caribe	1997	100	18	50	99	183
Grande Mariner	1998	100	18	50	99	183
Niagara Prince	1994	60	17	30	99	166

American Safari Cruises

19101 36th Ave. West, Suite 201, Lynnwood, WA 98036; ☎ *888-862-8881;* www.am safari.com

> ✔ **Type of cruise:** Adventure/educational, gourmet
>
> ✔ **Ship size/style:** Small, luxurious yachts

For those who can afford it, American Safari offers truly adventurous cruises on its fleet of tiny, but very cushy yachts. Carrying only 12 and 22 passengers apiece in plush comfort, the line's three vessels have homey lounges, ocean-view hot tubs, and large cabins. Fares include spirits, wine, and shore excursions (but not tips).

An American Safari cruise is best suited for hands-on types, attracting a well-traveled group of 40- to 60-somethings. Some days are spent kayaking in the wilderness and others visiting small ports of call, sometimes overnighting there for a taste of the local nightlife. A passenger-crew ratio of about two to one ensures that a cold drink, a clever meal, or a sharp eagle-spotting eye is never more than a request away. During the day passengers have a lot of flexibility: If some want to kayak and others want to go wildlife-watching in an inflatable, no problem; your wish is their command. American Safari itineraries and sample fares are shown in Table 13-3.

Professional naturalists sail on all Alaska, Pacific Northwest, and Baja itineraries leading off-vessel explorations and answering questions on board.

Dining

Crewmembers cheerfully fuss over you, adjusting lunchtime dishes and making elaborate cocktails from the free open bar (they may even call ahead to the next port for your favorite beer), and the chef indulges guests with multiple-course meals (cuisine is finer than you may expect to find on small ships) and clever snacks when he isn't bartering with a fishing boat for the catch of the day. All meals are served family-style and dress is always casual. Special dietary requests (vegetarian, and so forth) can be accommodated with advance notice. Snacks such as

Table 13-3 American Safari Itineraries and Sample Fares

Ship/Fares (per person/day)	Itineraries
Safari Escape $399 inside; $685 outside; no suites	**7-night Pacific Northwest/British Columbia:** Round-trip from San Juan Island, WA, Oct 2005 and Sept–Oct; **8-night Alaska Inside Passage:** North- or southbound between Juneau, AK, and Prince Rupert, BC, May–Sept
Safari Quest $574 inside; $624 outside; no suites	**8-night Mexico Sea of Cortez:** Round-trip from La Paz, Baja California Sur, with guests transferring overland from Los Cabos at beginning and end of cruise, Dec 2005–Apr; **7-night Alaska Inside Passage:** North- or southbound between Juneau, AK, and Sitka, AK, May–Sept (includes two full consecutive days in Glacier Bay National Park); **11-night Pacific Northwest (Columbia/Snake Rivers):** East- or westbound between Astoria, OR, and Lewiston, ID, Sept–Oct; **3- and 4-night California Wine Country:** Round-trip from San Francisco, CA, Oct–Nov
Safari Spirit $428 inside; $685 outside; no suites	**7-night Pacific Northwest:** Round-trip from San Juan Island, WA, Oct 2005 and Sept–Oct; **7-night Alaska Inside Passage:** Round-trip from Juneau, AK, May–Aug

Gorgonzola and brie with pears, walnuts, and table crackers are set out between meals.

Activities and entertainment

If you like staying active on vacation as much as you like being pampered, ASC is surprisingly outdoorsy, with expedition leaders accompanying passengers on off-vessel exploration. In Alaska, you may take out a Zodiac boat or kayak to investigate shoreline black bears or river otters, or to navigate fjords packed with ice floes and lolling seals. Expeditions include trips to boardwalked cannery towns, Tlingit villages, and tiny villages such as Meyer's Chuck, population about 50, give or take. Activities throughout the day are well spaced, and there are many opportunities to see wildlife.

In California, Wine Country cruises include private tours and tastings.

The main lounge is the social center of each ship, a place for guests to relax, listen to an informal lecture by the ship's naturalist, play a game of cards or Scrabble, or watch a movie from the ship's library on the big-screen TV. From time to time, the ship docks at a town with a measure of nightlife — at the least, you get to shoot a game of pool; at best, the passengers all head out together for a pub crawl.

For kids

Most sailings have no programs or facilities whatsoever for kids, but occasional sailings in Alaska and the Sea of Cortez are targeted to families (and called Kids in Nature, or KIN, cruises), with naturalists giving kids lessons in the region's flora and fauna. At the end of the trip, kids get a few "graduation gifts," including a video documenting their week on board and a "University of Whales" diploma.

(Photo: American Safari Cruises)

Figure 13-2: *Safari Quest*

Fleet facts

Safari Escape, Safari Quest (see Figure 13-2), and ***Safari Spirit*** resemble private yachts more than cruise ships, and they have the cabins to match, with televisions, VCRs, and roomy bathrooms with showers (and a shower-tub combo on the *Spirit*). The *Spirit* has the largest cabins, and after its overhaul in 2005, is considered the most luxurious of the fleet. The Admiral's Cabins have large picture windows, a small sitting area, plus other features such as a cedar-lined sauna or a small balcony. Otherwise, cabins have windows, but those on the lower deck are elevated, meaning sunlight comes in but you have no view. All public rooms have generous panoramic views. See Table 13-4 for fleet specifications.

Table 13-4	American Safari Fleet Specifications					
Ship	*Entered Service*	*Passengers*	*Crew*	*Total Cabins*	*Tonnage*	*Length in Feet*
Safari Escape	1983	12	6	6	*	112
Safari Quest	1992	22	9	11	*	120
Safari Spirit	1992	12	6	11	*	105

* Tonnage statistics are unavailable, but suffice to say the ships are really small, although roomy enough for the number of passengers they carry.

American West Steamboat Company

2101 Fourth Ave., Suite 1150, Seattle, WA 98121; ☎ **800-434-1232;** www.american weststeamboat.com

- ✔ **Type of Cruise:** Nostalgic river and coastal cruises
- ✔ **Ship size/style:** Two small, beautifully-designed sternwheelers, built in the fashion of the ships of the 1800s and early 1900s

Designed after the great paddlewheel riverboats of the late 19th and early 20th centuries, the *Empress of the North* and the *Queen of the West* offer an experience heavy on history and charm, taking passengers back in time while sailing in Alaska and on the Pacific Northwest's Columbia and Snake Rivers. The accommodations are plush, the atmosphere one of nostalgia, and the onboard artwork a feast of Americana, with cowboy bronzes, silver buckles and ornate spurs, paintings and artifacts of the Lewis and Clark expedition, Alaska Native art, and other items.

The two ships are all about nostalgia, offering cruises that mix port calls with time spent cruising wild areas. Guests — mostly early-to-bed types between ages 65 and 70 (though there are sometimes extended families with kids cruising together) — are attracted by the ships' historic feel and are equally interested in the history of the ports. All cruises feature lecturers who discuss the sailing region, and one shore excursion is complimentary in every port.

The crew is enthusiastic and helpful. Most are young, but some of them — the bartenders, for example — tend to be more mature and quite accomplished. Unlike the kids who work the dining rooms, these guys have had many years of experience in their craft. Table 13-5 displays American West's itineraries and sample fares.

Some itineraries — especially Alaska cruises — come with airfare bundled into the rates, providing a big cost savings.

Dining

Food on board is served family style: good and solid, but don't expect gourmet. One main restaurant serves all three very filling meals, but it can become a bit crowded, to the point where you sometimes pass dishes to your neighbor, as the server can't get through.

You can also get continental breakfast and burgers, hot dogs, sandwiches, and homemade chili and soup at lunch in a casual spot called the Calliope Bar & Grill.

Activities and entertainment

As aboard other small ships, organized activities are limited. Guest lecturers come aboard to talk about the history and culture of the areas through which the ships sail, and if you don't feel like showing up in

Table 13-5   American West Itineraries and Sample Fares

Ship/Fares (per person/day)	Itineraries
Empress of the North No inside cabins; $246 outside; $448 suite	**7-night Pacific Northwest (Columbia/Snake Rivers):** Round-trip from Portland, OR, Feb–Apr and Oct–Dec; **7-night Alaska Inside Passage:** Round-trip from Juneau, AK, May–Sept; **7-night Pacific Puget Sound/Canada:** Round-trip from Seattle, WA, Sept
Queen of the West No inside cabins; $168 outside; $437 suite	**7-night Pacific Northwest (Columbia/Snake Rivers):** Round-trip from Portland, OR, Mar–Nov

person, you can listen to the talks in your cabin, via an audio feed. In the evening, the main lounge programs various small-scale entertainments, including jazz soloists, small song-and-dance revues, and occasional movie screenings.

For kids

You don't find many kids on board, and those that do sail this line must find their own amusement.

(Photo: American West Steamboat Company)

Figure 13-3: *Empress of the North*

Fleet facts

Queen of the West, the smaller of the line's two ships, was built in 1995 and has operated in the Columbia and Snake Rivers ever since. Its bigger sister, ***Empress of the North*** (see Figure 13-3), debuted in 2003. The ships are more spacious than you may think when you first see them from shore, with public rooms that evoke a bygone era. Our favorite is definitely the Paddlewheel Lounge, where you can sip a cocktail to the thrum of the huge propulsion wheel, visible through the room-wide window at the back. Snacks are served here before dinner.

Both ships are fitted with bow landing ramps, which let them cozy up to shore so passengers can walk easily on and off the vessel, even in secluded spots that lack docking facilities.

All cabins on both ships are decorated like cozy bedrooms, with dark wood tones, flowery bedspreads, and lace curtains. The majority of suites and staterooms have verandas, the rest large picture windows. See Table 13-6 for fleet specifications.

Table 13-6	American West Fleet Specifications					
Ship	*Entered Service*	*Passengers*	*Crew*	*Total Cabins*	*Tonnage*	*Length in Feet*
Queen of the West	1995	136	60	71	1,308	212
Empress of the North	2003	235	84	112	3,388	360

Clipper Cruise Line

11969 Westline Dr., St. Louis, MO 63146-3220; ☎ *800-325-0010;* www.clipper cruise.com

> ✔ **Type of cruise:** River, coastal, and open-sea small-ship cruises

> ✔ **Ship size/style:** Mixed fleet of casual coastal cruisers and more elaborate oceangoing vessels

Passengers on Clipper ships get to explore rivers, sparsely inhabited islands, and deep fjords, yet these cruises are hardly about roughing it. Instead, they represent low-fuss vacations for low-fuss people who want to learn something about the places they visit. The line caters to mature, easygoing, relatively affluent, and well-traveled older passengers (average age 69) who want a casual and educational vacation experience heavy on nature, history, and culture. It's an ideal choice for travelers who've sailed the mainstream or premium lines and want to try a small-ship cruise.

One of the more wide-ranging small-ship lines, Clipper covers a huge variety of destinations, from river, lake, and coastal cruises on the U.S. east coast, the Great Lakes, and Alaska, to ocean voyages visiting Asia, Russia, Antarctica, Australia and New Zealand, Scandinavia and Greenland, Europe, South America, and the South Pacific. Naturalists, historians, and other experts sail on all itineraries to offer informal lectures and lead expeditions to sites of interest. Stops at the ports may also include a guided hike in a wildlife preserve or along the coast, a museum visit, swimming and snorkeling, or other options, including shore excursions similar to those offered by the mainstream lines. Occasional nights spent in port offer a chance to mingle with the locals. For Clipper itineraries and sample fares, see Table 13-7.

Dining

Clipper's cuisine is generally straightforward, prepared by chefs from the Culinary Institute of America. Though not terribly adventurous (beyond using local ingredients wherever possible), it's very well prepared, focusing on meat, seafood, and pasta. All meals are served in the main dining room, and light breakfast and lunch items are served buffet-style in a public lounge. Weather and time permitting, a barbecue is on deck at least once per weeklong cruise. There's no dress code.

Activities and entertainment

As aboard the other small-ship lines, Clipper's activities all revolve around the ships' destinations, with most days spent in port. In the evenings, resident naturalists and historians deliver informal lectures, which on our last cruise included talks on the nature and geology of the Caribbean islands, reef fish identification, and plant life.

For kids

Clipper offers no children's programs.

(Photo: Clipper Cruise Line)

Figure 13-4: _Clipper Adventurer_

Fleet facts

Clipper operates both small coastal cruisers and larger, more substantial vessels for expeditionary ocean voyages.

**Clipper Adventurer** (see Figure 13-4) is one of our very favorite small ships. Its interior (all new in 1998) is almost plush on the inside (in a clubby, comfortable, seagoing way) and tough as nails on the outside, with an ice-hardened hull that allows it to sail exotic itineraries in the Arctic and Antarctica. _**Clipper Odyssey**_ is Clipper's other oceangoing ship, holding down the fort on the Pacific the way _Adventurer_ does in the Atlantic. Sleek and yachtlike, she offers more than the average small

Table 13-7	Clipper Itineraries and Sample Fares
Ship/Fares (per person/day)	*Itineraries*
Clipper Adventurer No inside cabins; $351 outside; $601 suite	**16- and 23-night Antarctica/Falkland Islands:** Ushuaia, Argentina, to Buenos Aires, Argentina, Jan–Feb and Dec (23-night Dec sailing includes south Georgia); **12-night Mediterranean/Aegean:** Rome, Italy, to Athens, Greece, Mar; **13-night Greek Isles/North Africa:** Athens to Valletta, Malta, Mar–Apr; **10-night Adriatic:** Dubrovnik, Croatia, to Valletta, May; **10-night "World War II Campaign" cruise:** Valletta to Rome, May; **15-night Portugal/France/UK:** Lisbon, Portugal, to London, UK, May; **14-night Scottish Isles/Iceland:** Edinburgh, Scotland, to Reykjavik, Iceland, June; **16-night Iceland/ Greenland:** Reykjavik to Ottawa, ON, July; **20-night "Route of the Vikings":** Ottawa to Oslo, Norway, Aug; **14-night Arctic Circle/Norwegian fjords:** Oslo to Bergen, Norway, Aug; **11-night Norway/Ireland:** Bergen to Dublin, Ireland, Aug; **12-night British Isles:** Dublin to Greenock, Scotland, Sept; **18-night Argentina:** Buenos Aires to Ushuaia, Nov
Clipper Odyssey No inside cabins; $369 outside; $583 suite	**14-night New Zealand:** Queenstown, New Zealand, to Auckland, New Zealand, Jan–Feb and Dec; **19-night New Zealand/Australia:** Queenstown to Sydney, Australia, Feb; **16-night "World War II/South Pacific":** Sydney to Guam, Mar; **14-night Japan:** Himeji, Japan, to Tokyo, Japan, May–June; **14-night Russian Far East:** Tokyo to Anchorage, AK, June; **16-night Bering Sea:** Round-trip from Anchorage, June; **19-night Asia:** Yokohama, Japan, to Ho Chi Minh City, Vietnam, Aug; **13-night Vietnam:** Ho Chi Minh City to Hanoi, Vietnam, Sept; **17-night Pacific Islands:** New Caledonia to Auckland, Nov
Nantucket Clipper No inside cabins; $279 outside; no suites	**7-night eastern/southern Caribbean:** Round-trip from St. Thomas, USVI, Jan and Dec; **7-night Central America:** Belize City, Belize, to Puerto Cortes, Honduras, Feb; **7-night Intracoastal Waterway:** North- or southbound between Jacksonville, FL, and Charleston, SC, Mar–Apr and Nov; **11-night "Colonial and Civil War" U.S. east coast:** North- or southbound between Alexandria, VA, and Charleston, May and Nov; **10-night Chesapeake Bay/Hudson River:** North- or southbound between Alexandria and New York, NY, May and Nov; **7-night coastal Maine:** North- or southbound between Boston, MA, and Bangor, ME, May–June and Oct; **8-night St. Lawrence Seaway/Thousand Islands:** North- or southbound between Quebec City, QB, and Buffalo, NY, June–July; **14-night French Canada/Great Lakes:** Between Quebec City and Chicago, IL, July and Sept; **7-night Lake Michigan:** Round-trip from Chicago, Aug–Sept; **7-night Hudson River fall foliage:** Round-trip from New York, Oct

Ship/Fares (per person/day)	Itineraries
Yorktown Clipper No inside cabins; $364 outside; no suites	**7-night eastern/southern Caribbean:** Round-trip from St. Thomas, USVI, Jan and Dec; **7-night Central America/ Panama Canal:** Between San José, Costa Rica, and Panama City, Panama, Feb, Nov, and Dec; **7-night Mexico Sea of Cortez:** Round-trip from La Paz, Baja California Sur, Feb and Mar; **7-night California Wine Country:** Round-trip from Redwood City, CA, Apr–May and Oct–Nov; **7-night Alaska Inside Passage:** Round-trip from Juneau, AK, May–Sept; **7-night Pacific Northwest:** North- or southbound between Seattle, WA, and Vancouver, BC, Sept–Oct

ship, including two lounges, a library, a small pool, an elevator, and even a jogging track. All cabins have sitting areas with sofas, and eight deluxe cabins and one suite boast private verandas.

Nantucket Clipper and *Yorktown Clipper* are both simple coastal cruisers with simple layouts: one large lounge that can accommodate all guests, a single dining room, and several outside deck areas for sunning, relaxing, and wildlife-viewing. All the well-designed, smallish cabins are outside and most have picture windows and good amounts of storage space. Some have doors that open to the Promenade Deck rather than to an inside corridor. See Table 13-8 for fleet specifications.

Table 13-8   Clipper Fleet Specifications

Ship	Entered Service	Passengers	Crew	Total Cabins	Tonnage	Length in Feet
Clipper Adventurer	1975	122	72	61	4,364	330
Clipper Odyssey	1989	128	72	64	5,218	338
Nantucket Clipper	1984	100	32	51	1,471	207
Yorktown Clipper	1988	138	40	69	2,354	257

Cruise West

2301 5th Ave., Suite 401, Seattle, WA 98121; ☎ ***888-851-8133;*** www.cruisewest. com

> ✔ **Type of cruise:** River, coastal, and open-sea small-ship cruises

> ✔ **Ship size/style:** Mostly casual, coastal cruisers plus one elaborate oceangoing vessel

Alaska legend Charles "Chuck" West founded Cruise West in the late 1980s to present a genuine and close-up view of Alaska. Today, the company is still in the West family and its mission remains the same, even though its geographic reach has expanded to include destinations such as Mexico, Costa Rica, Panama, California's Wine Country, the rivers of Oregon and Idaho, Arctic Russia, the South Pacific, and Japan.

Cruise West passengers tend to be older (generally in the upper end of the 50–75 age range), well educated, independent-minded, and insistent upon a casual and relaxed onboard atmosphere. Every aspect of the trip is destination-oriented, with itineraries dividing their time between sailing in gorgeous natural areas and visiting ports of call — both large, popular ports and smaller, lesser-known ones. Because these ships are small, they can navigate tight areas (such as Alaska's Misty Fjords and Resolution Sound, Costa Rica's Manuel Antonio National Park, and Los Islotes and Isla Partida in the Sea of Cortez) and scoot close to wildlife without causing alarm. When the ship is sailing, many passengers congregate on the open bow or the open Top, Port, and Starboard Decks to scan for wildlife or just take in the views. Table 13-9 shows Cruise West's varied itineraries and some sample fares.

Dining

All meals are served in single open seatings at each ship's main restaurant, with an early-riser's buffet also available in the lounge. Cuisine is fairly average home-style American, varied but not over-fancy. Chefs make a point of stocking up on fresh seafood while in port. *Spirit of Oceanus* has a buffet option at breakfast and lunch, and all ships try to serve at least one lunch and/or dinner outdoors.

Activities and entertainment

The ships provide binoculars for guest use and carry naturalists who help guests spot and identify wildlife and geological features, usually announcing good sightings over the intercom. Forest Service rangers, fishermen, and members of local tribes sometimes come aboard to speak and/or accompany guests in port. Occasionally, expedition leaders take passengers for a spin in the ships' inflatable launches, getting close to shore. Kayaking is also available on some itineraries. At least one shore excursion is included for each port of call, ranging from short performances or driving tours to full-day odysseys.

Aside from these destination-oriented activities, the most you can expect is an occasional movie screening in the lounge (and even that is probably destination-oriented!) or sometimes a very silly crew talent show. The larger *Spirit of Oceanus* has a small gym, but on the other ships the only exercise option is walking around the outside deck.

For kids

Cruise West offers no children's program.

Table 13-9   Cruise West Itineraries and Sample Fares

Ship/Fares (per person/day)	Itineraries
Pacific Explorer No inside cabins; $246 outside; no suites	**7-night Costa Rica and Panama:** Round-trip from San José, Costa Rica, June–July and Nov–Dec; **9-night Costa Rica and Panama:** Between Panama City, Panama, and San José, Jan–Apr and Dec
Sheltered Seas $437 (includes cruise and hotel stays)	**4- and 5-night Alaska daylight cruise:** North- or southbound between Ketchikan, AK, and Juneau, AK, May–Aug
Spirit of '98 No inside cabins; $500 outside; $843 suite	**8-night Alaska Inside Passage:** North- or southbound between Juneau, AK, and Ketchikan, AK, May–Aug; **7-night Pacific Northwest (Columbia/Snake Rivers):** Round-trip from Portland, OR, Apr and Sept–Oct
Spirit of Alaska $169 inside; $246 outside; no suites	**3- and 4-night Glacier Bay:** Round-trip from Juneau, AK, May–Aug; **8-night Alaska Inside Passage:** Round-trip from Juneau, May–Aug; 7-night Pacific Northwest (Columbia/Snake Rivers): Round-trip from Portland, OR, September or Oct
Spirit of Columbia $214 inside; $291 outside; no suites	**3- and 4-night Prince William Sound:** Round-trip from Anchorage, AK, May–Aug; **7-night British Columbia:** Round-trip from Seattle, WA, Apr and Sept–Oct
Spirit of Discovery No inside cabins; $325 outside; no suites	**8-night Alaska Inside Passage:** Round-trip from Juneau, AK, May–Aug; **7-night Pacific Northwest (Columbia/Snake Rivers):** Round-trip from Portland, OR, Apr and Sept–Oct
Spirit of Endeavor No inside cabins; $362 outside; no suites	**8-night Alaska Inside Passage:** North- or southbound between Juneau, AK, and Ketchikan, AK, May–Aug; **7-night Mexico Sea of Cortez:** Round-trip from Cabo San Lucas, Baja California Sur, Dec 2005–Mar; **7-night British Columbia:** Round-trip from Seattle, WA, Apr and Sept–Oct; **3- and 4-night California Wine Country:** Round-trip from San Francisco, CA, Oct–Nov
Spirit of Glacier Bay Rates not available	**3- and 4-night Glacier Bay:** Round-trip from Juneau, AK, May–Aug
Spirit of Oceanus No inside cabins; $460 outside; $640 suite	**12-, 14-, and 19-night South Pacific:** Round-trip from Papeete, Tahiti; Papeete to Fiji; and Fiji to Guam, Jan–Feb; **14-night Japan:** North- or southbound between Kobe, Japan, and Niigata, Japan, Mar and Oct; **11-night Alaska Inside Passage:** North- or southbound between Vancouver, BC, and Anchorage, AK, May–Aug; **13-night Bering Sea:** Round-trip from Anchorage, June–Aug

Figure 13-5: *Spirit of '98*

(Photo: Cruise West)

Fleet facts

Spirit of Oceanus is one of our favorite small ships, a spacious and well-designed vessel with interiors reminiscent of 19th-century yachts. Wood-paneled staterooms are huge, most with a large sitting area and extra-large bathroom. Cabins on Sun and Sports Decks trade interior space for private teak balconies. Public areas include two lounges, a small gym, an outdoor buffet restaurant, and an outdoor hot tub.

Spirit of '98 (see Figure 13-5) is charming, designed to resemble a 19th-century coastal steamer. There's even a player piano in the lounge, plus period-looking balloon-back chairs, pressed tin (er, aluminum) ceilings, ruffled drapery, and plenty of polished woodwork and brass.

Spirit of Endeavor is very similar to Clipper's *Nantucket Clipper* and *Yorktown Clipper,* with the same kind of low-key, comfortable feel, which makes sense, since she formerly sailed for Clipper, as *Newport Clipper.* Similar in style is *Pacific Explorer,* which offers comfortable cabins as well as a fleet of Zodiacs, kayaks, snorkel gear, and banana boats for off-vessel exploration and fun.

The line's most unusual itineraries may be those offered by its cabinless day cruiser *Sheltered Seas,* which visits Alaska's great natural areas by day and then delivers passengers to shore every evening for dinner and a stay at a local hotel. It's like a road trip, but without the road. The vessel is equipped with a dining lounge (and a galley for preparing lunch), a viewing lounge, a bar, and two outside viewing decks.

Cruise West's remaining vessels, *Spirit of Alaska, Spirit of Columbia, Spirit of Discovery,* and *Spirit of Glacier Bay,* are all utilitarian small ships from the 1970s. They all offer an intimate cruise experience and the usual small-ship arrangement of two public rooms (a main lounge and a single dining room), plus outdoor viewing decks to take in the scenery. Expect décor and design to be spartan.

Spirit of '98 and *Spirit of Oceanus* have elevators — a rarity in the small-ship world. *Spirit of '98* also has one completely wheelchair-accessible cabin. See Table 13-10 for fleet specifications.

Table 13-10	Cruise West Fleet Specifications					
Ship	*Entered Service*	*Passengers*	*Crew*	*Total Cabins*	*Tonnage*	*Length in Feet*
Pacific Explorer	1995	100	33	50	102	185
Sheltered Seas	1986	70	8	0	98	90
Spirit of Alaska	1980	78	21	39	97	143
Spirit of Columbia	1979	78	21	39	97	143
Spirit of Discovery	1976	84	21	43	94	125
Spirit of Endeavor	1983	102	28	51	99	207
Spirit of Glacier Bay	1971	46	16	25	96	115
Spirit of '98	1984	96	23	49	96	192
Spirit of Oceanus	1991	114	59	57	4,500	295

Delta Queen Steamboat Company

Robin Street Wharf, 1380 Port of New Orleans Pl., New Orleans, LA 70130; ☎ *800-543-1949;* www.deltaqueen.com

> ✔ **Type of cruise:** Nostalgic river cruises
>
> ✔ **Ship size/style:** Three beautifully-designed sternwheelers, one an original from the 1920s, the others larger recreations

Wanna cruise like Mark Twain? Delta Queen is your best bet, offering a time-travel option that re-creates what it was like to sail the Mississippi River system back in the old days. The small, wooden *Delta Queen* was actually there. Built in 1927, she's a direct link to the old days, and even has National Historic Landmark status. The larger *Mississippi Queen* and *American Queen* (see Figure 13-6) were built in 1976 and 1995, respectively, and offer a combination of old-style décor and a few cruise ship amenities.

On board all three ships, the main activity is watching the river go by while a resident historian known as a "riverlorian" talks about life and history along its muddy banks. Porch swings and rocking chairs provide the best perches out on deck, and when it's time to go ashore, the boat may just tie up to a tree and let passengers off right on the river's edge. Who needs a pier?

All around, Delta Queen offers more lavishing décor and better food and service than you can find on most of the other ships discussed in this chapter, and its boats have an intimacy and personality that bigger cruise ships lack. Many crewmembers have been with the company a decade or more and really get into their roles. The same can be said for some passengers, many of whom have sailed with the line before. Table 13-11 shows Delta Queen's itineraries and sample fares.

Table 13-11 Delta Queen Itineraries and Sample Fares

Ship/Fares (per person/day)	Itineraries
American Queen $208 inside; $335 outside; $503 suite	**3- and 4-night Mississippi River:** Round-trip from New Orleans, LA, Oct 2005–June 2006*; **6- and 7-night Mississippi River:** Round-trip from New Orleans or between New Orleans and Memphis, TN, June–Aug*
Delta Queen No inside cabins; $278 outside; $670 suite	**4-, 5-, 6-, 7-, 11-, and 12-night river cruises (multiple routes):** Sailing between Cincinnati, OH, and Pittsburgh, PA; Cincinnati and Nashville, TN; Nashville and Chattanooga, TN; Chattanooga and Cincinnati; Pittsburgh and New Orleans, LA; New Orleans and Galveston, TX; New Orleans and Mobile, AL; New Orleans and Pensacola, FL; New Orleans and St. Louis, MO; round-trip from New Orleans; and round-trip from Galveston, year-round*
Mississippi Queen $271 inside; $418 outside; $669 suite	**5-, 6-, 7-, and 11-night river cruises (multiple routes):** Sailing between St. Louis, MO, and St. Paul, MN; St. Louis and New Orleans, LA; New Orleans and Memphis, TN; New Orleans and St. Louis; Memphis and Nashville, TN; and round-trip from New Orleans, year-round*

* Deployment affected by Hurricane Katrina disaster. Contact cruise line for updates.

Dining

Delta Queen serves some of the most varied and tasty menus among the small-ship lines, with cuisine tilted toward Southern, Cajun, and middle-American dishes. Meals are served in traditional style, with passengers assigned to a set table for lunch and dinner. Expect dishes such as crab-stuffed catfish, seafood gumbo, prime rib, Mississippi Mud Pie, and maybe even fried alligator at a late-night buffet. Between meals you can snack on a bottomless supply of popcorn.

Activities and entertainment

Learning about the Mississippi and its tributaries is the focus of most days, with the onboard historian offering both formal talks and less formal interaction — describing passing areas, showing you where you are on a chart, and so on. Other low-key activities include film screenings, calliope concerts (each boat has one), and kite flying from the top deck. In the evenings, Delta Queen's entertainment program is heavy on Dixieland jazz and swing. Because of Louisiana state law, currently no casinos are on any of the vessels.

For kids

Mississippi Queen and *American Queen* offer summer and holiday "river-bonding" cruises, offering activities for the whole family as well as unplugged kids' activities such as knot tying. The *Delta Queen* does not offer this program and does not have any facilities for kids.

(Photo: Delta Queen Steamboat Company)

Figure 13-6: *American Queen*

Fleet facts

Built in 1927 for service between San Francisco and Sacramento, **Delta Queen** is an authentic river steamboat, oozing personality from the fluted columns and potted plants of her Cabin Lounge to the polished brass and gauges of its engine room. Victorian and period American furnishings fill its several lounges, its Orleans Room restaurant, and its cabins, which feature stained-glass windows, acres of wood paneling, and (in most cases) doors that open up directly onto the Promenade Decks, with rocking chairs just outside.

American Queen and **Mississippi Queen** are much larger vessels built to offer a period feel as well as modern amenities such as plunge pools, a gym, and private balconies. The largest sternwheeler in history, *American Queen* was designed on a grand scale, full of filigree and curlicue ornamentation and crowned with two huge fluted smokestacks. *Mississippi Queen* was, amazingly enough, designed by the same architect who created Cunard's *Queen Elizabeth 2* in the 1960s. She was given a new Victorian interior in 1996, with a *trompe l'oeil* ceiling hovering over her grand staircase and period furnishings in her public rooms, such as the Paddlewheel Lounge (with views from two-story windows) and the Wheel House, where passengers can read the charts to track their progress on the river. See Table 13-12 for fleet specifications.

Table 13-12		Delta Queen Fleet Specifications				
Ship	*Entered Service*	*Passengers*	*Crew*	*Total Cabins*	*Tonnage*	*Length in Feet*
American Queen	1995	436	167	222	3,707	418
Delta Queen	1927	174	80	80	3,360	285
Mississippi Queen	1976	414	157	206	3,364	382

easyCruise

The Rotunda, 42/43 Gloucester Crescent, London NW1 7DL, United Kingdom; ☎ *0906-292-9000 in the U.K., 011-44-1895-651191 from the U.S. and elsewhere;* www.easycruise.com

> ✔ **Type of cruise:** Casual, easy, party, and *cheap*

> ✔ **Ship size/style:** Small, no-frills

easyCruise, a new line launched by U.K.-based entrepreneur Stelios Haji-Ioannou (the brains behind easyJet, easyHotel, easyCar, and a dozen other "easy" companies), has a niche all its own in the cruise business — neither mainstream, luxury, nor your usual small-ship cruise either. The idea is actually pretty simple: Throw out everything people expect a cruise to be and start over.

People accustomed to treating their ship like a home away from home? Not here, where the ship is just a combo transportation device and sleeping compartment. People accustomed to traveling in a bubble, with the cruise line arranging activities, entertainment, and excursions? Not here, where you're completely on your own, with a concierge to suggest the best restaurants and clubs in port. People accustomed to itineraries that start somewhere, go somewhere, and end up back at the beginning a week or so later? Not here, where passengers have the option of boarding and debarking at any of the ports and sailing as many or as few nights as they want, with the only rule being a minimum two-night stay. People accustomed to paying a single price for their whole trip, everything included? Not here, where the rates are per-day and only cover the cabin charge. Everything else costs extra: meals, daily service by a cabin steward, and niceties like beach towels. Sound expensive? *NOT!* EasyCruise's rates are actually fantastically low, averaging $57 per person, per day, double occupancy, with all bookings made through the company's Web site. And if you feel like traveling at the last minute, you can book up to 48 hours before sailing as long as cabins are still available.

Essentially, easyCruise is a Eurail Pass for the 25- to 50-year-old set: cheap, flexible, and easy, and they don't hold your hand. "I don't expect a lot of my customers to spend much time in their cabins," says Haji-Ioannou. "This is about making the destination the destination, not the ship."

Currently, the line is operating only one itinerary — a repeating 7-night French and Italian Riviera loop, sailing round-trip from Nice each Friday, visiting Cannes and St. Tropez (France); Genoa, Portofino, and Imperia/San Remo (Italy); and Monaco. Passengers may start and end their trip anywhere along the route. Because all these ports are close together (the route is less than 200 miles from end to end), the ship can stay late and still make it to the next stop by morning, giving passengers time to enjoy the Riviera nightlife. You never have to be back aboard before 4 a.m., and if you miss the boat, you can just hop a taxi and catch up in the next town.

If the easyCruise idea flies, Haji-Ioannou plans to add more ships to the itinerary and expand into other regions where the port-a-day concept could work, such as the Greek Isles, Spain's Balearic Islands, and the Italian coast around Capri and Naples. At press time, the company was also exploring plans to sail the Caribbean for the winter, offering 7-night cruises from Barbados. Table 13-13 shows easyCruise's current lone itinerary and sample fares.

Table 13-13	easyCruise Itineraries and Sample Fares
Ship/Fares (per person/day)	*Itineraries*
easyCruiseOne $16 inside; no outside cabins; $60 suite	**7-night French/Italian Riviera:** Round-trip from Nice, May–Oct. Check the line's Web site for additional itineraries, which may be announced after this book goes to press

Dining

Meals are available from three casual areas on board: a tapas bar, a sports bar with burgers, and an Italian-style cafe. All meals are charged restaurant-style, with prices listed on the menu. The expectation is that most passengers dine on shore, and the ship carries a concierge who can direct passengers to the best restaurants in each port.

Activities and entertainment

As with everything else in the easyCruise world, it's expected that passengers find their entertainment in port and only return to the ship to sleep. Consequently, the onboard experience offers very little: a hot tub, a small workout room, a gift shop, and a DJ in the tapas bar some evenings — and that's it.

For kids

None. The *easyCruiseOne* (see Figure 13-7) is adults only, with a minimum age of 18.

Figure 13-7: *easyCruiseOne*

Fleet facts

easyCruiseOne, the fledgling line's first ship, was built in 1990. As part of its easy-fication, the ship's hull, cabins, and public areas were painted orange and white (the official colors of all "easy" companies); its interior walls were moved to fit more cabins (increasing its passenger load from 114 to 170); and its cabin windows were sealed over, creating rooms that really are just places to sleep. Average cabin size is a tiny 100 square feet, with four larger staterooms at 258 square feet. All cabins have simple platform beds and a private bathroom with shower, but not much else. See Table 13-14 for fleet specifications.

Table 13-14	easyCruise Fleet Specifications					
Ship	Entered Service	Passengers	Crew	Total Cabins	Tonnage	Length in Feet
easyCruiseOne	1990	170	54	85	4,077	290

Glacier Bay Cruiseline

2101 4th Ave., Suite 2200, Seattle, WA 98121; ☎ ***800-451-5952;*** www.glacierbay cruiseline.com

> ✔ **Type of cruise:** Small-ship adventure cruises
>
> ✔ **Ship size/style:** Small expedition ships plus one fancier catamaran-style cruiser

Glacier Bay Cruiseline is your top choice in Alaska for a cruise heavy on active outdoor experiences at several different levels, from hardly active at all to so active you should probably get in shape before you go.

The *Wilderness Explorer* offers the most active adventure cruises, spending 5 days of her 6-day itineraries in Glacier Bay and the surrounding waterways, with passengers kayaking and hiking every day. (Day six is spent mostly aboard ship, with a brief stop at Glacier Bay Lodge.) The *Wilderness Adventurer* (see Figure 13-8) and *Wilderness Discoverer* offer medium-adventure cruises, spending most days in wilderness areas, either off-vessel for kayaking, hiking, or beachcombing, or on board for scenic cruising. The *Executive Explorer* offers cruises on a par with Cruise West and Clipper, combining cruising in natural areas such as Glacier Bay, Tracy Arm, and Misty Fjords with visits to small Alaska towns such as Sitka, Petersburg, Wrangell, and Metlakatla.

The adventure cruises attract younger guests as well as outdoors-oriented older passengers, with as many couples in their 40s and 50s as in their 60s and 70s. When we sailed, we even met one couple in their 90s who took advantage of every opportunity to kayak and hike. The *Executive Explorer* attracts a generally older, less active crowd. See Table 13-15 for Glacier Bay itineraries and sample fares.

 Cruise fares include shore excursions at the ports and/or exploration of wilderness areas. The *Wilderness Explorer* itineraries include a pre-cruise hotel night. Every once in a while the line also offers free airfare.

Dining

Glacier Bay's cuisine is pretty basic American fare, with dinners including a choice of two entrees, typically a fresh fish such as halibut or salmon and a chicken or beef dish. All meals are served at single open seatings in each vessel's one restaurant, but in good weather the chefs sometimes do a barbecue outside on the top deck.

Activities and entertainment

The adventure-oriented ships are outfitted like cruising base camps, with Zodiac landing craft for going ashore in places without port facilities and a fleet of stable, two-person sea kayaks that allow quiet and unobtrusive observation in wildlife areas. Two naturalists sail with each vessel, leading shore excursions and sharing information on the region's wildlife and history. Guest lecturers sometimes sail as well, or come aboard to give readings of Alaskan stories or presentations on glaciers, marine life, whales, and other natural topics. All ships offer a comfortable and casual environment, with meals served family style at one seating on an unassigned basis. The vessels' windowed observation lounges and large observation decks serve as the main gathering places, with binoculars provided for guest use. Expect little more.

For kids

Nothing for kids on most sailings, though the line does offer several family-oriented cruises every summer, with supervised kids' activities and half-off rates for passengers 18 and under.

Table 13-15   Glacier Bay Itineraries and Sample Fares

Ship/Fares (per person/day)	Itineraries
Executive Explorer No inside cabins; $330 outside; no suites	**7-night Alaska Inside Passage:** North- or southbound between Juneau, AK, and Ketchikan, AK, May–Aug
Wilderness Adventurer $375 inside; $434 outside; no suites	**7-night Alaska Inside Passage:** Round-trip from Juneau, AK, May and Aug–Sept; **8-night Prince William Sound:** Round-trip from Anchorage, AK, June–Aug
Wilderness Discoverer $171 inside; $228 outside; no suites	**7-night Alaska Inside Passage:** North- or southbound between Juneau, AK, and Sitka, AK, June–Aug; **7-night Pacific Northwest (Columbia/Snake Rivers):** East- or westbound between Portland, OR, and Richland, WA, Sept–Oct
Wilderness Explorer No inside cabins; $244 outside; no suites	**6-night Alaska Glacier Bay/Icy Strait:** Round-trip from Juneau, AK, May–Aug

(Photo: Glacier Bay Cruiseline)

Figure 13-8: *Wilderness Adventurer*

Fleet facts

Wilderness Adventurer and *Wilderness Discoverer* are very similar vessels that sailed originally for ACCL. Like all ACCL ships, they were built long and low, with a shallow draught (the amount of hull below the waterline) to sail into places few other ships can go. When Glacier Bay purchased the ships, it outfitted them with a fleet of stable two-person sea kayaks and a dry-launch platform in the stern that allows passengers to take off right from the ship. Glacier Bay also gussied both ships up over the past few years, though cabins remain small and spartan. Cabin bathrooms are amazingly tiny. Just consider it part of the adventure.

The tiny *Wilderness Explorer* raises the bar on spartan accommodations even higher, with miniscule cabins with upper and lower berths (bunk beds), one small lounge/bar, and a topside Observation Deck. If you've got the bucks, you can book the one sizable cabin on board, located right behind the wheelhouse, with windows to port and starboard.

Heads up? We mean "Duck!" *Wilderness Adventurer, Explorer,* and *Discoverer* share a drawback: low ceilings. If you're 6 feet 4 inches or more, you'll bump your head.

Executive Explorer is the most comfortable of the Glacier Bay vessels, with decent-size cabins (though still small bathrooms); a pair of state-rooms on the upper deck, with huge windows on two sides; and the usual small-ship arrangement of a single comfortable main lounge/bar and a single dining room. An open top deck and a covered area on the middle deck are the best spots for wildlife viewing. Weirdest thing about this ship? She's a catamaran, with four decks perched atop twin pontoon hulls. She's speedy, too, able to travel at 16 knots. See Table 13-16 for fleet specifications.

Table 13-16	Glacier Bay Fleet Specifications					
Ship	*Entered Service*	*Passengers*	*Crew*	*Total Cabins*	*Tonnage*	*Length in Feet*
Executive Explorer	1986	49	18	24	98	104
Wilderness Adventurer	1984	63	22	32	89	157
Wilderness Discoverer	1992	82	22	41	95	169
Wilderness Explorer	1969	31	13	18	98	112

Lindblad Expeditions

96 Morton St., New York, NY 10014; ☎ *800-397-3348;* www.expeditions.com

> ✔ **Type of cruise:** Small-ship adventure/educational cruises

> ✔ **Ship size/style:** Coastal and open-sea expedition vessels

Lindblad Expeditions specializes in environmentally sensitive soft-adventure cruises, offering an experience more oriented toward real learning and exploration than any competing line. It's our top pick for trips to real adventure destinations such as Antarctica and the Galapagos, and it also offers great adventure-learning trips in closer destinations, such as Baja and Alaska.

The line's cruises are truly exploratory in nature. Most days are spent off the ship aboard Zodiac boats and/or on land excursions, learning about the destinations first-hand, with a team of four to five naturalists, one historian, and an undersea specialist along to help you understand what you're seeing. That's the highest number of experts carried by any of the small-ship lines. As part of a 2004 agreement with the **National Geographic Society,** Geographic scientists, photographers, and film crews sail aboard Lindblad's ships, providing guests with an enhanced experience but also conducting actual research on land and undersea. The line's most adventure-oriented vessel was rechristened *National Geographic Endeavour* and fitted with advanced research equipment, and an advisory group is helping develop research, conservation, and educational initiatives for the Lindblad fleet.

Passengers tend to be physically active as well as intellectually curious and are generally in the over-55 range. They're also the types who can afford Lindblad's high rates, though the inclusive nature of the product makes those prices a little easier to swallow. Shore excursions are all included, for example, as is airfare on some itineraries and sailing dates. For more details about Lindblad's itineraries and fares, check out Table 13-17.

If you're flexible about your departure date, you can get a discount of $500 on many sailings. Just select the month you want to travel (as well as the cabin category), and then, one month prior to the selected month, Lindblad determines availability. If space is available, you get your sailing. If not, you get a travel certificate worth $250 per person, applicable to any future sailing.

Dining

Hearty buffet breakfasts and lunches and sit-down dinners often reflect regional culture and tastes, made from local, seasonal ingredients purchased in ports along the way, as part of Lindblad's commitment to promoting sustainable agriculture and fishing practices.

Activities and entertainment

While on board, passengers entertain themselves with the usual small-ship activities: wildlife watching, reading, and attending onboard lectures and slide presentations by resident naturalists and *National Geographic* experts. Each evening, the naturalists lead discussions recapping the day's events, and after dinner, a documentary or feature film may be screened in the main lounge. In some regions, local musicians may come aboard to entertain.

All ships carry exploration essentials such as Zodiac landing craft, sea kayaks, snorkeling gear, wet suits, and other low- and high-tech underwater equipment. On the *Islander,* a certified massage therapist sails on board, offering massage and wellness treatments and leading exercise classes, and the *Sea Voyager* has a small fitness room.

Table 13-17	Lindblad Itineraries and Sample Fares
Ship/Fares (per person/day)	**Itineraries**
Islander No inside cabins; $438 outside; $628 suite	**9-night Galapagos:** Round-trip from Baltra, Galapagos, Ecuador, Apr–May, July–Sept, and Nov–Dec
National Geographic Endeavour No inside cabins; $566 outside; $950 suite	**12-night Antarctica:** Round-trip from Ushuaia, Argentina, Jan; **22-night Antarctica/South Georgia/Falkland Islands:** Round-trip from Ushuaia, Feb; **13-night Patagonia/Chilean Fjords:** Ushuaia to Puerto Montt, Chile, Mar; **7-night South Pacific:** Papeete, Tahiti, to Raratonga, Cook Islands, May, July–Sept; **16-night South Pacific:** Easter Island to Papeete (Apr, May, and Oct), or Lautkoka, Fiji, to Port Moresby, Papua New Guinea (May, June, Aug, and Sept); **11-night South Pacific:** Raratonga, Cook Islands, to Lautkoka, May–Sept; **13-night South Pacific:** Round-trip from Papeete, July and Sept
Polaris No inside cabins; $249 outside; $374 suite	**9-night Galapagos:** Round-trip from Baltra, Galapagos, Ecuador, Apr–Dec
Sea Bird $356 inside; $563 outside; no suites	**6-night Pacific Northwest (Columbia/Snake Rivers):** Round-trip from Portland, OR, May and Sept–Nov; **7-night Mexico Sea of Cortez:** Round-trip from La Paz, Baja California Sur (Jan–Mar) or between Guaymas and La Paz (May–July); **7-night Alaska Inside Passage:** North- or southbound between Juneau, AK, and Sitka, AK, May–Aug
Sea Lion $569 inside; $836 outside; no suites	**6-night Pacific Northwest (Columbia/Snake Rivers):** Round-trip from Portland, OR, May and Sept–Nov; **7-night Mexico Sea of Cortez:** Round-trip from La Paz, Baja California Sur (Jan–Mar) or between Guaymas and La Paz (May–July); **7-night Alaska Inside Passage:** North- or southbound between Juneau, AK, and Sitka, AK, May–Aug
Sea Voyager No inside cabins; $425 outside; no suites	**7-night Central America:** Round-trip from San José, Costa Rica (July–Aug), and north- or southbound between San José and Panama City, Panama (Jan–Apr and Nov–Dec)
Triton No inside cabins; $399 outside; $599 suite	**9-night Egypt:** Round-trip from Cairo, Jan–Mar

For kids

None of the Lindblad ships has any organized children's programs, though designated "Family Expeditions" are offered annually in Costa Rica, Baja, Alaska, and the Galapagos.

Figure 13-9: *Sea Lion*

Fleet facts

National Geographic Endeavour is Lindblad's flagship and also the flagship of its partnership with the National Geographic Society. Built tough, with a reinforced hull and stabilizers to enable sailing in rough regions from the Arctic to the Antarctic, the vessel is also sizable and comfortable, with niceties such as a fitness center, sauna, small swimming pool, wood-paneled library, and even a hair salon, in addition to the usual main lounge and dining room. Cabins are sufficiently roomy. Cabins on the upper deck have picture windows but those on the lower decks make due with portholes — which is just fine except during rough seas, when the porthole covers are bolted shut for safety reasons. Two suites on the upper deck have separate sleeping and living areas.

The smaller, shallow-draft *Sea Lion* (see Figure 13-9) and *Sea Bird* are identical twins, right down to their décor schemes and furniture. Both ships have two public rooms (the observation lounge/bar and the dining room) and all cabins are outsides, with picture windows that open to let in breezes and fresh air.

The cabins, dining room, and lounge area on the *Sea Voyager* are almost plush by expedition standards. The *Polaris* is a homey expedition ship with a classic seagoing look, full of polished wood and brass, with teak decking and a comfortably laid-back vibe. Public areas include the main lounge, single dining room, and a cozy library, as well as a covered outside deck with chairs and tables. Cabins are all outsides with windows or (on A Deck) portholes. The *Islander* is a sturdy twin-hulled vessel designed for year-round service in the Galapagos, with all outside cabins and a comfortable lounge and dining room. See Table 13-18 for fleet specifications.

Table 13-18 Lindblad Expeditions Fleet Specifications

Ship	Entered Service	Passengers	Crew	Total Cabins	Tonnage	Length in Feet
Islander	1985	48	26	24	1,065	164
National Geographic Endeavour	1966	110	65	62	3,132	295
Polaris	1960	80	60	41	2,214	238
Sea Bird	1982	70	22	36	100	152
Sea Lion	1981	70	22	36	100	152
Sea Voyager	1982	62	22	33	1,195	175

Maine Windjammer Association

P.O. Box 317, Augusta, ME 04332-0317; ☎ *800-807-WIND;* www.sailmainecoast.com

> ✔ **Type of cruise:** Adventure/educational, rustic

> ✔ **Ship size/style:** Classic schooners

The Maine Windjammer Association isn't a cruise line at all, but rather a marketing group for 14 owner-operated classic schooners, some dating as far back as 1871. All of them sail — and we do mean sail, using sail power exclusively or almost exclusively — in and around mid-Maine's Penobscot Bay from late May to mid-October, providing an absolutely perfect way to see one of the country's most beautiful stretches of coast. This is one of the greatest small-ship experiences you can get — and the prices are right, too.

With no engines (on most vessels), little electricity, and only the most basic accommodations, these ships offer their passengers the chance to get off the grid for a while, away from mechanized society and constant bustle. Days are filled with the demands of sailing (which passengers can help out with if they choose), walks around quaint Maine towns, quiet reading time on deck, and sometimes an impromptu race with one of the other schooners. Service, such as it is, is provided by the same folks who trim the sails and keep the boat on course — which means you shouldn't expect much beyond a set of fresh sheets when you board. They're terrifically friendly, though.

Typical passengers run the gamut, age-wise, though most tend to fall between 30 and 80. A huge percentage are repeaters, with some returning to vacation on the same schooner year after year. They're individualists, sometimes luddites, and most are well-educated. For more information on itineraries and rates, check out Table 13-19.

You can request information for all ships from the address and phone number above and get basic information on the individual schooners (and links to their Web pages) through the association Web site. Actual bookings must be made directly with the captain of each schooner.

Many of the schooners offer early-booking rates during their winter off-season. Check their individual Web sites for details. As an additional cost-saver, all the ships are BYOB, providing coolers and ice with which passengers can chill their beer, wine, or whatever.

Dining

Fleetwide, meals are prepared on wood stoves in rustic galleys and served out on deck, picnic style. Expect traditional New England staples such as fresh seafood, chowder, roasts, and Irish soda bread. Dinners often coincide with sunset, making a beautiful tableau. In inclement weather, all passengers pack into the galley for meals. Once per cruise, most of the ships debark passengers onto a quiet, rocky beach for a traditional lobster bake.

Activities and entertainment

Aside from sailing itself, and visiting small Maine islands and towns by launch, there's not much. On many ships the captain and/or members of the crew are musicians, and will perform in the evenings. Passengers may also bring along acoustic instruments.

For kids

None of the Windjammers have kids' programs, and many actively discourage children from sailing. Most have minimum age requirements ranging from 10 to 16, though *Timberwind* (see Figure 13-10) accepts children as young as 5, and *Isaac H. Evans* accepts kids as young as 6 years old. Most ships make exceptions for children of past passengers.

(Photo: Maine Windjammer Association)

Figure 13-10: *Timberwind*

Table 13-19	Maine Windjammer Itineraries and Sample Fares
Ship/Fares (per person/day)	*Itineraries*
Whole fleet $140 inside; no outside cabins; no suites	**2- to 6-night Maine coastal cruises:** The whole fleet sails from Rockland, Rockport, and Camden, ME, late May through mid-Oct

Fleet facts

The Maine Windjammer Association includes classic vessels more than 130 years old as well as newer vessels created in a traditional style. Many vessels are either listed on the National Register or designated a National Historic Landmark; the oldest date from 1871, and the youngest launched in 1983. You can find out more details about each individual schooner through the Maine Windjammer Association Web site. See Table 13-20 for fleet specifications.

Table 13-20   Maine Windjammer Fleet Specifications

Ship	Entered Service	Passengers	Crew	Total Cabins	Tonnage	Length in Feet
American Eagle	1930	26	5	14	107	92
Angelique	1980	29	5	15	140	95
Grace Bailey	1882	29	5	16	80	80
Heritage	1983	30	8	16	153	95
Isaac H. Evans	1886	22	4	11	68	65
J & E Riggin	1927	24	6	12	75	89
Lewis R. French	1871	22	4	13	56	64
Mary Day	1962	30	5	15	90	90
Mercantile	1916	29	5	16	80	78
Mistress	1960	6	2	3	17	46
Nathaniel Bowditch	1922	24	4	13	150	82
Stephen Taber	1871	22	5	12	73	68
Timberwind	1931	20	4	9	85	70
Victory Chimes	1900	40	9	20	395	132

Star Clippers

4101 Salzedo St., Coral Gables, FL 33146; ☎ *800-442-0553;* www.starclippers.com

> ✔ **Type of cruise:** Adventure/educational, romantic
>
> ✔ **Ship size/style:** Classic-style sailing ships

 Wanna play pirate without roughing it? These three replicas of 19th-century clipper ships have the sails and rigging of classic tall ships, but also the creature comforts of today. Pools, a piano bar and deck bar, a bright and pleasant dining room serving tasty food, and a clubby, wood-paneled library balance out the swashbuckling spirit. *Royal Clipper* also boasts a gym, a small spa, and marble bathrooms.

Passengers are an international mix of active, intelligent 30- to 60-somethings with a penchant for the sea. The vibe is casual and chatty, and you're free to explore, whether climbing the masts (with a harness, of course), helping raise the sails, crawling into the bow netting, or chatting with the captain on the open-air bridge. Of course you can choose to do nothing but sunbathe, sip cold drinks at the bar, or listen to the captain's daily talk about the next port of call, the history of sailing, or some other nautical subject. When you cruise into a port, whether Bequia or Langkawi, you feel like you're on ships that belong there (as opposed to those big white megaships barreling into port).

 These ships aren't just pretty to look at; they're a treasure for old salts and history buffs. Mikael Krafft, the wealthy Swedish-born businessman who built the three ships, spared little expense to create the replicas. For the *Star Flyer* and *Star Clipper,* Krafft procured original drawings and specifications of Scottish-born Donald McKay, a leading naval architect of 19th-century clipper-ship technology, and employed his own team of naval architects to solve such engineering problems as adapting the square-rigged, four-masted clipper design to modern materials and construction. In mid-2000, Krafft went a step further, launching the *Royal Clipper,* a five-masted, fully rigged sailing ship inspired by the famed *Preussen,* a German clipper built in 1902. The *Royal Clipper* now claims the title of the largest clipper ship in the world, and is considered the tallest and among the fastest clipper ships ever built — they're a stunning sight. Table 13-21 shows itineraries and sample rates for Star Clippers.

 You can find frequent deals on back-to-back cruises — either a percentage discount or a dollar amount, such as $300 or more off.

Dining

The food is tasty, though don't expect gourmet. All meals are open seating, with tables for four, six, and eight in the restaurant; the dress code is always casual (though some guests don jackets on the night of the captain's cocktail party). Breakfast and lunch are served buffet style and are

Table 13-21   Star Clippers Itineraries and Sample Fares

Ship/Fares (per person/day)	Itineraries
Royal Clipper $254 inside; $300 outside; $543 suite	**7-night southern Caribbean:** Round-trip from Barbados, Jan–Apr and Nov–Dec; **5-night Mediterranean:** Malaga, Spain, to Rome, Italy, May; **6- and 7-night Mediterranean:** Round-trip from Rome, May–June; **10- and 11-night western Mediterranean:** East- or westbound between Rome and Venice, Italy, June–Sept
Star Clipper $246 inside; $275 outside; $521 suite	**7-night eastern Caribbean:** Round-trip from St. Martin, Jan–Apr and Nov–Dec; **10-night western Mediterranean:** Lisbon, Portugal, to Cannes, France, May; **7-night western Mediterranean:** Round-trip from Cannes, May–Oct; **10- and 11-night western Mediterranean:** East- or westbound between Cannes and Dubrovnik, Croatia (July–Aug), and Cannes to Lisbon (Oct)
Star Flyer $175 inside; $235 outside; $378 suite	**7-night Asia:** Round-trip from Phuket, Thailand; or north- or southbound between Phuket and Singapore, Jan–Mar and Nov–Dec; **10- and 11-night Asia:** North- or southbound between Phuket and Singapore, Dec; **37-night Indian Ocean:** East- or westbound between Phuket and Athens, Greece, Mar and Oct; **5-night Mediterranean:** Round-trip from Athens, May and Sept; **7-night eastern Mediterranean:** Round-trip from Athens (May–Sept); Athens to Istanbul, Turkey (May and Sept); or Istanbul to Athens (June and Sept)

the best meals of the day. The continental cuisine reflects the line's large European clientele and is dominated at breakfast and lunch by cheeses, as well as marinated fish and meats. Breakfasts also include a hot-and-cold buffet spread and an omelet station. Late-afternoon snacks served at the Tropical Bar include such munchies as crudités, cheeses, and chicken wings.

Friendly waiters serve sit-down dinners. Menus typically offer five main entree choices, plus appetizers, soup, salad, and dessert courses. Only the *Royal Clipper* offers 24-hour room service, and only for passengers staying in the 14 suites and Owner's Suites.

Activities and entertainment

For most people, just being on these ships is entertainment enough. Enjoying the sailing experience and socializing with fellow passengers and crewmembers is the main activity, as it is on most any ship this size. That, plus the ships are in port every single day, with few exceptions, so boredom is hardly an issue. Still there are a few things scheduled, including informal talks by the captain on maritime themes, and, at least once a day, the cruise director gives a brief spiel about the upcoming ports and shipboard events (if we had one complaint, it would be these talks aren't meaty enough). Weather and conditions permitting, passengers can lend a hand with deck duties, climb the masts, and have a token try at handling the wheel.

Each ship maintains an open-bridge policy, allowing passengers to wander up to the humble-looking navigation center at any hour of the day or night (you may have to ask to actually go into the chart room, though).

There may also be a brief engine-room tour, morning exercise classes on deck, ever-popular excursions via tender to photograph the ship under sail, and hanging out by the pools (three on *Royal Clipper,* two on *Star Clipper*). On all three ships, you can borrow DVDs from the library or watch the movies that are shown each day on cabin TVs in English, German, and French.

Activities in port revolve around beaches and watersports, and all are complimentary, including snorkeling, water-skiing, windsurfing, sailing, and banana boat rides. For an extra fee, the ships offer PADI-approved scuba diving, including resort instruction.

After-dinner entertainment takes place nightly by the open-air Tropical Bar, and runs the gamut from a crew talent show to a trivia contest, dance games, or a performance by local entertainers (such as a steel-drum band) who come on board for the evening. A keyboard player (who seems out of place on ships like these) is on hand to sing pop songs before and after dinner. Most nights, disco music is put on the sound system and a section of the deck serves as an impromptu dance floor, with the action usually quieting down by about 1 a.m.

Ships tend to depart from their ports early so that they can be under full sail during sunset. Trust us on this one: nothing is more romantic. Position yourselves at the ship's rail or dawdle over drinks at the deck bar to watch the sun melt into the horizon behind the silhouetted ships' masts and ropes. If only every day of your life was this good.

For kids

Not a line for young kids (though the line has no age restrictions). There are no supervised activities and no babysitting unless a crewmember agrees to volunteer his or her off-duty hours. The exception is during holiday seasons such as Christmas, when families are accommodated and some children's activities are organized by the watersports staff, including treasure hunts, beach games, and arts and crafts. For well-behaved, intellectually curious kids over 10 or 12, a Star Clippers cruise any time of the year could be a fun and educational experience.

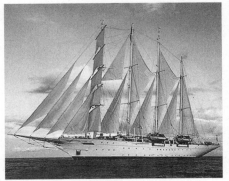

(Photo: Star Clippers/Harvey Lloyd)

Figure 13-11: *Star Clipper*

Fleet facts

Décor on Star Clippers ships is conservative, with touches of mahogany and brass. Public rooms on the *Star Clipper* (see Figure 13-11) and *Star Flyer* are comfortable and almost cushy. Cabins are small (but okay for a ship of this size), and the teak Sun Deck space gives you much more room to spread out and enjoy the sea breeze than what you can usually find on small ships.

The *Royal Clipper's* cabins are larger and have marble bathrooms and nautical décor, plus you can find 14 veranda suites with butler service. *Royal* has a neat lounge that offers underwater viewing while the ship is at anchor, plus there's a small gym, spa, and larger, more plush restaurant. See Table 13-22 for fleet specifications.

Table 13-22	Star Clippers Fleet Specifications					
Ship	*Entered Service*	*Passengers*	*Crew*	*Total Cabins*	*Tonnage*	*Length in Feet*
Royal Clipper	2000	227	106	114	5,000	439
Star Clipper	1992	170	72	85	2,298	360
Star Flyer	1991	170	72	85	2,298	360

Windjammer Barefoot Cruises

P.O. Box 190120, Miami Beach, FL 33119-0120; ☎ **800-327-2601** or **305-672-6453**; www.
windjammer.com

  ✓ **Type of cruise:** Adventure/educational, family, party

  ✓ **Ship size/style:** Old-style sailing ships

Weee whoooo, these ships sure are fun. Ultracasual (shorts and T-shirts are the order of every day — even at dinner and at the bar) and refreshingly carefree, leave your inhibitions (and your shoes) at home. This eclectic fleet of cozy, rebuilt sailing ships lures passengers into a fantasy world of pirates-and-rum-punch adventure. With the sails flapping above the ample wooden decks, you feel like you're a glorious million miles from reality. Passengers and crew mingle on the cozy decks and bond over free rum swizzles and homemade snacks at happy hour. The cute captains come right out of Central Casting, with their deep tans, shorts, and sunglasses, while passengers are an all-ages mix of eccentric non-conformists attracted to the totally unpretentious vibe, low rates, and cloak of adventure.

Windjammer strays off the beaten track when at all possible. The closest thing you get to a good old-fashioned Caribbean adventure, the ships head for quiet, out-of-the-way Caribbean islands such as Bequia, Les Saintes, and Jost van Dyke, places that couldn't be further away from the commercial tourist fray. The ships are ultra-informal and hokey, yet endearing rituals make the experience feel like summer camp for adults.

Captain Mike Burke — also known as Cap'n Mike — founded the company in 1947 with one ship. For years, the sailor-turned-playboy ran down-and-dirty party cruises popular with singles (the lines used to advertise in magazines like *Hustler* — you get the picture), purchasing sailing ships rich in history but otherwise destined for the scrap yard and transforming them into one-of-a-kind vessels. Things have tamed a bit since those early days; the company is now run by Burke's daughter Susan. Table 13-23 offers more information on Windjammer itineraries and rates.

Sure the cabins are closet-sized, but you pay way less for a Windjammer cruise than you would on Star Clippers and Windstar, and bar drinks are a steal. Plus, one child between 6 and 11 sails free May through early August when sharing a cabin with parents.

Dining

Elbows are allowed and so are bathing suits; just try and remember to say *please* when you're asking for more of that free cheap wine. Family style and informal, there's nothing gourmet about the food, though usually it's tasty enough. All breads and pastries are homemade, and at the two open dinner seatings, after soup and salad are served, passengers can choose from two main entrees, such as curried shrimp and roast pork with garlic sauce. Breakfasts and lunches are typically served buffet style. At certain islands, the crew lugs ashore a picnic lunch for an afternoon beach party, and each sailing usually includes one evening on-deck barbecue. The chef accommodates special diets, including vegetarian and low-salt. And don't be shy if it's your birthday: The chef will make you a free cake and serve it at dinner.

Table 13-23   Windjammer Itineraries and Sample Fares

Ship/Fares (per person/day)	Itineraries
Amazing Grace No inside cabins; $101 outside; $280 suite	**7-night eastern/southern Caribbean (several routes):** Between Trinidad and Antigua, Antigua and Tortola, and Antigua and Trinidad, Oct–Jan; **13-night eastern/southern Caribbean:** North- or southbound between Freeport, Bahamas, and Trinidad, Jan–Apr; **7-night Central America:** Between Balboa, Panama, and Playa Herradura, Costa Rica, June–Aug
Legacy No inside cabins; $184 outside; $234 suite	**6-night eastern/southern Caribbean:** Round-trip from St. Thomas, USVI, Dec–May; **4-, 5-, and 8-night Bahamas:** Between Miami, FL, and Nassau, Bahamas, summer
Mandalay $172 inside; $195 outside; $226 suite	**13-night eastern/southern Caribbean:** Between Grenada and Antigua, Nov–May; **6-night British Virgin Islands:** Round-trip from Tortola, Apr–Sept
Polynesia No inside cabins; $230 outside; $247 suite	**6-night eastern/southern Caribbean:** Round-trip from Sint Maarten, Dec–May; **6-night ABC Islands (Aruba, Bonaire, Curaçao):** Round-trip from Aruba, May–Oct
Yankee Clipper $150 inside; $193 outside; $227 suite	**6-night eastern/southern Caribbean:** Round-trip from Grenada, year-round

Aside from that free wine with dinner, Bloody Marys are free at breakfast, and each evening at about 5 p.m., gallons of complimentary rum swizzles are dispensed along with hors d'oeuvres that may include homemade plantain chips and salsa or cheese and crackers. Guests gather on deck, often still in their sarongs and shorts, mingling in the fresh sea air as island music plays in the background.

Activities and entertainment

In a nutshell, goofy. (And just our cup of tea!) It all starts with the Captain's "Story Time" each morning, where the boss offers a rundown of the day's schedule with some ribald jokes thrown in for good measure. Passengers are trained to lovingly shout back "Good morning, Captain SIR!" Then there's that beloved Windjammer tradition, the weekly costume party. Passengers (along with the captain and crew) get all decked out as cross-dressers, pirates, and other characters. Just about everything happens on the top open decks, including a passenger talent show and a local band brought on for the evening. Plus, the ships often stay late in one or two ports so that passengers can head ashore to an island watering hole.

Aside from all the free drinks, you can also buy 'em for peanuts: just $2 for an imported brew and $3.50 for a piña colada.

By day, you're likely to wander around some port or sunbathe on deck (or sleep off a hangover). A few inane activities may be offered on deck late mornings and late afternoons, from crab races to a knot-tying demo. If conditions are right and the captain amenable, passengers can jump overboard, literally, and go for a swim when the ship is anchored offshore. Just about every day is spent in port somewhere. Generally at least once per cruise, on one of the ships' beach visits — to Jost Van Dyke, perhaps — beach games are arranged and sometimes a barbeque or organized hike around the island. You can also rent snorkeling or scuba gear (and sign up for lessons, too).

Of course there's nothing better to do on a Windjammer cruise than cuddle with your special someone and watch a dreamy sunset melt into the horizon. What's more romantic than the swoosh swoosh swoosh of a sailing ship slicing through the sea, elbows on the railings and cold beer in hand?

If you're unattached, Windjammer offers about six wild-and-crazy singles cruises a year, plus a handful of other theme cruises every year. The line also occasionally charters its ships for gays, nudists, Parrot Heads, and other groups.

For kids

For curious kids with a love of the outdoors, Windjammer can work for families with older kids (no children under 6 are allowed to sail aboard any of the ships). The *Legacy, Polynesia,* and *Grace* have a "Junior Jammers" kids' program for ages 6 to 17 that can draw as many as 40 kids a cruise in the summer. There are youth counselors for two main age groups (6–11 and 12–17) who supervise a roster of complimentary summer-camp-style activities all day. Though there aren't any organized activities on *Mandalay* and *Yankee Clipper,* teens may enjoy the experience if they're the kind that can part with e-mail and cellphones for a week. There is no babysitting of any kind.

Unlike most megaship lines, which require passengers to be at least 21 years old unless accompanied by parents, Windjammer's minimum unaccompanied age is 17 and the drinking age is 18.

Fleet facts

The **Legacy, Mandalay, Polynesia,** and **Yankee Clipper** (see Figure 13-12) are all tall ships that operate by a combination of sail and engine power, while the **Amazing Grace** is best described as a motorized banana boat, carrying passengers and supplies for the other Windjammer ships (cargo areas of this ship are off-limits to passengers). The *Grace* tends to attract an older clientele.

(Photo: Windjammer Barefoot Cruises)

Figure 13-12: *Yankee Clipper*

The sailing ships are rustic — all polished rails, brass trimmings, and well-trod teak decks — and chances are you may grow quite attached to yours by week's end despite the close quarters below decks. Each ship has a single dining room, but all other onboard activities are out on the roomy open decks and the open-air bars. Cabins are tiny and offer no frills; many have bunk-style beds (the *Polynesia* and *Legacy* even have some four-passenger dorm-style cabins). Some cabins on the *Amazing Grace* don't have private shower and toilet facilities, so passengers share with neighboring cabins; the other ships provide individual showers in the cabins. The *Legacy,* which is much larger and more modern than the other ships, has somewhat larger cabins and bathrooms, wider corridors, and a small television room/library that gets little use. See Table 13-24 for fleet specifications.

Table 13-24	Windjammer Fleet Specifications					
Ship	**Entered Service**	**Passengers**	**Crew**	**Total Cabins**	**Tonnage**	**Length in Feet**
Amazing Grace	1955	92	40	46	1,525	254
Legacy	1959	122	43	61	1,165	294
Mandalay	1923	72	28	36	420	236
Polynesia	1938	112	45	50	430	248
Yankee Clipper	1927	64	29	32	327	197

Windstar Cruises

300 Elliott Ave. West, Seattle, WA 98119; ☎ *800-258-7245;* www.windstar cruises.com

> ✔ **Type of cruise:** Adventure, gourmet, romantic
>
> ✔ **Ship size/style:** Modern, smallish ships with sails (and engines, too)

It's simple: If you're looking for a high-end sailing ship experience that manages to be casual and down-to-earth, yet also elegant in a yachty sort of way, Windstar's for you. The food and service are really good, cabins are very comfortable, and the ships hit a lot of great out-of-the-way ports of call. Are you in love yet? We are.

The sailing ship thing is always romantic, and Windstar is particularly hot. Lounge by the pool under full sails as the ship cuts through the surf to the next exotic port of call. Retire to your cabin and enjoy room service or just drinks from the minibar. Have a cocktail under the stars, then enjoy chef Joachim Splichal's delicious cuisine in open-seating restaurants where you can always get a cozy table for two. No wonder Windstar's so popular with honeymooners.

The sophisticated, well-traveled crowd who's attracted to Windstar appreciates the classic, nautical surroundings, all stained teak, brass details, and navy-blue fabrics. And while the ships' proud masts and white sails cut a traditional profile, they're also ultra-state-of-the-art, controlled by a computer so that they can be furled or unfurled at the touch of a button (though the ships' diesel engines are used often too).

As you see a Windstar ship approaching port, with its long, graceful hull and masts the height of 20-story buildings, you forget all about the giant megaships moored nearby and think, *Now that's a ship.*

Beyond "don't wear shorts in the dining rooms," there's no real dress code here, and most men don't even bother with a sport jacket at dinner. The Windstar crowd, a casually elegant group of 30- to 60-somethings, wouldn't want to vacation any other way. Table 13-25 offers Windstar itineraries and lists sample rates.

The line operates under a tipping-not-required policy, although generally guests do tip staff as much as on other ships; on Windstar, as on Holland America, there's just less pressure to do so.

Windstar often offers two-for-one deals and discounted or free airfares.

Dining

Great cuisine is a high point of a Windstar cruise, and you can find it offered in two or three open-seating, always-casual restaurants on board the line's three ships. The cuisine here was created by award-winning chef/restaurateur Joachim Splichal, of Los Angeles' Patina, who at press

Table 13-25	Windstar Itineraries and Sample Fares
Ship/Fares (per person/day)	**Itineraries**
Wind Spirit No inside cabins; $291 outside; $428 suite	**7-night eastern Caribbean:** Round-trip from St. Thomas, USVI, Jan–Mar and Dec; **7-night Mediterranean:** Lisbon, Portugal, to Barcelona, Spain; Barcelona to Rome, Italy; Rome to Athens, Greece; Athens to Istanbul, Turkey; Istanbul to Athens; Athens to Rome; Rome to Barcelona; Barcelona to Lisbon, Apr–Nov
Wind Star No inside cabins; $379 outside; $725 suite	**7-night Costa Rica:** Round-trip from Puerto Caldera, Costa Rica, Jan–Mar and Dec; **7-night Mediterranean:** Lisbon, Portugal, to Barcelona, Spain; Rome, Italy, to Athens, Greece; Athens to Istanbul, Turkey; Istanbul to Athens; Athens to Venice, Italy; Venice to Athens; Athens to Rome; Rome to Barcelona; Barcelona to Lisbon, Apr–Nov; **14-night southern Caribbean/Central America:** Barbados to Puerto Caldera, Nov
Wind Surf No inside cabins; $280 outside; $441 suite	**7-night eastern/southern Caribbean:** Round-trip from Barbados, Jan–Apr and Dec; **7-night Mediterranean:** Lisbon, Portugal, to Malaga, Spain; Malaga to Marseille, France; Marseille to Rome, Italy; Rome to Nice, France; Nice to Rome; Rome to Barcelona, Spain; Barcelona to Lisbon; Lisbon to Barcelona; Barcelona to Rome; and Rome to Barcelona, Apr–Nov; **14-night Mediterranean:** Rome to Nice, May; **8-night southern Caribbean:** Round-trip from Barbados, Dec

time, was about to introduce 70 new recipes. His yummy dishes are straightforward, yet incorporate regional touches and surprising twists. The wine list is also impressive. Vegetarian dishes and healthy "Sail Light" choices designed by light-cooking expert Jeanne Jones are available for breakfast, lunch, and dinner; fat and calorie content is listed on the menu.

Restaurants aboard all three ships are set up with an unusual number of tables for two (proving that Windstar is serious about its romantic image), and there's rarely a wait.

Generous spreads at breakfast and lunch are available at the buffet-style Veranda on all three ships. Windstar's largest ship, the *Wind Surf,* also offers alternative dining at the casual, 128-seat Bistro, an intimate space with a pretty garden motif and slightly more eclectic menu choices. Reservations are required, but there's no additional fee.

The once-a-week evening barbecues on the Pool Decks of the *Star* and *Spirit* are wonderful parties under the stars, with a beautifully designed buffet spread and (often) a Caribbean-style band adding ambience. On the *Wind Surf,* there's a gala buffet dinner once per cruise in the main lounge, and all three ships also offer weekly barbeque lunches on deck.

The ships' pool bars offer pizza and hot dogs afternoons, and the 24-hour room service includes the standards plus seafood and steaks from 11 a.m. to 10 p.m.; during restaurant hours you can have anything from the restaurant's menu served in your cabin.

Activities and entertainment

There are zippo rah-rah activities, keeping days loose and languid: explore ashore (the itineraries visit a port almost every day) or kick back and relax aboard ship without a lot of distraction. The few things scheduled during the day include ho-hum stuff such as casino gaming lessons, walk-a-mile and stretch classes on deck, and maybe a vegetable-carving demo.

At ports where the ships anchor offshore, passengers can enjoy complimentary kayaking, sailing, water-skiing, snorkeling, windsurfing, and banana-boat rides, all from a watersports platform that's lowered from the stern, weather and sea conditions permitting. For a fee, you can also go scuba diving. You can also swim off of the platform on *Wind Spirit* and *Star,* though not on the larger *Wind Surf* for safety reasons. Up top, the Pool Deck offers a small pool and hot tub, deck chairs, and an open-air bar.

Come evenings, the low-key Windstar crowd enjoys dinner and pre- and post-cocktails. Several musicians are aboard each sailing to provide tunes for evening dancing and background. Most evenings, passengers either retire to their cabins; head for the modest casino; or go up to the pool bar for a nightcap under the stars. Sometimes after 10 or 11 p.m., disco/pop music is played in the lounge if guests are in a dancing mood, and once per cruise is a crew talent show.

The ships each maintain an open-bridge policy, so at most times you're free to walk right in to chat with the captain and officers on duty.

If you consider a massage to be an important cruise activity, you'll love the *Wind Surf.* Considering its intimate, 308-passenger size, she has a surprisingly large and well-accoutered spa facility, totally outclassing most facilities on other similar-size ships. Spa packages geared to men and women can be purchased in advance through your travel agent, with appointment times made once you're on board, or you can simply book individual treatments. The ship's totally glass-walled ocean-view gym and separate aerobics room are also as good as it gets on a small ship.

For kids

As you may expect, these are not kiddy ships. There are no organized activities or playrooms. The kids that do appear aboard are generally age 10 and up (the official age minimum is 2), but there are rarely more than six or seven kids on any sailing, and those only during school breaks. The ships' DVD libraries stock some children's films.

(Photo: Windstar Cruises)

Figure 13-13: *Wind Spirit*

Fleet facts

Although Windstar ships have tens of thousands of square feet of Dacron flying from their masts, they operate as smoothly as the very best modern yachts, owing to the computers that control the sails and stabilizers. The *Wind Spirit* (see Figure 13-13) and *Wind Star* are identical, with all outside cabins (featuring large portholes) and impressive teakwood-decked, recently refurbished bathrooms. The *Wind Surf* was built at the same shipyard and has the same sail-ship concept as the others, but being larger, it also boasts a bunch of suites, more lounges and dining venues, and plenty of excellent outside sitting and walking areas.

All cabins fleetwide have flat-screen TVs, DVD/CD players, and minibars. The ships offer an extensive DVD and CD collection.

At press time, Windstar was gearing up to announce a fleetwide refurbishment program called "Degrees of Difference." Similar to parent company Holland America's recent "Signature of Excellence" initiative, it will address all aspects of the passenger experience. See Table 13-26 for fleet specifications.

Table 13-26		Windstar Fleet Specifications				
Ship	**Entered Service**	**Passengers**	**Crew**	**Total Cabins**	**Tonnage**	**Length in Feet**
Wind Star/Spirit	1986/88	148	90	74	5,350	440
Wind Surf	1990	308	190	154	14,745	614

Part V
Calling All Ports: Where to Go and Why

It's a group of local musicians here to play for you. It's the customary greeting for new arrivals here on Jackhammer Island.

In this part . . .

A lot of cruise lines (and cruise passengers) behave as if the amenities and other hoo-ha's aboard ship are the be-all and end-all of the cruise experience. Not so. The *destinations* are what it's all about. In this part, we give you a good overview of the major (and some of the minor) ports of embarkation and ports of call in the Caribbean, Alaska, and the Mediterranean, and let you know what to expect on cruises in more than a dozen other destinations, from Tahiti to Arctic Scandinavia. We offer hints on the best shore excursions you can book through the cruise lines and also tell you what you can see on your own, whether you want to investigate natural wonders and historic sites or just grab a snow globe souvenir and hit the beach.

Chapter 14

Preparing for Ports of Call

A s the old Cunard slogan put it, "Getting there is half the fun," but the other half of a cruise's fun is *being* there, seeing the sights and getting a taste of local culture at the ports of call. Aside from some transatlantic sailings and 2-night party cruises, pretty much every cruise includes time in port, with some itineraries more port-intensive than others. It's just a matter of letting the ship take you there — but when you get there you have a few little decisions to make. This chapter walks you through the practical ins and outs of doing just that.

Signing Up for Excursions — or Not

At almost every port of call, you have three options: join one of the ship's organized shore excursions, strike out on your own, or remain on the ship and take it easy.

Gimme the whole truth about excursions

Shore excursions usually mean piling into a tour bus, although at some locations, you may take some other mode of transportation — minivan, jet boat, kayak, horse cart, helicopter, plane, or your own two feet. The excursion cost includes admission to any attractions visited, sometimes a meal, dance, and/or musical performance, and (oy vey) often a stop at a "preferred" souvenir store. A guide typically provides running commentary that's usually a combination of informative and corny.

For cruise passengers, most shore excursions (which we preview throughout the chapters in this part) are all about providing convenience and a sense of security. The excursion's staff picks you up right at the pier, drive you to your destination, give you a tour, and then drop you back off at the ship. Zip, boom, bang: done. Other excursions take things a little further, providing adventure and educational opportunities, sometimes near the port, sometimes at a considerable distance away.

In most cases, shore excursions are run by local tour operators with whom the cruise lines have an established business relationship. That means more "sense of security" for you, and a cut of the profits for the cruise lines — because remember, in almost all cases you pay for excursions over and above the cost of your cruise.

When do shore excursions make sense?

In ports where you can best reach the sights on foot, beating your own path is often less expensive and more exciting. However, in locales where most attractions are far from the docks — and taxis or other local modes of transportation are scarce, expensive, or dubious — you may be better off going with the flow and booking an organized excursion.

Other shore excursions that are generally worth the money are sports and adventure offerings, such as kayaking, biking, golfing, fishing, snorkeling, scuba diving, and flightseeing tours. These expeditions take smaller groups of passengers at a time, so you feel like part of the team rather than part of the herd. You can book most of these activities on your own, but by booking through the cruise line you're trading extra cost for lack of hassle, and assurance that the tour operator is reliable.

Are shore excursions for you?

Choosing an excursion is a matter of both personal preference and pocketbook concerns, and comes down to a few basic questions:

- ✔ Do you enjoy the company of a group (even on a crowded bus) and a sometimes perky tour guide to tell you what you're seeing, or do you prefer exploring quietly by yourself, even if you get lost occasionally?

- ✔ Are the sights you want to see close to the docks, or some distance away? In some ports, the most interesting sights are just a few blocks from the dock, but if they're far off it may cost you just as much to go on your own. Of course, going on your own also gives you more freedom to pursue your own interests, but you're also responsible for getting back to the ship on time. If an excursion's late in returning, the ship will wait for it. Not necessarily so if one or two passengers haven't returned by all-aboard time.

- ✔ How easy is it to find a cab, bus, or rental car to tour on your own, and how reliable is that transportation?

- ✔ Does the tour include all the things you definitely want to see and do? Some tour descriptions (especially of longer tours) read as if you can spend hours seeing everything there is to see, but in reality they move at a snail's pace to accommodate slow-walking passengers, and take hours getting to and from the destination. If the tour doesn't hit everything you want to see, will you still have time to see or do them before or after the tour?

- ✔ Does the activity you want to do require advance reservations (such as tee times for golf)?

✔ How much do the attractions you want to see cost? If they're near the dock, it may make sense to just go on your own, rather than pay the cruise line an extra amount to arrange tickets and a bus transfer. However, sometimes groups get priority entry to popular sights, such as La Sagrada Familia cathedral in Barcelona.

In the chapters that follow, we provide more detailed information on each port, making it easier for you to answer these questions.

How much do shore excursions cost?

Costs for prearranged shore excursions vary widely: You may pay $30 for a short bus or walking tour or $300 or more for a flightseeing trip via helicopter or plane. Prices listed in this book are adult rates; kids' prices are also usually available for all tours.

Guides expect tips, although the amount is up to you. Around 5 percent of the per-person excursion cost is about right if you enjoyed the tour.

How do you sign up?

Until recently, you always had to book shore excursions aboard ship, but recently a lot of lines have begun taking reservations early, usually via the Web. Excursions are listed on the lines' Web sites, along with descriptions, durations, and usually prices.

If you wait till you get aboard to sign up, do so early, especially if you intend to book the more specialized tours, which sometimes can only accept a limited number of guests.

Order forms for excursions may be waiting in your cabin on arrival. If not, you can find them at the main reception desk or shore excursions desk, or at a shore excursions talk that many lines give on the first day of the cruise. After you sign up, your account is charged for any cost, and the meeting time and place for your tour is written on the tickets delivered to your cabin before your first scheduled tour. Usually groups meet in the ship's theater or lounge and then debark the ship together.

Make sure that you really want to take all the tours you sign up for. The cruise lines usually tell the local tour operators how many have signed up so that the appropriate number of vehicles and guides can be arranged. If you change your mind after they've called, you'll probably pay the cost of the excursion anyway, even if you don't go.

Can I just sightsee on my own?

If you decide to just take in the port on your own, you can go the loose and easy route — just wandering around and seeing what strikes you — or you can plan your visit like Eisenhower planned D-Day. We're big fans of the former, though certain ports just have so many sights that a little bit of the latter may be in order, too. Here are some tips:

✔ **Prioritize:** Create a must-see list and calculate how much time you need to get there and how much it costs to get in when you do. You can ask the ship's shore excursions staff for assistance here.

✔ **Study up on adventures:** Even if you don't want to book a shore excursion through the cruise line, you may want to consult with the excursion staff for activities such as horseback riding, diving, tennis, and golf. They can recommend reliable operators and tell you if you need a reservation. Keep in mind that facilities and operators ashore may get booked up, not only by cruise passengers but also with land-based vacationers.

✔ **Avoid unmarked taxis:** That nice guy beckoning you over to his car promising a cheap tour may really be a nice guy . . . or he may not. Official, marked taxis are more likely to be legit, and often have to abide by city- or state-mandated rates.

✔ **Keep your cabbie:** If you find a reliable cab driver that gets you where you want to go, you may be able to have him pick you up when it's time to go back to the ship. This is especially important if you head to an out-of-the-way beach area (you may not find cabs waiting when you're ready to go).

✔ **Consider cost-sharing:** Share the cost of a cab with a couple of cruisemates, even if you all want to split up when you get to your destinations. And when you negotiate the cost, make sure you and the cab driver are talking in the same currency.

✔ **Reserve a table:** If you want to dine at a highly rated restaurant, make a reservation before you leave home.

✔ **Eat (and drink) smart:** Keep your wits about you when snacking ashore. What vibe do you get from that street vendor's cart: "Looks okay to me" or "Looks like salmonella central"? Likewise, bottled water may be a better option than tap in some places. If you're suspicious of the water quality, remember that the ice in your drink could be dodgy, too.

✔ **Don't dawdle:** Make sure you get back to the dock by all-aboard time. Make a note of it, or carry your ship's daily program with you ashore: The time is always listed there.

Prices listed for attractions are adult rates; kids prices are frequently available.

Why get off at all?

You're a paying guest on this cruise. Nobody can tell you what you can and can't do. If you want to stay on board the whole time, that's your right. But seriously, it's an option, especially if the port doesn't thrill you, or you've been there before, or you're just plain tired. The restaurants remain open, a limited range of activities are still offered, ship spas typically offer discounts on port-day appointments, and the ship is just generally quieter when everyone else is gone.

Starting your vacation before you embark

With few exceptions, a cruise's port of embarkation is a destination of its own. Most lines offer pre- and post-cruise packages for cruisers who want to stretch their trip by two to four days, or more. In Alaska, the Mediterranean, and some other destinations, cruise lines offer escorted tours that take you away from the coastal areas, traveling by bus, train, and sometimes boat and small plane to sights inland. These cruisetour packages include hotel stays and transportation. If you want to make your own hotel arrangements, we suggest properties in the main embarkation cities in the chapters that follow.

Most ships don't start boarding until the afternoon and don't depart until after 4 p.m., so even if you arrive on departure day, you may still be able to fit in some sightseeing at your city of embarkation. You can normally leave your luggage at the pier.

Getting from Ship to Shore: All about Debarking

You can't start sashaying down the gangway as soon as your ship ties up to the dock. Nope. You have to wait for local authorities to stamp all kinds of paperwork first. This may be a short process or it may take up to two hours, so relax. Have breakfast, look at the view, and study your city guide until the captain announces the all-clear over the ship's PA.

Docking versus anchoring

When a ship comes to port, it either docks at a pier or anchors offshore, depending on the size of the ship (sometimes the dock isn't deep enough or long enough to accommodate it) or the popularity of the port that day (other ships may have gotten dibs on the docks first). Docking is easy, at least for passengers: You just go to the gangway, swipe your onboard ID, and you're off. Things are a little more complicated when you're anchored. In these situations, passengers transit back and forth to shore via small boats called *launches* or *tenders*.

Tender debarkation usually works like this: Everyone who wants to go ashore goes to one of the public lounges and is given a number. Shore-excursion parties debark first. If you're not taking an excursion, you may get an early tender assignment by being first in line, though you still may have to wait a while.

When it's time for you to go, report to the lower deck where the tenders are loading. You have to descend a stairway outside the ship to a launch platform. There, crewmembers will be ready to help you onto the tender. Sometimes choppy waves make the boats bob like corks, so you may need to jump a bit to get on board. If you have a disability or just require special assistance getting in and out of the tender, alert the crew in advance so that they can better prepare to assist you.

The ride to shore, although usually short, can sometimes be rough. If you suffer from seasickness, try to sit near an open area and/or use a seasickness remedy.

The tenders run all day, so you can return to the ship at any time (including for lunch). Tenders from several anchored ships may board from the same dock, so you have to show your ID to get aboard.

Filling your daypack

Be sure to tote the following essentials when you disembark:

- ✔ **Ship boarding pass and/or shipboard identification:** Without them, you'll have trouble getting back on board.

- ✔ **Cash:** Although your onboard expenses go on account, you still need cash and maybe credit cards ashore. (Chapter 5 has the details on getting the right currency in countries where the dollar doesn't fly.) Make a special note of this: After you've spent a few days aboard ship, it's easy to forget that you need to carry cash.

- ✔ **Passport or other ID:** In foreign destinations, you should always keep your passport with you. If your ship is holding onto it for group-clearance purposes, get a photocopy of the main page to keep with you in port.

- ✔ **Sunblock/hat:** A few weeks ago, in Ibiza, we saw our 20,465th burnt-to-a-crisp tourist. Don't be number 20,466.

- ✔ **Bottled water:** Ships sell bottled water near the gangway, but you can probably get it more cheaply once you get ashore.

- ✔ **Beach towels:** Most ships hand them out for use ashore.

Getting from Shore to Ship: Don't Miss the Boat!

Cruise lines are very strict about sailing times, posting the schedules both in the daily bulletin and at the gangway. At ports where your ship is tendered offshore, the final tender departure time is also listed. You absolutely, positively need to be back at the dock at least a half-hour before the ship's scheduled departure — otherwise you may miss the boat. Shore excursions provide an exception to this rule. If they run late, the ship accepts responsibility and doesn't leave without you. If you travel on your own, however, you could get stuck.

If you do miss the boat, contact the cruise line's port agent immediately — they have offices near the docks, usually with a prominent sign, and their address is sometimes listed in the ship's daily program as well. They can help you catch your ship at the next port of call, but you have to pay your own way there.

Chapter 15

Landing in the Caribbean

In This Chapter

▶ Poking around the ports of embarkation
▶ Calling at the Caribbean's ports
▶ Enjoying the best excursions
▶ Exploring private islands

*W*hen most people think cruise, they think Caribbean, whether they mean to or not. It's almost creepy, like they've been programmed — and maybe they have. For a dog's age, the cruise industry focused laserlike on the region, and it's still the top cruise destination, for good reason. On the practical side, the Caribbean islands (and The Bahamas, which aren't technically on the Caribbean Sea but might as well be) are pretty much in Florida's backyard, and are so close to one another that it makes for easy sailing. On the unpractical side are white-sand beaches, swaying palms, clear turquoise waters, tropical fish, lush gardens, deep rain forests, waterfalls, mountains, rivers, and even volcanoes — plus rich Caribbean culture, spicy Caribbean food, European colonial history, and a big dollop of laid-back island living to top it all off. The multicultural history of the region creates a checkerboard blend, with the architecture, language, and customs of the Spanish, French, Dutch, Swedish, British, and Americans in their former (and current) colonies or possession. Pre-Columbian peoples, European explorers, pirates, and shipwrecked sailors all contributed to the stories behind numerous ruins, forts, churches, synagogues, historic homes, and museums.

Storming the Shore

Now granted, a lot of the islands are touristy, but often it's confined to the vicinity of the docks and other resort areas. If you tire of shopping for fine jewelry, local handicrafts, and duty-free items (or of tipping back the beers at an island bar), you can head to more isolated and frequently gorgeous spots along the coast or in the interior, either on your own or a shore excursion. In this chapter, we list a selection of the best excursions offered by cruise lines in all the ports.

Major sights on many of the islands are also perfectly accessible on your own, either on foot or with the aid of a taxi or other transportation. As is true everywhere, the cruise lines contract with local operators to run these tours, so you may be able to get the same trips cheaper by booking them yourself once you arrive. Of course, you may just want the ease of having the cruise line do it for you, figuring the extra few bucks they make off the top is worth it.

Shore excursions aren't what they used to be either. For every bland bus tour or mindless booze cruise, the cruise lines over the past few years have also been programming more and more active excursions, including rain forest hikes, mountain biking, golf, jungle canopy exploration, scuba, sport fishing, horseback riding, and more.

 The prices listed in this chapter are based on 2005 rates and may be slightly higher in 2006.

Boarding Ship for the Caribbean

The main port cities for Caribbean cruises remain in Florida — Miami, Fort Lauderdale, Cape Canaveral/Cocoa Beach, and Tampa — plus San Juan (Puerto Rico). In recent years, though, cruises have been leaving from **alternative homeports** such as Galveston and Houston, Texas; Charleston, South Carolina; Norfolk, Virginia; Jacksonville, Florida; and even as far north as Baltimore, Philadelphia, and New York. Beyond Puerto Rico, other Caribbean islands also serve as homeports, including St. Thomas and Barbados.

In this chapter, we cover the most heavily trafficked ports of embarkation for Caribbean cruises — Miami, Fort Lauderdale, Cape Canaveral/ Cocoa Beach, Tampa, and Galveston — hitting the see-and-do highlights, whether you only have a few hours before or after your cruise or are planning an extra couple days. (Prior to Hurricane Katrina, New Orleans served as a popular port — and may again — but cleanup from the devastation could take months or even years.) The cruise lines typically offer pre- and post-cruise packages for hotels, sometimes with a rental car, admission to local attractions, and/or organized tours.

San Juan, which is a port of embarkation *and* a popular port of call, is covered in the ports of call section.

Miami

Maybe more than anyplace else in the U.S., Miami seems to embody the cultural mash-up of fashion, celebrity, design, and wealth that is America in 2006. It's the most Latin city in the country, with a stylin' club scene that's utterly replaced the retirement condo lifestyle that predominated in the 1970s. It's like the Rat Pack era has returned, only now it's got a Latino accent.

The Gulf of Mexico & the Caribbean

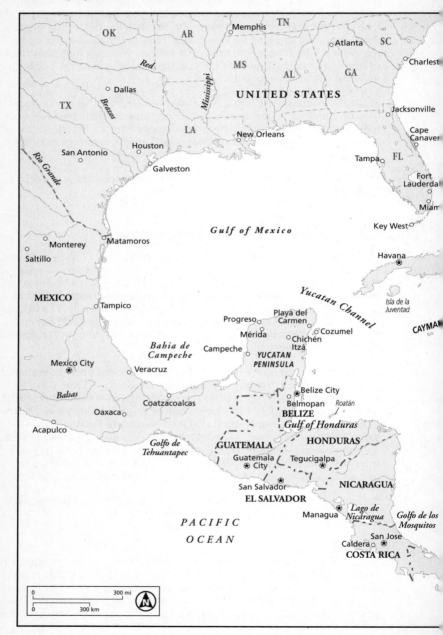

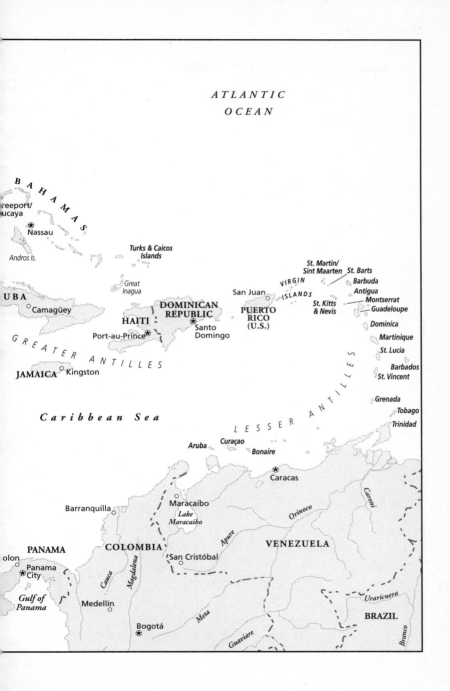

Florida Homeports

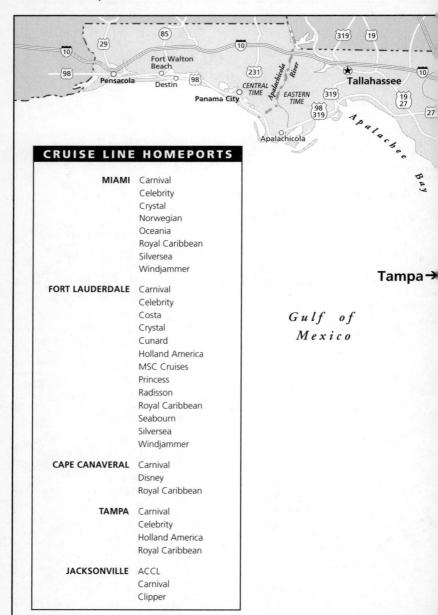

CRUISE LINE HOMEPORTS

MIAMI	Carnival
	Celebrity
	Crystal
	Norwegian
	Oceania
	Royal Caribbean
	Silversea
	Windjammer
FORT LAUDERDALE	Carnival
	Celebrity
	Costa
	Crystal
	Cunard
	Holland America
	MSC Cruises
	Princess
	Radisson
	Royal Caribbean
	Seabourn
	Silversea
	Windjammer
CAPE CANAVERAL	Carnival
	Disney
	Royal Caribbean
TAMPA	Carnival
	Celebrity
	Holland America
	Royal Caribbean
JACKSONVILLE	ACCL
	Carnival
	Clipper

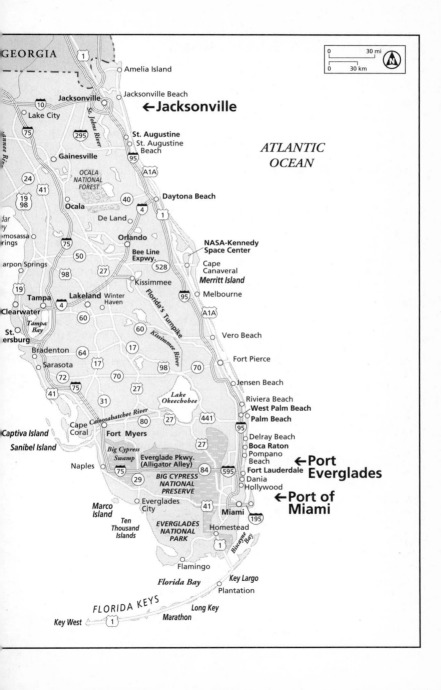

Of course, all the stuff that made Miami a resort destination in the first place is still there too: sparkling beaches, crystal clear waters, palm fronds, and that particularly Miami style of resort hotel, jutting up right from the beach's edge. And it's the undisputed cruise capital of the world, with nearly 4 million passengers embarking here annually.

Cruising into port

Miami International Airport (☎ **305-876-7000;** www.miami-airport. com) is about 8 miles (or 15 minutes) west of downtown Miami and the port. If you've arranged air transportation and/or transfers through the cruise line, a cruise line rep directs you to shuttle buses to the port. Taxis are also available for a fare of about $21 (plus tip) to the port. **SuperShuttle** (☎ **305-871-2000**) charges $12 per person to the port, with two pieces of luggage.

If you're arriving by car from the north, take I-95 to I-395 and head east on I-395, exiting at Biscayne Boulevard. Make a right and go south to Port Boulevard. Make a left and go over the Port Bridge. Coming in from the northwest, take Interstate 75 to State Road 826 (Palmetto Expwy.) south to State Road 836 east. Exit at Biscayne Boulevard. Make a right and go south to Port Boulevard. Make a left and go over the Port Bridge. Parking lots at street level face the cruise terminals. Parking runs $12 per day.

A five-lane bridge from the downtown district of Miami provides access to the number-one cruise port in the world, the **Port of Miami** (1015 N. America Way; ☎ **305-371-7678;** www.miamidade.gov/portofmiami). To accommodate the enormous amount of cruise traffic, a dozen bi-level terminals offer easy car access (as you're coming) and quick Customs clearance (as you're going).

Scoring the best excursions

Everglades Airboat Ride: The Seminole Indians called the Everglades *Pahay Okee,* the "grassy water," and on this 40-minute airboat ride you get to see some of the area's indigenous wildlife, including water birds and American alligators (4 hours; $45).

Exploring on your own

You probably need a taxi to hit most of the attractions in Miami.

Go to the beach! You can beachcomb along 10 miles of glorious sand and surf between the south of **Miami Beach** and **Haulover Beach Park** at the north end. Behind the surf, South Beach's renowned **Art Deco district** spreads out over a full square mile. All in all, it's the largest concentration of 1920s and 1930s resort architecture in the U.S. The district stretches from 6th to 23rd streets, and from the Atlantic Ocean to Lennox Court. Ocean Drive boasts many premier Art Deco hotels, while other buildings house chic shops, clubs, restaurants, and cafes.

Miami at a Glance

Pro Player Stadium

Palmetto Expwy.

NW 57th Ave.

817

9

NE 167th St.

NE 163rd St.

SUNNY ISLES

NORTH MIAMI

95

Gratigny Pkwy.

Red Rd.

916

NW 119th St.

NE 125th St.

Haulover Beach Park

BAL HARBOUR

Collins Ave.

HIALEAH

955

W 4th Ave.

Le Jeune Rd.

Amtrak Station

934

North-South Expwy.

N. Miami Ave.

915

Biscayne Blvd.

Bal Harbour Beach

SURFSIDE

A1A

Hialeah Racetrack

NW 79th St.

441

79th St. Cswy.

85th Street Beach

Okeechobee Rd.

944

953

LITTLE HAITI

95

Pelican Island

Airport Expwy.

112

Julia Tuttle Cswy.

195

MIAMI BEACH

Bass Museum of Art

Miami International Airport

NW 42nd Ave.

MIAMI

Biscayne Blvd.

South Beach Art Deco District

Venetian Cswy.

Lummus Park Beach

Collins Ave.

836

Dolphin Expwy.

Bayside Marketplace

Orange Bowl

DOWN-TOWN

MacArthur Cswy.

SOUTH BEACH

W. Flagler Rd.

LITTLE HAVANA

SW 8th St.

41

S. Miami Ave.

Miami Children's Museum/Parrot Jungle Island

First Street Beach

Tamiami Trail

9

SW 22nd St.

Port of Miami

Fisher Island

972

Miracle Mile

Hobie Beach

Brickell Ave.

VIRGINIA KEY

CORAL GABLES

COCONUT GROVE

S. Bayshore Dr.

Rickenbacker Cswy.

Miami Seaquarium

S. Dixie Hwy.

Le Jeune Rd.

Douglas Rd.

Vizcaya Museum & Gardens

Main Hwy.

Biscayne Bay

KEY BISCAYNE

Crandon Blvd.

Crandon Park Beach

ATLANTIC OCEAN

Old Cutler Rd.

Fairchild Tropical Garden

BILL BAGGS CAPE FLORIDA STATE PARK

Cape Florida

0   3 mi
0   3 km

✈ Airport

🏖 Beach

🚢 Cruise ship dock

Near the port, **Bayside Marketplace** (401 Biscayne Blvd.; ☎ 305-577-3344; www.baysidemarketplace.com) is a vibrant shopping and entertainment complex with many bayside restaurants and cafes offering outdoor seating, plus live musicians in the evenings. Regular shuttle service is available from the port, or you can walk over the Port Bridge.

If oil paintings turn you on more than tanning oil, the **Bass Museum of Art** (2121 Park Ave.; ☎ 305-673-7530; www.bassmuseum.org) houses old masters and then some. Admission is $6. Farther afield, the 70-room Italian Renaissance-style villa now known as **Vizcaya Museum & Gardens** (3251 S. Miami Ave., Coconut Grove; ☎ 305-250-9133; www.vizcayamuseum.com) has been called "the Hearst Castle of the East." Industrialist James Deering employed more than a thousand artisans and laborers from Europe and the Caribbean to build his dream house, which was completed in 1916 but designed to look as if it had stood for centuries. Inside, you can visit 42 rooms filled with furniture, paintings, sculpture, tapestries, wall panels, and decorative arts brought from Europe by Deering and his designers. Admission to the villa and gardens is $12. It's about a mile from downtown Miami.

Take the kids to the **Miami Children's Museum** (980 MacArthur Causeway; ☎ 305-373-KIDS; www.miamichildrensmuseum.org), which offers hundreds of interactive exhibits plus programs, classes, and learning materials related to arts, culture, community, and communication, including a mock TV studio, a music studio that exposes kids to music from other cultures, and (how Miami!) a mini Carnival cruise ship where kids see how a ship works, from navigating to limbo dancing. Admission is $10; kids under 12 months free.

Across the MacArthur Causeway from the kids' museum, 19-acre **Parrot Jungle Island** (1111 Parrot Jungle Trail; ☎ 305-2-Jungle; www.parrotjungle.com) features an Everglades exhibit, a petting zoo, and several theaters, jungle trails, and aviaries. Hundreds of parrots, macaws, peacocks, cockatoos, and flamingos fly overhead, while the Serpentarium houses the park's reptile and amphibian collection, including a 20-foot long saltwater crocodile. Eek! Continuous shows star roller-skating cockatoos, card-playing macaws, and stunt-happy parrots. Admission is $24.95 adults, $19.95 kids 3 to 10, free under 3.

To see sea critters in action, head to the **Miami Seaquarium** (4400 Rickenbacker Causeway, Key Biscayne; ☎ 305-361-5705; www.miamiseaquarium.com), where Flipper, TV's greatest sea mammal, performs along with Lolita the Killer Whale. You can also see endangered manatees, sea lions, tropical-theme aquariums, and a gruesome shark feeding. Admission is $26 adults, $21 kids.

Fort Lauderdale

Fort Lauderdale's **Port Everglades** is nearly as busy as the Port of Miami, drawing more than 3.5 million cruise passengers a year. It boasts the deepest harbor on the eastern seaboard south of Norfolk, 12

Fort Lauderdale at a Glance

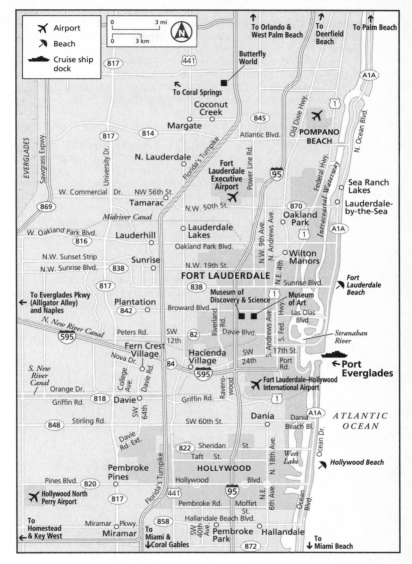

ultramodern cruise terminals, and easy access to the Fort Lauderdale–Hollywood International Airport. Unlike Miami, though, Port Everglades doesn't offer much nearby activity — just comfortable cruise terminals with snack bars and seating areas.

Fort Lauderdale and its well-known strip of beaches, restaurants, bars, and souvenir shops was once infamous for the annual mayhem that descended every spring break, but yesterday's students have been replaced by a far more affluent and definitely quieter yachting crowd. Boating isn't just a hobby here; it's a lifestyle, with more than 300 miles of navigable waterways and innumerable canals criss-crossing this city called "The Venice of America." Visitors can easily get on the water too by grabbing one of the **water taxis** (☎ 954-467-6677; www.watertaxi.com), which sail between Oakland Park Boulevard and Southeast 17th Street along the Intracoastal Waterway, and west along the New River into downtown Fort Lauderdale. All-day passes are $5.

Cruising into port

Port Everglades (☎ 954-523-3404) is located on State Road 84, east of U.S. 1, about a 2-mile/5-minute drive from the **Fort Lauderdale—Hollywood International Airport.** It's the easiest airport-to-cruise port trip in Florida. If you've booked air or transfers through the cruise line, a representative shows you to your shuttle after you land. If you haven't, taking a taxi costs less than $10 to the port or $12 to the city. If you're driving to Port Everglades, you enter via Spangler Boulevard, Eisenhower Boulevard, or Eller Drive. Parking is available in two large garages for $12 a day.

Scoring the best excursions

Everglades Airboat Ride: A longer version of this tour that we discuss in the preceding "Miami" section also visits the Flamingo Gardens and Wildlife Sanctuary, an old homestead that now houses a free-flight aviary (2½ hours; $36–$48).

Exploring on your own

You need transportation (taxi or otherwise) to get around Fort Lauderdale.

Backed by an endless row of hotels, the **Fort Lauderdale Beach** is located along Fort Lauderdale Beach Boulevard between SE 17th Street and Sunrise Boulevard. The **Fort Lauderdale Beach Promenade** is ideal for rollerblading, biking, or just strolling.

In the walk-through, screened-in aviary at **Butterfly World** (Tradewinds Park South, 3600 W. Sample Rd., Coconut Creek, west of the Florida Turnpike; ☎ 954-977-4400; www.butterflyworld.com), visitors can see 150 different varieties of the colorful insects performing butterfly ballet all summer long. Admission is $17.95 adults, $12.95 kids 4 to 12, free for kids 3 and under. In downtown Fort Lauderdale, the **Museum of Discovery & Science** (401 SW Second St.; ☎ 954-467-6637; www.mods.org) is an excellent interactive science museum with an IMAX theater and more than a dozen themed, hands-on exhibitions. Admission for both IMAX and exhibits is $14 adults, $12 kids 3 to 12, free for 2 and under.

The **Museum of Art** (downtown at 1 E. Las Olas Blvd.; ☎ 954-763-6464; www.moafl.org) is a terrific small museum with a permanent collection of 20th-century European and American art that includes works by

Picasso, Calder, Warhol, Mapplethorpe, and Dalí. African, South Pacific, pre-Columbian, Native American, and Cuban art are also on display. Admission is $7; closed Mondays.

Cape Canaveral/Cocoa Beach

Known as the "Space Coast" because of nearby Kennedy Space Center, the Cape Canaveral/Cocoa Beach/Melbourne area is really anything but space-age looking. Stretched out along 72 miles of beachfront, it's primarily a string of hotels, malls, and suburban homes on little side streets (one of them called "I Dream of Jeannie Lane," in honor of the old TV show set in Cocoa Beach). Because the area is only about an hour west of Orlando's theme parks, it's become a major port of embarkation for cruise ships, especially ones offering 3- and 4-night cruises that can be paired with 4- and 3-night stays at the Orlando resorts, to make a full week's vacation.

Once fairly quiet, the port got a big boost when Disney Cruise Line started up, building a gorgeous new port facility in 1998. Both of Disney's ships are normally based here year-round. Recently, the area has also begun to benefit from the industry trend of homeporting cruise ships in northerly cities and running them down the coast to The Bahamas. NCL's *Norwegian Dawn,* for example, includes Port Canaveral as a stop on her weekly round-trip Florida/Bahamas cruises from New York, giving passengers access to Orlando and to the Space Center's visitors complex.

Cruising into port

Port Canaveral is located at the eastern end of the Bennett Causeway, just off State Road 528 (the Bee Line Expwy.), the direct route from **Orlando International,** the nearest airport, about 45 minutes away. Cruise line representatives meet you if you've booked air and/or transfers through the line. If not, the **Cocoa Beach Shuttle** (☎ **800-633-0427** or 321-784-3831) offers shuttle service for $27 per person each way. By car, the area is accessible from virtually every interstate highway along the East Coast. Most visitors arrive via Route 1, Interstate 95, or S.R. 528. Parking at the port costs $10 a day.

Exploring on your own

You need a car or taxis to explore the area, which is very spread out.

Although some folks prefer to dash over to Disney World or Universal Studios, we're bigger fans of the **John F. Kennedy Space Center Visitor Complex** (State Road 405 E., Titusville; ☎ **321-449-4444;** www.kennedy spacecenter.com), home to American space flight since the unmanned Bumper 8 research rocket launch in 1950. The complex has real NASA rockets, the actual Mercury Mission Control Room from the 1960s, and exhibits and films (including IMAX) that look at space exploration from the 1950s to today. Tours explore various parts of the huge space center complex, with the complimentary hop-on/hop-off bus tour taking in the **LC-39 Observation Gantry** (with a view of where the space shuttles lift

Cape Canaveral at a Glance

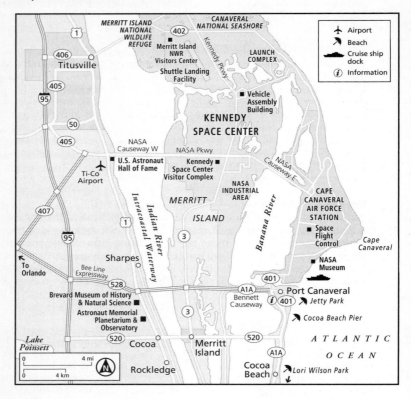

off) and the impressive **Apollo/Saturn V Center,** which includes artifacts, photos, interactive exhibits, and an actual 363-foot **Saturn V rocket.** Buses for this tour operate continuously, leaving every 15 minutes from the visitor center. Extra-cost tours allow you to visit parts of the space center where rockets and shuttles are prepared and launched. Down the road from the visitor complex, near the intersection of Routes 1 and 405, the **U.S. Astronaut Hall of Fame** has an extraordinary museum of space history, and several simulator rides that let you experience high G-forces, weightlessness, and the ups and downs of space flight. Admission (including all exhibits, Astronaut Encounter, IMAX space films, the KSC tour, and the Astronaut Hall of Fame) is $34 adults, $24 kids 3 to 11, free for kids under 3. Note that the last tour departs at 2:15 p.m. from the visitor complex, so get there early and spend the day — it will take that long to see everything.

If you prefer hanging out at the beach, you have a lot to choose from. Right near the port, **Jetty Park** (400 E. Jetty Rd; ☎ **321-783-7111**) is the most elaborate and best-landscaped of the local beaches, with picnic areas, a snack bar, bathrooms, showers, a children's playground, and fishing available. Farther along the A1A, at Meade Avenue, the **Cocoa Beach Pier** is more of a partying spot, with volleyball, surfing, and an open-air bar. **Lori Wilson Park,** farther south at 1500 N. Atlantic Ave., is another nicely landscaped area with bathrooms and showers, and a rustic boardwalk with shaded picnic areas and benches.

Tampa

On the other side of Florida from the rest of the cruise ports, Tampa was a sleepy little town until Cuban immigrants began arriving in the 1880s and founded the local cigar industry. A few years later, magnate Henry B. Plant put Tampa on the tourist map by building a railroad into town. Teddy Roosevelt trained his Rough Riders here during the Spanish-American War, and various economic booms gave the city both its charming, Victorian-style Hyde Park suburb and its towering downtown skyline. The seaport area is under redevelopment, with the **Florida Aquarium** and the **Garrison Seaport Center** (a 30-acre complex of shops, restaurants, and entertainment, including an IMAX theater) being joined by office buildings, apartment complexes, and another major shopping/dining/entertainment center called **Channelside.**

On the western shore of Tampa Bay, St. Petersburg is the picturesque and pleasant flip side of Tampa's busy busy-ness. Originally conceived and built primarily for tourists and wintering snowbirds, it's got a nice downtown area, some quality museums, and a few good restaurants.

More than 810,000 passengers head out to sea from Tampa annually. Ships sailing from here head primarily to the western Caribbean, Mexico's Yucatán Peninsula, and Central America.

Cruising into port

The Port of Tampa is set amid a complicated network of channels and harbors near the historic Cuban enclave of Ybor City and its deep-water Ybor Channel. The cruise terminals are all located along Channelside Drive, close to the heart of things. If you're flying, you'll probably arrive at **Tampa International Airport,** approximately 5 miles from downtown near the junction of Florida 60 and Memorial Highway. If you haven't arranged transfers with the cruise line, the port is an easy 30-minute taxi ride away, with a set fare of $20 per car for up to four people. By car, all roads — or at least I-275, I-75, I-4, U.S. 41, U.S. 92, and U.S. 301 — lead to Tampa. Parking at the port is $12 per day.

Scoring the best excursions

Tampa City Tour: A bus-tour overview of Tampa, with 90 minutes in Ybor City (including the Ybor State Museum), and visits to the University of Tampa, opulent Bayshore Drive, and Hyde Park (4 hours; $34).

Exploring on your own

Tampa is best explored by car, as only the commercial district can be covered on foot. Most interesting, culturally, is the old Latin enclave of **Ybor City,** located about a mile from the docks. Once known as the cigar capital of the world and now one of three national historic districts in Florida, it offers Spanish architecture, antique street lamps, cigar shops, boutiques, nightclubs, and great Cuban food. Most restaurants are spread out along 7th Avenue, the main artery, which is closed to traffic at night. The **Ybor City Museum State Park** (1818 9th Ave., between 18th and 19th streets; ☎ 813-247-6323; www.ybormuseum.org) has displays on the area's cigar history. Admission is $3.

You can get a glimpse of another culture — the Gilded Age tourist kind — at the **Henry B. Plant Museum** (401 W. Kennedy Blvd.; ☎ 813-254-1891; www.plantmuseum.com), easily identified on the Tampa skyline by its 13 silver minarets and distinctive Moorish architecture. It opened in 1891 as the Tampa Bay Hotel, a magnet for wintering society types; it's now filled with European and Oriental furnishings and decorative arts from the original hotel collection. Admission is $5; closed Mondays. The permanent collection of the **Tampa Museum of Art** (600 N. Ashley Dr.; ☎ 813-274-8732; www.tampamuseum.com) is especially strong in ancient Greek, Etruscan, and Roman artifacts, as well as 20th-century art. The museum grounds, fronting the Hillsborough River, contain a sculpture garden and a decorative fountain. Admission is $7; closed Mondays.

Kid-friendly but not wallet-friendly, **Busch Gardens and Adventure Island** (3605 E. Bougainvilla Ave., north of downtown; ☎ 888-800-5447; www.buschgardens.com) is still Tampa Bay's most popular attraction, offering thrill rides, themed "lands" (including Egypt, Timbuktu, Morocco, and the Congo), live entertainment, shops, restaurants, games, and a zoo with nearly 3,400 animals and numerous animal habitats. Admission is reeeeeaaaaaalllly high: $56 for adults, $50 for kids 3 to 9, free for kids 2 and under. Oh, and there's a 7 percent tax on top of that, and parking costs $7.

Near the docks, the **Florida Aquarium** (701 Channelside Dr.; ☎ 813-273-4000; www.flaquarium.org) displays more than 10,000 aquatic plants and animals in a state-of-the-art setting.

If you want to go to the beach, you have to head to neighboring St. Petersburg, which has a north-to-south string of interconnected white sandy shores. While you're there, grab a skein of surrealism at the **Salvador Dalí Museum** (1000 Third St. S., St. Petersburg; ☎ 727-823-3767; www.salvadordalimuseum.org), which contains the world's largest collection of Dalí's work, including 95 oil paintings; more than 100 watercolors and drawings; and 1,300 sketches, sculptures, photographs, and objects d'art.

Tampa at a Glance

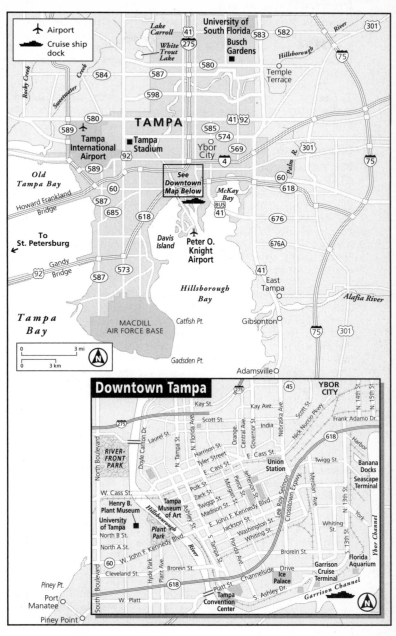

Galveston

Galveston was one of the first ports to which the cruise industry spread when it decided Florida just wasn't enough anymore. Located on a 30-by-2-mile barrier island off the Texas mainland, it's an ideal port from which to sail for the western Caribbean, letting ships reach open sea quickly and be on their way.

The port city's main attractions are its historic districts, full of Victorian architecture, and its beaches, which draw crowds of Houstonians and other Texans during the summer.

Cruising into port

The **Texas Cruise Ship Terminal** at the Port of Galveston (☎ **409-766-6113;** www.portofgalveston.com) is at Harborside Drive and 25th Street, on Galveston Island. It's reached via I-45 south from Houston. If you're flying in, you'll land at one of two Houston airports: **William P. Hobby Airport** (south of downtown Houston, and about 31 miles, or a 45-minute drive, from the terminal) or **George Bush Intercontinental Airport** (just north of downtown Houston, and about 54 miles, or an 80-min. drive, from the terminal). Information on both is available at the Houston Airport System Web site, www.houstonairportsystem.org.

If you've arranged air transportation and/or transfers through the cruise line, a representative directs you to shuttle buses that take you to the port. Taxis are also available, but the price is steep: about $80 per car-load from Hobby or $125 from Bush. If you're driving to the port, I-45 is the main artery for those arriving from the north. To get to the terminal, follow I-45 South to Exit 1C (at Harborside Dr./Hwy. 275); it's the first exit after the causeway. Turn left (east) onto Harborside Drive and continue for about 5 miles to the cruise terminal. Parking rates are based on length of cruise, with 4-day prices starting at $45.

Scoring the best excursions

City Tour: This basic bus tour visits the historic Strand District before heading on to Houston's downtown theater and museum districts, Hermann Park (home to the Houston Zoo), and River Oaks, Houston's most prestigious residential neighborhood. The tour ends at the airport, making it easy for departing passengers (3½ hours; $47).

Exploring on your own

If you've only got a few hours before you have to board your cruise, focus on the **Strand National Historic Landmark District,** the heart of commercial Galveston in the late 1800s and early 1900s, and just steps from the cruise terminals, running from 19th to 25th Streets between Church Street and the piers. Galveston was a booming commercial port back when cotton was king, and the Strand was its Wall Street. Today, its restored three- and four-story buildings, many with decorative ironwork facades, house shopping and dining.

Galveston at a Glance

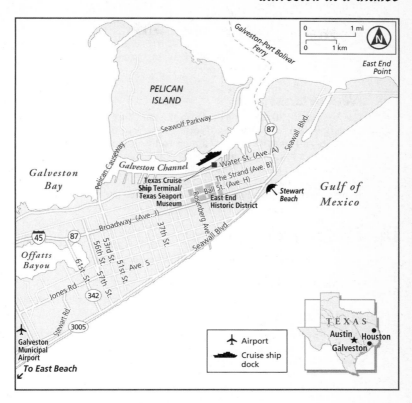

The **East End Historic District** is Galveston's old silk-stocking neighborhood, running from 9th to 19th Streets between Broadway and Church Street. It has many lovely houses that have been completely restored. Three large mansions-turned-museums have regular tours: **Ashton Villa** (2328 Broadway; ☎ 409-762-3933; www.galvestonhistory.com); the **Moody Mansion** (2618 Broadway; ☎ 409-762-7668); and the **Bishop's Palace** (1402 Broadway; ☎ 409-762-2475), the most interesting of the bunch. Admission to each is $6.

For a different take on cruising before you head out on your megaship, visit the *Elissa,* a three-masted, iron-hulled sailing ship built in 1877 and now the main attraction at the **Texas Seaport Museum** (Pier 21, ☎ 409-763-1877; www.tsm-elissa.org). Admission is $6 adults, $4 kids 7 to 18, free ages 6 and under.

While Galveston's beaches may not be as great as, say, Miami's, a good beach is better than no beach at all. **East Beach** and **Stewart Beach** both have pavilions with dressing rooms, showers, and restrooms, and are good for day-trippers. Stewart Beach is located at the end of Broadway, and East Beach is about a mile east of Stewart Beach. Locals and visitors alike also enjoy walking, skating, or biking along Seawall Boulevard, built after the giant September 1900 storm that killed 6,000 of the island's residents — one out of every six. The Seawall stretches for 10 miles along Galveston's shoreline from its eastern edge, providing a kind of low-key boardwalk atmosphere.

New Orleans

On August 29, 2005, just as this book was going to press, Hurricane Katrina smashed into New Orleans, flooding the city and causing catastrophic damage. At this writing, the human toll was still unknown, as were losses to the city's historical and cultural patrimony. Cleanup will take months, if not years. The authors and editors of this book would like to express their condolences to the families and friends of all those who were lost. Our hearts go out to all those struggling still with the storm's aftermath.

The Ports of Call

This section details most of the Caribbean islands visited by cruise ships, as well as some popular ports in the Florida Keys, The Bahamas, and Mexico's Yucatán Peninsula.

Antigua

Antigua (an-*tee*-gah) is the largest of the British Leeward Islands, once the home to Britain's most important Caribbean naval base (Nelson's Dockyard) and now mostly the home of warm tradewinds, powder-white sand beaches, scuba-friendly coral reefs, and about 68,000 Antiguans. St. John's, the island's capital and main town, is a quiet place full of cobblestone sidewalks and weather-beaten wooden houses. Close to port, you can shop in restored warehouses. Away from town, the rolling, rustic island boasts important historic sites and a laid-back vibe.

The language here in **English.** The **Eastern Caribbean dollar** (EC$2.72 = US$1; EC$1 = US37¢) is Antigua's official currency, but the U.S. dollar is accepted everywhere.

Cruising into port

Most cruise ships dock at the **Nevis Street Pier** or **Heritage Quay** (pronounced "key"), both located in St. John's, the island's only town of any size. From there, you can either walk or take a short taxi ride into town. A handful of smaller vessels drop anchor at **English Harbour,** near Nelson's Dockyard on the south coast.

Scoring the best excursions

Nelson's Dockyard National Park Tour: After heading across the island, you'll visit the site of the planet's last surviving, working

Antigua

Georgian dockyard, with original colonial structures including forts, residences, and barracks (3–4½ hours; $46–$59).

Helicopter to Montserrat Volcano: In December 1997, the Soufriere Hills Volcano on the nearby island of Montserrat erupted, burying much of the island in lava. This trip takes you over both the volcano and the lunar highlights of Montserrat's exclusion zone, the area declared off-limits to ground transportation (2 hours; $240–$261).

Off Road 4×4 Jeep Safari Adventure: Tour the island's only remaining rain forest via a four-wheel-drive vehicle, and stop at the ruins of forts, sugar mills, and plantation houses. The excursion includes beach time (3½–4 hours; $52–$67).

Hiking Safari Adventure: This 4-mile uphill/downhill hike takes you through Antigua's rain forest and up to a 1,200-foot lookout for panoramic views (3 hours; $49).

Exploring on your own

Most of the major attractions here are beyond walking distance. **Taxis** meet every cruise ship, and taxi drivers are qualified tour guides, charging fixed fares of around $20 per hour for sightseeing trips (for up to four people, with a 2-hour minimum). For a scenic 20-mile circular route across Antigua's main mountain range, ask your driver to take you along the steep and sometimes bumpy **Fig Tree Drive** for fantastic views of tropical forests and fishing villages. In the local lingo, *fig tree* actually means *banana tree*.

You can find the **Antigua and Barbuda Department of Tourism** at Nevis Street and Friendly Alley in St. John's.

Within walking distance: Apart from duty-free shopping close to the docks at Heritage Quay and Redcliffe Quay, St. John's itself is a little rusty, attractions-wise. Near the main docks, at the intersection of Market and Long Streets, the old 1750s Court House building now contains the **Museum of Antigua and Barbuda** (☎ **268-462-1469;** www. antiguamuseums.org), which traces the nation's history from its geological birth to the present day. Admission is free, but a donation of $3 is requested. Closed Sundays. While you're there, pick up one of the two brochures that detail a self-guided walking tour past the historic buildings along **Redcliffe Quay,** one of the oldest parts of town, with restored, Pez-colored Georgian buildings. Once a trade center for slaves, rum, sugar, and coffee, it now has a yacht marina, cafes, and boutiques. Top off the tour with a rum punch at **Redcliffe Tavern.** A couple of blocks uphill from the museum, **St. John's Anglican Cathedral** (between Long and Newgate Streets at Church Street) dominates St. John's skyline with its twin spires. The current cathedral was built in 1847, replacing an earlier structure lost to an earthquake. The whole interior is paneled in pitch pine.

If your ship is in town on a Friday or Saturday morning, the market at the lower end of Market Street gives a little taste of the local lifestyle, with residents bartering goods and gossip.

Beyond walking distance: From St. John's, take an excursion or taxi 11 miles to **Nelson's Dockyard National Park** (☎ **268-460-1379;** www. antiguamuseums.org), once headquarters to British Admiral Horatio Nelson (1784–87) and now one of the most historic sites in the eastern Caribbean. At the heart of this landmark is the **Dockyard Museum,** where you discover the facility's links to the era of privateers, pirates, and great sea battles. A number of other historic structures are dotted around the park, as well as numerous artifacts related to 17th- and 18th-century maritime life, and even some sailors' graffiti dating back to the 1740s. The park grounds are well worth exploring, full of sandy beaches, tropical vegetation, and a number of nature trails, which can take anywhere from 30 minutes to five hours to explore. Admission to the whole park is $5. Free guided tours last 15 to 20 minutes.

Uphill and east of the Dockyard, the **Dows Hill Interpretation Center** (☎ **268-481-5045**) is part of the Shirley Heights military complex, which dates to the mid-18th century. It features a multimedia review of Antigua's history, from the British military occupation to the island's role in the slave trade. Admission is $5 for adults, free for children under 12. Continue up the hill to see a number of other military structures and the **Shirley Heights Lookout,** once the main signal station used to warn of approaching bad guys, now just a great view of the harbor below and the French island of Guadeloupe in the distance.

You can reach the best beaches by taxi, but remember to arrange for your driver to pick you up later so that you don't get stranded. **Fort James Beach** is the closest to St. John's, about 5 minutes ($7 by taxi) from the cruise dock. It's popular with both locals and tourists, and often has games of volleyball and cricket going on, plus umbrellas and beach chairs for rent. Just a little farther north (a $10 cab ride away), **Runaway Bay** and **Dickenson Bay** are the island's busiest beaches, with numerous resort hotels, restaurants, and watersports vendors. The water is calm, and chairs and umbrellas are available for rent. If you crave complete peace and quiet, head to **Half Moon Bay,** which is as far as you can get from St. John's and still be in Antigua.

Aruba

Way down in the southernmost southern Caribbean, Aruba is one of the so-called ABC islands — Aruba, Bonaire, and Curaçao — that lie just 20 miles or so off the South American coast. Blessed with perpetually sunny skies (annual rainfall is only 17 inches), warm temperatures, and cool breezes, the island also has some of the best beaches in the Caribbean, plus great snorkeling, scuba diving, windsurfing, and pretty much anything else you can do on the water. Inland, all that dryness means a stark landscape full of cacti and iguanas.

The island is legally part of the Netherlands, so expect a Dutch feel. Oranjestad, the island's capital and the location of the cruise docks, has Dutch- and Spanish-influenced architecture (the latter owing to the proximity of Venezuela), great shopping, casinos, restaurants, bars, and yachting marinas, many right along **Lloyd G. Smith Boulevard,** the main drag, which runs along the waterfront.

The official language is **Dutch,** but nearly everybody speaks English. You also hear Spanish and Papiamento, a regional dialect that combines Dutch, Spanish, and English with Amerindian and African words. The **Aruba florin** (AFl) is the official currency (1.77 AFl = US$1; 1 AFl = US56¢), but U.S. dollars are as widely accepted.

Cruising into port

Cruise ships arrive at the **Aruba Port Authority,** a modern terminal on the island's southern coast, in the capital city of Oranjestad. From the pier, it's a five-minute walk to the downtown shopping districts.

Scoring the best excursions

In addition to the tours described here, cruise lines typically offer about a dozen snorkeling, diving, sailing, and other water-oriented tours.

Off-Road Jeep Adventure: If you like the idea of exploring the island by four-wheel-drive but don't want to go it alone, this tour puts you in a convoy of other like-minded souls. A guide stays in touch with you by radio, and schedules a stop for lunch and swimming (4½–5 hours; $65–$74).

Mountain Biking on the North Coast: Bike along 10 miles of Aruba's wild north coast, visiting a gold mine, a natural bridge cut by the sea and wind, the little Alto Vista Chapel (dating to 1750), and the California Lighthouse at the island's northwesternmost point (3½ hours; $47).

Aruba Bar and Pub Crawl: What you're doing here, basically, is paying for a designated driver, who'll shuttle you to five local pubs (in the capital, on the coast, and in the countryside), with one free drink included at each (4 hours; $52).

Atlantis Submarine Adventure: Cruise 150 feet below the ocean in a submarine to see coral reefs, shipwrecks, and hundreds of curious tropical fish (1½ hours; $89).

Exploring on your own

Shopping, a couple casinos, and a few museums are within walking distance of the port. To get to anything else you need wheels. **Taxis** line up at the dock and operate on a fixed-fare basis, with every driver carrying a copy of the official rate schedule (to the beach resorts, it's generally $8–$10). For about $35, you can book a one-hour taxi tour for up to four people at the dispatch office (☎ 297-8-22116) in Oranjestad on Sands Street between the bowling alley and Taco Bell. Another option is riding the **bus,** which stops across the street from the cruise terminal (on L. G. Smith Boulevard) and takes you to the casinos, hotel resorts, and beaches of Aruba's west coast. Fares are inexpensive — about $2 round-trip.

Excellent roads connect major tourist attractions, so many people rent **mopeds** (for about $30–$40 a day). You can get further information on rentals at the cruise terminal or at the many bike shops on Lloyd G. Smith Boulevard. You can also **rent a car** or four-wheel-drive vehicle from Hertz, Budget, Avis, or one of the other rental-car companies, all of which have offices here.

Keep safety in mind when you drive here: The roads get very slippery when even slightly wet or when sand blows across them. You drive on the right.

Within walking distance: One of your first welcoming sights is the row of colorful boats docked at **Schooner Harbor,** where locals set up open

Aruba

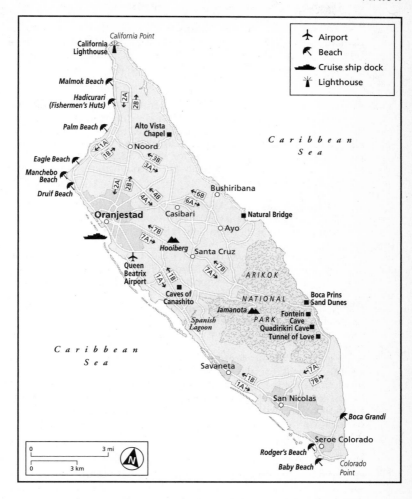

stalls to display their goods. Up the beach, you can buy fresh seafood right off the boat. **Wilhelmina Park,** with a statue honoring Queen Wilhelmina of the Netherlands, shows the island's Dutch influences and includes a tropical garden.

From the port facility, walk about five minutes up **Lloyd G. Smith Boulevard,** the main road that runs from Queen Beatrix Airport along the waterfront up to Palm Beach. This is where your shopping spree starts, should you have that kind of thing in mind. For quality items such as French perfume, Swiss watches, German and Japanese cameras, English bone china, and other quality goods, cross the street to **Caya**

GF Betico Croes. Delft blue pottery and Edam and Gouda cheeses from Holland are especially good buys.

Two **casinos** are located just steps from the dock: the elegant, 24-hour **Crystal Casino** (at the Aruba Renaissance Beach Resort, L. G. Smith Blvd. 82; ☎ **297-58-36000**), and the less assuming **Seaport Casino** (L. G. Smith Blvd. 9; ☎ **297-58-36000**). Both get crowded when ships are in port.

Beyond walking distance: If you're renting wheels or taking a taxi tour, you can scope the whole range of Aruba's desert island landscape in a day. You can reach two of the best beaches on the island, **Palm Beach** and **Eagle Beach** (both along the **Turquoise Coast,** west of Oranjestad) via taxi from the cruise terminal for about $8. All of Aruba's beaches are public, but chairs and shade huts are hotel property. If you use them, expect to be charged.

The **Alhambra Casino & Aladdin Theatre** (J. E. Irausquin Blvd. 47; ☎ **297-58-35000**) is the island's busiest casino, with a Moorish theme. It's located at the Manchebo Beach Resort, west of Oranjestad.

About 15 miles southeast of Oranjestad, in the center of the island, the 541-foot **Hooiberg** hill (also known as The Haystack) offers views of Venezuela if the visibility is good. And you only have to climb 600 steps to reach the top. Beyond, further into the island's interior, the building-size **Ayo and Casibari rock formations** served Aruba's early inhabitants as dwellings or religious sites — nobody's sure which, though the reddish-brown petroglyphs on the boulders suggest mystical significance.

Keep going to the northern (Caribbean side) coast to see the **Natural Bridge,** a coral formation more than 100 feet long and 25 feet above sea level. Crashing surf and whipping wind formed the bridge over the centuries, and now it's Aruba's most photographed site. A little to the west, the hulking ruins of the **Bushiribana Gold Smelter** offer another photo-op for folks interested in industrial design. It was built in 1872, and today its multitiered interior offers great sea views.

Head east on the northern coast to see Arikok National Park, which covers a full 20 percent of the island. Its most popular attraction is a series of caves, foremost of which is **Fontein Cave,** with its brownish-red drawings left by Amerindians and graffiti etched by early European settlers. Nearby **Quadirikiri Cave** has two large chambers with roof openings that allow sunlight in, making flashlights unnecessary. Hundreds of small bats use the 100-foot tunnel to reach their nests deeper in the cave. Another area cave, 300-foot Baranca Sunu, is more commonly known as the **Tunnel of Love** because of its heart-shaped entrance. You need a flashlight (for rent for $6) to explore.

You can see caves decorated with **Arawak artwork** — the oldest traces of human existence on the island — in Savaneta, on the south side of the island about 25 minutes east of Oranjestad by taxi. The area was also a

19th-century industrial center for phosphate mining. Until 1985, an Exxon oil subsidiary refinery operated here. To the east, San Nicolas is home to **Charlie's Bar and Restaurant** (Main Street; ☎ **297-8-45086**), which has served two-fisted drinks and decent food since 1941 in a nostalgic setting crammed with pennants, banners, trophies, and other memorabilia.

The Bahamas

Exotic they're not. Nassau and Freeport are some of the busiest cruise ports on the Caribbean circuit, even though technically The Bahamas aren't in the Caribbean at all — they're in the Atlantic, north of the Caribbean and fewer than 100 miles from Miami. Though holdovers from Great Britain's long colonial occupation linger in some architecture and culture, the vibe here isn't all that much different from parts of Florida, and the ports are totally tourist-oriented, with more shopping than at the Mall of America, all surrounded by beaches, casinos, and golf courses.

English is the official language of The Bahamas. Its legal tender is the **Bahamian dollar** (B$1), whose value is always the same as that of the U.S. dollar. Both currencies are accepted everywhere on the islands.

Cruising into port

In Freeport, ships dock at a dreary port in the middle of nowhere, a $15 taxi ride from Freeport and the International Bazaar, center of most of the action.

In Nassau, the cruise ship docks are at **Prince George Wharf** in the center of town at Rawson Square, in the middle of Nassau's shopping frenzy.

Scoring the best excursions

In addition to the excursions below, cruise lines typically offer a variety of snorkeling, diving, and boat tours.

Dolphin Encounter: Pat a dolphin on the nose! On this excursion from Freeport, you can watch, touch, and photograph Flipper, or at least one of his relatives. Organized by Unexso Dolphin Encounter (at Sanctuary Bay) (3¼ hours; $80–$89).

Kayak Nature Tour: Visit a protected island creek, kayak through a mangrove forest, explore the island's caves, and take a guided nature walk into Lucayan National Park. This Freeport excursion includes lunch and beach time (6 hours; $70–$75).

Harbor Cruise and Atlantis Resort: A tour boat with a local guide shows you the sights (such as they are) from the water, then drops you at the fanciful Atlantis Resort in Nassau for a brief tour that includes a visit to Predator Lagoon, home to sharks, barracuda, and other toothy fish (2½ hours; $42).

Thriller Powerboat Tour: A thrill-seeker's excursion, with high-speed boats roaring around the waters off Nassau, scaring the hell out of the fish. Not our personal favorite way to see . . . well, anything, but it sure is fast (1 hour; $50).

Exploring on your own in Freeport/Lucaya

Freeport/Lucaya on Grand Bahama Island is visited by far fewer ships than Nassau. Originally intended as two separate developments, Freeport (the landlocked section of town) and Lucaya (which hugs the waterfront) have grown together over the years, offering a mix of sun, surf, golf, tennis, and watersports.

Once you get to Freeport by **taxi,** you can explore the center of town on foot. Taxis can also take you to farther-flung attractions. The government sets taxi rates, which start at $3 and increase 40¢ for each additional ¼-mile (plus $3 extra per passenger).

Within walking distance: Nothing of note is within walking distance of the port. You must take a cab for all attractions.

Beyond walking distance: One of the island's prime attractions, the 12-acre **Garden of the Groves** (☎ 242-373-5668 or 242-373-1456; www. gardenofthegroves.com) was once the private meditation garden of Freeport's founder, Wallace Groves. The tranquil park features waterfalls, flowering shrubs, about 10,000 trees, tropical birds, Bahamian raccoons, Vietnamese potbellied pigs, and West African pygmy goats. It's located at the intersection of Midshipman Road and Magellan Drive. Admission is $10.

A couple of miles east of downtown Freeport on East Settlers Way, the 100-acre **Rand Nature Centre** (☎ 242-352-5438) serves as the regional headquarters of The Bahamas National Trust. Pineland nature trails meander past native flora and wild birds, including the Bahama parrot. Admission is $5. Closed weekends.

If you'd like a taste of The Bahamas the way they used to be, head for the **Star Club** on the island's west end (Bayshore Road; ☎ 242-346-6207). Built in the 1940s, the Star was Grand Bahama's first hotel, and over the years it's hosted many famous guests. Come for the good times and to mix with the locals, not for the food. Lunch costs $8. Next door, **Austin's Calypso Bar** is a colorful old dive if ever there was one.

Your best bet at this port is to head for the beach. **Xanadu,** immediately east of Freeport at the Xanadu Beach Resort, is the premier stretch in the Lucaya area, offering most watersports equipment. It can get crowded at times. **Taíno Beach, Churchill Beach,** and **Fortune Beach** are all conveniently located on the Lucaya oceanfront. A 20-minute ride east of Lucaya, **Gold Rock Beach** may be the island's best. Secluded in Lucayan National Park, it has barbecue pits, picnic tables, and a spectacular low tide. **Barbary Beach,** slightly closer to Lucaya, is great for seashell hunters, and in May and June white spider lilies in the area bloom spectacularly.

Freeport/Lucaya

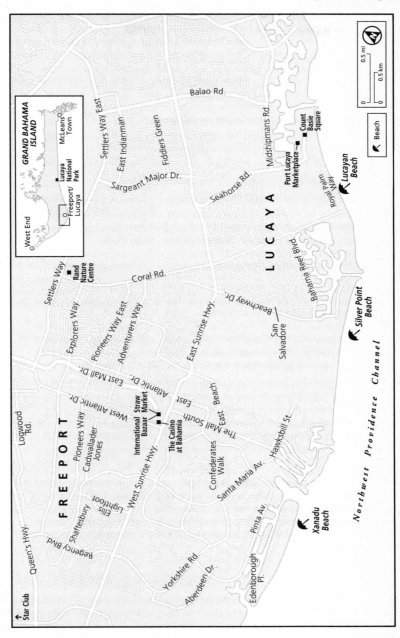

Then again, maybe shopping is the top draw (just shows you how blah this island is). The **International Bazaar,** at East Mall Drive and East Sunrise Highway, next to the Casino at Bahamia, is pure 1960s Bahamian kitsch, and though relentlessly cheerful, it's a little long in the tooth. Each area of the 10-acre, 100-shop complex attempts to capture the ambience of a different region of the globe. Stereotypes abound. Next door, the **Straw Market** features, you guessed it, straw baskets, hats, handbags, and placemats. The **Port Lucaya Marketplace,** on Seahorse Road, is a large shopping-and-dining complex much like the International Bazaar.

Exploring on your own in Nassau

The Nassau/Paradise Island area comprises two separate islands. Nassau is on the northeastern shore of 21-mile New Providence Island, while tiny Paradise Island is linked to New Providence by bridges, and protects Nassau harbor for a 3-mile stretch.

The major attractions and stores are pretty concentrated near the piers, and if you're really fit you can even trek over to Cable Beach or Paradise Island. (Otherwise, you'll have no problem finding taxis — they'll find you.) There's no good reason to rent a car here.

Within walking distance: As you exit from the cruise ship wharf into the main port area, you have no choice but to pass through **Festival Place,** a barnlike hall full of little shops and stalls. Outside, hawkers encourage you to have your hair braided at the government-sponsored **Hairbraider's Centre.**

Shopping is *the* thing here, but there are a few other sites of interest. Just across Bay Street from Rawson Square (inland from the wharf) are the flamingo-pink government buildings of **Parliament Square,** constructed in 1815. The House of Assembly, old colonial Secretary's Office, and Supreme Court flank a statue of Queen Victoria, while a bust on the north side of the square honors Sir Milo B. Butler, The Bahamas' first governor-general. One block inland, the pink, octagonal **Nassau Public Library** was built as a prison in 1798, and today it holds a collection of books, historical prints, and more.

Slaves carved the **Queen's Staircase** out of a solid limestone cliff in 1793. Originally designed as an escape route for soldiers, each step now represents a year in Queen Victoria's 65-year reign. Lush plants and a waterfall stand guard over the staircase, which is located a few blocks up from the library on East Street and leads to **Fort Fincastle,** Elizabeth Avenue, built in 1793 by Lord Dunmore, the royal governor. An elevator climbs a 38m (126-ft.) water tower, where you can look down on the fort. Walk around on your own or hire a guide.

If you have kids in tow, the **Pirates of Nassau Museum** (King and George Streets; ☎ 242-356-3759; www.pirates-of-nassau.com) is worthwhile. Admission is a steep $12 for adults — only worth it if you're with kids, as each adult may bring two children under 12 free; each additional child is $6.

Nassau

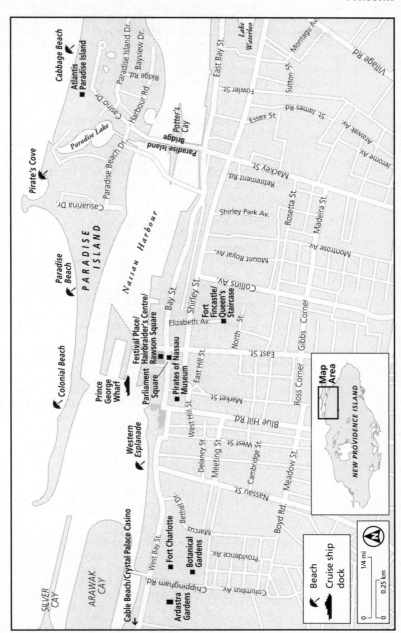

Beyond walking distance: About a mile west of downtown Nassau, just off West Bay Street, **Fort Charlotte** is The Bahamas' largest fort. Built in 1788, it covers more than 100 hilltop acres and offers impressive views of Paradise Island, Nassau, and the harbor. Nearby, parading pink flamingos are the main attraction at the lush, 5-acre **Ardastra Gardens** (Chippingham Road; ☎ 242-323-5806; www.ardastra.com). The graceful birds obey the drillmaster's orders daily at 10:30 a.m., 2:10 p.m., and 4:10 p.m. daily — kids think the whole thing is a hoot. Admission is $12, $6 children 4 to 12.

If you're in the mood for some conch, head for **Arawak Cay,** a small man-made island across West Bay Street from Ardastra Gardens and Fort Charlotte. Join the locals in sampling conch with hot sauce, and wash it down with a cocktail made from coconut water and gin. Farther to the west, the 3,252-sq.-m (35,000-sq.-ft.) **Crystal Palace Casino** (West Bay Street, Cable Beach; ☎ 800-222-7466 or 242-327-6200) is the only casino on New Providence Island.

On Paradise Island, the towering, fancifully designed **Atlantis Paradise Island** megaresort (☎ 242-363-3000; www.atlantis.com) is the largest gaming and entertainment complex in the Caribbean, all tied together with a "Lost City of Atlantis" theme. Outside, the resort's sprawling 11-million-gallon lagoon system boasts more than 200 sea species and 50,000 individual creatures. **The Dig** is a fantastic world of faux Atlantis ruins flooded by the sea. The interconnected passageways, boulevards, and chambers, now inhabited by piranhas, hammerhead sharks, stingrays, and morays, are visible through huge glass windows.

In general, cruise ship passengers can check out the casino and shops, but are not permitted in certain areas of the resort (namely the beaches, the pools, and the breathtaking water slides). If you sign up for the guided "Discovery Tour," you can explore The Dig. Tickets, available at the resort's guest services desks, are $29 for adults, $21 for children 4 to 12 (3 and under free). Disney and Royal Caribbean passengers only are also offered a special day-pass to use Atlantis's beaches.

Other non-Atlantis beaches are on Paradise Island, all just a ferry ride away from Prince George Wharf. **Paradise Beach** is $3 for adults and $1 for children, and includes use of a shower and locker. You may also want to check out smaller beaches as well, including **Pirate's Cove Beach** and **Cabbage Beach,** the latter of which often fills up with guests of the nearby resorts.

Five miles from town is **Cable Beach,** which offers various watersports and easy access to shops, a casino, bars, and restaurants. Not on the same level but more convenient for cruise ship passengers, the **Western Esplanade** sweeps westward from the Hilton British Colonial hotel, with changing facilities, restrooms, and a snack bar.

Barbados

In the former British colony of Barbados, cricket is the national pastime, fish and chips appears on local menus, and people drive on the wrong — oops, sorry, we mean the left — side of the road. The island is also one of the most gorgeous in the southern Caribbean, with seemingly endless stretches of pink- and white-sand beaches, small cottages with well-kept gardens, and historic parish churches. The most easterly of the Caribbean islands, its topography varies from rolling hills and savage waves on the Atlantic coast to densely populated flatlands and the sheltered beach/resort areas of the southwest. The northeast part of the island is hilly, with a morning mist that helped it earn the nickname "The Scotland District."

Predictably, the shopping area near the cruise port in **Bridgetown** can get crowded and noisy. You're better off making a beeline for the beaches of the **Gold Coast,** the island's western side, with luxury resorts fronting its calm waters.

English is spoken with an island lilt. The **Barbados dollar** (BD$) is the official currency (BD$2.08 = US$1; BD$1 = US50¢), but U.S. dollars are commonly accepted.

Cruising into port

The island's cruise terminal is located about a mile from the capital, Bridgetown, and is a veritable shopping mall, with 25 stores and a fleet of pushcart vendors selling all the usual: jewelry, watches, electronics, china, crystal, perfumes, blah blah blah. Goods made on Barbados, including rum, liquors, and jewelry, are duty-free.

You can walk to town in 15 or 20 minutes via the shoreline park. Otherwise it's a $4 taxi ride.

Scoring the best excursions

To get to the best locations in Barbados, you need to catch an excursion or a taxi.

Harrison's Cave: Barbados's most popular attraction, all cruise lines offer various tours here. See "Exploring on your own" for details (2 hours; $49).

Kayak and Turtle Encounter: A boat ride along the west coast brings you to the beach, where you clamber into your kayak for a 45-minute paddle along the shore. Once at the snorkel site, you can swim with and feed sea turtles (3½ hours; $69).

Rainforest Hike and Cave Adventure: A guide leads your group through one of Barbados's rain forest gullies, then down into a natural cave (4 hours; $74).

Jolly Roger Booze Cruise: Board the wooden schooner *Jolly Roger* for a sail along Barbados's west coast, with a pirate crew, beach stop, lots of goofiness (wanna walk the plank?), and lots of booze courtesy of the open bar (3½ hours; $49).

Atlantis Submarine Adventure: Sail aboard an air-conditioned submersible to view underwater life, including tropical fish, plants, and an intact shipwreck (2½ hours; $99 adults, $50 kids).

Exploring on your own

Taxis and car rentals are all available at the cruise terminal. Taxis aren't metered, but their rates are fixed by the government. Settle on the fare before getting in. **Buses** are frequent and inexpensive (the fare is about 75¢), but they can get crowded at rush hour. As an alternative, look for **minibuses** with a "ZR" license plate, which zoom around the island picking up tourists and locals for about the same price as the bus.

Within walking distance: For some, Bridgetown is within walking distance; others may opt to take a taxi. Either way, you won't spend much time here. For some history, stop in at the **Synagogue** (Synagogue Lane, Bridgetown; ☎ 246-432-0840), one of the oldest Jewish houses of worship in the western hemisphere. Brazilian Jews built the first temple on this site in 1654; the current building dates to 1833.

Beyond walking distance: The most popular tourist attraction on the island is **Harrison's Cave** (Welchman Hall, St. Thomas; ☎ 246-438-6640). Electric trams take you down into a series of beautiful coral limestone caverns, full of stalactites, stalagmites, streams, and waterfalls. It's about a $20 cab ride from the cruise terminal, and admission costs $13 for adults and $6 for children. Cruise lines typically offer a couple different tours that stop here.

Only about a mile from the cave, the **Flower Forest** (Richmond Plantation, St. Joseph; ☎ 246-433-8152) is a former sugar plantation that's now a junglelike botanical garden, with paths winding among huge tropical flowers and plants. Admission is $7.50.

You can take a bus to reach the lush, tropical garden known as **Welchman Hall Gully,** about 8 miles from St. Thomas (☎ 246-438-6671). Some of the plant specimens date back to 1627, when English settlers first arrived. For example, they say the ancient breadfruit trees grew from seedlings brought over by Captain Bligh of *Mutiny on the Bounty* fame. Many of the plants are labeled and occasionally you can spot a wild monkey. Admission is $10.

The 300-year-old **Sunbury Plantation House** (25 minutes from Bridgetown along Highway 5; ☎ 246-423-6270) is the only plantation house on Barbados whose rooms are all open for viewing, featuring mahogany antiques, old prints, and a collection of horse-drawn carriages. Admission is $10.

Barbados

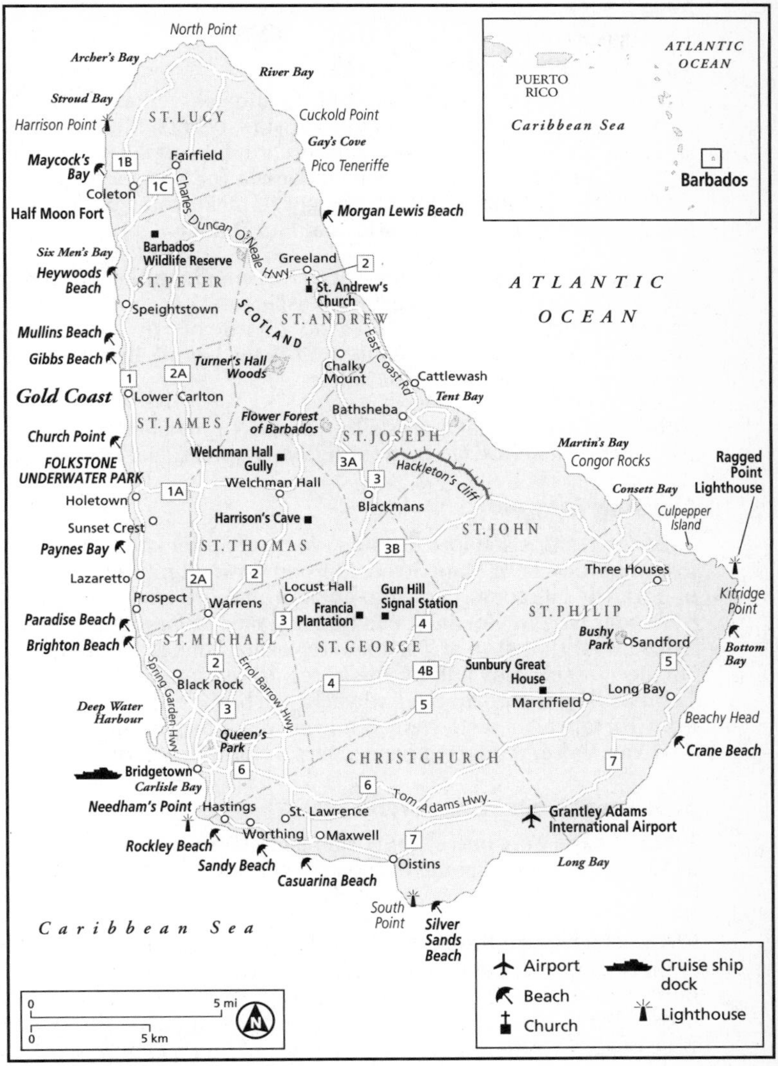
North Point
Archer's Bay
River Bay
Stroud Bay
Harrison Point
ST. LUCY
Cuckold Point
Gay's Cove
Maycock's Bay
1B
Fairfield
Pico Teneriffe
1C
Coleton
Charles Duncan O'Neale Hwy.
Half Moon Fort
Morgan Lewis Beach
Six Men's Bay
Barbados Wildlife Reserve
Greeland
2
Heywoods Beach
ST. PETER
St. Andrew's Church
ATLANTIC OCEAN
Speightstown
SCOTLAND
ST. ANDREW
Mullins Beach
East Coast Rd
Gibbs Beach
Turner's Hall Woods
Chalky Mount
1
2A
Cattlewash
Gold Coast
Lower Carlton
Tent Bay
Bathsheba
ST. JAMES
Flower Forest of Barbados
ST. JOSEPH
Church Point
Martin's Bay
Welchman Hall Gully
3A
Hackleton's Cliff
Congor Rocks
Ragged Point Lighthouse
FOLKSTONE UNDERWATER PARK
3
1A
Welchman Hall
Consett Bay
Holetown
Blackmans
Culpepper Island
Sunset Crest
Harrison's Cave
ST. JOHN
Paynes Bay
ST. THOMAS
3B
Lazaretto
2A
2
Three Houses
Locust Hall
Gun Hill Signal Station
Kitridge Point
Prospect
Warrens
Francia Plantation
ST. PHILIP
Paradise Beach
3
4
Bushy Park
Sandford
Brighton Beach
ST. MICHAEL
ST. GEORGE
Bottom Bay
2
Errol Barrow Hwy.
Sunbury Great House
5
Spring Garden Hwy
Black Rock
4B
4
Long Bay
Deep Water Harbour
3
Marchfield
5
Beachy Head
Queen's Park
Crane Beach
CHRISTCHURCH
7
Bridgetown
6
Carlisle Bay
6
Tom Adams Hwy.
Needham's Point
Hastings
St. Lawrence
Grantley Adams International Airport
Worthing
Maxwell
7
Rockley Beach
Oistins
Long Bay
Sandy Beach
Casuarina Beach
South Point
Silver Sands Beach
Caribbean Sea
ATLANTIC OCEAN
PUERTO RICO
Caribbean Sea
Barbados
Airport
Cruise ship dock
Beach
Lighthouse
Church
0 5 mi
0 5 km
N

All beaches in Barbados are open to the public, though those on the Gold Coast (north of Bridgetown) have calmer waters, and are closer to the port to boot. **Paynes Bay,** about an $8 cab ride from the port, is excellent for swimming, snorkeling, and other watersports, but can get crowded. Directly south of Paynes Bay, even closer to the port, **Brighton Beach, Brandon's Beach,** and **Paradise Beach** are all fine alternatives, clustered around Fresh Water Bay. Farther north, **Church Point** can get crowded, but it's one of the most scenic bays in Barbados, and the swimming is ideal.

The British Virgin Islands

Once upon a time, the British Virgin Islands served as a haven for pirates, but today they're a haven for sun-seekers. Most of the 40-some islands that make up the island group are quite small. Cruise ships stop at the largest three: **Tortola, Virgin Gorda** (or "Fat Virgin," so named by Christopher Columbus, which has got to make you wonder), and the less-frequented and very rustic **Jost Van Dyke.**

Treasure Island fans get a kick out of **Norman Island,** said to be the setting for Robert Louis Stevenson's classic tale. Legend holds that the notorious pirate Blackbeard stashed a bottle of rum and marooned 15 men at Deadman Bay on neighboring **Peter Island,** inspiring the famous "yo-ho-ho and a bottle of rum" ditty.

Although their official name is the *British* Virgin Islands, the **U.S. dollar** is the official currency. Go figure. **English** is the official language.

Cruising into port

Most large ships sail into **Tortola,** docking at Wickhams Cay, a pleasant five-minute walk to Main Street in Road Town. If more than two ships are in port, the latecomers have to anchor offshore and bring passengers in by tender. **Virgin Gorda** doesn't have a pier or landing facilities for large ships. Most that stop at Tortola offer excursions to Virgin Gorda instead. Smaller vessels may anchor offshore and tender passengers in to St. Thomas Bay, the port area and yacht harbor for Spanish Town. Ferries from Tortola also berth here. Some small ships visit hilly, 4-square-mile **Jost Van Dyke,** tendering passengers in for a beach day.

Scoring the best excursions

Tortola is the only one of the Virgin Islands where it makes sense to take an excursion — and some of those excursions go to the *other* Virgin Islands.

Virgin Gorda and the Baths: Travel by boat from Tortola across the Sir Francis Drake Channel to Spanish Town, on Virgin Gorda, then board open-air buses to the Baths for sunning, swimming, and snorkeling amid mammoth boulders and sea caves (for more details, see "Exploring on your own in Virgin Gorda," later in this chapter). Includes a Caribbean-style buffet lunch (4 hours; $62).

Town and Country Excursion: Tour Tortola in an open-air minibus, visiting the Botanical Gardens, Cane Garden Bay, Bomba's Full Moon Party Shack, and Soper's Hole (for more description, see the next section, "Exploring on your own in Tortola") (3½ hours; $34).

The British Virgin Islands

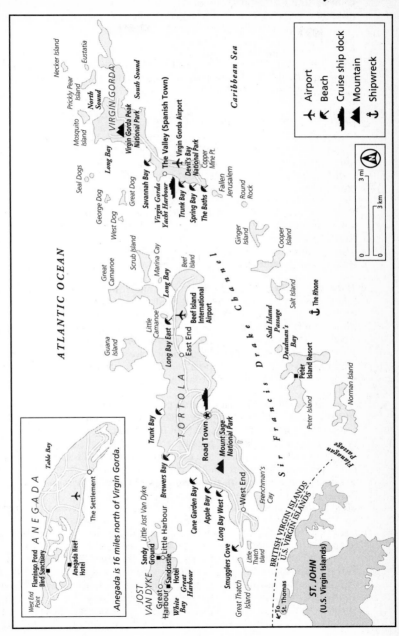

The British Virgin Islands

Legend:
- ✈ Airport
- 🏖 Beach
- Cruise ship dock
- ▲ Mountain
- ⚓ Shipwreck

Caribbean Sea

ATLANTIC OCEAN

3 mi
3 km

Necker Island
Eustatia
Prickly Pear Island
Mosquito Island
North Sound
South Sound
VIRGIN GORDA
Virgin Gorda Peak National Park
Long Bay
The Valley (Spanish Town)
Virgin Gorda Airport
Seal Dogs
Copper Mine Pt.
George Dog
Savannah Bay
Devil's Bay National Park
West Dog
Great Dog
Virgin Gorda Yacht Harbour
Trunk Bay
Spring Bay
The Baths
Fallen Jerusalem
Round Rock
Great Camanoe
Scrub Island
Marina Cay
Long Bay
Beef Island
Ginger Island
Cooper Island
Guana Island
Little Camanoe
Long Bay East
East End
Beef Island International Airport
Salt Island
Salt Island Passage
The Rhone
Drake Channel
Deadman's Bay
Peter Island Resort
Trunk Bay
TORTOLA
Road Town
Mount Sage National Park
Sir Francis
Peter Island
Norman Island
Brewers Bay
West End
Frenchman's Cay
Cane Garden Bay
Apple Bay
Long Bay West
Smugglers Cove
West End Point
Flamingo Pond Bird Sanctuary
A N E G A D A
Table Bay
The Settlement
Anegada Reef Hotel
Anegada is 16 miles north of Virgin Gorda.
JOST VAN DYKE
Sandy Ground
Little Jost Van Dyke
Great Harbour
Little Harbour
White Bay
Sandcastle Hotel
Great Harbour
Little Thatch Island
Great Thatch Island
BRITISH VIRGIN ISLANDS
U.S. VIRGIN ISLANDS
Flanagan Passage
ST. JOHN (U.S. Virgin Islands)
To St. Thomas/ St. John

Tortola Snorkeling Adventure: Cross the Sir Frances Drake Channel by boat to Norman Island, one of the BVI's prime snorkel sites, full of coral formations, colorful fish, and a group of caves at Treasure Point, where pirate loot is said to have been hidden (2½ hours; $48).

Forest Walk and Beach Tour: Safari buses take you to Tortola's interior for a mile-long hike through the Sage Mountain rain forest to the highest point in the Virgin Islands, followed by a brief stop at the Botanical Gardens (3½ hours; $35).

Exploring on your own in Tortola

Tortola is the largest and busiest of the British Virgin Islands. Its capital, **Road Town,** is a popular yachting center as well as the port for cruise ships. The rest of the southern coast is characterized by rugged mountain peaks, while the north coast has beautiful white-sand beaches fringed with palm trees, bananas, and mangoes.

Whether your ship docks or tenders passengers in, you end up right in town, about a five-minute walk to Main Street. Open-air and sedan-style **taxis** meet every arriving ship to carry passengers to the beaches and other attractions. Fares are set, so ask what you'll pay before you get in. If you want to **rent a car,** Budget, Hertz, and Avis all have offices here.

Within walking distance: You can walk from the pier to Tortola's **Main Street,** which has a relatively quiet shopping area by Caribbean standards, although you can get some good bargains on duty-free British goods such as English china. Across from the dock on the waterfront is **Pusser's Road Town Pub** (☎ 284-494-3897), with an extensive menu and the infamous Pusser's Rum, which was served aboard British Navy ships for over 300 years. The attached company store offers a selection of clothing and other logo items, some pretty cool.

Beyond walking distance: Drive or take a taxi to 92-acre **Mount Sage National Park,** where the namesake mountain soars to a magnificent 1,780 feet amid a lush tropical rain forest setting, which you can explore via nature trails. (You can pick up a trail map at the tourist office in the center of Road Town near the dock just south of **Wickhams Cay.**) The park was established in 1964 to protect what was left of Tortola's original forests, following the depredations of the plantation era.

Most of Tortola's beaches are a 20-minute taxi ride from the cruise dock, costing about $15 per person each way. Discuss price with the driver before setting out, and ask him to pick you up later, in time to get back to the ship. The best beach is at **Cane Garden Bay** on the island's northwest side, across the mountains from Road Town but worth the trip. Surfers like **Apple Bay,** also on the northwest side, while next-door Cappoon's Bay is known more for **Bomba's Surfside Shack** (☎ 284-495-4148), a legendary island bar built from what looks like scrap lumber and covered in day-glo graffiti. Painkillers — one of the Caribbean's legendary rum drinks — are a specialty. If you want to snorkel, the best beaches on Tortola are **Smugglers Cove,** on the western tip, and **Brewer's Bay,** on the northwest side.

Exploring on your own in Virgin Gorda

Instead of heading for Tortola, some smaller ships anchor outside of Virgin Gorda and bring visitors ashore by tender. You have to take a taxi to get there, but **The Baths** is the most popular beach destination on the island, looking like something Frank Gehry would have designed had he lived during the Neolithic age. It's a group of house-sized boulders, which geologists believe toppled onto one another as a result of ice-age eruptions, forming the dramatic shapes and saltwater grottoes we see today. It's an enormously fun area to swim around and explore, crawling under and between huuuuge boulders that you just know are going to fall over and crush you, but of course don't. A cafe sits just above the beach.

Spring Bay, just north of The Baths, is a great white-sand beach with clear water and good snorkeling. Farther north still, **Trunk Bay** is a wide sand beach reachable via a rough path from Spring Bay. **Devil's Bay,** just south of The Baths, is a less crowded swimming option.

Exploring on your own in Jost Van Dyke

Jost Van Dyke is visited mostly by private yachts and a few small cruise ships such as those of Windjammer Barefoot Cruises, which often throws afternoon beach parties on the beach at White Bay. If your ship stays late, head to **Foxy's** (☎ **284-495-9258**), a legendary beach bar at the far end of Great Harbour. It's a scene.

Cozumel and Playa del Carmen, Mexico

Woooo-ey, is **Cozumel** ever a busy place. Located just off Mexico's Yucatán coast, it gets up to 16 ships visiting *every single day* during high season. Do the math; that's something like 25,000 cruise passengers tromping down the gangways. Zowie. The island's main town, San Miguel (located on the island's western shore, where the best resorts and beaches are also found), is tourist central, with hundreds of stores, bars, and restaurants strung out along its waterfront and side streets. Get beyond the tourist zone, though, and things calm way down.

Playa del Carmen, on the mainland, is much quieter, with a small but expanding shopping district, some trendy boutiques and hip restaurants, and beaches. Mostly it's a jumping-off point for excursions and treks to the mainland's main draws: the Mayan ruins of **Tulum, Chichén Itzá,** and **Cobá,** plus a couple of water parks. Some ships spend one day in Cozumel and the next in Playa, though more frequently they just run boats from Cozumel to the mainland, 45 minutes away. There's also a regular ferry service, if you want to go on your own.

In recent years, a handful of other Yucatán ports have come onto the scene, including **Calica,** just south of Playa; **Costa Maya,** about 161km (100 miles) south near the sleepy fishing village of Mahajual; and

Progreso, on the Gulf coast of the Yucatán, making it the closest to both Chichén Itzá and the city of Merida. Costa Maya is the most elaborate of the three, with shopping, entertainment, beaches and beach bars, and activities. The others are little more than piers giving easier access to the other Yucatán attractions.

Spanish is the language of Mexico, although English is spoken by nearly everyone you deal with in the tourist zone. The Mexican currency is the **nuevo peso** (new peso). Its symbol is the "$" sign, but the exchange rate is about $11 pesos to US$1 ($1 peso = about US9¢). The main tourist stores accept U.S. dollars.

Cruising into port

Cruise ship berths are scattered all along the coast of San Miguel. The newest is **Punta Langosta,** in the center of town, just steps from the action and about a quarter mile from the ferries to Playa del Carmen. Other berths are at the **International Pier** (2 miles south of San Miguel) or the **Puerto Maya pier** (a little farther still). Both are about a $6 taxi ride from town. Beaches are closest to the International Pier.

Scoring the best excursions

The Mayan ruins on the mainland are, in our opinion, an absolute must. Because all ruins involve some traveling (especially from Cozumel), we recommend visiting as part of an excursion. In addition to the ruins, cruise lines always offer snorkeling, horseback riding, booze-cruising, folkloric shows, dolphin swims, submarine and scuba dives, ATV off-roading, bicycle treks, parasailing, kayaking, fishing, and more.

Tulum Mayan Ruins/Xel-Ha: About a 30-minute drive from Playa del Carmen, the small walled city of Tulum is usually the only ruin of conse-quence you can visit if you're coming from Cozumel. It was the only Mayan city built right on the coast (it's backed by sea cliffs) and the only one still inhabited when the Spanish conquistadors arrived in the 1500s. In the company of a trained guide, you visit some of the 60 individual structures, including a temple to Kukulkán, the primary Mayan/Olmec god. The Tulum tour is sold either on its own (6½ hours; $75) or in com-bination with a visit to the **Xel-Ha Eco Park** (8 hours; $99), a natural lagoon where you can drift from one end to the other in an inner tube, accompanied by schools of tropical fish. Snorkeling gear is available, as is a swim-with-dolphins option (for an extra cost).

Chichén Itzá: The most fabled of the Yucatán ruins, Chichén Itzá was founded in A.D. 445 and at its height was home to about 50,000 residents. All told, it's absolutely huge, covering an area of 7 square miles, though tours visit only a fraction of that, which is enough. The best known of Chichén Itzá's ruins is the magnificent El Castillo pyramid (also called the Pyramid of Kukulkán), with four 91-step outside stairways leading up to a central platform. Do the math and the steps add up to the number of days in the solar year (91×4 = 364, plus one for the central platform).

Cozumel/Playa del Carmen Area

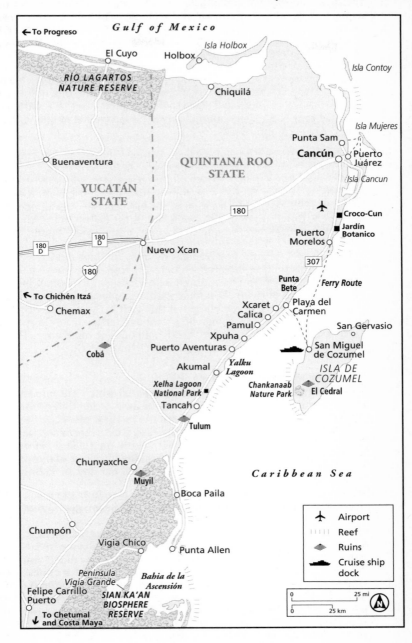

← To Progreso

Gulf of Mexico

El Cuyo

Isla Holbox

Holbox

Isla Contoy

RÍO LAGARTOS
NATURE RESERVE

Chiquilá

Isla Mujeres

Punta Sam

Cancún

Puerto
Juárez

Buenaventura

QUINTANA ROO
STATE

Isla Cancun

YUCATÁN
STATE

✈

Croco-Cun

180

Jardín
Botanico

180
D

Puerto
Morelos

180
D

Nuevo Xcan

307

180

← To Chichén Itzá

Chemax

Punta
Bete

Ferry Route

Xcaret
Calica

Playa del
Carmen

Pamul

San Gervasio

Xpuha

Cobá

Puerto Aventuras

San Miguel
de Cozumel

Akumal

Yalku
Lagoon

ISLA DE
COZUMEL

Xelha Lagoon
National Park

Chankanaab
Nature Park

El Cedral

Tancah

Tulum

Chunyaxche

Caribbean Sea

Muyil

Boca Paila

Chumpón

Vigia Chico

Punta Allen

Peninsula
Vigia Grande

Bahia de la
Ascensión

Felipe Carrillo
Puerto

SIAN KA'AN
BIOSPHERE
RESERVE

↓ To Chetumal
and Costa Maya

✈ Airport

| | | | | Reef

◆ Ruins

⬛ Cruise ship
dock

0 — 25 mi
0 — 25 km

N

On the spring and fall equinoxes, light striking the pyramid gives the illusion of a snake slithering down the steps to join its gigantic stone head mounted at the base. Those Mayans knew what they were doing. Typical tours also visit a sports court where the captain of the losing (or winning — nobody knows) team was sacrificed to the gods. Other stops include a well where virgins were sacrificed, and a temple where (guess!) other folks were sacrificed. They were big on sacrifices, those Mayans. Kidding aside, it's an absolutely incredible place, and one of the best excursions we've ever taken. Due to its distance into the Yucatán interior, this tour is typically offered only by ships calling at one of the mainland ports (12 hours; $149).

Cobá: A 35-minute drive inland from Tulum puts you at Cobá, once the commercial hub of the Mayan civilization, flourishing from A.D. 300 to 1000. Today, more than 3,500 structures have been identified on its grounds, which are bounded by four natural lakes. Excavation work began in 1972, but only a fraction of the city has been reclaimed from the jungle. Cobá's pyramid, Nohoch Mul, is the tallest in the Yucatán. Excursions travel here from both Cozumel and Playa (8 hours; $89).

Xcaret: From Cozumel, you transfer by ferry to Playa del Carmen then by bus to this unique eco-archaeological theme park, whose name is pronounced ish-car-*et*. You have about 3½ hours on site to enjoy the park's blue lagoons, lazy rivers, botanical gardens, aviary, aquarium, and cultural performances. The highlight of this visit is the underground river tour, which involves donning a float-vest and letting a gentle current carry you along a crystal river through an underground cave. This tour is offered from both Cozumel and Playa (8 hours; $88).

Exploring on your own in Cozumel

Depending on where you dock, you can either walk right into the tourist throng or take a short **taxi** ride to it — or away from it, depending on your preference. The typical fare from the farthest piers to downtown San Miguel is about $6. From San Miguel to most resorts and beaches is usually between $10 and $15. Be sure to settle on the fare before you start out. Many passengers also rent **mopeds** from one of many, many vendors. The cost is usually about $30 to $35 per day, including helmet.

To get far away, you can take the ferry from Cozumel and Playa del Carmen for $9 per person. The crossing takes approximately 45 minutes.

Within walking distance: The things to do in central San Miguel are shopping and drinking, both of which can easily be done on foot — either solidly or canted sideways, depending on how much you imbibe. **Avenida Rafael Melgar** runs along the waterfront and is chockablock with shops, bars, and restaurants. Ditto for the streets around the **Plaza del Sol,** which lies just behind Avenida Melgar, at the foot of the ferry pier. Shops sell the usual tourist goods, Mexican crafts, and especially **silver jewelry,** which is generally sold by weight. Prices are relatively high, but you can and should bargain. If you dock at the International

Pier, a bunch of nice shops in the terminal sell everything from Mexican blankets to jewelry, T-shirts, and handicrafts of all kinds. The pier at Puerta Maya also has a number of well-stocked gift shops.

The most iconic of the downtown bars — for better or worse — is **Carlos 'n Charlie's** (Av. Rafael Melgar 551; ☎ **987-869-1446;** www. carlosn-charlies.com). It's like a Mexican Hard Rock Cafe, with about as much authenticity.

If that's not your scene, you can drop into the small **Museo de la Isla de Cozumel** (on Rafael Melgar between Calles 4 and 6 N; ☎ **987-872-1475**). The building, which began life as Cozumel's first luxury hotel, houses two floors of historical exhibits, from pre-Hispanic times to the present. Admission is $3.

Beyond walking distance: The **Chankanaab Nature Park** (www. cozumelparks.com.mx) is a wildlife sanctuary, archaeological park, cultural park, and water park all in one. Just 10 minutes from the downtown pier by taxi (about $10–$12), you can swim in a saltwater lagoon with a beautiful powder-white beach, snorkel or scuba among fish-filled offshore reefs (equipment rentals are available), stroll through the botanical garden (home to more than 800 plant species), walk around a replica Mayan village, go to the interactive archaeological museum, take in a sea lion show, or see dolphins perform at the Dolphinarium. To swim with the dolphins, make reservations in advance at **Dolphin Discovery** in Cancún (☎ **998-849-4757;** www.dolphindiscovery.com/cozumel). Park admission is $12 adults, $6 kids 3 to 11. Dolphin swims are $119.

Mayan ruins on Cozumel are very minor compared to those on the mainland, but if you're driving around you can visit **San Gervasio** (north of San Miguel), once a ceremonial center and capital, and **El Cedral** (to the south), site of a Mayan arch and a few small ruins covered in heavy growth. Cozumel's best beach, **Playa San Francisco,** is only 2 miles from El Cedral. Another mile or so south is **Playa del Sol,** one of the island's more popular and crowded beaches.

Exploring on your own in Playa del Carmen

Within walking distance: Playa del Carmen is much more low-key than Cozumel. From the ferry dock you can walk to the white-sand beach or explore the ever-expanding shopping district, which has numerous shops, bars, and restaurants. For shopping, stroll the **Rincon del Sol,** a tree-lined Mexican colonial-style courtyard with some appealing local handicrafts stores.

Beyond walking distance: For all attractions beyond town, see "Scoring the best excursions," earlier in this section.

Curaçao, Netherlands Antilles

Curaçao (pronounced coo-ra-*sow*) is the largest and most populous of the Netherlands Antilles — the so-called ABC islands (Aruba, Bonaire,

Curaçao) located about 35 miles north of the Venezuelan coast. A Dutch possession since the 17th century, it has served over the years as a trading post, oil-refining center, and tourist destination. Today, it retains its Dutch flavor, especially in the capital of **Willemstad.** When your ship arrives at Willemstad's harbor, you can watch the town's famous floating bridge swing aside and invite you into a narrow channel, where rows of centuries-old pastel-colored homes create a fairy-tale effect. According to local lore, the houses were originally painted white, but were so blindingly bright in the hot Caribbean sun that the first Dutch colonial governors ordered them painted in softer, vibrant colors. Contrasting with this quaint and colorful architecture, the rest of the desertlike island may remind you of the southwestern United States.

Dutch, Spanish, and **English** are all spoken on Curaçao. The official currency is the **Netherlands Antillean florin** (NAf), also called a guilder (US$1 = 1.77 NAf; 1 NAf = US56¢). Most places accept U.S. dollars for purchases.

Cruising into port

Cruise ships dock in Willemstad at a megapier just beyond the Queen Emma pontoon bridge. It has a tourist information booth, car rental agencies, duty-free shopping, and workshop space for local artists. Just beyond the bridge is the famous **Floating Market** (see below). The adjacent fort houses **Riffort Village,** a shopping/entertainment complex.

Scoring the best excursions

Animal Encounter Scuba Adventure: Suit up in scuba gear and explore a shallow natural tidal pool at the edge of a colorful reef. There's a fence between you and those sharks and sea turtles, but you can feed them through holes. Meanwhile, on your side of the fence, you can interact with stingrays, parrotfish, and other marine life. Because the water is so shallow, scuba certification isn't required (4 hours; $89)

Spanish Water Canoe and Snorkeling: Board canoes at Caracas Bay Island for a 45-minute paddle alongside mangroves and rock formations. At Baya Beach, instructors lead snorkeling excursions over a sunken tugboat (3½ hours; $69).

Exploring on your own

From the pier, it's just a five- to ten-minute walk across the **Queen Emma pontoon bridge** to the city's principal shopping and business areas. You can "do" Willemstad on foot in two or three hours. which leaves you plenty of time for beaches or watersports. **Taxi** drivers waiting at the cruise dock can take you to any of the beaches. Fares are fixed, so ask the driver what the rate to your destination is before you set out. If you want him to pick you up again later, just inquire. If you want a taxi tour, you can share with up to four passengers total for about $30 per hour.

You can also get around the island by two kinds of buses. Take either a van (easily recognizable by the word BUS on the license plate) or one of the yellow or blue buses called *konvoi.* Yellow buses run from **Wilhelmina**

Curaçao

Plein (near the shopping center) to most parts of the island. Fares to any point are under $2.

Within walking distance: Boats from Venezuela, Colombia, and other Caribbean islands dock at the **Floating Market,** a short walk from the Queen Emma pontoon bridge. Here, amid a bustling crowd, vendors sell fresh fish, tropical fruits, spices, and crafts. Nearby, you can trace the island's history through the exhibits at the **Curaçao Maritime Museum** (Van den Brandhof Street; ☎ **5999-465-2327;** www.curacaomaritime. com). Admission is about $6. A guided harbor tour by boat is $12, including museum admission.

The oldest Jewish congregation in the New World gathers in the 1651 **Mikve Israel Emanuel Synagogue** (at the corner of Columbusstraat and Hanchi Snog). White sand covers the floor, symbolic of the desert that the early Israelites roamed. Next door, the **Jewish Cultural Historical Museum** (Hanchi Snoa 29; ☎ 599-9-461-1633; www.snoa.com) is housed in two buildings dating from 1728. They were the rabbi's residence and the *mikvah* (bath) for religious purification purposes. Entry is through the synagogue and admission is about $2.

The **Curaçao Museum** (Van Leeuwenhoekstraat; ☎ 599-9-462-3873) is housed in a restored 1853 building constructed by the Royal Dutch Army as a military hospital. Today, it displays paintings, objets d'art, and antique furniture, as well as a large collection from the Caiquetio tribes. Admission is about $3.

Housed in a former slave yard and prison, **Museum Kura Hulanda** (Klipstraat 9; ☎ 5999-434-7765; www.kurahulanda.com) is an anthropological museum that focuses on the predominant cultures of Curaçao, chronicling the African slave trade, West African empires, pre-Colombian gold, Mesopotamian relics, and Antillean art. You reach the museum via small boats that cross the harbor. Admission is about $5.50.

Beyond walking distance: Home to more than 400 species of fish and plant life, the **Curaçao Seaquarium** (off Bhpor Kibra, just east of Willemstad; ☎ 599-9-465-8900; www.curacao-sea-aquarium.com) offers divers, snorkelers, and experienced swimmers a chance to feed, film, and photograph sharks, stingrays, lobsters, and other marine life in a controlled environment. If you don't swim, a 46-foot semi-submersible observatory enables you to watch the underwater action. If you don't do semi-submersibles, the Seaquarium also maintains the island's only full-facility, palm-shaded, sugar-white beach. The facility is about a ten-minute, $8 cab ride from Queen Emma pontoon bridge. Admission is $15 for adults and $7.50 for children under 14.

A 40-minute taxi ride west of Willemstad, you can see cacti, bromeliads, rare orchids, iguanas, donkeys, wild goats, and many species of birds in 4,500-acre **Christoffel National Park** (near the northwestern tip of Curaçao; ☎ 599-9-864-0363). The park rises from flat, arid countryside to 1,230-foot **St. Christoffelberg,** the tallest point in the Dutch Leewards. Hiking along several trails to the top of the mountain, you find Arawak paintings and the **Piedra di Monton,** a rock heap piled by African slaves who cleared this former plantation. Legend says slaves could climb to the top of the rock pile, jump off, and fly back home across the Atlantic to Africa. The park has 20 miles of one-way trail-like roads for driving tours and several hiking trails that go to the top of the mountain. It takes about 1½ hours to walk to the top. Admission is $9.

Next to Christoffel National Park, **National Park Shete Boka** (Seven Inlets in the Papiamentu language) encompasses rugged seaside cliffs carved in dramatic patterns. The highlight is Boka Tabla, a wide cavern carved by millions of years of pounding surf. The place is also a turtle sanctuary. Admission is about $1.50.

If you want to explore the island's deeper side, head to **Hato Caves** (F. D. Rooseveltweg; ☎ 599-9-868-0379). Originally a coral reef, the limestone formations were created over thousands of years by water seeping through the coral and pushing it upward. After crossing the lake, you enter two caverns known as "The Cathedral" and La Ventana ("The Window"), where you see samples of ancient Indian petroglyphs. Local guides take visitors through every hour. Admission is $6.25 for adults, $4.75 for kids under 13.

Honeymooners and other couples can snuggle on a blanket at one of Curaçao's 38 beautiful beaches. The better ones are **Santa Barbara Beach,** south of Willemstad; **Blauwbaai** (Blue Bay), just west of the city; and **Playa Abao, Knip Bay,** and other stretches way up near the island's western tip.

Dominica

Tiny Dominica (pronounced dome-ee-*nee*-ka), sandwiched between Guadeloupe and Martinique, is the most lush and mountainous island in the eastern Caribbean. About 29 miles long and 16 wide, it's blessed with astonishing natural wonders, including lush rain forests, crystal-pure rivers, and dramatic waterfalls. Volcanic coral reefs, every bit as biologically complex as the rain forests onshore, ring the island, and a bit farther from land, whales mate and calve. No wonder they call this "the nature island of the Caribbean." On the downside, the island's capital, Roseau, is a little rough around the edges, and the island's shore lacks the kind of sugar-white beaches many folks associate with the Caribbean. That isn't the point of Dominica, though. Here, it's all about nature, with a little bit of the most authentic Caribbean culture mixed in: up in the island's northeast live about 3,000 Carib Indians, the last remaining descendants of the people who dominated the region when Europeans arrived, and gave it its name.

The **Eastern Caribbean dollar** (EC$2.72 = US$1; EC$1 = US37¢) is the official currency, but merchants accept the U.S. dollar virtually everywhere. The official language is **English,** but most people also speak Creole.

Cruising into port

Dominica has two cruise ship ports. The most frequented is in the heart of **Roseau,** the country's capital and largest town, with banks, restaurants, a market, a tourism office, and the Dominica Museum all within spitting distance. The other is near the northwestern town of **Portsmouth,** closer to attractions such as Cabrits National Park and Fort Shirley (see "Exploring on your own," later in this chapter).

Scoring the best excursions

Trafalgar Falls and Emerald Pool Nature Tour: Drive to Morne Bruce for a panoramic view of Roseau and visit the Botanical Gardens. Proceed to a lookout point for a fantastic view of Trafalgar Falls before driving into the interior, where you walk 15 minutes along a relatively easy trail to the **Emerald Pool,** named for the moss-covered boulders that enclose it. You can swim if you like, floating on your back under the rain forest canopy and 50-foot waterfall (3½ hours; $45).

Home of the Carib Indians: Located on Dominica's northeastern coast, the 3,700-acre Carib Territory is home to the world's last surviving population of Carib Indians. The Caribs today live like most other rural islanders — growing bananas and coconuts, fishing, and operating small shops — but they maintain cultural and artistic traditions that bind them to their past. On your visit, the tribe's chief will acquaint you with Carib history, and you'll see a performance by the Karifuna Cultural Group (5 hours; $54).

Dominica by Jeep and Swimming at the Titou Gorge: A jeep convoy heads up Morne Bruce for a picturesque view, stopping at the Botanical Gardens and the Wotten Waven Sulpher Springs before arriving at the volcanic Titou Gorge for a swim among sheer 20-foot black walls, rock outcrops, caves, and a thundering waterfall (3½ hours; $99).

Layou Gorge River Tubing: Tubing guides take you downriver through the Layou Valley, lined with tall, overhanging cliffs and lush vegetation (3 hours; $64).

Kayak and Snorkel Safari: A guided kayaking trip takes you from Soufrière to your snorkeling site at Scotts Head. The bay here is home to an amazing amount of marine life and coral, and it's common to see dolphins and frigate birds feeding (3½ hours; $59).

Exploring on your own

Fleets of **taxis** and **public minivans** await cruise ship passengers at the dock. All are designated by a "HA" or "H" on the license plate. Drivers are generally knowledgeable about sites and history, and the standard sightseeing rate is from $20 per site per person. The vehicles are unmetered, so negotiate a price in advance.

Within walking distance: On the bay front at the dock in Roseau is the **Dominica Museum,** located in an old market house dating from 1810. Its permanent exhibit illustrates the island's geology, history, archeology, economy, and culture. Admission is $3. Behind the museum is **Old Market Square,** where merchants have gathered for centuries. At one time, it was also the site for executions, slave auctions, and political rallies. Now, you find Dominican crafts and souvenirs for sale. The **Public Market Place,** at the mouth of the Roseau River and to your left as you leave the ship, is the town's commercial hub. Expect it to be especially jumping on Saturday mornings when farmers and countryside vendors display fruits, vegetables, and flowers.

On the eastern edge of Roseau, also within walking distance of the docks, the **Botanical Gardens** lie at the base of Morne Bruce, the mountain overlooking the town. The gardens were established at the end of the 19th century, and about 150 of the 500 original species of trees and

Dominica

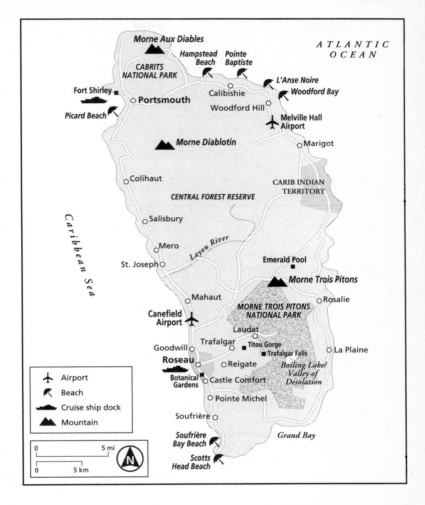

shrubs remain. Keep your eyes out for the Carib Wood tree, whose red blossom is the island's national flower (in bloom Mar–May).

The cruise ship dock at Portsmouth leads directly to the 260-acre **Cabrits National Park** (it takes 45–60 minutes to drive here from the Roseau dock, and a cab is $60). The park boasts dazzling mountain scenery, tropical forests, swamplands, volcanic sand beaches, coral reefs, and the ruins of **Fort Shirley,** an 18th-century garrison. Some of the park has been partly reconstructed, and look for stone walls and cannons hidden among vegetation along the trails. Previous visitors to the area have included Christopher Columbus, Sir Francis Drake,

Admiral Horatio Nelson, and John Smith, who stopped here on his way to Virginia to found Jamestown. You can spend a whole day touring the park, so wear good walking shoes. Admission is $2.

Beyond walking distance: About 15 to 20 minutes by cab from Roseau is **Trafalgar Falls,** two separate cascades that tumble side by side. A short trail from the road brings you to a viewing platform where you see the two falls converge into rocky pools. You can take a dip in the brisk water at the base of the falls, but be careful, the rocks are slippery.

Emerald Pool is located deep in the rain forest, not far from the center of the island. Expect about a 40-minute drive from Roseau. After you walk 15 minutes along a flat trail shaded by magnificent trees, you reach a 50-foot waterfall that crashes into the pool, which is named for the moss-covered boulders that enclose it. It's like a natural cathedral — except you can't swim around in most cathedrals.

Another swimming spot that beckons visitors is **Titou Gorge,** near the village of Laudat, northeast of Roseau. The water-filled canyon snakes along to the base of a waterfall. The flow is quite strong, and at times, you may feel like a salmon swimming upstream. A hot mineral cascade at the canyon's mouth relieves sore muscles. From Roseau to Laudat is about a 30-minute drive.

Beaches — featuring plenty of rocks and dark, volcanic sand — are not Dominica's strong point, but the island's top choices are **Hampstead Beach, Hodges Beach, L'Ance Noire,** and **Woodford Bay,** all on the northern coast, about 20 minutes from Roseau.

Grand Cayman, Cayman Islands

Mostly scrubland and swamp, Grand Cayman and its sister islands (Cayman Brac and Little Cayman) are anything but lush. Still, the island boasts its share of upscale, expensive private homes and condos, owned by millionaire expatriates from all over who come because of the tiny nation's lenient tax and banking laws. For tourists, Grand Cayman is known most for what's offshore — spectacular coral reefs that make for some really great **diving and snorkeling.** The island also has a nice stretch of sand, **Seven Mile Beach,** that fronts a strip of high-rise hotels. If all you care about is shopping, you're in luck. George Town, the British colony's capital and place where you'll land when your ship calls here, has its fair share of brand-name stores.

In 2004, Hurricane Ivan tore through Grand Cayman, causing substantial flooding, destroying many homes and businesses, and severely damaging power and sewage networks. Things were such a mess that the island was officially closed to tourists for two months. However, with tourism accounting for some 45 percent of the Caymans' GDP, cleanup was swift. Ships began returning in late November, and at press time things were more or less back to normal.

Grand Cayman

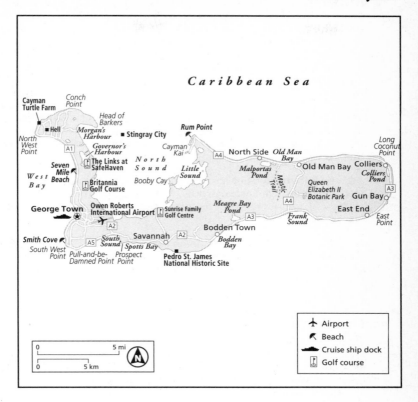

English is the official language of the islands. The legal tender is the **Cayman Islands dollar** (CI82¢ = US$1; CI$1 = US$1.22), but U.S. dollars are commonly accepted. Be sure to note which currency price tags refer to before making a purchase.

Cruising into port

Cruise ships anchor off George Town and ferry their passengers to a pier on Harbour Drive, right in the midst of George Town's thriving shopping district.

If seas are choppy, which happens fairly often, the piers may be closed and your cruise may be forced to skip the port altogether.

Scoring the best excursions

Stingray City: The waters off Grand Cayman are home to Stingray City, one of the world's wackiest underwater attractions. Set in the very shallow waters of North Sound, about 2 miles east of the island's northwestern tip, the site was discovered in the mid-1980s when local fishermen noticed that scores of stingrays were showing up to feed on the offal they dumped overboard. Today, anywhere from 30 to 100 relatively tame stingrays swarm around the hundreds of oohing and aahing snorkelers like so many aquatic basset hounds, eager for handouts. Stingrays are terribly gentle creatures, and love to have their bellies rubbed, but never try to grab one by the tail — their barbed stingers can inflict a lot of pain (2–3 hours; $49–$59).

Atlantis Deep-Dive Submarine: A real research sub takes two passengers at a time down to 800 feet to explore the Cayman Wall through a 3-foot viewing window. Powerful lights illuminate the sponge belt at 400 feet, and delicate coral and deep-sea creatures can be sighted even farther down (1½ hours, including a 55-minute dive; $399).

Atlantis Submarine: For less dough, a 48-passenger sub takes you down to 100 feet through coral canyons, with an automatic fish feeder drawing swarms of colorful marine creatures (1½ hours, including a 45-minute dive; $95).

Grand Cayman by Bicycle: Hop on a bike to work off all that cruise food, and check out the island's coastline to boot. Pick up your touring mountain bike at the Beach Club Colony Hotel, ride along the coastline for views of Seven Mile Beach, and then journey inland en route to the north side of the island to ride along the coast again (3 hours; $59).

Exploring on your own

Taxis line up at the pier to meet cruise ship passengers. Fares are fixed; typical one-way fares range from $12 to $20. **Motor scooters** and **bicycles** are another way to get around. Soto Scooters Ltd. (Seven Mile Beach at Coconut Place; ☎ 345-945-4465) offers Honda Elite scooters and bicycles for about $30 and $15 daily.

Within walking distance: Hey, like, it isn't only about shopping. In George Town, check out the small but interesting **Cayman Islands National Museum** (Harbour Drive; ☎ 345-949-8368; www.museum.ky). Exhibits include Caymanian artifacts collected by Ira Thompson (beginning in the 1930s), and other items relating to the natural, social, and cultural history of the Caymans. Admission is $5 ($2.50 seniors); closed Sundays.

Beyond walking distance: The only green-sea-turtle farm of its kind in the world, **Cayman Turtle Farm,** at Northwest Point, just beyond the town of Hell (☎ 345-949-3894; www.turtle.ky), is the island's most popular land-based tourist attraction. Once a multitude of turtles lived in the waters surrounding the Cayman Islands (in fact, Christopher Columbus called the islands Las Tortugas because there were so many), but today these creatures are endangered. The turtle farm's purpose is twofold: to replenish the waters with hatchlings and yearling turtles, and to provide the local market with edible turtle meat. You can peer into

100 circular concrete tanks containing turtles ranging in size from
6 ounces to 600 pounds, and sample turtle dishes at a snack bar and
restaurant. Admission is $6.

And now, we'd like to tell you to go to **Hell!** Now don't get all offended
on us; it's actually the name of a little town and a great place to buy
some souvenir T-shirts for your most despised friends back home. You
can also mail your postcards from here for the snarky postmark.

If you just want to flop on a towel and fry your skin, head for **Seven Mile
Beach,** a strip of white sand just north of George Town. Lined with con-
dominiums and plush resorts, it's an easy taxi ride from the cruise dock.
Watersports are available, and so are lots of lunch places.

Do the right thing and don't purchase turtle or black-coral products.
You'll see them everywhere, but it's illegal to bring them back into the
United States and most other Western nations.

Grenada

One of Heidi's favorite Caribbean ports of call, this one-time British
Crown Colony offers a little bit of everything — history, lush jungles, and
great beaches. And it's not overrun with tourists. Plus, maybe you didn't
know Grenada (pronounced gre-*nay*-dah) produces more spices than
anywhere else in the world — including clove, cinnamon, mace, cocoa,
tonka beans, ginger, and a third of the world's nutmeg — and thus its
nickname, the Spice Island. **St. George's,** the country's capital, is one of
the most colorful ports in the West Indies, nearly landlocked in the deep
crater of a long-dead volcano, full of charming Georgian colonial buildings, and flanked by old forts. The island's coast is white and sandy; its
interior is a jungle of palms, oleander, bougainvillea, and other tropical
foliage, crisscrossed by roads and trails.

Grenada was one of the hardest hit Caribbean islands during 2004's
devastating hurricane season. Almost every building sustained some
level of damage, but you can't keep a good island down. Known for its
lushness and most extravagant fertility (results of a gentle climate and
volcanic soil), Grenada started springing back almost immediately, its
coastal greenery growing back rapidly and its rain forests filling out a
little more slowly.

English is commonly spoken on this island, and the official currency is
the **Eastern Caribbean dollar** (EC$2.70 = US$1; EC$1 = US37¢), though
dollars are accepted commonly. Always determine which dollars — EC
or U.S. — you're talking about when discussing a price.

You might remember when the U.S. military invaded the island in 1983 in
one of its more bizarre Cold War excursions. But no worries, the likeli-
hood of a superpower invading this tiny, harmless Grenada any time
soon is pretty darn low.

Cruising into port

Ships either dock at a pier right in St. George's or anchor in the much-photographed harbor and send their passengers to the pier by tender. **The Carenage** (St. George's main street) is only a short walk away from the pier.

Scoring the best excursions

Because of Grenada's lush landscape, we recommend spending at least a few hours touring its interior, one of the most scenic in the West Indies.

Hike to Seven Sisters Waterfalls: After a 40-minute hike along a muddy path in the lush Grand Etang rain forest, passengers are free to take a swim in the natural pools or hop off the edge of the cascading waterfalls. It's gorgeous and lots of fun. Don't forget to wear your bathing suit and maybe a pair of water-friendly sandals (3½ hours; $59).

Island Tour, Grand Etang Lake, and Fort Frederick: This is a great way to experience Grenada's lush, cool, dripping-wet tropical interior. Via bus, you travel past the red-tiled roofs of St. George's en route to the bright blue Grand Etang Lake, within an extinct volcanic crater some 570m (1,900 ft.) above sea level. On the way, you drive through rain forests and stop at a spice estate. Some tours include a visit to Annandale Falls and Fort Frederick (4½ hours; $44).

Exploring on your own

Taxi fares are set by the government. A one-way taxi to Grand Anse (one of the Caribbean's best beaches) is about $15 for up to four passengers. You can also tap most taxi drivers as a guide for a day's sightseeing, for about $25 per hour. **Water taxis** also head from the cruise ship welcome center to Grand Anse. Round-trip fare is about $4.

Within walking distance: If you're up for a good hike and some awesome photo ops, walk around the historical Carenage from the cruise terminal in St. George's and head up to **Fort George,** built in 1705 by the French and originally called Fort Royal. While the fort ruins and the 200- to 300-year-old cannons are worth a peek, the 360-degree panoramic views of the entire harbor area are spectacular. You can pick up a rudimentary walking-tour map from the cruise terminal to help you find interesting sites along the way.

In town, you can also visit the **Grenada National Museum** (Young and Monckton Streets; ☎ 473-440-3725), set in the foundations of an old French army barracks and prison built in 1704. Small but interesting, check out stuff such as Joséphine Bonaparte's bathtub from her girlhood in Martinique. Admission is $1.

Church Street, which leads right to the fort, has lots of quaint 18th- and 19th-century architecture as well as several 19th-century cathedrals and the island's Houses of Parliament.

Grenada

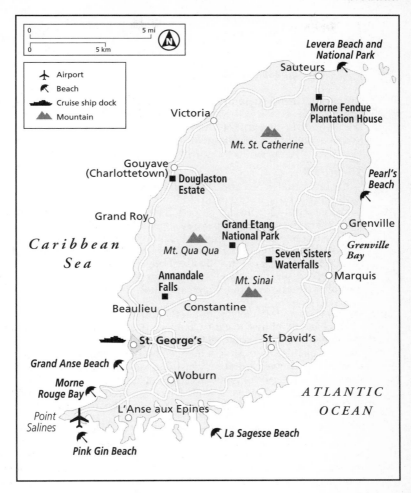

Beyond walking distance: You can take a taxi up Richmond Hill to **Fort Frederick,** which the French began in 1779. The British retook the island in 1783 and completed the fort in 1791. From its battlements, you'll have a panoramic view of the harbor and the yacht marina.

Don't miss the mountains northeast of St. George's. If you don't have much time, 15m (50-ft.) **Annandale Falls** is just a 15-minute drive away, on the outskirts of the **Grand Etang Forest Reserve.** You can swim and picnic surrounded by liana vines, elephant ears, and other tropical flora and spices — you'll swear you landed in Tahiti. If you have more time and want a less crowded spot, **Seven Sisters Waterfalls** are farther into

Grand Etang, an approximately 30-minute drive and then a mile hike through the beautiful tropical forest to the falls.

About 25 miles north of St. George's, at the 1912 **Morne Fendue Plantation House** (also known as Betty's) at St. Patrick's (☎ 473-442-9330), you can enjoy old-time island recipes while you dine as an upper-class family would have in the 1920s. A fixed-price ($16) lunch is served Monday to Saturday from 12:30 to 3 p.m. Call for reservations.

Grenada's **Grand Anse Beach,** with its 3.2km (2 miles) of wide sugar-white sands, is one of the best in the Caribbean, with calm waters and a great view of St. George's. There are several restaurants beachside, and you can also join a banana-boat ride or rent a Sunfish sailboat.

Jamaica

Yah mon. Jamaica is a cool, racy place as islands go, and real popular with cruise ships, not to mention honeymooners and couples who flock to the island's all-inclusive resorts. The third largest of the Caribbean islands after Cuba and Hispaniola, Jamaica has dense jungle in its interior, mountains rising as high as 2,220m (7,400 ft.), and many beautiful white-sand beaches along its northern coast, where the cruise ships dock. Most head for **Ocho Rios,** although more are opting to call at the city of **Montego Bay** ("Mo Bay"), 108km (67 miles) to the west, with comparable attractions, excursions, and shopping possibilities.

One of the most densely populated nations in the Caribbean, with a vivid sense of its own identity, Jamaica has a history rooted in the plantation economy and some of the most impassioned politics in the Western Hemisphere, all of which leads to a sometimes turbulent day-to-day reality. You've probably heard, for example, that the island's vendors and hawkers can be pushy and the locals not always the most welcoming to tourists, and while there's definitely some truth to this, we've had mostly positive experiences, so keep an open mind.

The official language is **English,** but most Jamaicans speak a richly nuanced patois. The unit of currency is the **Jamaican dollar,** designated by the same symbol as the U.S. dollar (US$1 = J$61; J$1 = US2¢). Visitors can pay in U.S. dollars, but always find out if a price is being quoted in Jamaican or U.S. dollars — though the huge difference probably makes it obvious.

Cruising into port

Cruise ships dock at either the **Port of Ocho Rios,** near Dunn's River Falls and adjacent to Island Village and several shopping options, or at **Montego Bay,** where there's a modern cruise dock with the usual duty-free stores and tourist information.

You can walk to the shopping, but otherwise **taxis** are your best means of getting around on your own (definitely don't rent a car here). They'll be waiting for you at the pier. Taxis licensed by the government — and

Jamaica

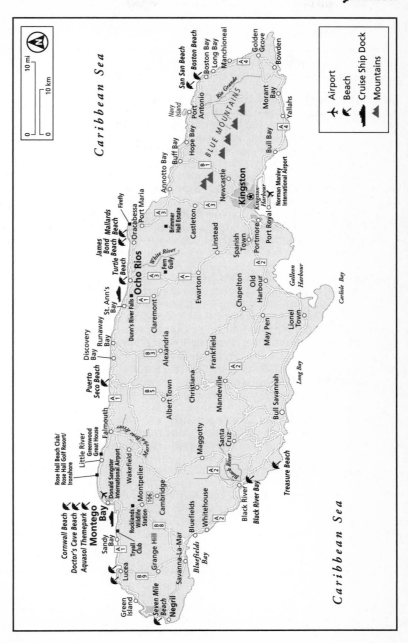

Caribbean Sea

10 mi
10 km
0
0

Airport
Beach
Cruise Ship Dock
Mountains

San San Beach
Boston Beach
Boston Bay
Long Bay
Manchioneal
Golden Grove
Bowden

Rio Grande
BLUE MOUNTAINS

Navy Island
Port Antonio
Morant Bay
Yallahs

A 4

Hope Bay
Buff Bay
Bull Bay

A B 1

Annotto Bay
Newcastle
Kingston
Norman Manley International Airport

A 3

Firefly
Port Maria
Oracabessa
Brimmer Hall Estate
Castleton
Linstead
Spanish Town
Portmore
Port Royal

A 2

Kingston Harbour

Mallards Beach
James Bond Beach
Turtle Beach
Ocho Rios

A 3

White River
Fern Gully

A 1

St. Ann's Bay
Dunn's River Falls

A 1

Claremont
Ewarton
Chapelton
Old Harbour
Lionel Town
May Pen

Gallows Harbour

Carlisle Bay

Runaway Bay
Discovery Bay

B 3

Alexandria
Frankfield

Puerto Seco Beach

A 1

Albert Town
Christiana
Mandeville
Bull Savannah

B 5

A 2

Long Bay

Falmouth
Little River
Greenwood Great House
Rose Hall Beach Club/
Rose Hall Golf Resort/
Ironshore

Maggotty
Santa Cruz

Martha Brae River

Wakefield
Montpelier
106
Cambridge
Whitehouse
Bluefields

Black River
Treasure Beach

Donald Sangster International Airport
Montego Bay

A 2

Cornwall Beach
Doctor's Cave Beach
Aquasol Themepark

Sandy Bay
Rodlands Wildlife Station

A 1

Tryall Club
Grange Hill
Savanna-La-Mar
Bluefields Bay

B 8

A 2

Lucea
Green Island

B 9

Seven Mile Beach
Negril

Caribbean Sea

Caribbean Sea

you should only use one of these — display **JTB** decals, indicating they're official Jamaican Tourist Board taxis. Fixed rates are posted.

Scoring the best excursions

Because there's little besides shopping near the docks at either Ocho Rios or Montego Bay, most passengers sign up for shore excursions. The following are usually offered from both ports.

Dunn's River Falls Tour: Okay, they're totally touristy, crowded, and over-hyped, but we have to admit, climbing the falls is totally fun. Cascading 180m (600 ft.) to the beach, it's a ball to slip and slide your way up the falls with hundreds of others, forming a human chain of sorts. Wear a bathing suit under your clothes, and don't forget your waterproof camera and your aqua-socks. (If you do forget, most cruise lines rent aqua-socks for an extra $5 or so.) The prettiest part of the falls, known as the Laughing Waters, was used in the James Bond classics *Dr. No* and *Live and Let Die.* Tour options often include visits to other sites and/or shopping. *Note:* The falls are much closer to Ocho Rios than to Mo Bay, so tours from the latter typically cost around $70 and require a 2¼-hour drive each way, for a total of 7½ hours (4–4½ hours; $45).

River Tubing Safari: This is one of the best excursions we've ever taken. After a scenic van ride deep into the pristine jungles, the group of 20 or so passengers and a couple of guides sit back into big black inner tubes and glide a few miles downriver, passing by gorgeous, towering bamboo trees and other lush foliage. The rapids are very tame; do this for the scenery and the fun of floating downstream on your bum! If you're docking in Ocho Rios, this tour is usually on the White River. If in Montego Bay, it's on the Great River. This trip is totally better than the **Martha Brae River Rafting,** which takes you down the river on two-seat bamboo rafts for about the same price (3½ hours; $58).

Horseback-Riding Excursion: After a 45-minute ride from the stables through fields, you can gallop along the beach and take your horse bareback into the surf for a thrilling ride (3–3½ hours; $89).

The following two popular excursions are typically offered from Mo Bay:

Rose Hall Great House: This is the most famous plantation home in Jamaica. Built about two centuries ago by John Palmer, it gained notoriety from the doings of "Infamous Annie" Palmer, wife of the builder's grandnephew, who supposedly dabbled in witchcraft and murder. Many Jamaicans insist the house is haunted (3 hours; $43).

Greenwood Great House and Town Drive: More interesting to some than Rose Hall, this Georgian-style building was the residence of Richard Barrett, a first cousin of Elizabeth Barrett Browning. On display are the family's library, portraits, antiques, and period musical instruments (3½ hours; $39).

Exploring on your own in Ocho Rios

The port at Ocho Rios is just a mile away from the major shopping area, Ocean Village Shopping Centre.

Once a small banana and fishing port, Ocho Rios is now Jamaica's cruise ship capital, welcoming a couple of ships every day during high season. Though the area has some of the Caribbean's most fabled resorts, and Dunn's River is just a five-minute taxi ride away, the town itself is not much to see, including the outdoor markets within walking distance. Don't expect to shop in the markets without a lot of hassle and a lot of very pushy hawking of merchandise — some of which is likely to be ganja (the wacky weed). In recent years, a fleet of blue-uniformed "resort patrol" on bikes has been helping keep order.

Within walking distance: Adjacent to the cruise pier, **Island Village** (www.islandjamaica.com) is a 4-acre entertainment and shopping complex developed by Island Records' Chris Blackwell. Attractions include the ReggaeXplosion museum, a museum of Jamaican art, a casino, an outdoor concert venue and indoor theater, a beach with watersports, and shopping (lots of it).

Beyond walking distance: Shore excursions are the best way to see popular sights such as **Dunn's River Falls** (see "Scoring the best excursions," earlier in this section).

The 1817 **Brimmer Hall Estate,** Port Maria, St. Mary's (☎ 876-994-2309), 34km (21 miles) east of Ocho Rios, is a working plantation where you're driven around in a tractor-drawn jitney to see the tropical fruit trees and coffee plants. It's really touristy, but a lot of people seem to like it. Most ships sell organized excursions here, or call ahead and arrange your own. Admission is $15.

In the same general area, toward the coast, **Firefly,** Grants Pen, above Oracabessa (☎ 876-997-7201), was the home of Sir Noël Coward and his longtime companion, Graham Payn, who, as executor of Coward's estate, donated it to the Jamaica National Heritage Trust. The recently restored house is as it was on the day Sir Noël died in 1973. It's open Monday to Thursday from 9 a.m. to 5 p.m. Admission is $10.

The cruise and hotel hordes descend upon **Mallards Beach,** at the Sunset Jamaica Grande (☎ 876-974-2201) on Main Street. Locals may steer you to the good and less-crowded **Turtle Beach,** southwest of Mallards. You may also want to check out the big **James Bond Beach** in Oracabessa, about 20 minutes from town. Bond author Ian Fleming's home, Goldeneye, is located nearby.

Exploring on your own in Montego Bay

Mo Bay, as it's called by insiders, has better beaches, shopping, and restaurants than Ocho Rios, as well as some of the best golf courses in the Caribbean — though it also has Ocho Rios' crime and traffic.

Within walking distance: One of the main shopping hubs is **Montego Freeport,** and it's within easy walking distance of the pier. Otherwise, you have to take a taxi or book an organized tour to see anything.

Beyond walking distance: If you're not taking a shore excursion, consider a visit to **Rocklands Wildlife Station,** Anchovy, St. James (☎ 876-952-2009). Lisa Salmon, known as the "Bird Lady of Anchovy," established this sanctuary, which is perfect for nature lovers and bird-watchers. You can feed small doves and finches from your hand, and with luck you can coax a Jamaican doctor bird to perch on your finger and drink syrup. Rocklands is about 1.2km (¾ mile) outside Anchovy on the road from Montego Bay. Admission is $8.

To beach it, head for **Doctor's Cave Beach** (Gloucester Avenue across from the Doctor's Cave Beach Hotel; ☎ 876-952-4355; www.doctors cave.com), which helped launch Mo Bay as a resort in the 1940s. One of the premier beaches of Jamaica, **Aquasol Theme Park** (formerly Walter Fletcher Beach), is in the heart of Mo Bay; its tranquil waters are very family friendly. On the main road 18km (11 miles) east of Montego Bay, the half-mile **Rose Hall Beach Club** (☎ 876-680-0969) is a secure, secluded, white sandy beach, offering crystal-clear water, a full restaurant, two beach bars, and more. All of these beaches charge admission, which runs between about $4 and $8.

If you'd rather eat than roast in the sun, beeline it to **The Pork Pit** (27 Gloucester Ave.; ☎ 876-952-1046), the best place to go for the famous Jamaican jerk pork and jerk chicken. Prices are very reasonable. Lunch costs $10.

If golf is your bag, there are several excellent 18-hole, par-71 or -72 courses, some with ocean views. If your ship doesn't have an excursion there, call ahead and then get there via taxi. Courses include **Tryall Club** (☎ 876-956-5660; www.tryallclub.com; greens fees $145), 19km (12 miles) from Montego Bay; ultrascenic **Wyndham Rose Hall Golf & Beach Resort,** Rose Hall (☎ 876-953-2650; greens fees $125), once featured in a James Bond movie; **Half Moon,** at Rose Hall (☎ 876-953-2560; www.halfmoon-resort.com/golf; greens fees $130); and **Ironshore Golf & Country Club,** Ironshore, St. James, Montego Bay (☎ 876-953-3681; greens fees $30–$50).

Key West, Florida

If you like booz'n and browsing for tacky souvenirs, with a little history thrown in for good measure, then cool Key West will do you just fine. Located at the very end of the Florida Keys, Key West is America's southernmost city and one of its most fun-loving and goofy. It's part Caribbean outpost with a dash of New Orleans–style high life. There are plenty of Hemingway look-alikes, a large gay community, and tons of tourists shuffling around with smiles on their faces. The proximity of most attractions to the cruise docks means there's little sense in taking an excursion here unless you have mobility problems. Wander around

Key West

touristy Mallory Square and Duval Street, check out some of the theme bars, and then take a walk down some of the quieter side streets, maybe visiting Truman's Little White House or the Hemingway House museum. Or spend your day playing golf, diving, or snorkeling. Several raw bars near the dock area offer seafood, including oysters and clams, although the king here is conch — served grilled, ground into burgers, made into chowder, fried in batter as fritters, or served raw in a salad.

You're in Florida, so the U.S. dollar is the official currency and English is the language.

Cruising into port

Ships dock at **Mallory Square** (Old Town's tourist central), at the nearby Hilton Resort's **Pier B,** and at the U.S. Navy base's **"Outer Mole" pier.** All are on the Gulf side of the island. Passengers arriving at the Navy pier must take an official shuttle bus the short distance to and from Mallory Square, as individuals are not permitted to transit the base on their own.

Scoring the best excursions

In addition to the Conch Tour Train described in the next section, most lines offer walking tours and sometimes bike tours for those who like the services of a guide. But, this is really a port to explore on your own, with the exception of booze cruises.

Key West Catamaran Sail and Snorkel Tour: The popular Fury catamarans take passengers to a reef for some snorkeling and then finish the trip back to shore with music, booze, and a good time (3–3½ hours; $44).

Exploring on your own

Within walking distance: The flat island is only 4 miles long and 2 miles wide, so getting around is easy. The most popular attractions are within walking distance of Mallory Square, at most a 20-minute walk. The farthest is Hemingway House, about a mile down Duval. Many passengers opt for one of the island's tram tours, which are sold as shore excursions but are also available on a walk-up basis. Shopping is available everywhere you look, and mostly of the flamingo snow globes, T-shirt, and floppy straw hats variety.

The **Conch Tour Train** (☎ 305-296-4444; www.conchtourtrain.com) is a narrated 90-minute tour that offers commentary on 100 local sites. The depot is located at Mallory Square, and trains depart every 30 minutes ($20 adults, $10 children 4–12, free 3 and under). The trip has only one stop where passengers can get on and off (at the Historic Seaport). If you want more flexibility, try the **Old Town Trolley** (☎ 305-296-6688; www.trolleytours.com), which allows you to hop on and off its trains to explore on your own. Prices are the same as the Conch Train, and pickup stops are signposted around town.

If you want wheels of your own, **bicycles and motor scooters** are a good bet here, and are widely available, with daily rates hovering around $12 and $45, respectively.

Depending on your degree of thirst, the most important sightseeing may be Key West's many bars. They're big, are often packed, and typically feature someone playing guitar and singing the hits in one corner. Most serve basic chow too. **Captain Tony's Saloon** (428 Greene St.; ☎ 305-294-1838) is the oldest active bar in Florida — Hemingway drank here and Jimmy Buffett got his start here, what better drinking credentials could you have? **Sloppy Joe's** (201 Duval St.; ☎ 305-294-5717) is the most touristy bar in Key West. **Jimmy Buffett's Margaritaville** (500 Duval St.; ☎ 305-296-3070) is kind of a refugee from Branson, Missouri, but if you've got a hankering for a cheeseburger from paradise or want to waste away again on margaritas, this is your place. Much less commercial is the open-air — and raucous and loud — **Hog's Breath Saloon** (400 Front St.; ☎ 305-296-4222) near the cruise docks.

The **Harry S. Truman Little White House** (111 Front St.; ☎ 305-294-9911; www.trumanlittlewhitehouse.com) served as Truman's vacation home during his presidency and remains just as he left it, decorated in late 1940s style. Guides lead a well-organized hour-long tour. Admission is $10.

Hemingway Home (907 Whitehead St.; ☎ **305-294-1136;** www.hemingway home.com) provides a similar if less formal look back at the island's old days. "Papa" lived here with his second wife, Pauline, completing *For Whom the Bell Tolls* and *A Farewell to Arms* in the studio annex out back. Hemingway had some 60 polydactyl (many-toed) cats, whose descendants still live on the grounds. Admission is $11.

Audubon House and Tropical Garden (205 Whitehead St., at Greene St.; ☎ **877-281-2473** or 305-294-2116; www.audubonhouse.com) is dedicated to the 1832 Key West sojourn of the famous naturalist John James Audubon. The main reason to visit is to see how wealthy sailors lived in Key West in the 19th century, and the lush tropical gardens surrounding the house. Admission is $10.

The Heritage House Museum and Robert Frost Cottage (410 Caroline St.; ☎ **305-296-3573;** www.heritagehousemuseum.org) was the home of Jessie Porter Newton, the grande dame of Key West. Today her home is filled with mementos of the illustrious guests who partook of her hospitality, including Tennessee Williams, Gloria Swanson, and Robert Frost, who stayed in a cottage out back.

On the waterfront at Mallory Square, the **Key West Aquarium** (1 Whitehead St.; ☎ **305-296-2051;** www.keywestaquarium.com), in operation since 1932, was the first tourist attraction built in the Florida Keys. Admission is $9.

Near the docks, the **Mel Fisher Maritime Heritage Society Museum** (200 Greene St.; ☎ **305-294-2633;** www.melfisher.com) contains some of the more than $400 million in gold jewelry, doubloons, and other artifacts the late treasure hunter Mel Fisher plucked from the Spanish galleon *Nuestra Señora de Atocha,* which sunk off the Keys in 1622. Admission is $10.

Nancy Forrester's Secret Garden (1 Free School Lane, off Simonton between Southard and Fleming Streets; ☎ **305-294-0015**) is the most lavish and verdant garden in town, with some 150 species of palms and thousands of orchids, climbing vines, and ground covers. Admission is $6.

This town is not known for beaches, but if you insist, the best of the mediocre is **Fort Zachary Taylor State Beach** (☎ **305-292-6713**), a 12-minute walk from the docks. To get there, go through the gates leading into the Truman Annex (site of the Little White House).

Martinique

Frenchies and Francophiles will appreciate Martinque's history. The island, an overseas department of France since 1946, was the birthplace and childhood home of Empress Joséphine, sweetheart and wife of

Napoleon. Martinique is also on the map for a horrific volcano that devastated St-Pierre in 1902. Within minutes, some 30,000 souls perished. Love and death make quite a one-two punch, but they're just the hook. Look a bit deeper to appreciate Martinique's subtler attractions — quaint seaside villages, colonial ruins dating to when France and England vied for the island, and captivatingly beautiful rain forests and beaches.

French is Martinique's official language, but you can get by with **English** at most restaurants and tourist sites. Martinique is an overseas region of France, so the **euro** (€) is the official currency (1€ = US$1.30; US$1 = .77€). U.S. dollars are commonly accepted in tourist areas.

Cruising into port

Most cruise ships dock in the heart of Fort-de-France, at the **Pointe Simon Cruise Dock,** which has quays for two large vessels. Because Martinique is a popular port of call, ships may also dock at the **Passenger Terminal** at the main harbor, a nondescript cargo port on the north side of the bay, a $10 cab ride from the center of town.

Scoring the best excursions

Rainforest and Plantations 4WD Safari: Take your off-road vehicle through tropical forests and sugar-cane plantations (stopping to sample the crop) to a banana plantation and a distillery where you do short tours (4 hours; $84).

Martinique Snorkeling: Across the bay from Fort-de-France, the reef at Anse Dufour offers excellent snorkeling for experts and novices. The reef is filled with marine animals, including French grunts, blackbar soldierfish, and silversides. Snorkeling equipment is provided, as are professional instruction, supervision, and transportation (3 hours; $49).

Exploring on your own

Travel by **taxi** is convenient but expensive. Most cabs are metered, and you can find them waiting at the cruise pier. To cross the bay to La Pagerie (Empress Joséphine's birthplace) and the resort area of Pointe du Bout, take one of the blue **ferries** that sail from east of the cruise dock in Fort-de-France at least once per hour. Round-trip tickets cost about 6€ ($7.80). Avis, Budget, and Hertz all offer **rental cars,** too.

Within walking distance: A bustling town of 100,000 residents, **Fort-de-France** is a sea of ochre buildings, cascading flowers, and tall palm trees. The town's narrow streets, cluttered with boutiques and cafes, climb from the bowl of the sea to the surrounding hills, forming a great urban amphitheater. There's plenty here to keep you busy.

At the eastern end of downtown, **La Savane** is a broad formal park with palms, mangoes, and manicured lawns, perfect for a promenade or rest in the shade. Its most famous feature is the **Statue of Empress Joséphine,** carved in 1858 by Vital Dubray and unceremoniously decapitated in 1995

Martinique

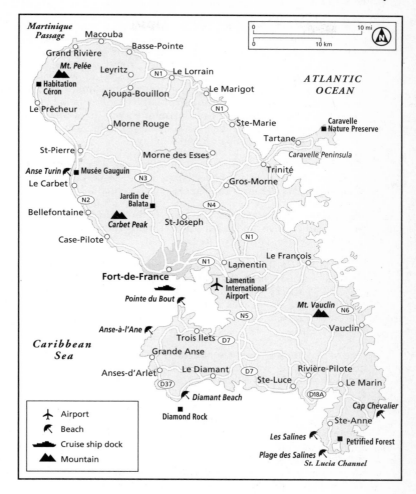

Martinique Passage

Macouba

Basse-Pointe

Grand Rivière

Mt. Pelée   Leyritz   N1   Le Lorrain

■ Habitation Céron   Le Marigot

Ajoupa-Bouillon   N1

Le Prêcheur

ATLANTIC OCEAN

Morne Rouge   Ste-Marie

Caravelle ■ Nature Preserve

Tartane

St-Pierre   Morne des Esses   Caravelle Peninsula

Anse Turin ≮ ■ Musée Gauguin   N3   Trinité

Le Carbet   Gros-Morne

N2   Jardin de Balata ■

Bellefontaine   N4

Carbet Peak   St-Joseph

Case-Pilote   N1

Le François

N1   Lamentin

Fort-de-France

Lamentin International Airport

Pointe du Bout ≮

Mt. Vauclin   N6

N5

Anse-à-l'Ane ≮   Vauclin

Caribbean Sea

Trois Ilets   D7

Grande Anse

Anses-d'Arlet   Le Diamant   D7   Rivière-Pilote

D37   Ste-Luce   Le Marin

≮ Diamant Beach   D18A

✈ Airport   Cap Chevalier

≮ Beach   ■ Diamond Rock   Ste-Anne

⛴ Cruise ship dock   Les Salines ≮   ■ Petrified Forest

▲▲ Mountain   Plage des Salines ≮

St. Lucia Channel

0 ——————— 10 mi
0 ——————— 10 km

in commemoration of her role in reinstating slavery on the island in the early 1800s.

Across the street, **Bibliothèque Schoelcher** (Schoelcher Library; ☎ 596-70-26-67) is one of Fort-de-France's great Belle Epoque buildings. Named in honor of Victor Schoelcher, one of France's most influential abolitionists, it houses his books and other documents. Admission is free; closed Sunday.

Another Henri Pick masterpiece, **St. Louis Cathedral,** on rue Victor Schoelcher at rue Blénac, was built in 1895. Check out the organ, stained-glass windows, and ornamented interior walls. They can be viewed every morning except Saturday.

Built in 1640, **Fort St. Louis,** Boulevard Alfassa, dominates the rocky promontory east of La Savane. It first defended Fort-de-France in 1674 against Dutch invaders, and today, remains the French navy's headquarters in the Caribbean. It is open to visitors only on special occasions.

The best of Fort-de-France's many museums, the **Musée Départemental d'Archéologie Précolombienne Préhistoire** (9 rue de la Liberté; ☎ 596-71-57-05), traces 2,000 years of Martinique's pre-Columbian past with more than a thousand relics from the Arawak and Carib cultures. Admission is 3.45€ ($4.50); closed Sunday.

You can expect to find great food all over town if you want to stop for lunch, and more than any other island in the French West Indies, Martinique gives French and Creole cuisine equal billing.

Beyond walking distance: Too large to tackle in a single day, you have to pick and choose among the island's many museums, plantations, floral parks, and natural wonders to visit.

Martinique's Carib name, Madiana, means "island of flowers." To see what the Caribs were talking about, stroll through the **Jardin de Balata** (☎ 596-64-48-73). Located about 8km (5 miles) north of town, this lush, Edenic garden showcases 200 species of plants, trees, and tropical flowers, as well as resident hummingbirds, frogs, and lizards. Admission is 6.50€ ($8.45).

One of Martinique's must-see attractions, the village of **St-Pierre** on the northwest coast, was the cultural and economic capital of the island until 8 a.m. on May 8, 1902, when the **Mount Pelée** volcano exploded in fire and lava. Three minutes later, all but one of St-Pierre's 30,000 inhabitants had been incinerated, buried in ash and lava, or asphyxiated by poisonous gas. The town once hailed as the "Paris of the Antilles" became "the Pompeii of the Caribbean," and today it's no more than a sleepy fishing village, home to fewer than 5,000 souls. Ruins of a church, theater, and other buildings punctuate the town, memorials to St-Pierre's former glory. The one-room **Musée Volcanologique** (rue Victor Hugo; ☎ 596-78-15-16) traces the story of the cataclysm through pictures and relics excavated from the debris. Admission is 2€ ($3.60).

Part sugar-plantation ruins, part tropical paradise, **Habitation Céron** (☎ 596-52-94-53) is the most evocative of Martinique's historical agricultural sites. This sprawling 17th-century estate, 15 minutes north of St-Pierre, is almost as wild and tranquil as the surrounding rain forest, but its verdigris cisterns, moss-covered stone buildings, and archaic, still functioning water mill are all haunted with the ghosts of a time when sugar was king. Admission is 6€ ($7.80).

A few miles south of St-Pierre, **Le Carbet** is where Columbus landed in 1502, where the first French settlers arrived in 1635, and where the French painter Paul Gauguin lived for five months in 1887. At the site is the tiny **Musée Paul Gauguin,** Anse Turin (☎ 596-78-22-66), though there are no original paintings. Admission is 4€ ($5.20).

Marie Josèphe Rose Tascher de la Pagerie was born in 1763 in the quaint little village of **Trois Ilets,** across the bay from Fort-de-France. As Joséphine, she became the wife of Napoleon Bonaparte in 1796 and Empress of France in 1804. A small museum, the **Musée de la Pagerie** (☎ 596-68-33-06), sits in the former estate kitchen building, where Joséphine gossiped with her slaves. Admission costs 3€ ($3.90).

You'll have passed through a number of quaint coastal villages by this time but none sweeter than **Ste-Luce.** Absurdly picturesque with its blindingly white stucco walls, red-tile roofs, turquoise sea, and multi-colored fishing boats, swim or snorkel off the small, pleasant beach, or just chill out.

Other beaches for bumming around include **Grand Anse des Salines,** just south of Fort-de-France and widely regarded as Martinique's nicest strand. To get to the island's main **gay beach,** turn right at the entrance to Grand Anse des Salines and drive to the far end of the parking lot, near the sign for Petite Anse des Salines. Follow the path through the woods and then veer left till you find the quiet section with the good-looking guys.

Conveniently located across the bay from Fort-de-France, **Pointe du Bout** is Martinique's most lavish resort area. Aside from a marina and a variety of watersports, the area has some modest man-made, white-sand beaches. The sandy, natural beaches at nearby **Anse Mitan** and **Anses d'Arlet** are popular with both swimmers and snorkelers.

Beaches north of Fort-de-France have mostly gray (they like to call it silver) volcanic sand. The best of the bunch is **Anse Turin,** just to the side of the main Caribbean coastal road, between St-Pierre and Le Carbet. Extremely popular with locals and shaded by palms, it's where Gauguin swam when he called the island home.

Martinique has no legal nudist beaches, but toplessness is as common here as anywhere in France.

Puerto Rico

San Juan, the capital of Puerto Rico, is a bustling port that easily sees five to ten ships a day. Many ships use San Juan as an embarkation port; others visit as a port of call. The San Juan metropolitan area, home to about a third of Puerto Rico's 3.8 million people, is one of the largest and most sophisticated urban centers in the Caribbean. The docks are right at the foot of **Old San Juan,** which is popular with cruise passengers also because it's the most beautiful, historic part of town. The neighborhood's hilly cobblestone streets are lined with brightly painted colonial townhouses, colonial churches, intimate parks, and sun-drenched plazas as well as restaurants and shops (U.S. citizens don't pay taxes here). Like the pyramids of Egypt and the Great Wall of China, Old San Juan's Spanish colonial forts and city walls are United Nations World Heritage Sites, and our top pick here.

Spanish is the native tongue, but most people on the island also speak **English** (both are official languages here). The farther you venture from San Juan, the more likely it is you'll have to practice your Spanish. Because Puerto Rico is part of the United States, the U.S. dollar is the coin of the realm.

Cruising into port

Almost all cruise ships dock at Old San Juan, but during periods of heavy volume, you may dock at one of the much less convenient cargo piers across the water from the old town, requiring a short taxi ride.

Scoring the best excursions

Unless you want a guide to offer historical perspective (2½ hours; $33), don't bother with organized walking tours of Old San Juan — it's easy enough to get around on your own (pick up a walking tour map in the terminal). On the other hand, if you explore somewhere farther afield, an organized tour is a good idea.

El Yunque Rainforest: Though you wouldn't know it from San Juan's hustle-bustle, Puerto Rico has a natural side too. After arriving at Baño Grande, a natural swimming hole, hike half an hour along the Caimitillo Trail and see parrot nests, giant ferns, orchids, and palms. Listen for the song of Puerto Rico's national symbol, the tiny coquí tree frog (4–5 hours; $35).

Rainforest Horseback Adventure: Meet your horse, briefly learn the ropes, and then ride along a beautiful beach. Take a quick swim during the refreshment stop (3½ hours; $79–$82).

City Tour and Bacardi Rum Distillery: After a tour of the old city, with a stop at Fort San Cristóbal, you'll travel to the Bacardi distillery to learn about the Puerto Rican sugar and rum industries, watch giant fermenting tanks transform sugar cane into rum, learn how to pronounce the product's name (baa-carrrr-*di!*), and then get a taste for yourself (4 hours; $30).

Exploring on your own

Old San Juan beckons the walker to explore its hilly streets. **Taxis** operated by the Tourist Transportation Division are available at the piers. They're metered in San Juan, but the fare structure between major tourism zones is standardized.

Hotel *

Old San Juan

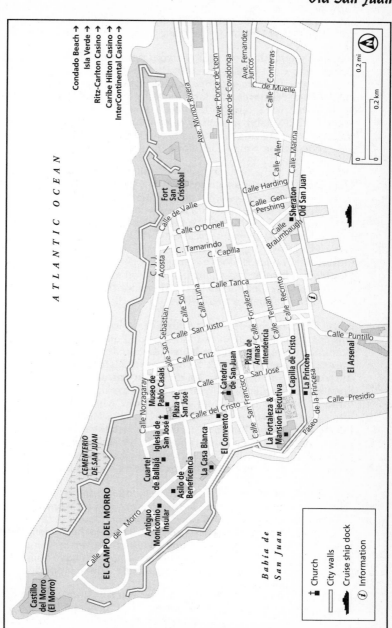

Condado Beach →
Isla Verde →
Ritz-Carlton Casino →
Caribe Hilton Casino →
InterContinental Casino →

Ave. Fernández Juncos
C. de Muelle
Calle Contreras
Calle Muelle
Ave. Ponce de León
Paseo de Covadonga
Ave. Muñoz Rivera
Calle Marina
Calle Allen
Calle Harding
Calle Gen. Pershing
Sheraton Old San Juan
Calle Braumbaugh
Fort San Cristóbal
Calle de Valle
Calle O'Donell
C. Tamarindo
C. Capilla
C.J.J. Acosta
Calle Tanca
Calle Sol
Calle Luna
Calle San Sebastián
Calle San Justo
Calle Cruz
Calle Recinto
Calle Tetuan
Calle Fortaleza
Intendencia
Plaza de Armas/ Calle
San José
Calle Puntillo
El Arsenal
Calle Norzagaray
Museo de Pablo Casals
Iglesia de San José
Plaza de San José
Catedral de San Juan
Calle San Francisco
Calle
Calle del Cristo
El Convento
Capilla de Cristo
La Princesa
La Princesa
Calle de la Princesa
Calle Presidio
La Fortaleza & Mansion Ejecutiva
Cuartel de Ballajá
Asilo de Beneficencia
La Casa Blanca
Antiguo Monicomio Insular
EL CAMPO DEL MORRO
Calle del Morro
Castillo del Morro (El Morro)
CEMENTERIO DE SAN JUAN

ATLANTIC OCEAN

Bahía de San Juan

0.2 mi
0.2 km

✝ Church
City walls
Cruise ship dock
ⓘ Information

Within walking distance: Walking the cobblestone streets of the historic landmark area of Old San Juan, you sense five centuries of history as you pass many of Puerto Rico's top historical attractions. You also find shops and cafes on any walking tour.

One must-see attraction is **El Morro** (Castillo de San Felipe del Morro) — indeed, you can't miss it as it sits at the top of a hill at the tip of the city. Its walls are part of a network of defenses that made San Juan a walled city, and for centuries, the fortress was considered impregnable. Here, Spanish Puerto Rico defended itself against the navies of Great Britain, France, and Holland, as well as against hundreds of pirate ships. The National Park Service maintains both El Morro and **Fort San Cristóbal,** located less than a mile east along the north coast.

Other varied and interesting sites include **La Fortaleza and Mansion Ejecutiva,** the centuries-old residence of the Puerto Rican governor; **Plaza de Armas,** the most beautiful of the squares in Old Town, flanked by the neoclassic **Intendencia,** which houses offices of the State Department and San Juan's historic City Hall; **La Casa Blanca,** which the son-in-law of Juan Ponce de León built as the great explorer's island home (although he never lived there); and **La Princesa,** once the most-feared prison in the Caribbean. The *Puerto Rican Academy of Fine Arts* is at the **Antiguo Monicomio Insular** (originally built in 1854 as an insane asylum). The nearby **Asilo de Beneficencia,** or "Home for the Poor," is a stately neoclassical building dating to the 1840s.

In the **Plaza de San José,** the statue of explorer Juan Ponce de León was cast from an English cannon captured during a naval battle in 1797. Dominicans established the **Iglesia de San José,** the church for which the plaza is named, in 1523. Several other historic buildings surround the plaza, including the **Museo de Pablo Casals,** which honors the Spanish-born cellist who lived his final years in Puerto Rico, and a former 17th-century convent, **El Convento,** which has been converted into one of the few hotels within the Old City. The **Catedral de San Juan,** Puerto Rico's most famous church, is across the street. You can also visit **Capilla de Cristo,** a tiny chapel with a silver altar dedicated to the Christ of Miracles. Also not far from the plaza, the **Cuartel de Ballajá** houses the **Museum of the Americas** on its second floor.

Beyond walking distance: Perhaps the most famous beach in the Caribbean, **Condado Beach,** at the western end of Ashford Avenue, is the backyard playground of Condado's resort hotels. A favorite of families, it can get pretty crowded in winter. The beaches of **Isla Verde,** behind the hotels and condominiums along Isla Verde Avenue, are less rocky and are excellent for people-watching. Both have white sand, palm trees, watersports, and plenty of eating and drinking options.

If you're more of a gambler than a sunbather, casinos are one of San Juan's biggest draws, and most large hotels have one. They're generally open daily from noon to 4 a.m., but some never close. There's the plush **Casino at the Ritz-Carlton** (6961 State Rd., Isla Verde; ☎ 800-241-3333 or 787-253-1700); the elegant **InterContinental San Juan** (187 Isla Verde Ave.; ☎ **800-303-1758** or 787-791-6100); and, the most convenient for cruise ship passengers, the **Sheraton Old San Juan Hotel & Casino** (100 Brumbaugh St.; ☎ **800-325-3535** or 787-721-5100), is directly across from Pier 3 and often bustling.

Golf is also an option, just be sure to sign up for a ship excursion or plan on renting a car to get to the courses, which include the well-regarded **Hyatt Dorado Beach Resort & Country Club** (☎ **787-796-8961;** www. hyatt.com), **Palmas del Mar & Villas Golf Club** (☎ **787-285-2256;** www.palmascountryclub.com), and **The Westin Rio Mar Golf Resort & Spa** (☎ **787-888-6000;** www.westinriomar.com). Greens fees at each range from $130 to $190.

St. Barthélemy (St. Barts)

Chic, sophisticated St. Barts (or, technically, St. Barthélemy, a name no one ever uses) is internationally renowned as one of the ritziest refuges in the Caribbean, rivaled only by Mustique as the preferred island retreat of the rich and famous. Yet despite all the hoopla, St. Barts retains its charm, serenity, natural beauty, and incredibly French flavor — in contrast to most Caribbean islands, where descendants of African slaves form the majority, St. Barts's 7,000 year-round residents are primarily of French ancestry. Gustavia, the main port (whose name harks back to the 19th century, when Sweden controlled the island), is full of French restaurants and semi-chic, semi-boho nightspots. Many of the small luxe ships that call here stay into the evening so that passengers can get a night out. Away from town, the island is full of dramatic hills and pristine white-sand beaches.

French is the official language, but virtually everyone speaks **English** as well. St. Barts is part of the French overseas region of Guadeloupe, so the **euro** (€) is the official currency (1€ = US$1.30; $1 = .77€). U.S. dollars are commonly accepted.

Cruising into port

Cruise ships anchor off **Gustavia,** the main town, and ferry passengers to the dollhouse-size harbor and town via tenders.

Scoring the best excursions

Jet-Set Boat and Beach Excursion: Circumnavigate St. Barts in a 40-foot cruiser, then tender ashore at St. Jean Beach for a swim, snorkel, and/or drinks from the open bar (4 hours; $200–$400).

St. Barts on Horseback: Travel to northern St. Barts for a relaxed guided ride through the island's outback (2 hours; $65).

Exploring on your own

Taxis congregate at Gustavia's harbor to take cruise passengers to the beaches. If you want some adventure, rent a **Smart Car,** the latest toys

St. Barthélemy (St. Barts)

on the island — they come in all kinds of bright colors — for a ride up and down St. Barts's picturesque, hilly roads. Budget, Avis, Hertz, and National have offices here.

Within walking distance: For a taste of the island's celeb vibe, make a beeline to **Le Select** (rue de la France at rue du Général de Gaulle; ☎ 590-27-86-87), the epicenter of Gustavia's social life for more than 50 years. This cafe's tables rest in a tree-shaded garden a block from the harbor. The classic, funky ambience inspired Jimmy Buffett's "Cheeseburger in Paradise," and a mix of salty locals, celebrities, and chic tourists typically make up the clientele. Aside from hanging out, shopping, and eating, cruisers sticking close to port can also visit Gustavia's modest points of interest: **St. Bartholomew's Church,** rue Samuel Fahlberg, dates from the 1850s, and the **Municipal Museum,** on rue Duquesne, across from the dock (☎ 590-29-71-55), is an unfocused but respectable introduction to the island. Admission is 2€ ($2.60); closed Saturday afternoon and Monday morning.

Beyond walking distance: For a little culture, the tiny fishing village of **Corossol** is a step back in time. About 10 minutes by taxi from the dock, this quaint, totally un-chic hamlet is home to traditional folk who still live off the sea. On the town's waterfront, just to the left of the road from Gustavia, the **Inter Oceans Museum** (☎ **590-27-62-97**) catalogs thousands of shells, corals, sand dollars, sea horses, sea urchins, and fish from around the world, all displayed in endearingly homemade style. Admission is 3€ ($3.90); closed Mondays.

The most famous of the island's 22 beaches is **St-Jean,** where you can enjoy watersports, beach restaurants, and a few hotels. **Grand Cul de Sac** offers a similar active vibe. If you want peace and privacy, the best secluded beaches include **Marigot** and **Colombier** to the north, and **Grande Saline** and **Gouverneur** to the south (which is very remote). Topless sunbathing is quite common and at Saline, you may also see a lot of people in their altogether, even though nudity is officially forbidden).

St. Kitts

St. Kitts is almost ridiculously lush and fertile, dotted with rain forests and waterfalls and boasting some lovely beaches along its southeast coastline, but it's also extremely poor, still dependent on the same sugar-cane crop that brought its English plantation owners riches (and its slaves hot misery) back in colonial days. Cane fields climb the slopes of its volcanic mountain range, and you'll see ruins of old mills and plantation houses as you drive around the island. Basseterre, the capital city, is full of old-time colonial architecture, but it's a small-scale place with little to offer visitors beyond a pleasant walk-around. The island's most impressive landmark, **Brimstone Hill Fortress,** is about 15km (9 miles) west of town. St. Kitts forms the larger and more populated half of the combined Federation of St. Kitts and Nevis, two islands separated by only about 3.2km (2 miles) of ocean.

English is the language of both islands. The local currency is the **Eastern Caribbean dollar** (US$1 = EC$2.70; EC$1 = US37¢). Many shops and restaurants quote prices in U.S. dollars. Always determine which currency locals are talking about.

Cruising into port

Port Zante stretches from the center of town into the deep waters offshore, with shopping, restaurants, and a welcome center on-site. New additions to the facility, including a second pier and expanded shopping, were due to be completed soon after this book hit the shelves.

Scoring the best excursions

Brimstone Hill Fortress and Romney Gardens: Among the largest and best-preserved forts in the Caribbean, **Brimstone Hill Fortress National Park** (www.brimstonehillfortress.org) dates from 1690, when the British fortified the hill to help recapture Fort Charles from the French.

St. Kitts

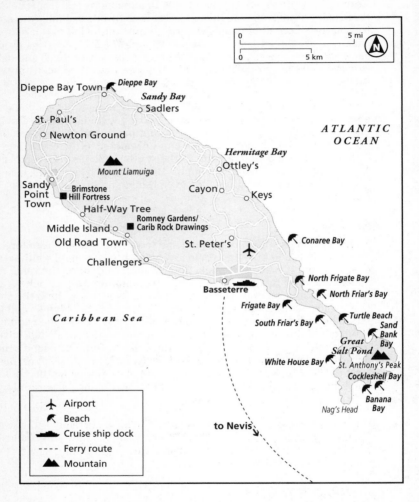

In 1782, an invading force of 8,000 French troops bombarded the fortress for a month before its small British garrison, supplemented by local militia, surrendered. When the British took the island back the next year, they proceeded to enlarge the fort into "The Gibraltar of the West Indies." In all, the structure took 104 years to complete. Today it's the centerpiece of a national park crisscrossed by nature trails, with a population of green vervet monkeys to keep things lively. Tours typically include a visit to the beautiful **Romney Gardens,** located amidst the ruins of a sugar estate between Basseterre and the fort. You can check out the lush hillside gardens, featuring giant ferns, orchids, poinsettias, and "The Tree," a 350-year-old Saman tree (3 hours; $46).

Mountain Biking and Beach Tour: From the pier, you ride through Basseterre then out through sugar-cane fields and up 450m (1,500-ft.) Olivees Mountain for views and refreshments. After the ride down, you stop at Friar's Bay for a swim and snack. It's a nice way to see this lush island (4 hours; $71).

Rainforest and Gardens Hiking Safari: Departing from Romney Gardens, you hike along a loop of trails through lush rain forest. With luck, you can catch sight of some of the island's resident monkeys (4 hours; $59).

Exploring on your own

You can walk around Basseterre, but you need a **taxi** to get anywhere else. They greet cruise passengers (loudly) at the docks and also around the Circus, a public square near the docks at the intersection of Bank and Fort streets. Taxis aren't metered, so you must agree on the price before heading out. Always ask if the rates quoted are in U.S. dollars or Eastern Caribbean dollars.

Within walking distance: The capital city of Basseterre, where the docks are located, has typical British colonial architecture and some quaint buildings, a few shops, and a market where locals display fruits and flowers — but even this description may give you the wrong idea about this place. The truth is, it's a very poor town, with few attractions aimed at visitors. When we were last there, there were chickens walking around in front of the government buildings. **St. George's Anglican Church,** on Cayon Street (walk straight up Church St. or Fort St. from the dock) is the oldest church in town and is worth a look. **Independence Square,** a stone's throw from the docks along Bank Street, is pretty, with its central fountain and old church, but there's no good reason to linger unless it's to sit in the shade and toss back a bottle of Ting, the local grapefruit-based soda.

The narrow peninsula in the southeast is where you find the best beaches and swimming, including **Conaree Beach,** 4.8km (3 miles) from Basseterre; **Frigate Bay,** with its talcum-powder-fine sand; the twin beaches of **Banana Bay** and **Cockleshell Bay,** at the southeast corner of the island; and **Friar's Bay,** a peninsula beach opening onto both the Atlantic and the Caribbean.

Beyond walking distance: All the best stuff to do outside of town is covered in "Scoring the best excursions," earlier in this section.

 To experience the sweeter side of St. Kitts, try a stalk of sugar cane. Buy one from any farmer, peel it, and chew the inner reeds to enjoy the sweet juice. Try it with ice and a splash of rum.

St. Lucia

Of all the islands in the Caribbean, St. Lucia is most likely to make you think you're in the South Pacific, with its green mountains, the peaks of **Petit Piton** and **Gros Piton,** and the brilliant white sandy beaches along

St. Lucia

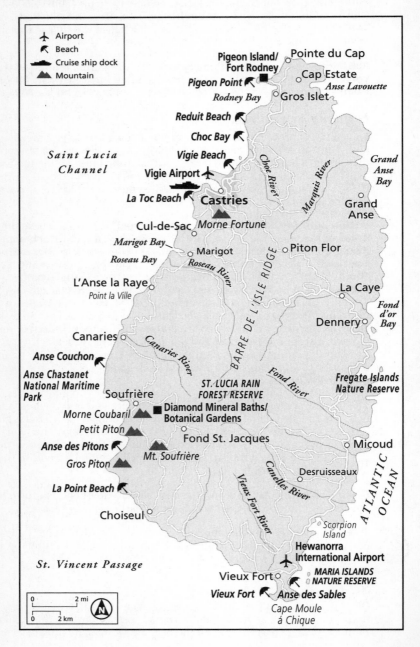

Airport
Beach
Cruise ship dock
Mountain

Saint Lucia Channel

Pigeon Island/ Fort Rodney
Pointe du Cap
Cap Estate
Pigeon Point
Anse Lavouette
Rodney Bay
Gros Islet
Reduit Beach
Choc Bay
Choc River
Marquis River
Grand Anse Bay
Vigie Beach
Vigie Airport
La Toc Beach
Castries
Morne Fortune
Grand Anse
Cul-de-Sac
Marigot Bay
Marigot
Roseau Bay
Roseau River
Piton Flor
BARRE DE L'ISLE RIDGE
L'Anse la Raye
Point la Ville
La Caye
Fond d'or Bay
Canaries
Canaries River
Dennery
Anse Couchon
Anse Chastanet National Maritime Park
Soufrière
ST. LUCIA RAIN FOREST RESERVE
Fond River
Fregate Islands Nature Reserve
Morne Coubaril
Diamond Mineral Baths/ Botanical Gardens
Petit Piton
Fond St. Jacques
Anse des Pitons
Gros Piton
Mt. Soufrière
Micoud
La Point Beach
Vieux Fort River
Canelles River
Desruisseaux
Choiseul
ATLANTIC OCEAN
Scorpion Island
St. Vincent Passage
Hewanorra International Airport
Vieux Fort
MARIA ISLANDS NATURE RESERVE
Vieux Fort
Anse des Sables
Cape Moule á Chique

0   2 mi
0   2 km
N

the northwest coast. **Castries,** the capital, has grown up around an extinct volcanic crater that's now a large harbor surrounded by hills. It looks more modern than other regional capitals because fires destroyed many of the original French colonial and Victorian buildings typical of the region's architecture. But at its heart, Castries is still very traditional. The country women dress in traditional cotton headdresses to sell their luscious fruits and vegetables, while weather-beaten men sit close by playing warrie (a fast game played with pebbles on a carved board) or fleet games of dominoes using tiles the color of cherries.

English is the official language. The official currency is the **Eastern Caribbean dollar** (US$1 = EC$2.70; EC$1 = US37¢), though shops and restaurants commonly take the U.S. dollar as well. Be sure you know which currency a price is being quoted in before paying.

Cruising into port

Most cruise ships arrive at a fairly new pier at **Pointe Seraphine,** within walking distance of the center of Castries and boasting St. Lucia's best shopping. In the unlikely event that Pointe Seraphine is full, your ship may dock instead at **Port Castries** on the other side of the colorful harbor. There's a shopping terminal here called La Place Carenage. Some smaller lines, such as Star Clippers, Seabourn, and Clipper, visit other sites around the island, anchoring off **Rodney Bay** to the north or **Soufrière** to the south and carrying passengers ashore by tender.

Scoring the best excursions

Pigeon Island Sea Kayaking: After transferring to Rodney Bay, you make the approximately 30-minute paddle out to the island, where you have time to swim, kayak some more, or make the steep climb up to Fort Rodney (3 hours; $65–$70).

Rainforest Bicycle Tour: Ride past banana plantations and the Errard Falls waterfall, and stop to sample various fruits that grow along the roadside (4½ hours; $69). A different tour, **Jungle Mountain Biking,** takes you by boat to the Jungle Biking facility, located on an 18th-century sugar plantation. There, you can explore 16km (10 miles) of trails at your own pace (4½ hours; $99).

Soody Nature Hike and Mineral Waterfall: Drive along the west coast through fishing villages and banana plantations, before arriving at Soufrière, location of the Pitons and the Diamond Botanical Gardens, Waterfall, and Mineral Baths. A guided hour-long hike through the volcanic forest introduces you to the island's flora and fauna, and ends up at a therapeutic sulphuric waterfall where you can take a dip to cure what ails ya. Lunch at a Creole restaurant is included (7 hours; $55).

Exploring on your own

There is an official **taxi** association servicing both Pointe Seraphine and La Place Carenage, with standard fares posted. You can hire a taxi to go to Soufrière on your own, too. Many taxi drivers offer two- to three-hour tours, with a stop at the beach, for $60. Be sure you're talking U.S. or EC dollars before agreeing on a price.

Within walking distance: The principal streets of Castries are **William Peter Boulevard** and **Bridge Street.** Don't miss a walk through town: People are very friendly, and Jeremie Street is chockablock with variety stores of the most authentic local kind, selling everything from spices to housewares. A Roman Catholic cathedral stands on **Columbus Square,** and take a gander at the enormous 400-year-old "rain" tree, also called a "no-name" tree, which grows in the square.

Beyond Government House lies **Morne Fortune,** which means "Hill of Good Luck." Actually, no one's had much luck here, certainly not the French and British soldiers who battled for **Fort Charlotte.** The fort switched between the two sides many times. You can visit the 18th-century barracks, complete with a military cemetery, a small museum, the Old Powder Magazine, and the "Four Apostles Battery," four grim muzzle-loading cannons. The view of the harbor of Castries is panoramic from this point. To reach Morne Fortune, head east on Bridge Street. Also worth a visit in Castries is a colorful market near the dock.

Beyond walking distance: St. Lucia's first national park, the 44-acre **Pigeon Island National Landmark** (☎ 758-450-0603), is ideal for picnics and nature walks, and is covered with lemongrass. It's joined to the mainland by a causeway, so you can take a taxi there. Stop by the **Captain's Cellar** pub, with seating out on the lawn just beyond the spray from the Atlantic waves. Two white-sand beaches lie on the island's west coast. Island admission is $5.

La Soufrière, a fishing port and St. Lucia's second largest settlement, is dominated by the **Pitons.** Near the town lies the famous "drive-in" volcano, **La Soufrière,** a rocky lunar landscape of bubbling mud and craters seething with fuming sulfur. You can literally drive into an old crater and walk between the sulfur springs and pools of hissing steam. Nearby are the **Diamond Mineral Baths,** dating back to 1784.

Leading beaches along the calm shores of the western coast include **Pigeon Island,** off the northern shore; **Vigie Beach,** north of Castries Harbour; **Marigot Beach,** south of Castries Harbour; and **Reduit Beach,** between Choc Bay and Pigeon Point. Just north of Soufrière is a beach connoisseur's delight, **Anse Chastanet** (☎ 758-459-7000), boasting an expanse of white sand at the foothills of lush, green mountains. This is a fantastic spot for snorkeling.

Sint Maarten & St. Martin

This 96-sq.-km (37-sq.-mile) island has two faces. It's been shared by France and the Netherlands for more than 350 years. Although the border between the two sides is virtually imperceptible — a monument along the road marks the change in administration — each side retains

Sint Maarten & St. Martin

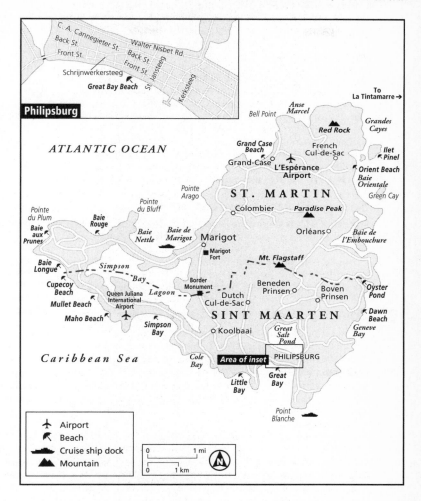

C. A. Cannegieter St.
Back St.
Front St.
Walter Nisbet Rd.
Back St.
Front St.
St. Jansteeg
Kerksteeg
Schrijnwerkersteeg
Great Bay Beach

Philipsburg

To
La Tintamarre →

Anse
Marcel
Bell Point

ATLANTIC OCEAN

Red Rock

*Grandes
Cayes*

Grand Case
Beach

French
Cul-de-Sac

*Ilet
Pinel*

Grand-Case
**L'Espérance
Airport**

*Orient Beach
Baie
Orientale*

Pointe
Arago

ST. MARTIN

Green Cay

Pointe
du Plum

Pointe
du Bluff

Colombier

Paradise Peak

Baie
Rouge

Baie
aux
Prunes

Baie
Nettle

Baie de
Marigot

Marigot

Orléans

*Baie de
l'Embouchure*

Baie
Longue

Simpson

Marigot
Fort

Mt. Flagstaff

Cupecoy
Beach

Bay

Border
Monument

Beneden
Prinsen

Boven
Prinsen

*Oyster
Pond*

Mullet Beach

Queen Juliana
International
Airport

Lagoon

Dutch
Cul-de-Sac

Maho Beach

Simpson
Bay

SINT MAARTEN

*Dawn
Beach*

Koolbaai

*Great
Salt
Pond*

Geneve
Bay

Caribbean Sea

Cole
Bay

Area of inset PHILIPSBURG

PHILIPSBURG

Little
Bay

*Great
Bay*

Point
Blanche

✈ Airport
🏖 Beach
🚢 Cruise ship dock
🏔 Mountain

0 — 1 mi
0 — 1 km
N

elements of its own heritage. The French side (St. Martin), with some of
the best beaches and restaurants in the Caribbean, emphasizes quiet
elegance. The Dutch side (Sint Maarten) reflects Holland's anything-goes
philosophy: Development is much more widespread, flashy casinos
pepper the landscape, and strip malls make the larger towns look as
much like Anaheim as Amsterdam. The 100 percent duty-free shopping
has turned both sides of the island into a bargain-hunter's paradise.

Surprise, surprise: The official language on the Dutch side is **Dutch,** and
the official language on the French side is **French.** Most people on both
sides also speak **English.** The legal tender in Dutch Sint Maarten is the

Netherlands Antilles guilder, or NAf (NAf1.79 = US$1; NAf1 = US56¢), and the official currency on the French side is the **euro** (1€ = US$1.30; $1 = .77€). U.S. dollars are widely accepted on both sides, and most prices are quoted in U.S. dollars, too.

Cruising into port

All cruise ships dock on the Dutch side, at **A. C. Wathey Pier,** about 1.6km (1 mile) southeast of Philipsburg. The majority of passengers are then tendered to the smaller Captain Hodge Pier in Great Bay Harbour at the center of town, but others choose to walk the distance on a newly developed boardwalk or take a taxi. The new $40 million **Harbor Point Village** waterside complex at the port offers a host of shopping and entertainment venues housed in old West Indies–style architecture. Smaller vessels sometimes dock on the French side of the island, at **Marina Port la Royale,** adjacent to the heart of Marigot.

Scoring the best excursions

America's Cup Regatta: A sailing adventure aboard one of the yachts that competes in the America's Cup races (3 hours; $89).

Pinel Island Snorkeling Tour: Offered on the French side, take a scenic bus ride to the French side and catch a boat to this small offshore islet for some of St. Martin's best snorkeling (3½ hours; $39).

Exploring on your own in Sint Maarten

Taxis on both sides of the island are unmetered. Agree on a rate and currency before getting in. Dutch law requires that drivers list government-regulated fares based on two passengers. Privately owned and operated **minivans** have signs to indicate their destination, and can be hailed anywhere on the street. Fares are usually about $1.50. **Rental cars** are a great way to see both sides of the island. Avis, Budget, and Hertz all have offices here.

Within walking distance: Directly in front of the Philipsburg town pier, on Wathey Square, the 1793-built **Courthouse** combines northern European sobriety with Caribbean brightness. East of the Courthouse, at 7 Front St. (down a little shopping alley), is the tiny **Sint Maarten Museum** (☎ 599-542-4917). Admission is free; closes 2 p.m. Saturday and all day Sunday. Historically, **Fort Amsterdam** is the Dutch side's most important colonial site. Since 1631, the fort has looked out over Great Bay from the hill west of Philipsburg. The fort was the Netherlands' first military outpost in the Caribbean. The Spanish captured it two years later, making it their most significant bastion east of Puerto Rico. The site provides grand views of the bay, but ruins of the walls and a couple of rusty cannons are all that remain of the original fort.

From the center of town, you can walk to **Great Bay Beach;** this mile-long stretch is convenient and has calm water, but it lacks the tranquility of the more remote beaches.

Gambling is also big here, with several casinos clustered along Front Street in the heart of Philipsburg. All of them open early enough to snag cruisers.

Beyond walking distance: Just west of the airport, on the west side of the island, **Maho Beach** boasts a casino, shade palms, and a popular beachside bar and grill. It's a good snorkeling spot, too. Farther west, **Mullet Beach** borders the island's golf course. Shaded by palm trees and crowded on weekends, it's popular with swimmers and snorkelers. **Dawn Beach,** on the east coast, is the best snorkeling site on the island. Rent equipment from Busby's Beach Bar, which is right on the sand.

Exploring on your own in St. Martin

For taxi info, see the preceding section, "Exploring on your own in Sint Maarten."

Within walking distance: From the 1767-built **Fort St. Louis,** Marigot's answer to Fort Amsterdam, the short climb up top affords splendid vistas. As a respite from the sun, duck into Marigot's **Museum of Saint Martin** (☎ 590-29-22-84), next to the tourism office and adjacent to the marina. Much more thorough and scholarly than its Philipsburg counterpart, this institution boasts a first-rate collection of Ciboney, Arawak, and Carib artifacts excavated from the island's Amerindian sites. Admission costs $6.50; closed Sunday. For shoppers, an **open-air market** is in the center of town. Another busy center of activity is **Port La Royale,** the largest shopping arcade on the French side.

Petit Club is the oldest restaurant in Marigot, serving Creole and French specialties such as spicy conch stew and fresh fish.

Beyond walking distance: Top-rated beaches on the French side are **Baie Longue, Baie Rouge,** and **Pinel Island.** If you want a stripped-down adventure, visit the famous clothes-optional **Orient Beach.**

St. Thomas and St. John, U.S. Virgin Islands

Ever since Columbus discovered the Virgin Islands during his second voyage to the New World in 1493, they have proven irresistible to foreign powers seeking territory, at one time or another being governed by Denmark, Spain, France, England, Holland, and, since 1917, by the United States. Tourism and U.S. government programs have raised the standard of living to one of the highest in the Caribbean, and today the island is one of the busiest and most developed cruise ports in the Caribbean. On St. Thomas, **Charlotte Amalie** (pronounced ah-*mahl*-yah), named in 1691 in honor of the wife of Denmark's King Christian V, is the island's capital and has become the Caribbean's major shopping center and one of its busiest cruise ports — it's often downright jampacked (and not one of our favorite ports).

The most tranquil and unspoiled of the U.S. Virgin Islands is St. John, the smallest of the lot, more than half of which is preserved as the gorgeous

Virgin Islands National Park. A rocky coastline, forming crescent-shaped bays and white-sand beaches, rings the whole island, whose miles of serpentine hiking trails lead past the ruins of 18th-century Danish plantations and onto panoramic ocean views.

English is spoken on both islands, and the **U.S. dollar** is the currency. Americans get a break on shopping in the U.S. Virgin Islands, as they can bring home $1,200 worth of merchandise without paying duty, as opposed to $400 from most other Caribbean ports. You can also bring back more liquor from here. See Chapter 19 for more Customs information.

Cruising into port

Most cruise ships anchor at **West Indian Dock/Havensight Mall.** Located at the eastern end of Charlotte Amalie Harbor, 2½ miles from the town center, it's got its own restaurants, bookstores, banks, postal van, and lots of duty-free shops. Many people make the long, hot walk to the center of Charlotte Amalie, but it's not a scenic route in any way, so you may want to opt for one of the $3 per-person open-air taxis. If Havensight is clogged with cruise ships, your ship will dock at the **Crown Bay Marina,** to the west of Charlotte Amalie. A taxi is your best bet — the 30-minute-plus walk into Charlotte Amalie feels longer on a hot day, and isn't terribly picturesque. A taxi ride into town from here costs about $4.

Cruise ships cannot dock at either of St. John's piers. Instead, they moor off the coast at **Cruz Bay,** sending tenders to the National Park Service Dock, the larger of the piers. Most cruise ships docking at St. Thomas offer shore excursions to St. John's pristine interior and beaches; it's just a 45-minute ferry ride between Charlotte Amalie and Cruz Bay.

Seeking out the best shore excursions

Expect to snooze through the St. Thomas sightseeing trips that most ships offer. Here are a few better bets:

Coral World and Island Drive: Coral World Underwater Observatory and Marine Park is St. Thomas's top attraction (3 hours; $39–$42).

Kayaking the Marine Sanctuary: Kayak from the mouth of the marine sanctuary at Holmberg's Marina and spend nearly an hour paddling among the mangroves while a naturalist explains the mangrove and lagoon ecosystem. Includes a free half-hour to snorkel or walk along the coral beach at Bovoni Point (3½ hours; $72–$79).

Golfing at Mahogany Run: Designed by Tom and George Fazio, Mahogany Run is one of the most beautiful courses in the West Indies. This 18-hole, par-70 course rises and drops like a roller coaster on its journey to the sea. You can also make arrangements for play on your own (☎ **800-253-7103, ext. 1,** or 340-777-6250, ext. 1). Greens fees are $130, including cart; the 20- to 30-minute taxi ride costs you about $10 each way (5 hours; $170).

St. Thomas

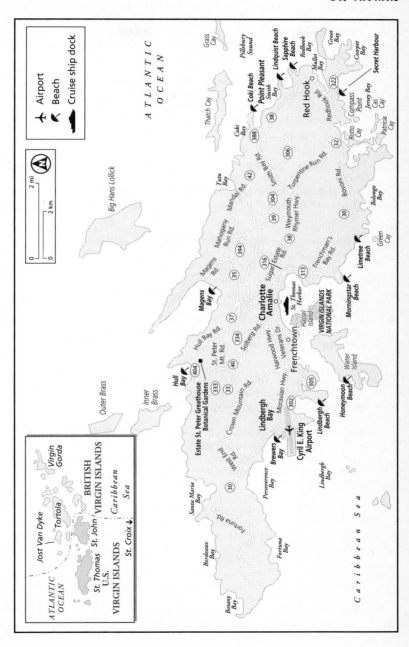

St. John Eco-Hike: Take the ferry to St. John for a walkabout through the Virgin Islands National Park. The Lind Point Trail ascends about 250 feet to the Lind Point Overlook for views of St. John, St. Thomas, and the surrounding islands. An expert guide discusses the park's ecosystem and St. John's cultural history while you walk to Honeymoon Beach for a little swimming (4 hours; $64).

Water Island Bike Trip and Beach Adventure: After a ferry ride to Water Island, a five-minute bus ride takes you to the island's highest point, from which you get a nice downhill ride. Your guide will point out various historic sites and wildlife en route to Honeymoon Beach (3½ hours; $79).

Exploring on your own in St. Thomas

Taxis are the chief means of transport here. They're unmetered, but a guide of point-to-point fares around the island is included in most tourist magazines. Less formal, privately owned **taxi vans** make unscheduled stops along major traffic arteries, charging less than a dollar for most rides.

Within walking distance: In days of yore, seafarers from all over the globe flocked to the old Danish town of Charlotte Amalie, including pirates and, during the Civil War, Confederate sailors. The main streets (called *Gades* here in honor of their Danish heritage) are a veritable shopping mall, especially close to the waterfront. Stray farther landward and you can find pockets of 19th-century houses and the truly charming, cozy, brick-and-stone **St. Thomas Synagogue,** built in 1833 by Sephardic Jews. There's a great view from here as well. It's located high on steep, sloping Crystal Gade.

Dating from 1672, **Fort Christian,** 32 Raadets Gade, rises from the harbor to dominate the center of town. Named after the Danish king Christian V, the structure has been everything from a governor's residence to a jail. Many pirates were hanged in its courtyard.

Seven Arches Museum, on Government Hill (☎ 340-774-9295), is a two-century-old Danish house completely restored to its original condition and furnished with antiques. You can walk through the yellow ballast arches and visit the great room with its view of the busy harbor. Admission is $5.

The **Paradise Point Tramway** (☎ 340-774-9809) affords visitors a dramatic view of Charlotte Amalie Harbor at a peak height of 697 feet. The tramways transport customers from the Havensight area to Paradise Point, where riders disembark to visit shops and a popular restaurant and bar. The cost is $16 round-trip.

Shopping is a main attraction in St. Thomas, and **Main Street** is the main shopping street. To the north is the fully stocked **Back Street.** The **Waterfront Highway** also sports stores, and you can always check out the side streets, alleys, and walkways between these principal streets.

St. John

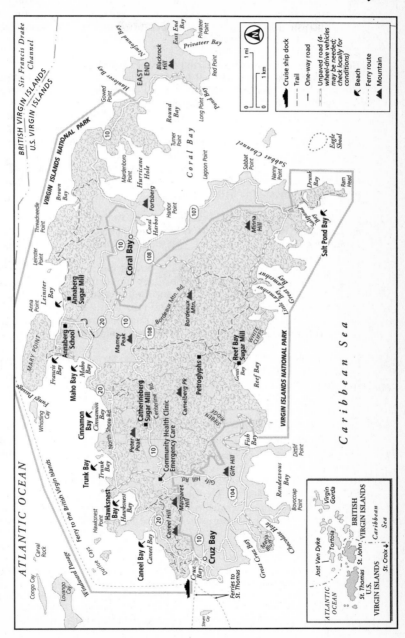

Dating back to 1672 and dominating the center of town, **Fort Christian** was named after the Danish monarch Christian V and has served as everything from a governor's residence to a prison. Some of the cells have become part of the **Virgin Islands Museum.** Historical artifacts are on display at the small facility.

Beyond walking distance: The lush **St. Peter Greathouse Estate and Gardens,** at the corner of St. Peter Mountain Road (Rte. 40) and Barrett Hill Road (☎ 340-774-4999), ornaments 11 acres on the volcanic peaks of the island's northern rim. It's the creation of Howard Lawson DeWolfe, a *Mayflower* descendant who, with his wife, Sylvie, bought the estate in 1987 and set about transforming it into a tropical paradise. It's filled with some 200 varieties of plants and trees, including an umbrella plant from Madagascar. There's also a rain forest, an orchid jungle, waterfalls, and reflecting ponds. From a panoramic deck you can see some 20 of the Virgin Islands. The house itself is worth a visit, its interior filled with local art. Admission is $10.

St. Thomas has some good beaches, all of which are easily reached by taxi. Arrange for your driver to return and pick you up at a designated time. If you're going to St. John, you may want to do your beaching there.

St. Thomas's beaches are open to the public, but some charge a fee. The most well known (and most popular for windsurfing) is **Sapphire Beach** on the east end of the island. Rent snorkeling gear or lounge chairs, or stretch out on its white-coral sand and take in the sun and the spectacular views of the bay. Other worthwhile beaches are **Magens Bay, Coki Beach** (at the Marine Park), and the **Morningstar,** just 2 miles from port.

If you check out the beaches on St. Thomas, be sure to protect your belongings — pickpockets and thieves have been known to strike. Also, to ensure that you don't miss the boat, arrange for a cab to pick you up at a specific time.

Exploring on your own in St. John

A tiny gem, lush St. John lies about 3 miles east of St. Thomas across Pillsbury Sound. It's the smallest and least populated of the U.S. Virgins, and since 1956, more than half of St. John's land mass, as well as its shoreline waters, have been set aside as the Virgin Islands National Park, and today the island leads the Caribbean in eco- (or "sustainable") tourism. Miles of winding hiking trails lead to panoramic views and the ruins of 18th-century Danish plantations. Because St. John is easy to reach from St. Thomas, and the beaches are spectacular, many cruise ship passengers spend their entire stay there.

Within walking distance: There are shopping, bars, and restaurants right by the docks. Otherwise, the most popular way to get around St. John is by **surrey-style taxi.** Typical fares from Cruz Bay are $5.50 to Trunk Bay, $7 to Cinnamon Bay, and $11 to Maho Bay. Taxis wait at the pier. You can also rent open-sided **jeeps.** Avis and Hertz both have offices here. Just remember to drive on the left, even though steering wheels are on the left, too. Go figure.

Beyond walking distance: At the **Virgin Islands National Park,** head to the **visitor center** (☎ 340-776-6201) right on the dock at St. Cruz, where you can view some exhibits and find out more about what you can see and do in the park. You can explore the park on the more than 20 miles of biking trails; rent your own car, Jeep, or Mini-Moke; or hike. The starting points of some trails are within walking distance while others can be reached by taxi for about $5 to $20. Within the park, try to see the **Annaberg Ruins,** Leinster Bay Road, where the Danes founded thriving plantations and a sugar mill in 1718. They're located off North Shore Road, east of Trunk Bay on the north shore.

To beach it, **Trunk Bay** is your best bet for the local beach experience, especially for snorkelers, who can rent gear and explore the underwater trail near the shore. Trunk Bay has amenities, such as showers, a snack shop, and lifeguards, but it also has crowds. **Hawksnest Beach, Cinnamon Bay, Honeymoon Beach, Maho Bay,** and **Salt Pond Bay** are all good beach choices.

Enjoying the Cruise Lines' Private Islands

Several cruise lines have spent millions to create their own fantasy islands (or at least beaches), giving passengers a beach day without the hassle of having to find the place. You normally get a whole day to bake on the beach, swim, snorkel, play beach games, go water-skiing or parasailing, or take advantage of whatever fancy facilities the cruise line has built. Children's activities may involve playground facilities, beach walks, and games. The islands typically have several beaches (the farthest off usually being the quietest), several bars, live music, and at least a few places to get lunch, usually of the barbecue variety.

Among the islands, only Disney's has docking facilities allowing passengers to just walk out onto the island. At all the others, you must ride a tender back and forth from the ship. Make sure to alert the crew if you require special assistance or a little "tender" loving care.

✔ **Costa Cruises:** Passengers on Costa's eastern Caribbean itineraries spend a day at **Catalina Island,** off the coast of the Dominican Republic, enjoying a long beach fringed by palm trees; opportunities for volleyball, beach Olympics, and snorkeling (plus jet skiing and banana-boat rides for a fee); and massages on the beach. Music and barbecue round out the day, and there's also a strip of shops hawking jewelry, beachwear, and other souvenirs.

 ✔ **Disney Cruise Line:** The 1,000-acre, 3×2-mile **Castaway Cay** (pronounced *key*) is a port of call on all Disney cruises, and is definitely the most elaborate of the private islands. Guests can swim and snorkel, rent bikes and boats, get their hair braided, shop, send postcards, go parasailing, have a massage, take a nature hike, or just lounge in a hammock or on the beach, snarfing barbecue. Families can head to their own beach, lined with lounge chairs and pastel-colored umbrellas, where they can swim, explore a 12-acre snorkeling course, climb around on the offshore water-play structures, or rent a kayak, paddle boat, banana boat, sailboat, or other beach equipment. Teens have a beach of their own, as do adults (on the far end of the island), and kids 3 to 12 can play at a supervised children's activity center whose highlight is an excavation site where kids can dig till they find something, then make plaster molds of whatever it might be.

✔ **Holland America:** Located on the Bahamian island of San Salvador, **Half Moon Cay** is a port of call on most of the line's Caribbean and Panama Canal cruises. Though the island is large, spreading out over 2,500 acres, Holland America has developed only 45 acres of it, maintaining the rest as a wild-bird reserve on behalf of the Bahamian National Trust. You can explore a network of hiking trails while keeping an eye out for all sorts of birds, including terns, shearwaters, and Bahamian pintails. Families can appreciate the new water park at one end of the beach, as well as the offshore play areas. Massages are available in huts along the beach, and big-spenders can also get air-conditioned beachfront cabanas with an open bar and butler service. La di da. Away from the main beach area, you can spend extra to go horseback riding, swim around with 26 resident stingrays, or go windsurfing, snorkeling, kayaking, scuba diving, deep-sea fishing, parasailing, sailboarding, or aqua-cycling.

✔ **Norwegian Cruise Line:** Norwegian bought the small, uninhabited Bahamian island of **Great Stirrup Cay** in 1977, making it the oldest of the private cruise line islands. Passengers can ride paddle boats, sail Sunfish, go snorkeling or parasailing, hop on a banana boat, join a game of volleyball, get a massage at one of the beachside stations, or do nothing more than sunbathe all day long. For kids, organized activities include volleyball tournaments and sandcastle building.

✔ **Princess Cruises:** Princess set up Princess Cays in 1992 on the southwest coast of Eleuthera in The Bahamas, and today makes it a stop on most eastern and western Caribbean itineraries. The half-mile of shoreline gives passengers room to swim, snorkel, and make use of Princess's fleet of Hobie Cats, Sunfish, banana boats, kayaks, and paddle-wheelers (bookable aboard ship before your visit). There's also live music, a dance area, and a beach barbecue, plus a strip of several dozen tree-shaded hammocks at the far end of the beach. For kids, there's a supervised play area with a sandbox and a pirate ship–themed playground.

✔ **Royal Caribbean (and Celebrity):** Sister lines Royal Caribbean and Celebrity have two different private spots, which often figure into their itineraries. **CocoCay** (also known as Little Stirrup Cay) is a small, 140-acre dot in The Bahamas' Berry Islands. You can find lots of beach, hammocks, food, drink, and watersports, plus such activities as limbo contests, water-balloon tosses, relay races, and volleyball tournaments. Kids get an aqua park that includes a floating trampoline, water slides, and a sunken airplane and schooner for snorkelers. For something quieter there's Wanderer's Beach, with calm surf and ultrasoft sand. The line's other beach stop is **Labadee,** an isolated, very private 270-acre peninsula along Haiti's north coast. Five beaches are spread around the peninsula, and are progressively less crowded the farther you walk from the dock. In the Columbus Cove area, a children's aqua park called Arawak Cay is full of floating trampolines, inflatable iceberg-shaped slides, and water seesaws. Kayaking and parasailing are offered from a dock nearby. A big plus at Labadee is the authentic and high-quality music and dance. On both Labadee and CocoCay, organized children's activities include beach parties, volleyball, seashell collecting, and sand-castle building.

Chapter 16

Doing Alaska in Style

● ●

In This Chapter

▶ Investigating much (but not all) of Alaska by sea

▶ Getting a gander at Alaska's whale population

▶ Exploring the cruisetour option

▶ IDing the best attractions and shopping at the major ports of call

▶ Sussing out the best shore excursions

● ●

*W*hy visit Alaska? Conjure up some postcard images: towering mountains, mountainous glaciers, sky-blue icebergs, leaping whales, lumbering moose, rain-forested fjords, endless tundra, bears and bald eagles, ravens as big as pug dogs, ice fields as big as cities, lumberjacks as big as . . . lumberjacks.

Sail the Caribbean and your megaship may completely dwarf the islands it visits, visible from miles away. Sail Alaska and that same megaship looks like a matchstick, completely overawed by the mountains, the expansive sky, and wilderness that seems to go on forever.

Visit the towns and meet people who embody the frontier spirit that brought them or their ancestors here. (You can also meet thousands of seasonal workers who come to serve all you cruise passengers, but that's a different story — see the upcoming sidebar, "Cruise ships in Alaska: Angel or devil?") Add Alaska's rich Native culture, its Russian colonial history, its gold rush mythology, and its "North to the Future" attitude, and you have one of the world's great cruise destinations.

Boarding Ship for Alaska

Most Alaska cruises concentrate on the Southeast Alaska panhandle, a string of islands linked by the waterway known as the **Inside Passage**. Some stay entirely within this region, sailing round-trip from Vancouver, British Columbia, or Seattle, Washington. Others sail north- or south-bound cruises between one of those ports and the northern towns of Seward or Whittier, the ports nearest to Alaska's biggest city, Anchorage. In addition to the Inside Passage, those cruises also sail through the **Gulf of Alaska** and sometimes Prince William Sound.

Cruise ships in Alaska: Angel or devil?

The 49th state is one of the top cruise destinations in the world, with about 750,000 people cruising there annually. That may not sound like much in the abstract — after all, Alaska's a huge state, right? — but two facts make it actually a pretty big figure: (1) Even though Alaska has more coastline than the rest of the United States combined, cruise ships sail in only about 20 percent of that area (and really concentrate on about half that); and (2) the cruise season is incredibly short, only lasting from late May to mid-September. That leads to crowding in the biggest ports of call, and also to some backlash, with local critics decrying excessive pedestrian traffic on their city streets, heavy bus traffic on outlying roads, and environmental damage to the air and seas.

Some towns, particularly Juneau, Ketchikan, and Skagway, really can get overwhelmed by cruise passengers at the height of high season, with a potential for more than 6,000 people floating in daily. The delicate balancing act between the resulting congestion and the plain fact that tourism provides the state's second largest pool of jobs has led to debate in recent years over imposing head taxes on cruise passengers, with the proceeds going to infrastructure support, conservation efforts, and other initiatives. The latest effort, which would have slapped a $46 tax on every passenger sailing state waters, was defeated in the Alaska legislature in May 2005, but don't expect debate to end.

On the environmental front, several well-publicized cases of illegal dumping over the past decade have led the cruise industry to institute in-house and industry-wide compliance and monitoring — after all, they can't sell cruises to pristine Alaska if they're perceived as making it less pristine. State and local governments also have a hand in minimizing cruise ships' impact in some of Alaska's most famous wild places. Glacier Bay, for example, has a strict permit system that allows in only two large cruise ships and several smaller vessels on any given day.

Luxury lines Crystal and Silversea offer Alaska cruises that sail round-trip from San Francisco. Most of the small-ship lines sail from one of the port towns in southeast Alaska (primarily Juneau, but also Ketchikan and Sitka), though some also operate out of Anchorage and Seattle.

 If possible, plan to arrive a day or two before your sailing date, especially if you have to travel a long distance. You can use that extra day to recover from jet lag and explore your port of embarkation, all of which have much to recommend them.

Storming the Shore

All the port towns along the Inside Passage have downtown areas compact enough to tour by foot if you choose — though as in almost every place that relies heavily on the tourist industry, they have their share of kitsch. In the most-visited cruise ports, expect a lot of tourist shops

Alaska Homeports

CRUISE LINE HOMEPORTS

ANCHORAGE	Clipper	**SAN**	Princess
	Cruise West	**FRANCISCO**	Silversea
	Glacier Bay		
	Silversea	**SEATTLE**	Celebrity
			Cruise West
ANCHORAGE	Celebrity		Holland America
(SEWARD)	Holland America		Norwegian
	Royal Caribbean		Princess
			Royal Caribbean
ANCHORAGE	Carnival		Silversea
(WHITTIER)	Princess		
	Radisson Seven Seas	**SITKA**	American Safari
			Glacier Bay
JUNEAU	American Safari		Lindblad
	American West		
	Clipper	**VANCOUVER,**	Carnival
	Cruise West	**BC**	Celebrity
	Glacier Bay		Cruise West
	Lindblad		Holland America
			Norwegian
KETCHIKAN	Cruise West		Princess
	Glacier Bay		Radisson Seven Seas
			Royal Caribbean
PRINCE	American Safari		Silversea
RUPERT, BC			

Chukchi Sea

RUSSIA

Little Diomede Island

Nome ○
Norton Sound

St. Lawrence Island

Yukon Delta Nat'l Wildlife Refuge

B e r i n g S e a

Nunivak Island

Bethel ○
Yukon Delta Nat'l Wildlife Refuge

~ *Attu Island*

Pribilof Islands

Bristol Bay

Cape
St. Stephen · *Rat Islands*

Alaska Peninsula

Unimak Island Cold Bay ○

Dutch Harbor

Adak
Adak Island

Atka Island
○**Atka**

Fort Glen ○○

○ **Unimak**
Unalaska

A l e u t i a n I s l a n d s

P A C I F I C

0	100 mi
0	100 km

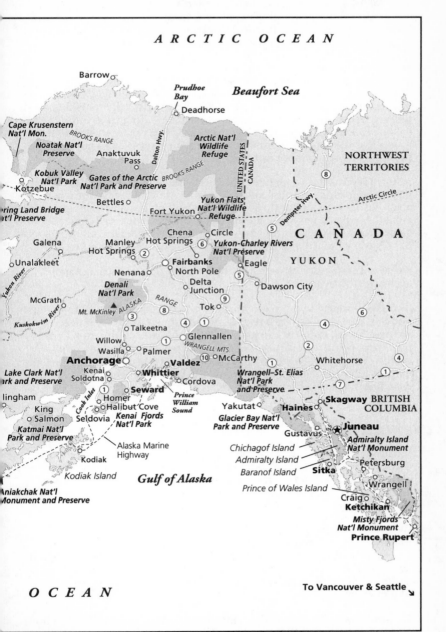

ARCTIC OCEAN

Barrow

Prudhoe
Bay
Deadhorse

Beaufort Sea

Cape Krusenstern
Nat'l Mon.   BROOKS RANGE

Noatak Nat'l
Preserve   Anaktuvuk
Pass

Arctic Nat'l
Wildlife
Refuge

NORTHWEST
TERRITORIES

Kobuk Valley
Nat'l Park   Gates of the Arctic   BROOKS RANGE
Kotzebue   Nat'l Park and Preserve

Dalton Hwy.

UNITED STATES
CANADA

Dempster Hwy.

Arctic Circle

ring Land Bridge   Bettles
't'l Preserve   Fort Yukon

Yukon Flats
Nat'l Wildlife
Refuge

Galena
Unalakleet

Yukon River

Chena
Manley   Hot Springs
Hot Springs

Circle
Yukon-Charley Rivers
Nat'l Preserve

CANADA

YUKON

Nenana   Fairbanks
North Pole
Eagle

Denali
Nat'l Park   RANGE   Delta
Junction
McGrath   Mt. McKinley   ALASKA   Tok

Dawson City

Kuskokwim River

Talkeetna

Willow   Glennallen
Wasilla   Palmer   WRANGELL MTS.
Anchorage   McCarthy

Whitehorse

Lake Clark Nat'l   Kenai   Valdez
ark and Preserve   Soldotna   Whittier
Wrangell–St. Elias
Nat'l Park
and Preserve

lingham   Homer   Prince
King   Halibut Cove   William
Salmon   Seldovia   Sound
Kenai Fjords
Katmai Nat'l   Nat'l Park
Park and Preserve

Yakutat   Haines   Skagway BRITISH
COLUMBIA

Glacier Bay Nat'l
Park and Preserve

Juneau

Alaska Marine
Highway   Gustavus
Kodiak   Chichagof Island
Admiralty Island
Kodiak Island   Baranof Island
Gulf of Alaska

Admiralty Island
Nat'l Monument
Petersburg
Sitka   Wrangell

niakchak Nat'l
Monument and Preserve   Prince of Wales Island   Craig
Ketchikan
Misty Fjords
Nat'l Monument
Prince Rupert

OCEAN

To Vancouver & Seattle

owned by out-of-state merchants, staffed by seasonal workers, and stocked with "Alaskan" merchandise that's actually made in China or Indonesia. Yuck, we say. Yuck. Luckily, no matter how crowded and touristy the area around the docks, all ports also offer ways of seeing some of the real Alaska, either on your own or via shore excursions.

In addition to the standard walking tours, bus tours, and even a few horse-drawn carriage tours, cruise lines also offer a slew of active, adventurous, and sometimes educational excursions. You can choose among mountain-biking, hiking, and kayaking trips; salmon fishing expeditions; helicopter and floatplane flightseeing; rafting trips through wildlife refuges; dogsled trips and workshops; visits to Alaska Native towns and tribal houses; brewery tours (who says they're not educational!?); and many other options.

At the adventurous (and expensive) extreme of excursion offerings, flightseeing trips show the vast and varied Alaskan landscape from the air. Tour operators offer these trips via small planes and helicopters, and sometimes pair them with unforgettable options such as landing on a glacier for a trek across the ice — an option we took recently which was, bar none, one of the top experiences we've ever had on a cruise.

Shore excursion prices we list in this chapter are for 2005 and may increase slightly in 2006.

If you're touring on your own, you need a taxi or shuttle to get to the more outlying attractions — for example, **Mendenhall Glacier** in Juneau or **Saxman Totem Pole Park** in Ketchikan. We provide information in each port write-up on which attractions you can walk to and which require wheels. You probably need to avail yourself of transportation in the large embarkation ports (such as Anchorage, Seattle, and Vancouver), though each has a walkable downtown core.

Watching Whales

Whales are a *huge* draw on Alaska cruises, ranking right up there with calving glaciers and Alaska Amber beer. On most large cruise ships, the captain or officer on watch makes an announcement when he or she spots a whale, at which point half the people on board crane their necks in the same direction.

We'll be honest with you: Whale-watching takes patience, because frankly, whales spend a lot of time underwater. What the spotter is seeing is typically the curve of the whale's back as he slides through the water, or the flash of his tail as he makes a deep sounding dive. It can be minutes before he comes up again, and you never know exactly where that may happen.

Humpbacks are definitely the stars of the Alaska whale-watching show, easily recognized by their huge, mottled tails; by the hump on their back, just forward of its dorsal fin; and by their armlike flippers, which can grow to be 14 feet long. These migratory whales spend all their summers in Alaska, feeding on small fish and other tiny creatures that they filter through strips of stiff, fibrous baleen — the material that humpbacks have instead of teeth. Most humpback sightings are of the whales' humped backs as they cruise along the surface, resting, and of the flukes of the tail as they dive. Feeding dives can last a long time and often mean you won't see that particular whale again, but if you're lucky, the whale may be just dipping down for a few minutes before breaching — leaping straight out of the water, twisting around in midair before falling back with a gigantic *kersploosh!* No one knows for sure why they do this, though to look at them it seems obvious: They're enjoying themselves.

Orcas, or **"killer whales,"** are probably the next most frequently sighted. Easily identified by their stark black-and-white patches, they're the ocean's top predator, moving like wolves in highly structured family groups called pods and swimming at up to 25 knots (about 29 mph) in pursuit of salmon, porpoises, seals, sea lions, and almost anything else that moves — except man, oddly enough. Like dolphins, orcas often pop above the surface in a flashing, graceful arc when they travel, giving viewers a glance at their sleek shape, markings, and tall dorsal fin. On a recent trip, we spotted a pod of Orcas coming straight toward our ship. As passengers watched, the group — at least ten strong, the younger whales flanked by their parents — turned and sliced through the water no more than 20 feet off the ship's port side, the sun shining off their sleek, angular dorsal fins and panda-colored backs. It was "a moment."

You may also spot **Beluga whales** and **Minke whales.** Belugas are the small, white whales with the cute rounded beaks. More likely to be confused for a dolphin than any other whale, belugas are larger and fatter than a dolphin and lack the dolphin's dorsal fin. Adults are all white, while juveniles are gray, and they swim in large packs that can number in the dozens, feeding on salmon. Minkes are the smallest of the baleen whales, generally under 26 feet long, with a blackish-gray body, a white stomach, a narrow, triangular head, and white bands on its flippers. When breaching, minkes leap something like dolphins, gracefully reentering the water headfirst — unlike humpbacks, which smash down on their sides. Also unlike the humpbacks, they don't raise their flukes clear of the water when they dive.

Choosing a Cruisetour

If you have additional time and dough, consider booking a cruisetour package that combines a cruise with a land tour via bus, train, and sometimes boat and plane. That's the only way you get to see some of the Alaskan Interior, which is vastly different from the rain forest ecosystem of Southeast Alaska. Holland America, Princess, Royal Caribbean, and Celebrity Cruises are the bigwigs in the cruisetour market, each with their own transportation infrastructure. Holland America and Princess also own their own hotels and lodges.

Cruise lines typically offer a number of different cruisetour options, concentrating on different regions.

A typical **Anchorage/Denali/Fairbanks cruisetour** package may include a 7-night Vancouver–Anchorage cruise, followed by 2 nights in Anchorage and a private railcar ride to **Denali National Park** for a full day in the park and a 2-night stay at one of the cruise line's lodges. If you're lucky, the cloud gods will part to give you a look at **Mount McKinley,** North America's highest peak at 20,320 feet. From there, you go by train to **Fairbanks,** spending two more days on activities that may include day cruises on the Chena and Tanana Rivers, jet boat rides, and excursions to gold mines and dredges. Passengers typically fly home from Fairbanks. A shorter variation of that itinerary may skip Fairbanks and return to Anchorage for departure.

Other cruisetours hop the border into Canada's huge **Yukon Territory,** combining a 3- or 4-day cruise between Vancouver and Juneau/Skagway with a land program into the Klondike. Passengers travel by rail, riverboat, motor coach, and sometimes air, with overnight stops in the territorial capital of **Whitehorse** and the picturesque Gold Rush town of **Dawson City.** From there it's back to Fairbanks, then through Denali to Anchorage and home. The tour can be taken in either direction.

Other cruisetour options include an add-on to **Wrangell–St. Elias National Park,** east of Anchorage, and a **Canadian Rockies cruisetour** offers some of the finest mountain scenery on earth, visiting Canada's Banff National Park, Jasper National Park, and other national and provincial parks. The beautiful **Lake Louise,** colored deep green from its mineral content, is located 35 miles north of Banff.

The cost of a cruisetour typically includes hotel stays, transportation (usually train and/or bus and sometimes a plane or ferry), and a limited number of meals (usually only while in transit).

The Ports of Embarkation

You have to start somewhere, and for an Alaska cruise you'll likely start in Vancouver, Seattle, or Seward/Whittier (which serve as ports for nearby Anchorage). Some small ships also sail itineraries that begin and/or end in Juneau and Ketchikan.

Anchorage

No, Anchorage isn't the capital of Alaska, though a lot of people think it should be. It's the state's largest city and one of the newest big cities in the U.S., only really taking off as a population center after World War II. The city was badly beaten up by the great quake and resulting tsunami of 1964, which rivaled in strength the one that hit South Asia 40 years later, though with far less loss of life. Today it's a modern city with good

Downtown Anchorage

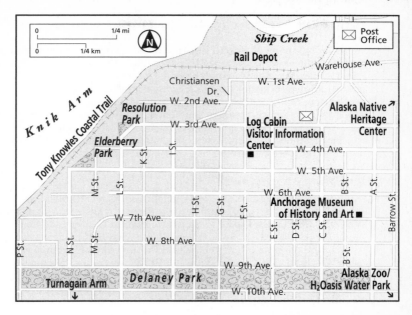

restaurants, good museums, a nice little zoo, and several major **attrac-tions** right outside town.

Cruising into port

Though Anchorage is the official northern embarkation and debarkation port on Gulf of Alaska cruises, it actually isn't. It's located on the wrong side of the Kenai Peninsula from the usual cruise ship routes, so ships typically dock instead in the towns of Seward or Whittier, both located on the southeast side. The switcheroo saves a whole day of sailing, let-ting the ships concentrate more of their sea time on the Inside Passage, then bus passengers overland to Anchorage itself (2–3 hours from Seward, about 90 minutes from Whittier).

Neither Seward nor Whittier offers much to hold visitor interest, and most people tend to head right from bus to ship, or the other way around. Cruise lines also offer several shore excursions from each port: sportfishing in Seward, for example, or sea kayaking near Whittier in Prince William Sound. Other excursions tour Anchorage before dropping passengers off at the international airport.

If you have time in Seward, visit the **Alaska SeaLife Center,** on the water-front at Mile 0 of the Seward Highway (☎ **800-224-2525;** www.alaska sealife.org). A major research aquarium founded with Exxon restitu-tions following the infamous *Exxon Valdez* oil spill, the center allows scientists and visitors (the latter through windows) to study sea lions, porpoises, sea otters, harbor seals, fish, and other forms of marine life that abound in the area, as well as many species of local seabirds. Admission is $14 adults, $11 ages 7 to 12, free 6 and under.

Whittier's only real attraction is that it's Anchorage's closest gateway to the wilderness splendor of Prince William Sound, accessible by both road and rail via the 2½-mile Anton Anderson Memorial Tunnel. Born as an army town, Whittier retains its barracks-like ambience, with almost every resident (and the grocery store, and the medical center) living in the 14-story **Begich Towers.** You heard that right: Almost everyone in town lives in that one building. An underground walkway links it with the local school so that the kids don't have to plough through the 14 feet of snow Whittier endures every year.

Exploring on your own

Anchorage's downtown area is a manageable 8-by-20 blocks, with some areas catering strictly to tourists and others obviously for locals only. The Visitor Bureau's **Log Cabin Visitor Information Center** is at 4th Avenue and F Street (☎ **907-274-3531;** www.anchorage.net). Across the intersection, in the old post office, the **Alaska Public Lands Information Center** (605 W. 4th Ave., Suite 105; ☎ **907-271-2737;** www.nps.gov/aplic) can help anyone planning to spend time outdoors anywhere in Alaska.

Within walking distance: If you visit town on a weekday from June to August, you can join one of the historic tours hosted by **Alaska Historic Properties** (☎ **907-274-3600**). Meet in the lobby of the old City Hall (524 W. 4th Ave.; next to the Log Cabin Visitor Information Center) at 1 p.m. The one-hour tours cover about 2 miles and cost $5.

You can view contemporary Alaskan art and a large collection covering Alaskan history and anthropology in the galleries of the **Anchorage Museum of History and Art** (121 W. 7th Ave., between A and C streets; ☎ **907-343-4326;** www.anchoragemuseum.org).

If you want a dose of the outdoors, stretch your legs along the paved, 11-mile **Tony Knowles Coastal Trail,** which follows the water from the western end of 2nd Avenue to Kincaid Park. You can hop on the trail at several points, including **Elderberry Park** at the western end of 5th Avenue. You can also rent a bike from **Downtown Bicycle Rental** (333 W. 4th Ave.; ☎ **907-279-5293;** www.alaska-bike-rentals.com) for $15 for the first three hours and $2.50 for each hour thereafter, up to a total of $29 for a 24-hour rental.

Most of the shopping is very kitschy, but there are a few goodies in the mix. The **Cook Island Book Company** (415 W. 5th Ave.; ☎ **907-258-4544;** www.cookinlet.com) has a huge and in-depth stock of Alaska-oriented books. The **Oomingmak Musk Ox Producers' Co-operative** (604 H St. at 6th Ave.; ☎ **888-360-9665;** www.qiviut.com) is a co-op owned by Alaska Native women in villages across the state. All of their products are knitted from *qiviut* (*kiv*-ee-oot), the light, warm, silky — and rare — underhair of the musk ox.

Beyond walking distance: **The Alaska Native Heritage Center** (8800 Heritage Center Dr.; ☎ 800-315-6608; www.alaskanative.net) is located about 15 minutes from downtown Anchorage and provides a great introduction to the lives and cultures of the state's five major Native groups: Southeast Alaska's Tlingit, Eyak, Haida, and Tsimshian tribes; the Athabascans of the Interior; the Inupiat and St. Lawrence Island Yupik Natives of the far north; the Aleuts and Alutiiqs of the Aleutian Islands; and the Yup'ik and Cup'ik tribes of the extreme west. The center features reconstructions of traditional Native dwellings, Native interpreters to explain what life was like in traditional communities; a small museum displaying some remarkable carvings and masks; a workshop for Native craftspeople; a theater presenting a rotating series of films on Native culture; and a rotunda for storytelling, dance, and music performances. Admission is $21. A free shuttle leaves regularly from the Anchorage Museum, the Anchorage Visitors Center at 4th Avenue and F Street, and several other sites. Times are posted at all pickup points, or call ☎ 907-330-8000.

If you're traveling with kids, Anchorage offers a few kid-centric options, including the **H2Oasis Water Park** (1520 O'Malley Rd.; ☎ 888-H2OASIS; www.h2oasiswaterpark.com), which offers a wave pool that generates 3-to-4-foot waves, a 150-foot long enclosed body slide, a children's lagoon, a pirate's ship, water cannons, and other fun. A day pass for an adult (13 and older) costs $20; children under 13 pay $15. About 8 miles south of downtown, the **Alaska Zoo** (4731 O'Malley Rd.; ☎ 907-346-3242; www.alaskazoo.org) affords you a closer look at many Alaskan animal species and some non-native varieties. Admission is $9 adults, $5 kids.

If you want to head out of town and into the wild, the **Alaska Public Lands Information Center** can show you a good route to the easily accessible and scenic **Chugach Mountains.** Or you can take a drive along **Turnagain Arm,** which stretches roughly 50 miles south of Anchorage to the funky little town of Girdwood. The road provides breathtaking mountain views and the possibility of wildlife sightings, including moose, Dall sheep, and occasionally beluga whales, all right from your car window. You can rent a car in Anchorage (see the appendix for toll-free numbers of rental firms) or take one of the seven- or ten-hour tours offered by **Gray Line of Alaska** (☎ 800-544-2206; http://graylinealaska.com), which include Turnagain Arm and a boat ride to **Portage Glacier.**

Vancouver, British Columbia

Most cruise ships that explore the Inside Passage and Gulf of Alaska use Vancouver as the main southern embarkation and debarkation port. Originally scouted out by the Spanish (uh, after Canada's First Nations people had already been there 12,000 years or so, we mean), Vancouver was named for Captain George Vancouver, who led a British expedition to the region in 1792, beginning the era of British control. Fur traders really got things rolling here in the early and mid-19th century, with more people arriving during the gold fever of the 1850s and 60s, but it wasn't until the Canadian Pacific Railway set up a terminus here in 1884 that the city really began to boom. Today it's a lovely, friendly city surrounded by mountains and ocean, with a rich vein of Northwest Coast Native culture, a thriving Asian community, a great arts scene, and a blatantly friendly populace.

The **Canadian dollar** (C$1.25 = US$1; C$1 = US80¢) is Canada's official currency (this exchange rate was during a period when the U.S. dollar's value was the pits; let's hope it's better when you read this!). We quote all prices in this section in U.S. dollars.

Cruising into port

Most cruise ships dock at **Canada Place** (☎ 604-666-7200; www.canada place.ca) at the end of Burrard Street. The pier terminal is a landmark in the city, noted for its five-sail structure, which reaches into the harbor like a ship setting off. It's located at the edge of the downtown district and is just a quick stroll from the **Gastown** area (see below) and other area attractions. Some ships may dock at the **Ballantyne** cruise terminal, about five minutes away by taxi.

Scoring the best excursions

Coastal Rainforest Adventure: This bus tour acquaints you with Vancouver's downtown area before continuing out to Capilano Canyon, where you go on a 2-mile walk through the rain forest. A naturalist guide provides insight as you go (3½ hours; $73).

Capilano Suspension Bridge and Grouse Mountain Skyride: Afraid of heights? Don't go on this tour, which visits the historic Capilano Suspension Bridge, a walkway that sways 230 feet above the canyon below. From here, you take the Grouse Mountain Skyride to the 4,000-foot summit, where you can hike one of the nature trails or grab lunch (3½ hours; $63).

Exploring on your own

The **Tourism Vancouver Infocentre** is near the piers, as are hotels, restaurants, and shops.

Within walking distance: So close to the ship pier that you can't miss it, **Gastown** is a charming area of historic buildings, cobblestone streets, and gaslights (although the area's name actually comes from a 19th-century saloon-owner, "Gassy" Jack Deighton). Tourists enjoy the bohemian atmosphere, complete with street musicians, antiques and art shops, boutiques, cafes, and clubs.

Besides featuring delicious Asian cuisine and shops selling Chinese goods, Vancouver's **Chinatown** is also a historic district, and one of the

Downtown Vancouver

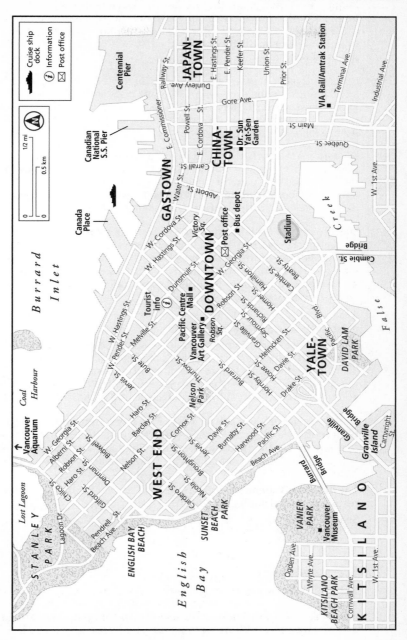

largest Chinese neighborhoods in North America. The area's most famous attraction is the **Dr. Sun Yat-Sen Garden** (578 Carrall St.; ☎ 604-689-7133; www.vancouverchinesegarden.com), a perfectly traditional Chinese garden based on the yin-yang principle. Admission is $6.60. Check out **Robson Street** and the **Pacific Centre Mall** for trendy fashions and bargains.

Cruise passengers may be particularly interested in visiting an exhibit of a 19th-century immigrant ship's steerage deck at the **Vancouver Museum** (1100 Chestnut St.; ☎ 604-736-4431; www.vanmuseum.bc.ca), which covers the history of the city from prehistoric times to the present. Admission is $8.

Beyond walking distance: Just a few miles from downtown Vancouver, northwest of the cruise ship terminal, the 1,000 acres of **Stanley Park** contain gorgeous rose gardens, hiking trails, totem poles, a kids' water park, and the **Vancouver Aquarium** (☎ 604-659-FISH; www.vanaqua.org), one of the largest in North America. Admission to the aquarium is $14.

Downtown, not far inland from the cruise docks, **Robson Street** is full of boutiques, souvenir shops, coffeehouses, and bistros. About 15 minutes' walk from downtown across False Creek, **Granville Island** (www.granvilleisland.com) is a former industrial site whose warehouses and factories now house galleries, artist studios, restaurants, theaters, and lots of shopping.

Seattle, Washington

A longtime embarkation port for small ships, Seattle is now home base for some of Norwegian Cruise Line's and Holland America's big ships. Seattle has shopping, fine restaurants, attractions galore, good air service, and culture. It is very much a water-oriented city, set between Puget Sound and Lake Washington, with Lake Union in the center.

Similar to Fisherman's Wharf in San Francisco, the **Seattle waterfront** is both touristy and home to some great restaurants and shops, as well as the popular **Seattle Aquarium.** It runs along Alaskan Way from Yesler Way North to Bay Street and Myrtle Edwards Park.

Cruising into port

Cruise ships dock at Pier 66 (the Bell St. Terminal), right in downtown Seattle, or at the new Pier 30 terminal, 2431 East Marginal Way S., at the south end of Seattle's downtown waterfront, just a few minutes away by car or taxi.

Scoring the best excursions

Seattle Duck Tour: Explore Seattle in a WWII-era amphibious tour bus, which explores the Seattle waterfront, historic Pioneer Square, Safeco Field, Pike Place Market, and the downtown shopping district before driving right into Lake Union (1½ hours; $23).

Downtown Seattle

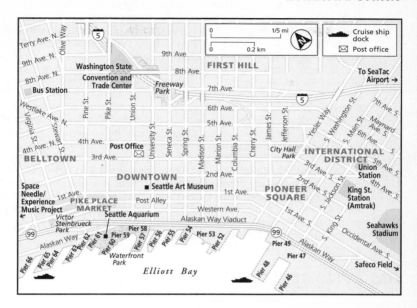

Bus Tour: A standard bus tour that includes the Space Needle and shopping time at Pike Place Market (3 hours; $45).

Exploring on your own

The Visitors Bureau's **Citywide Concierge Center** is located at the Washington State Convention and Trade Center, on Pike Street between 7th and 8th Avenues, on the Galleria level.

Within walking distance: A National Historic District, **Pike Place Market** (between Pike and Pine Streets at First Avenue; ☎ 206-682-7453; www.pikeplacemarket.org) provides a venue for some 200 local artisans and fine artists to display and sell their wares, and for countless street performers, restaurants, and literally hundreds of shops. Two blocks from the market, the **Seattle Art Museum** (100 University St; ☎ 206-654-3100; www.seattleartmuseum.org) has a great collection of Northwest Coast Indian art and diverse exhibits ranging from Andy Warhol to African masks. Admission is $7; closed Mondays.

If the huge octopus at the **Seattle Aquarium** (1483 Alaskan Way, in Waterfront Park; ☎ 206-386-4320; www.seattleaquarium.org) doesn't pull you in, its well-designed exhibits about **Puget Sound** sea life will. Admission is $12 adults, $8 kids 3 to 5, free for 2 and under.

Built for the 1962 World's Fair, the 600-foot **Space Needle** (400 Broad St.; ☎ 206-443-2111; www.spaceneedle.com) has become a symbol of

Seattle, pointing to the architectural trends of some Jetsonian future that may or may not arrive. You can enjoy fantastic views from the observation deck or dine in either of two equally expensive restaurants inside. Admission is $13. Next door, the newish, bizarro-looking **Experience Music Project** (☎ 877-367-5483; www.emplive.com) is a combination museum, performance center, and school, with displays, interactive music rooms, performance spaces, galleries, and research facilities dedicated to all aspects of American popular music. Admission is $20.

Beyond walking distance: Across Puget Sound in Blake Island State Marine Park is **Tillicum Village,** another surprising legacy of the 1962 World's Fair. You arrive by boat to this incredibly scenic spot where totem poles guard a traditional Northwest Coast Indian longhouse surrounded by forest (which is pretty much the whole "village," despite the name). Inside the longhouse is a large restaurant and performance hall where you can watch traditional masked dances while you enjoy an alder-smoked salmon dinner. **Tillicum Village Tours** (Pier 56; ☎ 206-933-8600; www.tillicumvillage.com) operates visits that include round-trip boat transportation to the village, an elegant dinner, and dance performance. The cost is $69.

The Ports of Call

Generally, a ship visits three or four ports of call during a 7-night Alaska itinerary, plus the ports of embarkation and debarkation and several outstanding natural areas. The ports and areas in this section are the most popular.

Haines

Surrounded by snowcapped mountains, Haines is the quintessential quiet, small Alaska town, the kind of place where you wouldn't be surprised to see a moose wandering down Main Street. It was established in 1879 not as a gold rush town like Skagway (its neighbor 15 miles up the Lynn Canal) but as a missionary town. The U.S. military arrived in the early 20th century and built **Fort William Seward,** a very unmilitary-looking military base, which was deactivated after World War II and is now a local tourist attraction, with a replica of a Tlingit clan house on its 9-acre parade grounds. The surrounding buildings, once barracks and officers' quarters, have been converted to private homes, B&Bs, and arts-and-performance spaces.

Downtown Haines has an almost totally local character, with an assortment of shops and museums mixed in. Only a few large ships dock here (plus a number of small ships), partially due to the lack of a large, deep-water dock, partly because there are few big local attractions. But that's just what makes Haines appealing: It's not just a tourist town.

Haines

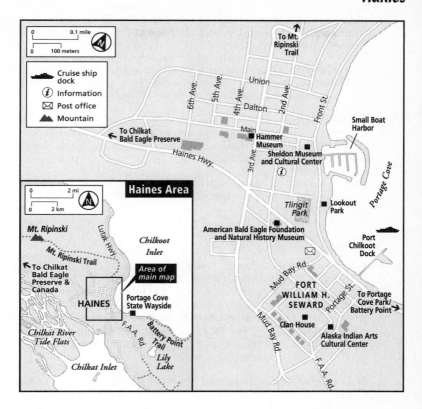

Cruising into port

Small ships tie up to the Port Chilkoot Dock, directly opposite Fort William Seward, about a half-mile from downtown. Larger vessels must anchor offshore and bring passengers in by tender, arriving either at Port Chilkoot or at the small-boat harbor in the downtown area. Visitor information is available at the dock. Most ships provide shuttle service to Main Street, or you can walk down Front Street to Main.

Scoring the best excursions

Chilkat Bald Eagle Preserve Float Trip: Haines is one of the best places on earth to see bald eagles, and the Chilkat Bald Eagle Preserve, about 20 miles outside town, is probably the best place to see them near Haines. An expert guide rows your rubber raft and provides commentary on the area's natural environment, keeping an eye out for eagles, moose, bears, and wolves (4 hours; $99).

Chilkoot Lake Bicycle Adventure: After driving to your start point, you can ride 8 miles along the shore of Lutak Inlet, where the river meets the sea. Highlights include some amazing views of the lake, glaciers, waterfalls, and mountains, and a chance at spotting eagles and bears (3 hours; $87).

Chilkat Nature Hike: A guide tells you all about Alaskan rain forests as you hike this moderately difficult 5-mile trail. With any luck, you may catch a glimpse of a bald eagle (4 hours; $65).

Taste of Haines Tour: Visit the Haines Brewing Company, the smallest brewery in Alaska, for a sample and a talk with the brewmaster. Then head to a local smoked-salmon shop to sample and learn how that stuff is prepared (2 hours; $55).

Best of Haines by Classic Car: Explore Haines in a 1930s- or 1940s-vintage car while your driver shares the history of the area and gives you a peek into how the townsfolk live when the tourists have gone home (1 hour; $54).

Exploring on your own

Within walking distance: Just above the dock, at Fort William Seward, the **Alaska Indian Arts Cultural Center** (☎ 907-766-2160) has a small gallery selling traditional artwork and prints, plus a carvers' workshop where you may see totem-carving in progress. Between the fort and the town center, the **American Bald Eagle Foundation and Natural History Museum** (Haines Highway at 2nd Avenue; ☎ 907-766-3094; http://baldeagles.org) has a huge diorama with more than 180 stuffed eagles and other critters. Admission is $3.

Main Street has two museums. The **Sheldon Museum and Cultural Center,** near the small-boat harbor (☎ 907-766-2366; www.sheldonmuseum.org), has been around since 1925, displaying a collection of local items and Tlingit art begun by local shopkeepers Steve and Bess Sheldon. Admission is $3. A more recent addition to the local scene is Dave and Carol Pohl's **Hammer Museum** (108 Main St.; ☎ 907-766-2374; www.hammermuseum.org), which is exactly what it sounds like, displaying more than 1,200 different hammers from around the globe. Admission is $2.

Beyond walking distance: Not much except the **Chilkat Bald Eagle Preserve,** and that's best visited on a shore excursion (see "Scoring the best excursions," earlier in this section).

Juneau

Juneau, Alaska's state capital and third-largest city (after Anchorage and Fairbanks), is surrounded by ice fields on three sides and water on the fourth, which makes it the only U.S. state capital that you can't drive to. Another weird fact: Although Juneau's downtown area looks relatively small, the greater city encompasses 3,108 square miles, making it

Juneau

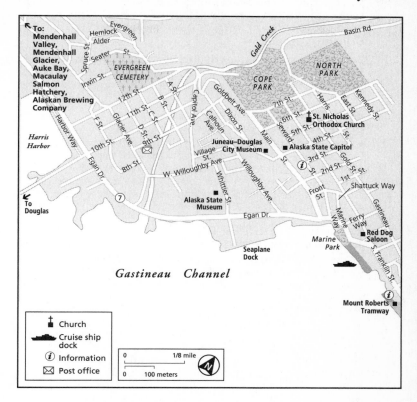

To:
Mendenhall
Valley,
Mendenhall
Glacier,
Auke Bay,
Macaulay
Salmon
Hatchery,
Alaskan Brewing
Company

*Harris
Harbor*

To
Douglas

Evergreen
Hemlock
Alder
Seater
Spruce St.
Irwin St.
EVERGREEN
CEMETERY
12th St.
11th St.
F St.
Glacier Ave.
10th St.
Harbor Way
Egan Dr.
8th St.
9th St.
D St.
C St.
B St.
A St.
Capitol Ave.
Calhoun Ave.
Dixon St.
Goldbelt Ave.
Gold Creek

NORTH
PARK

COPE
PARK

Basin Rd.

7th St.
6th St.
5th St.
4th St.
3rd St.
2nd St.
1st St.
Harris
Seward St.
Main St.
Gold St.
Willoughby Ave.
Whittier St.
W. Willoughby Ave.
Village St.
Juneau–Douglas
City Museum ■

■ St. Nicholas
Orthodox Church

■ Alaska State Capitol

(i)

Front
St.

Shattuck Way

East St.
Kennedy St.

Alaska State
Museum ■

Egan Dr.

Seaplane
Dock

Marine
Way
Ferry
Way

Marine
Park

■ Red Dog
Saloon

S. Franklin St.
Gastineau Ave.

Gastineau Channel

Mount Roberts ■
Tramway
(i)

✝ Church
⬛ Cruise ship
dock
(i) Information
✉ Post office

0   1/8 mile
0   100 meters

simultaneously the largest state capital in terms of mass and probably the only one that includes ice fields within its city limits. In spite of all this, Juneau is actually a fairly cosmopolitan city (by Alaskan standards, certainly) and one of the most-visited ports for cruise ships, with four or five ships making port here virtually every day during the summer season. If you're sailing an Inside Passage itinerary, you'll almost certainly stop here.

Juneau had its foundations in gold mining, beginning when Chief Kowee of the Auk Tlingit clan led miners Joe Juneau and Richard Harris to a local strike. As soon as you disembark ship, look up along the Mount Roberts Tramway to spot the ruins of the **Alaska-Juneau Mill** on the mountainside. Known locally as the A-J, it produced a whopping 3.5 million ounces of gold before it closed in 1944, effectively closing the book on Juneau's mining economy.

In town, right beyond the end of the dock, you find tourist shops, a great museum, and wonderful historical architecture, including the **State**

Capitol Building and a couple of genuine saloons. Various forest hiking trails, the blue-white **Mendenhall Glacier,** and several other attractions are located a short drive out of town.

Cruising into port

Both large and small ships dock right in the downtown area, along Marine Way. Every once in a while, overcrowding may mean a ship has to anchor in the channel and tender its passengers to shore.

Scoring the best excursions

Glacier Helicopter Tour: Glaciers are impressive when seen from the water, but you ain't seen nothing till you get up above, into the mountains, and see just how unbelievably massive they really are. This helicopter tour lands you right on either the **Norris** or the **Mendenhall Glacier,** where you have time to get out and walk around on the surface. This is one of the best shore excursions we've ever taken, anywhere (2½–6½ hours; $215–$375).

Mendenhall Glacier Float Trip: An experienced rafter steers your ten-person raft across Mendenhall Lake and past icebergs until you get to the **Mendenhall River** and its beautiful scenery. You encounter moderate rapids and stunning views, and get a snack of smoked salmon and reindeer sausage somewhere along the way (4 hours; $105).

Mendenhall Glacier and City Highlights Tour: Travel by bus from downtown Juneau to the glacier and its U.S. Forest Service Observatory. There, as time allows, you can follow one of the nature trails or hike to within a half-mile of the glacier — which sounds far, but the ice face is so enormous you'd think you're within spitting distance. A visit to the University of Alaska campus and the Gastineau Salmon Hatchery round out your tour (3 hours; $39). Other tours pair the glacier and hatchery with an outdoor all-you-can-eat salmon bake, with music and the possibility of beer, though you have to pay extra for that (4 hours; $65).

Bike and Brew Tour: Speaking of beer, this 11-mile bicycle tour takes you from town along Fritz Cove Road, offers views of picturesque Auke Bay and the Mendenhall Glacier, then ends at the Alaska Brewing Company for a tour and sampling of the brew (4½ hours; $80).

Wilderness Lodge Flightseeing Adventure: This tour combines flightseeing over an ice field and glaciers with a salmon bake at the Taku Glacier Lodge, and enough time for a short nature trail hike (3½ hours; $240).

Exploring on your own

You can find walking maps and visitors' guides at the **visitor information center,** located right on the dock, in a green building near the base of the Mount Roberts Tram. Downtown begins right at the end of the docks, but there's also a shuttle that circuits the town throughout the day. The **Davis Log Cabin Visitor Center** is located farther up in town, on Seward Street (☎ 907-586-2201). It's a replica of the city's first schoolhouse.

Within walking distance: Right on the docks, you can hop on board the **Mount Roberts Tramway** (490 S. Franklin St.; ☎ 888-461-TRAM; www. goldbelttours.com) for a six-minute ride 1,760 feet straight up Mount Roberts. At the top you'll find an observation area, a restaurant, shops, and a series of nature trails through the alpine ecosystem, offering great views of the Gastineau Channel below. If the sky is overcast, you won't get the views, though the trails can still be great — as long as you bring bug repellent. Tickets are $22.

The **Red Dog Saloon** (278 S. Franklin St.; ☎ 907-463-3658; www.reddog saloon.cc) sits right at the intersection just beyond the docks and is a virtual magnet for cruise passengers. Its self-created legend is that it's a wild frontier bar, but actually it's pretty Disney, but still fun, with a sawdust-covered floor, live music, and walls full of memorabilia. The more authentic **Alaskan Bar** is across the street at 167 S. Franklin (☎ 907-586-1000).

The state's Russian and Native cultures are well represented at the **Alaska State Museum** (395 Whittier St., ☎ 907-465-2901; www.museums.state. ak.us), which showcases Alaskan art and artifacts. Admission is $5. You can take a free tour of the **Alaska State Capitol** (on 4th Street between Main and Seward; closed Sat afternoon and Sun), which has photomurals depicting the early days of Juneau. A couple blocks to the north, the octagonal chapel of **St. Nicholas Orthodox Church** (Fifth and Gold Streets) was built by the Tlingits in 1893 and remains an active parish to this day. It's open daily during tourist season. A small donation is requested.

Specializing in children's programs, the small but engaging **Juneau-Douglas City Museum** (Fourth and Main Streets; ☎ 907-586-3572; www. juneau.org/parksrec/museum) displays artifacts from the city's history and gold-mining past. Admission is $4 for adults, free for students and children 18 and under.

Beyond walking distance: About 3 miles from downtown along the Egan Expressway, you can visit the **Macaulay Salmon Hatchery** (2697 Channel Dr.; ☎ 877-463-2486), where you get to see every step of the harvesting and fertilizing of salmon eggs. The resultant offspring are later released back into the wild. Admission is $3.25. Nearby, off Egan at Vanderbilt Hill Road (then right on Anka St. and right again on Shaune Dr.), the **Alaskan Brewing Company** (5429 Shaune Dr.; ☎ 907-780-5866; www.alaskanbeer.com) makes that great Alaskan Amber you see everywhere in the state. They offer free daily tours with a sampling of beer at the end.

Keep going down Egan Expressway to **Mendenhall Glacier,** about 13 miles from downtown at the head of Mendenhall Valley. The visitor center here

(☎ **907-789-0097;** www.fs.fed.us/r10/tongass/districts/ mendenhall) contains a glacier museum with excellent explanatory models, computerized displays, and ranger talks. Admission is $3. Trails of various lengths get you closer to the glacier, the easiest being a half-mile nature trail.

Ketchikan

Because Ketchikan is the southernmost port of call for Southeast Alaska, residents call it the "first city" — the first port ships from Vancouver or Seattle stop on northbound cruises. Although it is Alaska's fifth-largest city (with about 8,000 residents!), it likes to project a quirky/quaint frontier image, complete with a quirky/quaint old-time red-light district, **Creek Street,** which was in full schving until the 1950s. To cater to tourists, Ketchikan offers plenty of shopping near the docks, but you can walk past all that and watch fishing boats set out from the harbor, or head to several sites that interpret the local Native culture (Ketchikan has the largest concentration of Tlingit, Haida, and Tsimshian people in Alaska, and the world's largest collection of totem poles).

You may be able to find wetter places than Ketchikan, with its average rainfall of 13 feet per year, but at a certain point you become too damp to tell the difference. Suffice to say, it's wet. Carry a folding umbrella.

Cruising into port

Ships dock right at the pier in Ketchikan's downtown.

Scoring the best excursions

Misty Fjords Flightseeing: The 2.3-million-acre, Connecticut-size area of Misty Fjords looks like something out of *The Lord of the Rings,* with volcanic cliffs rising up to 3,150 feet, dense hemlock and spruce forests, high ridges covered in alpine grass, and a watery passage through it all that's so narrow only small ships can get any significant distance in. That's why the big ships offer these shore excursions, which fly from Ketchikan by floatplane. Some do a water landing and then fly out again. Others bring you to an excursion boat for exploration of the monument, then make the short cruise back to Ketchikan (2–4½ hours; $220–$285).

Saxman Native Village Tour: Not just another tourist attraction, this arts and cultural center, situated about 2½ miles outside Ketchikan, is home to hundreds of Tlingit, Tsimshian, and Haida Natives and is a center for the revival of Native arts and culture. On this excursion, you tour the grounds, see a performance by the Cape Fox Dancers at the Beaver Clan House, and listen to traditional Native stories. You may also watch artisans demonstrate totem carving (2½ hours; $49).

Sportfishing: You may never get a better chance to catch salmon than on a chartered fishing boat excursion in this region. The boat crew supplies your fishing gear, tackle, and bait; you catch the fish, and they ship

Ketchikan

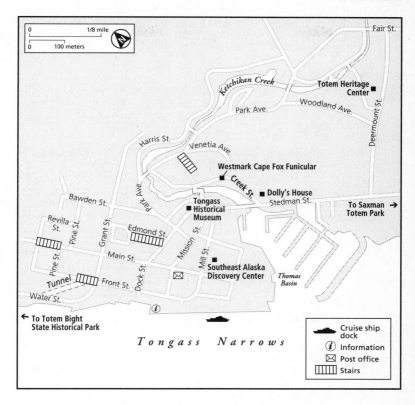

it home for you, for an added fee (4–6 hours; $169 plus $10 for a fishing license and another $10 for a king-salmon tag).

Totem Bight Historical Park Tour: A bus takes you through the Tongass National Forest to this historic Native fish camp, where you can view the totem poles and a ceremonial clan house. Some tours also visit points of interest in Ketchikan (2½ hours; $39).

Rainforest Wildlife Sanctuary: After an 8-mile coastal drive, you do a half-mile hike with a naturalist guide, trying to spot eagles, bear, seals, and various birdlife. Afterward, you can feed Alaskan reindeer, watch a totem pole carver at work, and take a tour of a historic sawmill (2½ hours; $79).

Tatoosh Island Sea Kayaking: After a trip to the island by van and motorboat, you get a quick orientation before heading out on your 90-minute paddle, where you see some great scenery and (maybe) spot a few bald eagles and harbor seals (4½ hours; $125).

The Great Alaskan Lumberjack Show: Located a few blocks from the docks, the show features lumberjack types competing in logrolling, speed climbing, tree topping, chainsaw carving, and all the other skills every lumberjack needs. If you don't book this as an excursion, you can still buy tickets at the door for the same price (1½ hours; $29).

Exploring on your own

Ketchikan's downtown port area is completely flat and walkable. Pick up a walking-tour map at the **Ketchikan Visitor Information Center** on the pier. Taxis are also available at the pier if you want to go to Saxman Indian Village or Totem Bight Park on your own.

Within walking distance: Don't miss the **Southeast Alaska Discovery Center** (50 Main St., only a block from the pier; ☎ 907-228-6214), which contains an amazing series of dioramas depicting local historical, environmental, and cultural themes. Admission is $4. On a smaller scale, the one-room **Tongass Historical Museum** (629 Dock St.; ☎ 907-225-5600) focuses on the Native heritage and history of the city. Admission is $2.

The centerpiece of downtown Ketchikan is **Creek Street,** a row of quirky/quaint wooden houses built on pilings above a busy salmon stream. Once upon a not-so-long-ago time, this was the city's red-light district, with more than 30 semi-legal brothels lining the waterway. That all came to an end in the mid-1950s, and today the houses contain boutiques, restaurants, and galleries featuring the work of local artists. **Dolly's House,** at #24 (☎ 907-225-2279), preserves one of the last of the brothels, with tours costing $4. At the end of Creek Street, a **funicular** takes you uphill to the Westmark Cape Fox Lodge, which offers nice views and a small collection of Native carvings out back. Walk through the lobby and follow the signs to the **Married Men's Trail,** allegedly a route taken by local men to get to Creek Street, back in the day. It makes for a nice little hike back into town.

You can find totem poles all over town, but you can admire the biggest collection of 19th-century totem poles in the world indoors at the **Totem Heritage Center** (601 Deermount St., a bit of a hike from the lodge and town; ☎ 907-225-5900). Built by the city in 1976, the place has 33 original totems retrieved from several Native villages, kept in their original, unrestored condition, sometimes with moss still attached. Traditionally, totem poles are meant to disintegrate naturally, usually lasting about 70 years, but these were preserved to help keep the culture alive. Admission is $4.

Beyond walking distance: The Alaska Division of Parks maintains **Totem Bight State Historical Park** (☎ 907-247-8574), about 10 miles outside of town on the North Tongass Highway (a short walk through the woods is involved), for the preservation of Tlingit totem poles, clan house, and other artifacts, carved beginning in 1938 as part of a New Deal/Civilian Conservation Corps project for Native craftsmen. Admission is free.

Visitors can also view Native artifacts at **Saxman Totem Park** (☎ **907-225-4846;** www.capefoxtours.com), located about 2½ miles south of Ketchikan on the South Tongass Highway in the Saxman Native Village. The place is really set up more for people on excursions (see "Scoring the best excursions," earlier in this section), but you can also see totem poles and the carving studio without joining a tour, using a pamphlet that costs $1.50 (note, however, that interpretive materials are scant compared to those at Totem Bight).

Sitka

Sitka is our favorite port in Southeast Alaska, with a perfect blend of a gorgeous location, genuinely fascinating historical attractions, and a neighborly small-city vibe that hasn't been touristed out of existence. (Main reason for that? Sitka isn't on the Inside Passage, sitting instead on the Pacific coast of Baranof Island, sheltered by a fringe of out islands. Big ships have to go all the way around to reach it, and then bring passengers in by tender — so not too many do.)

History is the big draw here. The rich, powerful, and sophisticated Kiksadi Tlingit clan called this part of Baranof Island home for centuries, but in 1799, the Russians arrived, intent on extending their trade empire. War flared, with the Tlingit initially getting the upper hand, but by 1804 they'd been forced from the town area. From then until the American purchase of Alaska in 1867, Sitka was the capital of Russia in the New World.

Cruising into port

Most passengers arrive in Sitka by tender because the harbor is too small to accommodate large ships. Tenders drop you right in the downtown area, where small ships can also dock. Maps are available at the volunteer-staffed visitor information desk at **Harrigan Centennial Hall,** which also houses the Isabel Miller Museum and the auditorium where the New Archangel Dancers perform. The other docking facility is at the nearby O'Connell Bridge, where you can pick up maps from a volunteer at the information kiosk (mornings only). Map boards are located near both docking facilities. You can take a free shuttle bus around town, though the downtown area begins right at the water.

Scoring the best excursions

Sitka Historical Tour: On this bus tour, you visit the city's main historical attractions, including St. Michael's Cathedral, the Russian Cemetery, Castle Hill, and Sitka's National Historic Park with its totem poles and forest trails. The tour is often combined with a performance by the New Archangel Dancers and/or a visit to the Alaska Raptor Rehabilitation Center (3 hours; $40–$50).

Sea Otter and Wildlife Quest: For a chance to spot wildlife ranging from otters to bears, visit Salisbury Sound by jet boat, with a naturalist along

Sitka

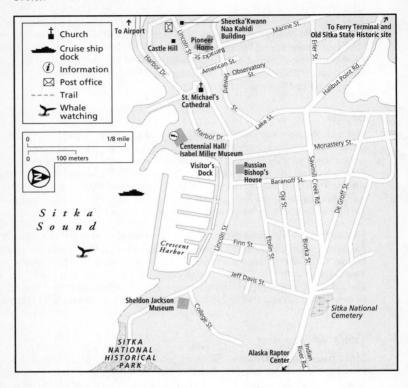

who explains the area's marine ecosystem and points out critters along the way (3 hours; $105).

Sport-Fishing: An experienced captain guides your fully equipped boat to a good spot for halibut and salmon; the rest is up to you. Your catch can be frozen or smoked and shipped to your home, if you wish (4 hours; $179 plus $10 for a fishing license and another $10 for a king-salmon tag).

Exploring on your own

Sitka is easy to explore on your own. Maps are available at the **Centennial Hall** (see "Cruising into port" above).

Within walking distance: You can't miss **St. Michael's Cathedral,** sitting right in the center of town and adorned with a striking onion-shaped dome. Though originally built in the 1840s by Russian bishop Innocent Veniaminov, the current structure is actually an exact replica, the first church having burned to the ground in 1966. Sitkans saved the icons, paintings, and other treasures, though, which you can see after you drop $2 in the collection box.

Bishop Innocent's 1842 home, called (duh) the **Russian Bishop's House** (☎ **907-747-6281**), is located a few blocks east at Lincoln and Monastery Streets. A fascinating place, it's owned and operated by the National Park Service, with ranger-led tours of the upstairs living quarters and a self-guided museum downstairs. Bishop Innocent was one impressive dude, an expert in architecture, carpentry (he built some of the furniture on display), ethnography, clock-making, and linguistics. Admission costs $4.

A little farther down Lincoln, on the grounds of Sheldon Jackson College, the **Sheldon Jackson Museum** (☎ **907-747-8981;** www.museums.state. ak.us) contains a fine collection of Native artifacts, from the Tlingit, Aleut, Athabascan, Haida, and Tsimshian peoples, as well as the Native peoples of the Arctic. Admission is $4.

Continue down Lincoln till you come to the **Sitka National Historical Park** (☎ **907-747-6281;** www.nps.gov/sitk). This is where, in 1804, the Tlingit made their stand against Russia, holding off imperial gunboats and Aleut mercenaries for six days before finally melting away one night after taking heavy losses. Today it's a National Historic Park, with historical and cultural exhibits indoors at the visitor center and a rain forest trail that winds along the coast of the 113-acre park, passing an amazing collection of towering totem poles. Admission is $4.

Back downtown, **Castle Hill** (up the stairs near the intersection of Lincoln and Katlian Streets) was where the first U.S. flag was raised on Alaska soil, after the U.S. and Russia held a transfer ceremony here in 1867. You get a great panoramic view of town from the top. Across the street, next to the Sitka Pioneers retirement home, the **Sheetka'Kwaan Naa Kahidi Building** (200 Katlian St.; ☎ **888-270-8687;** www.sitka tribal.com) is a modern version of a traditional Tlingit tribal house, hosting regular performances of traditional Tlingit dance. Show times are posted here and at the Centennial Hall, where another troupe, the **New Archangel Dancers,** performs traditional Russian and Ukrainian dance, with an all-woman company. Admission is $7.

 Beyond walking distance (just about): At the **Alaska Raptor Center** (1101 Sawmill Creek Blvd.; ☎ **907-747-8662;** www.alaskaraptor.org), visitors can observe owls, hawks, and bald eagles from just a few feet away. The center was opened in 1980 to treat sick or injured birds of prey (primarily eagles), and to provide an educational experience for visitors. Birds that cannot be returned to the wild are sent to zoos or housed here permanently. Admission is $12 for adults, $6 for kids under 12.

Skagway

Skagway was once a rootin' tootin', six-gun-shootin' wild west town where thousands of wanna-be prospectors played cards, slugged booze, spit tobacco juice, and generally wreaked havoc before heading up the Chilkoot Trail or the White Pass toward the Yukon, where they'd either (a) strike it rich, (b) strike out, or (c) give up and head back before ever getting to their destination.

Skagway

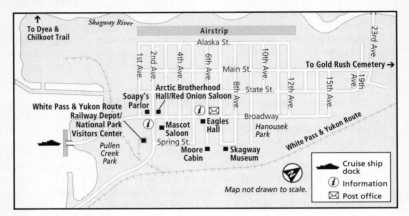

The boom eventually went bust, as booms do, but the people who remained had the good sense to recognize the historic value of their town rather than knocking it all down to "modernize." Today the whole downtown is run by the National Park Service as a historic district, but don't expect a pristine museum. Instead, most of those historic buildings house shops that sell hokey T-shirts, souvenirs, and even (eek) Starbucks coffee. It's the Gold Rush all over again, but this time the gold's in your wallet, and they want it bad.

If you're like us, you'll make a quick pass through a few of the tourist shops and then concentrate on the really worthwhile attractions, of which there are several.

Cruising into port

The cruise piers lie at the foot of Broadway or off Congress or Terminal Way. Though the docks are in sight of downtown, it's about a 20-minute walk, so take one of the frequent shuttle buses if you don't feel like hoofing it.

Scoring the best excursions

White Pass and Yukon Route Railway: From the dock, ride this famous narrow-gauge railway — complete with vintage parlor cars — past parts of the old prospectors' trail and stunning waterfalls to the **White Pass Summit,** which marks the U.S./Canadian border. Now the caveat: Don't bother going on an overcast day — you won't see anything. For that reason, you may want to try getting tickets when you get to town rather than booking the tour. Schedule info is available at www.wpyr.com (3½ hours; $97).

Dyea Ghost Town Bicycle Tour: Dyea, about 9 miles west, was established around the same time as Skagway but was abandoned completely after the Gold Rush. On this tour, you go partway by van before gearing up for a 6-mile ride through the remains of the town, past coastal tidal flats and wildflower fields (3 hours; $80).

Sled Dog Musher's Camp: An introduction to the sled-dog life, with a tour of a musher's camp, a 20-minute ride through the forest on a wheeled sled, and best of all, a chance to cuddle (awwwww!) husky pups (2¾ hours; $109).

Klondike Bicycle Tour: After vanning it to the White Pass summit, you ride down the Klondike Highway, 15 miles from peak to sea, pausing along the way for photos (2½ hours; $80).

Skagway by Streetcar: This tour makes for an entertaining theater experience. Guides in period costume (and loads of theatricality) drive you around town, telling stories about the good old days and showing you the highlights both inside and just outside town, including the old Gold Rush Cemetery. Sore feet and a high tolerance for hokum? Sign here (2 hours; $36–$40).

Exploring on your own

You can take a shuttle bus or walk pretty easily to downtown. You can find everything on the main street, Broadway, or on branches just off it. **Walking maps** describing the historic buildings and **trail maps** of the surrounding area (with hikes from 1–10 miles, departing from trailheads right in town) are available at the **Arctic Brotherhood Hall** on Broadway (between 2nd and 3rd) and at the National Historic Park Visitor Center (www.nps.gov/klgo), located next to the **White Pass & Yukon Route railroad depot,** just off the corner of 2nd and Broadway.

Within walking distance: Although you can certainly explore any of the historic downtown buildings on your own, you may want to take one of the short tours from the **Historic Park Visitor Center** (see above). Offered several times a day, these tours show you around the **White Pass & Yukon Railway Depot; Soapy's Parlor,** a preserved saloon once owned by notorious Gold Rush shyster and all-around badman Soapy Smith; the **Moore Cabin,** Skagway's original homestead; and the **Mascot Saloon,** a museum that simulates a 19th-century tavern.

Across Broadway from the visitor center, the **Arctic Brotherhood Hall** (see above) is one of the more photographed buildings in Southeast Alaska, its facade covered in thousands of pieces of driftwood. On the same block, the **Red Onion Saloon** (☎ 907-983-2222) was originally a dance hall and honky-tonk. Today, bartenders still serve drinks over the same mahogany bar they used a century ago and waitresses dress in busty period dance-hall outfits. Upstairs was once a bordello, and now offers a really interesting tour for $5, led by yet more young women in flouncy outfits. The rooms have been re-created to look as they did in the 1890s.

At the other end of town, the **Skagway Museum** (at Seventh Avenue and Spring Street; ☎ **907-983-2420**) is a very professional display offering a look at Skagway's history through artifacts, photographs, and historical records. Admission is $2. Back on Broadway, at the Eagles Hall, the old-timey *Days of '98 Show* has been playing since 1927, featuring 1890s-style dancing girls, ragtime music, a recitation of Robert Service poetry, and a reenactment of the famous shootout between bad guy Soapy Smith and good guy Frank Reid. The show is almost always offered as part of a shore excursion, but you can buy tickets at the door for $14. Two shows are scheduled during the day (10:30 a.m. and 2:30 p.m.) while ships are in port.

If you're up for a little walk, walk down Seventh then about a mile up State Street to the old **Gold Rush Cemetery,** where Smith and Reid are both buried — Reid within the cemetery, Smith just outside.

Victoria, British Columbia

Alaskan cruises that start in San Francisco or Seattle frequently call at Victoria, the capital of British Columbia. Located on Vancouver Island, this lovely little city boasts gorgeous Victorian architecture, lovely gardens, and an atmosphere that's almost more British than Britain, albeit with more evergreens.

The **Canadian dollar** (C$1.25 = US$1; C$1 = US80¢) is Canada's official currency. We quote all prices in this section in U.S. dollars.

Cruising into port

Cruise ships dock at the **Ogden Point cruise ship terminal** on Juan De Fuca Strait, about a mile southwest of the Inner Harbour and the Downtown/Old Town area, where most attractions are located.

Scoring the best excursions

City Tour and Butchart Gardens: After a quick bus tour of the city sights, a short ride out to the Saanich Peninsula takes you to the world-renowned 130-acre **Butchart Gardens** (see "Exploring on your own," below) (4 hours; $60–$65).

City Tour with High Tea and Craigdarroch Castle: After a bus tour of the major sights, this tour heads out to Craigdarroch Castle, an 1880s mansion built by a Scottish coal baron. The tour concludes with high tea at the Fairmont Empress Hotel (4 hours; $79).

Victoria Pub Crawl: Visit three of the city's finest pubs and sample its best local brews (3½ hours; $59).

Orca- and Wildlife-Watching Adventure: Sail by catamaran off southern Vancouver Island for probable sightings of killer whales, seals, and porpoises (3½ hours; $99).

Victoria, British Columbia

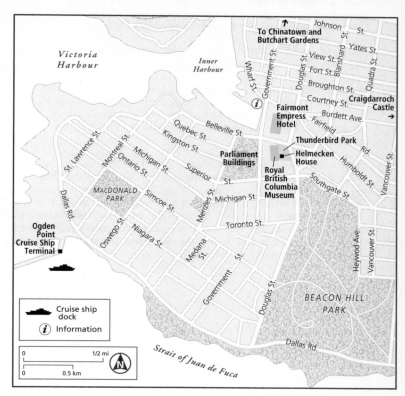

Exploring on your own

Shuttles are available from Ogden Point to the **Inner Harbor,** the center of Victoria. You can find walking maps right on the waterfront at the **Visitors Information Center** (812 Wharf St.).

Within walking distance: For afternoon tea, including perfect scones and genuine clotted cream (at a stiff $34 a head), visit the elegant **Fairmont Empress Hotel** (721 Government St.; ☎ **250-384-8111;** www. fairmont.com/empress), dating to 1908. Many shore excursions include tea here, but if you plan to go on your own, call two weeks before your cruise for reservations and be sure to follow the dress code: no sleeveless shirts, tank tops, short-shorts, or cut-offs.

Just to the east sits the **Royal British Columbia Museum** (675 Belleville St.; ☎ **888-447-7977;** http://rbcm1.rbcm.gov.bc.ca), offering exhibits highlighting British Columbia's natural history, First People's history, and Victoria's recent past. Admission is $8. Adjacent is **Thunderbird Park,** displaying totem poles and a ceremonial house. **Helmecken House** (10 Elliot St.), next to the park, was once the home of a pioneer doctor's home, and now displays some pioneering medical devices that remind you how painful life on the frontier could be.

Beyond walking distance: **Craigdarroch Castle** (1050 Joan Crescent; ☎ 250-592-5323; www.craigdarrochcastle.com) was built in the 1880s as the home of millionaire Scottish coal magnate Robert Dunsmuir. Four stories high and containing 39 rooms, it's topped with stone turrets and furnished in opulent Victoria splendor. Admission is $7.50. City bus routes 11 and 14 drop you off at the foot of Joan Crescent, a two-minute walk to the castle's doorstep, or you can get there by taxi in less than ten minutes.

For a more floral take on Victoria, visit the 130-acre **Butchart Gardens** (800 Benevenuto Ave., in Brentwood Bay; ☎ **250-652-5256;** www.butchartgardens.com), about 13 miles north of downtown Victoria on the Saanich Peninsula. Started as a beautification project by the wife of a quarry owner, it eventually became the couple's passion, and today features English, Italian, and Japanese gardens, water gardens, and rose gardens. Admission is $16. You can catch a public bus from downtown, or a cab, or visit as part of a shore excursion.

Chapter 17

Meandering in the Mediterranean

*T*he Mediterranean is a hot, hot, hot cruise destination these days. Lines sent lots of ships there for the summer 2005 season, and at press time things looked equally busy for 2006.

A Mediterranean cruise vacation appeals to people who want more than fun in the sun. Sure, you find glistening beaches with semi-nude bodies (in the French Riviera anyway) and such diversions as shopping and casinos (as in Monte Carlo). But in the Med, you also find incredible scenery, medieval ramparts, archaeological finds, and some of the best museums in the world. History lurks around every corner, and ancient sites such as Ephesus in Turkey can leave you drop-jawed. Cultural and culinary opportunities also abound; a lunch or dinner ashore is a must. The Mediterranean ports are close together, too, so you can generally visit several European countries — typically Spain, France, and Italy on a western itinerary, and Greece, Turkey, and sometimes Italy on an eastern itinerary.

Unlike Alaskan and Caribbean cruises — which, despite the rise of many alternative options, still tend to sail round-trip from a few major homeports — Mediterranean and other European cruises are mostly open-jawed: sailing from any of a dozen different port cities and ending in another. The most popular ports of embarkation and debarkation in the Mediterranean include most of those covered later in this chapter, plus Genoa, Italy, and Dover and Southampton, UK.

Another big draw of a Europe cruise is the price. With the euro sky high these days, booking a cruise and pre-paying in U.S. dollars is a great hedge against currency fluctuations. Plus, with meals and entertainment included in the cruise fare, there's no question you can spend less for a Europe vacation at sea than one on land.

When you plan a Mediterranean cruise, keep up on current events and consult with your travel agent as to possible itinerary changes in the event a volatile geopolitical situation heats up.

Hitting the Town

There's nothing like cruising into a European port; many are right in the old historic part of town. Leaning against the ship's railing, you'll have front row seats for the dramatic approach. Coming into Istanbul, for example, you'll be treated to views of the ancient minarets and domes of the shimmering Blue Mosque, the 1,500-year-old St. Sophia cathedral, and the outrageously ornate Topaki Palace. Entering Malta's Grand Harbour at a snail's pace affords breathtaking views of the honey-colored stone fortifications that rise up like ornate sand castles from the shoreline. It sure beats the view from a train!

Once you arrive, you'll want to do some exploring. You can either venture off on your own, which sometimes is the best way to handle your day, or sign up for your ship's organized tours.

Shore excursions at Mediterranean ports usually focus on educating you about the region and involve buses with English-speaking guides. As in the Caribbean and Alaska, local contractors, rather than the cruise lines, conduct the tours. Some of the more upscale and educational lines have expert lecturers that accompany shore excursions. And some lines offer tours in limos and minivans rather than in big buses.

In some countries, including Greece and Turkey, the guides must be licensed and very knowledgeable about their subject matter. Elsewhere, we have been generally impressed with the quality of the tours offered, with a few notable exceptions. We had a guide from Monaco, for example, who tried to entertain us on our way to St-Paul-de-Vence with a combination of inane commentary on the scenery ("Oh, look at the sea, isn't it blue?") and gossip about Monaco's royal family.

 The prices we list for shore excursions are for 2005 and may go up slightly in 2006. We convert admission fees to U.S. dollars.

If touring on your own, in some ports you can walk to the best sights from the docks, but in others the major attractions are some distance away. In most ports, renting a car is both a hassle and expensive, so you're better off hiring a car and driver. By getting together a small group, you can split the price of the cab and save money. Your ship's tour office can usually offer tips about taxis. In some ports, public transportation, such as buses, subways, and trains, is also an option.

 At many famed sites, such as Pompeii, you can rent audio tour headsets, so you can tour on your own and still learn something.

For touring, keep in mind that some churches, mosques, and other religious sites are more conservative than others, so both men and women should wear long pants or skirts (shorts and short skirts are a no-no) and avoid wearing sleeveless shirts.

Boarding Ship in Europe

As with cruise ship departures in the Caribbean, Alaska, and elsewhere, ships typically start boarding passengers in the early afternoon on the first day and then depart in the early evening. If you fly into the port of embarkation that day, however, the ship may allow you to board earlier — the cruise lines know people are generally exhausted after an overseas flight.

Minding Your Money

If you want to buy something at the ports in the Mediterranean, you have to exchange your dollars for local currency (on the ship, at a bank, or at a currency exchange), get money from a local ATM, or use your charge card. In most cases in the Mediterranean, the official currency is now the euro (Turkey is the exception). Trust us, this new inter-Europe currency makes buying a whole lot easier, especially for cruise travelers, because you don't have to keep switching currency for each country you visit. At press time, the euro exchange rate was US$1 = .77€ or 1€ = US$1.30. Turkey has the Turkish new lira; the exchange at press time was US$1 = 1.35 lira or 1 lira = US74¢. However, because exchange rates fluctuate, you should check an international newspaper or an online currency converter to get the most up-to-date rates. Try the handy currency calculator at www.bloomberg.com.

The French Riviera

Ahhh, what conjures up a more romantic locale? The French Riviera is the place of dreams, the **Côte d'Azur** (meaning the part of the Riviera in France), where beautiful mountains and a very blue sea combine with yachts and high culture to create a playground for the rich and famous (and for us mortal folk, too). Artists once drawn to the landscape included Matisse, Cocteau, Picasso, Leger, Renoir, and Bonnard, and their legacy remains in a host of wonderful museums. Medieval cities are within easy reach, as are numerous shopping opportunities. Cannes, Monte Carlo, Nice, St-Tropez, and Villefranche are all strung along the Riviera, and are so close together geographically that they offer nearly the same shore excursions.

Cannes is a bustling commercial center, famous for the international **Cannes Film Festival** held there every year in mid-May. The city offers

European Homeports

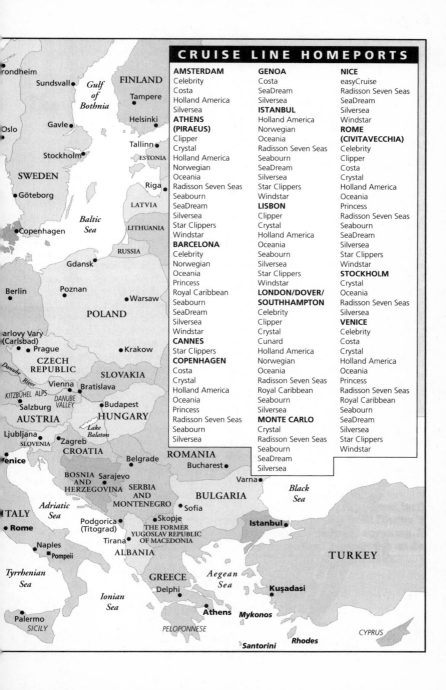

CRUISE LINE HOMEPORTS

AMSTERDAM	GENOA	NICE
Celebrity	Costa	easyCruise
Costa	SeaDream	Radisson Seven Seas
Holland America	Silversea	SeaDream
Silversea	**ISTANBUL**	Silversea
ATHENS	Holland America	Windstar
(PIRAEUS)	Norwegian	**ROME**
Clipper	Oceania	**(CIVITAVECCHIA)**
Crystal	Radisson Seven Seas	Celebrity
Holland America	Seabourn	Clipper
Norwegian	SeaDream	Costa
Oceania	Silversea	Crystal
Radisson Seven Seas	Star Clippers	Holland America
Seabourn	Windstar	Oceania
SeaDream	**LISBON**	Princess
Silversea	Clipper	Radisson Seven Seas
Star Clippers	Crystal	Seabourn
Windstar	Holland America	SeaDream
BARCELONA	Oceania	Silversea
Celebrity	Seabourn	Star Clippers
Norwegian	Silversea	Windstar
Oceania	Star Clippers	**STOCKHOLM**
Princess	Windstar	Crystal
Royal Caribbean	**LONDON/DOVER/**	Oceania
Seabourn	**SOUTHHAMPTON**	Radisson Seven Seas
SeaDream	Celebrity	Silversea
Silversea	Clipper	**VENICE**
Windstar	Crystal	Celebrity
CANNES	Cunard	Costa
Star Clippers	Holland America	Crystal
COPENHAGEN	Norwegian	Holland America
Costa	Oceania	Oceania
Crystal	Radisson Seven Seas	Princess
Holland America	Royal Caribbean	Radisson Seven Seas
Oceania	Seabourn	Royal Caribbean
Princess	Silversea	Seabourn
Radisson Seven Seas	**MONTE CARLO**	SeaDream
Seabourn	Crystal	Silversea
Silversea	Radisson Seven Seas	Star Clippers
	Seabourn	Windstar
	SeaDream	
	Silversea	

easily accessible beaches and plenty of shopping prospects. The 370-acre municipality of **Monaco** has symbolized glamour for centuries — the 1956 marriage of Prince Rainier and American actress Grace Kelly after their meeting at the Cannes film festival enhanced that renown.

Nice is nice. It really is. What was once a Victorian playground for the aristocracy is now a big middle-class city with much to offer tourists, including great art museums and shopping opportunities. Actress Brigitte Bardot made **St-Tropez** famous, and fun-in-the-sun still thrives in this artist colony. Although residents and visitors proudly uphold its reputation for hedonism (topless and even bottomless sunbathers bask at beaches outside of town), you can find some quaint mixed in. **Villefranche** is a lovely little port town that houses artists and is home to the U.S. Sixth Fleet. The quiet mood definitely changes when the fleet's in town.

Cruising into port

Only the smallest ships can dock at piers in these towns — for example, the 110-passenger SeaDream yachts and 208-passenger Seabourn ships can dock in Cannes, Monte Carlo, and Nice, and the Silversea ships can dock in Nice and Monte Carlo — otherwise you'll anchor offshore and tender in. The plus side is that the views of the Riviera are awesome from the ships' anchorages, which are never that far offshore, making for speedy jaunts into town. Many ships, including the largest ones, anchor offshore from Villefranche, and once on land, passengers are free to explore the coast. The ship and/or tender piers are all located right in town at each of the French Riviera ports, so you can walk right into the thick of things. If you don't sign up for a tour, you can take a taxi (expensive) if you want to go to another spot on the Riviera, or hop on one of the trains that run along the coastline (cheap and fun). Monte Carlo, for example, is just about a 20-minute ride from Villefranche.

Scoring the best excursions

The best way to explore the French Riviera ports is on your own. You needn't book an excursion unless you have problems with walking or you want to travel to a port other than the one your ship visits. But some outlying areas are worth exploring by tour, including the following:

St-Paul-de-Vence: This walled medieval city offers art galleries and shops, cobblestone streets, cafes, and gorgeous country views, as well as a world-renowned modern art museum, **Fondation Maeght** (4 hours; $80).

Medieval Eze: The French medieval town of Eze literally clings to the rocks above the sea. A guided walk takes you on narrow streets past lovely restored houses with stunning ocean views. Tours also allot some time for you to check out boutiques and artists' studios (3–4 hours; $45–$68).

The French Riviera

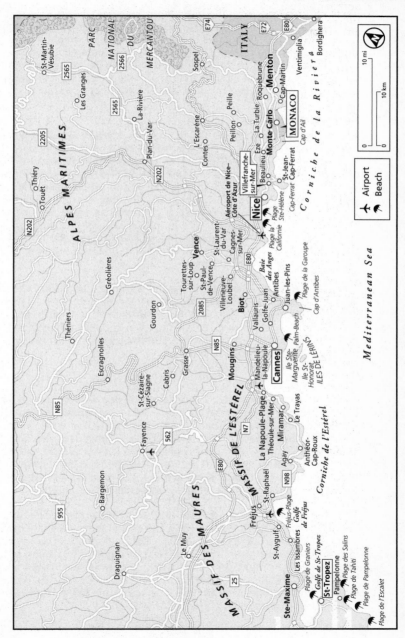

Exploring on your own

Taxis are available at all the piers, but they are expensive. (You may want to double up with other passengers if you plan to go any long distance.) You can walk from all the ports to many of the main local attractions. You can also take the great train service between cities on the Côte d'Azur, as well as the local bus service. In St-Tropez, you can rent bikes (for about $10 an hour) to get to the more daring beaches; the biggest bicycle outfitter is **Louis Mas** at 5 rue Josef-Quaranta.

Cannes, France

Within walking distance: Those glamorous grand hotels you see on television during the annual Cannes Film Festival are located on the seafront, close to the ship pier. Also within walking distance of the pier are free public beaches, including **Plage du Midi,** where exhibitionism and voyeurism are likely both in full view, and private beach areas where you pay a fee (about $18 or more) that includes the rental of a beach mattress and sun umbrella. You can shop near the pier at world-famous boutiques, including major Paris brands such as Saint Laurent, Rykiel, and Hermès, which you can find on **La Croisette,** the main drag facing the sea. More affordable, but still quite fashionable, shopping is a few blocks inland on **rue d'Antibes.**

Beyond walking distance: Across the bay from Cannes are the Lérins Islands, including **Ile Ste-Marguerite,** where the unlucky man immortalized in *The Man in the Iron Mask* was imprisoned. You can visit his cell. The island also boasts a maritime museum and nice family-run restaurants. The trip is about 15 minutes and the ferries depart every half-hour. The round-trip fare is $10.

Monte Carlo, Monaco

Within walking distance: There's nothing like a walk through Monte Carlo; you really do see playboys in sports cars zipping around the streets (when they're not hanging out in their million-dollar yachts moored in the harbor). They obviously don't have day jobs. When exploring this city, you walk up some steep hills or use the municipality's rather bizarre system of public elevators to be lifted from, say, the harbor to the casino area. Keep in mind that laws prohibit you from walking around town in swimsuits, bare-chested, or barefoot.

The **Monte Carlo Casino** at Place du Casino lets you put on your finery and play James Bond. Built in 1878, the casino is wonderfully ornate but surprisingly small. Admission is $9 to $18.50, depending on where in the casino you go, and you must show your passport. The casino admits no one under 18. At night, men must wear a jacket and tie. To get a whiff of the Monte Carlo lifestyle, check out the gazillion-dollar cars parked outside the casino. The more casual, American-style **Salle Américaine** casino (where admission is free) is next door.

Beyond walking distance: You can walk from the harbor to the city's historic area, but because the uphill hike is only for the vigorous (although the elevators help), we put it in this section. Try taking a cab uphill, and then take a walk back down.

The **Place du Palais** is the Italianate home of the Grimaldis, the royal family of Monaco. Tours of **Les Grands Appartements du Palais** include the throne room and art collection and a combined admission to a separate museum with many Napoleonic items. Admission is $8.25 for adults, $5 for children 8 to 14, and free for children under 7. At 11:55 a.m., a ten-minute changing-of-the-guard ceremony takes place outside.

The **Oceanographic Museum,** on avenue St-Martin, fascinates visitors with over 90 fish tanks that exhibit many species new to North Americans. Admission is $14 for adults, $9 for children 6 to 18, and free for children 5 and under.

Nice, France

Within walking distance: Don your designer sandals and latest bag (never, never wear your white sneakers here . . . way too gauche in these parts), and stroll from the harbor to old town, where colorful houses line narrow streets, and to the **Flower Market** area, full of outdoor cafes and great places for people-watching. (On Mondays, you can browse a wonderful antiques market here.) A few blocks inland, you find plenty of shopping opportunities for high fashion, Provencal wares, and more, especially on **rue Masséna, place Magenta,** and **rue Paradis.** You may also find it worth a trek uphill (you can use the elevator option here, too) to the old graveyard of Nice in **Le Château Park,** where both great views and lavishly sculpted monuments delight you at the top (the park is also home to a Naval museum).

Also within walking distance of the ship pier is **promenade des Anglais,** a wide boulevard stretching several miles on the bay, with beaches (where teeny bikinis rule), cafes, and historic buildings, including Victorian hotels.

Beyond walking distance: Nice boasts so many great museums that you can hardly go wrong in choosing one. But a must-see for modern art fans is **Musée Matisse,** located in a lovely setting in Cimiez on a hill above Nice. Matisse and his heirs donated all the works in the museum, which include *Nude in an Armchair with a Green Plant* and other famous paintings along with practice sketches, designs, and items from the artist's own collection and home. Admission is $5.25 for adults and $4 for children. About a 15-minute walk away, also in Cimiez, the **Musée National Message Biblique Marc-Chagall** features a collection donated by Chagall and his wife that includes oils, gouaches, drawings, pastels, lithographs, and sculptures, as well as a mosaic and stained-glass windows. A brochure is available in English to help you understand the biblical themes the artworks depict. Admission is $6.35 for adults, $4.60 for students and seniors, and free for children (rates may be higher for special exhibitions).

St-Tropez, France

Within walking distance: Family beaches, including **Plage de la Bouillabaisse** and **Plage des Graniers,** are close to the center of town. You can find good shopping at a wealth of antiques and art galleries in the city's old town. Celebrities visit here often, so keep your eyes peeled: You may bump into Oprah Winfrey or even Brad and Angelina (with *People* magazine photographers on their tails, of course). **L'Annonciade Musée St-Tropez,** at Place Georges-Grammont, is an art museum located in a former chapel with a renowned modern art collection. Admission is $6.75 for adults and $4.50 for children.

Beyond walking distance: The most daring beaches — **Plage des Salins, Plage de Pampellone,** and **Plage de Tahiti** — are located a few miles from town.

Villefranche, France

Within walking distance: This little town provides a nice setting for a walk, if you don't head into Nice (4 miles away) or Monte Carlo (about 10 miles away). Jean Cocteau left his legacy here in the form of frescoes on the 14th-century walls of the Romanesque **Chapelle St-Pierre** on Quai de al Douane/rue des Mariniéres. Admission is $3.50; closed Mondays.

Beyond walking distance: Head to nearby Nice, about 4 miles away. Check out the previous section on Nice for info on the sites.

Greece

Ancient sites and architectural treasures join forces with the sun, scenery, and food to make Greece one of the best vacation spots on Earth. Be ready for a feast for the mind and the senses, a place that is exotic but at the same time friendly and familiar, where something always reminds you of the past.

Athens

This fabled metropolis, home of the original and the 2004 Olympic Games, intersperses ancient monuments, tavernas, and neoclassical buildings with high rises, fast-food outlets, and souvenir shops, especially at the **Pláka,** the oldest continuously inhabited section of the city. The **Parthenon** and the treasures on display at the **National Archaeological Museum** best reflect the image most of us have of ancient Greece. But in reality, modern Athens is crowded, teems with taxis and cars, and is a hard place to get around. The city is also polluted and very hot during the summer. An organized tour is a good bet here. If you do spend the day on your own, check out the **Acropolis,** have lunch in the Pláka, and accept that you don't have time to see everything, so pick the places most important to you.

Cruising into port

Ships dock in **Piraeus,** located about 7 miles southwest of Athens, but the trip may seem much longer due to traffic. You can take a metro train or taxi into the city or hop the bus service that most cruise lines offer for a fee. We recommend the train, which you can walk to from the pier and ride for about $1.

Scoring the best excursions

Half-Day Athens City Tour: Includes a guided tour of the **Acropolis;** a drive past other Athens highlights, including **Constitution Square,** the **Parliament, the Temple of Zeus, Hadrian's Arch,** and **Olympic Stadium;** plus time for souvenir shopping (4 hours; $56).

Full-day Athens Tours: Full-day tours also include a visit to the National Archaeological Museum, time to shop in the Pláka, and lunch (7–9 hours; $65–$110).

Exploring on your own

If you want to take a taxi, the average meter fare from Piraeus to Syntagma Square in Athens should be around $10, but many drivers may quote a flat rate as high as $25. Try bargaining or find another taxi driver willing to turn on the meter.

Greek taxi drivers don't always accept you as a fare. They usually ask where you want to go and are free to decline if they don't want to go your way; consequently, allow a fair amount of time to find a cab. Also, a driver may stop and pick up two or three different parties to fill the cab. If this happens, you're responsible only for your leg of the journey. Also, check for a meter and for your driver's photo ID (an increasing number of gypsy cabs have found their way into the city).

Within walking distance: Piraeus is a gritty port city without the kind of ancient attractions that you find in Athens. Ship aficionados may enjoy a walk around the huge dock area, but everyone else should head into Athens.

In the summer, start out as early as possible in the morning, when the sun isn't at its strongest and the crowds aren't as overwhelming.

Beyond walking distance: For many centuries, the **Acropolis** was the religious center of Athens. At various periods, it served as the seat of a king and the "home" of gods and goddesses. Because it rests on a hilltop, you can glimpse it from many parts of the city. The most striking structures are the **Parthenon** (the most recognized Greek monument; a temple dedicated to Athena), the **Propylaea** (the gateway to the Acropolis), the

Athens

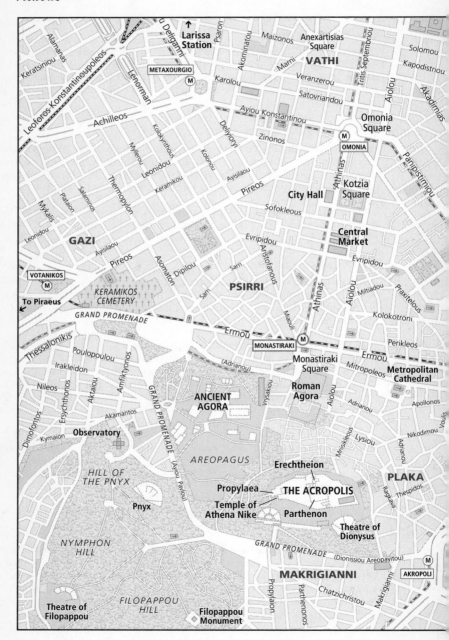

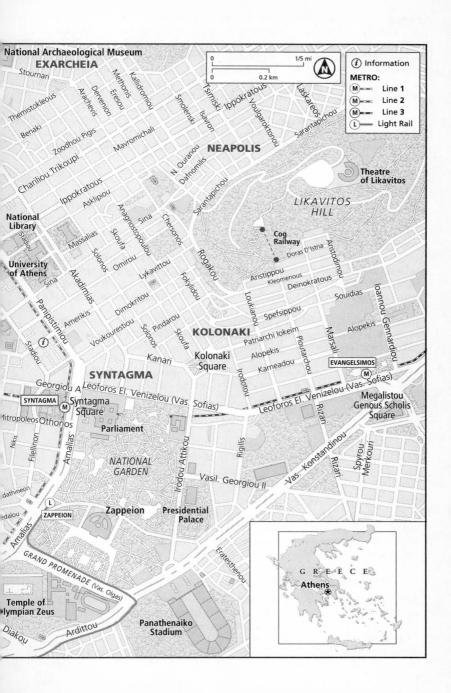

Temple of Athena Nike (built in the fifth century B.C. and restored in the 1930s), and the **Erechtheion** (the main temple, divided into two sections — one devoted to Athena and the other to Poseidon). You can't enter the Parthenon for preservation and restoration reasons. Admission to the Acropolis complex is $14 for adults, $7.50 for students, and free for kids under age 18 (includes same-day admission to the Acropolis Museum and the National Archeological Museum); free on Sundays.

The **National Archeological Museum** has one of the richest collections of ancient Greek art in the world and was renovated for the 2004 Olympics. Admission is $8.75 for adults, $5.25 for students, and free for kids under age 18.

Mykonos

Think picture-postcard perfect. **Hora,** Mykonos's main town, dazzles with white-washed homes, their doors and window frames painted brightly, and a harbor lined with fishing boats. Pelicans, the mascots of Mykonos, greet you at the pier, and as you explore the cobblestone streets you encounter windmills, outdoor cafes, and small churches with blue domes, all within easy walking distance of the pier. It's a very quaint atmosphere, despite the large numbers of sun-seekers, the town's well-deserved party reputation (especially in July and Aug), and the inevitable souvenir shops.

Unlike other Greek islands that cruise ships visit, Mykonos has no ancient ruins. Passengers starving for sacred sites of note can catch a shore excursion to nearby **Delos,** the birthplace of Apollo.

Mykonos is the best place for diving in the Aegean, especially in September. The most well-established diving center is at **Psarou Beach** (☎ and fax **30-22890-24-808**).

Cruising into port

Your ship's tender delivers you to the main harbor area along the Esplanade in Hora right in the center of things.

Scoring the best excursions

Delos Apollo Sanctuary: Travel by small boat from Mykonos harbor to Delos for a two-hour guided walking tour of this tiny island that once served as the religious and commercial hub of the Aegean Sea. Now the sanctuary is home only to ancient ruins and their caretakers. Also visit the Archaeological Museum (4 hours; $60).

Exploring on your own

The central bus station is located off the left of the harbor, and the bus service is quite good, heading to all the beaches. Still, the best way to get around town is to walk. Or, you can choose from two types of taxis. The standard cab, which you can find at Taxi (Mavro) Square, can take you outside of town. A notice board at the square displays rates. Smaller

The Greek Isles

scooter taxis with a cart for passengers also zip through the narrow streets of Hora — you find them at the pier.

Within walking distance: Hora is the main attraction here. The best activity is to simply wander. You can browse in plenty of art galleries and souvenir shops (some may say too many), and this is a great place to sit at a cafe and people-watch. You can also stop by the **Archaeological Museum** near the harbor to view finds from Delos. Admission is $3.25 for adults, $1.25 for students, and free for those under 18 and for all on Sunday.

Mykonos Town

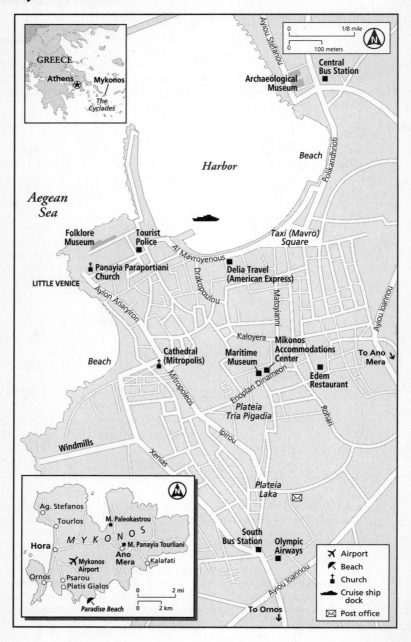

GREECE

Athens ✪ ⎯ Mykonos

The Cyclades

Ayiou Stefanou

Archaeological Museum

Central Bus Station

0   1/8 mile
0   100 meters

N

Harbor

Beach

Polikandhrioti

Aegean Sea

Folklore Museum

Tourist Police

Taxi (Mavro) Square

✝ Panayia Paraportiani Church

Al Mavroyenous

Delia Travel (American Express)

LITTLE VENICE

Ayion Anayiron

Drakopoulou

Matoyianni

Ayiou Ioannou

Kaloyera

Mikonos Accommodations Center

Beach

Cathedral (Mitropolis)

Maritime Museum

To Ano Mera

Mitropoleos

Enoplan Dinameon

Edem Restaurant

Plateia Tria Pigadia

Rohari

Ipirou

Windmills

Xenias

Plateia Laka

⊠

South Bus Station

Olympic Airways

Ayiou Ioannou

To Ornos

Ag. Stefanos

Tourlos

M. Paleokastrou

M Y K O N O S

Hora

✈ Mykonos Airport

M. Panayia Tourliani

Ano Mera

Kalafati

Ornos

Psarou

Platis Gialos

0   2 mi
0   2 km

Paradise Beach

✈ Airport
⚓ Beach
✝ Church
⛴ Cruise ship dock
⊠ Post office

Check out the local cuisine at **Edem** restaurant in Hora (follow the signposts off Matoyanni Street, near the Panahrandou church; ☎ **0289-22-855**). The food is tasty and the service is great.

Beyond walking distance: About 4 miles east of Hora lies Mykonos's second town, **Ano Mera,** which has a more traditional ambience and some religious sites of note. The **Monastery of Panayia Tourliani** dates to 1580 and has a handsomely carved steeple, as well as a small religious museum inside. You can also visit the 12th-century **Monastery of Paleokastro** nearby.

Rhodes

Imagine that the Colossus of Rhodes, the giant bronze statue of sun god Helios, towered over the very same harbor that now welcomes cruise ships. Wow. Rich in history, Rhodes is blessed with beautiful beaches, mountain villages, and fertile plains. The island's most famous inhabitants were the Knights of St. John, who came in 1291 after fleeing Jerusalem. They reigned for more than two centuries, and their treasures remain within the medieval walls of the old town of Rhodes (the city shares its name with the island). Lindos, a picturesque village about 50 minutes from Rhodes city, boasts the **Acropolis at Lindos,** which rises about 400 feet above a beautiful bay (though the beauty can be somewhat diminished on days the place gets terribly crowded).

Cruising into port

Ships dock at the commercial harbor, which is within walking distance of Rhodes's old section. The new town is also within walking distance, but the old town offers more sights of interest.

Scoring the best excursions

Rhodes and Lindos: Travel by bus through the scenic countryside to Lindos, a medieval walled city with a history that dates to ancient times. Walk or take a donkey up to the ancient Acropolis to see ruins and great views (you pass souvenir shops on the way). The trip may include a walking tour of old town Rhodes; a stop at a workshop selling Rhodian ceramics; and/or a visit to the ruins of ancient Rhodes, the Temple of Apollo, and Diagoras Stadium (4–4½ hours; $50–$65).

Exploring on your own

The best way to explore both the old and new sections of Rhodes is on foot. If you want to see other parts of the island, you can find taxis at the end of the pier. Negotiate fares with taxi drivers for sightseeing. Public buses are also available.

Within walking distance: The **old town of Rhodes** is the oldest medieval town in Europe and offers plenty of beauty. Be forewarned, though: You can easily get lost in the maze of streets (few of which have names). The 15th-century **Hospital of the Knights,** now home of the

Rhodes Town

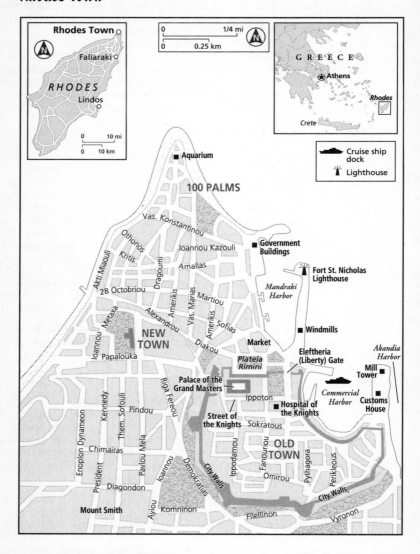

Archaeological Museum, features fine works from the Mycenaean and Roman eras. Admission is $12 for adults, $6.75 for students, and free for kids under 18 (this price also includes admission into three other local museums). Stroll the cobblestone **Street of the Knights** (*Ippoton* on the maps) to see medieval inns that served as clubs and meeting places for the multinational Knights of St. John; their facades mirror the architecture of the various countries the knights came from.

The famous **Colossus of Rhodes,** a 100-foot-tall bronze statue of the sun god Helios, considered one of the Seven Wonders of the Ancient World, was erected somewhere on **Mandraki Harbor** — legend says that it straddled the harbor. Nothing remains of the statue today.

You can find plenty of places to stop for a bite in old town and new town; seafood restaurants are your best bet. One of the best is **Alexis Taverna** (Odos Sokratous 18, in old town; ☎ **0241-29-347**), where the likes of Winston Churchill and Jackie O once dined. Dinners run about $60 per person, and reservations are recommended.

Beyond walking distance: Rhodes is also known for its great beaches, many of which lie on the east coast. **Faliaraki,** about 20 minutes from Rhodes, is one of the most popular.

If you want to visit **Lindos,** you should book a shore excursion (Lindos is 50 minutes away from Rhodes, and the excursion guarantees that you get back in time), though be prepared for mucho crowds if you're there in July or August.

Santoríni

Whitewashed homes, black-pebble beaches, rich vineyards, and ancient ruins dot one of the most breathtaking islands in the world: Santoríni. Approaching its volcanic cliffs by sea is a dramatic experience. Ships enter the *caldera,* a central crater formed when a volcano erupted in 1500 B.C. Ash fell on the remaining land, burying the ancient city of Akrotiri — an event that some believe may have sparked the legend of Atlantis.

Fira, the capital, perches about 1,000 feet above sea level. Along its winding streets, you find shops, cafes, and art galleries. **Ia,** about 10 to 15 minutes away by cab, is a quiet and picturesque artist colony.

Cruising into port

The ship's tender takes you to the port of **Skala,** where you have three options to reach Fira: donkey, cable car, or foot.

Scoring the best excursions

Akrotiri Excavations and Fira Town: This tour takes you to Akrotiri, an excavation site that dates back to the second millennium B.C. After the tour, you have time to explore Fira and make your own way back to the ship (3 hours; $60–$70).

Village of Oia and Winery: Walk on the picturesque narrow cobblestone streets of the small village of Oia, perched on a cliff. Stop at a local winery in a nearby village for a tasting. The tour ends in Fira (4 hours; $60).

Santoríni

Exploring on your own

From Skala, the donkey and cable car rides to the top cost about $5 each way. The walk up the 587 steps is the same route the donkeys take. Word to the wise: Donkeys are fed at the bottom of the hill, so they tend to run down whether carrying someone or not. They also smell. Donkey rides take about 20 to 30 minutes depending on traffic and availability. Cable cars run every 20 minutes; walking takes about 30 minutes (depending on the individual).

You can easily explore the town of Fira on foot, and you can take taxis (not cheap and not always easy to find) or buses to other parts of the island. If you hike regularly, you may want to try the 6.2-mile pedestrian path from Fira to Ia that follows the edge of the caldera and offers stunning views. Along the way, you pass several churches and climb two substantial hills.

Within walking distance: Fira offers shops and art galleries. If your ship stays late enough in port, watch the sunset from a cafe for a classic

Greek Isles experience. In addition, Fira has one of the best restaurants in Greece: **Selene,** located in the passageway between the **Atlantis** and **Aressana Hotels** (☎ **22860-22-249**). Local produce is the star, with main courses ranging from $10 to $18; reservations are suggested. (The restaurant also offers cooking classes that start at 10:30 a.m. and conclude with lunch at 2 p.m.)

Beyond walking distance: **Ia** is quieter than Fira and offers charming homes and galleries that showcase modern and folk art and traditional handicrafts. To visit Ancient **Akrotiri,** located about 5 miles from Fira, we recommend that you take a shore excursion with a guide to get expert commentary.

You want to explore the excavation at Akrotiri in the morning because its enclosing metal shed magnifies the afternoon heat.

Italy

If you ask ten people to name their favorite country in Europe, chances are eight or nine of them are going to say Italy — a beautiful and diverse country with an incredible cultural heritage. You can eat great food, talk to friendly people, shop for the latest fashions, see some of the ancient world's most famous ruins (such as the **Forum** in Rome and the ancient city of **Pompeii**), immerse yourself in the Renaissance in **Florence,** and be part of living history in **Venice.**

This is the land of Leonardo (da Vinci, not DiCaprio) and Michelangelo, of caesars and popes. And whether you feel drawn by the art, incredible architecture, religious significance, gorgeous scenery, wonderful pasta, or all of the above, Italy delivers your heart's desires.

Civitavecchia and Rome

The name Civitavecchia probably has you shaking your head wondering *Civita-who?* But Civitavecchia has actually served as the port of Rome since A.D. 108. Cruise ships shuttle passengers from here to Rome, about 90 minutes away. Rome, of course, is Italy's largest city, where you find incomparable sights such as the **Vatican** and the **Forum,** as well as other cultural opportunities, diverse restaurants, and great shopping.

Cruising into port

Ships pull alongside the docks in Civitavecchia, though don't expect to be bowled over. You're not in Rome, remember.

Scoring the best excursions

In addition to the following recommended excursion, most ships offer a bus transfer, for $55 to $70, allowing you easy transportation to explore Rome on your own. Some also offer the option of a half-day tour followed by a half-day on your own for $75 to $92.

Rome

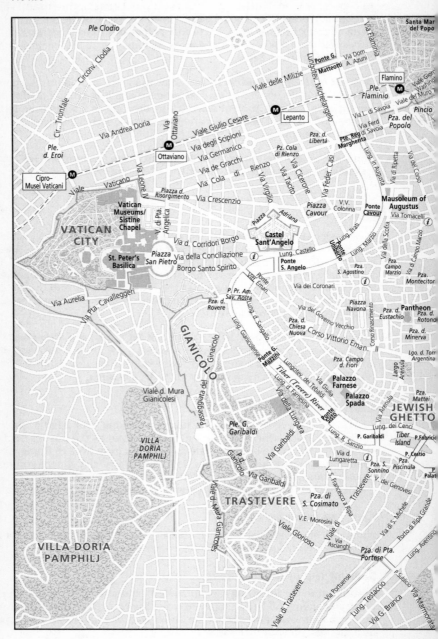

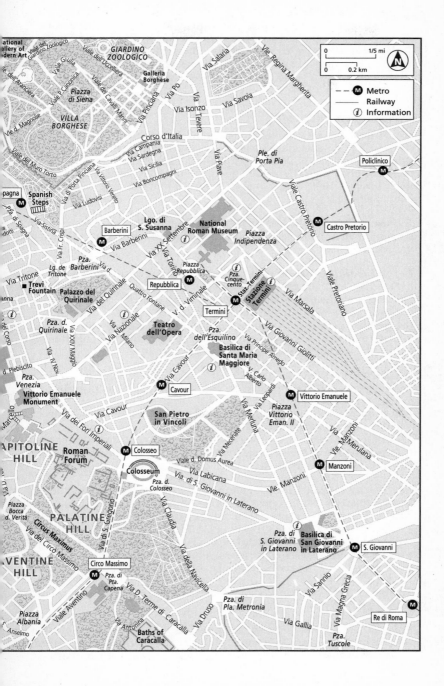

Rome City Tour: This comprehensive excursion includes a visit to the **Colosseum, St. Peter's Basilica,** the **Vatican Museum,** and the **Sistine Chapel.** The driver also passes such landmarks as the **Roman Forum, Trajan's Column,** the **Arch of Constantine,** and the **Circus Maximus.** The tour may also include a short walk to see **Trevi Fountain** and definitely includes lunch and time to shop for souvenirs (9½–10½ hours; about $180).

Exploring on your own

From the pier, you can take a 15-minute walk or 5-minute cab ride into the town of Civitavecchia. Taxis are usually available at the pier, and the ride to Rome is about 90 minutes. You can also take a train, and the ride takes about an hour (depending on the time of day, service is hourly or twice hourly); Heidi's done this and found it much more pleasant than a long bus ride.

Within walking distance: We highly recommend taking a shore excursion to Rome or going to Rome on your own because you can't see much in Civitavecchia.

Beyond walking distance: In Rome, the **Basilica di San Pietro** (St. Peter's Basilica), the earthly locus of the Roman Catholic Church, is amazing both inside and out and well worth a visit. The church is magnificent and so is the square on which it stands. Admission is free to the basilica; getting to the dome costs $4 by stairs, $5 by elevator; and guided tours of St. Peter's Tomb (children under 15 aren't admitted) are about $10. During the summer, be prepared for lines.

Women visiting the Vatican must wear pants or skirts that cover their knees. Men cannot wear shorts. No one is allowed to wear sleeveless tops.

American priests studying in Rome offer excellent, free tours of the Basilica. The tours last about two hours and are highly informative about the architecture and the religious significance of various parts of the area. Inquire at the Vatican Tourist Office (in the building to the left when you face the Basilica).

Nearby, the **Vatican Museum** and the **Sistine Chapel** are where the Vatican displays its gigantic collection of treasures. The museum is massive, so you need to choose a route based on four color-coded itineraries, which range from 1½ to 5 hours. All four itineraries culminate in the Sistine Chapel, where Michelangelo labored for four years (1509–12) to paint the famous ceiling frescoes. Admission is normally $14.50 and free for everyone the last Sunday of each month (be ready for a crowd).

The best way to view the Sistine Chapel's ceiling is to bring along binoculars.

Rome boasts so many other must-see sights that choosing among them is hard, but try to catch a glimpse of the **Roman Forum,** the **Colosseum,** and the **Pantheon.** A must-do stop for many is the **Trevi Fountain,** a lavish Baroque creation; according to legend, if you toss in a coin, you'll return to Rome (you may have to make your way through crowds to get close enough to drop your money, however). The famous **Spanish Steps** take their name from the Spanish Embassy, which used to be headquartered at the site. The steps are always packed with crowds of people browsing the carts of the flower and jewelry vendors or just people-watching. Shoppers also love the neighborhood, so check out the posh shops on **Via Borgognona** and **Via Condotti.** For a less-expensive alternative, head to **Via Sistina** and **Via Francesco Crispi.**

Venice

As beautiful as you could imagine, this old city of canals and narrow streets is in a category by itself. Even on a crowded August day, the place is special, and you can still find a quiet, quaint alleyway to explore, away from the hordes. Built at the waterline, spectacular Venice rises straight out of the Gulf of Venice. Everywhere you look in this living museum you see something artistic or otherwise fascinating, including amazing numbers of Gothic and Renaissance structures and construction projects aimed at stopping buildings from sinking into the sea.

Be prepared to get lost exploring the city's mazelike frenzy of canals, side streets, and medieval bridges — scratching your head is part of the fun. But don't worry; you can't get too lost because yellow signs everywhere point you to major landmarks such as **St. Mark's Square** and the **Rialto Bridge.**

Getting out on the **Grand Canal,** a watery version of a main city boulevard, is a must-do, whether you take the touristy route of paying for a gondola (negotiate up front with the driver and expect to pay through the nose) or an equally overpriced water taxi. You can also do like the Venetians: ride a *vaporetto* (water bus). Any way you go, you pass historic buildings, ornate bridges, and waterfront palaces, and you share the waterway with ambulance boats, delivery barges, and other vessels reminding you that the canal is the byway for ordinary life in Venice — the city has no cars (or streets wide enough to drive on).

Venice also has a treasure trove of paintings, statues, and frescoes in its churches and palaces. Check out the cafes and shops, with their glassware and wonderful Italian design items (including designer clothes).

Cruising into port

Ships generally dock at terminals about 15 to 20 minutes by boat from St. Mark's Square, though some of the small ships, like the SeaDream yachts, dock right in the downtown area.

Scoring the best excursions

Venice City Sightseeing: Take a motor launch to St. Mark's Square for a guided walking tour of **St. Mark's Cathedral** and a visit to **Doge's Palace,** the former residence of the Duke of Venice. The itinerary also includes

Venice

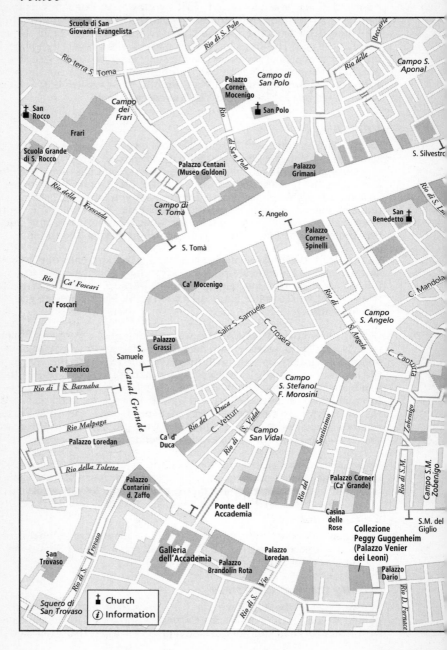

Scuola di San Giovanni Evangelista

Rio di S. Polo

Rio delle

Beccarie

Campo S. Aponal

Rio terra S. Toma

Rio delle

Campo di San Polo

Palazzo Corner Mocenigo

San Polo

Campo dei Frari

Rio

San Rocco

di San Polo

S. Silvestro

Frari

Scuola Grande di S. Rocco

Palazzo Centani (Museo Goldoni)

Palazzo Grimani

Rio di S. Lu

Rio della Frescada

Campo di S. Tomà

S. Angelo

San Benedetto

S. Tomà

Palazzo Corner-Spinelli

Rio

Ca' Foscari

Ca' Mocenigo

Rio di

C. Mandola

Ca' Foscari

Saliz S. Samuele

C. Crosera

Campo S. Angelo

S. Angelo

C. Caoturta

Palazzo Grassi

S.
Samuele

Ca' Rezzonico

Rio di S. Barnaba

Canal Grande

Rio del Duca

C. Vetturi

Campo S. Stefano/ F. Morosini

Rio Malpaga

Ca' d'
Duca

Rio di

S. Vidal

Campo San Vidal

Santissimo

Palazzo Loredan

Rio della Toletta

Zobenigo

Palazzo Contarini d. Zaffo

Palazzo Corner (Ca' Grande)

Rio del

Rio di S.M.

Campo S.M. Zobenigo

Ponte dell' Accademia

Casina delle Rose

S.M. del Giglio

San Trovaso

Galleria dell'Accademia

Palazzo Brandolin Rota

Palazzo Loredan

Collezione Peggy Guggenheim (Palazzo Venier dei Leoni)

Palazzo Dario

Rio di S. Vio

Squero di San Trovaso

‡ Church

ⓘ Information

Rio D. Fornace

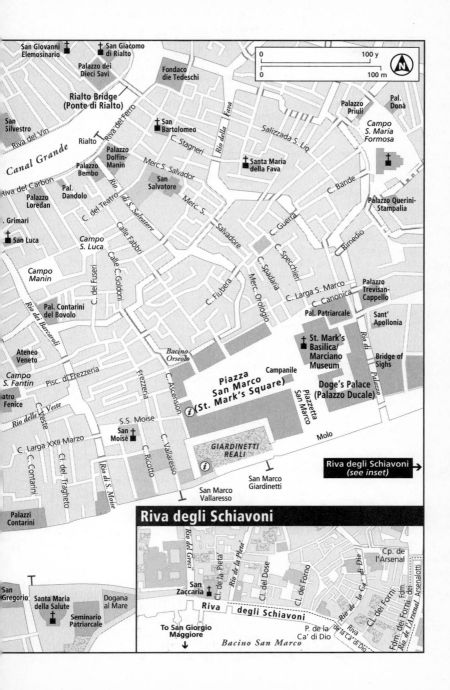

San Giovanni Elemosinario

† San Giacomo di Rialto

Palazzo dei Dieci Savi

Rialto Bridge (Ponte di Rialto)

Fondaco die Tedeschi

Palazzo Priuli

Pal. Donà

San Silvestro

Riva del Vin

Canal Grande

Rialto

Riva del Ferro

† San Bartolomeo

C. Stagneri

Salizzada S. Lio

Campo S. Maria Formosa

Palazzo Dolfin-Manin

Palazzo Bembo

Merc S. Salvador

Rio della Fava

† Santa Maria della Fava

Riva del Carbon

Pal. Dandolo

San Salvatore

Merc. S.

C. Bande

Palazzo Loredan

Rio d. S. Salvatore

Palazzo Querini-Stampalia

. Grimari

† San Luca

Campo S. Luca

C. del Teatro

Calle Fabbri

Salvadore

C. Guerra

Rimedio

Campo Manin

Calle C. Goldoni

C. dei Fuseri

C. Fijbera

Merc. Orologio

C. Spadaria

C. Specchieri

C. Larga S. Marco

C. Canonica

Palazzo Trevisan-Cappello

Sant' Apollonia

Pal. Contarini del Bovolo

Rio dei Barcaroli

Pal. Patriarcale

Rio di

Ateneo Veneto

Bacino Orseolo

† St. Mark's Basilica/ Marciano Museum

Bridge of Sighs

Campo S. Fantin

Pisc. di Frezzeria

Frezzeria

C. Ascension

Piazza San Marco (St. Mark's Square)

Campanile

Piazzetta San Marco

Doge's Palace (Palazzo Ducale)

Palazzo

atro Fenice

Rio delle Veste

S.S. Moise

San Moisè †

C. Vallaresso

GIARDINETTI REALI

Molo

Riva degli Schiavoni (see inset) →

C. Larga XXII Marzo

Cl. Contarini

Cl. del Traghetto

Rio di S. Moise

C. Ricotto

San Marco Vallaresso

San Marco Giardinetti

Palazzi Contarini

Riva degli Schiavoni

Rio dei Greci

Cl. de la Pietà

Rio de la Pietà

Cl. de Dose

Cl. del Forno

Cp. de l'Arsenal

San Gregorio

Santa Maria della Salute

Dogana al Mare

Seminario Patriarcale

San Zaccaria

Riva degli Schiavoni

Rio de la Ca' di Dio

Rio de la Ca' di Dio

Fdm. dei Forni

Fdm. dell'Arsenale

Fdm. dell'Arsenale Arsenalotti

To San Giorgio Maggiore ↓

P. de la Ca' di Dio

Bacino San Marco

0   100 y
0   100 m
N

the **Golden Staircase,** where you can enjoy the views of St. Mark's Basin. You also cross the famous **Bridge of Sighs** and stop at the small workshops of glass manufacturers (3 hours; $50–$99).

The Grand Canal and the Inside Canal: Travel by motorboat with a guide to find out how the city works — the police, fire brigade, even wedding and funeral processions travel by boat. From the water, you get a wonderful view of St. Mark's Square and other sights, including palaces and the **Guggenheim Museum.** You also go under the famous **Rialto Bridge** (2½ hours; $90–$110).

Evening Gondola Ride with Serenade: It may sound hokey, but we think you'll find something magical about exploring the canals of this romantic city on these black pointy vessels, with a gondolier singing in Italian (2 hours; $105).

Exploring on your own

Assuming your ship isn't docked right in the downtown, you'll have to take a boat to get to St. Mark's Square and the heart of Venice. Your choices are taking the ship's arranged boats, a private water taxi (which is pricey), or a public water bus called a *vaporetto* (which is cheap).

Within walking distance: Take a boat to **St. Mark's Square.** From there, you can walk to the rest of the attractions that we list here. The square is the cultural hub of the city, and you can easily spend hours here watching people feed the pigeons, sitting with the fashionable in a cafe, visiting the **Basilica** and **Doge's Palace,** and shopping. As a tourist hub, however, the square is very crowded during the day, particularly in the summer high season. To avoid the crowds, go in the early morning or in the evening. At night, you may catch free musical performances by chamber orchestras and other groups.

St. Mark's Basilica, located on the square, is nicknamed the "Church of Gold" and is one of the most elaborate churches in the world. You can see the Basilica's dome as your ship moves down the Grand Canal. The **Marciano Museum** contains the Triumphal Quadriga — four famous horse statues looted from Constantinople by Venetian crusaders in 1204. Admission to the Basilica is free, treasury $2.50, presbytery $2, and Marciano Museum $2.

Men and women are banned from wearing shorts or exposing bare arms or shoulders in the Basilica, and women may not wear skirts above the knee. Silence is required, and no photos are allowed.

Near the **bell tower of St. Mark's** (which at press time wasn't open to visitors wanting the bird's-eye view from the top), is **Palazzo Ducale** (Doge's Palace), Italy's grandest civic structure. Admission is $13 for adults, $6 for students, $4 for children 6 to 13, and free for kids under 5.

You can shop right on the square and on the streets between the square and the Rialto Bridge. A favorite shopping street is Salizzida San Moisé, where you find designer shops such as Prada. Generally, the farther away from St. Mark's you go, the more reasonable the prices.

Beyond walking distance: A must-see attraction for lovers of modern art is the **Collezione Peggy Guggenheim,** located in a waterfront palazzo on the other side of the canal from St. Mark's (you can get there by water taxi or water bus, or take a long walk, crossing at the Ponte dell' Accademia bridge). The impressive palazzo, which was art patron Mrs. Guggenheim's home, houses works by Pollock, Ernst, Picasso, Braque, Magritte, Duchamp, Chagall, Mondrian, Brancusi, Dalí, Giacometti, Moore, and others. Admission is $9.50 for adults and $6.50 for students and children 16 and under.

Near the Ponte dell'Accademia bridge is the **Galleria dell'Accademia,** a museum where the glory of old Venice lives on in a remarkable collection of paintings from the 14th to the 18th centuries. Admission is $7 for adults, $4 for students, and free for children 12 and under.

Portugal

First off, we know that Portugal isn't on the Mediterranean. Even so, the country's capital city, **Lisbon,** is the starting point for some Mediterranean itineraries.

Lisbon is Europe's smallest capital, but it gives the impression of a cosmopolitan city, boasting seven hills and a pleasing combination of history, cultural arts, modern amenities, and visual treats. Some areas may remind some visitors of Paris (with street painters and the like), others of hilly San Francisco, and still others — such as the old Moorish Alfama section — of a small, colorful town. Lisbon is a walking city, and you can easily get around, although the hills may prove challenging to some.

Cruising into port

Cruise ships dock at the Port of Lisbon, about 15 minutes by car from the city center.

Scoring the best excursions

Lisbon City Tour: Ride by bus around Lisbon to see a number of city highlights, including **Avenida da Liberdade,** with its mosaic-lined sidewalks and the magnificent views of the River Tagus at **Black Horse Square.** Tour the impressive **Jerónimos Monastery.** Also visit the **National Coach Museum** or the **Convent of Madre de Deus,** founded in 1509, which contains samples of religious architecture (3½ hours; $44–$60).

Sintra and Estoril: This tour along the famous and scenic Estoril coast includes such memorable highlights as **Sintra** — a serene historic resort nestled in the forested hills of Serra de Sintra and the summer residence of kings and nobility. Continue inland to **Queluz** to tour the magnificent

Lisbon

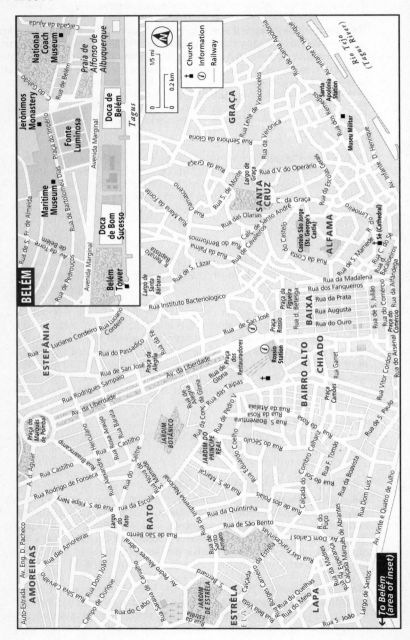

18th-century palace built in the style of Versailles. Some tours also include the well-known seaside resort of **Cascais** (4 hours; $44–$64).

Fatima and Batalha: Located 100 miles from Lisbon is the place known to Roman Catholics as the "Lourdes of Portugal." At Fatima, according to legend, three young shepherds in 1917 claimed they saw the Virgin Mary in an oak tree. Lunch is served at a local restaurant or hotel. The tour continues on to Batalha for a visit to the impressive gothic church of **Santa Maria da Victoria** (8–9 hours; $72–$130).

Exploring on your own

Taxis (usually diesel-engine Mercedes) are generally available outside the terminal building to take you into the city center. The ride to the central sightseeing and shopping districts is between $8 and $12. Traffic can be congested, so give yourself extra time. The city also has a good bus and tram service, as well as a subway, to get around. A *funicular* (elevator) connects the **Baixa** area, where you find shopping (between the Rossio, which is the city's main square, and the River Tagus), with the **Bairro Alto,** where you find nightlife.

Within walking distance: You need to take a taxi to the Alfama, the Belém area, and other sights.

Beyond walking distance: Houses in the alleys of the old **Alfama** district are so close together that you can't stretch your arms fully in some places. Visit the 12th-century **Sé** (cathedral), check out the goods at the markets, and climb up to the **Castelo São Jorge** (St. George's Castle) to enjoy the views. The fortress predates the Romans, and the Moors erected many of the walls that still stand. On the grounds, you may encounter a swan or rare white peacock. Admission is free.

Belém, where the River Tagus meets the sea, is where Portuguese explorers such as Magellan launched their missions. **Belém Tower** is a 16th-century monument to Portugal's age of discovery and its famous seafarers. Admission is $4 for adults, $2.25 for children, and free for seniors. Nearby **Jerónimos Monastery,** built in 1502, stands as a masterpiece of Manueline architecture. Admission to the church is free; admission to the secluded monastery is $4.25 adults, $2.50 students, and free for children and seniors. The **Maritime Museum,** located in the Jerónimos Monastery's west wing, is one of the most important of its kind in Europe. It contains hundreds of ship models, ranging from 15th-century sailing ships to 20th-century warships. Admission is $4 for adults, $2.25 for students, and free for seniors and children under 9.

Spain

Spain offers fascinating history, pretty beaches, Moorish palaces, quaint villages, and, of course, Picasso. But you also feel the beat of the country's modern-day vitality. Spain began to change with the death of

Barcelona

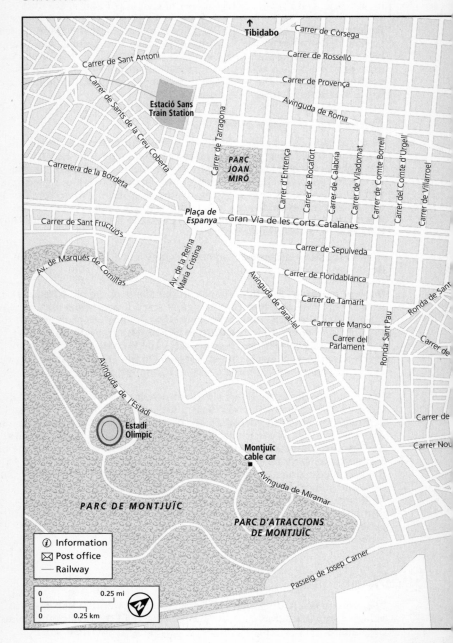

Carrer de Sant Antoni

Carrer de Sants de la Creu Coberta

Tibidabo

Carrer de Còrsega

Carrer de Rosselló

Carrer de Provença

Avinguda de Roma

Estació Sans
Train Station

Carrer de Tarragona

PARC
JOAN
MIRÓ

Carretera de la Bordeta

Carrer d'Entença

Carrer de Rocafort

Carrer de Calàbria

Carrer de Viladomat

Carrer de Comte Borrell

Carrer del Comte d'Urgell

Carrer de Villarroel

Carrer de Sant Fructuós

Plaça de
Espanya

Gran Vía de les Corts Catalanes

Av. de Marqués de Comillas

Av. de la Reina Maria Cristina

Carrer de Sepulveda

Carrer de Floridablanca

Avinguda de Paral·lel

Carrer de Tamarit

Ronda de Sant

Carrer de Manso

Ronda Sant Pau

Carrer del
Parlament

Carrer de

Avinguda de l'Estadi

Estadi
Olímpic

Montjuïc
cable car

Carrer de

Carrer Nou

Avinguda de Miramar

PARC DE MONTJUÏC

PARC D'ATRACCIONS
DE MONTJUÏC

ⓘ Information
✉ Post office
— Railway

Passeig de Josep Carner

0   0.25 mi

0   0.25 km

Generalissimo Francisco Franco and the country's entry into the European Union; today the nation is undergoing a cultural renaissance. Visitors delight in the energy of newly prosperous cities such as **Barcelona.**

The Romans developed Barcelona as a port, and it has long been a Mediterranean center of commerce. More recently, cruise lines, attracted by the city's prime location on the Iberian Peninsula, rediscovered its historical, cultural, and artistic treasures.

Once home to artists such as Picasso, Miró, Dalí, and Casals, Barcelona is renowned for its architecture, which mixes ancient Roman ruins and buildings from the 13th and 15th centuries with startlingly modern creations by Antoni Gaudí and I. M. Pei. You can find great museums, friendly people, pleasant cafes, and a very active nightlife. And Barcelona even has sandy beaches thanks to a recently reclaimed waterfront.

Cruising into port

Ships dock in an industrial-looking port near the heart of Barcelona. Depending on exactly where your ship ties up, you're just a five-minute walk from **La Rambla** (the Rambles), the part of Barcelona you want to be in, or you're 1 or 2 miles away — you may want to hop on the cruise line's shuttle service or jump in a cab.

Scoring the best excursions

City Highlights: This bus and walking tour includes the **Gothic Quarter,** a stop at **Montjuïc** for the views, the Olympic Stadium, **Gaudí's La Sagrada Familia, Les Ramblas,** and **Catalunya Square** (3½–4 hours; $32–$52).

Museums Tour: This tour visits the **Picasso Museum** and may include a drive to Montjuïc for the impressive views, the **Miró Foundation Museum,** and/or a drive past buildings created by Antoni Gaudí (3½–4 hours; $48–$62).

Pilgrimage to Montserrat: Head 36 miles north of Barcelona to the sacred **Mountain of Montserrat,** one of Spain's natural wonders. About halfway up the mountain, the Montserrat Monastery is famous for its shrine of the Virgin Mary, Our Lady of Montserrat. Back in Barcelona, enjoy a brief tour of the city before you return to the ship. Lunch is included in the longer tours (5–7 hours; $69–$126); some tours provide transportation only, and once there you're on your own (4 hours, $44).

Exploring on your own

Taxis are available outside the terminal. They're metered and the fare begins at $3, plus about $1 per kilometer and an extra charge if the taxi goes into the pier area (keep in mind, there are different rates for days and evenings). The city also has a good Metro and bus system.

In summer, **Bus Turistic** passes a dozen of the most popular sights, and you can get on and off as you please. Or ride the **Tibidabo funicular** and the **Montjuïc cable car and funicular** (both for panoramic city views) for the price of a single ticket (about $18 per day). Purchase tickets on the bus or at the transportation booth at Placa de Catalunya.

Within walking distance: Although you may be able to hoof it from the docks to Barri Gòtic or La Rambla — both good starting points for a walk — if your ship docks more than a five- or ten-minute walk away, there's nothing scenic about the route and we recommend that you get a taxi or take the cruise line's shuttle to get there faster. Upon arrival you can easily reach many interesting sights on foot.

Beyond walking distance: In the **Barri Gòtic** (Gothic Quarter), you can wander for hours — getting lost is part of the fun. Stop in at the **Gothic Cathedral de Barcelona** (admission to the church is free; the museum costs $1.25) and saunter the cobblestone streets past fountains, vintage stores, and cafes. Stroll **La Rambla** (the Rambles); Victor Hugo called it "the most beautiful street in the world." A tree-lined boulevard, the street runs from Placa de Catalunya to the sea and bustles with 24-hour street performers, flower vendors, birds in cages, cafes, and shops.

Watch out for pickpockets in the Barri Gòtic at night.

Two Gothic palaces house the **Museu Picasso,** which boasts an impressive collection of the artist's work. Pablo Picasso himself donated some 2,500 of his paintings to the collection, including a piece he painted at the age of nine. Admission is $5.75 for adults, $3 for students, and free for kids 12 and under. A must-do is a glimpse at the fantastical work of Antoni Gaudí. The designer's creations in Barcelona include **La Sagrada Familia** (Church of the Holy Family), a truly bizarre architectural wonder. You can climb the spires if you're not a claustrophobe. Admission is $9.25 for adults, $5.75 for students and seniors, and free for kids under nine.

Shoppers delight in the offerings on **Passeig de Gràcia,** the main shopping street, as well as on streets in the old quarter (including the Rambles).

Turkey

Turkey is literally where East meets West (Istanbul sits where Europe and Asia touch). Very likely, this imaginary gateway is the most exotic country you can visit on a Mediterranean cruise — a land of mosques and minarets, sultans' treasures, crowded bazaars, Greek and Roman archaeological sites, and holy Christian landmarks. Although its cities teem with the energy of a modern nation looking to the West, its villages remain much as they've been for hundreds of years.

Because of the wide fluctuation of Turkish currency, only exchange the amount that you intend to spend. The rug shops and some other vendors often deal in U.S. dollars.

Istanbul

The city where the continents of Asia and Europe meet is chaotic, congested, fascinating, and exciting. Cars careen (literally) past museums, churches, palaces, grand mosques, and other historic monuments that reveal a rich and ancient history. Among the many treats for your senses are the smells of a spice market, the sound of prayer, the taste of traditional Turkish dishes, the feel of a Turkish carpet, and the treasures left by rulers past.

Cruising into port

Ships drop anchor on the **Bosporus** (the strait between the Black Sea and the Sea of Marmara) on the European side of the city; coming and going, the views of Old Istanbul quite spectacular — minarets and domes pierce the skyline. Taxis are relatively inexpensive and wait at the pier (you can also find plenty throughout the city).

Scoring the best excursions

Highlights of Istanbul: This tour typically includes the **Hippodrome,** once the largest chariot race grounds of the Byzantine Empire; the **Sultan Ahmet Mosque,** also known as the Blue Mosque for its 21,000 blue Iznik tiles; the famous **St. Sophia,** once the largest church of the Christian world; and **Topkapi Palace,** the official residence of the Ottoman Sultans and home to treasures that include **Spoonmaker's Diamond,** one of the biggest in the world. The tour also visits the **Grand Bazaar** and its 4,000 shops. Some tours bring you back to the ship for lunch and others include lunch in a first-class restaurant. You can also take shorter tours that include some of the features of the full tour (7–10 hours; $90–$110).

Exploring on your own

It takes a healthy walk to get from the pier to the Blue Mosque. Your best bet is to take the cruise line's shuttle or a cab. The starting taxi fare is about $1, and drivers apply a surcharge after midnight. The best way to explore the old section is on foot.

Within walking distance: After you're dropped off, visit the **Ahmet Mosque,** built in the 17th century; admission is free. It features dazzling blue and white Iznik tiles and six minarets. Guests must remove their shoes at the entrance. The park in front of the Blue Mosque, the **Hippodrome,** once held great chariot races. Nearby is **Hagia Sophia,** the sixth-century basilica famous for its gigantic domes and magnificent mosaics. Historians regard the church as one of the best examples of Byzantine architecture. Admission to Hagia Sophia is $6.

From the 15th century to the mid-19th century, **Topkapi Palace,** located at Kennedy Cad. Sultanahment, served as the residence of sultans. The complex includes the chamber of the Sacred Mantle, harem quarters, crown jewels, holy relics, and the throne room. Admission is $9; the guided harem tour costs $7.50.

Old Istanbul

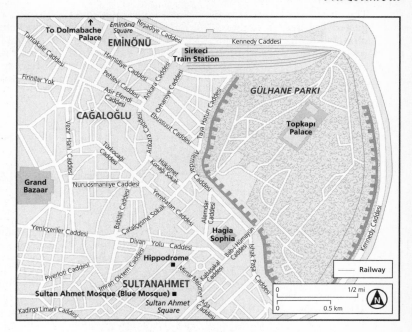

The **Grand Bazaar** (Kapalı Çarşısı), with your best bet for entrance at the Beyazit Gate or the Nuruosmaniye Gate, is the world's largest covered market. More than 4,000 vendors sell carpets, leather goods, jewelry, antique reproductions, and other items. You can buy maps of the Bazaar at newsstands for $6. The setting is a trip in itself, even if you buy nothing. If you want to buy, make sure you bargain.

Beyond walking distance: The **Dolmabache Palace,** Dolmabache Cad, is sometimes called the Ottoman Versailles. The extravagance includes a 4-ton Baccarat chandelier that was a gift from Queen Victoria. Admission is $7 for a long tour (including the Sultan's Quarters and Harem) or $6 for a short tour (of one room or the other). You must pay a fee of $13 to use your video camera.

Kuşadasi

A favorite port for travelers interested in history, the once sleepy little village of Kuşadasi is now a bustling seaside resort. The reason? Its proximity to **Ephesus,** one of the most fascinating and best-preserved ancient historical sites in the world, as well as other major early Christian and historical locales. If the past isn't your bag, you can stay in town and shop (the best place in Turkey to bargain for Turkish rugs) or go to one of the excellent nearby beaches for a swim.

Kuşadasi/Ephesus Region

Cruising into port

Ships dock right in downtown, so you can walk to stores and restaurants.

Scoring the best excursions

Ephesus: One of the world's best-preserved ancient cities. Your guide leads you down marble streets to the remains of the Baths, the theater, and the incredible library building. Along the way, you pass columns, mosaics, monuments, and ruins. The tour may include a stop at a rug shop (3–4 hours; $40–$46).

Ephesus and The House of The Virgin Mary: This tour combines a visit to Ephesus with a trip to the House of the Virgin Mary, a humble chapel in the valley of **Bulbuldagi** on the spot where historians believe the Virgin Mary spent her last days. The site was officially sanctioned for pilgrimage in 1892 (3½–4½ hours; $44–$52).

Ephesus, St. John's Basilica, and House of the Virgin Mary: This tour combines the two preceding tours with a visit to St. John's Basilica, another holy pilgrimage site. Some believe that St. John wrote the fourth book of the New Testament at this site (4½ hours; $56). Tour operators may also offer the tour as a full-day excursion, including lunch in a local restaurant and a visit to the museum of Ephesus (7½ hours; $72–$98).

Three Ancient Cities: This tour takes in the ruins of the region, including Priene, known for its **Athena Temple** (bankrolled by Alexander the Great); Didyma, known for the **Temple of Apollo;** and Miletus, which includes a stadium the Greeks built and the Romans expanded to hold 15,000 spectators. A light lunch is included (6–8 hours; $68–$89).

Exploring on your own

Though you can do a little shopping or have lunch in town, sign up for one of your ship's tours to Ephesus. Minibuses (available from the town center) and taxis (yellow and metered) can get you to the beach.

Within walking distance: You can find plenty of places to shop and haggle.

Vendors generally bump up prices when cruise ships are in port, and they expect you to bargain. Shopkeepers often offer you tea or soft drinks as negotiations get underway as part of Turkish hospitality; accepting their hospitality in no way obligates you to buy.

Beyond walking distance: Book a shore excursion to tour Ephesus or the other historic sites to get the most out of your visit. Law requires Turkish guides to be licensed, so you can expect guides who are quite knowledgeable about their subject matter.

Kadinlar Denizi is Kuşadasi's most popular beach, located about 5 miles from the port. Also known as *Ladies Beach,* the small stretch attracts a large crowd, including women who like to sunbathe topless and macho posers.

Kuşadasi isn't known for culinary artistry. Still, if you want to try the local cuisine, check out the restaurants along the harbor that specialize in the catch of the day.

Chapter 18

Exploring Other Destinations

*H*ave a yen to sail off the beaten path? The Caribbean, Alaska, and the Mediterranean are all fine and good, but sometimes you really want to do something a little different. In this chapter, we tell you about some of the other options. Some cruise lines that sail in these regions are also covered in the ship-review chapters of this book (Chapters 11–13). In instances where the lines didn't make the cruise-review chapters — because they don't operate in any big way in the Caribbean, Alaska, or the Mediterranean — we include contact information that you can use to get more details.

The American South and Midwest

Mark Twain discovered America's heartland while traveling down the Mississippi River, which he described as "the great Mississippi, the majestic, the magnificent Mississippi, rolling its mile-wide tide along, shining in the sun." You can explore the America that so enticed the writer by traveling down the very same river and in the very same way as Twain: aboard a real paddlewheel steamboat.

Delta Queen (see Chapter 13), with its lovely 1927-built *Delta Queen* (an actual National Landmark) and two newer steamboats, is the big cheese is this region. The **Mississippi River system** (www.nps.gov/miss) consists of some 50 rivers and tributaries, seven of which — the Atchafalaya, Arkansas, Ohio, Tennessee, Cumberland, Missouri, and Illinois — are navigable for considerable distances. From the rural plantation homes and stately mansions of the antebellum south to the farmlands and Victorian-era homes of the more northern reaches of the region, the experience is pure Americana. Principal embarkation ports are Memphis, Nashville, Cincinnati, and St. Louis.

RiverBarge Excursions (☎ 888-GO-BARGE; www.riverbarge.com) also operates year-round river cruises on waterways including the Mississippi, Cumberland, Ohio, and Missouri. The company offers 4- to 10-day cruises on the *River Explorer* that combines two hotel barges propelled by a tugboat.

If you want to feel like you're sailing the ocean without being on the ocean, you can also cruise on the Great Lakes with American Canadian Caribbean (ACCL) and Clipper Cruises (see Chapter 13). The Traverse City, Michigan-based **Traverse Tall Ship Company** (☎ 800-678-0383; www.tallshipsailing.com) also offers sailings on Lake Michigan and Lake Huron aboard Windjammer sailing ships.

If you're hankering for a more offbeat river experience than you'll find on Mississippi and Great Lakes itineraries, **American Cruise Lines** (☎ 800-814-6880; www.americancruiselines.com), based in Haddam, Connecticut, operates three small ships on weeklong itineraries that include Chesapeake Bay, the St. Johns and Tolomato rivers in Florida, and the Intracoastal Waterway (between Charleston, South Carolina, and Jacksonville, Florida). The line also offers New England cruises (see "New England and Canada," later in this chapter).

The Columbia and Snake Rivers

So, reading *Undaunted Courage* by Stephen Ambrose sparked an ambition to copy Lewis and Clark? You're in luck — several cruise lines tread the Columbia and Snake Rivers in the U.S. northwest. As the second-largest river in the United States (only the Mississippi is bigger), the Columbia River winds between the Cascade Mountains and past the Columbia River Gorge's waterfalls and lush forests. Cruises depart from Portland and follow the Columbia River east between Oregon and Washington, sometimes going as far east as Idaho. Visits can include **Bonneville Dam, Hood River** (the windsurfing capital of the world), **Hell's Canyon,** and the historic towns of the **Oregon Trail.**

American West Steamboat Company offers cruises that depart from Portland year-round. Cruise West, Lindblad Expeditions, and American Safari (see Chapter 13 for more on these lines) also offer small-ship Columbia and Snake River cruises in the spring and fall.

New England and Canada

If you're looking for a slow, easy meander past quaint, often un-touristy towns — and couldn't give a hoot about sunbathing and conga lines — book a cruise along the coast of New England and eastern Canada. The folksy vibe and the striking natural beauty of the northeastern Atlantic coast are quite appealing, and we highly recommend taking a fall cruise and feasting your eyes on the turning foliage. Attractions on the 7- to 14-day cruises typically include stops in Boston, with its historic Freedom Trail; Newport, Rhode Island, with its gorgeous mansions; Bar Harbor, Maine, with its splendid hiking trails and scenic vistas; the trendy and picturesque island of Martha's Vineyard, Massachusetts, where notables (including the Clintons) have been known to summer; the Canadian coastal provinces of Nova Scotia, New Brunswick, and Newfoundland; and Quebec City or Montreal, two historic Canadian cities in bilingual Quebec. Shorter cruises out of New York City, with lines such as Carnival, may make just a stop or two in the Canadian provinces.

Cruises generally depart from New York or Boston and travel northward, but you can also board in Montreal or Quebec City and sail south. Some smaller ships sail in Canada's St. Lawrence and Saguenay rivers, or up the coast to Labrador.

American Canadian Caribbean, American Cruise Lines, Carnival, Celebrity, Clipper, Crystal, Cunard, Holland America, Norwegian, Princess, Radisson Seven Seas, Royal Caribbean, Seabourn, and Silversea all have ships with New England itineraries. Look for more detail on all these lines in Chapters 11 through 13.

For a totally different New England experience, you can take a rustic, fun cruise vacation on board a schooner. A fleet of tall ships based in Rockland or Camden, Maine, sail from May to October in Maine's scenic Penobscot Bay, with itineraries dependent on the weather. The fleet of schooners includes the historic *Stephen Taber* (☎ **800-999-7352**) and *Victory Chimes* (☎ **800-745-5651**), and other members of the Maine Windjammer Association (see Chapter 13).

Bermuda

Cruises to Bermuda, that neat and tidy British colony in the Atlantic Ocean where it's normal to pair brightly colored shorts with knee highs and a jacket, usually combine several relaxing days at sea with several relaxing days on the island. You can spend your island time exploring by the preferred and fabulously fun means of transport — mopeds or scooters (rental cars are banned here) — and enjoy activities such as golf, sunbathing on the island's famous pink-sand shores, snorkeling, scuba diving, joining glass-bottom boat tours, visiting museums and historic homes, and savoring very proper High Tea. Opportunities abound for shopping, too, especially for British goods such as wool sweaters and Wedgwood china.

Bermuda's ports of call are Hamilton, King's Wharf, and St. George's.

Celebrity, Norwegian, Royal Caribbean, and Radisson Seven Seas have ships that sail Bermuda routes weekly, from late April to October, with most of the cruises departing from New York, New Jersey, or Boston on Saturday or Sunday. Norwegian also has Bermuda cruises from Philadelphia and Charleston, and Royal Caribbean does Bermuda from Baltimore. Radisson does a handful of Bermuda sailings from Florida and from Norfolk. One-off- or two-off Bermuda cruises are offered by Costa (from Florida) and Carnival (from New York). Cunard, Princess, Seabourn, and Silversea also visit Bermuda as part of transatlantic crossings or in combination with coastal Atlantic itineraries. We offer more detail on all these cruise lines in Chapters 11 through 13.

Costa Rica

Most cruises to lush, green Costa Rica ("rich coast" in Spanish) explore this Central American country's natural wonders, offering tours of beaches, rain forests, and mountains. Highlights include the indigenous plant and animal life, including thousands of varieties of butterflies. In addition to the numerous national parks, you can visit historic sites and ruins.

Costa Rican ports of call include Bahia Herradura, Cano Island, Corcovado National Park, Curu, Golfito, Golfo Dulce, Manuel Antonio Park, Marenco Reserve, Playa Flamingo, Puerto Caldera, Puerto Limón, Puntarenas, Quepos, and Tortuga.

Cruise West operates 7-day cruises in Costa Rica nearly year-round, and the line also offers longer sailings that combine Costa Rica with a trip through the Panama Canal (see the next section). Lindblad Expeditions operates 7-day Costa Rican and Panama Canal cruises in the winter, summer, and fall. See Chapter 13 for info on both lines.

Also cruising from Costa Rican ports (but on an occasional basis) are Clipper, Crystal, Seabourn, Silversea, Windjammer, and Windstar. Celebrity, Crystal, Holland America, Norwegian, Oceania, Princess, Radisson Seven Seas, and Royal Caribbean all have ships that visit Costa Rica as part of Caribbean, Panama Canal, or Central American itineraries, stopping at Puerto Caldera or Puntarenas on the Pacific coast or Puerto Limón on the Caribbean coast. Chapters 11 through 13 have more about these cruise lines.

The Panama Canal

Ships pass through this eighth wonder of the world as part of one-way repositioning cruises in the late fall and early spring as the cruise lines move their vessels from the Alaskan market to the Caribbean market and vice versa. Some lines also include the Panama Canal as part of longer Caribbean, Central American, and South American itineraries in the winter.

The reasons are both practical and scenic. Use of the canal trims some 8,000 nautical miles off a trip from, say, New York to San Francisco, because without the continental passageway, ships must go south around Cape Horn, the tip of South America. Traversing the 50-mile canal takes just eight hours and provides a unique and fascinating experience. The water level lifts and lowers your ship 85 feet through a series of locks, gates, and dams.

Panama Canal cruises can include stops at Central American ports such as Cartagena, Colombia; Puerto Caldera, Puerto Limón, and Puntarenas (all in Costa Rica); and Panama's San Blas Islands — home of the Cuna Indians, known for their colorful needlework. Itineraries often last ten days or more, and may also include Caribbean or Mexican Riviera stops.

Cruise lines that make full or partial Panama Canal crossings include American Canadian Caribbean, Celebrity, Clipper, Cruise West, Crystal, Cunard, Holland America, Lindblad, Norwegian, Oceania, Princess, Radisson Seven Seas, Royal Caribbean, Seabourn, and Silversea, all of which we cover in Chapters 11 through 13.

The Mexican Riviera

The so-called Mexican Riviera — the stretch of port cities and resorts extending from Mazatlán in the north to Acapulco in the south — is the Caribbean of the west coast, offering gorgeous beaches, perfect weather, beautiful scenery, and a good helping of rich Mexican culture. The glorious beaches are the main attraction, along with the accessibility of golf, tennis, deep-sea fishing, and water sports. Seven-day cruises leave year-round from Los Angeles, Long Beach, or San Diego, visiting ports such as Cabo San Lucas (a partying town and beach heaven at the southern tip of Baja California) and the mainland cities of Mazatlán and Puerto Vallarta, both of which combine beach resorts with historical and cultural sites. Shorter 3- or 4-night cruises call at Catalina Island and Ensenada, both in Baja, while longer cruises usually include a stop in Acapulco. Some lines also visit the region as part of longer itineraries that include the Panama Canal.

Carnival, Celebrity, Crystal, Holland America, Norwegian, Oceania, Princess, and Royal Caribbean all have ships that sail in the area (see Chapters 11 and 12).

Baja and the Sea of Cortez

Many small ships sail this region, which is sometimes referred to as Mexico's Galapagos for its rugged, arid scenery and its remarkable wildlife, which includes gray whales in winter. Cruises typically mix visits to the region's cities and towns with stops at protected islands in the Sea of Cortez. One day you're in Cabo San Lucas, with its beach scene and touristy bars, and the next you're walking along the shore of an uninhabited island, with no trace of human civilization in sight. Whale- and wildlife-watching are major attractions, and you can also hike, kayak, snorkel, and swim from beautiful, isolated beaches.

American Safari Cruises, Clipper Cruise Line, Cruise West, and Lindblad Expeditions (see Chapter 13) all offer cruises in the region. Pre- and post-cruise tours can take you to the great **Copper Canyon** — four times larger than the Grand Canyon in the U.S., with four of its six individual canyons deeper than the Grand too, some by more than 1,000 feet.

The Hawaiian Islands

Oh, right, Hawaii. That's another word for paradise, right? Pretty much. It's got rugged coastlines, majestic volcanoes (some still active and spewing lava), dramatic waterfalls, lush forests, abundant orchids and other tropical flowers, and magnificent beaches — plus gorgeous hula girls, hunky Polynesian men, and some of the most perfect weather you can imagine, putting both locals and visitors in a friendly, mellow mood.

Cruising around the Hawaiian Islands gives you the chance to experience **Hawaiian culture** and food at a traditional luau, explore ancient sacred places on land, snorkel or scuba around underwater reefs, golf on picture-perfect courses, hike around a volcano's crater (or even right through it!), go bird-watching, learn to surf, or just hang on the beach and be, you know, mellow. Hawaiians are fiercely proud of their culture, which survives alongside the modern world in a vibrant arts scene that includes traditional Polynesian dance, music, painting, sculpture, and crafts. **Pearl Harbor** is another important attraction.

There's an interesting caveat to sailing in Hawaii, though: The itineraries are often wacky. See, U.S. law prohibits ships not built, registered, and staffed in the United States from sailing directly to Hawaii from the contiguous 48 states, or even from sailing within the islands themselves unless they also make a stop in another country. The rules were originally written to protect U.S. shipbuilding and maritime industries, and we won't try to say whether they work or not. What we will say is that they make it really difficult for most cruise lines to sail here, since nearly everyone builds, registers, and staffs their ships abroad to keep costs down. Some ships sail to the islands from Mexican ports such as Ensenada. Others sail round-trip from Honolulu but make a detour to one of the Polynesian nations in the middle of the cruise, while still others visit in April/May and September/October, on their way between seasons in Alaska and the Caribbean.

Norwegian Cruise Line (NCL) took a different tack in 2003, agreeing to play by most of the rules in exchange for a little government flexibility on others. A special Congressional provision allows the Malaysian-owned line to cruise the islands without calling at a foreign port, as long as NCL flags its ships American, pays U.S. taxes, hires an all-American crew, and abides by U.S. laws. The line began all-Hawaii cruises in July 2004 when it introduced the first of its new NCL America brand ships, *Pride of Aloha.* Another, *Pride of America,* just launched as this book was in production. Both offer weeklong cruises round-trip from Honolulu, visiting a Hawaiian port every single day. For that reason, NCL rules the Hawaiian roost for the foreseeable future. If you sail here, it'll probably be on one of the *Pride* ships. A third vessel, *Pride of Hawai'i,* is due in summer 2006.

NCL sails the islands year-round. Other lines, including Carnival, Celebrity, Holland America, Princess, Radisson Seven Seas, and Royal Caribbean, offer cruises at different points of the year. See Chapters 11 and 12 for more about all of these lines.

Tahiti and the South Pacific

Cruising here is like spending a week in paradise — and we don't mean some kind of phony "Calgon, take me away" kind of paradise either. No, we mean the kind where the weather is always perfect, the beaches are always clean and uncrowded, the water is always crystal blue, and the people all look like angels. Up above, volcanic peaks poke holes in perfect blue skies, while down below, scuba divers and snorkelers swim among thousands of species of fish and even humpback whales. If you're not into water activities, you can find plenty to do at visits to ports such as Huahine, Moorea, Raiatea, and Bora Bora, including helicopter tours, visits to black pearl farms, and Jeep safaris. Or you can just rent a bike and explore.

Radisson Seven Seas (see Chapter 12) has its chartered ship *Paul Gauguin* in Tahiti year-round at least through January 2007. Princess (see Chapter 11) also has its small, 654-passenger *Tahitian Princess* there throughout the year. All the cruises sail from Papeete, on the island of Tahiti. Holland America (also reviewed in Chapter 11) also occasionally offers Tahiti sailings, and other lines visit as part of longer itineraries (sometimes world cruises).

Transatlantic Cruises

Most cruise lines offer transatlantic cruises simply because the Atlantic is between the Caribbean and Europe, so why not put some passengers on board when they move their ships between the two markets? The actual crossings can take anywhere from six days to two weeks. The shorter itineraries are usually just a straight sail across, with no port calls; the longer ones include several ports before or after the crossing, either on the Europe side or in the Caribbean or New England/Canada, depending where the vessel is sailing from.

Cunard (see Chapter 12) is the only line that offers a regular schedule of 6-day transatlantic crossings from April through November aboard the gigantic *Queen Mary 2,* which was built extra-tough, specifically for this purpose. Other lines sail transatlantic on repositioning cruises, for which good deals are often available.

The British Isles and Northern Capitals

A number of ships sail from England, either focusing entirely on ports in England, Scotland, Ireland, and Wales, or linking some of those ports with visits to the capitals of France, Belgium, the Netherlands, Denmark, and Germany. Cruise passengers get the city life of London and Dublin, the golf of Scotland, the natural beauty of the coasts, and the charm of the Channel Islands. The main season is April through October, with most ships sailing from Southampton or Dover.

Celebrity, Princess, Oceania, Royal Caribbean, Norwegian, Radisson Seven Seas, and Silversea offer cruises from and around the British Isles, as do small-ship lines Clipper and Lindblad — the former on the great expedition ship *Clipper Adventurer,* the latter aboard the 54-passenger *Lord of the Glens,* which cruises in the highlands via the inland waterway that links the country's famed lochs. Cunard's fabled **QE2** is based in Southampton for most of the year, offering cruises in the isles and the Continent. You can find more detail on each of these lines in Chapters 11 through 13.

The Scandinavian Fjords

We never met a fjord we didn't like, so how can we not like Norway (not to mention Denmark and Sweden, the other two Scandinavian nations visited regularly by cruise ships). Cruises lasting one to three weeks typically depart from Southampton, Amsterdam, or Stockholm, sailing up the Norwegian coast with its never-ending string of deep fjords, small fishing villages, wildflowers, and medieval cathedrals. Some ships sail up above the Arctic Circle into the land of the midnight sun. Many routes include Norway's southern towns of Bergen and Oslo, as well as Copenhagen, Stockholm, and ports along the Baltic Sea, such as Helsinki and St. Petersburg.

Celebrity, Clipper, Costa, Crystal, Cunard, Holland America, Lindblad, MSC, Oceania, Princess, Radisson Seven Seas, Royal Caribbean, Seabourn, and Silversea all offer cruises in the region (and we cover all in Chapters 11 through 13). Although the main cruise season is May to September, **Norwegian Coastal Voyage** (☎ 800-323-7436; www.coastalvoyage.com) operates a fleet of working ships here year-round, bringing passengers and cargo up and down the Norwegian coast, with dozens of stops along the way.

European River and Canal Cruises

Cruising on Europe's rivers and canals gets you inland without having to take bus tours or car treks, and gives you a close-up view of the countries you visit. The pace is leisurely and the ambience informal — like booking a B&B or country inn that just happens to float.

River cruises are aboard 100- to 200-passenger vessels that sail the Danube, Rhine, Rhone, Moselle, Elbe, Seine, and other rivers in Germany, Switzerland, Hungary, Holland, France, Austria, the Czech Republic, and sometimes Russia. **Canal cruises** are on intimate barges that usually carry between 6 and 24 passengers, sailing the back waterways of France (including Burgundy, Provence, the upper Loire, and the Loire Valley), Italy, Ireland, the Netherlands, Belgium, and so on. The season generally runs from mid-March through early November.

Top operators include **Abercrombie & Kent** (☎ 800-554-7016; www.abercrombiekent.com); **The Barge Lady** (☎ 800-880-0071; www.bargelady.com); **French Country Waterways** (☎ 800-222-1236; www.fcwl.com); **Peter Deilmann Cruises** (☎ 800-348-8287; www.deilmann-cruises.com); **Uniworld** (☎ 800-733-7820; www.uniworld.com); and **Viking River Cruises** (☎ 877-668-4546; www.vikingrivercruises.com).

Antarctica

Got a hankering to head to the bottom of the earth? Got a hankering to see waddling penguins, towering icebergs, giant albatrosses, and more seals than you can count? A tour of the Great White Continent may be for you, visiting scientific research stations and islands reachable only by small landing craft.

Most Antarctica cruises depart from Ushuaia, Argentina, although some sail from ports in Chile or from Port Stanley in the Falkland Islands. The cruise season is January and February, and the offerings mostly range from 8 to 15 nights.

Adventure cruise pioneer Lars-Eric Lindblad was the first to bring travelers to the southern end of the world in 1965, and the company his son founded, **Lindblad Expeditions** (see Chapter 13), maintains a big presence here, frequently visiting Lindblad Cove, named for Lars-Eric in honor of his achievements. Upscale tour operator **Abercrombie & Kent** (☎ 800-554-7016; www.abercrombiekent.com), extreme adventure operator **Quark Expeditions** (☎ 800-356-5699; www.quarkexpeditions. com), **Norwegian Coastal Voyage** (☎ 800-323-7436; www.coastalvoyage. com), and **Orient Lines** (☎ 800-333-7300; www.orientlines.com) all cruise here as well, as do Clipper Cruise Line, Holland America, and Radisson Seven Seas Cruises (see Chapters 11 and 12).

Part VI
The Part of Tens

The 5th Wave   By Rich Tennant

"Oh Ted, this Alaskan cruise is everything I'd ever imagined! The sweeping vista of the salad bar, the breathtaking dessert tray, the majesty of the carving station..."

In this part . . .

Get ready, the book is about to end! In this part, we wrap it all up by telling you what you need to do on debarkation day (oh, stop crying — you can take another cruise next year), and then have some fun by running through things we personally like about cruising, and recommend you try, too.

Chapter 19

Ten Things to Do When Your Cruise Ends

In This Chapter

▶ Getting a grip

▶ Drying those tears

▶ Leaving your tips

▶ Checking your gear

▶ Getting through Customs

▶ Departing the pier

▶ And (if you can afford it) making plans for next year

*F*ace facts: It's over. Your vacation: kaput. Over. Done. Finished. You have to go back to work tomorrow. Yes, you. And don't give us that sad face, either, 'cause we have to be back at our desks at 9 a.m. too, writing this book.

Before you leave the ship, there are a few things you have to get settled. In this chapter, we walk you through them, and try to make the whole process as painless as possible.

Settling Your Bill

On the last night of your cruise, an itemized account of all you've charged up to that point will be left in your cabin. Look it over. If you agree with the charges, they'll automatically be billed to the credit card you registered at the start of your cruise. If you'd rather pay in cash or with a different card — or if you dispute any of the charges — you need to stop by the reception desk and hash it out with the purser's staff.

Leaving Your Tips

Most cruise lines pay their service staff low base wages with the under-standing that the bulk of their income will come from tips. In the old days, the last hours of a cruise were a flurry of little white envelopes, as passengers slipped cash to their cabin steward, waiter, assistant waiter, and sometimes maitre d' and favorite bartender.

That's still the way of it on some lines, but these days a lot of others (Carnival, Costa, Holland America, Norwegian, Oceania, and Princess, for example) are automatically adding tips to passengers' onboard accounts, with the amount adjustable up or down if you request it at the purser's desk before the end of the cruise. The base amount varies by cruise line, but expect to pay between $8.50 and $11.50 per person, per day.

Some lines, such as Royal Caribbean and Disney, give you the option of paying cash directly to staff or adding the gratuities onto your account. Most small-ship lines pool the tips and divide them up among all crewmembers after you're gone.

And then there are the real ultraluxury lines, such as Silversea, Seabourn, SeaDream, and Radisson, where tips are included in your up-front cost.

Windstar promotes its "tipping not required" policy, but "required" is the operative word: Tipping really is expected.

Each line has clear guidelines, which you'll usually find out about in each line's brochures, Web sites, cruise documents, daily program for the last day, and/or debarkation briefing.

On lines that follow traditional person-to-person gratuity policies, tip your waiter and assistant waiter during the cruise's final dinner, and leave your cabin steward his or her tip on the final night or morning, just before you disembark. Generally, expect to tip between $9 and $13 total per person, per day (half that for kids). We usually divide it up as $3.50 per day for the cabin steward, $3.50 for the dining room waiter, and about $2 for the assistant waiter. Some lines suggest you tip the maitre d' about $5 per person for the week and slip another couple bucks to the chief housekeeper, but we'll leave that up to you. Guests staying in suites with butler service should slip the gent $3.50 per day. A 15 percent gratuity is usually included on every bar bill, so you don't have to tip your bartender with every drink. (The exception is on NCL's Hawaii ships.)

Packing Up

A day or two before the end of the cruise, you'll receive color-coded or numbered luggage tags based on your cabin category and flight time. These determine the order you'll disembark ship on the last day. Attach them to any bags you want the ship's staff to carry off the ship for you.

Plan to pack your bags before dinner on your final night aboard. You'll be asked to leave your luggage outside your cabin door by midnight or thereafter so that staff can carry it all to a central offloading location. First-time cruisers always worry about leaving their bags out in public, but we've never heard an instance of anything being stolen.

Especially on megaships, where ship staff collect and offload upwards of 5,000 or 6,000 pieces of luggage in just a few hours, don't expect that your luggage will be treated gently. If you've bought anything breakable on your trip — pottery, glass, or bottles of duty-free liquor, for example — carry them off the ship yourself rather than packing them in your checked luggage.

Disembarking, Whether You Want to or Not

Big ships typically offload passengers based on a color or number code that matches the one on your luggage tags. Ships normally arrive in port on the final day before 8 a.m., but usually need at least 90 minutes to complete docking formalities, get cleared by authorities, and unload baggage. No one disembarks much before 9 a.m., and even then you may have to wait a while before your color code is called. Passengers with early flights and passengers who've paid the most (suite passengers, for example) are typically allowed off first.

 So they have time to clean up before the next group of passengers arrive, cruise lines usually ask that you vacate your cabin early, have breakfast, and wait in a lounge for your color or number to be called. If your hand luggage is heavy or unwieldy, though, you can leave it in your cabin and go back for it before you disembark.

If you're sailing on a small or very high-end ship, you can usually just get off when the captain gives the all-clear. Them's the virtues of smallness.

Once you disembark, you'll find your bags waiting for you in the terminal, organized by the colored or numbered tags you attached. Attendants are standing by to help you should your bag not be where it's supposed to be. Claim your luggage, head through Customs (see below), then board whatever transportation you've arranged — your car, a taxi, a cruise line bus transfer to the airport, or "other."

Understanding Immigration (We Wish)

 U.S. passport requirements were in flux as this book was being prepared, with a new initiative set to mandate passports for all travel outside the U.S. by 2008. (Previously, U.S. citizens didn't need passports for travel to Mexico, Canada, and most Caribbean countries.) Depending on the implementation schedule for this initiative — and the process the Department of Homeland Security comes up with for cruise passengers — you may have to pass through **Immigration** and have your passport stamped as you leave the ship.

Non-U.S. citizens and green card holders definitely have to see an immigration official. Your ship will give you details about the where and when.

Getting Through Customs

When you leave the ship after visiting a foreign country (or when you arrive home after flying from a ship that disembarks you in a foreign country), you must fill out a Customs declaration form. In the United States, rules for what you can and can't bring back are enforced by the U.S. Customs and Border Protection, and although inspectors don't check each and every bag that comes back into the country, you don't want to get caught breaking the rules — say, for trying to sneak in Cuban cigars. Customs applies stiff fines for doing so.

If you take a cruise that sails from the U.S. and visits foreign ports (in the Caribbean, Canada, Central America, Mexico, or The Bahamas, for example), you'll receive a Customs form the last night of your sailing and clear Customs at the pier when you arrive. If you get off the ship in another country, you clear Customs at the airport when you get back to the United States (or at a border point, if you drive).

Read and review your Customs form thoroughly. Make sure that you fill in the spaces correctly (if you mess up, ask for another form). You need to fill out only one form per family. You must declare all items you acquired abroad and are bringing back into the U.S., including purchases (for yourself and/or others), gifts, and duty-free items. On your Customs form, state the price you paid for all items, including tax.

All Americans returning from abroad get a **duty-free exemption,** also called a *personal exemption.* That's the total value of merchandise you may bring back to the States without having to pay duty — otherwise known as tax. You can bring back more than your exemption, but if you do, you'll have to pay the taxes on it.

When you see the term *duty free* at all those shops in the Caribbean, Europe, and elsewhere (including in the shops on your ship), it doesn't mean you won't pay tax on it ever; it just means you won't pay tax when you buy it. Duty-free items *do* count toward your personal exemption.

In most cases, the **personal exemption** is $800, but depending on which countries you visited, your exemption may be as little as $200 or as much as $1,600. There are also limits on the amount of alcoholic beverages (usually 1 liter), cigarettes (1 carton), cigars (100 total, and no Cubans!), and other tobacco products you may include in your personal duty-free exemption.

The $200 exemption applies to people who have been out of the country more than once in a 30-day period, and to people who've been out of the country less than 48 hours before returning.

The $1,600 exemption applies to people who are traveling to a Caribbean Basin or Andean country or countries *and* to a U.S. insular possession, such as the U.S. Virgin Islands, American Samoa, or Guam. But only $800 worth of your items may come from the Caribbean Basin or Andean countries.

Confused yet?

Family members who live in the same home and return to the country together may combine their personal exemptions into a **joint declaration.** For example, if while traveling abroad Mr. Scnozzlehammer buys a $600 guitar and Mrs. Scnozzlehammer buys a $1,000 sculpture, they can combine their $800 exemptions on a joint declaration and not have to pay duty.

For more specifics, visit the **U.S. Customs and Border Protection** Web site at `www.cpb.gov`. Canadian citizens should look at the **Canada Border Services Agency** site (`www.cbsa.gc.ca`), and citizens of the U.K. should visit the **U.K. Customs and Excise** site (`www.hmce.gov.uk`).

If you go over your exemptions (dollar-wise and amount of liquor and cigarettes wise), the next $1,000 worth of goods bought in most countries will be taxed at a flat rate of 3 percent (1.5 percent for U.S. insular possessions). Above that, the Customs officer will levy duties at whatever duty rates apply. That sounds vague, right? Well it is (for us) and isn't (for the government). See, under what's know as its "301" authority, the U.S. Trade Representative is authorized to impose different duty rates for different items from different countries — sometimes up to 100 percent of an item's value. Most of these items aren't things travelers would be bringing back with them, but some are: diamonds from the Ukraine, for example.

You can pay in cash (U.S. dollars only), by personal check, or, at most airports, by MasterCard or Visa.

Mailing Goods to Yourself

You can mail items you purchase abroad home to yourself, but in general they'll be subject to duty when they arrive, and cannot be counted toward your personal exemption. One loophole in this is that goods from the Caribbean and U.S. insular possessions (including the U.S. Virgin Islands) carry an $800 and $1,600 duty-free exemption, respectively. Duty is charged at a flat rate for the next $1,000 of value (3 percent for Caribbean Basin countries, 1.5 percent for U.S. possessions).

Knowing What's Prohibited or Restricted

When you read all the rules, you discover how complex this whole Customs business is. For example, the following list includes some things you can't bring back into the United States (or whose importation is subject to limits). For restrictions for Canadian or U.K. citizens, check the appropriate Web site (listed in the preceding section).

✔ **Cuban cigars:** Number-one on the banned-articles hit parade! You'll see Cuban cigars for sale in Canada, Mexico, Europe, and elsewhere, but Uncle Sam will come down on you in righteous 1960s-era Bay of Pigs fury if you try to bring them back to the U.S. Smoke 'em while you got 'em.

✔ **Meat and many other food products:** Customs is very strict about food products. Any fruits or vegetables you're carrying must be declared to the Customs officer and be presented for inspection — even that apple you put in your pocket at the ship's buffet on debarkation morning. Meats, livestock, poultry, and their by-products are either totally prohibited or restricted from entering the country, depending on the animal-disease condition in the country of origin. Fresh meat from most countries is generally prohibited, while canned, cured, or dried meat is severely restricted. Ditto for almost anything containing meat products, such as bouillon, soup mixes, and so on. Bakery items and all cured cheeses are generally admissible, as are most condiments, vinegars, oils, packaged spices, honey, coffee, and tea.

✔ **National treasures:** Most countries have laws that protect culturally important antiquities such as art, artifacts, and other archaeological and ethnological materials. Such laws include export controls and/or national ownership of cultural property. Even if purchased from a business in the country of origin or in another country, legal ownership of such artifacts may be in question if you try to bring them into the United States. It's unlikely you'll buy anything that would fall under this category on your cruise, but it's something to keep in mind if you're shopping for high-priced antiquities, particularly in places such as Greece or the Middle East. U.S. law also restricts the importation of specific categories of art/artifacts/antiquities, including any pre-Columbian monumental and architectural sculpture and murals from Central and South American countries; First Nations (Native American) artifacts from Canada; Mayan pre-Columbian archaeological objects from Guatemala; pre-Columbian archaeological objects from El Salvador and Peru; archaeological objects (such as terracotta statues) from Mali; Colonial-period objects (such as paintings and ritual objects) from Peru; Byzantine-period ritual and ecclesiastic objects (including religious icons) from Cyprus; and Khmer stone archaeological sculpture from Cambodia.

✔ **Live animals:** Sorry, you can't bring home that cute little dog who befriended you in Mexico. Don't take it so hard. You've heard that old story anyway, right, about the family who adopted the Mexican street dog, got it home, and had the vet tell them it was actually a rat?

✔ **Some wildlife products:** This is one you may actually run up against while you're cruising. Following international prohibitions on products made from endangered species, the U.S. prohibits importation of elephant ivory (unless you have documentation showing it to be more than 100 years old), sea turtle products (including turtle leather boots, tortoiseshell jewelry, and sea turtle oil cosmetics), coral (including all that black coral jewelry you see in the Caribbean), crocodile or caiman leather, feathers and feather products from wild birds, fur from spotted cats, and other less common items. If you try to sneak in any of these souvenirs, Customs inspectors can confiscate them and issue a fine. Ditto for products made from dog or cat fur.

✔ **Plants and seeds:** Some plants, cuttings, seeds that are capable of propagation, unprocessed plant products, and certain endangered species are allowed into the United States if you have the proper import permits, while others are prohibited entirely. Every plant or plant product (including handicraft items made of straw), must be declared to Customs and presented for inspection.

✔ **Bootleg and pirated goods:** Travelers arriving back in the United States are allowed to import one copy each of any pirated work or object, as long as it's for your personal use, not for resale. This applies to CDs, DVDs, books, handbags, $12 "Rolex" watches, $18 "Armani" jeans, and other fakes.

✔ **More than $10,000 in currency:** You can bring in or take out of the country as much cash as you like, but if it's more than $10,000, you have to report it to Customs.

✔ **Drugs and medicines:** Narcotics and certain other drugs with a high potential for abuse — including Rohypnol, GHB, and Fen-Phen — may not be brought into the United States. Medications that can be legally prescribed in the United States may be imported for personal use, but restrictions apply. Contact Customs for details.

✔ **Absinthe:** Strange but true: In the 21st century, Customs actually lists absinthe as one of the items you can't bring back into the United States (since its active ingredient, Thujone, has a similar chemical structure to Tetrahydrocannabinol — the thing that makes marijuana marijuana). Lord Byron would be appalled.

Taking Back Value-Added Tax and Goods-and-Services Tax

As if dealing with Customs restrictions isn't confusing enough, other countries have tax oddities that may actually get you some money back.

European countries, for example, levy a tax called the **value-added tax** (VAT) on all items. Unlike American taxes, it's already included in the price of the item. The tax ranges from 15 to 35 percent (varying by country), but you may be able to get it refunded if you spend a designated amount (normally between $50 and $200) in a single store.

By far the easiest way to get your money back is to go through the store's *refund affiliate,* which you can identify by a decal in the store window. The biggest of these services is **Global Refund,** which has its "Tax Free Shopping" sticker in more than 225,000 stores in 35 countries. Using them as an example, all you do is shop where you see their sign; ask for your Global Refund Cheque; when leaving the country (let's say at the airport), show your purchases, receipts, and passport to Customs officials and have your cheques export validated; then collect your refund in cash at the airport's Global Refund Office or send the cheques to the company to get your money back.

A number of other companies operate the same way, with their own networks of retail outlets and airport offices.

Be aware that an administrative fee is deducted from your refund.

In Canada, a **goods and services tax (GST)** of 7 percent applies to most goods and services sold in Alberta, British Columbia, Manitoba, Ontario, Prince Edward Island, Quebec, Saskatchewan, the Northwest Territories, Nunavut, and the Yukon. A **harmonized sales tax (HST)** of 15 percent is applied to the same goods and services as the GST in New Brunswick, Newfoundland, Labrador, and Nova Scotia. Non-resident visitors can claim a refund for accommodation and goods as long as each item is worth more than C$50 and the total is at least C$200 (before taxes). Keep your receipts and pick up a *Tax Refund Application for Visitors* at any Customs office or at most visitor centers, duty-free shops, department stores, and some hotels. Also, keep your airline boarding passes, which you may have to mail in with the form. If you leave the country by plane, car, or motor coach, you have to show your goods at the border (or airport) and get your receipts validated, or you can't get a refund.

You can find more information on Canadian tax refunds at www. cra-arc.gc.ca.

Dealing with Departure Tax

Something to remember if your cruise ends in a foreign country from which you plan to fly home: Some countries levy a departure tax on everyone who leaves. It normally, but not always, costs you less than $20. When you depart from Vancouver Airport, for example, you incur an airport improvement fee of C$10 (about US$8), payable in U.S. or Canadian dollars. So don't spend every penny you have before you get to the airport. The airline can tell you the exact tax amount in advance.

Chapter 20

Matt and Heidi's Ten Favorite Cruise Experiences

In This Chapter
▶ Sailing, exploring, cruising, and tipping back a few
▶ Gaping, dining, luxuriating, and reboarding

*W*e practically make a living out of arguing. In fact, we do a regular "He Said–She Said" column in *Porthole* cruise magazine about our opinions on various aspects of cruising. Though we shamelessly enjoy bickering, we really aren't always at odds. In fact we often agree. And so, in this chapter, we share our favorite cruise experiences, which touch on some similar themes.

Matt's Top Five Cruise Experiences

First, a little background: Living in Brooklyn, New York, Matt is a writer and musician, early 40-something, and newly married as you read this. His tastes tend toward high culture, low culture, and pretty much nothing in the middle. He's equal parts curmudgeon, booster, anarchist, and detail-oriented wonk. If he likes something, he'll tell you. If he doesn't, he'll tell you that, too. Here are some of his cruise ship–related faves.

Appreciating the art of sailing

Ships are amazing things, whether they're great, hulking megas or small, graceful schooners. Human civilization would never have gotten where it is today without them, and without the people who pilot them. Take some time to appreciate the work and dedication that goes into designing and building your vessel, guiding it across the ocean, and making it run smoothly and safely. Think of all the people who have sailed before you. That sense of history is why there's a **romance to sea travel** that you'll never get if you just fly everywhere.

Walking the ports of call

Sure, shore excursions can be fun, and sometimes they really are the best way to see the sights, but if you're in a walkable historic town — whether it be New York, Barcelona, Mazatlan, San Juan, Bordeaux, Sitka, or any one of a thousand others — I can think of few better ways to get acquainted than by just stepping off your ship and walking around. You'll see and smell things from ground level — and at a human pace rather than a bus-view fly-by — and get a much better sense of the town's character. Try to get beyond the typical tourist areas, too, out to where people live, and try to find some of the local oddities that give a place its character — little local museums, community gardens, well-kept residential streets. The people who maintain them are your neighbors on this planet. Go say hello.

Exploring the smaller, more niche-oriented cruise lines

For a lot of destinations — including Alaska, the Pacific Northwest, the U.S. East Coast, and of course the world's rivers — I think small ships are a far better option than large cruise ships. Why? Fewer things to distract you from the scenery; an ability to sail into narrower, shallow waters and ports; a low-key vibe; and fellow passengers who want to keep the focus on nature, history, and culture. Sure, the small ships are more expensive, but doing a cost-benefit analysis may make that pill easier to swallow (see Chapter 13 for more info about these ships).

Seeking out traditional culture

As a cruise passenger, you start with a few limitations if you really want to learn about the place you're visiting. For one thing, you're usually only able to visit the coast, and the culture of port towns is usually different from that in the heartland. For another thing, you're usually only in port for eight or ten hours. Still, with a little effort, you can learn at least a few things about the local culture and traditions that'll give you something more to take home than just a miniature made-in-China totem pole. In Alaska, many ports have Native community houses where local tribes put on shows of traditional dance and music. In the Yucatán, you can visit ruins that show the complexity of Mayan culture. In Honduras, you can visit with local Indian tribes and learn how they live. Know how they say travel broadens the mind? This is what they're talking about.

Sipping brews on ship and shore

One of the ways I judge a ship is by its beer selection. Ditto for port towns — hell, for whole countries for that matter. Some ships have bars that are particularly well stocked — *Queen Mary 2,* for example, as well as the British P&O ships, and Royal Caribbean isn't bad either. In some ports (Juneau, Halifax, Dublin, Amsterdam, Copenhagen, and so on), you can tour the local and, in some cases, world-famous breweries. At the very least, most cities have at least a few great bars. Mark this down as another opportunity to get a "taste" of the local culture.

Heidi's Top Five Cruise Experiences

Okay, Heidi's story: She's a not-quite 40-year-old writer living in Manhattan who also wears the hat of wife and mother. She considers herself somewhat of a chameleon. She can blend into the crowd at a fancy dinner party or play pool in an old-man bar down on the corner. She can duck fistfuls of macaroni and cheese while sipping a glass of Verve Cliquot. This mother of 3-year-old twin boys is used to going with the flow. While she now lugs her adorable twosome on most cruises, she can still remember what it was like *before,* when only her selfish needs mattered. Here are her favorite cruise moments.

People-watching

Few places offer such perfect conditions for the sport. Ships big and small offer prime peeking opportunities, though the bigger they are, the more players in the show. My nightly routine goes like this: Find a comfy bar stool in the middle of the hubbub, an hour or so before the dinner rush. Here's when you realize what a melting pot the megaships really are. You see all kinds, from dumpy couples in matching Hawaiian shirts strolling hand-in-hand, to hip families dressed in black, and showy botoxed types sportin' major bling bling.

Getting into the glamorous dining scene

Allow me to qualify this: There are plenty of loud, crowded restaurants on ships, but I'm talking about those few intimate venues that cater to adults with a penchant for gorgeous atmosphere, excellent cuisine and wine, impeccable service, and dressing up. The alternative restaurants on Celebrity's *Millennium, Infinity, Constellation,* and *Summit* are like something out of a 1940s Cary Grant movie. The Edwardian-style Olympic restaurant on the *Millennium,* for example, takes your breath away with its décor alone: several dozen hand-carved and gilded French walnut wall panels that come straight from an ocean liner that sailed more than 70 years ago.

Agreeing (finally) that small ships are priceless

Sure, Heidi the chameleon changes her spots when she's on a megaship and can enjoy the Vegas thing (it's a tough job, but someone's got to do it), but her heart belongs to small ships. You get cozy with the crew and your fellow shipmates fast, and you feel like you're all in a vacation adventure together. And you sure can't beat a small-ship itinerary; they're always way more interesting and offbeat. In places such as Jost Van Dyke or Monte Carlo or Santoríni, you'll feel like you're on a ship that belongs there.

Soaking up the tradition — tradition!

Okay, these days you may have to look hard to find it, but it's there. Vestiges of a more elegant, refined, and formal time. Officers still look ultrasmart in their crisp white or black uniforms. The captain is still commander of the ship and almost godlike when he walks the decks and nods hello to passengers. I get all sentimental when I hear a big band playing oldies in a lounge. The warm fuzzies hit when I'm sitting in a darkened theater, enjoying the pleasant buzz from wine at dinner, as a troupe of singers and dancers do Cole Porter and Steven Sondheim classics. It's all against the backdrop of those wooden decks and polished railings and that haunting ship's horn . . . sigh.

Coming back . . . to the mother ship

After a particularly satisfying day doing something totally cool and exhausting — such as climbing the narrow spires of Antonio Gaudi's Sagrada Familia in Barcelona, or hopping on a six-seater pontoon plane for a totally breathtaking, white-knuckle ride over glaciers and snowy peaks in Alaska — coming back to the ship is like coming back to a cozy, nurturing nest. A place to unwind and regroup and reboot. Your cabin's all made up, the bathroom's stocked with fresh towels, and a cool drink and a tasty dinner are just a few decks away.

Appendix

Quick Concierge

● ●

This appendix offers some helpful resources that you can use with this book to begin planning your cruise.

Cruise Lines

All numbers are for the United States unless otherwise noted.

Abercrombie & Kent
1520 Kensington Rd., Suite 212
Oak Brook, IL 60523-2156
☎ 800-554-7016
www.abercrombiekent.com

American Canadian Caribbean Line
461 Water St.
Warren, RI 02885
☎ 800-556-7450
www.accl-smallships.com

American Safari Cruises
19101 36th Ave. West, Suite 201
Lynnwood, WA 98036
☎ 888-862-8881
www.amsafari.com

American West Steamboat Company
2101 Fourth Ave., Suite 1150
Seattle, WA 98121
☎ 800-434-1232
www.americanweststeamboat.com

The Barge Lady
101 West Grand Ave., Suite 200
Chicago, IL 60610
☎ 800-880-0071
www.bargelady.com

Carnival Cruise Lines
3655 NW 87th Ave.
Miami, FL 33178-2428

☎ 800-CARNIVAL
www.carnival.com

Celebrity Cruises
1050 Caribbean Way
Miami, FL 33132
☎ 800-437-3111
www.celebrity.com

Clipper Cruise Line
11969 Westline Dr.
St. Louis, MO 63146-3220
☎ 800-325-0010
www.clippercruise.com

Costa Cruises
200 South Park Rd., Suite 200
Hollywood, FL 33021-8541
☎ 800-462-6782
www.costacruises.com

Cruise West
2301 5th Ave., Suite 401
Seattle, WA 98121
☎ 888-851-8133
www.cruisewest.com

Crystal Cruises
2049 Century Park East, Suite 1400
Los Angeles, CA 90067
☎ 800-446-6620
www.crystalcruises.com

Cunard Line
24303 Town Center Dr., Suite 200
Valencia, CA 91355-0908
☎ 800-7CUNARD
www.cunard.com

Delta Queen Steamboat Company
Robin Street Wharf
1380 Port of New Orleans Pl.
New Orleans, LA 70130
☎ 800-543-1949
www.deltaqueen.com

Disney Cruise Line
P.O. Box 10210
Lake Buena Vista, FL 32830
☎ 888-325-2500
www.disneycruise.com

easyCruise
The Rotunda
42/43 Gloucester Crescent
London NW1 7DL, United Kingdom
☎ 0906-292-9000 in the UK
011-44-1895-651191 from the U.S. and
elsewhere
www.easycruise.com

French Country Waterways
P.O. Box 2195
Duxbury, MA 02331
☎ 800-222-1236
www.fcwl.com

Glacier Bay Cruiseline
2101 4th Ave., Suite 2200
Seattle, WA 98121
☎ 800-451-5952
www.glacierbaycruiseline.com

Holland America Line
300 Elliot Ave. West
Seattle, WA 98119
☎ 800-426-0327
www.hollandamerica.com

Lindblad Expeditions
96 Morton St.
New York, NY 10014
☎ 800-397-3348
www.expeditions.com

Maine Windjammer Association
P.O. Box 317
Augusta, ME 04332-0317
☎ 800-807-WIND
www.sailmainecoast.com

MSC Cruises
6750 N. Andrews Ave.
Fort Lauderdale, FL 33309
☎ 800-666-9333
www.msccruises.com

Norwegian Coastal Voyage
405 Park Ave.
New York, NY 10022
☎ 800-323-7436
www.coastalvoyage.com

Norwegian Cruise Line
7665 Corporate Center Dr.
Miami, FL 33126
☎ 800-327-7030
www.ncl.com

Oceania Cruises
8300 NW 33rd St., Suite 308
Miami, FL 33122
☎ 800-531-5658
www.oceaniacruises.com

Orient Lines
7665 Corporate Center Dr.
Miami, FL 33126
☎ 800-333-7300
www.orientlines.com

Peter Deilmann Cruises
1800 Diagonal Rd., Suite 170
Alexandria, VA 22314
☎ 800-348-8287
www.deilmann-cruises.com

Princess Cruises
24305 Town Center Dr.
Santa Clarita, CA 91355
☎ 800-PRINCESS
www.princess.com

Quark Expeditions
1019 Post Rd.
Darien, CT 06820

☎ 800-356-5699
www.quarkexpeditions.com

Radisson Seven Seas Cruises
600 Corporate Dr., Suite 410
Fort Lauderdale, FL 33334
☎ 800-477-7500
www.rssc.com

Royal Caribbean International
1050 Caribbean Way
Miami, FL 33132
☎ 800-327-6700
www.royalcaribbean.com

Seabourn Cruise Line
6100 Blue Lagoon Dr., Suite 400
Miami, FL 33126
☎ 800-929-9391
www.seabourn.com

SeaDream Yacht Club
2601 S. Bayshore Dr., Penthouse 1B
Coconut Grove, FL 33133
☎ 800-707-4911
www.seadreamyachtclub.com

Silversea Cruises
110 E. Broward Blvd.
Fort Lauderdale, FL 33301
☎ 800-722-9055
www.silversea.com

Star Clippers
4101 Salzedo St.
Coral Gables, FL 33146
☎ 800-442-0553
www.starclippers.com

Uniworld
Uniworld Plaza
17323 Ventura Blvd.
Los Angeles, CA 91316
☎ 800-733-7820
www.uniworld.com

Viking River Cruises
21820 Burbank Blvd.
Woodland Hills, CA 91367
☎ 877-668-4546
www.vikingrivercruises.com

Windjammer Barefoot Cruises
P.O. Box 190120
Miami Beach, FL 33119-0120
☎ 800-327-2601
www.windjammer.com

Windstar Cruises
300 Elliott Ave. West
Seattle, WA 98119
☎ 800-258-7245
www.windstarcruises.com

Cruise Agencies

The following sections include some of the top cruise agencies in the United States. The Web-based agencies take bookings online and over the telephone, and they all allow users to search for cruises in a number of ways (for example, by dates, itineraries, length of cruise, and more).

The bricks-and-mortar agencies aren't specifically Web-based (although some have a significant Web presence). We list only the main offices.

Top Web-based cruise agencies

Cruise.com
☎ 800-303-3337

Cruise411.com
☎ 800-553-7090

eCruises.com
☎ 800-438-2686

Expedia.com
☎ 800-397-3342

Icruise.com
☎ 866-942-7847

Travelocity.com
☎ 877-815-5446

Top bricks-and-mortar cruise agencies

Cruise Professionals
130 Dundas St. E., Suite 103
Mississauga, ON L5A 3V8 Canada
☎ 800-265-3838
www.cruiseprofessionals.com

Just Cruisin' Plus
5640 Nolensville Rd.
Nashville, TN 37211
☎ 800-888-0922
www.justcruisinplus.com

Cruises Only
100 Sylvan Rd., Suite 600
Woburn, MA 01801
☎ 800-278-4737
www.cruisesonly.com

Largay Travel
625 Wolcott St.
Waterbury, CT 06705
☎ 800-322-9481
www.largaytravel.com

Cruise Value Center
6 Edgeboro Rd., Suite 400
East Brunswick, NJ 08816
☎ 800-231-7447
www.cruisevalue.com

Mann Travel & Cruises/123Travel
4400 Park Rd.
Charlotte, NC 28209
☎ 800-835-9828
www.123Travel.com

Travel agency consortiums

Another way to find a reputable travel agency in your town is by contacting one of a handful of agency groups or consortiums that screen their members. The following groups all maintain Web sites that allow you to search for local agencies within your zip code or city. The latter two specialize in luxury cruises.

Carlson Wagonlit Travel
www.CarlsonTravel.com

TravelSavers
www.travelsavers.com

Cruise Holidays
www.cruiseholidays.com

Vacation.com
www.vacation.com

Cruise Ship Centers (Canada based)
www.cruiseshipcenters.com

Virtuoso
☎ 800-401-4274
www.virtuoso.com

Signature Travel Network
☎ 800-339-0868
www.signaturetravel.com

Web Directory

Here are some great Web sites to help you research your cruise.

✔ **http://travel.state.gov/:** The section of the U.S. State Department's site offers information on the travel situations in every country.

✔ **www.cdc.gov/travel:** The Centers for Disease Control's site details their Vessel Sanitation program and offers other health-related travel information.

✔ **www.cruisecritic.com:** Cruise Critic features reader and expert reviews, chat, and cruise advice.

✔ **www.cruisemates.com:** Cruisemates offers an online cruise community, expert reviews, chat, news updates, message boards, and links to special deals.

✔ **www.cruising.org:** The site of Cruise Lines International Association, the industry's marketing group, offers contact info for accredited travel agents, information on cruise lines, articles, and statistics.

✔ **www.cruise-news.com:** Check here for industry news.

✔ **www.frommers.com:** Features reviews, cruise tips, round-ups, news, and deals.

Index

• *T* •

BUSINESS, CAREERS & PERSONAL FINANCE

Grant Writing FOR DUMMIES

Home Buying FOR DUMMIES

0-7645-5307-0 0-7645-5331-3 *†

Also available:
- Accounting For Dummies †
  0-7645-5314-3
- Business Plans Kit For Dummies †
  0-7645-5365-8
- Cover Letters For Dummies
  0-7645-5224-4
- Frugal Living For Dummies
  0-7645-5403-4
- Leadership For Dummies
  0-7645-5176-0
- Managing For Dummies
  0-7645-1771-6

- Marketing For Dummies
  0-7645-5600-2
- Personal Finance For Dummies *
  0-7645-2590-5
- Project Management
  For Dummies
  0-7645-5283-X
- Resumes For Dummies †
  0-7645-5471-9
- Selling For Dummies
  0-7645-5363-1
- Small Business Kit For Dummies *†
  0-7645-5093-4

HOME & BUSINESS COMPUTER BASICS

Windows XP FOR DUMMIES

Excel 2003 FOR DUMMIES

0-7645-4074-2 0-7645-3758-X

Also available:
- ACT! 6 For Dummies
  0-7645-2645-6
- iLife '04 All-in-One Desk Reference
  For Dummies
  0-7645-7347-0
- iPAQ For Dummies
  0-7645-6769-1
- Mac OS X Panther Timesaving
  Techniques For Dummies
  0-7645-5812-9
- Macs For Dummies
  0-7645-5656-8
- Microsoft Money 2004 For Dummies
  0-7645-4195-1

- Office 2003 All-in-One Desk
  Reference For Dummies
  0-7645-3883-7
- Outlook 2003 For Dummies
  0-7645-3759-8
- PCs For Dummies
  0-7645-4074-2
- TiVo For Dummies
  0-7645-6923-6
- Upgrading and Fixing PCs
  For Dummies
  0-7645-1665-5
- Windows XP Timesaving
  Techniques For Dummies
  0-7645-3748-2

FOOD, HOME, GARDEN, HOBBIES, MUSIC & PETS

Feng Shui FOR DUMMIES

Poker FOR DUMMIES

0-7645-5295-3 0-7645-5232-5

Also available:
- Bass Guitar For Dummies
  0-7645-2487-9
- Diabetes Cookbook For Dummies
  0-7645-5230-9
- Gardening For Dummies *
  0-7645-5130-2
- Guitar For Dummies
  0-7645-5106-X
- Holiday Decorating For Dummies
  0-7645-2570-0
- Home Improvement All-in-One
  For Dummies
  0-7645-5680-0

- Knitting For Dummies
  0-7645-5395-X
- Piano For Dummies
  0-7645-5105-1
- Puppies For Dummies
  0-7645-5255-4
- Scrapbooking For Dummies
  0-7645-7208-3
- Senior Dogs For Dummies
  0-7645-5818-8
- Singing For Dummies
  0-7645-2475-5
- 30-Minute Meals For Dummies
  0-7645-2589-1

INTERNET & DIGITAL MEDIA

Digital Photography FOR DUMMIES

Starting an eBay Business FOR DUMMIES

0-7645-1664-7 0-7645-6924-4

Also available:
- 2005 Online Shopping Directory
  For Dummies
  0-7645-7495-7
- CD & DVD Recording For Dummies
  0-7645-5956-7
- eBay For Dummies
  0-7645-5654-1
- Fighting Spam For Dummies
  0-7645-5965-6
- Genealogy Online For Dummies
  0-7645-5964-8
- Google For Dummies
  0-7645-4420-9

- Home Recording For Musicians
  For Dummies
  0-7645-1634-5
- The Internet For Dummies
  0-7645-4173-0
- iPod & iTunes For Dummies
  0-7645-7772-7
- Preventing Identity Theft
  For Dummies
  0-7645-7336-5
- Pro Tools All-in-One Desk
  Reference For Dummies
  0-7645-5714-9
- Roxio Easy Media Creator
  For Dummies
  0-7645-7131-1

* Separate Canadian edition also available
† Separate U.K. edition also available

Available wherever books are sold. For more information or to order direct: U.S. customers
visit www.dummies.com or call 1-877-762-2974.
U.K. customers visit www.wileyeurope.com or call 0800 243407. Canadian customers visit
www.wiley.ca or call 1-800-567-4797.

SPORTS, FITNESS, PARENTING, RELIGION & SPIRITUALITY

0-7645-5146-9

0-7645-5418-2

Also available:

- Adoption For Dummies
  0-7645-5488-3
- Basketball For Dummies
  0-7645-5248-1
- The Bible For Dummies
  0-7645-5296-1
- Buddhism For Dummies
  0-7645-5359-3
- Catholicism For Dummies
  0-7645-5391-7
- Hockey For Dummies
  0-7645-5228-7

- Judaism For Dummies
  0-7645-5299-6
- Martial Arts For Dummies
  0-7645-5358-5
- Pilates For Dummies
  0-7645-5397-6
- Religion For Dummies
  0-7645-5264-3
- Teaching Kids to Read
  For Dummies
  0-7645-4043-2
- Weight Training For Dummies
  0-7645-5168-X
- Yoga For Dummies
  0-7645-5117-5

TRAVEL

0-7645-5438-7

0-7645-5453-0

Also available:

- Alaska For Dummies
  0-7645-1761-9
- Arizona For Dummies
  0-7645-6938-4
- Cancún and the Yucatán
  For Dummies
  0-7645-2437-2
- Cruise Vacations For Dummies
  0-7645-6941-4
- Europe For Dummies
  0-7645-5456-5
- Ireland For Dummies
  0-7645-5455-7

- Las Vegas For Dummies
  0-7645-5448-4
- London For Dummies
  0-7645-4277-X
- New York City For Dummies
  0-7645-6945-7
- Paris For Dummies
  0-7645-5494-8
- RV Vacations For Dummies
  0-7645-5443-3
- Walt Disney World & Orlando
  For Dummies
  0-7645-6943-0

GRAPHICS, DESIGN & WEB DEVELOPMENT

0-7645-4345-8

0-7645-5589-8

Also available:

- Adobe Acrobat 6 PDF
  For Dummies
  0-7645-3760-1
- Building a Web Site For Dummies
  0-7645-7144-3
- Dreamweaver MX 2004
  For Dummies
  0-7645-4342-3
- FrontPage 2003 For Dummies
  0-7645-3882-9
- HTML 4 For Dummies
  0-7645-1995-6
- Illustrator CS For Dummies
  0-7645-4084-X

- Macromedia Flash MX 2004
  For Dummies
  0-7645-4358-X
- Photoshop 7 All-in-One Desk
  Reference For Dummies
  0-7645-1667-1
- Photoshop CS Timesaving
  Techniques For Dummies
  0-7645-6782-9
- PHP 5 For Dummies
  0-7645-4166-8
- PowerPoint 2003 For Dummies
  0-7645-3908-6
- QuarkXPress 6 For Dummies
  0-7645-2593-X

NETWORKING, SECURITY, PROGRAMMING & DATABASES

0-7645-6852-3

0-7645-5784-X

Also available:

- A+ Certification For Dummies
  0-7645-4187-0
- Access 2003 All-in-One Desk
  Reference For Dummies
  0-7645-3988-4
- Beginning Programming
  For Dummies
  0-7645-4997-9
- C For Dummies
  0-7645-7068-4
- Firewalls For Dummies
  0-7645-4048-3
- Home Networking For Dummies
  0-7645-42796

- Network Security For Dummies
  0-7645-1679-5
- Networking For Dummies
  0-7645-1677-9
- TCP/IP For Dummies
  0-7645-1760-0
- VBA For Dummies
  0-7645-3989-2
- Wireless All In-One Desk Referer
  For Dummies
  0-7645-7496-5
- Wireless Home Networking
  For Dummies
  0-7645-3910-8

-7645-6820-5 *†   0-7645-2566-2

Also available:
- Alzheimer's For Dummies
  0-7645-3899-3
- Asthma For Dummies
  0-7645-4233-8
- Controlling Cholesterol For Dummies
  0-7645-5440-9
- Depression For Dummies
  0-7645-3900-0
- Dieting For Dummies
  0-7645-4149-8
- Fertility For Dummies
  0-7645-2549-2

- Fibromyalgia For Dummies
  0-7645-5441-7
- Improving Your Memory For Dummies
  0-7645-5435-2
- Pregnancy For Dummies †
  0-7645-4483-7
- Quitting Smoking For Dummies
  0-7645-2629-4
- Relationships For Dummies
  0-7645-5384-4
- Thyroid For Dummies
  0-7645-5385-2

DUCATION, HISTORY, REFERENCE & TEST PREPARATION

0-7645-5194-9   0-7645-4186-2

Also available:
- Algebra For Dummies
  0-7645-5325-9
- British History For Dummies
  0-7645-7021-8
- Calculus For Dummies
  0-7645-2498-4
- English Grammar For Dummies
  0-7645-5322-4
- Forensics For Dummies
  0-7645-5580-4
- The GMAT For Dummies
  0-7645-5251-1
- Inglés Para Dummies
  0-7645-5427-1

- Italian For Dummies
  0-7645-5196-5
- Latin For Dummies
  0-7645-5431-X
- Lewis & Clark For Dummies
  0-7645-2545-X
- Research Papers For Dummies
  0-7645-5426-3
- The SAT I For Dummies
  0-7645-7193-1
- Science Fair Projects For Dummies
  0-7645-5460-3
- U.S. History For Dummies
  0-7645-5249-X

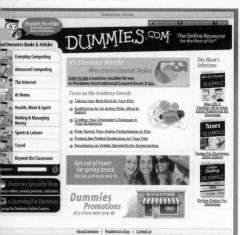

Get smart @ dummies.com®

- **Find a full list of Dummies titles**
- **Look into loads of FREE on-site articles**
- **Sign up for FREE eTips e-mailed to you weekly**
- **See what other products carry the Dummies name**
- **Shop directly from the Dummies bookstore**
- **Enter to win new prizes every month!**

Separate Canadian edition also available
Separate U.K. edition also available

ailable wherever books are sold. For more information or to order direct: U.S. customers
it www.dummies.com or call 1-877-762-2974.
K. customers visit www.wileyeurope.com or call 0800 243407. Canadian customers visit
ww.wiley.ca or call 1-800-567-4797.

Do More with Dummies

Products for the Rest of Us!

From hobbies to health, discover a wide variety of fun products

DVDs/Videos • Music CDs • Games
Consumer Electronics • Software
Craft Kits • Culinary Kits • and More!

Check out the Dummies Specialty Shop at
www.dummies.com for more information!